COLLECTED STUDIES SERIES

Monastic, Scholastic and Mystical Theologies from the Later Middle Ages

Professor Kent Emery, Jr.

Kent Emery, Jr.

Monastic, Scholastic and Mystical Theologies from the Later Middle Ages

VARIORUM
1996

This edition copyright © 1996 by Kent Emery, Jr.

Published by VARIORUM
Ashgate Publishing Limited
Gower House, Croft Road,
Aldershot, Hampshire GU11 3HR
Great Britain

Ashgate Publishing Company
Old Post Road,
Brookfield, Vermont 05036
USA

ISBN 0–86078–617 –X

British Library CIP Data

Emery, Kent, 1944–
Monastic, Scholastic and Mystical Theologies from the Later
Middle Ages. (Variorum Collected Studies Series; CS561).
1. Theology–History–Middle Ages, 600–1500.
I. Title.
230' .0902

US Library of Congress CIP Data

Emery, Kent, 1944–
Monastic, Scholastic and Mystical Theologies from the Later
Middle Ages/Kent Emery, Jr.
p. cm. – (Collected Studies Series; CS561).
Includes bibliographical references and index (cloth: alk. paper).
1. Theology, Doctrinal–History–Middle Ages, 600–1500.
2. Theology–History–Middle Ages, 600–1500.
I. Title. II. Series: Collected Studies Series; CS561.
BT26. E46   1997   96–35533
230' .2' 0902–dc20   CIP

Printed by Galliard (Printers) Ltd., Great Yarmouth, Norfolk, Great Britain.

COLLECTED STUDIES SERIES C561

CONTENTS

This volume contains xii + 362 pages

PREFACE

The essays in this volume treat theological writers and texts from the eleventh through seventeenth centuries, focusing mainly on the thirteenth through fifteenth centuries. They offer historical, rhetorical and doctrinal analyses of texts representing various kinds and different modes of medieval theological discourse: monastic topics, Scholastic treatises and commentaries, mystical theology strictly speaking, pastoral works (summas, sermons, etc.). In each essay I have striven to discover the philosophic and speculative thought that governs the organization and coherence of the texts considered, and I have attempted to show how theological writers employ grammatical, rhetorical and dialectic instruments of invention, analysis and exposition in their compositions.

Although several of these essays were written for specific ocassions, there is, I think, an overall pattern to them all. They illustrate the continuity of theological traditions, amidst differing historical circumstances, from the later Middle Ages through early modern times. The material foundation of this continuity is textual. (For reasons of space, I have excluded from this volume a number of my essays that treat manuscript and print transmissions of theological works, in the Middle Ages and beyond.) Moreover, each essay, implicitly or explicitly, tests historiographical concepts and categories commonly used by modern scholars in their study of medieval religious literature.

For decades, scholars have employed the terms 'monastic theology', 'spirituality', 'Scholastic theology' and 'mystical theology' to classify medieval theological writers and texts. These terms and categories have become *topoi* of interpretation. Their usage is often very elastic, or, contrariwise, imposes upon medieval writings 'clear and distinct' concepts more often than not confused by the textual and historical record.

The term 'monastic theology' usually designates the types and style of medieval monastic texts written before Scholastic dialectical and logical techniques, applied to theological subjects, came to dominate in the schools and universities in the thirteenth century. The contrast the term is meant to signify may be seen most clearly in the disputes between Bernard of Clairvaux and Peter Abelard, and in the broad differences between monastic and 'school' writings in the twelfth century. Even so, the writings of many twelfth-century monks (e.g., Isaac of Stella, the author of *Liber de spiritu et anima*, William of St.-Thierry, let alone the Canons of St.-Victor), are replete with philosophical speculations and learning, and they were received by later, Scholastic theologians as 'authorities' with which to be reckoned in argument.

The institutional and intellectual history of the change during the twelfth to thirteenth centuries in the method and style of theological inquiry, which involved the increasing knowledge of, and interest in, works of ancient and Arabic philosophy, has been studied extensively by the greatest masters of medieval studies. Their study was in large part inspired by the revival of Scholastic philosophy and theology in the nineteenth and twentieth centuries. The notions of 'monastic theology' and 'spirituality' (largely a modern coinage) were conceived in reaction to the dominating interest in Scholasticism, which often neglected vast stretches of medieval religious and theological literature. Yet, however useful the terms 'monastic theology' and 'spirituality' have been in delineating subject matters for scholarly study, they seem somewhat anachronistic when applied to theological writing in the late Middle Ages and beyond. Late-medieval monks often studied in the universities, or were taught by those who did. Thus, it is not surprising that Scholastic techniques and conceptions informed their writings on traditional ascetic, psychological and monastic topics. In the late Middle Ages, relations among universities, convent *studia* and monasteries were fluid; *abbreviationes*, for example, such as the one I study in essay II, transmitted Scholastic learning to the simpler brethren 'in the provinces.'

For its part, the term 'spirituality' comprehends nearly every kind of religious expression, and has been amplified even more by some to include almost anything. Its usage is especially favored by those who interpret medieval religious writings in modern psychological and phenomenological terms. The term 'spirituality' evidently opposes the strictly and artificially 'rational'. In the late Middle Ages, however, a text of 'pure spirituality', whatever that might mean, is elusive. In turn, the writings of Scholastic theologians were informed by a 'spirituality', as many articles in the *Dictionnaire de spiritualité*, for example, reveal.

In several important studies, Alain de Libera has questioned conventional categories in the analysis of medieval spiritual writings, and has demonstrated how closely related late-medieval 'mystical theology' was to Scholastic speculations concerning God and the soul.[1] Like 'monastic theology' and 'spirituality', the term 'mystical theology' is often applied elastically and anachronistically. The term, however, has a concrete, historical sense. Although the adjective 'mystic' and what we might call 'mystical themes' are everywhere present in Christian theological literature

---

[1] Alain de Libera, *Penser au Moyen Âge* (Paris, 1991) 299–308; *La mystique rhénane d'Albert le Grand à Maître Eckhart* (Paris, 1994).

from late antiquity onwards, the term 'mystical theology', signifying a specific mode of inquiry or genre of theological literature, emerged in the Latin west with the reception of the writings of pseudo-Dionysius in the twelfth and thirteenth centuries. The reception of these difficult writings was foremost among university theologians (e.g., Robert Grosseteste, Albert the Great, Bonaventure, Thomas Aquinas, Meister Eckhart). Late-medieval commentators on the works of pseudo-Dionysius and writers of treatises on mystical theology could scarcely avoid terms and concepts taught and learned in school, and they sought to reconcile the Areopagite's teaching with longstanding patristic and monastic authorities. Those like Hugh of Balma, who completely separated 'mystical' from Scholastic theology, necessarily presupposed the latter in order to define the former, and they established the difference between the two 'modes of theology' by way of Scholastic distinctions among the intellect, will and affections, and between the objects of 'the true' and 'the good'.

Seven of these essays treat Denys the Carthusian (Dionysius Cartusiensis, 1402-1471). Johan Huizinga considered Denys 'the perfect type of the powerful religious enthusiast produced by the waning Middle Ages . . . . It is as if through him the entire stream of medieval theology flows once again. *Qui Dionysium legit, nihil non legit*'.[2] Denys' voluminous writings, which embrace every genre of medieval theological discourse and hundreds of authors, are a fit subject for the general problematic addressed in these essays, and they offer a late-medieval perspective on the whole prior tradition of Christian thought. Denys reflects the distinctive religious and intellectual movements of his time and place: elite Carthusian monasticism; popular piety and the *Devotio moderna*; the revival of thirteenth-century Scholastic thought, notably of Albert the Great and Thomas Aquinas; a keen interest in 'Platonic' philosophy; visionary and speculative mysticism (as far as I know, Denys is the only Latin writer besides Albert the Great to comment on every writing in the *Corpus Dionysiacum*); an overriding concern for personal, ecclesiastical and social reform. At the same time, his synthesis is personal and singular, as I believe these essays show. While he formally defines the 'essence' and scope of each of his writings, materially they are 'mixed genres'. He introduces Scholastic distinctions and concepts in his pious works and adduces arguments of piety in his speculative writings; all of them tend towards, or culminate in, mystical contemplation. Denys' own terms for distinguishing and coordinating different modes of medieval discourse about God (natural wisdom naturally acquired, supernatural wisdom naturally acquired, supernatural wisdom supernaturally given), which I treat in several essays, seem to me as good as any we can conceive.

---

[2] Johan Huizinga, *The Autumn of the Middle Ages*, trans. Rodney J. Payton and Ulrich Mammitzche (Chicago, 1996), 218.

In sum, I hope that this collection of 'microstudies' yields some glimpse of the flexibility of theological discourse in the later Middle Ages, and of the nexus among 'symbolic, intelligible and mystical' modes of theology.

KENT EMERY, JR.

The Medieval Institute
University of Notre Dame
May 1996

PUBLISHER'S NOTE

The articles in this volume, as in all others in the Collected Studies Series, have not been given a new, continuous pagination. In order to avoid confusion, and to facilitate their use where these same studies have been referred to elsewhere, the original pagination has been maintained wherever possible.

Each article has been given a Roman number in order of appearance, as listed in the Contents. This number is repeated on each page and is quoted in the index entries.

Corrections noted in the Addenda and Corrigenda have been marked by an asterisk in the margin corresponding to the relevant text to be amended.

ACKNOWLEDGEMENTS

I am grateful to the following persons, journals and publishers for their permission to reproduce the articles included in this volume: the editors of *Traditio* and Fordham University Press (article I); Dom Guibert Michiels, OSB, the editor of *Recherches de Théologie ancienne et médiévale* (II); Dr. Rozanne Elder and the editors of Cistercian Publications (III); Dr. James Hogg, who allowed me to publish a revised, amplified version of an article originally published in the series, Analecta Cartusiana (IV); Dr. Alain Girard and les Éditions du Cerf (V); Duke University Press (VI); Dr. Andreas Speer, editor of the series *Miscellanea Mediaevalia* (VII); Professor Simo Knuuttila, for the Luther-Agricola-Society (VIII); the Director of the University of Notre Dame Press (IX); the editors of *Viator* and the University of California Press (X); the editors of the *Journal of the History of Ideas* and John Hopkins University Press (XI).

To Lucy

I

READING THE WORLD RIGHTLY AND SQUARELY: BONAVENTURE'S DOCTRINE OF THE CARDINAL VIRTUES

In an article concerning the seven deadly sins, Siegfried Wenzel[1] distinguishes one model for the traditional topic of vices and virtues which he calls 'cosmological' or 'symbolic.' This model develops the idea that 'man is a septenary,' a composite of three powers of the soul and four elements of the body.[2] The association of the three theological virtues with the three powers of the soul and the four cardinal virtues with the four elements of the body was current in the twelfth century.[3] In the first half of the thirteenth century, Robert Grosseteste developed the analogy in the context of a metaphysics of light, somewhat unexpectedly in a treatise on confession.[4] The 'connection between virtues and vices on one hand and physiology on the other,' Wenzel remarks, 'is an area that needs much further study.'[5] Perhaps the fullest development of the cosmological or symbolic model of the virtues was made in the last half of the thirteenth century by Bonaventure. Indeed, for him the cardinal virtues (the concern of this study) are the four poles of the created universe.

Interestingly, Grosseteste's teaching may be relevant to Bonaventure's doctrine of the cardinal virtues. The two authors shared the same sources of inspiration: Augustine, Anselm, pseudo-Dionysius Areopagita, and Hugh of St. Victor.[6] Moreover, the studies of Servus Gieben and others suggest that

---

[1] I wish to acknowledge Professor Wenzel's advice during the early stages of this study. Funds for my first research were provided through a fellowship from the National Endowment for the Humanities.

[2] S. Wenzel, 'The Seven Deadly Sins: Some Problems of Research,' *Speculum* 43 (1968) 8.

[3] See, for example, the anonymous *De septem septennis* (PL 199.945–64). On the sevenfold classification of man's powers of body and soul in the twelfth century, see the remarks of B. McGinn, *Three Treatises on Man: A Cistercian Anthropology* (Kalamazoo 1977) 19–20.

[4] S. Wenzel, 'Robert Grosseteste's Treatise on Confession "Deus Est",' *Franciscan Studies* 30 (1970) 218–93, esp. 239–42, 249. Grosseteste was accustomed to treat technical philosophic matters in pastoral works. He did so notably in a sermon or 'conference,' ed. by J. McEvoy, 'Robert Grosseteste's Theory of Human Nature with the Text of his Conference "Ecclesia Sancta Celebrat",' *RThAM* 47 (1980) 131–87. The setting of this work is suggestively the same as Bonaventure's *Collationes*, the primary text of this paper.

[5] Wenzel, 'The Seven Deadly Sins' 10.

[6] J.-G. Bougerol, 'Saint Bonaventure et le pseudo-Denys l'areopagite,' *Études franciscaines* suppl. ann. (1968) 33–123; 'Saint Bonaventure et la hiérarchie dionysienne,' *AHDLMA* 36 (1969) 131–67; 'Saint Bonaventure et Saint Anselme,' *Antonianum* 47 (1972) 333–61; G. Zinn, 'Book and Word: The Victorine Background of Bonaventure's Use of Symbols,' in: *S. Bonaventura, 1274–1974* (Grottaferrata 1973) II 143–69.

Grosseteste may have been an immediate source for Bonaventure on such crucial topics as the nature of light, the illumination of the intellect, and the notion that man is a *minor mundus*.[7] All of these ideas are central to Bonaventure's teaching on the virtues. For the sake of brevity, I shall do no more than allude, as occasion arises, to Grosseteste's possible influence upon Bonaventure.

Bonaventure's theology is, as he might have said, a created reflection of God himself, the 'intelligible sphere whose center is everywhere and circumference nowhere.'[8] Each point of Bonaventure's doctrine implicates all the others. This is both the beauty and the difficulty of his thought. One is unable, therefore, to discuss Bonaventure's teaching on the cardinal virtues without turning to other major themes in his works. The texts upon which we shall finally focus require a broad context.

Recently, Edward A. Synan has pointed out that Bonaventure's fullest, most mature treatment of the cardinal virtues is to be found in the *Collationes in Hexaëmeron sive illuminationes ecclesiae*.[9] The circumstances in which Bonaventure composed his *Collationes* are instructive. When Bonaventure delivered these conferences to his Franciscan brethren at Paris in 1273, he had been relieved for many years of what was for him the burden of university teaching.[10] As General of the Franciscan Order, Bonaventure was compelled to address the practical matters of the administration of religious life and at the same time was free to direct his attention to spiritual matters which he thought more urgent than the questions of the schools. Nonetheless, the affairs of the university remained a concern for Bonaventure until the end of his life (1274), since many of the brethren over whom he had charge attended the schools and were influenced by the movements that occurred there.

Indeed as Bougerol and Synan show, Bonaventure's *Collationes* were prompted by new ideas gaining ground at the University of Paris. Bonaventure was

---

[7] S. Gieben, 'Traces of God in Nature According to Robert Grosseteste,' *Franciscan Studies* 24 (1964) 144–58; 'The Pseudo-Bonaventurian Work "Symbolica Theologia",' in: *Miscellanea Melchior de Pobladura* (Rome 1964) I 173–95; C. Bérubé and S. Gieben, 'Guibert de Tournai et Robert Grosseteste: Sources inconnues de Saint Bonaventure, suivi de l'édition critique de trois chapitres du *Rudimentum Doctrinae* de Guibert de Tournai,' in: *S. Bonaventura, 1274–1974* II 627–54; D. Unger, 'Robert Grosseteste, Bishop of Lincoln, 1235–1253, on the Reasons for the Incarnation,' *Franciscan Studies* 16 (1956) 1–36. See also R. C. Dales, 'A Medieval View of Human Dignity,' *Journal of the History of Ideas* 38 (1977) 457–72 (a study of the Christian tradition of man as *minor mundus* culminating in Grosseteste).

[8] *Itinerarium mentis in Deum* V 8 (*S. Bonaventurae Opera omnia*, cura PP. Collegii S. Bonaventurae; 10 vols [Quaracchi 1882–1902] V 310). The editors, n. 3, cite Alan of Lille as Bonaventure's immediate source for this traditional maxim.

[9] E. A. Synan, 'Cardinal Virtues in the Cosmos of Saint Bonaventure,' in *S. Bonaventura, 1274–1974* III 21–38.

[10] J.-G. Bougerol, *Introduction to the Works of Bonaventure* (trans. José de Vinck; Paterson, N.J. 1964). See the chronology, pp. 171–77.

disturbed by recent presumptions of members of the Arts faculty, who, swept by enthusiasm for the philosophy of Aristotle, had stepped beyond their proper domain of dialectic and physics, and were addressing questions of theology — in effect judging the revealed wisdom of God according to the standards of a pagan's philosophy.[11] In Bonaventure's eyes, the artists and theologians influenced by them were reversing the order of wisdom established by Christ, thereby changing wine into water and bread into stones.[12] Joseph Ratzinger further argues that the above stated purpose of the *Collationes in Hexaëmeron* was closely related to another: Bonaventure's attempt to domesticate and construe in an orthodox manner the thought of Joachim of Fiore, which had penetrated to the heart of the Franciscan Order and had caused much dissension. The symbolic structure of the *Collationes* suggests Joachim's influence upon Bonaventure himself, and it may be true, as Ratzinger implies, that Bonaventure saw in Joachim a closer ally of Christian wisdom than Aristotle.[13] In any case, Bonaventure considered the mystical concordances of the kind discovered by Joachim to be the fabric of the Scriptures.

Bonaventure addressed his series of conferences to his Franciscan brethren and others at Paris between 9 April and 28 May 1273, the year before his death.[14] Bougerol notes the monastic origin of such conferences and their relation, in Bonaventure's time, to the university sermon.[15] Significantly, Bonaventure confronted the problem of pagan philosophy, not in the setting of university lectures or disputed questions, settings perhaps too congenial to strictly philosophic discourse, but in a setting traditionally reserved for the exposition of sacred Scripture and its practical meaning for the Christian life.

As he refused to meet the artists on their own ground, so Bonaventure refused, for reasons which will become evident, to speak to them in their own terms. The particular literary form of the *Collationes*, like the forum in which Bonaventure delivered them, is somewhat antique. Happily, the very ambiguity of the textual transmission of the *Collationes* serves to reveal the significance of their form. The text of the *Collationes* exists in two redactions, both of which are *reportationes* of the master's teaching made by auditors, and both of which have claims to authority. One of these, which the Quaracchi editors and Bougerol designate the 'official version,'[16] represents a more expanded account of Bonaventure's teaching, and the form in which it was most widely

[11] Synan 26; Bougerol, *Introduction* 136.
[12] *Collationes in Hexaëmeron sive illuminationes ecclesiae* XIX 14 (*Opera* V 422). We shall cite this edition as *In Hex.* (*Opera* V). See Synan 26–27.
[13] J. Ratzinger, *The Theology of History in St. Bonaventure* (trans. Z. Hayes; Chicago 1971) chapter 1, pp. 104ff., 117ff.
[14] Bougerol, *Introduction* 132.
[15] Bougerol, *Introduction* 125.
[16] See note 12; Bougerol, *Introduction* 131.

circulated within the Order. The second redaction is compressed and offers a somewhat different disposition of the text.[17] However, its composer claims — and there is no reason to doubt his words — that his version, bearing certain corrections, at one point was seen and approved by Bonaventure himself.[18] Whatever one may judge of the relative merits of the two redactions,[19] I think the opinion of Fr. Synan is correct. The divisions of the text in the compressed, 'corrected' version make clearer what is in fact the structure of the work: a commentary on the six days of creation narrated in Genesis, comprising a *principium* and six *visiones* or *illuminationes*, corresponding to the six days.[20] Each *visio* or *illuminatio*, in turn, includes a number of *collationes*. Of the work, alternatively titled *Collationes in Hexaëmeron* or *De septem visionibus sive illuminationibus*, Synan says:

> If the work is not a line by line commentary on the Genesis account of the Six Days of creation, its fundamental theme remains the thorough-going parallelism that the Saint discerned between the cosmos produced during those Six Days and the Christian life.[21]

There are reasons, we shall see, why the work does not offer a line-by-line commentary. Bonaventure was unable to complete the design of his work before his death. The three final illuminations required by the work's structure were never written. Bonaventure's intent in these, to treat the 'light of the soul sublimated by the spirit of prophecy . . . absorbed in God by mystical rapture . . . the light of the vision of glory,'[22] indicates that in the words of the book of Genesis he perceived not only the true account of the workings of nature, but also the signposts marking the path of the mind's journey into God. Bonaventure himself defines the relation: just as the world, the *maior mundus*, was created in six days, so man, the *minor mundus*, is perfected in contemplation in six days.[23] The correspondence between the four elements and the four cardinal virtues must be understood within the context of this overriding correspondence.

---

[17] *S. Bonaventurae Collationes in Hexaëmeron et Bonaventuriana quaedam selecta* (ed. F. M. Delorme; Quaracchi 1934). We shall cite this edition as *In Hex.* (ed. Delorme).

[18] *In Hex.* (ed. Delorme 274–75); *In Hex.* (*Opera* V *Additamentum* 449–50). Cf. Bougerol, *Introduction* 126.

[19] Since both texts have authority, which one a commentator prefers will depend upon his understanding of the work. I do not find the two texts significantly different conceptually. Generally, I shall cite the *Opera omnia* text. When its expression seems more apt, or amplifies in an interesting way a point common to both texts, I shall cite the redaction edited by Delorme.

[20] Synan 24–27.

[21] Synan 26.

[22] Bougerol, *Introduction* 133.

[23] *In Hex.* III 24 (*Opera* V 347); *In Hex.* Princ. Coll. I 9 (ed. Delorme 4). Cf. Synan (26 n. 17) who adduces these texts.

Rather than in the form of the scholastic question, then, which had arisen with the recovery of Aristotelian learning,[24] Bonaventure chose to assess the new understanding of nature through the old-fashioned hexaemeral commentary, originated by the ancient fathers and continued by medieval monks.[25] We may sense, I think, that Bonaventure judged that the very dialectical form of scholastic discourse prejudiced the understanding of nature (and hence of the cardinal virtues). Bonaventure, of course, was adept at such discourse, and we shall find that his teaching on the cardinal virtues is constant, whether expressed in a formally scholastic manner, as in his earlier works, or in the symbolic manner of his later ones. Concerning the *Itinerarium mentis in Deum*, written (1259) two years after Bonaventure had left university teaching to become General of the Order, Bougerol acutely observes that Bonaventure was then free 'from the patterns of the Schools,' that is, free to develop a form for his thought more concordant with his vision.[26] By the time of the *Collationes in Hexaëmeron* Bonaventure had fully developed an extravagantly symbolic mode of expression, wholly alien to the language of the schools. Nevertheless, the principles that determine Bonaventure's conclusions concerning the cardinal virtues are already stated clearly in earlier works, such as his commentary on the *Sentences* and the *Breviloquium*. According to the terms of the Augustinian scriptural exegesis which Bonaventure accepted, one may turn usefully to the 'plain' speaking of these texts as a means for deciphering the 'obscure' signs of the *In Hexaëmeron*.[27] Or, according to another analogy in the spirit of Bonaventure, one may find in the commentary on the *Sentences* 'seminal reasons' which receive a perfection of form, a beautiful adornment, through the 'illuminations' arising from a consideration of the six days of creation.[28]

Bonaventure's decision to scrutinize the new doctrines of nature through an hexaemeral commentary is consistent with his own doctrine. If one wishes to understand nature aright, he must partake the illumination of sacred Scripture. In other words, the proper starting place for a study of nature is a careful

---

[24] M.-D. Chenu, *Toward Understanding St. Thomas* (trans. A. M. Landry and D. Hughes; Chicago 1964) 79–99, 157–58.

[25] F. E. Robbins, *The Hexaemeral Literature: A Study of the Greek and Latin Commentaries* (Chicago 1912). On the difference between exegetical and scholastic treatment of the six days, see the remarks of Nicholas H. Steneck, *Science and Creation in the Middle Ages: Henry of Langenstein (d.1397) on Genesis* (Notre Dame 1976) 20–21.

[26] Bougerol, *Introduction* 123.

[27] Augustine, *De doctrina christiana* II 10–15, 30–31, III 83–86 (ed. G. M. Green, CSEL 80.36–37, 41–42, 101–102). For the direct influence of Augustine's *De doctrina* upon Bonaventure's exegesis, see, for example, *Breviloquium* Prol. 6 (*Opera* V 208–208).

[28] On the role of the 'seminal reasons' in Bonaventure's thought, see the lucid account in E. Gilson, *The Philosophy of St. Bonaventure* (trans. I. Trethowan and F. J. Sheed; Paterson, N.J. 1965) 265–83. I hope that the significance of these analogies will become clear in the course of my study.

reading of the book of Genesis. Even when students of natural philosophy do not presume to trespass theology, they cannot comprehend the workings of nature unless they are guided constantly by the light of revealed wisdom. It is precisely the philosophers' reversal of this order which Bonaventure attacks in *Collatio* XIX.[29] Turning first to the appearances of the natural world and only afterward, if at all, seeking to corroborate their opinions with Scripture, the philosophers turn wine into water.

Bonaventure's judgment on this matter was not new, nor does it seem to have been only a practical, cautious response to the excesses of the artists at the University of Paris in the 1270s. In a remarkable question in his commentary on the *Sentences* (1250–1252), Bonaventure fully expresses the reasons underlying his conviction that Scripture provides the only sure means for understanding nature. This question so directly anticipates his hexaemeral commentary, and so deeply penetrates to the heart of his teaching, that it requires close comment here. Moreover, the question is germane to Bonaventure's understanding of the correspondence between the greater and smaller, the material and spiritual worlds.

In II *Sent* d. 12 a. 1 q. 2,[30] Bonaventure addresses the question 'Utrum materia producta sit in perfecta actualitate?'; that is, were material things created in the full actuality of their specific forms, or was matter first created, in some sense, unformed? Within the context of Peter Lombard's *Sentences*, this question involves a more fundamental theological one: did God, as he was clearly able, create all things simultaneously or did he create them through an interval of time?[31] This question, in turn, entails an exegetical one: must one interpret the account of creation in Genesis literally, as having taken place over six temporal days? For the theologians of the schools, the questions of the formation of prime matter and the nature of divine revelation were inextricably bound up together.

In the dialectic manner of the schools, Bonaventure first cites sets of contrary opinions, in this instance first noting arguments which his conclusion will oppose (*ad oppositum*), and then those upon which he will base his determination (*fundamenta*). Thus, he first cites scriptural texts which would seem to affirm the simultaneous creation of things (*ad opp.* 1–3; for example, *ad opp.* 2: 'Qui vivit in aeternum creavit omnia simul,' Ecclesiasticus 18.1). Descending from authority to reason, Bonaventure refers to the following arguments. An effect ought to express the nature of its cause; the simultaneous creation of

---

[29] *In Hex.* XIX: title 'De tertia visione tractatio septima et ultima, quae agit de recta via et ratione, qua fructus Scripturae percipiantur, sive qua per scientiam et sanctitatem ad sapientiam perveniatur' (Opera V 419–24).

[30] *In II Sent.* d.12 a.1 q.2 (*Opera* II 295–98).

[31] Cf. Peter Lombard, II *Sent.* d.12 (*Bonaventurae Opera* II 290).

all things more befits the divine power than a successive creation of them (*ad opp.* 4). According to Aristotle, the mark of wisdom is perfect order; confusion, in this case the existence of matter lacking the distinctions of forms, is contrary to order, and therefore to wisdom (which we believe God to be) (*ad opp.* 5). The perfection of an effect attests the perfect goodness of its efficient cause; if God is perfect goodness, it would seem fitting that he create all material things fully perfected (actualized) in (specific) form, since he was able to do so, and matter required it (*ad opp.* 6). We should note that Bonaventure orders opposing arguments according to the triad: power, wisdom, and goodness.

All of these arguments presume an Aristotelian theory of the relation between form and matter, and all of them are argued in terms of what presumably most befits the divine nature, the omnipotence of the first cause. Bonaventure's contrary arguments (*fundamenta*) exactly balance their opposites. From authority he asserts the opinion held by many saints and doctors, Greek and Latin (Chrysostom, Ambrose, Jerome, Gregory, Dionysius, John Damascene), that 'quod simul exstitit per substantiam materiae non simul apparuit per speciem formae' (*fund.* 2). The name of Augustine is notably absent from Bonaventure's list of authorities. It is Bonaventure's first argument from authority (*fund.* 1), however, that defines what to his mind is the central issue of the question, an issue that goes far beyond philosophic questions about cause and effect, form and matter. To counter the more remote scriptural texts seeming to support a simultaneous creation (*ad opp.* 1–3), Bonaventure quotes the text of Genesis declaring 'quod per sex dierum spatium complevit Dominus opus, quod inchoaverat.' Ironically, it turns out, he cites Augustine, who said that the authority of sacred Scripture is greater than all of the keenness of human wit. Responding to what had become a commonplace among those with a philosophic turn of mind, Bonaventure says that it does no good to argue that the lawgiver Moses spoke to ignorant (*rudibus*) men and that he could not speak 'at once' what occurred 'at once.' In other words, neither the ignorance of the audience nor the sequential nature of human language can explain away the letter of Genesis. For precisely because he knew his auditors were ignorant, Moses needed to be careful not to deceive them, or to lead them into error. He knew full well that his words would be understood literally, and thus, if he had spoken otherwise, he would have knowingly risked being the occasion of deceit and error. Furthermore, although it is true that Moses could not speak 'at once' what was done 'at once,' nevertheless he could have said, without confusing his listeners, 'omnia simul facta esse' (*fund.* 1).

However remote from the question the above argument may seen, it contains the seed of Bonaventure's conclusion. Even the arguments which Bonaventure draws from reason (*fund.* 3–6), although they address questions of causality, matter and form more directly, continually circle around questions about revelation. Opposing the idea that the divine power is best expressed by the creation of matter fully actuated by forms, Bonaventure states that the power of God is expressed, not only *in productione formae,* but also, and even more, *in eductione materiae (fund.* 4). (The twofold cadence, here both verbal and conceptual, will run through Bonaventure's whole argument.) The greater the capacity of matter, the more it expresses the power of its efficient cause. Now if matter could subsist in some way unactualized by specific form, in a relatively unformed state *(informitas),* it would seem to have a greater intrinsic capacity, and thus would manifest the divine power more adequately *(fund.* 4). Contrary to the opinion of some,[32] Bonaventure, on this point at least, does not seem consciously to be limiting the inherent power of nature in order to magnify the power of God. Rather, he magnifies God's power by attributing more to nature.

In the above argument Bonaventure relates the question to the divine power; in another he relates it to the divine wisdom *(fund.* 3). Although God was able, Bonaventure says, to establish man immediately in his beatitude, and to arrange or set in place *(collocare)* the universe in its perfection, his wisdom was expressed better otherwise, since order is manifest, not simply in the existence of things, but more efficaciously *(efficacius)* in their course *(decursu)* through time. In the first going forth of things *(in primario rerum exitu),* order was served, not only in the order of their being, but in the order of their making *(fund.* 3).

The implications of this condensed argument are fertile. First, we should observe that Bonaventure relates the creation of unformed prime matter to the mystery of man's beatitude, a relation he will elucidate in the conclusion to the question. Second, we should remark Bonaventure's distinction between an order of existing and an order of making *(producere sive facere).* In distinguishing these orders, Bonaventure conceives God, now as the first cause of the order of being, now as an artist who follows an order of making. The philosopher exclusively attends the first order, the order of cause and effect. To conceive God only as the first cause of existence, however, is inadequate; indeed, his divine nature is revealed more fully in the manner of his creation. For, like a maker, a poet or an orator, God disposes and arranges *(collocare)* his creation to some desired effect. Bonaventure shows the likeness between God and an artist in *De reductione artium ad theologiam.* To produce his artifact, the human artist imitates forms in his mind derived from the natural world, and embodies them in matter disposed to receive them. In creating, the divine artist imitates the exemplars of all things existing in his mind, the Word, and his work of creation is completed and receives its final

---

[32] 'Of two possible conclusions, of which one attributes more to nature or free-will and less to God, while the other more to God at the expense of nature, he will always choose the second ...' (Gilson 432).

perfection when the Word itself becomes flesh.[33] The divine artist, of course, differs from the human artist. The forms which God imitates are not derived from without, and the matter in which he embodies them he has created *ex nihilo*. We might note, nevertheless, that according to Bonaventure's understanding of the sequence of creation, the matter with which God works in creation is in one sense pre-existent, since it exists in time before all other things.

Bonaventure expounds the more specific likeness between God and a poet or orator in the *Breviloquium*. Upon this likeness, we shall see presently, he founds his determination of the immediate question, and his criticism of the inadequacy of philosophy. In the *Breviloquium*, after having shown that the successive ages of the world are revealed in the successive days of creation, Bonaventure declares that the Scriptures and the stages of the world's history which they embrace are ordered like a beautifully composed poem. The great beauty of the *machina mundana*, and the greater beauty and adornment of the Church for which it is a sign, both made manifest in the Scriptures, are ordered to a purpose. Unlike philosophy, which is concerned primarily with truth as an object of the speculative intellect, the science of the Scriptures is ordained first of all to drawing the soul from evil and impelling it toward God. The Scriptures accomplish this by appealing to man's root passions, fear and love. For this purpose, Scripture takes up the book of creation and the diversity of created things, which in their ordered beauty are so many instruments whereby to persuade man to virtue. Because it intends chiefly to persuade, and to appeal to the different capacities of men's minds, Scripture eschews the definition, division, and composition of philosophic discourse, and proceeds instead by examples and the desirable images of future good.[34] In sum, the discourse of the Scriptures is the discourse of an orator, not that of a dialectician. In *De reductione*, Bonaventure subordinates grammar and dialectic to the persuasive end of rhetoric, and states that rhetoric achieves its end through order (*ordinem*) and adornment (*ornatum*).[35] Likewise, as we shall see, the whole world, by means of the ordering and embellishment it receives over the

---

[33] *De reductione artium ad theologiam* 12 (*Opera* V 322–23).

[34] *Breviloquium Prol.* 1–3 and 5 (*Opera* V 203–207).

[35] *De reductione artium* 4 and 17 (*Opera* V 321, 323–24). As we shall see, Bonaventure, *In II Sent.* d.12 a.1 q.2, will amplify his argument by the fourfold reasoning of the spiritual senses, as he does throughout his works. H. Caplan, 'The Four Senses of Scriptural Interpretation and the Medieval Theory of Preaching,' *Speculum* 4 (1929) 282–90, shows that the four senses served as a means both of rhetorical topical invention, and of *dilatatio* and adornment. See the *Ars concionandi* attributed to Bonaventure, cap. 34 (*Opera* IX 17). In composing the world in a persuasive way, God would seem to have amplified and adorned the *machina mundana* by bestowing a fourfold significance upon all of its elements. On Bonaventure's subordination of dialectic to rhetoric, see R. McKeon, 'Rhetoric in the Middle Ages,' *Speculum* 17 (1942) 23–25.

course of time, is an oration moving men to their perfection. Thus if the order of making is 'more efficacious' than the order of existing, it would seem to be so in the way in which a poem or oration is more effective than a philosopher's abstract discourse. Bonaventure's distinction, moreover, seems also to relate to an exegetical one. The order of existence, redundantly enough, pertains to the existence of 'things'; the order of making pertains to their natures as 'signs,' efficacious signs of future redemption.[36]

Finally, we shall note that by means of his distinction Bonaventure implicitly corrects those who, in a philosophic manner, would abstract the question of creation from the question of time. If, like Thomas Aquinas and others, one perceives the relation between creator and creature abstractly as a relation between self-subsistent and dependent being, he may entertain, at least 'philosophically,' the idea that the world is eternal. But the authority of Scripture, which as Augustine says is greater than all the keenness of human wit, flatly contradicts this.

Indeed, in *fundamenta* 5 and 6 Bonaventure redirects the argument to the question of revelation. In *fund.* 6 he again distinguishes among different orders so that he may specify the wisdom manifested in God's creating of the world in six days, literally understood. If God had wished only to express wisdom according to an order of dignity, that is, by establishing an order of being, he would have created man, not the void, on the first day. If he had wished only to express wisdom according to an order of nature, he would have produced the sun and moon before the plants and herbs. He did neither. Rather, following an order of duration, he produced man only on the sixth day, and the plants and herbs before the sun and moon (*fund.* 6). Thus, what we naturally observe — for example, that to grow plants requires the sun — is not necessarily a reliable guide to the manner in which God created the world. Moreover, neither does the hierarchy of being (the order of dignity) wholly reveal God's will; the order of theological *summae* is not the order of sacred Scripture.

It is the truth of Scripture, not so much the nature of matter, that is at stake in this question. This is evident in another argument Bonaventure puts forward (*fund.* 5), the one he takes up first in the conclusion. It is impossible,

---

[36] See *Breviloquium Prol.* 3: '. . . philosophia quidem agit de rebus, ut sunt in natura, seu in anima secundum notitiam naturaliter insitam, vel etiam acquisitam; sed theologia, tanquam scientia supra fidem fundata et per Spiritum sanctum revelata, agit et de eis quae spectant ad gratiam et gloriam et etiam ad Sapientiam aeternum . . . assumens de naturis rerum, quantum sibi opus est ad fabricandum speculum, per quod fiat repraesentatio divinorum' (*Opera* V 205). See also *Prol.* 4: 'Quoniam autem Deus non tantum loquitur per verba, verum etiam per facta, quia ipsius dicere facere est, et ipsius facere dicere; et omnia creata tanquam Dei effectus innuunt suam causam; ideo in Scriptura divinitus tradita non tantum debent significare verba, verum etiam facta' (*Opera* V 206). See the Appendix to this study for further comment on words and things.

Bonaventure says, for material days, by their very definition, to exist simultaneously. Therefore it is impossible to conceive how God could produce all things simultaneously, and likewise in six material days. In order to maintain that creation was at once produced simultaneously and in six days, one must needs, as a famous interpretation would have it, to interpret the six days spiritually (*spiritualiter*), in a way abstracted from time. One might, then, understand the work of the first day, the division of light from darkness, as the dividing between good and bad angels. But if this were true, good and bad angels in the first instant, as it were, would have been distinguished and there would have been no space of time (*mora*) between creation and the fall. Bonaventure ever insists upon the importance of time. He has already rejected the argument that the evil angels fell instantly; furthermore, he notes, this argument contradicts the authority of Augustine[37] (*fund.* 5).

Ironically, however, the spiritual interpretation of the six days which Bonaventure rejects is Augustine's in *De Genesi ad litteram*. In the *fundamenta* Bonaventure argues tacitly that Augustine in *De Genesi* contradicted his own principle: the authority of Scripture is greater than all of the keenness of human wit. The argument becomes explicit in the conclusion. Interpreters of Genesis, Bonaventure says, fall into two camps. Some, pre-eminent among whom is Augustine, follow a 'philosophic way' (*viam philosophicam*); others, some of whom preceded Augustine and some of whom came after him, follow a 'theological way' (*viam theologicam*). The arguments of those who follow a philosophic way, like Augustine, are reasonable and very subtle (*rationabilis et valde subtilis*). In a manner which we have observed, they argue that there was no usefulness or need for God to create the world over a period of six days, and that in truth it ill-suited his exceeding power (*summa potentia*) to do so. More appropriately, he created all things at once. Therefore, one must understand the six days of Genesis to be spiritual days, not material days (*conclusio*). Here the term 'spiritual,' one should note, is used in the philosophic sense, as that which by definition is opposed to matter.

Bonaventure allows that this interpretation seems more consonant with human reason than the interpretation of those who follow the theological way. Nonetheless it is deficient and in the end not truthful. Those following Augustine's philosophic way approve the words of Genesis only insofar as they accord with the judgment of human reason, that is, in the terms of the *In Hexaëmeron*, they reverse the order of wisdom and turn wine into water, bread into stones.[38] On the contrary, those following the theological way draw reason

---

[37] *In* II *Sent.* d. 3 q. 2 a. 1 qq. 1&2 (*Opera* II 112–17).

[38] This motif (see n. 122 below) seems to have Eucharistic overtones. In terms of Bonaventure's exegesis, the 'bread' and 'wine' of the letter are transformed into the 'body' and 'blood' of Christ in the allegorical sense, since the 'Opera reparationis [toward which the sense of allegory always points] cum sint multa, omnia ad Christi oblationem principalem

upward toward those things which are of faith. These submit themselves to the word of Scripture as it sounds. Thus, concerning the question at hand, they are directed to understand that 'omnia corporalia simul esse creata in materia, sed non simul, sed per senarium dierum, esse distincta in forma.'[39] It is the word of Genesis, obviously understood, that causes Bonaventure to reject the Aristotelian theory of the relation of matter and form, and to posit an 'unformed' prime matter (that is, without specific form).

Bonaventure's criticism of Augustine's exegesis could not be more fundamental. The whole enterprise of De Genesi ad litteram is ill-conceived. Augustine clearly conceived the literal in a philosophic way as that which is most compatible with human reasonings. He did not conceive the literal in a grammatical way as the clear, immediate sense of the sacred text. Thus he was constrained to neglect his own axiom concerning the authority of Scripture and the reason of men, and paradoxically did not produce a literal commentary but an accommodating one. His result is a rather good example of the ἁμαρτία of philosophic thought, a theme Bonaventure will develop in the In Hexaëmeron.

Bonaventure does not leave readers of the Sentences with a negative conclusion. Although the conclusion of the theological way, that matter became distinct in its specific forms over a course of six days, seems less reasonable than its philosophic contrary, nevertheless it can be sustained by reason, if one will consider the question under the light of faith (sub lumine fidei). In order to see the reasonableness of the successive formation and distinction of things, one must exercise a fourfold reasoning: literal, moral, allegorical, and anagogic.[40]

The form Bonaventure's argument will take is evident. Just as, according to a descending order of light and wisdom, the light of the letter of Scripture must illumine our reasonings about nature, so the letter of Scripture is itself determined or confirmed from above, by the spiritual senses. Only when the meaning of Genesis is considered in all its senses does the reasonableness of the letter, stating that God created the world in six material days, become manifest. Bonaventure's favorite scriptural text, 'Every good gift and every perfect gift is from above, coming down from the Father of Lights' (Jac. 1.17),[41] applies in every instance to the formation of matter, to the reading of Scripture. Even

---

habent aspectum' (Breviloquium Prol. 4 [Opera V 205]). The philosophers would seem then to 'desacramentalize' the letter, and thereby degrade the substance of bread into stones, wine into water. For the medieval theme of the 'two tables,' Scripture and the Eucharist, see J. Leclercq, F. Vandenbroucke, and L. Bouyer, The Spirituality of the Middle Ages (trans. the Benedictines of Holme Eden Abbey; London 1968) 303.

[39] In II Sent. d. 12 a. 1 q. 2 concl. (Opera II 296).

[40] In II Sent. d. 12 a. 1 q. 2 concl. (Opera II 297).

[41] For example, Itinerarium Prol. 1 (Opera V 295); Breviloquium Prol. (Opera V 201); De reductione artium 1 (Opera V 319 et passim); In Hex. II 1 (Opera V 336).

in the last half of the thirteenth century, in a school commentary on the *Sentences*, the theological way is said to be the way of the ancient exegesis. A literary critic has spoken of self-consuming artifacts;[42] Bonaventure's commentary on the *Sentences* would seem to be one of these.

Bonaventure proceeds to determine the various, yet concordant senses of the Genesis text. Literally, we should understand that God in creating the world intended to do not only what he was able (establish an order of being), but also to communicate (by means of an order of making) to the human creature what he was yet able to receive. Thus, even though God could have given man beatitude without his meriting it, nevertheless he did not choose to do so, but wished rather that man might freely choose and merit his beatitude. In the same way, God created matter lacking its final perfection of form, so that by reason of its lack of form and imperfection (*informitate et imperfectione*), matter might, as it were, cry out (*clamaret*)[43] for its perfection. God chose to effect this gradual perfection over a course of six days because six, the sum and multiple of its integers, is the perfect number.[44]

Bonaventure sustains his literal interpretation, referring to creation, by reference to the mystery of redemption. In other words, the allegorical sense confirms the reasonableness of the letter. Embedded in Bonaventure's argument is the notion, to which we have alluded, that God's purpose in creating was not simply metaphysical, to establish an order of being which he could have done in any manner, but rhetorical as well: to teach, move, and delight man in such a way as to persuade him to his final perfection. Elsewhere in his commentary on the *Sentences* Bonaventure says as much. Having stated philosophic reasons demonstrating that all sensible things were created on account of man (man's being mediates between God's being and the being of all other sensible creatures), Bonaventure enumerates further reasons of a different kind. In the state of innocence God subordinated sensible creatures to man *ad manifestandum eius imperium*, so that man might learn, by the creature's obedience, the nature of his sovereignty. Likewise, God subordinated sensible creatures to man *ad excitandum hominis sensum*, so that man might learn, by means of the diverse natures of animals, about the 'multiformity of the wisdom of the creator' (*multiformitatem sapientiae Conditoris*). Further, God subordinated sensible creatures to man

---

[42] S. E. Fish, *Self-Consuming Artifacts: The Experience of Seventeenth-Century Literature* (Berkeley 1972) esp. 21–43 for an analysis of Augustine on signs and things.

[43] Might this allude to Romans 8.22–23 ? 'Scimus enim quod omnis creatura ingemiscit et parturit usque adhuc; non solum autem illa, sed et nos ipsi primitias Spiritus habentes, et ipsi intra nos geminus adoptionem filiorum Dei expectantes, redemptionem corporis nostri.'

[44] *In* II *Sent.* d. 12 a. 1 q. 2 *concl.* (*Opera* II 297).

. . . ad movendum eius affectum, ut dum homo videret, animalia secundum rectitudinem suae naturae currere et amare illud ad quod naturaliter facta sunt, ex hoc excitaretur ad amandum Deum.

Again, God subordinated sensible creatures to man *ad decorandum hominis habitaculum*, so that man might delight in the manifold adornment of his abode.[45]

As we might expect, Bonaventure in his interpretation of the six days according to the moral sense again stresses the rhetorical purpose of God's creation. In that matter as matter (*per se*) existed first in an unformed state and then over a course of six days received through the divine goodness the perfection of various forms, man is instructed as to his own condition, wherein the soul *per se ipsam* is not able to attain its final perfection until God infuses in it his grace. The final form which perfects human nature, Bonaventure states, is the 'consummation of final grace,' and this perfection occurs gradually over time, according to the six ages of man's life in the present world.[46] On the one hand, according to the analogy with prime matter it would seem that the potency of human nature is not fully actualized until its perfection in grace; on the other, human nature, like prime matter, has a certain 'unformed' mode of existing *per se* before receiving the infusion of grace.

In his allegorical and anagogic interpretations of the six days, Bonaventure multiplies the concordances of the number six which will pervade the *In Hexaëmeron*. Allegorically, the six days of the world's first founding foreshadow the history of the world's redemption in six ages. Anagogically, one may at last accept Augustine's interpretation, whereby the distinction of the six days refers to the gradual perfection of knowledge in the beatified angelic nature. We are now able to understand better the error of Augustine's *De Genesi ad litteram*: what was in fact the anagogic sense Augustine called literal, turning the proper order of the senses, according to man's reception of them, upside down. In doing so, he seemed to forget what he himself had taught in the *Confessiones*: 'quod una et eadem Scriptura multipliciter potest intelligi, et in omnibus sensibus vere.'[47] In his 'philosophical' interpretation of Genesis Augustine anticipates the presumption of the artists in the thirteenth century. Bonaventure does not further specify Augustine's error, but it is apparent that Augustine did not seek to do what Bonaventure has done, achieve a concordance of the senses wherein no sense contradicts another, and wherein each sense is shown to be true in the way proper to it.

Bonaventure's *responsiones* to the initial arguments *ad oppositum* provide a kind of peroration to the question. The idea that God's purpose in creating

---

[45] *In* II *Sent.* d. 15 a. 2 q. 1 *concl.* (383).
[46] *In* II *Sent.* d. 12 a. 1 q. 2 *concl.* (297).
[47] *In* II *Sent.* d. 12 a. 1 q. 2 *concl.* (297). The editors cite *Confessiones* 12.18–32.

was rhetorical is again central. Responding to the argument that the divine power is best manifested through a simultaneous creation, Bonaventure replies that God's power was expressed in the production of being from non-being, not so much in its subsequent formation. The latter act manifested rather God's wisdom and goodness. After the *opus creationis*, manifesting his power, God wrought an *opus distinctionis*, showing forth his widom. Finally, he manifested his goodness in an *opus ornatus et decorationis*.[48] This is the Bonaventure of the symbolic works, who teaches that the images or *vestigia* of the Trinity, of the Father's power, the Son's wisdom, the Spirit's goodness, are everywhere stamped on the face of creation and are intrinsic to it.[49] The God whom Bonaventure sees at work in the six days is the God whose highest name is goodness, the God who reveals himself to man in the incarnate, crucified Christ and who perfects man in the Spirit. This is the vision of chapter 6 of the *Itinerarium*. At best, the philosophers attain only the vision of chapter 5, the vision of a God whose name is being and who is the one cause of many effects.[50] Bonaventure concludes his question by affirming that God indeed handed over the Scriptures to men in an unformed and, as it were, inappropriate way (*quasi rudi modo et inepto*). He did so because he wished that ignorant hearers of the word might be able to comprehend the *infiniti thesauri sapientiae et scientiae* in Christ. Likewise in the formation of things (first unformed) in his desire to communicate to men in the terms of their own temporal nature, God, like a good preacher, accommodated himself to his intended audience. In the creation of nature itself, as well as in the report of that act in Genesis, God 'condescendit modo naturae et etiam eruditioni rationalis creaturae.'[51]

---

[48] *In* II *Sent.* d. 12 a. 1 q. 2 *sol. opp.* 4, 5, 6 (298). Might these three orders correspond to the rhetorical *inventio* (the discovery of *res*), *dispositio* (see Appendix), and *elocutio* (where traditionally the figures of *ornatus* are treated)?

[49] See, for example, *Itinerarium* I 14 (*Opera* V 299); *Breviloquium* II 1 and 2 (*Opera* V 219, 220). The idea pervades the *Collationes*.

[50] *Itinerarium* V–VI (*Opera* V 308–12). God's nature is best expressed in his desire to communicate (*communicare*). He is the *summa communicabilitas*, the *summa communicatio et vera diffusio* (*Itinerarium* VI 3 [Opera V 311]). The latter phrase indicates the analogy between light and the divine goodness.

[51] *In* II *Sent.* d. 12 a. 1 q. 2 *sol. opp.* 4, 5, 6 (*Opera* II 298). Throughout this question, Bonaventure draws terms from rhetorical tradition. *Rudis* usually signifies uncultivated or formless speech. See Cicero, *Brutus* 85.294 (ed. Wilkins); *De oratore* 1.2.5 (ed. Wilkins); Quintilian, *Institutio oratoria* 3.1.5; 9.4.17–18 (ed. M. Winterbottom [Oxford 1970] 130, 538). The term *ineptus* is closely related to *rudis*. It refers to one whose speech is tactless and inappropriate. See Cicero *De oratore* 2.4.17–18 and *Orator* 67.226 (ed. Wilkins). Bonaventure's use of the term suggests that the manner of God's creation is inappropriate considered in relation to his power, but not inappropriate considered in relation to the audience. Throughout the rhetorical tradition, *eruditio* signifies the comprehensive knowledge of words and things necessary for one who would unite wisdom and eloquence, and one who possesses

I

Intervening between Augustine's and Bonaventure's literal interpretations is Hugh of St. Victor's *De sacramentis*, from which Bonaventure derived his method of exegesis as well as his resolution of this particular question (see Appendix). We must now summarize the teaching of Bonaventure in II *Sent.* d. 2 a. q. 2 in a way that looks forward to the *In Hexaëmeron* and its doctrine of the cardinal virtues. As unformed prime matter 'cries out' for its perfection through subsequent forms, and as the letter of Scripture awaits the completion of its meaning, even its confirmation as letter, by the spiritual sense, so reason awaits its illumination by revelation, the book of creatures awaits the light of the book of Scripture, and in general rational creatures await their perfection in grace. Moreover, as unformed matter is potent to a succession of higher forms and is first distinguished into the four elements, then into the mixtures of various bodies, and finally disposed to receive a spiritual soul,[52]

---

such encyclopaedic knowledge is *eruditus*. See Cicero, *De oratore* 1.22.102–103; *Brutus* 67.236; *De officiis* 1.33 (Loeb 120–21); Quintilian, *Inst. orat.* 1.4.6; 6.3.17 (ed. cit. 23, 339) (opposite to *rusticitas*). God's creative work conducts ignorant listeners (*rudes*) to knowledge (*eruditio*). For the rough eloquence of Scripture, which however instructs (*erudire*) to beatitude, see Augustine, *De doctrina* IV 27–28 (CSEL 80.124). The term *eruditio*, in its fullest significance, occurs in the title of Hugh of St. Victor's work, *Eruditio Didascalia*. On the influence of Hugh's *Didascalicon* upon Bonaventure's concept of wisdom, see Bougerol, *Introduction* 38, and Roger Baron, 'L'Influence d'Hugues de Saint-Victor,' *RThAM* 22 (1955) 56–71. Encyclopaedic erudition in the Middle Ages centered on the work of six days; see R. Collison, *Encyclopaedias: Their History Throughout the Ages* (New York 1964) 44–81. The word *thesaurus* is commonly used by rhetoricians to signify the abundance of words, things, and topics stored in the eloquent orator's memory. See Cicero, *De oratore* 1.5.18, and Quintilian, *Inst. orat.* 11.2.1–2 (ed. cit. 642). Bonaventure here quotes the term in a scriptural text, but Christian rhetoricians habitually accommodated this text to an analogy with abundance in rhetorical invention. See the introduction to my translation of Benet of Canfield, *The Rule of Perfection* (forthcoming). Bonaventure's term, *collocare (fund.* 3), also has strong rhetorical overtones. God's exact arrangement of created signs over a sequence of six days is similar to the rhetorician's *collocatio verborum*, wherein if a precise order of words is changed, a certain symmetry is lost, even though the *sententia* remains the same. See Cicero, *Orator* 24.80–81. Bonaventure several times states that God could have created the world in any manner (the fact remains), but that he ordered his effects carefully over six days in view of sixfold concordances. Cicero says that the *collocatio verborum* is one of the primary species of *ornatus*. Finally, in *De reductione artium* 16 (*Opera* V 323), Bonaventure explains God's ultimate 'condescension' to man by analogy to speech. As a speaker clothes the concept of his mind (*verbum mentis*) in material sound (*vox*) in order to communicate it to another, so the eternal Word became flesh, so that he might be known by men endowed with senses. In becoming flesh the Word does not depart from the bosom of the Father, any more than a concept when uttered in speech leaves the mind. See Augustine, *De doctrina* I 26 (CSEL 80. 14–15).

[52] *In* II *Sent* d. 12 a. 1 q. 3 *concl.*; d. 13 *div. text.*; d. 14 p. 1 *div. text.*; d. 15 a. 1 q. 1 *concl.*; d. 15 a. 1 q. 2; d. 17 a. 2 q. 2; d. 18 a. 1 q. 3 (*Opera* II 300, 310, 335, 374, 377–78, 414–26, 442).

a potency influenced at every stage by light,[53] so the human virtues are potent to, incomplete without, and await their perfection by higher forms of grace and charity. Bonaventure states the analogy expressly elsewhere in his commentary on the *Sentences*.[54] These correspondences between greater and smaller worlds, between the formation of matter and the perfection of the virtues in man's soul, are not imaginary. Their reality in the nature of things is guaranteed by God's revealed, creative purpose: to communicate with man, to teach, move, and delight him by means of his works and days.

The question from the *Sentences* which we have analyzed illumines the symbolic concordances, or 'beautiful pictures' as Anselm called them in a different but related context,[55] of the *In Hexaëmeron*. There Bonaventure discovers a profusion of likenesses for the cardinal virtues. One cannot treat these likenesses in isolation, for they are founded in the created natures of things and in the truth of the Word. In the first conference of the *In Hexaëmeron* Bonaventure declares:

> . . . haec est tota nostra metaphysica: de emanatione, de exemplaritate, de consummatione, scilicet illuminari per radios spirituales et reduci ad summam. Et sic eris verus metaphysicus.[56]

Bonaventure attributes this threefold activity to the three persons of the Trinity, emanation to the Father, exemplarity to the Son, and consummation to the Holy Spirit.[57] The second person is the mean between each of God's three operations and the created world. Christ is the *Verbum increatum*, in whom all things are made; the *Verbum inspiratum*, in whom the truth of all things shines and is known; and the *Verbum incarnatum*, through whom all things return to their origin in God.[58] Since true metaphysics consists in emanation, exemplarity, and consummation, and since Christ is the mean of all these operations, there is no true philosophy without its center in Christ. In his sermon *Christus unus omnium magister*, Bonaventure expresses God's relation to the world in different but parallel terms. As Augustine teaches, 'Deus est causa essendi, ratio intelligendi et ordo vivendi.'[59] Throughout his works, as

---

[53] *In II Sent.* d. 2 p. 2 a. 2 q. 1 *sol. opp.* 1, 2 (light of empyrean influences all below); d. 13 *div. text.* (light the form of prime matter); d. 13 a. 1 q. 1 *sol. opp.* 4; d. 13 a. 2 q. 2 *fund.* 4 (light educes the forms of animal and vegetable souls); d. 13 a. 3 q. 2 *concl.* (light educes the act of the senses, presides over generation of minerals) (*Opera* II 75, 310, 313, 319, 328); *Breviloquium* II 4 (*Opera* V 221).

[54] *In III Sent.* d. 27 a. 1 q. 3 *sol. opp.* 1 (*Opera* III 598).

[55] *Cur Deus homo* I 3–4 (*S. Anselmi Opera omnia* [ed. F. S. Schmitt; Edinburgh 1946] II 51 lines 3–18).

[56] *In Hex.* I 17 (*Opera* V 332).

[57] A. Schaefer, 'The Position and Function of Man in the Created World According to St. Bonaventure,' *Franciscan Studies* 20 (1960) 262–70.

[58] *In Hex.* III 2 (*Opera* V 343).

[59] *Sermo* IV 17 (*Opera* V 572).

we have seen in II *Sent.* d. 12 a. 1 q. 2, Bonaventure maintains a strict analogy among the orders of being, knowing, and right living. Intellectual truth conforms to the order of being and right living to the truth of the intellect, so that, as Augustine says, unless a creature conform to his exemplar in the divine mind, his life is a lie.[60] Within this network of reciprocal and dependent orders, the stones themselves speak to man's moral condition. Bonaventure places his discussion of the cardinal virtues in the *visio* of the first day, governed by the scriptural text 'God saw that the light was good. God separated the light from darkness' (Gen. 1.4–5). In *Collatio* VI Bonaventure establishes a series of correspondences pertaining to the cardinal virtues. Borrowing an analogy from Gregory the Great,[61] he asserts that human life revolves around the axes of the four virtues, just as the sun manifests itself differently in the four dimensions of the earth. The virtues also correspond to the four effects of light, which cleanses, illumines, reconciles, and confirms. Moreover, the cardinal virtues, as in Grosseteste, correspond to the four elements. Temperance, like the earth, is dry and adorned with flowers. Prudence, the virtue pertaining to the practical intellect, like water is translucent to light. Justice is sweet like the air, and fortitude, as a text from Canticles (8.6) suggests, is like fire.[62]

In most of these correspondences one may discern a common pattern, an interplay between material properties and light. For now, we shall focus attention upon the correspondence between the cardinal virtues and the four elements. With the aid of modern iconographical studies, one may see how this analogy developed within the exegetical tradition, in which authors discovered various relations among the four evangelists, the four rivers of paradise, the four elements, and the four virtues.[63] By the tenth century one writer had made all of these analogies in one encyclopedic chapter of tetrads.[64] For Bonaventure's analogy between virtues and elements, however, there would seem to be a more immediate source. Odon Lottin has demonstrated that Philip the Chancellor was the primary source for the scholastic treatment of the virtues by Bonaventure and two of his Franciscan predecessors, Odo Rigaud and John of La Rochelle. In his treatise on the virtues, Philip alludes to a certain Harialdus, whose works are unknown, who taught that just as the health of the body requires an agreement of equality among the four elements, so the health of the soul requires the same among the four virtues.[65]

---

[60] *In Hex.* III 8–9 (*Opera* V 344–45).

[61] Gregory the Great, *Hom. in Ezech.* 3 (PL 76.808–809).

[62] *In Hex.* VI 7 (*Opera* V 362–63).

[63] E. S. Greenhill, *Die geistigen Voraussetzungen der Bilderreiche des Speculum virginum: Versuch einer Deutung* (BGPhMA 39, 2; Münster 1962); R. E. McNally, 'The Evangelists in the Hiberno-Latin Tradition,' in *Festschrift Bernhard Bischoff* (Stuttgart 1971) 111–22.

[64] Radolphus Glaber, *Historiae sui temporis* (PL 142.613–14).

[65] O. Lottin, *Psychologie et morale aux XIIᵉ et XIIIᵉ siècles* III 1 (Gembloux 1949) 175–76.

Furthermore, Bonaventure, in his commentary on the *Sentences* and in the *Breviloquium*, also follows Philip's lead in teaching that whereas the theological virtues pertain to man's purely spiritual acts, the cardinal virtues pertain to his earthly and bodily acts.[66] Whence the appropriateness of analogies drawn from the properties of the material world.

Whatever one may think of them, Bonaventure, for reasons which we have stated, thought his correspondences to be real, inhering in the nature of things. He says that the cardinal virtues are so noble that the disposition of the world corresponds to them.[67] The reality of this correspondence, of course, presupposes the reality of the more general one between *maior* and *minor mundi*, as it did for Grosseteste. One can be guided in his moral life by the workings of creatures, then, but not without qualification. Adopting terms taken directly from Hugh of St. Victor, Bonaventure in the *Breviloquium* speaks of God's revelation to man in two books, the book of creatures and the book of Scripture. Before the fall, the book of creatures sufficed to reveal God to Adam. By nature Adam possessed three eyes, one of the flesh, one of reason, and one of contemplation. As a consequence of the fall, however, the eye of contemplation was shut and the eye of reason impaired. Thus, fallen man requires a more definitive revelation in the book of Scripture, since for him the book of creatures is as a work written in Hebrew letters. Only by means of the light shining in Scripture can man once again begin to decipher the signs of God in created nature. Consequently, reason without divine illumination, metaphysics without Christ, is bound to go awry. It is the book of Scripture that restores the book of creatures to our vision. It does so because even though Scripture refers primarily to the work of reparation, it nevertheless refers also to the work of foundation, since the restoration of all things cannot be understood adequately unless the manner of their creation be first understood.[68] In light of Bonaventure's careful argument in his commentary on the *Sentences*, the most obvious sense of these metaphoric terms cannot easily be dismissed. No less than Moses when speaking to the Hebrews, one must be careful never to mislead his readers, even when writing a simple *compendium* of doctrine.

We have remarked the imagery of light in Bonaventure's series of correspondences to the cardinal virtues. For Bonaventure, as for Grosseteste,[69]

---

[66] Lottin, *op. cit.* 180–83.

[67] 'Hae sunt tantae nobilitas, quod dispositio mundi his correspoṅdet,' *In Hex.* VI 20 (*Opera* V 363). Synan (32 n. 39) remarks that the other redaction states the reverse: 'Sunt iterum hae virtutes tantae veritatis et ordinis, ut mundi dispositionibus correspondeant,' *In Hex. Vis.* 1 *Coll.* III 20 (ed. Delorme 96).

[68] *Breviloquium* II 5, 12 (*Opera* V 222–24, 229–30). See Hugh of St. Victor, *De sacramentis christianae fidei* I pt. 6 5–6; pt. 10 2 (PL 176.266–68, 327–31).

[69] Grosseteste, *De luce seu inchoatione formarum* (ed. L. Baur, *Die philosophischen Werke des Robert Grosseteste* [BGPhMA 9; Münster 1912] esp. 51–52). For the influence of Grosssteste on Bonaventure's theory of light, see Gilson 251–59.

light is the underlying principle of the created world. By its nature, like the divine goodness for which it is an analogue, light is diffusive, spreading from the highest heavenly bodies, where it is in most act and least potency, to the lowest physical bodies, where it is most obscure, in least act and most potency.[70] Consistent with his rejection of Augustine's spiritual interpretation of the six days, Bonaventure holds that the light created on the first day is material.[71] This material light is not a body, but rather a certain form of all bodiliness.[72] It is this form that provides the minimal act of the prime matter created on the first day.[73] All subsequent corporeal bodies, then, possess at least two forms: light, the general form of all bodies, and one or more specific forms or compositions of the material elements. Within the hierarchy of being, the dignity of physical bodies is determined by the degree to which they participate in the common form of light. The greater the degree to which this common form is actualized within the body and not obscured by the potency of matter, the greater the dignity of the body.[74] Within the sequence of creation, the production of the four elements represents the first specifications of prime matter. In turn, more and more refined compositions of the elements represent greater and greater actualizations of matter's potency — greater and greater reflections of the light that binds together the universe.[75]

Like all other bodies, and in an especially dignified manner since it is ordained to the information of a rational soul, the human body participates in the common form of light. Moreover, like all sublunary bodies, the human body is composed of a mixture of the four elements. In this instance retaining Aristotle's cosmology, Bonaventure modifies Augustine's and Grosseteste's[76] teaching that light inheres in the human composite as a medium disposing the material elements for their union with the spiritual soul. Since light is the incorruptible quintessence of the universe, inhering properly in the heavenly bodies, it cannot enter into immediate composition with corruptible material elements. Nevertheless, since by their nature the four elements are contrary among themselves, they could not enter some form of unity unless they should be held in order by something that transcends their contrariety. This something is the light of the three heavenly spheres, which remotely influences the

---

[70] *In II Sent* d. 2 p. 2 a. 1 q. 1 *fund.* 4 *concl.*; d. 13 *div. text.*; d. 13 a. 2 q. 1 *fund.* 6 *concl. sol. opp.* 5, 6 (*Opera* II 310, 73–74, 310, 317–22); *Breviloquium* II 3 (*Opera* V 220–21).

[71] *In II Sent.* d. 13 a. 1 q. 1 *concl.* (*Opera* II 312–13).

[72] *In II Sent.* d. 13 *div. text.*; d. 13 a. 2 q. 1 (*Opera* II 310, 317–18).

[73] *In II Sent.* d. 12 a. 1 q. 3 *concl.*; d. 12 a. 2 q. 1 *arg. pro aff.* 1–4; d. 13 *div. text.* (*Opera* II 300–302, 310).

[74] *In II Sent.* d. 2 p. 2 q. 2 *fund.* 4 *concl.*; d. 13 a. 2 q. 1 *fund.* 6 *concl. sol. opp.* 5–6 (*Opera* II 73–74, 319–22).

[75] See notes 52 and 53.

[76] Grosseteste, *De intelligentiis* (ed. Baur 116).

four elements of the human body, reconciling them in a fit order. In this way the human body participates in the quintessence of light, for by its influence the light of the heavenly bodies produces in all terrestial bodies a certain proportion, or 'equality,' among the elements. This proportion becomes more perfect in bodies as they ascend the hierarchical order of being. The most perfect equality or balance of elements is found in the human body. Bonaventure points out that this equality must be construed not as one of weight, *a pondere*, but as one of justice, *a iustitia*, a certain right order.[77] The human body, comprising the four elements and partaking more than other bodies of the light of the three heavenly spheres, is the subject wherein all terrestrial bodies, as in an intelligible circle, find their end.[78]

In the composition of his body, man, the *minor mundus*, recapitulates the entire material universe. But the universe is not only material. As we shall see, the relation between light and the elements finds its analogue in the moral order of the virtues, the *ordo vivendi*. For now we should note that the justice reconciling the elements does not subsist properly in them, but is the effect of light descending from above. In the midst of his discourses concerning material light, Bonaventure states the principle which gives correspondences between material and spiritual orders their reality. The name 'light,' he says, is predicated properly of God and spiritual realities, but analogously of corporal things.[79] Physical reality, whose quintessence is light, is a metaphor for God, who is light *per se*, and for his spiritual creatures, including the rational human soul. What is said metaphorically about the light that effects justice among the elements is more true when predicated of the divine light which creates justice among the virtues. Bonaventure affirms the common scholastic adage that knowledge begins in the senses, but he does so less under the influence of Aristotle than under the influence of the pseudo-Dionysius Areopagita, who taught that through an understanding of material light one might rise to an understanding of the truer, spiritual light.[80]

Not surprisingly, the action of light in the material world has another analogue in the order of knowing, upon which the order of right living is based. We cannot here confront all the thorny questions concerning Bonaventure's controverted theory of intellectual illumination.[81] We shall attempt only to relate Bonaventure's teaching on this point to its analogues in the orders of being and right living. As a *minor mundus* of the material world, the human body

---

[77] *In* II *Sent.* d. 17 a. 2 q. 2 *concl.*; d. 17 a. 2 q. 3 (*Opera* II 422–23, 425); *Breviloquium* II 4 (*Opera* V 226).

[78] *Breviloquium* II 3 (*Opera* V 220–21).

[79] *In* II *Sent.* d. 13 a. 1 q. 1 *ad opp.* 3 *sol. opp.* 3 (*Opera* II 310, 313).

[80] *In* II *Sent.* d. 13 a. 1 q. 1 *sol. opp.* 3 (313).

[81] The most faithful account of Bonaventure's teaching on this point is C. Bérubé, *De la philosophie à la sagesse chez Saint Bonaventure et Roger Bacon* (Rome 1976).

is perfectly adapted for conducting the sensible realities of the greater world
to the soul. The material world enters the soul through the gates of the five
senses:

> Homo igitur, qui dicitur minor mundus, habet quinque sensus quasi quinque
> portas, per quas intrat cognitio omnium, quae sunt in mundo sensibili, in
> animam ipsius. Nam per visum intrant corpora sublimia et luminosa et
> cetera colorata, per tactum vero corpora solida et terrestria, per tres vero
> sensus intermedios intrant intermedia, ut per gustum aquea, per auditum
> aërea, per odoratum vaporabilia, quae aliquid habent de natura humida,
> aliquid de aërea, aliquid de ignea seu calida, sicut patet in fumo ex aromati-
> bus resoluto.

In this passage from the *Itinerarium*, as elsewhere,[82] Bonaventure achieves a
correspondence between the five substances of the universe, light and the four
elements, and the five senses. From the similitudes and phantasms of these
things entered through the senses, reason abstracts their essence, free from
particularity of place, time, and change. By its own light, however, human
reason is incapable of judging the truth of what it abstracts. This is so because
'nothing is absolutely immutable and unlimited in time and space unless it
is eternal, and everything that is eternal is either God or in God.'[83] Thus, only
in God, the light of truth, and in his divine ideas do all things shine forth in an
infallible way that admits no doubt or limitation of space and time.[84] The
divine ideas are the eternal art through which all things, in the order of being
(*opus conditionis*) and in the order of making (*opus distinctionis*) are created
and directed toward their end. Only in the light of the divine ideas can those
things which enter through the senses be judged correctly,

> quia, ut dicit Augustinus, 'nullus de eis iudicat, sed per illas': necesse est,
> eas esse incommutabiles et incorruptibiles tanquam necessarias, incoarcta-
> biles tanquam incircumscriptas, interminabiles tanquam aeternas, ac per
> hoc indivisibiles tanquam intellectuales et incorporeas, non factas, sed in-
> creatas, aeternaliter existentes in arte aeterna, a qua, per quam et secundum
> quam formantur formosa omnia; et ideo nec certitudinaliter iudicari possunt
> nisi per illam quae non tantum fuit forma cuncta producens, verum etiam
> cuncta conservans et distinguens, tanquam ens in omnibus formam tenens et
> regula dirigens, et per quam diiudicat mens nostra cuncta, quae per sensus
> intrant in ipsam.[85]

Every true act of knowledge, even of natural things, requires the illumination
of the divine ideas. As they cause and direct the things of the natural world,

---

[82] *Itinerarium* II 2 (*Opera* V 300) and *De reductione artium* 3 (*Opera* V 320). See the fine
article by J. McEvoy, 'Microcosm and Macrocosm in the Writings of St. Bonaventure,'
in *S. Bonaventura, 1274-1974* II 309–43.

[83] *Itinerarium* II 9 (*Opera* V 301–302).

[84] *Itinerarium* II 9 (302).

[85] *Itinerarium* II 9 (302).

so their light moves, regulates, measures, and directs our comprehension of them.[86] The light of the divine ideas, in short, is the *ratio intelligendi*. And just as the justice of the four elements in bodies is effected by a light from above, so the right measure or rectitude of our thought, abstracted from various compositions of the elements, is effected through illumination of the divine ideas.

Since divine illumination never ceases to influence the mind, and since it is the foundation of all intellectual knowledge, the problem of error is largely a moral one. Our understanding of natural things requires the illumination of the divine Word, just as our sight of many and varied colors requires the illumination of the sun.[87] Bonaventure borrows this simile, possibly through an intermediary, from Robert Grosseteste.[88] Grosseteste teaches that the morally impure see the light of truth only as it is dispersed in the multitude and variety of created things; only the pure of heart can see the light of truth in itself. In the *Itinerarium* Bonaventure transfers the moral emphasis, I believe, from personal to original sin, to the general condition of the fallen intellect:

> Mira igitur est caecitas intellectus, qui non considerat illud quod prius videt et sine quo nihil est potest cognoscere. Sed sicut oculus intentus in varias colorum differentias lucem, per quam videt cetera, non videt, et si videt, non advertit; sic oculus mentis nostrae, intentus in entia particularia et universalia, ipsum esse extra omne genus, licet primo occurrat menti, et per ipsum alia, tamen non advertit. Unde verissime apparet, quod 'sicut oculus vespertilionis se habet ad lucem, ita se habet oculus mentis nostrae ad manifestissima naturae': quia assuefactus ad tenebras entium et phantasmata sensibilium, cum ipsam lucem summi esse intuetur, videtur sibi nihil videre; non intelligens, quod ipsa caligo summa est mentis nostrae illuminatio, sicut, quando videt oculus puram lucem, videtur sibi nihil videre.[89]

We shall remember that as a consequence of the fall the eye of contemplation is closed. Later in the *Itinerarium* Bonaventure teaches that the darkness of mystical theology is in fact a superabundance of divine light,[90] or in the terms of this passage, the *pura lux* which we perceive as darkness or nothing. We shall also remember that as a consequence of the fall the eye of reason is impaired, because, as it would seem in the terms of this passage, it has become wholly habituated *ad tenebras entium et phantasmata sensibilium*. The only remedy to the impairment of reason's vision, let alone our contemplative blind-

---

[86] *Quaestiones disputatae de scientia Christi* IV 22–23 (*Opera* V 572).

[87] *In Hex.* III 8–9 (*Opera* V 344–45).

[88] Grosseteste, *De veritate* (ed. Baur 137–38). See Bérubé and Gieben, *art. cit.* 'Guibert de Tournai' (supra n. 7).

[89] *Itinerarium* V 5 (*Opera* V 309).

[90] *Itinerarium* VII 5 (*Opera* V 313). Bonaventure quotes Dionysius on this point.

ness, is the light of the incarnate Word, in whom the divine light is accommodated to our sensible nature. He is a book written without and within,
able to lead us from the visible things of the world to the invisible things of
God.[91] It should be clear that knowledge inattentive to the illumination of
divine light and without reference to Christ would be incapable of producing
virtues in the will dependent on it.

We are now prepared to understand why Bonaventure in the *In Hexaëmeron*
begins his discourse on the cardinal virtues by addressing the most crucial
philosophic issues of his day. He wonders why the pagan philosophers, despite
their natural gifts, followed darkness instead of light. Bonaventure had already said that true metaphysics consists in three things: emanation, exemplarity, and consummation. Aristotle and his followers, Bonaventure now
says, knew the first and last of these, that God is the first principle and final
end of all things. Aristotle, however, denied that God knew things through
divine ideas and he did so in a book concerning moral behavior, the *Nicomachean Ethics*. Denying exemplarity, the crucial middle term of all knowledge,
Aristotle introduced a new darkness into the world, obscuring what light of
truth had been glimpsed by Plato and his followers.[92] One may add that although Aristotle was able to grasp something of the order of existing, because
he denied exemplarity he was unable to grasp anything of the more efficacious
order of making.

The worst consequences of Aristotle's errors are moral ones. If God knows
only himself and does not know created things through divine ideas, he cannot
know particular creatures or judge their merits. Nor could God have fore-
knowledge of or providence for creatures. Hence, one must conclude, as
Aristotle's followers have, that the world is governed either by chance or by the
rule of the stars. If this is true, how could one be held responsible for his moral
acts? Another of Aristotle's errors yields the same conclusion. If there be
but a single agent intellect, shared in transiently by all men, one could not be
personally responsible for his intellectual errors nor for the immoral acts consequent on them. Furthermore, if there is one agent intellect, human souls are
not immortal. All of these teachings, implied by the denial of divine ideas,
lead to the conclusion that there is no devil, no hell, no heaven, no punishment,
no reward. Accordingly, Aristotle taught that the world is eternal.[93] We
recognize Bonaventure's Aristotle as the Aristotle of those of his contemporaries
who read the philosopher's works according to the letter and not according
to the spirit. In Bonaventure's mind, the denial of the divine exemplars leads
either to no morality at all or, at best, to a specious earthly morality determined

---

[91] *Breviloquium* II 11 (*Opera* V 229).
[92] *In Hex.* VI 2–5 (*Opera* V 360–61).
[93] *In Hex.* VI 4 (*Opera* V 361).

by the exigencies of political life, such as Aristotle taught in the *Nicomachean Ethics*.

Although his judgment of Aristotle is as severe as it could be, Bonaventure does not reject all the pagan philosophers. He praises other 'ancient and noble philosophers' (*antiqui et nobiles philosophi*), namely the Platonists, who knew of the divine ideas. In making the divine ideas their central teaching, these philosophers laid the foundation for a morality rooted in God, for as Plotinus said, 'Absurdum enim est . . . quod exemplaria aliarum rerum sint in Deo, et non exemplaria virtutum.'[94]

Bonaventure adduces the noble philosophers to show that the four cardinal virtues, which appear to originate in man, in truth originate in God. He cites the most learned philosopher among the Jews, Philo, to whom he ascribes authorship of the book of Wisdom. In a verse of that text (8.25–26), one may discern that God is the height of purity, the beauty of clarity, the strength of power, and the rectitude of diffusion in his light.[95] Bonaventure continues:

> Haec imprimuntur in anima per illam lucem exemplarem et descendit in cognitivam, in affectivam, in operativam. Ex celsitudine puritatis imprimitur sinceritas temperantiae; ex pulcritudine claritatis serenitas prudentiae; ex fortitudine virtutis stabilitas constantiae; ex rectitudine diffusionis suavitas iustitiae. — Hae sunt quatuor virtutes exemplares, de quibus tota sacra Scriptura agit; et Aristoteles nihil de his sensit, sed antiqui et nobiles philosophi.[96]

As the seminal reasons of material things, which first diversify into the four elements, are implanted in prime matter by the Father of lights,[97] so the four cardinal virtues are 'impressed' in the soul by the exemplary light descending from above.

At the end of his first conference on the cardinal virtues, Bonaventure closely paraphrases a long text from Macrobius' commentary on the *Somnium Scipionis*.[98] Interpreting Plotinus, Macrobius distinguishes four genera of the four virtues. The cardinal virtues participate in four ascending degrees of reality. First, they exist in man insofar as he is a social animal, and are called 'political.' Secondly, they pertain to man insofar as he is fit for God, and are called 'cleansing,' or 'purgatorial.' Thirdly, they reside in the souls of those al-

---

[94] *In Hex.* VI 6 (*Opera* V 361).

[95] *In Hex.* VI 7 (*Opera* V 361–62).

[96] *In Hex.* VI 10 (*Opera* V 362).

[97] *In* II *Sent.* d. 7 p. 2 a. 2 q. 1 *concl.* (*Opera* II 197–99); d. 7 p. 2 a. 2 q. 2 *concl.* (201–202).

[98] Macrobius, *Commentary on the Dream of Scipio* I 8 (trans. W. H. Stahl [New York 1952] 120–29). For the influence of Macrobius' scheme in the Middle Ages, see R. Tuve, 'Notes on the Virtues and Vices: Pt. 1, Two Fifteenth-Century Lines of Dependence on the Thirteenth and Twelfth Centuries,' *Journal of the Warburg and Courtauld Institutes* 26 (1963) 264–303. See also Ps.-Vincent of Beauvais, *Speculum morale* I d. 7 p. 3 ad 4 (*Speculum maius* [Douai 1624; repr. Graz 1964] III 187).

ready cleansed, 'washed of every stain of this world.' Finally, they subsist in the mind of God as exemplars.[99] According to this division, the cardinal virtues are clearly instruments of ἄσκησις and union with God. Bonaventure rephrases Macrobius' teaching in terms of his own Christian contemplative doctrine, and uses a characteristic analogy:

> Hae virtutes fluunt a luce aeterna in hemisphaerium nostrae mentis et reducunt animam in suam originem, sicut radius perpendicularis sive directus eadem via revertitur, qua incessit. Et haec est beatitudo. Unde primo sunt politicae, secundo purgatoriae, tertio animi iam purgati. Politicae sunt in actione, purgatoriae in contemplatione, animi iam purgati in lucis visione.[100]

The cardinal virtues subsist properly in God and are participated in by man in various degrees, in much the same way that light subsists properly in God, and is participated in by creatures, spiritual and material, in various ways.

Although the ancient and noble philosophers knew that the virtues subsist in God, and although they dreamed of union with the divine, their own errors prevented them from achieving such union. Bonaventure analyzes their helplessness in *Collatio* VII of the *In Hexaëmeron*. These philosophers imagined what Bonaventure calls a 'false circle of beatitude.' Augustine taught that a virtue is not true unless directed to God, the living fountain, as to its first end. In God, each virtue abides in a perfect eternity and peace. The ancient philosophers imagined a specious eternity, still bound to the visible universe. They conceived (here Bonaventure alludes to Macrobius[101]) a kind of ever recurring journey of the soul, wherein the soul descends and reascends through Capricorn, Cancer, and the Milky Way, now assuming, then escaping from a wretched body. They did not know that true peace is the perfect harmony of soul and body, accomplished in eternity through the resurrection of the body.[102] The effect of Bonaventure's words, which he does not elaborate further, is quite startling. Because they did not know an article of faith, he says, the philosophers could not discover the truth concerning a question they have always claimed as their own: the relationship between soul and body. Aristotle fared even worse than the Platonists, since he denied the soul's immortality and posited a single agent intellect. What does the philosophers' failure on this point bespeak of the rest of their knowledge of the natural world? Not knowing a true eternity and a true immortality, Plato himself taught that in the Great Year, when the heavenly spheres return to the original configuration whence they began, the same effects would again be produced in the temporal world.

---

[99] *In Hex.* VI 26–32 (*Opera* V 364).
[100] *In Hex.* VI 24 (*Opera* V 363).
[101] Macrobius, *Commentary* I 12 (tr. Stahl 133–37).
[102] *In Hex.* VII 5 (*Opera* V 366).

Hence, in another time, he would be teaching the same students in the same place in the same manner.[103] In the end, no more than Aristotle could the Platonists escape a cosmological determinism. Since they had glimpsed the source of beatitude their failure was all the more frustrating. Turning to Pliny's book of creatures for a moral example, Bonaventure says that these philosophers had wings like ostriches, and like ostriches their feet were planted firmly in the mud.[104]

The pagan philosophers could not know that the cosmos is radically Christian, a truth revealed only in Scripture. Lacking revelation, these philosophers could not understand their own imperfection. They could not know the source of their disease, original sin, which infects man with weakness, ignorance, malice, and concupiscence. In his commentary on the *Sentences* Bonaventure prescribes the cardinal virtues (fortitude, prudence, justice, temperance) as remedies to these effects of the fall.[105] The pagan philosophers knew these afflictions, but they blamed them on the flesh, having not heard that these are afflictions of the soul itself.[106] Moreover, they could not know the physician for their disease, the incarnate Christ. Finally, they could not know the proper medicine, the grace of the Holy Spirit. Unless illumined by the three virtues of faith, hope, and charity, the cardinal virtues are unable to attain their final perfection, incapable of actualizing their inherent potential.[107] In both the orders of knowing and right living, nature is frustrated without grace.

When the natural cardinal virtues are perfected by grace, the affective dispositions of the soul are rectified.[108] Throughout his writings Bonaventure develops the concept of *rectitudo*, which had already been richly developed by Augustine, Gregory the Great, Anselm, and Grosseteste. In these writers,and especially as systematized in the latter two, the principle of rectitude applies consistently in each of the orders of being, knowing, and right living.[109] It is worth noting that Bonaventure apparently adopted his term here, *rectificatio*, from Grosseteste.[110] Bonaventure discusses the rectification of the virtues more

---

[103] *In Hex.* Vis. 1 Coll. IV 12 (ed. Delorme 103). On the Great Year, see P. Duhem, *Le Système du monde* I (Paris 1913) 65–75 *passim*.

[104] *In Hex.* VII 12 (*Opera* V 367).

[105] *In III Sent.* d. 33 *art. unicus* q. 4 (*Opera* III 719–21). Lottin, *op. cit.* (supra n. 65) 158–59.

[106] *In Hex.* VII 8 (*Opera* V 366–67). For 'false opinions' concerning the relation between soul and body, for want of the revealed doctrine of the resurrection of the body, see Augustine, *De doctrina* I 48-53 (CSEL 80.20–22).

[107] *In Hex.* VII 9–11 (*Opera* V 367).

[108] *In Hex.* VII 7 (*Opera* V 366).

[109] R. Pouchet, *La Rectitudo chez saint Anselme: Un itinéraire augustinien de l'âme à Dieu* (Paris 1964) 252–58 for Grosseteste and Bonaventure.

[110] Grosseteste, *De veritate* (ed. Baur 135); J.-G. Bougeril, *Lexique de saint Bonaventure* (Paris 1969) 113.

I

amply in the *Breviloquium*. In that text he teaches that the soul must be rectified according to its twofold face, in its *portio superior* and in its *portio inferior*. Bonaventure uses these terms throughout his works to designate the soul in its purely 'celestial' and 'heavenly' operations on the one hand and in its lower 'earthly' and 'temporal' operations on the other.[111] In its 'superior face,' the soul is rectified in its higher faculties by the three theological virtues. In its 'inferior face,' the soul is rectified by the cardinal virtues,

> Nam prudentia rectificat rationalem, fortitudo irascibilem, temperantia concupiscibilem, iustitia vero rectificat omnes has vires in comparatione ad alterum.[112]

The virtue of justice has both a particular and a general character. Justice can be directed toward another person or to one's self as toward another. Likewise, it can be directed toward God. In the first two senses, justice is a specific, cardinal virtue. In the last sense, it is a general virtue *comprehendens totius animae rectitudinem* and it is called *rectitudo voluntatis*. Moral perfection lies in this rectitude of the will.[113] At once a particular and general virtue, justice is analogous to physical light, which is both a particular accident of bodies, and the common form embracing them all.[114] The many analogies we have been tracking are woven together in Bonaventure's concluding words about the cardinal virtues in the *Breviloquium*:

> Hinc est etiam, quod ceteri habitus virtutum possunt esse informes, sola caritate excepta, quae est virtutum forma. Cum enim habentur sine gratia et caritate, in quibus consistit vita virtutum, tunc sunt informes. Cum autem superinfunditur gratia, tunc formantur et decorantur et Deo acceptabiles fiunt; sicut et colores absque luce sunt invisibiles, superveniente autem lumine, fiunt lucidi, pulcri et aspectui complacentes. Unde quemadmodum ex luce et coloribus fit unum in ratione motivi, et una lux sufficit ad multos colores illuminandos; sic ex gratia et habitibus informibus, cum formantur, fit unum secundum rationem meritorii et gratuiti; et una nihilominus gratia sufficit ad informationem et gratificationem habituum diversorum.[115]

As unformed matter acquires its perfection by a gradual eduction of the potent forms ·mplanted in it by the Father of lights, as the sun's illumination exposes the diverse colors of bodies, as the divine illumination of the mind reveals the

---

[111] R. W. Mulligan, '*Portio superior* and *Portio inferior rationis* in the Writings of St. Bonaventure,' *Franciscan Studies* 15 (1955) 332–49.

[112] *Breviloquium* V 4 (*Opera* V 256–57).

[113] *Breviloquium* V 4 (*Opera* V 256).

[114] *In* II *Sent.* d. 13 a. 2 q. 2 (*Opera* II 319–20).

[115] *Breviloquium* V 3 (*Opera* V 257). *In* III *Sent.* d. 23 a. 2 a. 5 *concl.* (*Opera* III 498), Bonaventure develops the analogies among the eduction of forms from matter, light's reduction of color from potency to act, and grace's infusion of the virtues.

significance of the multiform wisdom expressed in the created world, so the
infused light of grace draws the cardinal virtues to their formal perfection.
And as created light, the image of God's diffusive goodness, binds together and
energizes being in every degree, and is the common form of all bodies, so the virtue of charity binds together and energizes the diverse virtues of the moral life,
and is the common form of them all. In the *In Hexaëmeron*, using yet another
metaphor drawn from rhetorical tradition, Bonaventure says that the virtues
of the philosophers, lacking charity, are *informes et nudae*. In contrast, the
virtues of Christians, informed by charity, are 'clothed' (*vestitae*). Thus, insofar as the cardinal virtues are informed by charity, they are decorously
signified by the *ornamenta*, the embroidered tapestries and varicolored skins
that drape the four sides of the tabernacle (Exodus 26).[116]

This is scarcely the only vesture the virtues receive. Viewed in the light of
faith, which restores the impaired sight of the eye of reason, the workings of the
natural world are adequate signs of the workings of grace. Thus we can understand how, as the light of the sun generates life in each of the twelve signs of the
zodiac, so the sun of wisdom, radiating over the hemisphere of the mind, gives
life to the twelve Ciceronian subspecies of the cardinal virtues.[117] In his commentary on the *Sentences*, Bonaventure amplified his interpretation of the six
days by a fourfold reasoning, confirming his literal understanding of natural
signs by relating them to the signs of man's redemption. Likewise, in moving
from *Collatio* VI to *Collatio* VII in the *In Hexaëmeron*, Bonaventure leaves
behind the 'natural' signs for the virtues drawn from the book of creatures for
their 'mystical' signs as found in the book of Scripture.[118] Thus, as had Philo,
Ambrose, Augustine, Honorius of Autun, and other discerners of a tropological
paradise,[119] Bonaventure signifies the cardinal virtues through the four rivers
of paradise. The river of paradise branches into four, Phison, Gehon, Tigris,
and Euphrates. Similarly, the grace of the Holy Spirit branches into temperance, prudence, fortitude, and justice. Like the river Euphrates, which encircles
many lands and whose final destination is unreported in Scripture, the virtue

---

[116] *In Hex.* VII 15, 17 (*Opera* V 367–68). 'To clothe' (*vestire*) speech with colors is synonymous with adorning (*ornare*) it. See Cicero, *De oratore* 1.31.142; Quintilian, *Inst. orat.* 8. praef.
20 (ed. cit. 422).

[117] *In Hex.* VI 14–19 (*Opera* V 362–63). Cicero, *De Inventione* 2.53–54 (Loeb ed. 326–33).
For the influence of Cicero's doctrine of the virtues in the Middle Ages, see P. Delhaye, 'Une
adaptation du "De Officiis" au XIIe siècle,' *RThAM* 15 (1949) 227–58; *id.*, 'L'enseignement
morale au XIIe siècle,' *Mediaeval Studies* 11 (1949) 77–99.

[118] *In Hex.* Vis. 1 coll. IV 15 (ed. Delorme 105).

[119] Philo, *Legum allegoria* 1.19–27 (Loeb ed. 187–205); Ambrose, *Liber de paradiso* 3 (PL
14.296–300); Augustine, *De Genesi contra Manichaeos* 1.9–10 (PL 34.202–204); Honorius of
Autun, *Expositio in Cantica Canticorum* vers. 13–14 (PL 172.420–30). See also *Speculum
virginum* (ed. Greenhill 52–58 and the ample notes).

of justice embraces all parts of the soul and extends to God, as Augustine had explained.[120] Added to the virtues of faith, hope, and charity, the cardinal virtues become seven like the heavenly Pleiades mentioned in the book of Job (28.1) as expounded by Gregory.[121] The complement of seven virtues, referred to the mystery of Christ in head and members, is signified allegorically in the strict sense. According to this sense, the seven virtues are signified by the seven loaves of the Gospel with which the whole body of the elect is fed (Mt. 15.32–39). Bonaventure adds that for the philosophers, who did not see their completion by the theological virtues, the cardinal virtues become stones, and not bread of life.[122] Moreover, multiplied thrice, the cardinal virtues become twelve, as signified by the anagogic temple of the soul, having four three-doored walls, in the Apocalypse (21.12ff.). In turn, these virtues are doubled in practical and speculative contemplation, thereby corresponding to the twenty-four wings of the four animals, each having six wings, standing before the face of God.[123] Like light, the virtues by nature multiply themselves. Truly, as Bonaventure taught interpreting Macrobius in *Collatio* VI, the cardinal virtues, planted in man's social nature, lead from moral purgation to contemplation to the light of the highest vision.

Against the false circle of pagan beatitude Bonaventure sets a true one. 'This alone,' he says, 'is eternal life, that the rational spirit, which proceeds from the blessed Trinity and is the image of the Trinity, returns in the manner of an intelligible circle into the most blessed Trinity, through memory, understanding, and will, through the deiformity of glory.'[124] This return is possible only through the incarnate Christ, who 'is the consummation of perfection, as appears in a circle, the most perfect of figures, which also is terminated in the same point from which it begins.'[125] Christ's cross is the lost center of this circle, since the lost center of a circle cannot be found except through intersecting two lines at right angles.[126] We too come full circle. The true nature of the cardinal virtues cannot be discovered without the divine illumination of the mind. But one's mind cannot be illumined unless his life be first illumined by the moral virtues. At least Socrates can be praised for knowing this, Bonaventure says.[127]

---

120 Augustine, *De Genesi contra Manichaeos* 1.10 (PL 34.204).

121 *In Hex.* VII 18 (*Opera* V 368). Gregory the Great, *Moralia in Job* 29.72 (PL 76.517.)

122 *In Hex.* VII 20 (*Opera* V 368). See note 38 above.

123 *In Hex.* VII 21 (*Opera* V 368).

124 *Quaestiones disputatae de mysterio Trinitatis* q. 8 ad 7 (*Opera* V 115).

125 *In III Sent.* d. 1 a. 2 q. 1 concl. (*Opera* III 20).

126 *In Hex.* I 22–24 (*Opera* V 333).

127 *In Hex.* V 33 (*Opera* V 359).

In criticizing Aristotle, Bonaventure was not simply cautious or jealous against better reason of the rights of God.[128] Bonaventure's criticism of Aristotle goes far beyond the Philosopher's particular conclusions or those of his thirteenth-century followers, reaching the substance of philosophy conceived as a distinct, autonomous science of unaided natural reason. Bonaventure judged that the very method of the *via philosophica* was inadequate to the discovery of the nature of things, and he thought that the fathers, monks, and canons had made this clear. In the *In Hexaëmeron*, Bonaventure equates the philosophers with the faithless Jews. A text from the *Ars concionandi* attributed to Bonaventure clarifies this typological comparison and draws together neatly many of the themes which we have investigated. The preacher who would be abundant in metaphors must know the many properties of things and know how to adapt them to the edification of souls. God created things not only for man's physical nourishment, but also for his spiritual instruction. Receiving instruction from and taking delight in the variety of things God has made, man is moved to love his maker more. The philosophers, because they fix their attention too narrowly on the things in themselves, and the Jews, because they fix their attention exclusively on the letter, are deceived about the true nature of things and have no desire to direct (*reducere*) them toward the edification of the soul.[129] Thus, the book of creatures is opaque to the philosophers and the book of Scripture is opaque to the Jews, because neither the philosophers nor the Jews understand that things are intrinsically signs. Bonaventure directs his theology immediately to the edification of souls and in so doing fulfills the charge of Francis to his friars: to preach the vices and virtues, pain and glory.[130]

If in continuing the grammatical and rhetorical tradition of theology in the late thirteenth century Bonaventure was old-fashioned, he was so only relatively. For if Aristotle was for the Middle Ages new in relation to the old scriptural commentaries, he was in fact old in relation to the Gospel which had given them birth. Finally, if Bonaventure teaches a Christian philosophy, it is in the sense that the lover of wisdom will find what he desires in the gracious self-revelation of God. And such a philosophy has its own convenient logic:

 . . . argumentum Christi fuit salvativum et destructivum argumenti diaboli. Ex quo enim diabolus fecerat hominem dissimilem Deo, cum tamen promisis-

---

[128] See these opinions in Gilson (286, 432 et passim). Expressed so eloquently, they have become scholarly commonplaces.

[129] *Ars concionandi* 44 (*Opera* IX 19). On the question of authorship, see the summary in H. C. H. Hazel, 'The Bonaventurian "Ars concionandi",' in *S. Bonaventura, 1274–1974* II 435–46. Hazel thinks Bonaventure's authorship probable and cites McKeon's acceptance. On the Jews in *In Hex.*, see Synan 29–31.

[130] R. C. Petry, ' *Verbum Abbreviatum*: St. Bonaventure's Interpretation of the Evangelical Preaching of St. Francis,' in *S. Bonaventura, 1274–1974* II 214, 219.

set, similem se facturum; necesse fuit, Christum esse similem homini, ut faceret hominem similem sibi sive Deo. . . . Maior propositio fuit ab aeterno; sed assumptio in cruce; conclusio vero in resurrectione. . . . Haec est logica nostra, haec est ratiocinatio nostra, quae habenda est contra diabolum, qui continuo contra nos disputat. Sed in assumptione minoris est tota vis facienda; quia nolumus pati, nolumus crucifigi. Tamen ad hoc est tota ratiocinatio nostra, ut simus similes Deo.[131]

APPENDIX

Bonaventure and Hugh of St. Victor:
Scripture, Prime Matter, and the
Illumination of the Virtues

Bonaventure is aware of seeming contradictions (what modern historians would call an evolution) in St. Augustine's thought. In the question from the *Sentences* we have examined, Bonaventure several times quotes Augustine against himself. Bonaventure's criticism of *De Genesi ad litteram*, however, does not obscure his general debt to Augustine or his specific debt to the program of Christian learning which Augustine puts forward in *De doctrina christiana*. Significantly, the ideal of learning which Augustine holds up in *De doctrina* is not a *via philosophica*, but rather a Christian transformation of the Ciceronian, rhetorical ideal of the union of wisdom and eloquence. Those who taught the art of rhetoric, Augustine says, knew that wisdom without eloquence little benefits the state, and that eloquence without wisdom profits nothing and is often positively injurious. How much more then should Christians, who possess the true wisdom descending from the Father of lights, strive for an eloquence founded on wisdom. And a man is more or less wise insofar as he knows sacred Scripture, not by having memorized it, but by having understood it and sought out its various senses.[1] The erudition of the Christian seeker of wisdom is ordered to the understanding of Scripture according to its spiritual senses.

Bonaventure read *De doctrina christiana* through the lens of Hugh of St. Victor's *De sacramentis christianae fidei*. Bonaventure's admiration for Hugh is well known. In his own work offering an encyclopaedic program of Christian learning, *De reductione artium ad theologiam*, Bonaventure specifies three modes of theology, each of which he personifies by certain theologians. Among the theologians he mentions, Hugh alone is praised for being a master of all three modes.[2] Scholars point out that Hugh made a singular contribution to Western theology by conflating Augustine's theory of signs, as taught in *De doctrina*, with

---

[131] *In Hex.* I 27, 28, 30 (*Opera* V 334).
[1] Augustine, *De doctrina christiana* IV 18–19 (CSEL 80.122).
[2] *De reductione artium* 5 (*Opera* V 321).

pseudo-Dionysius' teaching that everything in the created hierarchies is a sacrament or theophany of God.[3] Bonaventure inherited this conflation from Hugh.

In *De doctrina* Augustine observes that many of the 'things' narrated in sacred Scripture through verbal signs are themselves signs of other realities.[4] Augustine does not develop this idea fully, and he seems to reserve the principle to certain privileged events in Scripture. Under the influence of pseudo-Dionysius, Hugh of St. Victor in *De sacramentis* extends the principle to the whole of Scripture, and to the whole of created nature which it reflects.[5] Like Bonaventure who follows him, Hugh teaches that God's primary intent, both in his creation and in special revelation, is to speak to man about his condition and future perfection. Hugh distinguishes God's communications into his *opera conditionis* and his *opera restaurationis*. From the beginning the former, the *creatio mundi cum omnibus elementis suis*, was accomplished in view of the latter.[6] The works of foundation comprise those things which were done over the six days in the beginning of the world. The works of restoration are all those things which for man's reparation have been or will be accomplished over the entire six ages of the world. Strictly speaking, the works of restoration all pertain to the Incarnation of the Word, to all those things which prefigured it, to the Word's own acts in the flesh, and to all of those things which to the end of the world declare the Incarnation:

> De his loquitur omnis divina Scriptura, et de his et pro his facta est omnis divina Scriptura; quia, quemadmodum libri gentilium opera conditionis investigant, et tractant, sic divina eloquia ad opera restaurationis tractanda et commendanda maxime operamdant.[7]

The Scriptures take up the works of foundation in relation to the more comprehensive works of restoration. In the *libri gentilium* one will find something about God's works in the world's first age; only in *divina eloquia* will he discover his own and the world's destiny as signified in those works.

Thus, unless he sees them in relation to his final end, man will not grasp the full significance of the works of God's creation. The first man, Adam, was short-sighted in this way. Although he was created in grace (*gratia creatrix*), he was not yet confirmed in the grace which saves (*gratia salvatrix, gratia reparatrix*). The latter would have been granted to Adam if, instructed by the things around him, he would have responded to God's exhortation with a 'conversion of love to the creator.' This grace would have bestowed upon human nature the perfection of its form, raising it from simple *esse* to *esse pulchrum*.[8]

Hugh speaks of the instruction which God's work of creation imparts, and which should have persuaded Adam to a conversion of love, in a series of questions which we shall recognize: 'whether matter was made before form'; 'why God wished to bring his works to completion through intervals of time';

---

[3] M.-D. Chenu, *La Théologie au douzième siècle* (Paris 1957) 172–78: 'La mentalité symbolique'; Zinn, *art. cit.* (supra n. 6).

[4] For example, *De doctrina* I 4–6; II 6–7 (CSEL 80.9, 35).

[5] *De sacramentis christianae fidei Prol.* 5 (PL 176.185).

[6] *De sacr. Prol.* 1 (PL 176.183).

[7] *De sacr.* 1 pt. 1 28 (PL 176.204).

[8] *De sacr. Prol.* 3; I pt. 5 5; I pt. 6 17 (PL 176.189, 249, 273–74).

'whether there could have been matter without form.' Hugh's treatment of these questions is the immediate source of Bonaventure's.

Hugh recognizes that the first of these questions — 'whether matter was made before form' — involves more important questions concerning God's revelation. Should the account of Genesis, which suggests that matter somehow existed before receiving definite forms, be understood literally? Hugh acknowledges that the Fathers differ on this point. Some maintain that the creation took place over six successive days, as the letter of Genesis declares. Others (namely Augustine) maintain that God created all things at once in their matter and form, and that consequently the account of creation in Genesis must be understood 'mystically.' Those who hold this latter position argue that it would be unworthy of the creator's omnipotence to bring his work to perfection through intervals of time in the manner of human feebleness (*imbecillitas*). These also cite a text of Scripture: 'Qui vivit in aeternum, creavit omnia simul' (Ecclesiasticus 18.1).[9]

Hugh affirms the opposite opinion, allowing however that God could have created all things at once. Accordant with his broad notion of sacraments, Hugh's argument for the literal interpretation of Genesis is founded on the conviction that God's primary intention in creation was to communicate with his creature, man. Hugh's reasoning so closely resembles Bonaventure's that it merits quotation in full:

> Omnipotens etenim Deus (cujus voluntas sua bonitate nunquam privari potest) sicut propter rationalem creaturam caetera omnia fecit, ita etiam in eis omnibus faciendis illum praecipue modum servare debuit, qui ipsius rationalis creaturae commoditati ac causae magis congruus fuit. Hic autem ille erat in quo eidem creaturae rationali, scilicet non solum id quo ad obsequium indiguit, sed per illud etiam quod accipit agnosceret id quod fuit. Propterea in caeteris rebus prius informis materies facta est ac deinde formata, ut eo ipso demonstraretur quod ab illo prius non existentia accepissent essentiam, sine quo modo formam et ordinem non poterant habere confusa. Eodem modo ipsa rationalis creatura per id quod foris fiebat, in se cognosceret, et ab illo esse quod erat, atque ab illo expetendum esse quod futura erat, quatenus et pro eo quod acceperat in gratiarum actionem exsurgeret et in id quod acceptura erat obtinendum in ipsum affectum dilectionis dilitaret. Nam et ipsa rationalis creatura quodam suo modo prius informis facta est, postmodum per conversionem ad Creatorem suum formanda; et idcirco foris prius ei demonstrata est informis materia, postea formata, et quanta foret inter esse et pulchrum esse distantia discerneret. Ac per hoc admonita est ne contenta esset eo quod per conditionem a creatore esse acceperat, donec et pulchrum esse atque beatum esse adipisceretur, quod per amoris conversionem a Creatore acceptura erat.[10]

According to Hugh's own terms, God proceeds in creation by way of 'demonstration.' God's manner of demonstration is not the scientific demonstration of Aristotelian logic. Rather, God's manner of creation is analogous to the orator's *genus demonstrativum*, that adorning mode of discourse which exhorts man to virtue and dissuades him from vice by setting before his eyes vivid images of goods to be desired and emulated, and evils to be avoided, or, in the example

---

[9] *De sacr.* 1 pt. 1 2 (PL 176.188).
[10] *De sacr.* 1 pt. 1 3 (PL 176.188–89).

of prime matter, imperfections to be transformed.[11] We shall see also that the creation of prime matter is literally an 'illustration,' the close rhetorical synonym of 'demonstration.'[12]

In the above argument, Hugh confirms (as Bonaventure will do) the literal interpretation by reference to the more significant allegorical sense. Having affirmed the truth of the letter in the Genesis account, Hugh concludes that the matter created on the first day existed in an unformed state, but not wholly without form. Although matter could not exist lacking all form,

> tamen non absurde informam eam appellari posse, quod in confusione at permistione quaedam subsistens, nondum hanc in qua nunc cernitur, pulchram aptamque dispositionem et formam coeperit. Ergo ante formam fracta est materia, tamen in forma. In forma confusionis, ante formam dispositionis. In prima forma confusionis prius materialiter omnia corporalia simul et semel creata sunt; in secunda forma dispositionis postmodum per sex dierum intervalla ordinata.[13]

In his conclusion, exactly Bonaventure's, Hugh again assumes rhetorical terms and concepts. Like the invented matter (*materia*) of the orator, prime matter awaits the *dispositio*, the shaping and ordering, of apt and beautiful forms.[14] The difference between the orator's and God's persuasive discourse is this: God speaks in things, not words.

We have remarked the influence of Grosseteste's technical theory of light upon Bonaventure in the main part of our study. Nevertheless, Bonaventure was able to find the lineaments of his own doctrine in Hugh's *De sacramentis*. Following the order of Scripture, like Bonaventure Hugh teaches that light was the first thing made;[15] that light was the form of the prime matter created on the first day;[16] that this light was corporeal, since it was made to illlumine corporeal things;[17] that visible lights were made simultaneously, since from the beginning corporeal light was made to be an image of spiritual light, and the exemplars of God's work needed to be in harmony;[18] and that the first light was not the sun, since the confusion to be illumined was not yet worthy of full light, yet needed some illumination in order to discern how to proceed in its ordering and disposition.[19]

---

[11] Cicero, *De inventione* 1.5.7 (Loeb ed. 14–17); 1.9.12 (Loeb ed. 24–27); *Rhetorica ad Herennium* 4.55.68–69 (Loeb ed. 405–409) (*demonstratio*); 3.6.10–18.15 (Loeb ed. 172–85) (*genus demonstrativum*); Quintilian, *Inst. orat.* 2.10.11; 3.12–14 (ed. cit. 276–77, 394–97); Boethius, *De topicis differentiis* IV (PL 64.1207); Isidore of Seville, *Etymologiae* (ed. Lindsay) 2.4.1–8 (*genus demonstrativum*); 2.9.11–12 (the *ostensibile* kind of enthymeme); 2.21.33 (*energia* — Greek term equivalent to *demonstratio*). See Bonaventure, *In Hex.* IV 21–22 (*Opera* V 353).

[12] Cicero, *Partitiones oratoriae* 6.20 (ed. Wilkins); Quintilian, *Inst. orat.* 6.2.32–33 (ed. Winterbottom 434–37).

[13] *De sacr.* 1 pt. 1 4 (PL 176.189).

[14] Cicero, *De inventione* 1.5.7 (Loeb ed. 14–17).

[15] *De sacr.* 1 pt. 1 8 (PL 176.193).

[16] *De sacr.* 1 pt. 1 9 (PL 176.193–94).

[17] *De sacr.* 1 pt. 1 9 (PL 176.194).

[18] *De sacr.* 1 pt. 1 10 (PL 176.194–95).

[19] *De sacr.* 1 pt. 1 11 (PL 176.195).

Hugh sees a 'great sacrament' in the successive illumination of the world, as he did in its successive formation and beautification. The successive illumination of the world offers an instructive analogy to the gradual illumination of the 'world of the human heart' by the sun of justice, which gives rise first to purifying virtues and then to contemplation. Hugh's terms are strikingly similar to Bonaventure's:

> ... omnis anima quandiu in peccato est, quasi in tenebris est quibusdam et confusione. Sed non potest evadere confusionem suam et ad ordinem justitiae formamque disponi, nisi illuminetur primum videre mala sua, et discernere lucem a tenebris, hoc est virtutes a vitiis, ut se disponat ad ordinem et conformet veritati. Hoc igitur anima in confusione jacens sine luce facere non potest; et propterea necesse est primum ut lux fiat, ut videat semetipsam, et agnoscat horrorem et turpitudinem confusionis suae, et explicet se atque coaptet ad illam rationabilem dispositionem et ordinem veritatis. Postquam autem ordinata fuerint omnia ejus, et secundum exemplar rationis formamque sapientiae disposita, tunc statim incipiet ei lucere sol justitiae; quia sic in repromissione dictum est: Beati mundo corde; quoniam ipsi Deum videbunt (Matth. 5). Prius ergo in rationali illo mundo cordis humani creatur lux, et illuminatur confusio ut in ordinem redigatur. Post haec cum fuerint purificata interiora ejus, venit lumen solis clarum et illustrat eam. Non enim digna est contemplari lumen aeternitatis, donec munda et purificata fuerit; habent quodammodo et per materiam speciem, et per justitiam dispositionem.[20]

The first work of foundation illustrates the last work of restoration. The light which illumines sinners to justice precedes the light which illumines the justified to blessedness. Indeed, light everywhere precedes light.[21] Bonaventure too will teach that the light which establishes justice among the virtues in the soul disposes the soul to further illuminations of grace and glory.

Hugh's direct influence upon Bonaventure is suggestive in at least one way. Clearly, Hugh conceives the relation between matter and form in the manner of a rhetorician, and we have seen indications that Bonaventure follows him in this. Gilson succinctly observes:

> The term 'form' in St. Bonaventure has an Aristotelian origin, but the idea of form has not. For him the form has indeed the bestowing of a perfection as its chief function, but it does this by preparing the substance which it informs for other substantial perfections which it cannot itself confer upon it.[22]

But does Bonaventure's term, let alone his concept, originate in Aristotle? To what extent was Bonaventure laboring, in the language of the schools, to express concepts that in fact originated in Roman rhetoric?

---

[20] *De sacr.* 1 pt. 1 12 (PL 176.195–96).

[21] *De sacr.* 1 pt. 1 12 (PL 176.196).

[22] Gilson 253.

II

The 'Sentences' Abbreviation of William de Rothwell, O.P.

University of Pennsylvania, Lat. MS. 32

University of Pennsylvania Lat. MS. 32 contains the *Sentences* commentary of the English Dominican, William de Rothwell. Twelve other manuscripts of William's commentary are known to exist; three of these are from the thirteenth century. Two of the thirteenth-century manuscripts come from the monastery of Wettingen in Switzerland, one of which is a copy of the other. The original Wettingen manuscript yields the earliest precise date: although probably copied earlier, it came into the possession of the monastery in 1298. Interestingly, except for *University of Pennsylvania Lat. MS. 32* and two fourteenth-century copies, all of the manuscripts originated in the southern Germanies [1].

* I wish to thank Dr. David Dumville, Cambridge University, and Professors Leonard E. Boyle, OP, and James A. Weisheipl, OP, of the Pontifical Institute of Mediaeval Studies, Toronto, for the help they have given me in this study.
1. Martin GRABMANN, *Handschriftliche Mitteilungen über Abbreviationem des Sentenzenkommentars des seligen Papstes Innozenz V. (Petrus de Tarantasia O.P. † 1276)*, in *Divus Thomas* (Freiburg) 24 (1946) 109-112; F. STEGMÜLLER, *Repertorium Commentariorum in Sententias Petri Lombardi*, I (Würzburg 1947), p. 138, n. 301; W. A. HINNEBUSCH, *The Early English Friars Preachers* (Rome 1951), p. 415; V. DOUCET, *Commentaires sur les Sentences : Supplément au Répertoire de M. Frédéric Stegmüller*, in *Archivum franciscanum historicum* 27 (1954) 125; J. H. H. MARTIN, *A Study of the Writings of William Rothwell, A Thirteenth-Century Dominican*, (unpublished B. Litt. thesis, Oxford, date not given), pp. 41-55. None of these authors cites *University of Pennsylvania, Lat. MS. 32*. The other known mss. of William de Rothwell's commentary are : (1) *Aarau, Kantonsbibliothek, Wett. 15*, 107ᵛ-175ᵛ (13th c.); (2) *Aarau, Kantonsbibliothek, Wett. 14*, 111ᵛ-203ᵛ (13th. c., copied from *Wett. 15*); (3) *Copenhagen, Kongelige Bibliotek, Gl. Kgl. S. 1363*, 1ʳ-49ᵛ (14th-15th c.); (4) *Einsiedeln, Stiftsbibliothek, 243*, 3ʳ-266ʳ (15th c.); (5) *Erfurt, Amplonianischen Bibliothek, CA 4° 115*, 1ʳ-147ᵛ (14th c.); (6) *Heiligenkreuz, Stiftsbibliothek, 247* (14th c.); (7) *Karlsruhe, Landesbibliothek, Augs. perg. 258*, 3ʳ-143ᵛ (14th c.); (8) *London, British Library, Harley 3211*, 1ʳ-144ᵛ (14th c.); (9) *München, Staatsbibliothek, Clm 26359*, 123ʳ-231ᵛ (15th c.); (10) *St. Florian, Stiftsbibliothek, 125*, 1ʳ-160ᵛ (14th c.); (11) *Zürich, Universitätsbibliothek, Cod. 81*; (12) *Zwettl, Zisterzienserstift, 56*, 1ʳ-62ᵛ (13th c.). GRABMANN, 109-110, cites the Zürich ms., but he does not give an author for the work that it contains. It is William de Rothwell.

70

The precise origin of *University of Pennsylvania Lat. MS. 32* is unknown. The University of Pennsylvania purchased the manuscript from Bernard Quaritch booksellers. The Bernard Quaritch cataloguer (1952), who did not know that William de Rothwell was the author of the commentary, correctly dated the manuscript thirteenth-century, but probably guided by the manuscript's fine parchment, he mistakenly thought that it was Italian[2]. The University of Pennsylvania cataloguers identified William de Rothwell as the author of the commentary, and more correctly judged the manuscript to be French. However, misled by false information in Quétif-Échard, these cataloguers thought that William lived in the fourteenth century, and therefore concluded incorrectly that the manuscript must have been copied in the fourteenth century[3]. W. A. Hinnebusch's discovery of the thirteenth-century Wettingen manuscript makes it possible to correct William's biography in Quétif-Échard[4], and thus to confirm the Bernard Quaritch cataloguer's thirteenth-century date for the manuscript.

Biographical information concerning William de Rothwell is scant. J. Bale says that William belonged to the Dominican convent in London. A. B. Emden says that William probably received his D.Th. at Oxford, where he may have been a younger contemporary of Robert Kilwardby (ca. 1215-1279)[5]. There is no sure evidence for this judgment. However, for the record, Kilwardby was regent in theology at Oxford from 1256 to 1261; he became Prior Provincial of the English Dominicans in 1261, was elected Archbishop of Canterbury in 1272, and was named a Cardinal in 1278[6]. During his reign as Archbishop, Kilwardby was much involved with intellectual affairs at Oxford. For twenty years, therefore, Kilwardby

---

2. *Bernard Quaritch's Catalogue*, no. 699 (1952), p. 26, n. 86.

3. Norman P. Zacour and Rudolph Hirsch, *Catalogue of Manuscripts in the Libraries of the University of Pennsylvania to 1800* (Philadelphia 1965), p. 8; J. Quétif and J. Échard, *Scriptores Ordinis Praedicatorum*, I (Paris 1719), p. 648.

4. W. A. Hinnebusch, *The Early English Friars Preachers*, pp. 415-416.

5. A. B. Emden, *A Biographical Register of the University of Oxford*, III (Oxford 1959), p. 1596. Emden cites J. Bale, *Script. Illustr. Bryt.*, pt. 1, pp. 442-443, and *Index Brit. Script.*, pp. 146-147, 513.

6. I follow the chronology of Albert G. Judy, OP, ed., *Robert Kilwardby, O.P., De Ortu Scientiarum* (London-Toronto 1976), pp. XI-XVII.

exercised considerable intellectual influence among English Dominicans. There are no traces of Robert Kilwardby's immediate influence in William de Rothwell's commentary, but as we shall see, the evidence suggests that William did compose his work during the period of Kilwardby's authority. Besides his commentary, William wrote a number of other works, including a *De principiis naturae*[7] and several *postillae* on Scripture not yet found[8]. Until new information about William de Rothwell's life is discovered, any more than that given here is unfounded conjecture.

I. DESCRIPTION OF THE MANUSCRIPT

The manuscript has modern numbering 1-10, and usually once every five folios after that. The modern numerator has made two mistakes. He has skipped a folio between 1 and 3, numbering the third folio 2. I shall number the true second folio 2, and the third, now numbered 2, I shall number 2B. Likewise the numerator has skipped a folio between his 125 and 130; I shall number the folio immediately after the numerator's 125 : 125B. In this way our folio numbers otherwise accord.

Philadelphia, University of Pennsylvania, Lat. MS. 32.

Northern French—German Border Region (Old Low Countries?)
Last quarter, 13th century[9].

GUILELMUS ROTHWELLUS, O.P. EXCERPTUM SUPER QUATUOR LIBROS SENTENTIARUM (1ʳ-2B-125B-137ʳ).
1) 1ʳᵃ-2B-19ᵛᵇ : TABULA ARTICULORUM.
    1ʳ(*inc.*) : Queritur utrum theologia sit scientia/

---

7. This text is edited by J. H. H. Martin in his B. Litt. thesis, *A Study of the Writings of William Rothwell*, pp. 23-269. Martin has also transcribed from *Aarau, Wett. 15* several selections from William's "Super Sententias", pp. 1*-22*. I did not know of Fr. Martin's thesis until very recently, when Fr. Weisheipl alerted me to it. On the questions Fr. Martin and I have transcribed in common, I have checked *Penn. Lat. MS. 32* against *Aarau, Wett. 15*. The texts are the same; slight variances can be attributed to scribal error.
8. These are listed in EMDEN, p. 1596.
9. Fr. Leonard Boyle confirms my judgment about the date and provenance of the manuscript. This judgment must be based on paleographical and codicological evidence, which I give in the description.

72

19ᵛ(*exp.*): Vtrum carentia visionis que est pena dampni. sit grauior quam gehenna. — Amen Amen dico vobis etc.

20ʳ-22ᵛ : blank.

2) 23ʳᵃ-42ᵛᵇ : LIBER UNUS.

23ʳᵃ (*inc.*): *Queritur utrum theologia sit scientia* Respondeo : proprie loquendo debet dici sapientia. que secundum augustinum est de diuinis/ Sed scientia de humanis. tamen hec large etiam potest Scientia. quia licet non procedat secundum uiam rationis inferioris sicut alie scientie/ tamen procedit secundum uiam rationis superioris.

42ᵛᵇ(*exp.*): *Vtrum sancti uelint penas reproborum* ... sed ad gloriam eternam et beatitudinem creata/ est/ ad quam nos perducat. deus qui est benedictus in secula seculorum Amen/.

3) 42ᵛᵇ-67ʳᵇ : LIBER SECUNDUS.

42ᵛᵇ(*inc.*): *Queritur utrum creatio esse possit.* Respondeo. sic. secundum fidem. cum enim deus sit omnipotens/ non solum producit aliquid de sua substantia. quod est generatio. non solum de aliena substantia./ ut in facultate/ sed etiam de nichilo/ quod est creatio/ ...

67ʳᵇ(*exp.*): *Vtrum religiosi teneantur. prelatis suis in omnibus obedire* ... dei filius qui cum patre/ et spiritu sancto/ est benedictus in secula Amen.

4) 67ʳᵇ-104ᵛᵇ : LIBER TERTIUS.

67ʳᵇ(*inc.*): *Queritur utrum Incarnatio fuit possibilis.* Respondeo. sic et possibilitate congruitatis/ quia summi boni proprium est. summe se communicare/ ...

104ᵛᵇ(*exp.*): *Vtrum lex per ewangelium sit impleata* ... qui est benedictus in secula Amen. Amen.

5) 105ʳᵃ-125B-137ʳᵃ : LIBER QUARTUS.

105ʳᵃ(*inc.*): *Queritur quid sit sacramentum.* Respondeo Augustinus de ciuitate dei et in littera Sacramentum est. sacre rei signum hec est large. Item. augustinus de doctrina christiana. Sacramentum est inuisibilis gratie/ uisibilis forma ...

137ʳᵃ(*exp.*): *Vtrum carentia uisionis que est pena dampni. sit grauior quam gehenna* (136ᵛᵇ) ... ipso ad suscipiendum nos disponente qui est benedictus in secula seculorum Amen.

(Annotator): Explicit excerptum Magistri petri de tarantasia super quatuor libros sententiarum Qui postea fuit Magister *ordinis* electusque est in summum pontificem.

(Annotator, bottom 137ᵃ): In die dorothe lxij.

137ᵛ : blank.

Size, Material, and Composition. 139 ff. (misnumbered 137), 16.75 × 12.1 cm; parchment. The parchment is smooth and thin, nearly translucent. The ink of the text is dark brown, shading to black.

The book comprises 12 gatherings : i¹⁰(1-2B-9), ii¹³(10-22, originally 14), iii-viii¹²(23-94), ix¹⁰(95-104), x-xi¹²(105-125B-127), xii¹⁰(128-

137). Boxed catchwords are found at the foot of col. b on the last versos of iv (46^v), v(58^v), vi(70^v), vii(82^v),viii(94^v), x(116^v), xi(128^v). The remaining gatherings are distinguished adequately by other signs : i, the first gathering of the *tabula*, is distinguished by initials trimmed in red on its first three folios (1^r-2B-2^r); the last three folios of ii (20-22), the second gathering of the *tabula*, are blank; iii, which begins the text proper, is signaled by the decorated initial on its first folio (23ra); likewise x, which begins Book IV, bears a decorated initial on its first folio (105ra) that distinguishes it from the preceding gathering, lacking a catchword; xii ends the book.

Page Preparation and Format. This book was carefully made in a traditional scriptorium. The folios have been pricked and line-ruled throughout for two columns of writing. The pricking is made on the outer margins of each bifolio, and across the top and bottom. Although the number of pricks is sometimes different in different gatherings, the number is the same throughout any one gathering. The ruling is done in the ink of the text; sometimes the scribe rules extra lines beyond the number of pricks (see 116^v, the last verso of x which ends Book III). Evidently, the folios were pricked in gatherings, but ruled individually by the scribe.

Gatherings i-ii(1-22), containing the *tabula*, have been pricked and ruled 35 times for 34 lines of writing. Six pricks across top and bottom direct bounding lines for each column, and a single letter-space for initials running down the left margin of each column. The writing space is 12.5 × 9.0 cm, each column 4.3 cm wide, and center-space .4 cm.

The first gathering of the text proper (iii, 23-34) has been pricked 34 times for 33 lines; the next gathering (iv, 35-46), however, has been pricked 36 times for 35 lines, and thereafter the gatherings are pricked 35 times for 34 lines. These changes seem to indicate a decision to economize space : a regular pattern is established after the pricking of the second gathering of the text compensates for the "lost" space of the first. Moreover, at the midpoint of the second gathering of the text proper (iv, 40^v), the script changes to a less formal, less space consuming one which is used throughout the remainder of the manuscript. Four pricks across the top and bottom of the folios direct bounding lines for two columns of writing. The writing space is again 12.5 × 9.0 cm, each column 4.3 cm wide, and centerspace .4 cm.

Scripts and Scribes. Although it is possible that the same scribe alternatively raised and lowered the register of his script, we judge that this book was copied by two scribes. Among other reasons, even though the article titles throughout the manuscript are written in a gothic textual display script, they evince many of the same differences that otherwise distinguish the two scripts of the book.

Script (1) : 23ra-40rb. The first gathering and one half of the text proper is written in a rather remarkable *textualis formata* of the late thirteenth century. Although the space of the lines is small, the full angularity of the gothic letters is preserved, as it is not in the "pearl script" sometimes used in thirteenth-century books similarly small[10]. Because the carefully formed letters are so close together, the aspect of the writing is often difficult, and moreover, nearly every word is abbreviated. The writing has the usual features of the *textualis formata*. Double compartment *a* is regular; the tail of the *g* closes upon the letter's upper compartment. The finials of *i, l, m, n, r, s* are on the line; biting occurs where one would expect : *de, do, oc, oe, pc, pe, po*, etc. The script shows some features influenced by cursives : *v* alternates with *u* in initial position, and the abbreviation for *pro* is looped. This abbreviation is rather distinctive, for the loop is detached from the staff of the *p*, and thus the form is not made in a single stroke. The script bears a number of features which Harrison Thomson especially remarks in late thirteenth-century French manuscripts. The ascenders of *h, b*, and *l* are forked, the bow of the *h* is angular and bent sharply back, and *r* is broken. The crossed tironian note abbreviation for *et*, customary in French manuscripts, is invariable. Both erect and looped *s* occur in final position[11]. The scribe's regular abbreviation

10. For the "pearl script", see H. DEGERING, *Die Schrift : Atlas der Schrift-formen des Abendlandes vom Altertum bis zum Ausgang des 18 Jahrhunderts* (Berlin 1929), pl. 81; J. STIENNON, *Paléographie du Moyen Age* (Paris 1973), pp. 246-247.

11. For the Alphabet of this *textualis formata*, see J. KIRCHNER, *Scriptura latina libraria a saeculo primo usque ad finem medii aevi* (Munich-Vienna-Oldenbourg 1955), no. 45b. For the distinctively French, late thirteenth-century features, see the commentaries in Harrison THOMSON, *Latin Book Hands of the Later Middle Ages. 1100-1500* (Cambridge, Eng., 1969), pl. 11 (France, 1263, *re.* note); pl. 12 (France, 1277);

for *est* is *ē*, although the commonly germanic (ȝ) appears occasionally. Likewise germanic is the *con-* abbreviation looped at top and bottom, used invariably throughout this section of the manuscript.

Script (2) : 1^(ra)-19^(vb)(*tabula*), 40^(va)-137^(ra). The script of the text changes abruptly at 40^(va), and the new script, also the script of the *tabula*, continues for the rest of the manuscript. The script remains textual, but is more current; the letters lose their angularity and become more spread out. The finials on *i*, *l*, *m*, *n*, *r* and *s* virtually disappear, and erect *s* often dips below the line. Single compartment *a* is more frequent than the double compartment form. Ascenders, although sometimes forked (and occasionally looped), are usually straight. In general, this script shows more cursive borrowings than (1). The final minims of *m* and *n* in final position curve back and sink below the line, looped *s* is often an extravagent flourish, and the ligature *or*, the *r* springing away from the *o*, according to Thomson is characteristic of French cursives[12]. The tironian note abbreviation for *et* is invariable, but the *ē* abbreviation for *est* is never found, now replaced completely by the germanic form (ȝ). At the same time, the typically French abbreviation for *con-* (9)[13] completely supplants the double-looped form in the other part of the manuscript. The less angular letter forms of this script allow for a yet smaller hand. This script closely resembles what Thomson calls the "tight school gothic" frequently found in late thirteenth-century German manuscripts, and what Lieftinck names *littera textualis currens*, common in manuscripts between 1260 and 1300[14]. After this time, Lieftinck says, cursive bookhands generally replaced this script.

Script (3) : annotations. Annotations on the last folio (137^(rb)), on a paper paste-down on the inside front cover, and the colophon

---

pl. 13 (France, 1298). Some of the features which we have noted are borrowed from contemporary cursives, and are also evident in the second, less formal script of the ms.

12. See the remarks of Thomson, pl. 11, pl. 12.

13. See Thomson's remarks, pl. 13.

14. See Thomson, pl. 40 (Germany, 1279), and M. G. I. Lieftinck, *Pour une nomenclature de l'écriture livresque de la période dite gothique*, in *Nomenclature des écritures livresques du IXe au XVe siècle : Premier Colloque international de paléographie latine, Paris, 28-30 avril, 1953* (Paris 1954), p. 18, fig. 16 (Liège, St. Jacques, 13th c.).

76

(137^r) are written in a hand clearly later than the text of the manuscript. The script resembles what Lieftinck labels a *littera cursiva currens* of the fourteenth century, and also resembles closely the script of French examples in Harrison Thomson dated 1356 and 1367[15]. Most striking are the thick spiked descenders of *f*, *s*, *p*, and *q*. Ascenders of *b* and *h* are looped, and looped final *s* is circular; the *r* is sharply broken. An abbreviation for *con-* looped at the top alternates with one looped at the bottom. The abbreviation for *est* is the germanic form (ʒ). The inscription "In die dorothe lxij" (137ra) led the University of Pennsylvania cataloguers to date the manuscript 1362. This is a good date for the annotations, if not the manuscript itself.

Rubrication and Decoration. This small book is systematically rubricated and nicely decorated. The *tabula* (1^r-19^v) lists the questions in the order of their appearance but does not number them; nor are they numbered in the text. Arabic numerals at the top center or sometimes in the margin of the folios in the *tabula* indicate the Book location of the listed questions (1 = 1^v, 2^r, 3^r; 2= 4^r; 3 = 8^r; 4 = 12^v, 12va 1.27). Beginning with the commentary itself (23^v), the manuscript has original foliation. At the top center of each verso a Roman numeral numbers the folio; another Roman numeral at the top center of each recto numbers the Book of the *Sentences*. These Roman numerals are done in alternating red and blue ink; the original foliation runs I-CXVI (23^v-136^v). There are some errors : X is duplicated on 32^v and 33^v, but the misnumbering is corrected and XII is placed on 34^v; LX is mistakenly given to 83^r, where a Book number should be, but 83^v properly resumes LXI; 95^r is also given a folio number, LXIII, and the next verso is given LXIIII, thereby throwing the original foliation off by 1. Paragraph markers alternating in red and blue ink set off each question. Article titles are written by the scribes in a bolder, larger display script. The article titles are also underlined in red ink. All of these devices of indexing and text division were developed and applied to *Sentences* commentaries in the thirteenth century[16].

15. LIEFTINCK, p. 21, fig 21 (near Ghent, 1351); THOMSON, pl. 18 (1356), pl. 19 (1367).

16. Ignatius BRADY, OFM, *The Rubrics of Peter Lombard's Sentences*, in *Pier Lombardo* 6 (1962) 5-25; Richard ROUSE, *La diffusion en Occident au XIIIe siècle*

Red and blue decorated initials begin Books I, III, and IV of the commentary. The tail of the Q beginning Book I (23ra, 11.1-3) trails the entire left margin and ends in a "fish-spawn" flourish. A spindle-bar tops column a. The same Q begins Book III (67rb, 11.10-12)—here the tail and flourish above the letter fill the entire center-space—and Book IV (105ra, 11.1-3), where a fishspawn flourish tops column a. These flourishes frequently appear in the margins of Book IV, but not in the other books. The design of these initials is typical of manuscripts produced in the old southern Low Countries and the Rhineland[17].

A red bulged-tailed Q (42vb, 11.21-22) begins Book II. The first of these initials appears on 41vb, immediately after scribe (2) has taken over the copying, and thereafter they appear throughout the manuscript (52ra, 71ra, 81ra, 84ra, 85vb, 88va, 89va, 95vb, 104ra, 119ra, 128rb, 130vb, 134ra). A different form of this initial, ubiquitous in manuscripts of the Low Countries and Germany, occurs only twice in the section of the text copied by scribe (1) (25va, 26va). Moreover, whereas scribe (2) always leaves a letter to indicate rubrication of the initial, scribe (1) does not do so. Scribe (1), presumably, did his own initial rubrication; scribe (2) either left his Q's for someone else, or rubricated them himself later. In any case, this fact provides another indication that the manuscript was copied by two scribes, and not by one scribe using different registers of script.

Binding. The binding—red pigskin over boards—is contemporary with the manuscript. The spine has been anciently rebacked. The upper cover has a central leather strap, meant to buckle with a metal clasp now missing on the lower cover. A strip of pigskin is cut on the lower cover, leaving a rectangular space (.5 × 9.0 cm) for an inscription : *veritas hūa.* The rebacking covers the last part of the inscription.

des outils de travail facilitant l'accès aux textes autoritatifs, in *L'enseignement en Islam et en Occident au moyen âge : Medieval Education in Islam and the West (International Colloquy of La Napoule, 1976),* pp. 115-147, esp. pp. 134-138.

17. See THOMSON, pl. 14 (1298, Bolebec, Seine-Inférieure). As stated, the designs are common to manuscripts of the Low Countries; I have seen very similar ones in many mss. from Liège. I take the term "fish-spawn" from Alison STONES, *The Minnesota Vincent of Beauvais Manuscript and Cistercian Thirteenth-Century Book Decoration,* James Bell Ford Lecture 14 (Minneapolis 1977).

Provenance and History. The conflation of French and German features in the script and decoration suggest that the manuscript was made in a border region. I believe that it probably originated in the southeastern Low Countries. The colophon, which states that Peter of Tarentaise was "Magister *ordinis*", shows that the manuscript once belonged to Dominicans. The Quaritch catalogue indicates that the book belonged to J. P. R. Lyell, but gives no further information about origin.

Literature. Bernard Quaritch's Catalogue, no. 699 (1952) p. 26, n. 86; Norman P. Zacour and Rudolph Hirsch, *Catalogue of Manuscripts in the Libraries of the University of Pennsylvania to 1800* (Philadelphia 1965) p. 8.

II. THE METHOD AND CONTENT OF WILLIAM DE ROTHWELL'S COMMENTARY

The colophon to the manuscript (137^r) states that the book contains an "excerptum Magistri petri de tarantasia super quatuor libros sententiarum". Observing that the incipits of the work do not match those of Peter's commentary, the Bernard Quaritch cataloguer judged that the "writer who added the colophon was mistaken in his attribution"[18]. On the contrary, the writer of the colophon is precisely correct. William de Rothwell's work proves to be an *abbreviatio* of Peter of Tarentaise's commentary on the *Sentences* of Peter Lombard.

The Dominican Peter of Tarentaise (*ca.* 1224-1276), who became Pope for one day (Innocent V, 21-22 January, 1276), completed his commentary on the four books of Peter Lombard's *Sentences* during his first regency at Paris, 1259-1264[19]. For the moment, we can therefore establish the date 1264 as the *terminus post quem* for William de Rothwell's abbreviation, and 1298, the earliest exact

---

18. *Bernard Quaritch's Catalogue*, no. 699 (1952), p. 26, n. 86.
19. L. B. GILLON, *Sur les écrits de Pierre de Tarentaise et leur chronologie*, in *Le Bienheureux Innocent V (Pierre de Tarentaise) et son temps*, ed. P. GILLET (Vatican City 1947), p. 361.

date that appears concerning a manuscript of the work, as the *terminus a quo*. We shall remark here that William's work is not a *reportatio* concurrent with Peter of Tarentaise's lectures. William's verbatim extraction of formulae from Peter's commentary and his culling of them from different parts of the articles demonstrate that he had a completed written text before him[20].

In his commentary, Peter of Tarentaise draws largely upon the earlier commentaries of Bonaventure (1250-1252) and Thomas Aquinas (1254-1256)[21]. Peter's commentary is notably irenic. On most questions he reports opinions on both sides of the argument in the body of his article. Many times he answers objections against each of the contrary opinions. Sometimes he reveals a preference ("more probable", "easier", "more common"); at other times one may infer Peter's preference only from the set of objections he chooses to answer. The style of Peter's commentary suggests that he considered theological reasoning to be mainly a form of probable argumentation. When Peter does state a preference, he usually inclines more to the opinions which Bonaventure represents, but not always.

Despite its mediating approach, Peter of Tarentaise's commentary was the object of mild controversy within the Dominican Order. Sometime between 1264 and 1268, the Master of the Order John of Vercelli forwarded to Thomas Aquinas for comment a number of objections against Peter of Tarentaise's teaching made by another Dominican. To these objections Thomas wrote a *Responsio ad magistrum Ioannem de Vercelli de 108 articulis*[22]. Generally Thomas expounds the words of his fellow Dominican *reverenter*, saving the

---

20. All references in our study are to *Innocentii Quinti ... In IV Libros Sententiarum Commentaria*, 4 vols. corresponding to the 4 Books (Toulouse 1652; repr. 1964, The Gregg Press). This text was printed from a single manuscript, and in some places is clearly faulty; however, William's text corresponds well with this printed edition.

21. See H.-D. SIMONIN, *Les écrits de Pierre de Tarentaise*, in *Beatus Innocentius V (Petrus de Tarantasia O.P.) : Studia et documenta* (Rome 1943), pp. 163-335; R.-M. MARTIN, *Pour une réédition critique du commentaire de Pierre de Tarentaise sur le Livre des Sentences de Pierre Lombard*, in *Miscellanea Alb. De Meyer*, I (Louvain 1946), pp. 590-602.

22. Edited in *Sancti Thomae de Aquino Opera omnia iussu Leonis XIII P.M. edita*, cura et studia Fratrum Praedicatorum, t. XLII (Rome 1979), pp. 259-294.

appearances of Peter's arguments. At times Thomas reproves the understanding of the objector. In several instances, however, Thomas flatly disapproves of Peter's expression[23]. Dom Odon Lottin has shown that at least some Dominican readers of Peter of Tarentaise's commentary noted Thomas' "corrections", and that even Peter himself may have heeded them[24]. In relation to William de Rothwell's abbreviation, Thomas Aquinas' *Responsio* is interesting precisely because it chiefly concerns verbal formulae.

Peter of Tarentaise in his commentary employs the full dialectical technique of the schools. First arguments are put forward — these usually affirm the conclusion opposite to Peter's — and these are matched by arguments *contra*. A Response in which Peter determines the question follows, constituting the body of the article. Finally, Peter answers objecting arguments. Peter often saves the objections by means of a distinction; at other times, as we have said, Peter will sustain both sides of an argument, answering the first arguments according to one opinion and the arguments *contra* according to the other opinion. In such cases it seems that Peter thinks that each opinion can claim "probability" in relation to faith. For Peter, theology strictly speaking is a transcendent wisdom, and a science in only a faint, derivative sense[25].

In his abbreviation of Peter's commentary, William de Rothwell omits most of the dialectical argumentation. Customarily William excerpts from Peter's Response, often simply repeating the two or three opinions he finds there. Occasionally William draws material from other parts of Peter's article, or directly from the text of Peter Lombard. William's *sententiae* can be nearly unintelligible unless one refers them to the text from which they are drawn. William's method of abbreviating makes it difficult to ascertain his own

---

23. See the study, Benedictus M. SMERALDO, OP, *Intorno all'Opuscolo IX di S. Tomaso d'Aquino. Pietro da Tarantasia ha errato in Teologia?* (Rome 1945).

24. See Odon LOTTIN, *Pierre de Tarentaise a-t-il remanié son commentaire sur les Sentences?*, in *Recherches de Théologie ancienne et médiévale (RTAM)* 2 (1930) 420-433; *A propos du commentaire des Sentences de Pierre de Tarentaise*, in *RTAM* 13 (1946) 86-98, repr. in *Psychologie et morale aux XIIᵉ et XIIIᵉ siècles*, VI (Gembloux 1960), pp. 337-352.

25. See I *Sent.*, *Prol.*, q. unica, a.1, p. 3. For William's abbreviation, see the description of the manuscript, 23ʳᵃ (inc.).

opinion. However, the material from Peter's questions which William chooses to extract—or omit—and the way he disposes it can be revealing. Moreover, Peter sometimes abandons Peter's text altogether; such variations are clearly significant. Finally, in a few noteworthy instances Peter declares his opinion firmly.

We shall test William de Rothwell's abbreviation of Peter of Tarentaise's commentary on the *Sentences* against a number of urgent questions concerning (A) God's knowledge and divine ideas, (B) creation and the composition of creatures, and (C) the soul and its powers. Afterwards, we shall decide the intent and significance of William's abbreviation. On this last point, manuscript evidence will be helpful.

A. — *God's Knowledge and Divine Ideas.*

In his *Collationes in Hexaëmeron* (1273), Bonaventure preached severely against the "philosophers" in the arts faculty at Paris. Bonaventure traced the philosophers' many errors to Aristotle's denial of Plato's Ideas, which Augustine had placed correctly in the divine mind. If, as Aristotle and his followers taught, God knows only himself and does not know creatures through exemplar reasons in his mind, he cannot foreknow the actions of creatures, judge their merits, or provide for their good. Moreover, the denial of divine ideas leads ultimately to the conclusions that there is no devil, no hell, no punishment, no heaven, no reward, and that the world is eternal [26]. For Bonaventure, the doctrine of divine exemplars, according to which God created everything in his vestige, image and likeness, is synonymous with Christian wisdom. By means of philosophic reasoning, one can discover that there is a first cause to the universe. This knowledge, however, is inadequate, since it reveals little about the purpose and meaning of creation. The full understanding of nature comes only through the revealed divine Word, the exemplar cause of all things. As the eternal reasons in the Word measure the being of creatures, so they are the standards of truth which regulate the human mind. The human

---

26. *Collationes in Hexaëmeron, S. Bonaventurae Opera omnia*, cura PP. Collegii a S. Bonaventura, V (Quaracchi 1891), *Coll.* 6, 2-5, pp. 360-361.

mind is regulated by the eternal reasons through a divine illumination, without which human reasoning is blind. The eternal reasons are also the exemplars of human virtues, since the order of right living follows the orders of being and understanding[27]. Within the context established by Bonaventure, the doctrine of divine ideas, based squarely on the teachings of Augustine, is a touchstone to one's thought concerning the relationships between faith and reason, theology and philosophy.

(1) *An Pater genuit Filium secundum rationem exemplaritatis vel ideae.*
Peter of Tarentaise, I *Sent.*, d.6, q. unica, a.4 (p. 61).

Thomas Aquinas' commentary on the *Sentences* lacks an article corresponding to this title. Peter of Tarentaise draws both the question and his solution from the commentary of Bonaventure. Like Bonaventure[28], Peter says that something can proceed by way of exemplarity either as a thing *exemplatum*, or as the *ratio exemplandi*. Creatures proceed from God in the first way, the Son proceeds from the Father in the second.

William de Rothwell repeats the distinction. To the distinction he adds the strong words of Augustine quoted by Peter in his argument *contra* 3 : "he who denies the existence of the ideas denies the existence of the Son of God".

William de Rothwell, I, 25[va] :

> *Vtrum genuit eum secundum rationem exemplaris vel ydee* Respondeo procedere secundum rationem exemplaris. vel ydee. dupliciter potest intelligi. vel ut exemplatum. uel ut ratio exemplandi alia/. primo modo procedit creaturam. secundo modo filius ut augustinus. qui negat ydeas esse/ negat filium dei esse[29].

27. For a detailed treatment of these matters, see the author's *Reading the World Rightly and Squarely : Bonaventure's Doctrine of the Cardinal Virtues*, in *Traditio* (1983-in press).
28. BONAVENTURE, I *Sent.*, d.6, a. unicus q.3, in corpore, *Opera omnia*, I (Quaracchi 1882), pp. 129-130.
29. PETER OF TARENTAISE, I *Sent.*, d.6, q. unica, a.4, p. 61 : "(Contra 3) Filius est idea, vnde dicit Augustinus, quod qui negat ideas esse, negat Filium Dei esse ... (R.) secundum rationem ideae vel exemplaris potest dici aliquid dupliciter : vel vt exemplatum, vel vt ratio exemplandi alia : primo modo procedit creatura secundum rationem ideae, id est, per ideam; secundo modo Filius, ita vt sit idea".

(2) *An verbum importat respectum ad creaturam vel non.*
Peter of Tarentaise, I *Sent.*, d.27, q.2, a.3 (pp. 226-227).

Thomas Aquinas and Bonaventure resolve this question similarly. According to Bonaventure, God knows himself and all things in one and the same glance (*aspectu*)[30]; or, as Thomas Aquinas says, God knows all things in the Word which is the "species or similitude of the Father or the divine essence"[31]. Peter of Tarentaise states the principle in Thomas Aquinas' terms[32]. However, he bases his conclusion on a distinction made by Bonaventure: the Word does not have a relation to creatures according to his act, by which he is an image of the Father, but according to his habit, by which he is their exemplar.

William de Rothwell excerpts the conclusion which Peter draws from Bonaventure.
William de Rothwell, I, 34[rb]:

> *Vtrum inportet respectum ad creaturam.* Respondeo. sic. secundum augustinum super Ioannem. habitualem. scilicet. non actualem de necessitate quia habet similitudinem cum patre inquantum est ymago eius. cum creaturas/ inquantum exemplar earum[33].

(3) *An vna sola sit veritas in omnibus.*
Peter of Tarentaise, I *Sent.*, d.8, q.2, a.2 (pp. 72-73).

Peter of Tarentaise again takes his question and his solution from Bonaventure's commentary. Following Bonaventure[34], Peter says that truth may be considered in relation "to the subject which it informs; to the principle which it imitates and represents, namely the divine intellect; and to the human intellect, which it excites

---

30. BONAVENTURE, I *Sent.*, d.27, pt.2, a. unicus, q.2, in corpore, p. 485.
31. THOMAS AQUINAS, I *Sent.*, d.27, q.2, a.3, in corpore, *Scriptum super Libros Sententiarum*, ed. P. MANDONNET, OP, I (Paris 1929), p. 663.
32. PETER OF TARENTAISE, I *Sent.*, d.27, q.2, a.3, R., p. 227: "Deus Pater in eadem specie, scilicet seipso, seu essentia sua, se & omnia intelligit".
33. *Ibid.*: "Hinc est quod verbum eius habet quidem similitudinem cum ipso, inquantum est imago eius: habet etiam cum omnibus quae ab ipso fiunt, inquantum est exemplar eorum: sed primus respectus inest ei secundum actum, alius secundum habitum". For Augustine, see arg. 2, p. 226.
34. BONAVENTURE, I *Sent.*, d.8, pt.1, a.1, q.1, in corpore, p. 151.

and illumines" (*in corpore*). According to the first and third relations, there are many truths; according to the second, there is one truth of all truths.

Thomas Aquinas was asked to comment upon Peter's proposition that "Veritatés rerum comparate ad subiectum diuerse sunt, sed secundum quod comparantur ad intellectum diuinum una est ueritas". In his *Responsio*, Thomas says that this proposition is "most true", if it be understood that the one truth is uncreated, not created. Thomas remarks that the objector has understood Peter of Tarentaise to mean one created truth[35]. Peter, however, makes his meaning clear. Responding to Anselm's statement that "as there is one time of all temporal things, so there is one truth of all true things", Peter specifies (ad 1) that the one exemplary and efficient truth of all things is not created.

As if aware of the objection against Peter's words, William de Rothwell incorporates into his response both Anselm's statement and Peter's clarification. William then refers to the threefold aspect of truth upon which Peter bases his conclusion.

William de Rothwell, I, 26[ra] :

> *Vtrum vna sola sit ueritas in omnibus ueris* Respondeo tantum una est efficiens et exemplaris de qua anselmus in littera. determinatur. Sicut vnum est tempus omnium temporalium. sic una est ueritas/ omnium uerorum Sed non vna est vna (*read*: veritas) comparata ad subiectum quod informat/ similiter non secundum quod comparatur ad intellectum quem excitat et illuminat. immo plures[36].

(4) *An Deus cognoscat singularia.*
Peter of Tarentaise, I *Sent.*, d.36, q.1, a.2 (p. 289).

---

35. THOMAS AQUINAS, *Responsio*, 17, p. 282.
36. PETER OF TARENTAISE, *I Sent.*, d.8, q.2, a.2, pp. 72-73 : "(arg. 1) Dicit Anselmus lib. De veritate, quod sicut est vnum tempus omnium temporalium, sic est vna veritas omnium verorum ... (R.) Veritas comparatur ad tria, ad subjectum quod informat, ad principium quod imitatur & repraesentat, scilicet intellectum diuinum; & ad intellectum humanum quem excitat & illuminat ... vel per comparationem ad subjectum, & sic sunt plures simpliciter veritates; vel per comparationem ad intellectum diuinum, & sic est vna veritas omnium ... vel ad intellectum creatum, & sic sunt plures ... (Ad 1.) Ex Anselmo. Resp. Vna est veritas omnium efficiens & exemplaris, non creata".

Peter of Tarentaise takes his argument from the commentary of Thomas Aquinas[37]. Philosophers argue that since God is not the immediate cause of matter, which individuates particular things, he cannot know singulars except in a universal way. On the contrary, however, God is the immediate cause of all causes, including the material. Thus, through his essence God knows the universal, singular, and particular causes of things, just as an artificer would know the whole chest which he wishes to make if his idea (like God's) were the cause of all the formal and material principles that concur in the chest's production.

William de Rothwell's abbreviation of Peter's argument is elliptical, omitting the analogy but declaring its principle. William further alludes to a quotation from Aristotle with which Peter begins his Response, and refers the reader to a previous question.

William de Rothwell, I, 36[vb]-37[ra] :

> *Vtrum cognoscat singularia.* Respondeo. Sic quia causa est omnium causarum concurrentium ad constitutionem rei et immediata causa. sed tunc arbitramur scire etc. (Supra, d. 3.6. q.6)[38].

(5) *An ideae per quas Deus cognoscit, sint in ipso.*
Peter of Tarentaise, I *Sent.*, d.36, q.2, a.2 (p. 292).

Peter of Tarentaise continues to follow Thomas Aquinas closely on this question[39]. Like Thomas, Peter founds his determination on a distinction and analogy made by Averroes. As artificial forms have a twofold being, one in act as they are in matter, another in potency as they are in the mind of the artificer, so natural forms have a twofold being, one in act as they are in their own genus,

---

37. THOMAS AQUINAS, I *Sent.*, d.36, q.1, a.1, in corpore, p. 832.

38. PETER OF TARENTAISE, I *Sent*, d.36, q.1, q.1, R., p. 289 : "Vt ait Philosophus. 1. Post. Scire arbitramur vnumquodque cum causas cognoscimus & principia prima vsque ad elementa : Deus cogniscit per essentiam suam causas omnium singularium & uniuersales & particulares ... tanquam existens eorum tota causa & immediata, & ideo cognoscit seipso omnia singularia. Sicut si artifex per ideam arcae esset causa omnium quae concurrunt ad arcam & materialium & formalium principiorum, per illam ideam vniuersalium cognosceret totam arcam". William refers to his question, *Vtrum sit vniuersalis et particularis*, I, 36[vb], which corresponds to PETER OF TARENTAISE, I *Sent.*, d.35, q.2, a.6, pp. 284-285.

39 THOMAS AQUINAS, I *Sent.*, d.36, q.2, a.1, in corpore, p. 839.

another in active potency, as they are in the first mover, that is, God. To this distinction Peter adds another : whatever is in prime matter in a passive potency is in the first mover in an active potency. Elsewhere, we shall see, Peter develops a correspondence between forms in the mind of God and forms latent in matter. After relating Averroes' distinction to a text from pseudo-Dionysius ("Exemplaria dicimus substantificas rationes existentium in Deo vniformiter praeexistentes"), Peter concludes his Response by stating that the ideas or forms do not exist separately through themselves, as the Platonists thought, but in the mind of God.

William de Rothwell's abbreviation is an outline of Peter's Response.

William de Rothwell, I, 37ra :

> Vtrum ydee sint in deo per quas res cognoscat Respondeo. Sic secundum augustinum et boetium. oportet enim secundum commentatorem. super xi metaphysice primum agens prehabere omnes formas exemplares et in potentia actiua. sicut omnes sunt in materia in potentia passiua. quasi idem dicit dionysius v. capitulo. de. diuinis. nominibus. hec autem forme non per se subsistunt. ut dixerunt platonici. sed sunt in mente diuina. et sunt in ipso principium cognitionis rerum [40].

(6) *An sit in Deo plures ideae, vel vna.*
Peter of Tarentaise, I *Sent.*, d.36, q.2, a.3 (pp. 292-294).

Although they employ different terms, on this question Bonaventure and Thomas Aquinas reach substantially the same conclusion. Peter of Tarentaise uses some material from Bonaventure's commentary[41], but for the main argument in his Response he adopts

---

40. PETER OF TARENTAISE, I *Sent.*, d.36, q. 2, a.2, R., p. 292: "ita & formae naturales habent esse duplex vt ait Comment. super 11. Met. vnum in actu, secundum quod sunt in proprio genere : alterum in potentia actiua, secundum quod sunt in primo motore, id est in Deo. Nam quicquid est in prima materia in potentia passiua, est in primo motore in potentia actiua ... Vnde dicit Dionys. 5. Cap. de Diu. nomin ... Has autem formas seu ideas non separatas extra materiam & per se ponimus, vt Platonici, sed in mente Diuina, quae sunt in ipsa principium tam speculatiuae quam practicae cognitionis rerum". For Augustine and Boethius, see Peter's arg. 3-5.

41. Peter begins his Response with a distinction among the being of forms as they exist in matter (with opposition, composition, distinction), in the created intellect (with composition, distinction), and in the divine intellect (with distinction alone). See BONAVENTURE, I *Sent.*, d.35, a. unicus, q.2, in corpore, p. 605.

the express terms and conclusions of Thomas Aquinas. The completely simple perfection of God is imitated by creatures in diverse ways, as they are more or less imperfect. In God, to exist, to live, and to understand are one and the same thing; they are not in creatures, some of which only exist, some of which exist and live, and some of which exist, live, and understand. The object of God's knowledge is his divine essence; however, God knows his divine essence as the exemplar of the diverse creatures which imitate his being in diverse grades of perfection. Hence, although the divine essence which is the object of God's knowledge is one according to being, nevertheless it is said to have many ideas "because it is the similitude of the many things which imitate it in diverse ways". The many divine ideas, then, "are nothing other than the diverse modes of imitability (*imitabilitatis*) by which diverse things imitate the divine essence, existing in the divine intellect for the production and knowledge of creatures"[42].

Careful to stress the unity of the divine essence, Peter adds that the ideas in God are said to be many "secundum rationem, non secundum rem". But Peter does not wish to say, as these terms suggest, that a plurality of ideas has no foundation in God. Peter confronts this issue in reply to two arguments also cited and answered by Bonaventure. It is argued (arg. 6) that God is signified by a plurality of ideas either properly, as he is in himself, or connotatively, in terms of his relation to many creatures. God cannot be signified properly by a plurality of ideas, since the divine intellect is one. If he is signified connotatively by a plurality of ideas, this is either in respect to time or to eternity. If in respect to time, then either a plurality of ideas does not exist from eternity, or the temporal is the reason of the eternal. But a plurality of ideas cannot be predicated of God in respect to eternity, since there is no diversity in eternity; therefore, there is no reason in God upon which to found a plurality of ideas[43]. To this argument Peter replies that the

---

42. See THOMAS AQUINAS, I *Sent.*, d.36, q.2, a.2, in corpore, pp. 841-842.

43. See BONAVENTURE, I *Sent.*, d.35, a. unicus, q.3, ad opp. 3, ad (ad opp.) 3, p. 608. Bonaventure's terms are "non propter significatum, sed propter connotatum", and he concludes: "Quoniam igitur sic connotantur temporalia, ut futura sunt, et futura sunt multa ... tamen sic connotata, quamvis ab aeterno connotentur, non sunt ab aeterno, sed ex tempore; ita multitudo connotatorum, quamvis ab aeterno dicatur, tamen non ponit realem multitudinem nisi ex tempore".

divine ideas in God are many by reason of the connotative relation between the divine essence and many things, and this relation is eternal, although it is realized in the temporal future.

Again, it is argued (arg. 9) that a plurality of ideas in God "aut est secundum rem, aut secundum solam rationem". If the first, then a plurality of forms composes the divine intellect as it does the human intellect (which is impossible); if the plurality is posited only according to reason, then the notion is empty because it has no foundation (in an object)[44]. To this argument Peter replies (ad 9) that the distinction according to reason which posits a plurality of ideas "is not from the human or angelic intellect, but from the divine intellect, and this distinction is not empty, because it is founded in the plenitude of the divine essence imitable in diverse ways, and is realized in act in the future, different imitations of creatures".

John of Vercelli asked Thomas Aquinas to comment upon these two propositions of Peter's article, since the Dominican objector thought that they implied a real plurality and distinction in the divine essence. Thomas sustains both propositions, affirming that God from eternity "understood the multitude of relations between himself and creatures, and this suffices for a plurality of ideas, which are nothing other than the reasons of things as they are understood by God"[45]. Not surprisingly does Thomas sustain Peter's propositions, for Peter drew his arguments, and the very terms of one of the propositions questioned by the objector (67; Peter, ad 9), from Thomas' commentary on the *Sentences*: secundum quod est multiplex imitabilitas in essentia divina, propter plenitudinem suae perfectionis, est pluralitas idearum (Peter, ad 9) ... quamvis relationes quae sunt Dei ad creaturam, realiter in creatura

---

44. See BONAVENTURE, I *Sent.*, d.35, a. unicus, q.2, in corpore, p. 605; d.35, a. unicus, q.3, fund. 2, ad opp. 1, sol. opp. 1, pp. 607-608.

45. THOMAS AQUINAS, *Responsio*, 66-67, p. 289: "66 ... Deus enim ab aeterno sicut intellexit multitudinem creaturarum, ita intellexit multitudinem respectuum prout sunt inter ipsum et creaturas; et hoc sufficit ad pluralitatem ydearum, que nichil aliud sunt quam rationes rerum prout sunt intellecte a Deo"; "67. Quod uero LXVII proponitur 'Pluralitas ydearum est in Deo secundum rationem, non tamen intellectus humani uel angelici, sed diuini'. patet ex precedenti quomodo uerum est ...".

fundentur, tamen secundum rationem et intellectum in Deo etiam sunt; intellectum autem dico non tantum humanum, sed etiam angelicum et divinum (*Responsio*, 67; Peter ad 9): et ideo quamvis creaturae ab aeterno non fuerint, tamen intellectus divinus ab aeterno fuit intelligens essentiam suam diversimode a creaturis imitabilem; et propter hoc fuit ab aeterno pluralitas idearum in intellectu divino, non in natura ipsius (Peter, ad 6, ad 9)[46].

William de Rothwell composes his response from several parts of Peter of Tarentaise's article. Among the items he incorporates is the proposition, questioned by Peter's objector but affirmed by Thomas Aquinas, that a plurality of reasons is in the divine intellect by reason of the exemplar's "relation to the modes of future things". Like Thomas and Peter after him, William asserts that this reason is not empty, because founded in the "plenitude of the divine nature imitable in diverse ways".

William de Rothwell, I, 37[ra-b]:

> *Vtrum sint in deo plures ydee/ vel vna.* Respondeo quamuis essentia una sit que est exemplar. omnium rerum. tamen ydee plures sunt. quia secundum augustinum. non eadem ratione conditus est homo qua equus. Singula enim propriis creata sunt rationibus. Ille autem ydee plures. nihil aliud sunt quam modi diuersi immitabilitatis diuine essentie in rebus diuersis in intellectu diuino existentes ad diuersas creaturas producendum et cognoscendum vnde illa pluralitas rationum. quamuis in deo absolute nullo modo differat in creatura tamen differt re et ratione inquantum autem sunt in intellectu quocumque etiam diuino per modum exemplaris in comparatione ad modos rerum futuros. sic differunt ratione tantum/ quod ratio non est cassa/ sed fundatur super diuine nature plenitudinem. diuersis modis immitabilem. completur autem per operationem intellectus et terminatur ad creaturam diuersis modis immitantem[47].

46. Thomas Aquinas, I *Sent.*, d.36, q.2, a.2, ad 1-2, p. 842.

47. Peter of Tarentaise, I *Sent.*, d.36, q.2, a.3, pp. 292-294: "(Contra 1.) Augustinus lib. 83 quaest. Non eadem ratione conditus est homo, qua equus, singula enim creata sunt proprijs rationibus ... (R.) ... illae enim ideae plures nihil aliud sunt quam diuersi modi imitabilitatis Diuinae essentiae a, rebus diuersis, in intellectu Diuino existentes ad diuersas creaturas producendas & cognoscendas ... Si vero quaeritur vbi sit illa pluralitas rationum. Resp. Modi imitandi possunt considerari tripliciter : vel prout sunt absolute in natura Diuina imitabili, sic nullo modo distinguuntur : vel prout absolute erunt in rebus, sic differunt etiam re quando sunt : vel prout sunt in intellectu (diuino) per modum exemplaris in comparatione ad modos rerum futuros accipiente, sic differunt ratione ... Sed nunquid illa ratio

90

(7) *An in Deo sint ideae omnium rerum, & quomodo.*
Peter of Tarentaise, I *Sent.*, d.36, q.2, a.4 (pp. 295-296).

One's solution to this question depends upon his understanding of matter and the composition of created beings. Thomas Aquinas says that creatures have a perfect idea in God insofar as they have perfect being (*esse perfectum*). By reason of their (substantial) form, composites of matter and form have perfect being and a perfect idea in God. Matter in itself is pure potency and attains being only in composition with form. Thus, God does not know matter apart from composites; known indirectly, matter may be said to have an "imperfect idea" in God (and man). Evil is strictly privation and has no being; thus it has no idea in God, who knows it through the idea of its opposite good[48].

Peter of Tarentaise's solution is somewhat different, and bespeaks a different understanding of matter and the composition of created beings. "Whatever imitates the divine form in any way", Peter declares, "has an idea in God". Everything that participates in being imitates God more or less perfectly according to a hierarchy of actualized being. Thus, form alone, as act, has an idea in God; composites of matter and form are in complete act, and these have a more complete being (*esse completum*). The composite itself has the most complete being, and after that the substantial form of the composite. Other things have an incomplete being (*esse incompletum*). Matter in itself is only potency and is in act through another, namely form; things constantly in the process of change (e.g. time) have an act mixed with potency; certain things, like the infinite, can never be fully in act; certain others, like the vacuum, are in act contrary to their potency. Such incomplete beings can never be known completely by the human intellect. God, however, knows them completely, not through a form received from them, but through the idea which is their cause. Indeed, although creatures imitate God more or less perfectly, in God "every idea is perfect,

cassa est ... (Ad 4.) ... Illa ergo idearum pluralitas quodammodo fundatur super essentiae Diuinae plenitudinem, completur per operationem intellectus Diuini sub diuersis modis imitabilitatis eam apprehendentem, terminatur ad creaturam diuersis modis imitantem, vnde non causatur ab ea". See also ad 7,9.
48. THOMAS AQUINAS, I *Sent.*, d.36, q.2, a.3, ad 1,2, p. 844.

representing even the imperfect most perfectly". Since they have no being at all, evil and privation have no idea in God.

Peter's solution, which comes in part from Albert the Great[49], is not clear on every point. Unlike Thomas Aquinas, Peter says that matter has a perfect idea in God. In answer to an objection that prime matter can have no idea in God because it has no form (arg. 3), Peter replies that "although prime matter in itself has no intrinsic perfecting form, nevertheless it has an extrinsic exemplar", namely God, whose act of existence is the cause of its potency. This statement echoes the principle, stated before by Peter (see 5, above), that whatever is a passive potency in prime matter is an active potency in God. Although lacking an "intrinsic perfecting form", does matter, as an incomplete being, have some kind of act apart from the complete act it attains in composites of matter and form? Peter's terms *esse completum—esse incompletum* urge this interpretation, for elsewhere, as we shall see (10, 11 below), he speaks of prime matter's existence in an incomplete state deprived of complete form, and of the incomplete being of the seminal reasons in matter which dispose to the reception of completing forms. Moreover, Peter's distinction here between the complete being of the *ipsum compositum* and the *forma substantialis compositi* is clarified by another which he makes while arguing for the union of forms incomplete in themselves in the human composite (see 15, below).

William de Rothwell's excerpt faintly echoes Peter's graded hierarchy; one can discern, however, Peter's distinction between the complete composite and the substantial form ("postmodum forma substantialis"), and William alludes to the incomplete being of matter.

William de Rothwell, I, 37[rb]:

> *Vtrum in deo sint ydee omnium rerum et quomodo.* Respondeo. quia ydea nihil aliud est quam immitabilitas diuine essentie etc. Supra. proximo. Ideo omnia habent ydeam in deo/ que diuinam essentiam siue formam qualitercumque imitantur. non alia. vnde non malum. non

49. As reported in DIONYSIUS CARTUSIANUS, I *Sent.*, d.36, p.2, *Opera omnia*, XX (Tournai 1902), p. 411. Albert uses the distinction matter-time-infinite-vacuum (from Boethius), but he does not here use the term *esse incompletum*.

priuatio. ydeam habent. Sed omnia que naturam entis. participant. et eque perfectam ex parte dei. sed non ex parte creature. quia diuersimode imitantur. sed illa perfectiorem que perfectius habent esse. ut ex materia et forma. compositum. postmodum forma substantialis. sed materia incompletam similiter infinitum. vacuum. tempus. secundum id quod se habent ad esse. Deus tamen perfecte illa cognoscit per ydeam que est causa illorum quamuis nos ipsa imperfecte [50].

B.—*Creation and the Composition of Creatures*

As is well-known, questions concerning the nature of matter and the composition of creatures were hotly disputed in the last three decades of the thirteenth century. Thomas Aquinas' solutions to a number of theological problems follow from three philosophic principles. First, like Aristotle Thomas held that matter was purely passive. Thomas did not allow seeming theological difficulties to cause him to vary from this principle. Secondly, Thomas denied that spiritual creatures were composed of matter and form, or that there was any such thing as spiritual matter. Both sides of this argument had been upheld since the 1230s [51]. Thirdly, Thomas argued that every creature possessed one, and only one, substantial form. This position was more novel. Although several theologians in the first half of the century anticipated Thomas' teaching in regard to the human soul [52], Thomas seems to be the first to establish the unicity of substantial form as a metaphysical principle

50. PETER OF TARENTAISE, I *Sent.*, d.36, q.2, a.4, R., p. 295: "Quicquid ergo Diuinam illam formam qualitercumque imitatur, habet idea in Deo: id vero quod nullatenus imitatur, non habet. Quia ergo malum & priuatio Diuinam formam nullatenus imitatur, nullam habet in Deo ideam: quia vero omne quod naturam entis participat aliquo modo imitatur eam, ideo omne tale in Deo ideam habet ... ex parte Dei omnis idea perfecta est ... sed ex parte creaturarum aliqua perfectius, aliqua minus perfecte dicuntur habere in Deo ideam. Quaedam sunt ... in actu completo, vt compositum ex materia & forma; & haec habent esse magis completum, & hoc magis ipsum compositum, deinde forma substantialis compositi. Quaedam ... vt materia ... vt omnia de genere successiuorum ... vt infinitum ... vt vacuum ... habent esse incompletum: vnde & a nobis sciri complete non possunt: Deus tamen habet complete cognitionem eorum ... per idea quae est causa illorum".
51. Odon LOTTIN, *La simplicité de l'âme humaine avant saint Thomas d'Aquin*, in *Psych. et mor.*, I (2nd. ed., Gembloux 1957), pp. 425-460.
52. Odon LOTTIN, *L'unité de l'âme humaine avant saint Thomas d'Aquin*, in *Psych. et mor.*, I, pp. 461-479.

that applies to the entire order of created being[53]. In any case, it was his teaching that occasioned the controversy in the latter part of the century.

Thomas Aquinas' opponents, who thought themselves to uphold traditional doctrine, argued that matter had an incomplete act of its own—which some called a certain *forma corporeitatis*—and that all creatures, including the angels and the human soul, were composed of matter and form, since "matter" is the general principle of potency and mutability, and only the being of God is pure act and immutable. These doctrines entail a plurality of forms in the composition of creatures, since every creature will partake the general form of matter and at least one specific form. Scholars have shown that the theologians who maintained these doctrines were greatly influenced by the *Fons vitae* of the Jewish philosopher, Avicebron (Solomon ibn Gabirol, fl. 1020-1058). This text was made accessible to Latin thinkers through the late twelfth-century translation of Dominicus Gundissalinus[54]. Thomas Aquinas traced the ideas opposed to his to this work.

However, not all theologians who maintained that prime matter has some act of its own or that spiritual creatures are composed of matter and form argued exclusively from the principles of Avicebron. Those who used his terms doubtless found them useful for expounding traditional doctrines. For Augustine himself had

53. See Roberto ZAVALLONI, OFM, *Richard de Mediavilla et le controverse sur la pluralité des formes* (Louvain 1951), pp. 261-272, 497 *et passim*. I consider this book to be the most even-handed on the subject of this controversy. For a recent study of the controversy in the late thirteenth century, see John F. WIPPEL, *The Metaphysical Thought of Godfrey of Fontaines. A Study in Late Thirteenth-Century Philosophy* (Washington, D.C.).

54. *Avencebrolis (ibn Gebirol) Fons Vitae ex Arabico in Latinum translatus ab Iohanne Hispano et Dominico Gundissalino*, ed. Clemens BAEUMKER, *Beiträge zur Geschichte der Philosophie des Mittelalters (BGPM)*, I, 2-4 (Münster, 1892-95), pp. 1-339. M. WITTMANN, *Die Stellung des hl. Thomas von Aquin zu Avencebrol (Ibn Gebirol)*, BGPM, III, 3 (Münster 1900); G. THÉRY, *L'augustinisme médiéval et le problème de l'unité de la forme substantielle*, in *Acta Hebdomadae Augustinianae-Thomisticae* (Turin 1931), pp. 140-200; D. A. CALLUS, OP, *The Origins of the Problem of the Unity of Form*, repr. in *The Dignity of Science*, ed. J. A. WEISHEIPL, OP (Washington, D.C., 1961), pp. 121-149; J. A. WEISHEIPL, OP, *Albertus Magnus and Universal Hylomorphism: Avicebron. A Note on Thirteenth-Century Augustinianism*, in *The Southwestern Journal of Philosophy* 10 (1980) 239-260. See also ZAVALLONI, pp. 420-422.

said that angels and the human soul are composed of matter and form[55]. Moreover, Augustine's long-standing, almost canonical doctrine of "seminal reasons" implied that matter has some act of its own, and that incomplete forms are perfected by complete ones in composite creatures[56]. The centrality of the doctrine of seminal reasons to all the questions concerning matter and the composition of creatures is suggested by John Peckham's oft-quoted letter (1285) to the Bishop of Lincoln. Peckham laments the moderns' deviance from "what Augustine teaches concerning ... the seminal reasons included in matter and innumerable questions of the same kind"[57].

In the minds of Thomas' opponents, even more than the authority of Augustine was at stake. Augustine had adopted the doctrine of seminal reasons from ancient sources in order to accommodate the sequential, temporal account of creation in Genesis. It was in these terms that Bonaventure and others framed the question of prime matter, the resolution to which determines the resolutions to many other questions. Bonaventure distinguished those who interpret Genesis in a "theological way", in more obvious conformity with the letter of the text, from those who interpret it in a "philosophic way", according to the apparent requirements of human reason. Bonaventure did not refrain from challenging even Augustine on this matter; it is clear, however, that he had thirteenth-century "philosophers", including Thomas Aquinas, in mind[58]. The theological issue of revelation is far more fundamental than a number of individual items involved in the dispute over substantial form in creatures (e.g. transubstantiation, the identity of Christ's body before and after death, and even the immortality of the soul)[59].

55. *De Genesi ad litteram*, I, 19, 18-21, 41; VII, 6, 9; VII, 21, 31; VII, 27, 39; VII, 28, 43 (human soul); I, 9, 17 (angels); *PL* 34.260-262, 359, 366, 369-370, 372; 253. See Étienne GILSON, *The Christian Philosophy of St. Augustine*, trans. L. E. M. LYNCH (Vintage ed., New York 1967), pp. 208-209.

56. See GILSON, *The Christian Philosophy of St. Augustine*, pp. 206-208, and ZAVALLONI, pp. 436-440. See the texts cited by ZAVALLONI, p. 440, n. 67, p. 441, n. 69 for Augustine's use of the term "inchoate", which clearly justifies the thirteenth-century interpretation of seminal reasons as "inchoate forms" in matter.

57. *Registrum epistolarum fratris Johannis Peckham*, ed. C. T. MARTIN (London: Rolls Series), 3, p. 901.

58. BONAVENTURE, II *Sent.*, d.12, a.1, q.2, *Opera omnia*, II (Quaracchi 1885), pp. 295-298. For a full treatment of this question in Bonaventure, see the present author's *Reading the World Rightly and Squarely*, in *Traditio* (1983).

59. ZAVALLONI, pp. 317-319; Frederick J. ROENSCH, *Early Thomistic School* (Dubuque, Iowa, 1964), pp. 170-265, *passim*.

(8) *An Deo ab aeterno produxerit, vel producere potuerit mundum.*
Peter of Tarentaise, II *Sent.*, d.1, q.2, a.3 (pp. 10-12).

No question tested more obviously the relation between philosophic reasoning and revelation. The philosophers taught that the world is eternal; Scripture revealed that it began in time. In his commentary on the *Sentences*, Thomas Aquinas on this question sharply distinguishes the article of faith from philosophic reasoning. Philosophic arguments on both sides, Thomas says, are only "probable or sophistic"; neither the eternity of the world nor the beginning of the world in time can be demonstrated by reason. Thomas' solution allows one to entertain reasons on both sides impartially, and in effect, removes the philosophers from the immediate censure of Scripture[60]. Modern scholars dispute whether Thomas went further in his *De aeternitate mundi* (1270) by defending the possibility of an eternal world[61]. Contrary to Thomas, other theologians maintained that the impossibility of an eternal world can be demonstrated by reason.

Peter of Tarentaise treats the two questions of this article separately. Responding to the first—is the world eternal?—Peter cites three opinions, "Vna Platonis ... Altera Aristotelis ... Tertia Moysi". The opinions of the two philosophers, affirming the eternity of the world, are simply heretical. Responding to the second question, Peter says that it is impossible for the world to have been created from eternity because the very definition of a creature "est habere esse potest non esse". This is one of Bonaventure's arguments[62]. Dionysius the Carthusian observes that according to Peter of Tarentaise's solution, the beginning of the world in time is not only an article of faith, but can be demonstrated[63].

John of Vercelli asked Thomas Aquinas to comment upon Peter's first Response. Thomas objects to its formulation:

60. THOMAS AQUINAS, II *Sent.*, d.1, q.1, a.5, *Scrip. super Lib. Sent.*, ed. MANDONNET, II (Paris 1929), pp. 27-41, corpus, pp. 33-34.

61. See the recent article by John F. Wippel which reviews the scholarly opinion and delineates the textual and philosophic problems, "Did Thomas Aquinas Defend the Possibility of an Eternally Created World?" (*The "De aeternitate mundi" Revisited*), in *Journal of the History of Philosophy* 19 (1981) 21-37.

62. BONAVENTURE, II *Sent.*, d.1, pt. 1, a.1, q.2, fund. 6, p. 22.

63. DIONYSIUS CARTUSIANUS, II *Sent.*, d.1, q.4, *Opera omnia*, XXI (Tournai 1903), p. 71.

97. Quod uero XCVII proponitur "opinio Moysi fuit quod mundus non esset eternus", non satis reuerenter dictum est; nisi forte dicatur per comparationem ad opiniones aliorum, ut si diceretur 'Opinio Aristotilis talis fuit, sed opinio Moysi talis', ad significandum huius excellentiam super alios[64].

Thomas' quibble is as much philosophic as pious, for Peter's signification implies that Moses opposed the philosophers on their own ground. Consistent with his principle for resolving the question, Thomas wishes to separate Moses' teaching of faith from any philosophic opinion.

William de Rothwell repeats the three opinions stated by Peter of Tarentaise. Significantly, he sets off Moses' opinion by the *sed* (capitalized in the manuscript) which Thomas thought would ameliorate Peter's expression. Furthermore, William inserts the term *fides* into his response. These alterations suggest that William knew Thomas Aquinas' *Responsio.*

William de Rothwell, II, 43[rb] :

> *Vtrum mundus sit eternus/*. Respondeo in littera/ magister ponit tres positiones. plato enim eum dixit/ fuisse ab eterno in potentia. materie. solum./ et operatione diuina./ eductum./ de potentia. ad actum/ et hoc in tempore/ Aristotelis autem posuit eum fuisse/ ab eterno in statu generationis et corruptionis. ut nunc est. Sed moyses et fides ponit mundum nec in potentia materie. nec in actu. sed in sola potentia agentis. ab eterno fuisse/ et in tempore per creationem incepisse[65].

In his excerpt of Peter's Response to the second question, William gives the argument of reason "ex parte creaturae" against the possibility of an eternal world, and alludes to a further argument derived from Boethius.

---

64. THOMAS AQUINAS, *Responsio*, 97, p. 293.

65. PETER OF TARENTAISE, II *Sent.*, d.1, q.2, a.3, R. (1), p. 11 : "... triplex praecipue legitur circa mundi aeternitatem positio, quam tangit hic Magist. Vna Platonis, qui posuit mundum ab aeterno fuisse in potentia materiae, non in actu speciei : & operatione Diuina eductum de potentia in actum, non ab aeterno sed in tempore. Altera Arist. qui posuit mundum ab aeterno actu in materia, & in specie, & in statu generationis & corruptionis, sicut modo. Tertia Moysi qui posuit mundum non fuisse ab aeterno, nec in potentia materiae, nec in potentia materiae, nec in actu, sed in sola potentia agentis, & in tempore factum a Deo quoad materiam & speciem. Prima & secunda opinio indicatur haeretica : tertia sola vera est & tenenda". See PETER LOMBARD, II, d.1, pt.1, cc.1, 3, in *Bonaventurae Opera omnia* II, pp. 11-12.

William de Rothwell, II, 43rb-44va :

> *Vtrum aliqua creatura potuerit fieri ab eterno/.* Respondeo. licet deus potuit ab eterno/ non tamen creatura fieri ab eterno potuit/ quia est contra rationem creature. cum de eius ratione sit quod habet esse. post non esse/ Item deus creaturam duratione precedit/ sicut eternitas tempus/ boetius/ qui tempus ab euo etc. ergo etc.[66]

(9) *An ex eadem materia simul vel successiue omnia primitus sint producta.*

Peter of Tarentaise, II *Sent.*, d.12, q. unica, a.2 (pp. 101-102).

This question at once involves the principles of scriptural interpretation and the nature of matter. In his response to this question, Bonaventure attacks Augustine's interpretation *De Genesi ad litteram* which admits the conclusion that God created all things at once distinct in matter and form. Bonaventure says that Augustine's interpretation of the six days as "spiritual" is not at all literal, but anagogic. Augustine's "philosophic" interpretation of Genesis is "rationabilis et valde subtilis". Nevertheless, it does not conform to the plain sense of Scripture, which clearly states that God created things over six material days. The letter of Scripture requires that one understand all things to have been created at once in matter (on the first day), but to have been distinguished in form over the course of six days. This understanding, in turn, suggests that matter existed in a relatively unformed state (*informitas*) before it was actualized by specific forms[67]. Bonaventure's conclusion prepares the way for the doctrine of seminal reasons and a succession of forms in corporeal creatures. We should note that Augustine in *De Genesi ad litteram* does not conclude that everything was created distinct in form at the first instant, but only the angels, the heavenly bodies, the elements, and man's soul. At that time the

---

66. PETER OF TARENTAISE, II *Sent.*, d.1, q.2, a.3, R.(2), p. 12 : "Deus ab aeterno potuit creare creaturam, sed non potuit creare ab aeterno: non ex sui impotentia, sed creatura, de cuius natura est habere esse potest non esse". William alludes to BOETHIUS, *De consolatione philosophiae*, III, metr. 9, "Qui tempus ab aevo Ire jubes". Peter does not cite the text in his article; see the argument of THOMAS AQUINAS, II *Sent.*, d.2, q.1, a.1, arg. 2, p. 62.

67. BONAVENTURE, II *Sent.*, d.12, a.1, q.2, pp. 295-298, especially the *conclusio*, pp. 296-297. Again, see the author's study, *Reading the World Rightly and Squarely*, in *Traditio* (1983). This question is fundamental to Bonaventure's thought.

seeds of other species were implanted in matter, and these unfolded over time[68]. Bonaventure directs his criticism not so much against the conclusion as the principle of Augustine's interpretation, which was seized upon by thirteenth-century partisans of Aristotle.

One of whom was Thomas Aquinas. Thomas' understanding of matter does not permit Bonaventure's literal reading of Genesis. In order to avoid the implications of such a reading, Thomas distinguishes between the substance of faith, which requires one to believe that God created the world, and the accidents of faith, which are matters of probability. The manner in which God created the world is an accident of faith, as the saints' diverse interpretations of creation indicate. Thomas' distinction allows him to choose whichever interpretation accords best with his understanding of matter. Not surprisingly, he declares that Augustine's interpretation—which maintains that Scripture follows a rational instead of temporal order—"pleases him more" and is *rationabilior*. Thomas agrees with Augustine's statement that Moses divided his account of creation into six days in order to accommodate the intelligence of "rude listeners"[69]. Bonaventure sharply dismisses this idea, which, he notes, allows philosophers to submit Scripture to their own reasonings. On this crucial question Bonaventure and Thomas could not be more opposed, and their disagreement here leads to a series of further ones.

Peter of Tarentaise reports both opinions and answers objections against each. He remarks that Augustine "sometimes" follows the opinion that all things were created at once in matter but not in form. However, over Augustine's spiritual interpretation of the six days he recommends the interpretation of "other saints" as "securior ... quia auctoritati scripturae conuenientior".

William de Rothwell likewise reports both opinions, naming some of the saints who taught the more secure interpretation.

William de Rothwell, II, 49[va] :

> *Vtrum omnia sint simul producta* Respondeo due sunt opiniones. etiam in littera/ vna solius augustini. dicentis deum simul creasse in initio

---

68. See GILSON, and the texts he cites, *The Christian Philosophy of St. Augustine*, p. 206.
69. THOMAS AQUINAS, II *Sent.*, d.12, q.1, a.2, pp. 305-306.

temporis principales partes/ scilicet corpora celestia/ et species aliorum in materia. et specie distincta/ et quod vi. dies sunt vi. cognitiones/ angelice. secundum diuersa genera rerum. alia etiam aliorum sanctorum communiter. scilicet. bede. Gr(egorii). et iero(nymi) et in littera/ quod simul omnia facta in materia non specie[70].

(10) *An materia creata fuerit omnino informis.*
Peter of Tarentaise, II *Sent.*, d.12, q.unica, a.3 (pp. 102-103).

This question draws the philosophic inference of the previous one. Peter of Tarentaise denies that matter could exist without any form at all. However, the term "unformed" can be understood to mean "deprived of complete form, as is said of the unformed infant (*pauperium*), and in this way prime matter was unformed, and preceded the things to be formed in time, according to the more common opinion". Peter's example of the infant foreshadows allegiance to a doctrine of a plurality of forms in the human composite. The example of the embryo was a favorite argument among the "pluralists"[71].

The more common opinion is shared by Bonaventure. He also concludes that it is impossible for matter to exist deprived of every form. However, one may reasonably say that matter was made under some form. This form was not complete, nor did matter possess complete being (*esse completum*). Rather, in matter there was "a disposition to further forms, not a complete perfection". Furthermore, because of its appetite for diverse forms, prime matter possessed a certain imperfect diversity of forms. Thus, prime matter existed in a state "*permixta ... et confusa*". As an analogy, Bonaventure gives the example of the embryo, "which in act has the one form and figure of the mass of flesh, but a disposition for the figures

---

70. PETER OF TARENTAISE, II *Sent.*, d.12, q. unica, a.2, R., p. 101 : "Circa hoc duae leguntur sententiae Sanctorum. Vna videtur solius esse Augustini dicentis, quod Deus in primo instanti temporis simul fecit principales partes mundi, scilicet corpora celestia & species aliorum in materia & species distincta. Altera est aliorum sanctorum communis, quod simul facta sunt omnia opera sex dierum in materia, sed non in specie ... Secundum ergo Augustinum sex dies non sunt aliud nisi vna dies sex vicibus repetita secundum diuersa rerum genera. Rationem vero distinctae repetitionis facit differens cognitio angelica de rebus ipsis ...". For Bede, Gregory, and Jerome, see PETER LOMBARD, II, d.12, c.2, in *Bonaventurae Opera omnia* II, p. 290.

71. ZAVALLONI, p. 316, *et passim*; ROENSCH, p. 175 (Kilwardby).

of the other members of the body"[72]. Bonaventure's terms (*esse completum*, etc.) recall Peter's in a previous question (see 7, above).

By means of the imperative (*intellige*), William de Rothwell strongly affirms that matter was created in a state deprived of "complete form". William's conclusion that prime matter had a form "confusam et quasi commixtam" echoes Bonaventure.

William de Rothwell, II, 49[va] :

> *Vtrum materia creata fuit informis.*/ Respondeo sic secundum sanctos et magistrum in littera et hoc intellige a priuatione forme. complete/ non tamen potuit esse sine forma omnino/ quia esse est a forma secundum boetium/ vnde habuit formam confusam et quasi commixtam[73].

(11) *Quid sint rationales seminales.*
Peter of Tarentaise, II *Sent.*, d.18, q.1, a.3 (pp. 151-153).

Bonaventure expresses a conventional thirteenth-century understanding of Augustine's "seminal reasons". Seminal reasons are active powers—or intrinsic, inchoate virtues—implanted in matter which produce natural effects. Unlike other natural causes which produce their effects immediately (as a serpent engenders a serpent), the seminal reasons in matter produce the effects of which they are capable through mediating forms or acts. Thus, for example, by virtue of its seminal reason bread is potent to produce a human body; before this effect is produced, however, the bread is transformed into a humor and thence into the immediately productive seed. More generally, a seminal reason in matter is potent to produce a complex form (*forma complexionis*) mediated through prior elementary (*forma elementaris*) and compound (*forma mixtionis*) forms. A seminal reason, then, is the essence of a subsequent form; the essence of the form and the form itself differ as incomplete being differs from complete being. The seminal reasons are natural

---

72. BONAVENTURE, II *Sent.*, d.12, a.1, q.3, concl., p. 300; see also d.12, a.1, q.2, concl., p. 294.

73. PETER OF TARENTAISE, II *Sent.*, d.12, q. unica, a.3, R., p. 102: "Materia informis dupliciter dici potest : vel a priuatione omnis formae, hoc modo materia informis esse non potuit ... vel a priuatione formae completae ... & hoc modo materia prima informis fuit, & res formandas tempore praecessit, secundum opinionem communiorem".

forms that correspond to the uncreated ideal forms and exemplars in the mind of God [74].

Bonaventure's argument shows clearly how the common interpretation of Augustine's seminal reasons entails a plurality of forms in creatures composed from matter. The terms "incomplete-complete being", "incomplete-complete form", which we have seen Peter to use, were the signature of later defenders of the pluralist thesis, like Richard of Middleton [75]. Bonaventure's argument also reveals that the pluralist position does not depend strictly upon Avicebron's principle of universal hylemophism, but can rest solely on the doctrine of seminal reasons. Admittedly, many pluralists upheld both doctrines, but not all. We shall see (15, below) that Peter elsewhere takes over Bonaventure's terms *forma elementaris—mixtionis—complexionis*.

Thomas Aquinas' definition of matter and theory of substantial form is incompatible with Bonaventure's understanding of seminal reasons. Since matter is purely passive and has no active power, Thomas says, there can be no incomplete or inchoate forms pre-existing in matter which are excited to complete being by some exterior agent. Moreover, this idea is untrue because nothing can have a twofold substantial form; further, if the first form received by matter conferred substantial being, any subsequent forms would be accidental. Thus a thing's specific form would be accidental. Thomas saves Augustine's authoritative term by interpreting it largely and metaphorically. The term "seminal reasons" comprehends "virtues active as well as passive" in nature which are brought together in the production of natural things. They are called "seminal", not because they have some imperfect being as the formative virtue in a seed, but because natural things are multiplied from them "as if from certain seeds". They are called "reasons", not because they are in matter with some kind of intention, but because they are directed by the divine intellect. They are said to

---

74. BONAVENTURE, II *Sent.*, d.18, a.1, q.2 and q.3, pp. 434-443, especially the *conclusiones*, pp. 436-437, 440-442.

75. See, e.g., *Quaestio fratris Richardi De gradu formarum*, ed. in ZAVALLONI, pp. 47-48, 146-151, where the influence of Bonaventure is manifest. Zavalloni concludes (p. 352): "On le voit, Richard revient toujours à la distinction entre *perfection complète et perfection incomplète*", a "distinction capitale".

be "implanted in matter" not because they pre-exist in matter before the coming of complete form; rather, they are said to be "in matter" in the sense that matter has a capacity or a susceptibility to receive complete forms[76].

Peter of Tarentaise begins his Response by reporting the opinion which Thomas holds: "the seminal reason in matter is not some active form, but only a passive disposition to receive form". He then reports the contrary opinion, and following Bonaventure, he continues by asking whether the "certain form in matter" is universal or particular. Bonaventure concludes that the seminal reason may be considered a universal form in the sense that it is "indifferent to the many things able to come from it", but that properly speaking, it is a form of singular things. This opinion seems "more common and more intelligible"[77]. Peter likewise says that a seminal reason "has a certain likeness to a universal form by reason of its indistinction and potentiality, but nevertheless it is not truly universal, but particular". This last position Peter defends against objections. Peter concludes his Response with a precise definition and an example. A seminal reason is an incomplete form

> quasi initium quoddam seu seminarium formae completae in materia adeo, quod per actionem agentis naturalis de potentia ad actum educitur, fluit autem seu transit de vno esse ad aliud vsquequo perueniat ad esse formae vltimae complentis: sicut ratio seminalis quae est in semine animalis alicuius primo habet esse quasi lactis, deinde quasi sanguinis, .deinde carnis, deinde embrionis, deinde perfecti animalis.

Peter uses the same example in an answer to an objection (ad 1): the seminal reason of a particular complete form has a potential, incomplete, and confused being, as the form of a chicken in an egg. As these examples suggest, Peter specifies (ad 2) that a seminal reason precedes its complete form in time, not only in nature.

While Peter of Tarentaise's position on seminal reasons is clear, William de Rothwell's is somewhat ambiguous. William outlines the three opinions reported in Peter's Response, but he does not use any of Peter's examples or choose to quote Peter's definition of seminal reasons. In the previous question, indeed, William gives

---

76. THOMAS AQUINAS, II *Sent.*, d.18, q.1, a.2, in corpore, ad 1-2, pp. 451-453.
77. BONAVENTURE, II *Sent.*, d.18, a.1, q.3, concl., pp. 440-442.

his own definition of seminal reasons, and this definition echoes Thomas Aquinas':

> *Vtrum illa productio fuit secundum rationem seminalem*
> *Et quid sint rationes seminales. causales etc.* Respondeo iste rationes nihil aliud sunt quam uirtutes naturales. que sunt/ in ipsa natura dicuntur tamen rationes inquantum exemplate sunt a rationibus eternis · uerbi diuini ... (II,52ᵛᵃ)[78].

Whatever its echoes, William's definition here[79] is vague enough. William's previous affirmation of prime matter's creation in an unformed state but not divested of every form (see 10, above) would seem to entail a literal understanding of seminal reasons. Moreover, the new title which William gives to the next question presupposes seminal reasons to be certain forms in matter. In any case, such a question does not appear in the commentaries of those who, like Thomas Aquinas, "dicunt. quod ratio seminalis in materia. non est aliqua forma actiua/ sed solum dispositio passiua".

William de Rothwell, II, 52ᵛᵇ-53ʳᵃ :

> *Vtrum ratio seminalis. sit forma uniuersalis uel particularis/* Respondeo. triplex. circa hoc est opinio. quidam. dicunt. quod ratio seminalis in materia. non est aliqua forma actiua/ sed solum dispositio passiua/ ad recipiendum formam. quia ratio seminalis secundum eos dicit principium/ materiale/ Alia opinio dicit quod ratio seminalis est forma aliqua in materia/ Alioquin non esset naturalis productio/ sed potius artificialis et uiolenta/ cum forma nullo modo esset in materia. et ita nec de ea educeretur/ et horum quidam dicunt/ rationem seminalem esse formam uniuersalem. non particularem. et quod est forma totius/ non partis/ et hij distinguunt in qualibet re duplicem formam/ secundum rem/. scilicet. generis et speciei/ prima autem rationem seminalem. et secundam. semper recipi in materia mediante/ prima. que est quasi quedam inclinatio ad secundam. Alij. uerius dicunt quod non est alia secundum esse nature. forma uniuersalis. et particularis/ nec forma

---

78. Such a definition is not found in Peter of Tarentaise, II *Sent.*, d.18, q.1, a.2, p. 151, which William here excerpts. William's words seem to echo Thomas, d.18, q.1, a.2, in corpore and ad 1, p. 453 : "rationes seminales dicuntur virtutes activae completae in natura cum propriis passivis ... hujus modi virtutes activae in natura dicuntur rationes ... quia ab arte divina producuntur".

79. Peter of Tarentaise and William in this question distinguish primordial, causal, seminal, and obediential reasons in order to determine the precise causality by which Eve was produced from Adam's side.

uniuersalis in materia/ precedit formam particularem/ vnde non est prius ignis/ quam hic ignis. Alias cum adueniret post formam substantialem. esset accidentalis. dicunt ergo quod ratio seminalis est forma particularis non uniuersalis./ est tamen forma incompleta/ que continue par agens naturale educitur/ ad esse completum/ siue de potentia ad actum. Vniuersalis autem dicitur/ tantum secundum similitudinem ratione. scilicet. sue distinctionis (*read*: indistinctionis). et potentialitatis. uere est particularis[80].

(12) *An eadem sit materia spiritualium & corporalium.*
Peter of Tarentaise, II *Sent.*, d.3, q.1, a.3 (pp. 30-32).

In the 1230s, Phillip the Chancellor and Hugh of St. Cher noted that those who argued a composition of matter and form in spiritual creatures often posited a threefold matter : the matter of terrestrial bodies, endowed with substantial form, quantity, and contrariety; the matter of celestial bodies, endowed with substantial form and quantity, but free from contrariety; and the matter of spiritual creatures, endowed with substantial form, but without quantity and free from contrariety. Phillip and Hugh denied the existence of spiritual matter and, anticipating Thomas Aquinas, argued that the distinction between *id quod est* and *id quo est* in spiritual creatures suffices to establish their composition[81]. The Franciscan master

80. PETER OF TARENTAISE, II *Sent.*, d.18, q.1, a.3, R., p. 152 : "Circa hanc materiam triplex est opinio. Quidam enim dicunt, quod ratio seminalis in materia non est aliqua forma actiua, sed solum dispositio passiua ad recipiendam formam : quia ratio seminalis dicit principium materiale ... Alia opinio dicit quod ratio seminalis est forma quaedam in materia, alioquin non esset naturalis productio, sed potius artificialis vel violenta ... quia de nihilo educeretur forma, nam de materia educi non posset, cum nullo modo esset in ea ... Sed haec opinio diuiditur in duas. Quidam enim dicunt quod ratio seminalis est forma vniuersalis, non particularis, & forma totius non partis : dicunt enim quod alia est ... forma generis; & alia ... forma speciei; nec forma speciei recipitur in materia nisi mediante forma generis, quae ... est ratio seminalis, quia est quaedam inclinatio materiae ad recipiendam formam speciei in materia ... Alij vero dicunt quod non est alia secundum esse naturae forma vniuersalis & particularis, nec formam particularem in materia praecedit forma generis, sed eadem est forma ... per quam est ignis, siue hic ignis: alioquin cum forma quae aduenit post formam substantialem sit accidentalis ... Dicunt ergo quod ratio seminalis est forma particularis non vniuersalis ... est tamen forma incompleta ... quod per actionem agentis naturalis de potentia ad actum educitur. ideo similitudinem habet quandam formae vniuersalis ratione suae indistinctionis & potentialitatis, non tamen est vere vniuersalis, sed particularis". Note that William signifies his preference for the opinion that seminal reasons are particular forms : "alij *uerius* dicunt ...".

81. Odon LOTTIN, *La simplicité de l'âme*, in *Psych. et mor.* I, pp. 432-43, and for Odo Rigaud, pp. 447-49.

Odo Rigaud and the Dominican Robert Kilwardby (commentary on the *Sentences*, 1252-1254) [82] were among those who propounded the threefold distinction to which Phillip and Hugh refer.

Peter of Tarentaise's Response to the question—are corporeal and spiritual matter the same?—presents an elaborate outline of various arguments. Peter first observes that the question is irrelevant for those who do not posit matter in spiritual creatures. Among those who do, Peter says, (I) some consider matter in terms of its *esse*, as joined with form. These say that matter is one or diverse according to the unity or plurality of the individual, special, or general forms with which it is joined. Only when considered in relation to the "most general form"—substance in general—can matter be said to be one in every corporeal and spiritual creature. Others consider matter (II) in terms of its essence, as divested of every form. Some who consider matter in this way say (A) that the essence of matter is simple, having no parts, and that it is the same in every body and spirit; the essence of matter is replicated under diverse forms and multiplied in diverse beings. Others, however, say (B) that the essence of matter is one only according to a certain analogy. As gold is found to be more or less pure in things of the same genus, *a fortiori* matter is found to be more or less pure in the different genera, spiritual and corporeal. Thus, prime matter has substantially different parts, not evident to the senses but to the intellect, which become manifest through composition with different forms. In the same way, many seminal reasons exist simultaneously in one grain. Among those who thus argue that prime matter has many parts, some say (1) that these parts are infinite, any one of them sufficient to produce the whole world; others say (2) that the parts are finite, each able to become a body of determined magnitude, and no more. Although Bonaventure reports some of these opinions [83], Peter does not derive his Response from his usual sources. He has taken the argument entirely, its order and very words, from Ròbert Kilwardby's *De ortu scientiarum* (ca. 1250) [84]. Kilwardby sides with the opinion that matter is one

82. See D. E. SHARP, *Further Philosophical Doctrines of Kilwardby*, in *New Scholasticism* 9 (1935) 46-51.

83. BONAVENTURE, II *Sent.*, d.3, pt.1, a.1, q.2, pp. 94-98.

84. *De ortu scientiarum*, ed. JUDY, c.XXXI, 276-282, 285, pp. 101-104. Peter's text (see note 85) is itself an extract of Kilwardby's argument.

only through analogy. For matter is diverse not only when considered in terms of its *esse*, as joined to forms, but also when considered "in its naked and absolute essence". The matter of terrestrial bodies, celestial bodies, and spiritual creatures is essentially different. Peter of Tarentaise favors the same argument as "more probable and more intelligible".

William de Rothwell sketches the Response which Peter has borrowed from Kilwardby, but he does not indicate a preference for any of the opinions.

William de Rothwell, II, 44^{va-b} :

> *Vtrum vna et eadem. sit materia. spiritualium et corporalium.*/ Respondeo secundum vnam opinionem. patet quod non/ secundum aliam autem/. scilicet. que ponit materia in spiritualibus. tunc materiam considerata est. secundum esse non speciale. sed sub forma generalissima/. scilicet. substantie/ sic vna in genere/ est omnium substantiarum/. considerata autem secundum essentiam secundum quosdam. vna numero materia est in omni corpore. et in omni spiritu/ et in qualibet parte corporis. secundum alios non est vna numero. sed genere/ secundum analogiam quamdam. quia magis et minus plura (*read* : pura) est./ primi dicunt materiam esse simplicem nec habere partes./ Secundi quod habet partes substantialiter differentes sub inuicem contentas/ et inuolutas intelligibiliter/ sicut in vno grano multe rationes seminales. hec autem per formas/ aduenientes/ explicantur. Horum autem quidam dicunt/ uel ponunt/ materiam omnino primam. habere huiusmodi partes infinitas. Ita quod materia. cuiuscumque corporis./ sufficiens ad totum mundum faciendum. Alij quod finitas et quod corpus tantum inde fit solum secundum quantitatem materie[85].

85. PETER OF TARENTAISE, II *Sent.*, d.3, q.1, a.3, R., p. 31 : "Secundum opinionem quae non ponit materiam in spiritualibus, patet quod neque vna communis est materia spiritualium & corporalium ... Secundam opinionem vero quae ponit materiam in spiritualibus, dicendum quod est vna materia in aliquo modo communis & aliquo non. Nam materiam est considerare dupliciter : aut secundum essentiam, scilicet vt exutam omni forma : aut secundum esse, scilicet coniunctam cum forma. Secundo modo considerata recipit vnitatem vel pluralitatam, secundum quod vna est forma vel plures ... vnde hoc modo materia considerata cum forma generalissima, scilicet substantiae, est vna genere generalissimo tantum in omnibus substantijs ... Primo autem modo considerata, secundum quosdam est in omnibus vna etiam numero : vnde eadem essentia materiae est in omni corpore, & in omni spiritu, & in qualibet parte corporis : quae essentia simplex est, nec habet partes ... Secundum alios vero non est vna numero, sed genere quodammodo secundum analogiam quamdam. Nam sicut eadem materia auri in genere, alicubi reperitur purior, alicubi minus pura : ita eadem materia in genere spiritualium & corporalium, purior est ...

(13) *An substantia angeli sit composita ex materia et forma.*
Peter of Tarentaise, II *Sent.*, d.3, q.1, a.2 (pp. 29-30).

In his even-handed way, Peter here entertains both opinions. According to the first, the created rational spirit is composed not only of the being which it receives and the *quod est* which sustains it, but also of a spiritual matter and spiritual form which constitute the creature's *quod est* itself. According to the second opinion (held by Thomas Aquinas), the *quod est* of a spiritual creature is simple and not composed; thus spiritual creatures are composed only of their *quod est* and the *esse* which it receives. Since the *quod est* of spiritual creatures does not have being from itself but from another, it stands in relation to the giver of being as potency to act, and this suffices for the composition which distinguishes all creatures from God. Although Peter answers arguments against both opinions, he states that the first, affirming a composition of matter and form in angels, is *planior*.

William de Rothwell exemplifies the reasoning of the first opinion by alluding to one of Peter's beginning arguments : "Proprietas rei non est sine re : in angelo est proprietas materiae, scilicet subsistere accidentibus : ergo & materia" (arg. 5). At the end of his response, William alludes to the rejoinder which Peter gives on behalf of the second opinion : "Aliter substat angelus, aliter materia,. & non vniuoce omnino : quia materia cum possibilitate transmutationis, angelus non" (ad 5). Moreover, in support of the second opinion William supplies an argument "by reason of the angels' intellectuality" which he borrows from Thomas Aquinas[86]. William's

---

minus pura ... Isti ergo dicunt quod materia ... habet partes substantialiter differentes sub inuicem contentes & inuolutas, non sensibiliter, sed intelligibiliter : sicut in vno grano sunt inuariabiles rationes seminales simul omnes existentes ... hae partes per formas aduenientes explicantur. Et horum quidam ponunt quod materia omnino prima habet partes huiusmodi infinitas, ita quod materia cuiuscumque corpus accepta sufficiens est ad totum mundum faciendum : alij quod habet partes finitas, ita quod ex determinata parte materiae potest fieri corpus determinatae magnitudinis, & non amplius".

86. THOMAS AQUINAS, II *Sent.*, d.3, q.1, a.2, in corpore, p. 90 : "Ratiocinatur homo discurrendo et inquirendo lumine intellectuali per continuum et tempus obumbrato, ex hoc quod cognitionem a sensu et imagine accipit : quia, secundum Isaac in lib. *De definition.*, ratio oritur in umbra intelligentiae; sed angelus lumen intellectuale purum et impermixtum participat, unde etiam sine inquisitione deiformiter intelligit, secundum Dionysium".

108

arrangement of material implies that he favors the position against a composition of matter and form in angels.

William de Rothwell, II, 44[va] :

> *Vtrum sit compositus.* Respondeo. quidam dicunt quod sic/. scilicet. ex materia spirituali et forma et quod non tantum compositus sit/ ex quod est et esse/ sunt enim in eo/ ut dicunt proprietates materie ut substare et huiusmodi. Alij quod non/ ex materia et forma. cum sit in plena luce./ intellectuali/ materia autem obumbrat/ sed est compositus ex quod est et esse/ siue ex potentia et actu./ est enim in potentia respectu dei. a quo esse accepit/ essentia sua/ potentia etiam substare/ equiuoca hic et in materia[87].

(14) *An anima producta sit ex aliqua materia.*
Peter of Tarentaise, II *Sent.*, d.17, q.1, a.2 (pp. 141-142).

This question involves the same principles as the last one. To begin his Response, Peter of Tarentaise again cites a threefold distinction of matter, somewhat different than the one he cited before[88]. All agree that the soul does not have any kind of corporeal matter. However, there are two "celebrated opinions" as to whether the soul comprises a spiritual matter. Peter repeats the arguments he gave concerning the composition of angels. Some (like Thomas Aquinas) say that the human soul is composed only by its *quod est* and *esse*. The soul's essence or quiddity is one thing, the act of existence that it receives from God another. The soul's essence receives its being as potency receives act. Others say that although the human soul is composed by its essence and act of existence, nevertheless the soul's essence itself is composed of (spiritual) matter

---

87. PETER OF TARENTAISE, II *Sent.*, d.3, q.1, a.2, R., p. 29 : "Circa compositionem angeli, duae sunt opiniones. Prima dicit quod ... spiritus rationalis creatus componitur quasi ex materia spirituali, & quasi ex forma spirituali ... vnde non tantum compositus est angel ex quod est & esse ... Altera opinio dicit quod spiritus creatus compositus est ex quod est & esse tantum ... Ipsum ergo quod est non habet esse ex se, sed aliunde : habet ergo se in potentia ad ipsum datorem ipsius esse ..., & sic dicitur compositum ex potentia & actu : per primum recipit, per secundum agit".

88. "Aliquid habere materiam tribus modis potest intelligi : vel materiam in qua fiat, sic omnes formae corporales & accidentia ... vel ex qua fiat tanquam ex aliquo praejacenti, sic omnia corpora generabilia & corruptibilia ... vel materiam ex qua sit, sic prima corpora incorruptibilia, vt coelum empyreum & huiusmodi ..." (pp. 141-142).

and form, the former receiving and the latter conveying its act of existence. For just as corporeal matter receives corporeal forms, so spiritual matter receives spiritual forms. Peter answers objections against both arguments, but he says that whereas the first is *subtilior*, the second is *facilior*.

The greater difficulty of the first position arises from the problems it creates for the soul's individuality and immortality. Peter begins his article with an argument in favor of the soul's "materiality". If the soul were not composed from spiritual matter and form it would not be an individual *hoc aliquid* in nature, capable at once of subsisting apart from the body and of moving the body while united with it (arg. 1). If the soul were individuated by the corporeal matter of the body with which it is united, it would lose its individuality when the body dies, and thus as an individual it would not be immortal. In response to this worry, Peter, arguing on behalf of the soul's immateriality, cites an analogy of Avicenna also used by Thomas Aquinas[89] : as the wax receives its figure from a seal yet the impression remains after the seal is removed from contact, so the soul is individuated by the matter of the body yet retains its individual being after being separated from the body (ad. 1). Elsewhere Peter reports another argument that accounts for the individuality of wholly immaterial creatures : a form not receivable by any other suffices to determine and individuate such a creature[90].

Whatever its consequences may appear to be, Thomas Aquinas holds fast to the principle that only matter individuates, as is evident in his famous teaching concerning angelic species. Since things that agree in species are individuated by matter, and since angels are wholly immaterial, no two of them can agree in the same species, and hence each of them is a single species[91]. Étienne

89. THOMAS AQUINAS, I *Sent.*, d.8, q.5, a.2, ad 6, p. 232; II *Sent.*, d.17, q.1, a.2, in corpore, p. 418.

90. PETER OF TARENTAISE, II *Sent.*, d.3, q.2, a.1, ad 1, p. 33.

91. THOMAS AQUINAS, II *Sent.*, d.3, q.1, a.4, pp. 96-98. See PETER OF TARENTAISE, II *Sent.*, d.3, q.2, a.2, pp. 34-35. WILLIAM DE ROTHWELL, II, 44[vb]-45[ra], abbreviates Peter's Response : "*Vtrum differant in specie*. Respondeo quidam quod omnes eiusdem speciei/ Alij. quod omnes differant specie quia non habent materiam. ex qua indiuiduatio/ uel quia tota possibilitas. cuiuslibet perfecta est/ per actum proprium/ sicut possibilitas materie in celis per formam. Alij quod angeli eiusdem ordinis

Tempier condemned both the principle and the conclusion in 1277[92]. In order to insure the individuality and immortality of the soul, some of Thomas' later adversaries argued that forms alone can individuate within a species[93]. This opinion creates its own difficulties. Since it avoids dangers on both sides, the position that matter and form together in a *hoc aliquid* is the principle of the soul's individuation might well seem the "easier" solution. This is the solution of Bonaventure[94].

In his response, William de Rothwell does not at all raise the question of individuation. Indeed, he departs from Peter of Tarentaise's text entirely, and lists three inter-related arguments affirming the human soul's immateriality. We shall remember that William in his response concerning the composition of angels (see 13, above) inserted an argument favoring their immateriality by reason of their "intellectuality". This is the argument Thomas Aquinas develops in regard to the angels. When treating the composition of the human soul in his commentary on the *Sentences*, Thomas simply refers to his former argument, although in the *Summa theologiae* he applies it in full in regard to the human soul[95]. William de Rothwell, in turn, applies the argument "by reason of intellectuality" to the human soul, composing his response according to various principles established by Thomas Aquinas.

Peter of Tarentaise cites one of these : "Omne quod recipitur in aliquo, est in illo per modum recipientis, non rei receptae : omnes formes materiales recipiuntur in anima, & per modum immaterialem : ergo ipsa est immaterialis" (contra 2)[96]. Thomas Aquinas takes

sunt specie/ quia maior uidetur similitudo eorum sed non cum aliis". William takes the example of the heavenly bodies from the *sed contra* arguments in Thomas' article (p. 96), and inserts them into Peter's Response.

92. See WIPPEL, *The Metaphysical Thought of Godfrey of Fontaines*, p. 367. Wippel's discussion (pp. 349-369) of the problems of individuation is enlightening.

93. See the propositions and arguments of William de la Mare cited by ROENSCH, p. 186.

94. See the discussion of Étienne GILSON, *The Philosophy of St. Bonaventure*, trans. Illtyd TRETHOWAN and Frank J. SHEED (Paterson, N.J., 1965), pp. 226-229.

95. THOMAS AQUINAS, II *Sent.*, d.17, q.1, a.2, in corpore, p. 417; *ST*, I, q.75, a.5. The *Prima pars* of the *Summa* was finished in 1268. William's terms more exactly derive from the commentary on the *Sentences*.

96. This principle is not articulated expressly in the article from the *Sentences*, but it is in the question from the *Summa* (see n. 95).

great pains to distinguish the way in which prime matter receives forms from the way in which the intellect receives them. In short, he seeks to abolish the equivocation inherent in the analogy which Peter repeats: "just as corporeal matter receives corporeal forms, so spiritual matter receives spiritual forms"[97]. William de Rothwell's sentences are terse and elliptical, but his terms suggest that he refers to the following arguments deduced from Thomas Aquinas' articles on the angels. (I) If the possible intellect's potency to receive forms were the same as matter's, then it would not be in act through itself, but rather would attain its act from the forms which it receives; thus, these forms would define or "denominate" the intellect and its operation, since "omnis denominatio est a forma, quae dat esse et est principium operationis"[98]. (II) "Perfection is proportionate to the thing perfected"; the perfection of the intellect is a universal intelligible form; but if the potency of the intellect were like matter's, it would receive forms singularly, not universally "per vnam speciem"[99]. Thus, (III) the forms received by the intellect would be individuated, and the soul would know only individuals. But "the intellect receives a form insofar as it is simply form, not individuating it, because form in the intellect has universal being"[100].

William de Rothwell, II, 52rb:

> Vtrum producta sit ex aliqua materia. Respondeo non quia tunc potentia sua. esset potentia materialis. et ita. forme recepte intellectu possibili denominarent ipsum. quia darent ei formam/ et materiam. Item perfect(ius) per vnam speciem. aliam recipere non posset. Item forme in eo indiuiduarentur/ due tamen sunt opiniones circa compositionem anime. supra/ uidelicet d.8. q.12.

(15) An anima sit simplex, & quomodo.
Peter of Tarentaise, I Sent., d.8, q.6, a.2 (pp. 79-80).

In the above text William de Rothwell presumably refers to this question, the twelfth article in Peter of Tarentaise's Book I, d.8. Peter here once again recites the opinions for and against the soul's

---

97. THOMAS AQUINAS, II Sent., d.3, q.1, a.1, ad 3, pp. 88-89.
98. Ibid., d.9, q.1, a.4, in corpore, p. 239, where the principle of denomination is stated.
99. Ibid., d.3, q.1, a.1, in corpore, pp. 86-87, and d.3, q.1, a. 2, arg. 3, p. 90.
100. Ibid., d.3, q.1, a.1, ad 3, pp. 88-89.

composition from matter and form. This time he explicitly cites Avicebron's authority for the argument that since every passive principle is reduced to the nature of matter and every active principle to the nature of form, the soul must have "as it were a certain spiritual matter and a spiritual form". Again Peter defends each position against objections.

William de Rothwell refers to the two opinions recited in Peter's Response, and to them he adds a third. One must say that the soul is composed of prior and subsequent, determining and determined forms. William's use of the imperative (*dic*) signifies that this position is his own. Clearly, William affirms a plurality of forms in the human composite. His terms indicate that he conceives what Zavalloni calls a "subordination dispositive" of forms in the human being, whereby prior forms dispose the composite to receive more and more perfect determinations until it is fixed, by an ultimate form, in its species. Hence the human composite first exists, then vegetates, then senses by forms which prepare it for its specific form, the intellectual soul[101].

William de Rothwell, I, 26[va] :

> Vtrum anima sit simplex. Respondeo. duplex est opinio circa compositionem anime. quidam dicunt eam. compositam ex materia spirituali et forma. ut dicit auicebron. eo quod habet proprietates materie. ut recipere. Alii dicunt compositam ex quod est. id est quantitate (*read*: quidditate). et esse. scilicet. actuali./ Sed dic quod est composita/ compositione prioris forme et sequentis. id est. determinantis cum determinata. ut esse. uiuere. sentire. intelligere[102].

In this response, William signifies his distance from the hylemorphic doctrine of the soul; elsewhere, following Thomas Aquinas, he firmly denies it. At the same time, contrary to Thomas, William affirms a plurality of forms in the human composite. Questions concerning the soul's "simplicity" and its "unity" can be distin-

101. ZAVALLONI, pp. 313-314.
102. PETER OF TARENTAISE, I *Sent.*, d.8, q.6, a.2, R., p. 79 : "Circa compositionem animae rationalis duae sunt opiniones : nam quidam, vt patet ex Libro Fontis vitae, dicunt eam compositam quasi ex materia spirituali & forma spirituali, id est, ex aliquo quasi materiali principio, ex altero quasi formali ... Alij vero dicunt eam compositam ex quod est, & esse, id est, quidditate rei & esse eius actuali, Quod habet a Deo ...".

guished[103]. On the one hand, as Thomas Aquinas continually points out, a hylemorphic doctrine of the soul necessarily entails affirmation of a plurality of forms in the human composite. If the soul itself is a composite of matter and form, then the union between soul and body will be a union of two substances, however incomplete each may be. On the other hand, it is possible to maintain the immaterial simplicity of the intellectual soul, as William does, and simultaneously posit a plurality of forms in the body with which it unites. R. Zavalloni has shown that such a teaching was common before Thomas Aquinas[104]. Moreover, to say that there are several incomplete, predisposing forms in the human composite completed by a final specific form does not require one to posit a plurality of souls in the human being. Entered into composition with the body, the intellectual soul directs all of its operations. Pleading on behalf of the hylemorphic doctrine, Peter of Tarentaise produces an argument which illustrates how the doctrine entails a plurality of forms in the human composite. One may argue thus : if the soul is a composite of matter and form, and enters into a further composition with the body, man will then have a twofold being, which is impossible (arg. 2). Answering this argument (ad 2), Peter states that being belongs properly to the composite ultimate in composition, that is, the complete human nature, which subsists *per se*. The soul, although itself a composite, was not created to subsist *per se*, but in a body, just as the body was created to be united with a soul. As long as the soul is part of another composite ("pars est alterius"), it does not have complete being *per se*, but when it is separated from the body, it does. The argument easily preserves the immortality of the soul; it would seem also to imply numerical identity between the cadaver and the animated body, a position which later pluralists vigorously upheld[105]. In any case, Peter's argument here relies on a distinction, developed by Odo Rigaud, between the *forma partis* and the *forma totius* of the human com-

---

103. As Odon Lottin distinguishes them in his two essays in *Psych. et mor.*, I, pp. 424-460, 461-479.

104. See ZAVALLONI, pp. 405-419, and importantly, p. 437, n. 61.

105. *Ibid.*, p. 316. This a "common argument" among the pluralists. For the application of the argument to the problem of Christ's body after death, see ROENSCH, pp. 178-188 (Kilwardby, Peckham, William de la Mare).

posite. The *forma partis* is the soul, to which the body responds as its matter; the *forma totius* is the total "humanity" which results from the union of the soul and body. In respect to the *forma totius*, the composite of body and soul (*forma partis*) plays the role of matter[106]. This distinction clarifies the one Peter makes elsewhere between the substantial form and the form of the "complete composite itself" (see 7, above). This argument exemplifies yet another conception of the plurality of forms in the human composite; from a "subordination dispositive" Zavalloni distinguishes a "subordination essentielle", wherein the relation between inferior and superior forms is conceived as a relation between matter and form[107].

In another question ("An brutorum corpora ex quatuor elementis composita sint")[108], Peter of Tarentaise explicitly affirms a plurality of disposing forms in sensible bodies. Peter's terms and formulae come directly from Bonaventure[109]. The more noble the form the more posterior it is, and the more preceding forms it requires; since the sensible soul is more noble than compound (*forma mixtionis*) or complex (*forma complexionis*) forms, it is posterior to them and they must precede it. Again, the more noble the soul the more it requires a nature disposed and moderated (*contemperatum*) through many forms; whence the animal soul requires prior vegetable, compound, and complex forms. For his excerpt of this question William de Rothwell draws upon an argument Peter presents concerning the sense of touch, and likewise adduces the argument "propter nobilitatem forme"[110].

106. Odon LOTTIN, *La simplicité de l'âme*, in *Psych. et mor.*, I, pp. 449-450; ZAVALLONI, pp. 413-415.

107. ZAVALLONI, p. 313.

108. PETER OF TARENTAISE, II *Sent.*, d.15, q.1, a.2, contra 3, in corpore, p. 126.

109. BONAVENTURE, II *Sent.*, d.15, a.1, q.2, fund. 3-4, concl., ad 6, pp. 377-378; see also II *Sent.*, a.1, 2, a.1, q.3, concl., p. 300; II *Sent.*, d.17, a.2, q.2, ad 6, p. 423. The terms *forma mixtionis-forma complexionis*, in the sense used by Bonaventure and Peter, seem to have been devised by Phillip the Chancellor, and were taken up by John of Rochelle as well. See ZAVALLONI, p. 407.

110. WILLIAM DE ROTHWELL, II, 51vb: "*Vtrum corpora animalium ex quatuor. elementis composita sint*/ Respondeoque sic/ sensus enim constituit animal/ et precipue sensus tactus. ille autem cum discernant omnes qualitates. oportet quod omnes/ habeant in potentia ... vnde oportet corpus esse mixtum/ immo oportet etiam esse maximam contemperanciam/ propter nobilitatem forme/ et multiplicabilem in diuersis organis/ propter multas potentias anime". For the argument from

C.—*The Soul and its Powers*

William de Rothwell seems to have been especially interested in the powers of the soul and the relations among them. William composed treatises *De potentiis sensitivis* and *De intellectu*, now lost[111]; as we shall see presently, the longest question in his abbreviation of the *Sentences* concerns the order of powers and habits in the soul.

Questions concerning the soul's powers arise early in Peter Lombard's *Sentences*, in Book I, d.3, c.2, "De imagine et similitudine Trinitatis in anima". This chapter in Peter Lombard's text is made up entirely of passages from Augustine's *De Trinitate* which establish that the soul is an image of God in its three powers of memory, understanding, and love (or will). In the mind's acts of remembering, understanding, and loving itself, one can discern a certain trinity which is the image of the Trinity in God. Moreover, the soul is also the image of God's unity, for the three powers of the mind (*mens*) "are not three lives but one life, not three minds but one mind, and one essence"[112].

Aristotelian psychology, especially as it pertains to memory, created problems for Augustine's authoritative teaching. Furthermore, while all affirmed that the three powers constituted the image of God in the soul, commentators on the *Sentences* disputed whether the soul's powers are identical with its essence, as Augustine seemed to say, or whether they are really distinct from the soul's essence, as the difference between God and creatures on the one hand, and the definition of "powers" on the other, seemed to require.

(16) *Quomodo memoria, intelligentia, & voluntas se habeant, & distinguantur inter se.*
Peter of Tarentaise, I *Sent.*, d.3, q.5, a.1 (pp. 35-36).

For Augustine there can be no doubt that the memory is part of the image of God in the soul. The power of memory is so encom-

---

the sense of touch, see PETER OF TARENTAISE, II *Sent.*, d.15, q.1, a.2, contra 1, p. 126, and BONAVENTURE, II *Sent.*, d.15, a.1, q.2, fund. 1, p. 377.
111. EMDEN, *A Biographical Register*, III, p. 1596.
112. Peter Lombard, in *Bonaventurae Opera omnia* I, pp. 63-64.

passing that it might seem that "the image of the Trinity belongs alone to the memory"[113]. The memory is the "seat of the soul itself". Not only does it recollect and make present to the mind the image of sensible things; in it one also discovers laws and reasons not impressed by any bodily sense. Indeed, one discovers there the immutable standards of truth and right living which govern and judge all of our acts. One may even say that God himself resides in the memory, for it is there, beyond all sensible images and the mind itself, that one recalls the creator and preserver of his being, the lord God of the mind[114].

On the contrary, Peter of Tarentaise says, "Avicenna, Aristotle, and all of the philosophers who divide the powers of the soul number the memory among the parts of the sensible soul" because it receives sensible images and discerns differences of time, whereas only powers which abstract from the conditions of time belong to the rational part of the soul (arg. 1). Peter finds an answer to this challenge in Thomas Aquinas' commentary on the *Sentences*[115]. The power that receives material species is indeed bound to a material organ. However, the intellective part of the soul retains immaterial species, such as universals and the like. Referring to the intellect, Aristotle said that the soul is a "locus specierum". The intellect reflects upon the species it retains, and hence understanding arises, followed by the will. In this way Augustine's ordering of the powers may be sustained. Insofar as it retains immaterial species, the soul may be called memory; insofar as it affixes itself to the things understood, it is called will (Peter of Tarentaise, Response).

This initial solution does not fully satisfy a number of philosophic objections. First, the "memory" which retains immaterial species does not seem to be really distinct from the intellect, and thus the soul would seem to have two instead of three powers. Secondly, in retaining intelligible species the soul in some way makes past

113. *De Trinitate libri XV*, ed. W.J. Mountain auxiliante Fr. Glorie, *Corpus Christianorum, Series Latina* (*CCSL*), La (XIII-XV) (Turnhout 1968), XIV, 7, 10, p. 434.

114. *Confessionum libri XIII*, ed. L. Verheijen, *CCSL*, XXVII (Turnhout 1981), X, viii, 12-13, pp. 161-162; X, x, 17-xii, 19, pp. 163-165; X, xvii, 26, pp. 168-169; X, xxv, 36-xxvi, 37, pp. 174-175.

115. Thomas Aquinas, I *Sent.*, d.3, q.4, a.1, in corpore, pp. 112-113.

things present, and thus discerns a difference in time. Thirdly, the retention of intelligible species follows acts of understanding, and thus the act of the intellect does not proceed from memory, as Augustine teaches, nor should memory be appropriated to the Father, but to the Son[116].

Peter of Tarentaise does not state these arguments explicitly, although they are implicit in some of the arguments he presents. Moreover, he admits and answers them in a further solution by means of a hierarchical, threefold distinction of memory which at once accommodates Augustine's and the philosophers' understanding of the power. The distinction is implicit in Augustine's teaching, but Peter took the threefold scheme directly from Bonaventure. Robert Kilwardby developed a similar scheme[117]. The soul receives sensible species by way of a potency attached to an organ; it preserves acquired intelligible species which are received in the intellective part of the soul; but it also possesses innate species, similitudes of the true and the good, which are created with the soul. The sensible memory follows an order of time and contains things determined in time; the intellective memory contains things abstracted from time, but follows an order of time; the innate memory, however, neither contains anything determined in time nor follows any order of time. Strictly speaking, only the innate memory is part of the image of the Trinity in the soul (ad 1).

William de Rothwell carefully insinuates this latter distinction into his abbreviation of Peter's article, and makes it the center-piece of his excerpt.

William de Rothwell, I, 24rb :

> De distinctione parcium ymaginis. memorie. scilicet. intelligentie. et voluntatis. et de origine earum ab inuicem. ac consubstantialitate. Nota primo quod ymago assignatur penes potentias naturales./ et accipitur potentia large/ quelibet naturalis anime proprietas. siue in suscipiendo siue in retinendo. siue operando. vocatur ergo hic memoria virtus anime/

---

116. See BONAVENTURE, I Sent., d.3, pt.2, a.1, q.1, contra 3, pp. 80-81. Dionysius Cartusianus summarizes the standard objections in I Sent., d.3, a.8, Opera omnia, XIX (Tournai 1902), p. 254.

117. BONAVENTURE, loc. cit. in n. 116, ad 3, p. 81. For Kilwardby, see SHARP, Further Philosophical Doctrines of Kilwardby, 43-44.

continens species intelligibles quia intellectus secundum philosophum est locus specierum. proprie autem secundum quod continet species innatas. scilicet. similitudinem ueri et boni. que species concreate sunt. non autem acquisitorum specierum nisi large summendo./ quia uero intellectus immaterialis est/ reflectitur supra speciem receptam et sic oritur intellectiua./ huiusmodi vero reflexionem consequitur voluntas. secundum quam afficitur circa rem intellectam./ et sic patent partes ymaginis et ordo parcium/ et origo. actus etiam intuendi species et conseruandi eas/ cum uterque sit cognoscitiue potentie/ sunt eiusdem potentie secundum essentiam. differentis tantum siue distincte/ penes duo officia. voluntatis autem specialis potentia est [118].

(17) *Vtrum istae potentiae sint ipsa anima.*
Peter of Tarentaise, I *Sent.*, d.3, q.5, a.2 (pp. 36-38).

Since the three persons of the Trinity are one essence, it would seem that the three powers of the soul are not an image of the Trinity unless they are one essence of the soul (Peter of Tarentaise, arg. 8). Augustine seems clearly to say this in the text quoted by Peter Lombard: the powers "are not three lives but one life, not three minds but one mind, and one essence". Elsewhere in *De Trinitate* Augustine says that the mind (*mens*) is the undivided spiritual essence of the soul embracing knowledge and love of itself in one simultaneous, indistinguishable act; the mind binds together memory, understanding, and will in one substance, one essence [119].

---

118. PETER OF TARENTAISE, I *Sent.*, d.3, q.5, a.1, p.35: "Respondeo ad 1. quaest. imago in anima hic assignatur penes potentias naturales: accipitur autem hic large naturalis potentia quaelibet naturalis animae proprietas, vel officium, siue virtus, siue in concipiendo aliquid siue in conseruando, siue in operando. Notandum ergo quod cum potentia intellectiua sit immaterialis, sensitiuae vero alligatae sint organo materiali, oportet quod species immateriales, sicut vniuersalium & huiusmodi, suscipiantur & conseruantur in parte intellectiua: vnde secundum Philosophum lib de anima. Anima est locus specierum ... quia vero intellectus immaterialis est, reflectitur supra speciem receptam, & sic oritur intelligentia: huiusmodi vero reflexionem consequitur voluntas quae ... afficitur ad rem intellectam ... & sic patent tres partes imaginis, & ordo partium.

Ad. 1. De memoria. Respondeo memoria dupliciter accipitur: vno modo virtus conseruatiua specierum sensibilium ... altero modo conseruatiua specierum intelligibilium, & haec duobus modis dicitur; vel prout est conseruatiua specierum acquisitarum quae recipiuntur in ipsa parte intellectiua, vel specierum innatarum, scilicet naturalis similitudinis veri & bonae, quae concreatae sunt in anima ... secunda aliquo modo est pars imaginis; tertia proprie est pars imaginis ...".

119. See *De Trinitate*, IX, 4,4; IX, 4,7; IX, 5,8; X, 11,18, ed. MOUNTAIN and GLORIE, *CCSL*, L(I-XII) (Turnhout 1968), pp. 297, 299, 300-301, 330-331. See also XIV, 10, 13 and XV, 6,10 in *CCSL* La, pp. 440-441, 474.

The twelfth-century author (Alcher of Clairvaux?) of the *Liber de spiritu et anima*, attributed to Augustine in the Middle Ages, faithfully repeats and literally interprets Augustine's sayings[120]. Like Augustine, the author of *De spiritu et anima* uses the terms "essence" and "substance" synonymously. In an argument cited by Peter of Tarentaise (arg. 1), the author says that the "one, same substance" of the soul receives different names according to its diverse operations; hence it is called "sense" when it senses, the "rational soul" (*animus*) when it knows (*sapit*), "mind" when it understands, "reason" when it discourses, "memory" when it remembers, "will" when it desires[121]. In short, the soul is "simple in essence, manifold in duties"[122]. Several early thirteenth-century masters likewise concluded that there is no essential plurality among the soul's powers, and that they are diverse only by reason of their relations to many acts and operations. Robert Kilwardby later made the same argument[123].

A literal interpretation of Augustine's words was unacceptable to other thinkers for philosophic, but equally pious reasons. Bonaventure states an argument used by many. Only in God are essence, existence, and powers identical; if the *quo est* and *quod est* in creatures are distinct, how much more distinct will be the *quo potest* and *quod potest* in them[124]. Yet in order for the soul to be an image of the Trinity, its three powers must in some way be one. Peter Lombard himself laid the groundwork for other solutions. He observed that Augustine did not speak strictly when he said that the soul's powers are one in "essence"; rather, they should be said to be one in "substance", to exist, not as accidents in a subject, but substantially in the soul[125].

120. *Liber de spiritu et anima*, e.g., 11; 23-24, in *PL* 40.786, 801-804.

121. Peter of Tarentaise cites this text first in I *Sent.*, d.3, q.5, arg. 1, p. 36. He assigns the *De spiritu et anima* to Augustine.

122. *De spiritu et anima*, 24, *PL* 40.803: "In essentia namque est simplex, in officiis multiplex".

123. See Odon LOTTIN, *L'identité de l'âme et de ses facultés avant saint Thomas d'Aquin*, in *Psych. et mor.*, I, pp. 486-490 (Hugh of St. Cher, William of Auvergne, Phillip the Chancellor); SHARP, *Further Philosophical Doctrines of Kilwardby*, 43-44.

124. BONAVENTURE, I *Sent.*, d.3, pt.2, a.1, q.3, fund. 3, p. 85. LOTTIN, *L'identité de l'âme et de ses facultés*, in *Psych. et mor.*, I, pp. 484-485, 490-494, 497-499, shows that this argument was established by William of Auxerre, and was taken up by early Franciscan masters and Albert the Great.

125. PETER LOMBARD, II, d.3, pt.2, c.2, in *Bonaventurae Opera omnia* II, p. 64.

Peter of Tarentaise conflates Thomas Aquinas' solution with another first developed by Odo Rigaud[126]. The essence of a thing is that by which it is what it is; the substance of a thing is that by which it subsists in its natural properties; the subject of a thing is that by which it subsists in accidents. Thus, the soul may be considered as it is in essence, simple in itself; as a substance, having diverse powers that perfect it in being; and as a subject which supports accidents. In relation to the soul's essence, the powers are accidents. However, the powers are not accidents of the soul as accidents of a subject; rather, the powers flow from the natural principles of the soul and are connatural with it. In terms of the distinction essence-substance-subject, then, the soul and its powers are one in substance. Together they constitute a "potential whole", wherein the soul, simple in itself, is totally present in each of the powers that perfects it. When Augustine said that the soul and its powers were one in essence, he spoke broadly, using the term "essence" for "substance".

Addressing the question of the image of God in the soul (ad 8), Peter says that it is not necessary for the image to be in every way similar to the Trinity. It suffices that the powers be in one essence, not one essence. Peter then entertains an argument which appears to be contrary to his previous conclusion. The powers of the soul may be considered as they are *in radice*, and then they are the same as the substance and essence of the soul; or they may be considered by reason of their relation to different acts and duties, and then they differ from the soul and from each other. In the same way the beginning and ending of lines which converge in a point are identical with the point and with each other essentially, *in radice*; but considered in terms of their different functions as point of convergence, beginning point and ending point of different lines, three points may be distinguished from each other.

126. On this question Odo Rigaud codified the distinction essence-substance-subject of the soul, and like earlier Franciscan masters, argued that Augustine used the term "essence" broadly for "substance". See LOTTIN, *L'identité de l'âme et ses facultés*, in *Psych. et mor.*, I, pp. 494-495. Peter integrates Odo's distinction with Thomas Aquinas' argument that the powers are connatural accidents of the soul, forming with it a "potential whole". See THOMAS, I *Sent.*, d.3, q.4, a.2, in corpore, p. 116.

William de Rothwell includes this latter argument in his response as an alternative to the position that the powers are one in substance, in a "potential whole".

William de Rothwell, I, 24^{rb-va} :

> *Vtrum potentie anime sint idem quod anima*. Respondeo. secundum essentiam non sunt idem. quia potentia naturalis est accidens. sed substantia sunt idem. quia sic anima est totum potentiale (ejus) integratum ex omnibus potentiis et tota est sub qualibet potentia. in subiecto autem idem est anima cum omnibus suis accidentibus. alii vero dicunt. et potentias cum anima. et potentias inter se/ secundum id quod sunt. id est. in radice/ idem esse in essentia sed differe sub ratione qua potentie sunt. scilicet. ratione. id est. in comparatione ad actum. exemplum de puncto [127].

(18) *Synderesis, Conscience, and Free Choice.*

Peter of Tarentaise develops his teaching on conscience and synderesis by means of a series of analogies [128]. As the speculative intellect has two habits, a habit of universal principles called *intellectus*, and a habit of special conclusions called *scientia*, so the practical intellect has two habits, a universal habit of the principles of natural right called *lex naturalis*, and a special habit that makes particular decisions about particular cases called *conscientia*. Although associated with science, conscience is not a pure science since it is "joined to affection and is a practical knowledge ordered to a deed" (*ad opus*) [129].

Similarly, the affective part of the soul has two habits for govern-

---

127. PETER OF TARENTAISE, I *Sent.*, d.3, q.5, a.2, p. 37 : "Respondeo ... quod primo modo, scilicet essentia, potentiae non sunt idem cum anima, quia sunt accidentia ejus ... Secundo modo prout est totum potentiale, sic sunt idem, scilicet cum ipsa substantia ... tota adest sub qualibet potentia ...' Tertio modo alia accidentia suis possunt dici idem, cum ipsa anima, scilicet subjecto ... (ad 8) ... Alij vero dicunt, quod potentias est considerare dupliciter, vel secundum id quod sunt, scilicet in radice, sic omnes sunt idem quod ipsa animae substantia & essentia : vel ratione qua potentiae sunt, id est in comparatione ad actum : sic officio vel ratione differunt, & ab anima, sicut in puncto finem & principium linearum est considerare dupliciter ...".

128. See Odon LOTTIN, *Syndérèse et conscience aux XIIe et XIIIe siècles*, in *Psych. et mor.*, II (Louvain-Gembloux 1948), pp. 236-238.

129. PETER OF TARENTAISE, II *Sent.*, d.39, q.3, a.1, R., p. 328.

ing action ("regulante ad operandum"). One, called synderesis, is general and innate; the other, named according to the various virtues, is special and acquired. The subject of synderesis is the natural will, and the subject of the special habit is the deliberative will[130]. As Odon Lottin points out, in making conscience a special habit of the practical intellect and synderesis a universal habit of the natural will, Peter follows Bonaventure[131]. Conscience is informed partly by the natural law, which says that evil should be avoided, and partly by deliberative reason, which determines that this or that is evil. Insofar as conscience is informed by natural law it cannot err, but it can err in its deliberation. Synderesis acts according to the universal judgment of the conscience, not the particular, and hence it cannot err[132]. In Peter's scheme, conscience moves synderesis according to the general order of intellect and will.

In the corresponding articles of his abbreviation, William de Rothwell summarizes Peter's teaching.

William de Rothwell, II, 64[rb] :

Quid sit conscientia/. Respondeo. est dictamen rationis/ de aliquo faciendo uel non faciendo/ in particulari facto/ vnde est cognitio practica et ordinata. scilicet. ad opus/ supra. d.24. q.4.

William de Rothwell, II, 64[va] :

Quid sit synderesis. Respondeo synderesis est habitus generalis innatus/ Inclinans ad bonum naturaliter. existens in uoluntate. naturali. sicut uirtus est specialis/ inclinans uoluntatem deliberatiuam. secundum alios est potentia. habitu naturali perfecta/ vnde dicunt quod est idem quod uoluntas que tamen non differt essentialiter deliberatiua/ supra q.4.2. Item supra. d.24. q.4/[133].

130. *Ibid.*, q.4, a.1, R., pp. 329-330.
131. Lottin, *Syndérèse et conscience*, in *Psych. et mor.*, II, pp. 236, 238. See Bonaventure, II *Sent.*, d.39, a.2, q.1, pp. 909-911.
132. Peter of Tarentaise, II *Sent.*, d.39, q.4, a.2, ad. 4, p. 330.
133. William draws the second opinion he reports from Peter, *loc cit.*, n. 132, ad 3, p. 330: "Vel secundum quosdam, est potentia cum habitu naturali perfecta: est enim idem quod uoluntas naturalis ... non ... differat essentialiter a uoluntate deliberatiua rationali". The idea that synderesis is a *potentia habitualis* was first expressed by Phillip the Chancellor, and became a feature of the discussion thereafter. See Lottin, and texts, *Syndérèse et conscience*, in *Psych. et mor.*, II, pp. 138-142. At the end of his excerpt, William seems to refer to Peter of Tarentaise, II *Sent.*, d.39, q.2, a.1, p. 326, on the natural and deliberative will. We shall discuss the other question, "d.24, q.4", presently.

Thomas Aquinas' doctrine of synderesis and conscience is nearly opposite Peter of Tarentaise's. Thomas bases his teaching on Albert the Great's[134]. As the speculative reason possesses a habit of self-evident principles called *intellectus*, so the practical reason possesses a habit—or power with a habit—of self-evident principles of universal right (e.g., "evil should not be done", "the laws of God ought to be obeyed"). This habit of the practical intellect is called synderesis[135]. Albert says that the universal principles by means of which the practical intellect decides what is shameful and what is honorable (*honestum*) behavior are the natural law written in the human spirit (e.g. "one ought not to fornicate", "one ought not to murder")[136]. Thomas Aquinas carefully distinguishes between the universal principles and their habit in the soul : the principles themselves are the *lex naturalis*, their habit synderesis[137].

The habit of universal principles does not suffice for the performance of particular deeds. Following Albert closely[138], Thomas says that particular judgments about deeds proceed from universal principles as a conclusion proceeds from the premises of a syllogism. Synderesis provides the major premise of the moral syllogism of the practical intellect. Either the *ratio superior* or the *ratio inferior* supplies the minor premise. Thomas says that the superior and inferior reason are one power distinguished by different media. The superior reason consults the divine and eternal reasons ("this is against the precepts of God"), and the inferior reason consults the temporal reasons of things ("this is superfluous or insufficient, useful or honorable—*honestum*")[139]. From these premises one elicits a conclusion as to what one should do in this particular act.

134. See F.-M. HENQUINET, *Vingt-deux questions inédites d'Albert le Grand dans une manuscrit a l'usage de S. Thomas d'Aquin*, in *New Scholasticism* 9 (1955) 283-328. Henquinet presents the question "de synderesi" on 320-322. Extracts of the text are reprinted by LOTTIN, *Syndérèse et conscience*, in *Psych. et mor.*, II, pp. 218-221.
135. THOMAS AQUINAS, II *Sent.*, d.24, a.2, a.3, in corpore, p. 610. Thomas says that synderesis is a habit, strictly speaking. However, in II *Sent.*, d.24, q.2, a.4, in corpore, p. 613, he says that synderesis is a habit, "seu potentiam cum habitu".
136. This is the *Summa de homine*, text quoted in LOTTIN, *Syndérèse et conscience*, in *Psych. et mor.*, II, p. 213.
137. THOMAS AQUINAS, II *Sent.*, d.24, q.2, a.4, in corpore, p. 613.
138. See Albert, text cited from *Summa de homine* in LOTTIN, *Syndérèse et conscience*, in *Psych et mor.*, II, pp. 217-218, and from "de synderesi", p. 221.
139. THOMAS AQUINAS, II *Sent.*, d.24, q.2, a.2, in corpore, p. 606.

The dictate (*dictamen*) of reason that applies universal principles to particular deeds is called conscience. Conscience, then, is related to synderesis, not as reason to will, but as the conclusion of a syllogism to its major premise. Thomas gives an example of the moral syllogism of the practical reason. Synderesis proposes that "every evil must be avoided". Either the superior reason, which says that "adultery is evil because it is prohibited by the law of God", or the inferior reason, which says that adultery is evil because it is "unjust or dishonorable (*inhonestum*)", supplies the minor premise. From these premises conscience concludes that this adultery should be avoided. Synderesis cannot err in its universal principles, but reason can err in its judgments and conscience in its conclusions. Thus, for example, conscience dictates to the heretic that he should allow himself to be burned rather than take an oath; in this he errs because he wrongly believes in his superior reason that God has prohibited oath-taking without qualification [140].

Commenting upon Peter of Tarentaise's doctrine of conscience and synderesis, Dom Odon Lottin remarks that "in the ... Bonaventurian order ... one speaks first of conscience residing in the reason before treating the synderesis which affects the will. The contrary order imposes itself in the Thomist tradition, since the synderesis furnishes the major premise of a practical syllogism the conclusion of which is the conscience. By the order alone in which authors treat problems one is able to determine the school they represent" [141]. In his excerpts of Peter of Tarentaise's articles on conscience and synderesis, William de Rothwell twice refers to "d.24.q.4". Peter does not treat conscience and synderesis in II,d.24, but rather in II, d. 39, where he treats conscience first and then synderesis. Thomas Aquinas, on the other hand, treats both in II,d.24, first synderesis (q.2, a.3) and then conscience (q.2, a.4). Precisely at Peter's "d.24.a.4" (d.24, q.2, a.1—following q.1, aa. 1-3) William de Rothwell abandons Peter's text for several articles [142]. In their

---

140. *Ibid.*, a.4, in corpore, p. 613.

141. LOTTIN, *Syndérèse et conscience*, in *Psch. et mor.*, II, p. 236, n. 2.

142. William omits Peter of Tarentaise's questions II *Sent.*, d.24, q.2, aa.1-3; q.3, aa.1-3, pp. 203-209. These concern free choice, the superior and inferior reason, the possible and agent intellect. William incorporates these topics into his own treatment. William rejoins Peter's text at II *Sent.*, d.24, q.4, a.1, p. 208, "Qualiter peccatum habet fieri in sensualitate".

stead, William composes a small treatise concerning the order of habits and powers in the soul. Here William follows the order established by Albert the Great and Thomas Aquinas for treating synderesis and conscience. He also uses their definitions, terms, and examples.

In order to segregate the powers and habits of the soul, William adopts a classification elaborated by Albert the Great [143] which places synderesis among the intellectual powers and habits. Synderesis is one of the "moving and deciding" (*movens et discernens*) powers of the rational soul, as distinct from those which execute its movement towards a work (*faciens impetum in opus*, e.g., the will). Understood as the rectitude rooted naturally in the reason, synderesis is a habit; understood as the subject of the natural habit of universal principles, synderesis is a power. This distinction as well seems to be based on remarks made by Albert the Great [144]. Synderesis directs the movement of the soul according to the "universal natural right", which is a common, undetermined conception including all the particular rules of action. As a habit of universal principles, synderesis never errs.

There are further powers that determine the movement of the soul according to the natural law insofar as it is special and determined (e.g., "this or that ought not to be stolen"). The powers that direct according to the special and determined *lex naturalis* are the superior and inferior reason. These are in fact one power, distinguished only by their different media. The superior reason directs the soul according the divine right and divine rules (e.g., "this ought to be done or left undone because it pleases or displeases God, or because it is prohibited by the divine law"). The inferior reason directs the soul according to human and positive law (e.g.,

143. See the question "de sinderesi", ed. Henquinet, *solutio*, 320-21. Albert concludes that "sinderesis est potentia rationalis anime (320) ... est quedam potentia motiva per habitum universalium iuris et habet aliquid de cognitione et aliquid de appetitu, sed plus se tenet ex parte cognitivarum" (321). See the remarks of LOTTIN, *Syndérèse et conscience*, in *Psych et mor.*, II, p. 219.

144. In the *Summa de homine*, Albert speaks of synderesis as the "subject" of universal principles, and also speaks of the synderesis as the first rectitude remaining in the soul after the Fall. The latter idea was initiated by Phillip the Chancellor. See LOTTIN, *loc. cit.* in n. 143, pp. 146-47, 212-214.

"this ought to be done because it is praiseworthy and honorable—
honestum"). Like Thomas Aquinas [145], William says that the superior
reason pertains to *sapientia*, the inferior reason to *scientia*. Moreover,
the human and positive law derives from the natural law, and the
natural law derives from the divine law, which "in the first place
is just and right". William uses the term *lex naturalis* differently
than Thomas Aquinas, assigning it to special and determined rather
than to the most universal principles. The relation William makes
between the superior and inferior reason and a hierarchy of laws
seems to amplify terms of Albert the Great. Albert says that the
superior and inferior reason regulate the soul "particularibus regulis
determinatis ad speciale opus". If these are received from eternal
things, or the first rectitude, it is the superior reason which regulates;
if these are received from human things, or lower things which have
some rectitude reflecting ("rectitudinem aliquam exemplatam") the
first rectitude, it is the inferior reason which regulates the soul [146].
In any case, for William as for Albert the *lex naturalis* "is written
in the human spirit", and it mediates the exemplar rectitude of the
divine rules and human, positive law.

Conscience is a conclusion of the foresaid principles. As Thomas
says, it is a dictate (*dictamen*) of the reason which applies universal
principles to a particular deed. Whereas synderesis cannot err,
conscience can when it draws a faulty conclusion from the premises.
Thus from the premise "you should not kill" (a divine prohibition),
the heretic wrongly concludes that "you should not kill a worm".

William next turns to the "rational appetite", or the affective,
executing power of the soul. The rational appetite is twofold: in
itself and absolutely, it is called will (*voluntas*); in relation to the
reason which governs it, it is called free choice (*liberum arbitrium*).
On free choice, William resumes the teaching of Peter of Tarentaise,
which does not differ greatly from Thomas Aquinas' [147]. Essentially,
free choice is one power, namely will; but inasmuch as it is related

145. THOMAS AQUINAS, II *Sent.*, d.24, q.2, a.2, in corpore, p. 606.
146. See the question "de sinderesi" in LOTTIN, *Syndérèse et conscience*, p. 219,
ll. 5-13 (ed. HENQUINET, 320), and p. 221, ll. 23-26.
147. PETER OF TARENTAISE, II *Sent.*, d.24, q.2, a.3, pp. 204-205. On free choice in
Thomas Aquinas, see Odon LOTTIN, *Libre arbitre et liberté depuis saint Anselme
jusqu'à la fin du XIIIe siècle*, in *Psych. et mor.*, I, pp. 207-216.

to reason, one may say that it is a faculty of both reason and will. Related to both, free choice has two acts, counsel and election. Counsel is in the will as it is participated by reason; election, however, is made by the will alone[148].

William finishes his outline of the powers of the soul "which rule in life" with paragraphs concerning the various sensitive powers and the agent and possible intellects.

William de Rothwell, II, 56ra-57ra :

> De potentiis anime apprehensiuis et motiuis. precipue de hiis que regunt in uita. et de distinctione earum inter se/ propter solutionem plurium questionum/. Nota. ergo quod potentiarum distinctio accipi potest secundum quod sunt principium motus deliberatiui in homine/ Aut igitur sunt potentie. discernentes motum in motu. diliberato/. scilicet. secundum potentias rationalis anime/ Aut impetum facientes in opus/ Si primo modo uel hec fit/ secundum ius naturale/ vniuersale/ quod est communis conceptio/ et indeterminata de agendis in qua omnes particulares includuntur/ ut quod tibi non uis (56rb) fieri. Alij ne feceris et similia. sicut dicit apostolus. qui proximum diligit legem[149] impleuit. et hec potentia uocatur synderesis/ et quia vniuersaliora sunt ueriora/ ideo synderesis numquam errat/
>
> Hec igitur synderesis si accipitur pro ipsa rectitudine/ que naturaliter insita est ipsi rationi. sic est habitus. si autem accipitur pro potentia. subiecta illi habitu naturali. sic dicit potentia. Et idem sciendum est de omnibus potentiis et habitibus sequentibus
>
> uel est decernens secundum ius naturale speciale determinat(um). scilicet. per obiectum. hoc uel illud ut non furandum. non mechandum/. et huiusmodi/ sic dicit ius naturale. uel lex naturalis. que consistit in distinctione preceptorum diuersorum ordinatorum tamen ad eundem finem. sicut est in decalogo. uel est discernens. secundum ius diuinum/ quod est. quando sumit regimen ex regulis diuinis ut hoc faciendum. uel admittendum. quia deo placet uel displacet/ uel quia lege diuina prohibitum et huiusmodi/ et sic est ratio superior. que in legibus diuinis inherescit/ secundum Augustinum in littera. que etiam dicitur ratio sapientialis. eo quod sit subiectum sapientie/. Vel est discernens/ secundum ius humanum. quod dicitur positiuum ius. sicut statuta ecclesie. quedam. et legum. et principum/ sic dicitur ratio inferior sicut

---

148. PETER OF TARENTAISE, II *Sent.*, d.24, q.2, a.3, R., p. 205. Neither Peter nor Thomas make William's particular distinction between counsel and election. However, THOMAS, II *Sent.*, d.24, q.1, a.3, in corpore, p. 597, remarks that "counsel precedes election as a disputation a conclusion".

149. Scribe repeats *legem*.

si illud laudabile et honestum. ergo faciendurh et huiusmodi. fundatur autem hoc ius super ius naturale. vnde quando illi concordant (*read*: concordat)/ tenendum est. quando discordat a nullo tenendum est. etiam a quocumque homine illud statutum fiat/ Hec ratio inferior etiam dicitur ratio scientialis eo quod subiectum sit scientie/ que docet conuersari in medio/ praue et peruerse nationis./

Ex hiis autem patet quod eadem potentia est ratio superior et inferior. quia potentie non distinguntur penes diuersa media/ sed per actus/ et obiecta./ (56va) Rationis autem superioris et inferioris idem est actus. scilicet. discernere quid faciendum. et idem obiectum. quamuis per diuersa media. scilicet. ius diuinum et humanum/ Nota etiam secundum philosophum/ quod in potentiis istis debet esse ordo/ ut primam. scilicet. moueat. et regat omnes sequentes. et ideo oportet quod ius naturale deriuetur a Iure diuino/ quod primo iustum et rectum[150] est. Ab illo autem ius humanum uel positiuum.

Ex hiis autem omnibus sequitur alia potentia. movens et discernens. scilicet. conscientia que est conclusio/ ex quocumque predictorum/ principiorum que habetur cum assertione mentis quantum ad principium et dictamen uie rationis. quantum ad propriationem (*read*: ad applicationem)[151]/ad illud particulare factum/ et dicitur conscientia quasi cum alio scientia. scilicet. cum principio/ illo/ scientia enim proprie conclusionum est

hec autem ali(quando) est recta. scilicet. quando bene sumitur sub. ali(quando) erronea/ quando/ male sumitur sub./ ut cum dicitur/ non occides. dicit hereticus. ergo non uerminem occidas.

Si autem sit faciens impetum in opus. sicut dicitur appetitus rationalis. qui potest adhuc sumi dupliciter. uel per se et absolute/. sic dicitur uoluntas. uel in ordine ad rationem regentem. et sic dicitur liberum arbitrium. quod est facultas rationis et uoluntatis./ ut dicitur in littera/ et Ita patet/ quod liberum arbitrium est vna potentia. essentialiter. scilicet. uoluntas per ordinem tamen ad rationem. vnde et nomen habet utriusque/ et ideo etiam habet duos actus. scilicet. consilium/ et electionem. sed tamen diuersis respectibus. quia consilium est in uoluntate/ participata ratione. et habente in se uirtutum rationis. Sed electio est ab ipsa uoluntate

Si autem sumatur motus non deliberatiuus. scilicet. secundum potentias sensitiuas. tunc uel est decernens motum sic est forma (*read*: fantastica) et estimatiua. uel nuncians ipsum primum (56vb) mouens. et sic sunt sensus particulares qui nunciant ipsum sensibile primo mouens. vel etiam faciens impetum in opus. siue mouens/ quod dicitur. appetitus.

---

150. Scribe repeats *et rectum*.

151. *Applicatio* is Thomas Aquinas' term; II *Sent.*, d.24, q.2, a.4, in corpore, p. 613 : "inde dicitur conscientia ... quia scientia universalis ad actum particularem applicatur ... conscientia vero nominat applicationem quamdam legis naturalis ad aliquid faciendum".

et tunc ille appetitus mouens uel est motus ab appetibili primo mouente. et sic dicitur sensualitas. que mouet ad opus secundum sensibile ut sensibile est non habitu respectu. ad aliquid regimen cuiuscumque. et ideo etiam sempiterne peruersitatis dicitur/

Si autem mouet/ motus ab appetibili decernentem motum/. scilicet. a fantastica et estimatiua. que decernunt aliquid faciendum. siue persequendum uel fugiendum. et hoc uel secundum intentiones. ut estimatiua. uel etiam ipsas res ut fantastica. que concipit ipsas res. terribiles. uel delectabiles. sic dicitur appetitus sensibilis. qui alius est a sensualitate. Ille ergo appetitus uel est de delectabili secundum sensum/ per se. uel de contrario/ et sic est appetitus concupiscibilis. uel est de sensibili non per se/ sed quod per accidens sentitur/ sicut est gloria et altitudo. et huiusmodi uel de contrario. et sic est appetitus irrascibilis. vterque autem istorum. scilicet. concupiscibilis./ et irrascibilis. secundum quod in homine/ sic uocatur/ ratio participatiue dicta/ et alterior est in nobis quam in brutis/ quia rationi obedientialis est[152].

Nota etiam ratio et uoluntas/ diuerse potentie sunt in anima quia anima diuersas/ operationes secundum speciem agit per eas quarum necessario diuersa oportet esse principia./

De intellectu etiam agente et possibili sciendum est quod sunt due potentie intellectiue in anima/ per agente(m) quidem anima species/ a fantasmatibus abtrahit sicut lux a coloribus. per possibilem species abstractas (57ra) recipit. sicut oculus speciem coloris Vnde differunt sicut in uisione exteriori. lux et pupilla/

Hec de hiis potentiis sufficiant. obmissis multis erroribus et opinionibus circa predicta.

III. The Date and Significance of William de Rothwell's Abbreviation

As stated, Peter of Tarentaise's commentary on the four books of the *Sentences* was completed ca. 1264. Thomas Aquinas' *Responsio ... de 108 articulis*, which William de Rothwell seemingly knew, was composed between 1264 and 1268. These dates recommend a date for William's abbreviation at least very near 1270, and probably after. Other evidence strengthens the argument for a date after 1270.

---

152. On the difference between *sensualitas* and *sensibilitas*, and on the imaginative and estimative powers in relation to them, see THOMAS AQUINAS, II *Sent.*, d.24, q.2, a.1, pp. 601-604. This article covers the items of the sensitive powers treated here by William.

On the first question of Book III of the *Sentences*—"Was the Incarnation Possible?"—William de Rothwell again departs from Peter of Tarentaise's text. William's response recalls Albert the Great's solution "primo ex potentia Dei, secundo ex sapientia, tertio ex bonitate", and echoes Albert's particular argument: "infinitum bonum infinito modo se communicat, et non est infinitum nisi ipsum substantialiter: ergo seipsum communicabit creato"[153].

William de Rothwell, III, 67[rb]:

> *Queritur utrum Incarnatio fuit possibilis.* Respondeo. sic et possibilitate congruitatis/ quia summi bono proprium est. summe se communicare/ hec communicationem maior est per sui communicationem substantialem quam per similitudinem communem/ tantum/ et etiam possibilitate absoluta/ quantum ad potentiam efficientis quia non erit impossibile/ apud deum omne uerbum. sed non potentia materie (*read*: creature?) proprie. nisi large. scilicet. quantum ad potentiam obedientialem. facta est augustinus hec vnio non commixtione neque confusione naturarum sed per modum cuiusdem associationis. ut dicit augustinus in littera.

More exactly, William's response abbreviates the argument of Albert's disciple, Ulrich of Strasbourg, in his *Summa de bono*, Book V, tract. 1, a. 4[154]. Ulrich's argument is reported by Dionysius the Carthusian:

> Udalricus quoque hic loquitur: Deum carnem asumere, fuit possibile ex parte Dei, non solum potentia absoluta, sed etiam ordinata, quae est congruitatis. Nempe potentia absoluta non est impossibile apud Deum omne verbum, id est, id quo potest verbum formari, videlicet omne quod contradictionem non implicat ... Fuit etiam incarnatio Verbi possibilis potentia ordinata, quae est potentia congruitatis ... Porro ex parte creaturae non fuit possibilitas nisi secundum potentiam obedientialem, qua de creatura potest fieri quidquid Creator de ipsa velit facere, non remota dispositione congruitatis qua magis assumptibilis fuit natura humana quam quaecumque alia[155].

---

153. ALBERT THE GREAT, III *Sent.*, d.1, A., d.1, in *Opera omnia* XXVIII, ed. J. BORGNET (1894), pp. 3-7; see arg. 6, p. 5.

154. "De possibilitate Incarnationis et de modo hujus unionis, et an Deus incarnatus fuisset, si homo non peccasset" etc.; see Francis J. LESCOE, *God as First Principle in Ulrich of Strasbourg* (New York 1979), p. 27. This text from Ulrich's *Summa de bono* has not yet been edited.

155. DIONYSIUS CARTUSIANUS, III *Sent.*, d.1, q.1, *Opera omnia*, XXIII (Tournai 1904), pp. 38-49.

Ulrich of Strasbourg probably composed his *Summa de bono* between 1262 and 1272; one scholar dates the completion of the work as late as 1274-76[156]. In light of the combined evidence of William de Rothwell's sources, we believe it is conservative to date his abbreviation after 1270.

A later date increases the interest of William de Rothwell's abbreviation. William's sources are Dominican; if he sometimes states "Franciscan" opinions, these are mediated through the text of Peter of Tarentaise. William clearly knew Thomas Aquinas' commentary on the *Sentences* first hand, for when he parts from Peter's text he often turns to Thomas'. Against Peter of Tarentaise's preference, and contrary as well to the teaching of the Oxford Dominicans Richard Fishacre and Robert Kilwardby[157], William rejects a hylemorphic composition in the human soul and in angels. Early Dominican masters like Hugh of St. Cher (1230-35) had done likewise before the issue was greatly controversial, but William's arguments "by reason of the intellectuality" of spiritual creatures come directly from Thomas. William likewise subscribes to Thomas' "intellectualism" in his treatment of synderesis and conscience. Robert Kilwardby, like Bonaventure and Peter of Tarentaise, placed synderesis in the will, and consequently treated conscience before turning to synderesis[158].

At the same time, contrary to Thomas Aquinas, William affirms a plurality of prior and subsequent, incomplete and complete forms in the human composite. This issue became notably controversial after 1270, when John Peckham disputed Thomas Aquinas at Paris over a number of propositions relating to the principle. The controversy became especially heated at Oxford, where Robert Kilwardby on 18 March, 1277 condemned a number of propositions affirming the unicity of substantial form in creatures in general and

---

156. See LESCOE, p. 6. F. PELSTER, *Zur Datierung einiger Schriften Alberts des Grossen*, in *Zeitschrift für katholische Theologie* 47 (1923) 475-482, suggests the *terminus ad quem* 1274-76.

157. See D.E. SHARP, *The Philosophy of Richard Fishacre (D.1248)*, in *New Scholasticism* 7 (1933) 287-289, and *Further Philosophical Doctrines of Kilwardby*, 46-54.

158. M.-D. CHENU, OP, *Le 'De conscientia' de R. Kilwardby, O.P.,* †*1279*, in *Revue des Sciences philosophiques et théologiques* 16 (1927) 318-326; Odon LOTTIN, *Syndérèse et conscience*, in *Psych. et mor.*, II, pp. 313-332.

man in particular. Almost immediately, Oxford Dominicans rallied in support of the position of Thomas Aquinas, and over the next decade and thereafter Thomas' doctrine became officially Dominican[159]. As R. Zavalloni says, after 1270 no master could be indifferent to the question of a plurality of forms in man[160]. Nor was William de Rothwell. Even though his little work is not disputatious, and even though he seldom indicates his personal opinion, he is careful to signify his position on this question. We offer the judgment that William composed his abbreviation after 1270, when the question of substantial form became controversial, and before 1280, after which time Thomas Aquinas' opinion was nearly prescribed for Dominicans.

Except for the article which Peter of Tarentaise culled from *De ortu scientiarum*, the questions which we have examined in William's abbreviation reveal no immediate influence of Robert Kilwardby. However, William expresses his position on the plurality of forms in the question "An anima sit simplex", and it was under this title that Kilwardby condemned the Thomist thesis: "Quod vegetativa, sensitiva et intellectiva, sunt una forma simplex"[161]. Moreover, the "dispositive" form of the pluralist argument which William gives is the same type as that given by Kilwardby in his letter to Peter Conflans (1278). Kilwardby.too speaks of "forme priores" by which the human body first exists, then vegetates and senses before the "aduentus intellectus":

> cum non sit corpus nisi per formam corpoream, nec uegetatiuam nisi per formam uegetatiuam, nec sensitiuam nisi per formam sensitiuam, quod non esset in homine actio sentiendi uel uegetandi uel existentia corporis ... Scio tamen, quod unus homo unam habet formam, que non est una simplex, sed ex multis composita, ordinem ad inuicem

---

159. On Kilwardby's condemnations, See D. E. SHARP, *The 1277 Condemnation by Kilwardby*, in *New Scholasticism* 7 (1934) 306-318; D. A. CALLUS, *The Condemnation of St. Thomas at Oxford* (Aquinas Society of London, Aquinas Papers, no. 5: Oxford 1946). ROENSCH, *Early Thomist School*, gives a full account of the succession of English (and French) Dominican masters who defended Thomas' positions.

160. ZAVALLONI, p. 221.

161. Number 12; *Chartularium Universitatis Parisiensis*, ed. H. DENIFLE and E. CHÂTELAIN, I (Paris 1889), p. 559.

habentibus naturalem et sine quarum nulla perfectius homo esse potest, quarum ultima, completiua et perfectiua totius aggregati est intellectus [162].

The least one can say is that William de Rothwell's formula reflects an authoritative Oxford and Dominican teaching.

Even when he departs from the text of Peter of Tarentaise, William did not invent any of the arguments in his abbreviation. None the less, his selectivity and disposition of material suffices to reveal his own thinking. From what we have seen, we might conclude that William was somewhat independent, inasmuch as he did not adhere strictly to any given school within or without his Order. But such a conclusion is not precise enough, since it does not sufficiently consider the formal genre of William's text.

What was the purpose of William's *abbreviatio*, and of others like it? Clearly, it fulfilled no academic requirement, or served any academic end. William's text could not be judged a *reportatio*, since it evinces such a detailed use of written texts. Unlike theological *compendia*, it does not state arguments but rather alludes to them. We know that some abbreviations of the *Sentences* were made for brethren in religious houses remote from university life [163]. Indeed, more than anything else, William's abbreviation seems designed to supply its readers with *meditabilia*. William's responses are "sentences" which delineate considerations for the items of faith.

Most of the copies of William's abbreviation were owned by monasteries [164]. The "pretty", labored production of *University of Pennsylvania Lat. MS. 32* argues more a devotional than a pragmatic, intellectual use. Further, the manuscript's two annotations reveal a certain kind of reader. On the last written folio of the manuscript one finds a salient item :

> Sinderesis est vis anime que innata est figi in superioribus naturaliter mouens et stimulans ad bonum ac abhorens malum neque et in (i)stis numquam errat neque secundum synderesim contingit peccare (137rb).

---

162. *Der Brief Robert Kilwardbys an Peter von Conflans und die Streitschrift des Ägidius von Lessines*, ed. A. Birkenmajer, *BGPTM*, XX, Heft 5 (Münster 1922), pp. 61, 5-10; 62, 25-63, 5; 63, 30-35.

163. See Nicholas H. Stenick, *Science and Creation in the Middle Ages. Henry of Langenstein (d.1397) on Genesis* (South Bend 1976), pp. 9-10, 18, 25, 190, n. 2.

164. See Note 1.

The annotator has observed the composer's special preoccupation with the powers of the soul that "rule in life". Besides this note, the annotator has filled in the pastedown on the inside front cover. Here one finds "a curious magical invocation of angels and demons, with strings of names beginning, Lamech, Salmalaach, Helmahn ... etc."[165] The names of the good angels, which counteract the influence of evil ones, derive their power from the glorious and ineffable divine name, the "fons bonitatis et totius pietatis origo". In pious combat amidst principalities and powers, it must have been consoling to know that there was one power of the soul which was sure.

It is revealing that Bonaventure's commentary on the *Sentences* was often abbreviated, and that these abbreviations were widely copied throughout the late Middle Ages[166]. Bonaventure's theology was reliable, conducive to piety and free of the novelties that might arouse curiosity. Like Bonaventure, Peter of Tarentaise taught that theology was ordered to wisdom and affection, a *scientia pietatis*[167]. William de Rothwell was not the only one to abbreviate Peter of Tarentaise[168]. Among Dominicans, Peter was the most authoritative representative of the thirteenth-century *theologia communis*[169]. To William de Rothwell, Peter's commentary must have seemed best-suited to edify the Dominican brethren in the faith.

165. *Bernard Quaritch's Catalogue*, no. 699 (1952), p. 26, n. 86.

166. Z. ALZEGHY, *Abbreviationes Bonaventurae. Handschriftliche Auszüge aus dem Sentenzenkommentar des hl. Bonaventura in Mittelalter*, in *Gregorianum* 18 (1947) 474-510.

167. PETER OF TARENTAISE, I *Sent., prol.*, q. unica., a.4, p. 5. WILLIAM DE ROTHWELL, I, 23ra : "*Vtrum theologia sit scientia speculatiua. vel practica* Respondeo partim speculatiua. partim practica. quia de ipsa est sapientia/ que est habitus perficiens intellectum in extensione ad affectum est secundum quod excitat affectionem vnde potest de scientia affectiua. vnde apostolus dicit eam esse scientia pietatis".

168. GRABMANN, *Handschriftliche Mitteilungen über Abbreviationem des Sentenzenkommentars des seligen Papstes Innozenz V.*

169. The term is applied by Gilson to the thought of John Peckham, *History of Christian Philosophy in the Middle Ages* (New York 1955), p. 706, n. 80.

Summary

University of Pennsylvania Lat. MS. 32 contains one of the earliest copies of the *Sentences* commentary of the English Dominican, William de Rothwell. William's work, probably composed between 1270 and 1280, proves to be an *abbreviatio* of the *Sentences* commentary of Peter of Tarentaise. William sometimes departs from Peter's text, either adopting the solution of another Dominican master (e.g., Thomas Aquinas) or confecting his own. William's text serves as a mirror to the controversies of the time, and presents an interesting configuration of doctrines. In the end, however, the nature of the work's genre and the evidence of the MS. bespeak a pious rather than a speculative or disputatious intent. The teaching of Peter of Tarentaise which William de Rothwell abbreviates seems especially apt for this purpose.

III

THE CLOUD OF UNKNOWING AND MYSTICA THEOLOGIA

The Cloud of Unknowing is an anonymous fourteenth-century book written for someone about to enter a solitary form of monastic life. It treats elements of spiritual growth — sin, humility, grace, charity — and the ordering of human faculties — imagination, reason, and will — to God. Steeped in the western tradition of mystical theology, the unknown author of the Cloud distilled and made his own that rich tradition.

No MIDDLE ENGLISH work of spiritual doctrine has received more comment or met more enthusiasm than the anonymous *Cloud of Unknowing*. The work was composed in an East Midlands dialect in the last quarter of the fourteenth century, probably by a Carthusian monk.[1] The doctrine of *The Cloud* is highly distilled, or, as pseudo-Dionysius says mystical theology should be, *minimam . . . et rursus concisum . . . et brevium dictionum*.[2] Perhaps it is the distilled quality of *The Cloud*'s teaching which has made it susceptible to diverse interpretations. Among the most persistent of these is one which would relate *The Cloud* to eastern mysticisms. Several decades ago, for example, Aldous Huxley praised *The Cloud* for its 'pure Vedantic spirit' which transcends the narrow confines of a 'Christo-centric' dogmatism.[3] Today, *The Cloud*'s teaching is perceived to be similar to the practices of Zen Buddhism. Compatible with both of these is the interpretation which discovers in *The Cloud* fashionable psychological techniques, such as 'centering'.

However appealing such interpretations may be, however uncluttered *The Cloud*'s teaching may seem, and even though the author chooses not to display his authorities, *The Cloud* is full of medieval, Latin learning. We intend to show in this study that *The Cloud of Unknowing* is, according to a traditional and precise generic definition, a work of 'mystical theology', and to explore the implications of this definition for an understanding of the work.

To begin, we should remember that the author of *The Cloud* composed a small corpus of closely related works. He made an English translation, entitled *Deonise Hid Diuinite*, of pseudo-Dionysius' *De mystica theologia*, based upon a conflation of Johannes Sarracenus' Latin rendering and Thomas Gallus' paraphrases. He also adapted and translated into English parts of Richard of St Victor's *Benjamin minor (De duodecim patri-archis)* giving his work the title *A Tretyse of þe Stodye of Wysdome þat Men Clepen Beniamyn*.[4] The author's major works are *The Cloud* and its later companion piece, *The Book of Privy Counselling*, both probably addressed to the same person. Finally, the author of *The Cloud* composed three other small works, *A Pistle of Preir*, *A Pistle of Discrecioun of Stirings*, and *A Tretis of Discresyon of Spirites*.[5] In these works, the author applies the general teaching of *The Cloud* to particular matters of the spiritual life.

As their editor notes, four of these works, *The Cloud*, *The Book of Privy Counselling*, *A Pistle of Preir*, and *Pistle of Dis-crecioun of Stirings* 'are written in the form of letters', at times achieving a 'noticeably personal, and even intimate' tone.[6] This fact is significant. Medieval spiritual writers, especially in the more eremitic orders such as the Cistercians and Carthusians,[7] were fond of the epistolary genre. Their exemplar, of course, was Paul. One should also remark that pseudo-Dionysius, the presumed disciple of Paul, composed a series of letters, and cast his *De mystica theologia* in epistolary form (*Compresbytero Timotheo, Dionysius presbyter salutem*).[8]

Furthermore, ancient rhetorical theory suggested the appro-priateness of an epistolary style for spiritual teaching. Cicero distinguished a less adorned style, particularly suited for philo-sophic discourse, from the more abundant style suited for pub-lic forensic persuasion. Cicero designated the plainer, personal style *sermo* in contrast to the more adorned, public *oratio*. It was Seneca, however, who most clearly defined the 'idea' of

the *sermo* style, and developed its characteristic form, the personal letter to a like-minded friend. For many centuries his
Epistulae ad Lucilium were the model for the genre. Throughout the Middle Ages, admiring christian writers called Seneca
'our Seneca', 'the moral Seneca', a 'doctor of souls'. Seneca's
favoring of the personal epistle was consistent with his Stoic
beliefs, which recommended more the cultivation of an interior, private virtue than an outward, public one.

Indeed, the ends of the epistolary style, as taught and prac-
tised by Seneca, were easily accommodated to the purposes of
christian, especially monastic, spiritual writers. The major
themes of Seneca's letters — self-knowledge, reason's governance of the passions, conformity to the divine will, the joys of
solitude and fruitful leisure — are commonplaces of monastic
literature. Precisely because it urged man to a spiritual governing of himself, Seneca's rhetoric made sparing use of the figures
of sound, regretably necessary when one wished to move a
crowd swayed by every passion. Figures of thought were more
appropriate to a form designed to communicate mind to mind.
The primary purpose of the epistolary style, Seneca taught, is,
on the one hand, to reveal candidly the soul of the writer, and
on the other, to effect self-knowledge in the reader. The intimate style of the epistle, directed to a well-known, individual
recipient, allowed for another important effect. By means of
such personal communication, the writer could provide diag-
nosis and therapy for the exact condition of the recipient's soul,
preventing or curing any spiritual illness caused by disordered
passions, and establishing the soul's healthy condition of harmony.[9] In his *Epistola ad fratres de Monte Dei*, William of St
Thierry directly borrowed this theme from Seneca's letters.[10]
The author of *The Book of Privy Counselling*, in turn borrowing a metaphor from Augustine and William of St Thierry,[11]
likewise claims a therapeutic effect for his own doctrine:

> Take good gracyous God as he is, plat & pleyn as a plastre,
> & legge it to þi seek self as þou arte. Or, ȝif I oþer-wise
> schal sey, bere up þi seek self as þou arte & fonde for to

touche þi desire good gracious God as he is, þe touching of
whom is eendeless helþe by witnes of þe womman in þe
gospel: Si tetigero vel fimbriam vestimenti eius, salvo ero.
'If I touche but þe hemme of his cloþing, I shall be saa[f]!
Miche more schalt þou þan be maad hole of þi seeknes for
þis heiȝe heuenly touching of his own beyng, him owne
self. Step up þan stifly & taast of þat triacle.[12]

Since the epistolary, *sermo* style and the notion of its effects
were assimilated and transformed by christian fathers such as
Tertullian, Jerome, Augustine, and Gregory, and by medieval
monastic writers, we need not argue that the author of *The
Cloud* was directly influenced by Seneca. Walsh, interestingly,
remarks the close resemblance between the intent of William
of St Thierry's *Epistola aurea* and that of *The Cloud*.[13] Whatever his reading among the ancients, the author of *The Cloud*
knew the purpose and customary usage of the epistolary form.
The Cloud's form instructs the reader that he should pay close
attention to the one for whom the work was specifically intended, and to the recipient's particular spiritual condition as
diagnosed by the author. But even if *The Cloud* was not immediately addressed to a general audience, a larger audience was
not deprived of its teaching. Having described its arduous
material production, Jean Leclercq says of the monastic spiritual letter:

> a letter was a gift whose value was appreciated because
> everyone knew just how much it entailed. Even personal
> letters therefore are almost always somewhat public in
> quality. It is generally taken for granted that the letter's
> contents will fall under the eyes, or reach the ears, of sev-
> eral others and that the receiver will take pains to see that it
> is available. This explains how it can happen that the writer
> will tell his correspondent things that both already know.
> ... The writer of a letter took great pains with it because he
> knew it would be brought to the attention of a more or less
> extensive audience.[14]

The spiritual epistle, then, at once conceals and reveals.
Accordingly, *The Book of Privy Counselling*, as its title sug-

gests, is addressed to the particular spiritual condition of a personal friend. At the same time, the author is aware that his writing will find a larger audience:

> Goostly freende in God, as touching þin inward ocupacioun as me þink þee disposid, I speke at þis tyme in specyal to þi-self, & not to alle þoo þat þis writyng scholen here in general. For ʒif I schuld write vnto alle, þan I must write þing þat were acordyng to alle generaly. Bot siþ I at þis tyme shal write vnto þee in special, þerfore I write none oþer þing bot soche as me þink þat is moste speedful & acording to þin disposicion only. If eny oþer be so disposid as þou arte, to whom þis writing may profite as vnto þee, in so moche þe betir, for I am wel apaied. Neuerþeles, at þis tyme, þin owne inward disposicion is only by it-self, as I may conceiue it, þe poynte & þe prik of my beholdyng (p. 135).[15]

The author directs *The Cloud* in the same manner. In the prologue to the work, the author enjoins its recipient to keep the writing to himself, unless he should find another who would be 'a parfite folower of Criste, not only in actyue leuyng, bot in þe souereinnest pointe of contemplatife leuing.' He further charges his reader, under the authority of charity, to make sure that any other readers read it 'al ouer', lest any of them fall into error by heeding 'o mater & not anoþer.' The work must be kept not only from carnal and ignorant men, but also from 'corious lettred' men who take pride in their over-subtle speculations (prol., pp. 1-2).

In *The Cloud*'s first chapter the author specifies the spiritual state of his intended reader. He tells his 'goostly freende in God' that there are 'foure degrees & fourmes of Cristen mens leuyng . . . Comoun, Special, Singuler, & Parfite.' The first three begin and end in this life; the last (like the virtue of charity, we might add) begins in this life 'bot it schal euer laste wiþ-outen eende in þe blis of heuen.' Having specified these four degrees of christian living, the author tells his reader something he already knows, that he has already passed through the common form of life, wherein he was called to God through the divine love which 'made þee & wrouȝt þee when þou were nouȝt, & siþen bouȝt þee wiþ þe prise of his precious blood when þou were loste in Adam.' Pulled by the leash of God's longing for his soul, the reader has also passed through the special form of christian living, wherein he had become a servant of God's special servants. He has now entered into a solitary, singular form of living, wherein he will learn to ascend through love 'towardes þat state & degree of leuyng þat is parfite' (1, pp. 14-15).

What do these degrees signify? First of all, I think, they refer to outward christian vocations, determined by vows of the will. In this manner *The Cloud*'s fifteenth-century Latin translator, the Carthusian Richard Methley, understood them. Methley says that in this passage, the common degree signifies the state of the ordinary layman, the special degree that of a professed cleric or religious, and the singular degree that of a solitary, that is, a hermit or anchorite. Methley adds that in modern times, the terms 'hermit' or 'anchorite' usually refer to a Carthusian monk.[16] According to this understanding, the recipient of *The Cloud* has for some time been a professed religious, and has newly entered solitude, either by receiving permission from his superior to live the life of a hermit, or more likely by having taken up a new vocation in the 'wilderness' of the Charterhouse.[17] Perhaps this was the occasion of the epistle addressed to him. In any case, we need not accept Methley's interpretation as definitive to admit its general likelihood.

The author of *The Cloud* knows that a habit does not an interior perfection make, that outward professions are but signs and instruments of an inward progress. Actually, only three degrees of living are visible; the last degree, perfection and the anticipation of eternity, takes place within and by means of a singular form of life. In this passage, the author carefully indicates the inner graces corresponding to outward vocations. In the common form of christian life, one enters the general economy of christian salvation as explained by scriptural exegetes. Man, in his creation, was made for God. Through participation in Adam's human nature he shares in the Fall. Likewise, through the common christian sacrament of baptism, he participates in the life of the new Adam and shares in Christ's redemption. The divine acts of creation and redemption benefit all men. By a special act of love, God calls some men to serve him and his people in a particular way. Finally, a few, like the recipient of *The Cloud*, are called to be alone with God in a solitary state where nothing distracts. In this state one is more readily disposed to seek the highest perfection, to be, as it were, hidden with Christ in God.

Throughout *The Cloud*, the author speaks of a threefold order of interior perfection which corresponds with the three outward degrees of christian living delineated in the first chapter. The author of *The Cloud* derived his notion of a threefold spiritual order from a number of Latin works which by the fourteenth century constituted a fairly well-defined corpus of 'mystical theology.' This corpus crystallized around the synthesis of Augustine and pseudo-Dionysius accomplished, in large part, by the Victorine writers in the twelfth century.[18] Within the corpus of mystical theology, the works of pseudo-Dionysius, thought to have apostolic authority, held pride of place. His *De mystica theologia* defined the genre for writers of the late Middle Ages. Virtually as important, I believe, are Thomas Gallus' (*Vercellensis*, †1246) paraphrases of pseudo-Dionysius. It was he who established the standard, affective interpretation of pseudo-Dionysius' mystical union.[19] Included also within the corpus were works by Hugh of St Victor, notably his commentary on pseudo-Dionysius' *Celestial Hierarchy*, and the *Benjamin minor* and *Benjamin major* (*De arca mystica*) of Richard of St Victor. The corpus included two important later works. In his *Mystica theologia* (*Viae Syon lugent*), the Carthusian Hugh of Balma (fl. 1300) carried the priority of affection over understanding to its extreme, teaching that affective union with God required neither a preceding nor concomitant act of the intellect. Hugh hardened the distinction between mystical and scholastic theology, which had become traditional, and which perdured into modern times. He also is a primary source for the threefold purgative, illuminative, and unitive ways.[20]

In the middle of the fourteenth century, the Franciscan Rudolph of Biberach (†1362) defined and codified the basic canon of mystical theology. Rudolph's *De septem itineribus aeternitatis* is a convenient mystical encyclopaedia. Throughout, Rudolph generously excerpts works of Origen, Augustine, Gregory, the twelfth-century *Liber de spiritu et anima* falsely attributed to Augustine, Bernard, Hugh and Richard of St Victor, Thomas Gallus, and the Dionysian commentaries of Robert Grosseteste. He disposes the excerpts of these authors according to a threefold order of sensible, intellectual, and affective, mystical theology.[21] Especially in gathering germane texts from the wide-ranging works of earlier fathers, and accommodating them to well-known classifications among later writers, Rudolph's work was useful for anyone seeking authorities on points of mystical theology. Both Hugh of Balma's and Rudolph of Biberach's works circulated under the name of Bonaventure. This is not surprising, since Hugh's *Mystica theologia* and Rudolph of Biberach's *De septem itineribus* show clear signs of Bonaventure's influence. It is just to say that Bonaventure, in his *Itinerarium mentis in Deum* and other works, perfected the synthesis of Augustine and pseudo-Dionysius begun by the Victorines. In a chain of remarkable analogies, he unified the various threefold orders advanced by previous authors.

Two further points concerning the late medieval corpus of mystical theology should be made. First, since the later writers quote or allude to the same texts of the same earlier writers, it is difficult to determine exactly the source of their citations. Secondly, in the late Middle Ages Carthusian and Franciscan authors were generally the leading proponents of pseudo-Dionysius' mystical theology, interpreted affectively and always assimilated to the theology of Augustine. And Carthusian and Franciscan writers shared a particular point of interpretation: an emphasis upon the mediating role, within the spiritual ascent, of meditation on Christ's passion. Although pseudo-Dionysius stated that Christ was the head of every hierarchy and the mediator between spiritual and material worlds, such an emphasis upon Christ's passion cannot be found in his works. The *De contemplatione* of the Carthusian monk Guigo du Pont (†1297) is a typical example of late medieval mystical theology. Recently, James Walsh has argued for the influence of this work upon the author of *The Cloud*. Certainly, Guigo's particular variation of the threefold ascent — 'purification by means of contrition, union with Christ by means of meditation on his life and passion, and contemplation of the Divine Majesty' by means of affective aspiration[22] — is close to the teaching of *The Cloud*, as we shall see.

The preceding catalogue of authors and titles, although not exhaustive, is none the less meant to be restrictive. The author of *The Cloud*'s reading was within this library. From it he acquired his precise definition of mystical theology in relation to other kinds of theology. The *locus classicus* of what came to be called the three modes of theology[23] is pseudo-Dionysius' *De mystica theologia*. Of pseudo-Dionysius the author of *The Cloud* says:

> & trewly, who-so wil loke Denis bookes, he schal fynde þat his wordes wilen cleerly aferme al þat I have seyde or schal sey, fro þe beginnyng of þis tretis to þe ende (70, p. 125).

In chapter three of *De mystica theologia*, pseudo-Dionysius classifies the various works he has written. His *Symbolica theologia*[24] (not extant), Dionysius says, praises (I quote *The Cloud* author's translation)

> alle þe names þat ben applied vnto God from þees sensible þinges — as which ben þe godliche fourmes, which ben þe godliche figures . . . & what oþer sensible formes þat on any maner in Holy Scripture ben applied vnto God.[25]

In another work, 'þe booke of *Goddes Names* it is affermyngliche set & preised how þat he is namyd Good, how Beyng, how Liif, how Wisdome, & how Vertewe, & what oþer þat þei be of þe vnderstonable namynges (*intelligibilis . . . nominationis*) of God? Commentators generally understood that pseudo-Dionysius' two other major works, '*þe Ierarchies of Heuen* & . . . *þe Ierarchies of þis Fiʒtyng Chirche*', exemplified these two modes of theology, sensible and intelligible. The first shows how the angelic orders, the immaterial 'liʒtes of goodness', burst forth out of God, and the second how God's goodness is manifest in the sacraments of the visible world.[26]

These two kinds of theology differ from a third — mystical theology — in a fundamental way. Whereas the first two affirm God by assigning to him names derived from the properties of creatures, mystical theology denies all of these names, and entering '*þe derknes þat is aboven mynde* [*in caliginem quae est super mentem*]',[27] ascends to the creator himself. Within the context of these modes of theology — sensible or symbolic, intelligible, and mystical — medieval writers understood Dionysius' famous injunction to forsake

> þi bodely wittes (as heryng, seyng, smelling, taastyng, & touching), and also þi goostly wittes, þe whiche ben clepid þin vnderstondable worchings; and alle þoo þinges, þe whiche mowe be knowen wiþ any of the fyue bodely wittes without-forþe; and alle þoo þinges, þe whiche mow be knowen by þi goostly wittes wiþinne-forþ; and . . . rise . . . in a manner þat is þou woste neuer how, to be onid with hym þat is abouen alle substaunces and al manner knowyng.[28]

The Cloud author's rendering of this passage is faithful enough, but his paraphrase expansion of the single terms *sensibilia et intelligibilia* ('knowen . . . without-forþe; knowen . . . wiþinne-forþ') reveals the influence of later interpreters, namely, Richard of St Victor and Bonaventure.[29] In these texts from pseudo-Dionysius' *De mystica theologia*, one may discern the seeds of a threefold analogy among modes of being (sensible, intelligible, divine), modes of apprehension (imaginative, intellectual, above mind), and modes of theology (symbolic, intelligible, mystical). These analogies were amplified by the writers to whom we have alluded. What the apprehension

above mind is, Dionysius does not expressly say. The author of
The Cloud, however, in a sentence which he inserts in his translation, says that it is 'wiþ affecyon' that one rises 'abouen
mýnde.'[30] In so doing, he states his agreement with Thomas
Gallus, Bonaventure, Hugh of Balma, and a long line of commentators.

The analogy between modes of apprehension and modes of
theology becomes clearer by reference to works of Richard of
St Victor, whose *Benjamin minor* the author of *The Cloud*
translated in part. In the *Benjamin major*, Richard generally
distinguishes three kinds of contemplation. One, founded in
the imagination, perceives God in sensible things. Another,
founded in the reason, discerns God in intelligible things. The
highest, founded in the power (*intelligentia*) above reason, sees
God in invisible, incomprehensible things (*intellectibilibus*).[31]
This hierarchy is expressed allegorically in the *Benjamin minor*.
In Richard's allegory, Leah, who signifies the imagination
which brings the information of the senses to the soul, is replaced by the fairer Rachel, who signifies the abstract knowledge of reason. In turn, Rachel must herself die in giving birth
to her favored son, Benjamin. The author of *The Cloud* translates:

> For whi in what tyme þat a soule is rauished abouen him-
> self by habundaunce of desires & a greet multytude of loue,
> so þat it is enflawmyd with þe liзt of þe Godheed, sekerly
> þan dyзeþ al mans reson . . . so þat it be fulfillid in þee þat
> is wretyn in þe psalme: 'Ibi Beniamyn adolescentulus in
> mentis excessu.' Þat is: 'Þere is Beniamyn, þe зonge childe,
> in rauesching of mynde.'[32]

Before coming to such a rapture of the mind, Richard says, we
must 'þorow þe grace of God lyзtenyng oure reson' come 'to
þe parfite knowyng of our selfe and of God', insofar as it is possible in this life. One must not presume 'to knowe þe vnseable
þinges of þe spirit of God' before he knows 'þe vnseable
þinges of his owne spirit.'[33] The strands we have been following are woven together tightly by Bonaventure in the *Itinera-*

rium. Through symbolic theology we rightly use those sensible things outside of us; through the theology proper to our rational capacity we rightly use those intelligible things within us; finally, through mystical theology we are rapt *ad supermentales excessus*, to those divine things above us.[34]

These texts suffice to indicate that the work of mystical theology presupposes previous exercise of the imagination and reason. If the intended reader of *The Cloud* is a beginner,[35] he is so in the sense of the initiate who is prepared finally to enter the hidden mysteries of God.

The threefold order we have sketched informs many chapters of *The Cloud of Unknowing*. The author introduces it into his treatment of Martha and Mary, who according to traditional exegesis signify the active and contemplative lives. The author of *The Cloud* notes that Holy Church customarily speaks of only two lives. Nevertheless, the active and contemplative lives should be divided once more, since there is an intermediate life wherein the active flows into the contemplative. In the usual medieval way, the author seeks the justification for his new division in the text he is expounding. Martha and Mary may be considered singly and apart, or together as sisters. In the intermediate life 'is contemplatyue liif & actyue liif couplid to-geders in goostly sibreden & maad sistres', like Martha and Mary (21, p. 53). The active life, then, consists 'in good & onest bodily werkes of mercy & of charite'. The intermediate life 'liggeþ in good goostly meditacions of a mans owne wrechidnes, þe Passion of Criste, & of þe ioyes of heuen' (21, p. 53). The contemplative life, finally, 'hangeþ in þis derk cloude of vnknowyng, wiþ many a priue loue put to God by him-self' (21, p. 54). The author's terms mark the specific psychological character of each of the three lives. The first is concerned with 'bodily' things, the second with the just exercise of the discursive reason in good meditations, and the third with the work of the affections which reach beyond knowledge.

An earlier division of active and contemplative lives into four turns out to be, like this one, threefold. Both the active life and the contemplative life may be divided into higher and lower parts. However, the higher part of the active life and the lower part of the contemplative life are in fact the same (8, pp. 29-33). Again, the active life is said to consist of 'bodily werkes'. The intermediate life, as stated above, consists of 'goostly meditacions, & besy beholding' of Christ's passion and of 'þe wonderful ʒiftes, kyndnes, & werkes of God in alle his creatures' (8, pp. 31-32), or in other terms, of the *liber scripturae* and *liber creaturae*. The contemplative life, which *The Cloud* properly concerns, consists of 'a louyng steryng & a blind beholdyng vnto þe nakid beyng of God him-self only' (8, p. 32).

In the same chapter, the analogy between states of life and powers of the soul is explicit:

> In þe lower partye of actiue liif a man is wiþ-outen him-self & bineeþ him-self. In þe hiʒer party of actyue liif & þe lower party of contemplatiue liif, a man is wiþinne himself & euen wiþ himself. Bot in þe hiʒer partie of contemplatiue liif, a man is abouen him-self & vnder his God. Abouen him-self he is, for whi he purposeþ him to wynne þeder bi grace, wheþer he may not come bi kynde; that is to sey, to be knit to God in spirite, & in oneheed of loue & acordaunce of wile (8, p. 32).

A man is outside and beneath himself when he relies on the senses, which he shares with other animals beneath him in the order of creation. He is within and 'euen' with himself when he exercises what defines his specific human nature, the reason. He is above himself when through the affection of the will he dilates to embrace God. Then he is 'vnder his God'. I think this latter phrase refers to a famous teaching of Augustine, repeated by William of St Thierry, the author of *De spiritu et anima*, and others, stating that nothing, not even the angels, intervenes between God and the mind (*mens*), that highest and innermost part of human nature superior both to other animals and to other parts of the soul.[36]

Presently we shall comment upon the author of *The Cloud*'s use of the term 'mind'. For now we shall note that man's discursive reasoning, by exercise of which he is 'euen' with himself, can never, according to the author of *The Cloud*, attain to that which is purely spiritual. This is so because as long as the soul dwells in a mortal body,

> euermore is þe scharpness of oure vnderstanding in behold-ing of alle goostly þinges, bot most specialy of God, mede-lid wiþ sum maner of fantasie; for þe whiche oure werk schuld be vnclene (8, p. 33).

Therefore the author says, only 'loue may reche to God in þis liif, but not knowing.' On this point the author consciously parts way with Richard of St Victor and adheres more closely to the affective teaching of Thomas Gallus and Hugh of Balma. For not only does Richard teach a completely spiritual cogni-tion in the soul's highest power, which he calls *intelligentia*, but he also posits a contemplation 'formed in the reason according to reason', wherein the rational soul, 'far removed from every function of imagination, directs its attention toward those things alone which the imagination does not know but which the mind gathers from reasoning or understands by means of reason.'[37] Developments of the thirteenth century intervene between Richard and the author of *The Cloud* here. The latter accepts the scholastic adage that there is nothing in the under-standing which was not first in the senses. Consequently, all reasoning and meditation, however abstract, is rooted in sensi-bility, and one cannot attain God, who is pure spirit, by means of it. For this reason, the author of *The Cloud* associates medi-tation closely with the 'bodily' active life. The immediate source for the author's teaching is probably Hugh of Balma, who sharply distinguished scholastic theology, the abstract con-ceptions of which are always more or less remotely rooted in sense, from mystical theology, in which the affection of the will frees the soul from all attachment to the senses.[38]

The threefold order of the spiritual life finds a fit object in Christ who, having a sensible nature, rational soul, and a divine person, unites created and divine natures. Once more returning to the commonplace of Martha and Mary (16-17, pp. 44-48), the author of *The Cloud* points out that when Christ visited

their house, while Mary was engaged in contemplation Martha
was busy preparing food for Christ's flesh. Martha's business
was good; it corresponds to the work of the active life. However, the work of Mary, who sat attentively at Christ's feet, was
better. In fact, in terms of the threefold comparison good, better, best, it was the best. For Mary did not heed, as would one
in the intermediate life, the 'preciouste' of Christ's 'blessid body,'
or 'þe swete voyce & þe wordes of his Manheed.' Rather she be-
held 'þe souvereynest wisdom of his Godheed lappid in þe derk
words of his Manheed.' By means of a 'swete prive & a lysty
loue' Mary penetrated Christ's human words, which stood as a
'cloude of unknowing bitwix hir & hir God' (17, p. 47).

In the light of this passage, to rise from meditation to contemplation is to rise from Christ's humanity into his divinity,
which is as much concealed as revealed by the humanity. The
author's terms, 'the obscure human words that envelop the divine wisdom,' are taken from the tradition of exegesis. Usually
such terms refer to the allegorical sense, by which one discerns
the light of the spirit through the obscurity of the letter. The
allegorical sense, however, corresponds more to the author of
The Cloud's meditation. Mary's hearing of Christ's words is
anagogic, in the sense rather singularly defined by Hugh of
Balma. Hugh conflated the exegetical term 'anagogy' with the
Dionysian use of the term to mean 'a rising, an ascent,' and in
turn interpreted the latter as an affective aspiration. Each word
in the Old and New Testament, and each creature in the world,
referred to the 'point of love' (*ad punctum amoris*), is an occasion for union with God, Hugh says.[39] The author of *The
Cloud* develops his practice of the single-word prayer in relation to this notion of anagogy. Those in the active and medita-
tive lives, the beginners and the proficient, cannot pray without
having first heard or read the 'mirour' of God's word (35, pp.
71-72). However, the prayers of contemplatives, the author
says, echoing Hugh of Balma directly, 'risen euermore sodenly
vnto God, wiþ-outen any meenes or any premeditacion in special comyng before, or going þer-wiþ' (37, p. 74). For contem-

platives, a single word can be a syllabic instrument upon which
to affix an affective 'stering', 'a scharp darte of longing loue'
that pierces the cloud of unknowing (6, p. 36):

> Þerfore, what tyme þat þou purposest þee to þis werk . . .
> lift þan up þin herte vnto God wiþ a meek steryng of loue
> . . . & ȝif þee list have þis entent lappid & foulden in o
> worde, for þou schuldest have betir hold þer-apon, take þee
> bot a litel worde of o silable . . . & fasten þis worde to þin
> herte, so þat it neuer go þens for þing þat bifalleþ (7, p. 28;
> see also 26-40, pp. 72-79.)

On the one hand, to accommodate human souls God 'envelops'
('lappid', 17, p. 47) his unitive wisdom darkly in the glass of the
many words of Scripture. On the other hand, man returns to
the source of wisdom by enfolding ('lappid & foulden', 7, p. 28)
his dispersed powers in an undivided act of love.

In *The Book of Privy Counselling* the author relates the person of Christ to the active and contemplative lives in a similar
way. He does so by means of a scriptural interpretation which
he borrows from the *Liber de spiritu et anima*, and which is also
amply developed in Rudolph of Biberach's *De septem itineribus
aeternitatis*.[40] In John 10:9-10, Christ says: 'I am the door. If
anyone enters by me he shall be safe, and shall go in and out,
and shall find pastures. He who does not enter through the door
but climbs up another way is a thief and a robber.' In order to
be saved, the author of *The Cloud* says, all must enter through
the door of Christ's humanity, by meditating on his passion and
sorrowing for the sins which caused it. Whoever does not enter
the spiritual life through this door, preferring to humble meditation on the passion 'þe corious fantastic worchyng in his wilde
wantoun wittis', is a thief and will not be saved. 'Faire meditations' on the passion are the truest, the only way through which
a sinner may enter the spiritual life (p. 158). One must stand
patiently at this door until 'þe grete rust of his boistous bode-
lynes be in grete party rubbid awei' (p. 161). Then he may be
drawn within to Christ's divinity, to perfection and a 'more
special worching of grace'. If so drawn, one must enter, leaving

off consideration of Christ's humanity and passion in order to penetrate his divinity. The author opines that if there were no greater perfection available to men in this life than 'beholdyng & louing' Christ's humanity, Christ would not have ascended before the world ended and withdrawn his bodily presence from 'his specyal louers in erþe.' As he asked his disciples then to forego his bodily presence, so now he asks his special friends to forego their 'corious meditacions & queinte sotyl wittes' in order to taste the love of God (pp. 170-71). Presumably, those who forego such meditations will become, like the recipient of *The Cloud*, singular friends of God.

From the texts I have cited, it should be clear that the author of *The Cloud* does not slight the soul's sensible, imaginative, and rational powers, or the highest object of their attention and devotion, the humanity of Christ. Moreover, the degrees of active and contemplative living, and the corresponding hierarchy of the soul's powers, must be understood not only in relation to the person of Christ, but also in relation to the redemptive work of Christ accomplished through sanctifying grace. This relation is manifest in chapters sixty-two through sixty-seven of *The Cloud*, where the author, in part following Richard of St Victor, discusses the faculties of the soul and their perfection.

The author of *The Cloud* says that the 'mynde conteneþ & comprehendeþ in it-self' four major powers: 'reson & wille . . . ymaginacion & sensualite' (63, p. 115). The first two are independent and spiritual. The last two are dependent and bodily, and serve the former. By nature, imagination, through which the images of sensible things enter the soul, should serve reason. It works properly when it is disciplined by 'þe liȝt of grace in þe reson', as it is when it serves the meditation of spiritual things such as 'þe Passion & þe kyndenes of oure Lorde God' (65, pp. 117-18). Correspondingly, sensuality, or the appetite for necessary sensible things, should be governed by the spiritual appetite of the will (66, pp. 118-19). As a result of the Fall, however, this created order has been disturbed. The lower faculties have become insubordinate, and the mind's single focus is scattered. Undisciplined by reason, the imagination never ceases 'to portray dyuerse vnordeynd ymages of bodely creatures', turning the mind's attention downwards towards them (65, p. 117). Unable to govern easily the unruly imagination, the reason, which before the Fall was able naturally to discern good from evil, the good, better, best, can now do so only when illumined by grace (64, p. 116). Likewise, the rebellious sensual appetite thirsts after sensible things in an unrestrained, unmeasured way (66, p. 117). The will, which before the Fall was never deceived in its choice of the highest good, and by nature took delight in created things according to their relative measure of goodness, can now resist the lusts of the flesh only if anointed by grace (64, pp. 116-17).

In sum, man was made upright, (Ecclesiastes 7:30), pointed towards the heavens. Through the Fall he has become 'crokid', like the beasts bent towards the earth, towards sensible things (61, p. 113). The mystical doctrine of *The Cloud*, which urges man to rise above himself towards the heavens, teaches the final perfection, through grace, of the restoration of man's original rectitude, justice and integrity. The central teaching of the work is the regathering of the mind's dispersed powers into a single aspiration towards the highest good, God. The author of *The Cloud* summarizes his discussion of the soul's powers by arranging them according to his threefold order:

> euer whan þe mynde is ocupied wiþ any bodely þing . . .
> þou arte bineþe þi-self . . . & with-outen þi soule. & euer
> whan þou felist þi mynde ocupied wiþ þe sotil condicions
> of þe myȝtes of þi soule & þeire worchynges in goostly
> þinges . . . þat þou miȝtest by þis werke lerne to know þi-
> self . . . þou arte wiþ-inne þi-self & euen wiþ þi-self. Bot
> euer when þou felist þi mynde ocupyed wiþ no maner of
> þyng þat is bodely or goostly, bot only wiþ þe self sub-
> staunce of God, as it is & may be in þe preof of þe werk of
> þis book; þen þou arte abouen þi-self & vnder þi God . . .
> for whi þou atteynest to come þedir by grace wheþer þou
> mayst not come by kynde: þat is to sey, to be onyd to God

in spirit & in loue & in acordaunce of wille (67, pp. 119-20).

The author's use of the term 'mynde' in these texts deserves comment. Many of the authors whom we have cited used the term *mens* to designate the highest part or power of the soul.[41] It seems of no little significance, however, that the author's use of the term 'mynde' wholly agrees with Augustine's extended definition of *mens* in *De Trinitate*. The author of *The Cloud* says that 'mynde' the 'souereynest pointe of þe spirit' (37, p. 74) which comprehends all of the soul's powers, 'is soche a miȝte in it-self þat properly to speke & in maner it worcheþ not it-self . . . bot ȝif soche a comprehencion be a werke' (63, p. 115). This notion is identical with that of Augustine, for whom the term *mens* signifies the undivided, spiritual essence of the soul, embracing its powers of loving and knowing.[42] These powers are indistinct and simultaneous in the mind, since the mind knows and loves itself in an act identical with its very substance.[43] Whereas the mind is turned fixedly to the unchangeable truth, a rational power, deputed to govern inferior, temporal things, issues from it. This rational power does not depart from the mind in such a way as to sever its unity, but rather is related to mind as a helpmeet. Thus, just as Adam and Eve are embraced in one flesh, so the reason and the rational appetite are embraced in the one spiritual nature of the mind.[44] Finally, we should note that the *acies mentis*, as Augustine often calls it,[45] is nearly synonymous with the spiritual memory, which recollects the diverse powers of the soul in unity.[46]

There is no reason to doubt that the author of *The Cloud* read Augustine's *De Trinitate* immediately. However, Augustine's teaching concerning *mens* was echoed faithfully, if formulated more rigidly, in the handy *compendium, De spiritu et anima*.[47] Indeed, certain formulae of this text are especially close to those of *The Cloud*, for example, the terms of the relation between reason (*ratio*) and mind (*mens*).[48] Moreover, the author of *De spiritu et anima* speaks of the mind's capacity to sink below, retreat within, and rise above itself, to ascend from outward and lower things to its own level, and from thence above itself to God.[49] As a result of the Fall, the powers of the mind, 'manifold in duty but simple in essence,'[50] were scattered among the delights of the earth.[51] Thus, the mind must now 'collect itself within itself' by rejecting the images and phantasms of earthly things, and by coming to a certain forgetting of itself (*quodam modo in oblivionem sui veniat*).[52] This last phrase anticipates our author's 'cloude of forȝeting.'

Augustine's definition of *mens* illumines *The Cloud*'s central teaching, the recovery of the created soul's essential unity. This unity can only be accomplished in the soul's highest, undifferentiated power, the 'mynde,' where there is no distinction among being, knowing, and loving. The single word prayer is efficacious precisely because it gathers 'al þe myȝt . . . all þe wittis of þe spirit' in a single act (38, p. 75). Reason must be transcended not because it is inherently perverse or conducive to vanity. These it cannot be when illumined by grace. Rather, reason must be transcended because by nature it is discursive, and therefore, unlike mind, is not directly 'vnder God.'

We are now able to define narrowly the teaching of *The Cloud*. According to a traditional scheme of the genera of theology, *The Cloud* is a work of mystical theology, teaching one to rise above himself and all other creatures, after, however, he has learned to love God in sensible and intelligible revelations, and after he has exercised his sensible faculties in good works, and his reason in meditation. Having accomplished a certain perfection in these lower faculties, one may reach out with affection towards that which human understanding cannot grasp.

In mystical theology, however, considerations of before and after are inappropriate. Such considerations are the work of the sequential, discursive reason, that faculty which at once distinguishes man from what is beneath him and from God, who is above him. The author of *The Cloud* addresses this matter in chapter four, where he lays the philosophic foundation for his mystical, affective practice.

The contemplative work, in which one perceives in his will

nothing except 'a nakid entent vnto God' (3, pp. 16-17), reintegrates the soul's powers dispersed and scattered through the Fall. Elsewhere the author of *The Cloud* says that prayer is nothing else 'bot a deuoute entent directe vnto God' (39, p. 77), and that the substance of all perfection is nothing else 'bot a good & an acordyng wil vnto God' (49, p. 92). Once again, the author's teaching is nowise unique. Cassian in the *Conlationes*, the guidebook of the Latin eremitic tradition, speaks of the monk's intention and prayer in metaphors similar to those of *The Cloud*;[53] the notion of a rectified will as the means to perfection was a commonplace of Latin theological literature.[54] Rudolph of Biberach's *De septem itineribus* gives a comprehensive account of the way in which the *recta intentio* of the will is transformed into an *intentio . . . immediata, simplificata, & Deificata*, that is, into perfect union.[55] The forming of a 'nakid entent', the author of *The Cloud* says, is the shortest work imaginable to man. It is no longer or shorter than an atom, the smallest and indivisible unit of time. It is so short that it is nearly inconceivable. The author identifies these atoms of time with each stirring and desiring of the soul's principal faculty, the will:

> so many willinges or desiringes — & no mo ne no fewer —
> may be & aren in one oure in þe wille, as aren athomus in
> one oure. & ȝif þou were reformid bi grace to þe first state
> of mans soule, as it was bifore sinne, þan þou schuldest
> euer-more, bi help of þat grace, be lorde of þat stering or
> of þoo sterynges; so þat none ȝede forby, bot alle þei
> schulde streche in-to þe souerein desirable & into þe heiȝest
> wilnable þing, þe whiche is God (4, p. 18).

All of the soul's faculties are ordered to the will, each desire of which must be directed immediately towards God. If the faculties are dispersed in things beneath, or even equal with, itself, the soul's desires will not reach their destined mark. The reason, naturally discursive, cannot be the source of the soul's unity. Besides, the end which should order the soul's acts, God, is 'incomprehensible to alle create knowable miȝt' (4, p. 18). Only the 'blynde stering of loue' (4, p. 22), which outruns the objects presented to it by the understanding, can reach out to touch God. The author makes clear that human consciousness, by the necessity of human nature and as a result of sin, can never be free of images (10, pp. 35-37). However, the naked intent for the highest good never rests in or consents to the limited goods these images present, but continually pushes beyond them. The acts of the soul, then, must be united and directed towards God in what the author of *The Cloud* calls, interchangeably, 'naked intents', 'flaming darts', 'blind stirrings'. Such single, momentary acts of desire, even though they can have no ground in sensible images or rational concepts, are none the less, if not diverted, sure of their mark, because of the will's intrinsic ordering to God. As the author says, the human soul, by virtue of being created in his image and likeness, is measured by and proportioned to God (4, p. 18). Hence, the soul's desire is necessarily directed to the source of its created goodness.

The intrinsic proportion between God and the soul is the proportion between eternity and time. The source for the author of *The Cloud*'s conception is Augustine, this time the *Confessiones*. Augustine contrasts eternity with time by stating that whereas in eternity everything is present simultaneously, and nothing moves into the past, time is characterized exactly by a great number of movements flowing into the past.[56] And yet, after scrutinizing the division of time into past, present, and future, Augustine concludes that even for the human soul nothing exists except the present. The past has already ceased to exist, and the future does not yet exist. Any being they have derives only from the present memory or present desire of the soul. If this is so, how does time, which exists only in the present, differ from eternity, which is always present? Augustine distinguishes the two in terms of the being they possess, or more precisely, in terms of the being which one lacks:

> if the present is time only because it moves into the past, how can we say that even the present is, since the reason that it is is that it will not be? Thus, we can say truly that time is, only because it tends not to be.[57]

The creature is in time by virtue of being created: in making the heavens and the earth God made time, Augustine says, and there was no time before God made time.[58] The creature is in time because its wholly dependent, contingent being is always on the verge of the nothingness from which it was created. The precariousness of the creature's being, and its total dependence upon the being of God, is indicated by the fact that the creature's existence is measured out in the briefest moments. The present, in which the creature exists, is a moment so short that it cannot be divided into the most minute parts, and it passes so quickly from the future into the past that it has no extended duration.[59]

Augustine's reflections provide the sufficient reason for *The Cloud*'s practice. If created existence is only a moment, an atom, the duration of a single desire, then a single intention, a simple dart of love, a monosyllabic prayer wraps in itself the creature's whole existence. Such an undivided act pierces the cloud of unknowing and reaches the source of the soul's momentary, created being. This being is not dispersed into nonbeing as long as the soul does not dwell on the past or entertain created images of future happiness (10, pp. 35-37). Proper use of the indivisible atoms of time is a foretaste of the truly indivisible present, eternity.

In *The Book of Privy Counselling* the author likewise conceives the relation between creator and creature, although in somewhat more scholastic terms. Most affective mystics, like Bonaventure, follow pseudo-Dionysius in asserting that the highest name of God is Goodness. In *The Book of Privy Counselling*, however, the author follows the usual doctrine of the schools, saying that the highest name of God is 'IS' (p. 143). The proportion between God's being and the creature's is the same as that between eternity and time. As the indivisible atom of time is an image of eternity, so our 'nakid beyng', the indivisible source of our diverse acts, is an image of God's self-subsistent being. By a 'nakid beholdyng' and 'nakid blynde felyng' of our being in 'þe first poynte' of the spirit, we are led ineluctably to the being of God (p. 143, *et passim*). For the being of God is the source of our being; he is in us as our cause and as our being. In a sense, our undivided act of being and his being are the same, although whereas he is the cause of his own being, we are not the cause of ours, and are dependent on his (p. 136). When we worship God with the undivided substance of our being, we thereby worship him with himself:

> for þat þou arte þou hast of him & he it is. & þof al þou had-dest a biginnyng in þi substancyal creacion, þe whiche was sumtyme nouȝt, ȝit haþ þi being ben euer-more in hym wiþ-outyn beginning & euir schal be wiþ-outyn ending, as him-self is. & þerfore oft I crie, & euer upon one: 'Do wor-schip to þi God with þi substance' (p. 144).

In both *The Cloud of Unknowing* and *The Book of Privy Counselling* the reader is instructed to unite himself with the eternal source of his fleeting existence by means of single, con-centrated acts of the spirit that bear his whole being. Doing so, he will imitate Christ, who made a total sacrifice of himself for God and for all men through a single 'comon entent' (*Book of Privy Counselling*, p. 142).

If *The Cloud*'s teaching concerning the redemption of time through affective aspirations is consoling, it also seems discour-aging. What does one do about all of those past atoms of his existence which were not integrated and were dispersed into nothingness? The author foresees this anxiety in chapter four of *The Cloud*. These seemingly lost moments are redeemable through the mingling, by means of a renewed intent, of one's life with the life of Christ. One shares Christ's life through love, since love makes all things common. As God, Christ is the crea-tor and giver of time. As man, who came in the fullness of time, he is the preserver of all the time bestowed upon creatures. As God and man together, he will be the future judge of man's use of time. United to him, one is as well united to Mary, who was full of grace at every moment, and lost no time. Likewise, he is united to the angels, who having made the one instantaneous choice offered them, are confirmed in grace and can never more lose time. Finally, he is united 'with all þe seintes in heuen & in erþe, þat by þe grace of Ihesu kepen tyme ful iustly in vertewe of loue' (4, 21). In other words, through participation in the body of Christ, one is united to the single, eternal intention of Christ, and to the intention of all those confirmed in his grace, an intention which redeems and restores past acts. 'For,' as the author of *The Cloud* states, 'Crist is oure hede, & we ben þe lymes, if we be in charite' (25, pp. 60-61). By the same means, when one constantly renews the unified act of his mind, he offers to God not only the fullness of his own being, but the plenitude of all created being.

The Cloud of Unknowing presents a rich, coherent doctrine firmly rooted in theological tradition. Surely this tradition was not a closed book to *The Cloud*'s intended reader. Why then does the author of *The Cloud* conceal his learning, and why did he write in the vernacular? I suspect he does both for two related reasons. First, by writing in the vernacular, the author of *The Cloud* would not likely draw the attention of 'corious lettred or lewed men' not so spiritually advanced as they think themselves to be. For such men, the author often repeats, knowledge serves only to puff up. The author knows the kind of books such men read and write:

> somtyme men þouȝt it meekness to sey noȝt of þeire owne hedes, bot ȝif þei afermid it by Scripture & doctours wordes; & now it is turnid into corioustee & schewyng of kunnyng. To þee it nediþ not, & þerfore I do it nouȝt. For who-so haþ eren, lat him here (70, p. 125).

Secondly, the author hoped his reader would assimilate *The Cloud*'s teaching to his personal substance, as the author, clearly, had digested the teaching of others. And what better way to express one's own naked being than in the mother tongue? For, as Dante says, one's native tongue is intimately near his mind, and inasmuch as it was the language of his parents' conversation, it is, in a sense, the cause of his being in time.[60]

NOTES

1. I agree with James Walsh, trans., *The Cloud of Unknowing* (New York, 1981), intro. pp. 2-9, that none of the arguments adduced against Carthusian authorship is sufficient. Walsh has shown in what way the circumstances of the text's composition point to Carthusian authorship, and has brought forward the slight external evidence available. I think the configuration of *The Cloud's* sources suggest Carthusian authorship. This point, without special reference to the question of authorship, will be treated in this study.

2. References to pseudo-Dionysius' *De mystica theologia* will be to the Latin text assembled by the editor in *Deonise Hid Diuinite and other Treatises on Contemplative Prayer Related to The Cloud of Unknowing*, ed. Phyllis Hodgson, EETS 231 (Oxford 1955 for 1949, repr. 1958). See p. 95. In his translation of the work, the author of *The Cloud* renders these phrases, 'streite & litel . . . of short seiinges', p. 4.

3. Aldous Huxley, *Grey Eminence: A Study in Religion and Politics* (New York, 1941) pp. 62-66.

4. *Deonise Hid Diuinite* and *A Tretyse of þe Stodye of Wysdome* are edited by Hodgson in *Deonise Hid Diuinite*, pp. 2-10, 11-46, respectively.

5. These three works are edited by Hodgson in *Deonise Hid Diuinite*, pp. 47-59, 61-67, 79-93, respectively.

6. *Deonise Hid Diuinite*, p. xxxvii.

7. See Guigo II, *Scala claustralium*, ed. Edmund Colledge and James Walsh (*Lettre sur la vie contemplative*) (Paris, 1970). Colledge and Walsh restore the epistolary genre of this seminal monastic work. A Middle English translation of this work, *A Ladder of Foure Ronges by the which Men Mowe Wele Clyme to Heven*, is edited by Hodgson, *Deonise Hid Diuinite*, pp. 100-117. For remarks on this translation, see *Lettre*, ed. Colledge and Walsh, pp. 45-52.

8. *De mystica theologia*, p. 94.

9. For Cicero's distinction between *oratio* and *sermo*, see *Orator*, with trans. by H. M. Hubbell (Loeb Classical Series, 1942) 19, 63-64, pp. 352-53. For the themes in Seneca's letters to which I have referred, see *Ad Lucilium epistulae morales*, 3 vols., with trans. by R. M. Gummere (Loeb Classical Series, 1953) XXXVIII, I, pp. 256-59 (*sermo* creeps into the soul, appeals to reason rather than passion); XL, I, pp. 262-71 (letters suited to communication of like-minded friends; plain, unadorned style appropriate to speech that 'heals the mind', contrasted with speech that pleases a crowd; the spiritual *medicus*); XLI, I, pp. 272-78 (God is to be found within the soul); LV, I, pp. 365-73 (soli-

tude, tranquillity of spirit, fruitful leisure, spiritual friendship communicated by letters); LXXV, II, pp. 136-47 (the spiritual *medicus,* appropriateness of *sermo* for self-revelation, self-knowledge); XCII, II, pp. 446-70 (conformity of reason to divine reason, reason's control of the passions, tranquillity of spirit, the good lies in election of the will). XCV, III, pp. 58-104 (extended comparison between the art of medicine and philosophy of the soul; conformity with the divine will); XCVI, III, pp. 104-107 (conformity with the divine will). In XCV, 57, pp. 92-93, Seneca says 'Actio recta non erit, nisi recta fuerit voluntas, ab hac enim est actio. Rursus voluntas non erit recta, nisi habitus animi rectus fuerit, ab hoc enim est voluntas'; see note 54 below. On this aspect of the Stoics' thought in general and Seneca's in particular, see André-Jean Voelke, *L'Idée de volunté dans le stoicisme* (Paris, 1973). For the christian absorption of Seneca's thought, see José Antonio Franquiz, 'The Place of Seneca in the Curriculum of the Middle Ages', in *Arts libéraux et philosophie au moyen âge: Actes du Quartième Congrès International de Philosophie Médiévale* (Montreal, 1967) pp. 1065-72. For Seneca's theory of therapeutic speech, conducive to self-knowledge, see A. Guillemin, 'Sénèque directeur d'âmes: III. Les Théories littéraires', *Revue des études latines,* 32 (1954) 250-74.

10. *Epistola ad fratres de Monte Dei,* I, 9, 25-I, 9, 27; PL 184:323-25. See J. M: Déchanet, '*Seneca noster,* des Lettres à Lucilius à La Lettre aux Freres du Mont-Dieu', in *Mélanges de Ghellinck* (Gembloux, 1951) pp. 753-66. Since it was addressed to Carthusians, William's *Epistola* was a part of Carthusian literature. In the late Middle Ages, the work was usually attributed to Bernard of Clairvaux.

11. Augustine, *De doctrina christiana,* ed. G. M. Green, CSEL (Vienna, 1963) I, 14, pp. 15-16; William of St. Thierry, *Epistola ad fratres,* I, 9, 26; PL 184:324. For the therapeutic theme in Augustine, and its classical source, see Rudolph Arbesmann, 'The Concept of "Christus Medicus" in St. Augustine', *Traditio,* 10 (1954) 1-28.

12. *The Book of Privy Counselling,* in *The Cloud of Unknowing and The Book of Privy Counselling,* ed. Phyllis Hodgson, EETS, O.S. 218 (Oxford, 1944 for 1943, repr. 1958) pp. 139-39. All quotations from *The Cloud* and *The Book* are from this edition. Henceforward citations of these texts will be made in the body of the paper.

13. Walsh, trans., *The Cloud of Unknowing,* pp. 52-53.

14. Jean Leclercq, *The Love of Learning and the Desire for God,* trans. C. Misrahi (New York, 1961) p. 181.

15. The author's use of the term 'writing' perhaps echoes the *dictamen* of the *ars dictaminis,* the medieval art of letter writing.

16. See *The Cloud,* ed. Hodgson, p. 183 n. 14/13, where Methley's annotation is quoted. Edmund Colledge's and James Walsh's ' "The Cloud of Unknowing" and "The Mirror of Simple Souls" in the Latin Glossed Translations by Richard Methley of Mount Grace Charterhouse' is scheduled to appear in *Archivio italiano per la storia della pietà.*

17. On the eremitic tradition among the Carthusians, see Yves Gourdel, 'Chartreux', *Dictionnaire de spiritualité* 2 (Paris, 1955) especially 705-711. Gourdel quotes a fourteenth-century Carthusian author: 'La vie cartusienne,

quoiqu'elle doive être jugée érémetique en raison de la place préponderante et de la dignité plus grande de l'élément érémentique, est composée de la vie solitaire et de vie commune' (711).

18. See M.-D. Chenu, *La Theologie au douzième siècle* (Paris, 1957) pp. 172-78; Grover Zinn, 'Book and Word. The Victorine Background of Bonaventure's Use of Symbols', in *S. Bonaventura, 1274-1974*, II (Grottaferrata, 1973) pp. 143-69.

19. James Walsh, '*Sapientia christianorum:* The Doctrine of Thomas Gallus, Abbot of Vercelli, on Contemplation' (Ph.D. dissertation, Gregorian University, Rome, 1957). Robert Javelet, 'Thomas Gallus ou les Écritures dans une dialectique mystique', in *L'Homme devant Dieu: Mélanges offerts au pere Henri De Lubac*, 2 (Paris, 1964) pp. 99-110.

20. Hugh's *Mystica theologia* is printed in the *Opera omnia sancti Bonaventurae* (Rome, 1586-96) volume VII, pp. 699-730. See especially the *Quaestio unica*, pp. 726-30.

21. Rudolph's *De septem itineribus aeternitatis* is also printed in *Opera . . . Bonaventurae* (Rome, 1586-96) VII, pp. 145-96.

22. Walsh, trans., *The Cloud of Unknowing*, pp. 23-26. As Walsh points out, in lieu of an edition we are indebted to J. P. Grausem, 'Le "De contemplatione" de Guiges du Pont', *Revue d'ascetique et de mystique*, 10 (1929) 259-89.

23. For an extended treatment of the tradition of the three modes, see Kent Emery, Jr., 'Benet of Canfield: Counter-Reformation Spirituality and its Mediæval Origins' (Ph.D. dissertation, University of Toronto, 1976) pp. 148-249.

24. In *Deonise Hid Diuinite*, 3, the author translates the title *Symbolica theologia* '*þe Gadering of Deuine Sentence*', p. 7 (Latin text, p. 97). This rendering reflects Hugh of St Victor's definition of *symbolum*. We quote, because Hugh's contrasting term, *anagoge* is also illumining for *The Cloud*, as we shall see: 'Symbolum est collatio formarum visibilum ad invisibilium demonstrationem. Anagoge autem ascensio, sive elevatio mentis est ad superna contemplanda . . . Ex his vero duobis generibus visionum, duo quoque descriptionum genera in sacro eliquio sunt formata. Unum, quo formis, et figuris, et similitudinibus rerum occultarum veritas adumbratur. Alterum, quo nude et pure sicut est absque integumento exprimitur. Cum itaque formis, et signis, et similitudinibus manifestatur, quod occultum est, vel quod manifestum est, describitur, symbolica demonstratio est. Cum vero pura ett nuda revelatione ostenditur, vel plana et aperta narratione docetur, anagogica.' Hugh of St Victor, *Expositio in Hierarchiam Coelestem s. Dionysii Areopagitae; PL* 175-941.

25. *Deonise Hid Diuinite*, 3, pp. 7-8; *De mystica theologia*, 3, p. 97 (*In symbolica autem theologia, quae sunt a sensibilibus ad divina Dei nominationes*).

26. *Deonise Hid Diuinite*, 3, pp. 7-8.

27. *Deonise Hid Diuinite*, 3, p. 8; *De mystica theologia*, 3, p. 96.

28. *Deonise Hid Diuinite*, 1, p. 3. The Latin text of Sarracenus (pp. 94-95) reads: 'circa mysticas visiones forti contritione et sensus derelinque et intellectuales operationes, et omnia sensibilia et intelligibilia, et omnia non exsistencia et exsistentia; et sicut possibile, ignote consurge ad ejus unitionem qui est super omnem substantiam et cognitionem'.

29. For the distinction *infra rationem, supra rationem*, and implied *in ratione*

see Richard of St Victor, *Benjamin minor*, 74; PL 196:53; for the distinction *extra se, intra se et in se,* and *supra se,* see Bonaventure, *Itinerarium mentis in Deum, Opera omnia,* cura PP. Colegiia s. Bonaventura, V (Quaracchi, 1891), I, 4, p. 297.

30. *Deonise Hid Diuinite,* prol., p. 2, 11.25-28./ See the note by Hodgson, p. 121, n. 2/25.

31. *Benjamin major,* I, 7; PL 196: 72-73.

32. *A Tretyse of þe Stodye of Wysdome,* pp 54-6. Richard of St Victor, *Benjamin minor,* 73; PL 196:52: 'In tanta namque quotidiani conatus anxietate, in hujus modi doloris immensitate, et Benjamin nascitur, et Rachel moritur, quia cum mens hominis supra seipsam rapitur, omnes humanae ratiocinationis, angustias supergreditur. Ad illud enim quod supra se elevata, et in extasi rapta, de divinitatis lumine conspicit, omnis humanae ratio succumbit. Quod est enim Rachelis interitus, nisi rationis defectus?'

33. *A Tretyse of þe Stodye of Wysdome,* p. 42. See Richard of St Victor, *Benjamin minor,* 72, 78; PL 196:51-52, 55-56.

34. Bonaventure, *Itinerarium* I, 4, p. 297; I, 7, p. 298.

35. Walsh, trans., *The Cloud of Unknowing,* pp. 52-53, implies that *The Cloud* was written for a novice.

36. Augustine, *De Trinitate libri XV,* ed. W. J. Mountain auxiliante Fr. Glorie, *Corpus Christianorum* L (I-XII), La (XIII-XV) (Turnhout, 1968), XV, 27, 49, p. 531: 'Quantum uero attinet ad illam summam, ineffabilem, incorporalem immutabilemque naturam per intelligentiam utcumque cernendam, nusquam se melius regente dumtaxat fidei regla acies humanae mentis exerceat quam in eo quod ipse homo in sua natura melius ceteris animalibus, melius etiam ceteris animae suae partibus habet, quod est ipsa mens cui quidam rerum inuisibilium tributus est uisus, et cui tamquam in loco superiore atque interiore honorabiliter praesidenti iudicanda omnia nuntiat etiam corporis sensus, et qua non est superior cui regenda est nisi deus.'

William of St Thierry, *Epistola ad fratres de Monte Dei,* II, 2, 5; PL 184:341: 'Nullam vero dignius et utilius exercitium est homini eam habenti, quam in eo quod melius habet, et in quo caeteris animalibus, et caeteris partibus suis praeeminet, quae est ipsa mens vel animus. Menti vero vel animo, cui caetera pars hominis regenda subdita est, nec dignius est aliquid ad quaerendum, nec dulcius ad inveniendum, nec utilius ad habendum, quam quod solum ipsam mentem supereminet, qui est solus Deus.'

Liber de spiritu et anima, 11; PL 40:786: 'Rationale et intellectuale lumen, quo ratiocinamur, intelligimus et sapimus, mentem dicimus, quae ita facta est ad imaginem Dei, ut nulla interposita natura ab ipsa veritate formetur. Mens enim ex eo dicta est quod emineat in anima.'

37. Richard of St Victor, *Benjamin major,* I, 6; PL 196:71.

38. Hugh of Balma, *Mystica theologia,* pp. 726-30.

39. See Hugh, *Mystica theologia,* 2, 2, *De triplici anagogia,* pp. 704-710: 'Tantum autem per artem huius theoricae scientiae lumen acquiritur, & tanto sapientiae dilitatio in scripturis, ut quot verba in nova & veteri Testamento, quot creaturae in mundo, tot habeat anima intelligentias, vel sermones, totum ad Deum ad punctum amoris omnia referendo, ut postea apparebit' (p. 704).

40. *Liber de spiritu et anima*, 9; PL 40:785: 'Duplex est quidem vita animae; alia qua vivit in carne, et alia qua vivit in Deo. Duo siquidem in homine sensus sunt, unus interior reficitur in contemplatione divinitatis, sensus exterior in contemplatione humanitatis. Propterea enim Deus homo factus est, ut totum hominem in se beatificaret, et tota conversio hominis esset ad ipsum, et tota dilectio hominis esset in ipso, cum a sensu carnis videretur per carnem, et a sensu mentis videretur per divinitatis contemplationem. Hoc autem erat totum bonum hominis, ut sive ingrederetur sive agrederetur, pascua in factore suo inveniret (Jn 10:9); pascua foris in carne Salvatoris, et pascua intus in divinitate Creatoris.' See Rudolph of Biberach, *De septem itinerius aeternitatis, Prol.*, d. 1-6, pp. 145-50. Characteristically, Rudolph's progress is threefold (sensible, intelligible, affective-mystical): 'Ego sum ostium sensui, per corporale obiectum, Videte, inquit, manus meas, & pedes meos. Ego sum ostium intellectui, per fidem reseratum. Unde in Isaia dicitur: Nisi credideritis, non intelligitis. Ego sum ostium voluntati, per charitatem apertum. *Charitas non vult scire medium inter se & dilectum* immo, ut dicit Hugo, Amor sive charitas suo acumine omnia penetrat, donec ad dilectum veniat' (pp. 145-46). By such acute love, Mary penetrates the 'obscure' humanity to Christ's divinity (*The Cloud*, 17, p. 47).

41. **From the twelfth century on**, one discovers many terms, nearly synonymous but interpreted variously by different authors, for the highest part of the soul, for example, besides *mens, apex mentis, scintilla animae, synderesis, apex affectus* (Hugh of Balma). For William of St Thierry, *animus* and *mens* are synonymous (see note 36). The *Liber de spiritu et anima* equates *mens* and *spiritus*, distinguished from *anima* (see 10; PL 40:736). This equation was common; see M.-D. Chenu, 'SPIRITUS, Le vocabulaire de l'âme au XIIᵉ siècle', *Revue des sciences philosophiques et théologiques*, 41 (1957) 217-19. However, some, such as the author of the twelfth-century *De discretione animae, spiritus, et mentis*, sharply distinguished *spiritus* and *mens*. The author of this treatise founds his distinction on a scriptural passage, and identifies *spiritus* with *cor*: 'Inter spiritum enim et mentem manifeste dividit Apostolus in *Epistola* ad *Corinthos prima* . . . In Evangelio mens ab anima discernitur, ubi Deus *ex toto corde* et *ex tota anima* et *ex tota mente* diligi praecipitur. Si autem et nomine cordis spiritus ibi intelligitur, sic ipsius quoque ab utraque illarum discretio innuitur.' See the text edited by Nicholas M. Haring, 'Gilbert of Poitiers, Author of the "De discretione animae, spiritus et mentis" commonly attributed to Achard of Saint Victor', *Mediaeval Studies*, 22 (1960) 26, 179. The author of the treatise, who despite Haring's argument seems to be Achard of St Victor (J. Chatillon, 'Achard de saint Victor et le *De discretione animae spiritus et mentis*', *Archives d'histoire doctrinale et littéraire du Moyen Âge*, 31 (1964) 7-35), demotes *spiritus* and associates it with *imaginatio*; see *De discretione*, ed. Haring, 42, 183. The source for this association, is Augustine, *De Genesi ad Litteram*, XII, 24, 51; PL 34:474-75. Whoever wrote *De discretione*, Bonaventure seems to have used the text, while restoring *spiritus* to a purely spiritual power. See *Itinerarium*, I, 4, p. 297: 'Secundum hunc triplicem progressum mens nostra tres habet aspectus principales. Unus est ad corporalia exteriora, secundum quem vocatur *animalitas* seu sensualitas; *alias* intra se et

in se, secundum quem dicitur *spiritus*; tertius supra se, secundum quem dicitur *mens*. —Ex quibus omnibus disponere se debet ad conscendendum in Deum, ut ipsum diligat *ex tota mente, ex toto corde,* et *ex tota anima,* in que consistit perfecta legis observatio et simul cum hoc sapientia christiana.'
The author of *The Cloud* seems to use the terms 'spirit' and 'mind' synony-mously.
   42. See Augustine, *De Trinitate,* IX, 4, 4, p. 297, IX, 4, 7, p. 299, and IX, 5, 8, pp. 300-301, where he states that *mens* embraces *amor* and *notitia* in one indis-tiguishable act and is the one *essentia* of the soul. In X, II, 18, pp. 330-31, Augustine says that *mens* binds *memoria, intelligentia,* and *uoluntas* in one *substantia,* one *essentia. Memoria* is nearly identified with *mens* in this text.
   43. See the texts in note 42, and *De Trinitate,* XIV, 10, 13, pp. 440-41, and XV, 6, 10, p. 474.
   44. *De Trinitate,* XII, 3, pp. 357-58. In XV, 7, 11, p. 475, Augustine explains why 'non igitur anima sed quod excellit in anima mens uocatur.'
   45. *De Trinitate,* IV, 15, p. 187; XII, 14, 23, p. 376; XV, 1, 1, p. 460. In the last text, Augustine, as will William of St Thierry after him, identifies *mens* and *animus,* and distinguishes this higher part from *anima.*
   46. See *De Trinitate,* XIV, 7, 10, p. 434, where Augustine observes that the unified act of *mens* seems most like memory: 'Nam si nos referamus ad interi-orem intellegentiam qua se intellegit et interiorem uoluntatem qua se diligit, ubi haec tria simul sunt et simul semper fuerunt ex quo esse coeperunt siue cogitarentur siue non cogitarentur, uidebitur quidem imago illius trinitatis et ad solam memoriam pertinere.' Throughout book X of the *Confessiones,* Aug-ustine speaks of *memoria,* the *ipsius animi mei sedem* (X, 25, 36) in terms strik-ingly similar to those which define *mens.*
   47. See note 36. For *mens* knowing and loving itself in an indistinguishable, simultaneous act, see *Liber de spiritu et anima,* 23; PL 40:801; in this unified act *mens* is an image of the Trinity, 24; 804; *mens* embraces the soul's powers, and is especially related to memory ('Mens universorum capax, et omnium rerum similitudine insignita; Memoria etiam mens est ... Mens autem vocata est, quod emineat in anima, vel quod meminerit'), 11; 786, and 24; 803; *mens* distinguished from *anima* but identified with *spiritus,* 24; 803. Here the author quotes Augustine, *De Trinitate,* XII, 3, pp. 357-58 directly: 'Quapropter non anima, sed quod excellit in anima, mens vocatur, tanquam caput vel oculus' (803-804).
   The attribution of *De spiritu et anima* to Augustine is, of course, anachron-istic, but not perverse. At least medieval authors acknowledged, or recog-nized, their primary source of inspiration. On the question of authorship, see the discussion of Bernard McGinn, ed. *Three Treatises on Man: A Cistercian Anthropology,* CS24 (Kalamazoo, 1977) pp. 65-67.
   48. *Liber de spiritu et anima,* 11; PL 40:786.
   49. *Liber de spiritu et anima,* 11, 52; PL 40:786, 817.
   50. *Liber de spiritu et anima,* 24; PL 40:803 ('In essentia namque est simplex, in officiis multiplex').
   51. *Liber de spiritu et anima,* 52; PL 40:818.
   52. *Liber de spiritu et anima,* 24; PL 40:804.

53. *Iohannis Cassiani Conlationes XXIIII*, ed. Michael Petschenig, *CSEL* XIII (Vienna, 1886) I, 5, pp. 10-11. Cassian says that a monk should pursue his end (*finem* = eternal life) by directing his *intentio* in a straight line towards the proper 'fixed target' (*scopos* = purity of heart), as athletes aim their *iacula vel sagittas*. Cassian's distinction between the monk's 'end' and the 'fixed target' at which he should aim in order to attain it is based on the beatitude, 'Blessed are the pure in heart, for they shall see God.'

54. Robert Pouchet, *La Rectitudo chez saint Anselme: Un itinéraire augustinien de l'âme a Dieu* (Paris, 1964), *passim* (Augustine, Gregory, Anselm, Grosseteste, Bonaventure, etc.).

55. Rudolph of Biberach, *De septem itineribus aeternitatis, itin.* I, d. 1-6, pp. 150-54.

56. *Confessions*, Texte établi par Pierre de Labriolle, II (Livres IX-XIII, Paris, 1969), XI, 11, 13, p: 305. Since it is unavailable to me, I am unable to cite Luc Verheijen's new *Corpus Christianorum* edition of the *Confessiones*.

57. *Confessions*, XI, 14, 17, p. 308: 'Si ergo praesens, ut tempus sit, ideo fit, quia in praeteritum transit, quomodo et hoc dicimus, cui causa, ut sit, illa est, quia non erit, ut scilicet non uere dicamus tempus esse, nisi quia tendit non esse?'

58. *Confessions*, XI, 13, 15, p. 307.

59. *Confessions*, XI, 15, 20, p. 310: 'Si quid intellegitur temporis, quod in nullas iam uel minutissimas momentorum partes diuidi possit, id solum est, quod praesens dicatur; quod tamen ita raptim a futuro in praeteritum transuolat, ut nulla morula extendatur.'

60. *Il Convivio, Le opere di Dante Alighieri*, 4th ed. (Oxford, 1924), I, 12-13, pp. 249-50.

IV

DENYS THE CARTHUSIAN AND TRADITIONS OF MEDITATION:
Contra detestabilem cordis inordinationem

Among currents of religious thought in the late Middle Ages, modern historians are accustomed to distinguish "monastic theology,"[1] Scholasticism, speculative mysticism, and the Modern Devotion. Often, individual writers are classified according to these categories. The writings of Denys of Ryckel (Dionysius Cartusiensis, 1402-1471), however, reflect and partake of all of these currents. Denys has been praised generally for his monastic union of piety and learning, and particularly for the monastic character of his scriptural exegesis.[2] At the same time he has been called the "last Scholastic."[3] Denys' contacts with the Modern Devotion are well known. For a short time he attended the school at Zwolle.[4] Several of his treatises were influenced directly by Devout writers,[5] and in turn his works were read by the Devout. Indeed, a large number of the surviving manuscripts of Denys' writings were copied in houses of the Augustinian Canons of Windesheim and other groups associated with the Modern Devotion.[6] In a list of recommended readings, the Augustinian Canon, Jan Mombaer (ca. 1460-1502), besides naming several specific titles by Denys, commends "omnia opuscula... Dionysii Cartusiensis."[7] Denys read *De ornatu spiritualis disponsationis* by Jan van Ruusbroec in the Latin translation made by Geert Grote.[8] He defended the most daring mystical speculations of van Ruusbroec, whom he called *Doctor divinus*, against charges of heresy made by Jean Gerson.[9] Like his correspondent Nicholas of Cusa, he argued the

---

[1] Jean Leclercq, *The Love of Learning and the Desire for God*, trans. Catherine Misrahi (New York, 1961).

[2] See François Vandenbroucke, "Écriture sainte et vie spirituelle," *Dictionnaire de spiritualité ascétique et mystique* 4 (Paris, 1960): 201-3.

[3] K. Krogh-Tonning, *Der letzte Scholastiker: Eine Apologie* (Freiburg im Breisgau, 1904).

[4] K. Swenden, "Dionysius van Rijkel, Biographische nota," *Ons Geestelijk Erf* 24 (1950): 170-81. See Denys, *In librum II^m Sententiarum*, in *Doctoris Ecstatici D. Dionysii Cartusiani Opera omnia*, cura et labore monachorum sacri ordinis Cartusiensis, 42 in 44 vols. (Montreuil-sur-Mer/Tournai/Parkminster, 1896-1935), vol. 21: 493: "Proinde recolo me ante annos quadraginta, dum in pueritia Suollis studerem, vidisse ac legisse tractatum a S. Bernardo compositum..." The edition cited here will henceforward be abbreviated: *Op. om.*

[5] See Albert Gruijs, *Jean de Schoonhoven (1356-1432): Son intérpretation de I Jean 2,15, «N'aimez pas ce monde, ni ce qui est dans ce monde». De contemptu huius mundi*, 4 vols. (Nijmegen, 1967), 3: 36-40.

[6] See now Kent Emery, Jr., *Dionysii Cartusiensis Opera selecta (Prolegomena). Bibliotheca manuscripta 1A-1B: Studia bibliographica* (Corpus Christianorum Continuatio Mediaevalis 121-121a: Turnhout, 1991), esp. CCCM 121: 36-38.

[7] Pierre Debongnie, *Jean Mombaer de Bruxelles, Abbé de Livry: Ses écrits et ses réformes* (Louvain/Toulouse, 1927), 320-21, 324-27.

[8] Georgette Epiney-Burgard, *Gérard Groote (1340-1384) et les débuts de la dévotion moderne* (Wiesbaden, 1970), 125-27.

[9] Kent Emery, Jr., "The Carthusians, Intermediaries for the Teachings of John Ruysbroeck during the Period of Early Reform and the Counter-Reformation," *Analecta Cartusiana* 43 (Salzburg, 1979): 100-16.

priority of intellect in mystical union against those who preferred simple to learned ignorance.[10]

Denys' encyclopedic use of spiritual traditions is evident in his *Contra detestabilem cordis inordinationem in Dei laudibus horisque canonicis, vel Laus Cartusiana*, by his own testimony his "primum opusculum." He wrote the work about 1430 at the request of the Prior of the Charterhouse in Basel, Albert Buez, to whom he sent an autograph copy, perhaps the only manuscript of the work that ever existed.[11] Denys' first treatise concerns meditation in relation to the recitation of the Divine Office; likewise, his last treatise, written in 1469 when he was 67 years old, concerns meditation.[12] That his first and last writings treat meditation seems appropriate, for according to his overall teaching, meditation is the pivotal practice of the spiritual life.

In medieval monastic life, the practice of meditation was bound closely to the recitation of the liturgy. Denys' Carthusian predecessor, Guigo II (†1188), neatly formulated the place of meditation within a fourfold monastic activity of reading, meditation, prayer and contemplation. In his *Epistola de vita contemplativa (Scala claustralium)* he defined these respective acts: "lectio inquirit, meditatio invenit, oratio postulat, contemplatio degustat."[13] As we shall see, the term *invenit*, which distinguishes the practice of meditation, in many writers, including Denys, acquired a technical rhetorical sense. Following longstanding tradition, Guigo relates meditation to the Beatitude, "Beati mundo corde, quoniam ipsi Deum videbunt" (Matthew 5:8). Thus he associates meditation with moral purification and the elimination of impure, carnal thoughts.[14]

Denys preserves the place of meditation within Guigo's fourfold order of monastic life. Like Guigo, he bases meditation on reading, although, as I shall suggest, habits of reading changed greatly between Guigo's and Denys' times, with considerable effect upon the art of meditation. Moreover, like Guigo Denys emphasizes that meditation, in order to be fruitful and not empty, must issue in prayer and affection. Finally, he treats meditation as an intermediate step in the spiritual life, preparatory to a pure and naked union with God in contemplation.[15]

---

[10] For a study of these issues, see E. Vansteenberge, *Autour de la docte ignorance: Une controverse sur la théologie mystique au XVe siècle* (Beiträge zur Geschichte der Philosophie des Mittelalters 14: Münster, 1915).

[11] *Contra detestabilem* is printed in *Op. om.* 40: 191-259. See Prooemium, 194. For the date, see Anselme Stoelen, "Denys le Chartreux," *Dictionnaire de spiritualité* 3 (Paris, 1957): 434. To my knowledge, no manuscript of the work survives. The title is not cited in any of the early lists of Denys' writings, and seems to have been discovered for the first time by Dirk Loër in 1532; see Emery, *Dionysii Cartusiensis... Bibliotheca manuscripta* (CCCM 121: 113).

[12] *De meditatione (Op. om.* 41: 69-90). Denys himself gives the date of the treatise and states that it is his final writing (*Op. om.* 41: 90C'). The earliest list of his writings, which he made in 1466, does not cite the treatise; see Emery, *Dionysii Cartusiensis... Bibliotheca manuscripta* (CCCM 121: 56-60).

[13] Guigo II, *Lettre sur la vie contemplative (L'Échelle des moines). Douze méditations*, Latin text ed. Edmund Colledge, O.S.A. and James Walsh, S.J., with a French translation by a Carthusian monk (Sources Chretiennes 163: Paris, 1970), 84.

[14] Ibid., 88-92.

[15] *Contra detestabilem* a.27 (*Op. om.* 40: 252); *De meditatione* a.4 (*Op. om.* 41: 75D-B').

Before turning directly to Denys' first treatise, one may usefully consider works by Anselm of Canterbury (ca. 1033-1109) and Geert Grote (1340-84), which illustrate lineaments of the tradition of meditation that Denys received. Anselm's *Orationes sive meditationes* decisively influenced the course of later medieval piety.[16] Geert Grote was the founder of the Modern Devotion; his *De quattuor generibus meditabilium* lays a theoretical foundation for meditation, which was a central practice among the Devout.[17] I shall not argue that either of these works was a direct source for Denys' *Contra detestabilem cordis inordinationem*: there are enough of these. Denys knew Anselm's meditations, however, and in his treatises on meditation there are traces of Geert Grote's teaching.

As the title of his collection indicates, Anselm's prayers are meditations and his meditations are prayers. Like his speculative writings, to which they are closely related, they are governed by the general rubric: *Fides quaerens intellectum.*[18] In his meditations, Anselm associates faith with the soul's faculty of memory, with the recollection of God's creative and redemptive works recorded in Scripture. Faith is only a beginning to the knowledge of God. Understanding, which penetrates to the spirit or *ratio* of the letter recalled in memory, lies between faith and vision, and is the ground of man's hope: "Denique quoniam inter fidem et speciem intellectum quem in hac vita capimus esse medium intelligo: quanto aliquis ad illum proficit, tanto eum propinquare speciei, ad quam omnes anhelamus, existimo."[19] Nearly all of Anselm's meditations mark a rhetorically complex progress from initial despair to faith, hope and love. This progress in the theological virtues corresponds to a movement in the soul from memory to understanding to affection. This movement is especially evident in the *Oratio ad Christum cum mens vult eius amore fervore.* Recollection of the articles of faith (emphasized by the repetition of the word *memor*) leads to understanding, which lies between faith and the vision of God face to face, to which the soul aspires by affection. Within this movement, meditation corresponds to understanding:

> Converte, misericordissime, meum teporem in ferventissimum tui amorem. Ad hoc, clementissime, tendit haec oratio mea, haec memoria et meditatio beneficiorum tuorum, ut accendam in me tuum amorem.... Sic et ego non quantum debeo, sed quantum queo, memor passionis tuae, memor alaparum tuarum, memor flagellorum, memor crucis, memor vulnerum tuorum, memor qualiter pro me occisus es, qualiter conditus, qualiter sepultus, simul memor gloriosae tuae resurrectionis et admirabilis

---

[16] A. Wilmart, *Auteurs spirituels et textes dévots du moyen âge latin* (Paris, 1932), 147-216. I cite Anselm's *Orationes sive meditationes* from the edition of F.S. Schmitt in vol. 3 of *S. Anselmi Cantuariensis Archiepiscopi Opera omnia* (Edinburgh, 1946).

[17] I cite from Gerardo Groote, *Il Trattato «De quattuor generibus meditabilium»*, ed. with intro. and Italian trans. by Illario Tolomio. One should note that R.R. Post, *The Modern Devotion: Confrontation with Reformation and Humanism* (Leiden, 1968), 164-65, states that in Geert's treatise, one finds little of the "methodical meditation" developed by later Devout writers.

[18] Anselm's *Meditatio redemptionis humanae*, ed. Schmitt in *S. Anselmi... Op. om.* 3: 84-91, is obviously related to his treatise *Cur Deus Homo*, ed. Schmitt in *S. Anselmi... Op. om.* 2 (1946): 36-133. Other speculative treatises, such as *De veritate* and *De casu diaboli*, ed. Schmitt in *S. Anselmi... Op. om.* 4 (1949): 167-99, 227-76, illumine difficult passages in various prayers and meditations.

[19] *Cur Deus Homo*, Dedication to Pope Urban II, in *S. Anselmi... Op. om.* 2: 40.

4   *Denys the Carthusian*

ascensionis: haec indubitata fide teneo, exilii mei aerumnas defleo, spero tui adventus solam consolationem, ardeo tui vultus gloriosam contemplationem.[20]

In his *Meditatio redemptionis humanae*, Anselm tersely expresses the progress from memory (of creation and redemption), to understanding, to love:

> Certe, domine, quia me fecisti, debeo amori tuo me ipsum totum; quia me redimisti, debeo me ipsum totum; quia tanta promittis, debeo me ipsum totum.... Fac precor, domine, me gustare per amorem quod gusto per cognitionem. Sentiam per affectum quod sentio per intellectum.[21]

Truth and understanding yield hope, which engenders prayer and desire:

> Sic enim esse veritas ostendit, et tamen affectus non sentit. Sic ratio docet, et cor non dolat.... Si hoc possem, forsitan sperarem, sperando orarem, orando impetrarem... quomodo sine spe orabo, quid sine oratione impetrabo?[22]

Anselm's meditations likewise mark a corresponding progress in the verbal arts. Faith and memory are based on reading. Understanding comes through dialectic, or rather "speculative grammar," which distinguishes the proper sense of Scripture's human terms applied to God.[23] Finally, rhetorical figures are the instruments for expressing one's affection for God. The correspondence between meditation and understanding points to the relation between Anselm's devotional and speculative writings. The latter, as he says, provide abstract, "necessary reasons" that underlie Scripture's "beautiful pictures," or the concordances between Old and New Testaments.[24]

The personal, psychological and artful structure of Anselm's meditations is firmly attached to liturgical prayer. All of the prayers and meditations focus upon the the central point of liturgical celebration, the redemption of the old creation in Christ, the new creation. In the liturgical manner, Anselm weaves texts of the Old and New Testaments around this event. One should remark especially the aural quality of his recollection of scriptural texts. Nearly each sentence, explicitly or implicitly, refers to a scriptural verse. Such a memory is the product of repeated recitation. The rhythmic prose and verbal repetition of the meditations bespeak their oral composition, and serve the memory of those to whom they were read aloud. Anselm's meditations were meant to be a shared, "public" devotional experience. Oral and aural techniques of memory, composition and reading were practiced in monastic culture

---

[20] *Oratio II*, in *S. Anselmi... Op. om.* 3: 7.

[21] *Meditatio III*, in *S. Anselmi... Op. om.* 3: 91.

[22] *Oratio X* (*Oratio ad sanctum Paulum*), in *S. Anselmi... Op. om.* 3: 34.

[23] See Marcia L. Colish, *The Mirror of Language: A Study in the Medieval Theory of Knowledge* (New Haven, 1968), 92-160.

[24] See *Cur Deus Homo*, in *S. Anselmi... Op. om.* 4: 51-52.

through the twelfth century, but they increasingly disappeared in the later Middle Ages.[25] Then Anselm's meditations were collected and variously arranged in literary anthologies for private reading.

Anselm influenced later writers on meditation less by his style than by his conception of a regular movement, culminating in affection, from reading and memory to abstraction and understanding, which defines meditation precisely. Later writers also followed his example in developing an art of meditation by means of the techniques of the verbal arts. In Anselm's treatment of meditation according to an order of faculties in the soul and an order of the arts, one recognizes the seed of a tradition, passing through the Modern Devotion, which crystallizes in the *Exercises* of Ignatius of Loyola.[26]

***

Geert Grote's *De quattuor generibus meditabilium* dispels any lingering notion that the Modern Devotion is best characterized as anti-intellectual. In the happy phrase of Georgette Epiney-Burgard, Geert's treatise is "post-scholastique," in the sense that it presupposes the full development of Scholastic culture.[27]

As the title of his treatise indicates, Geert distinguishes four classes of things upon which one may meditate: the words and images of sacred Scripture, especially the life and death of Christ; revelations given to favored saints; the assertions of theological doctors; the phantasms of sensible things apprehended by the imagination. Although these classes follow a descending order of authority in terms of their objects, subjectively they may all be reduced to the last one. Even the "verisimilitudes, conjectures, and probable arguments" of the doctors, however abstract they may seem, are rooted in the imagination. Geert's terms for the speculations of the doctors cannot identify him, in any precise sense, as a philosophic "nominalist"; rather, they are drawn from Latin rhetorical discourse.[28]

Geert's treatise, at the beginning, purports to be a sermon on Christ's nativity, on the text "Parvulus natus est nobis" (Isaias 9:6). Epiney-Burgard finds this device clumsy, and R.R.

---

[25] For Anselm's memory and oral composition by dictation, see Mary Carruthers, *The Book of Memory: A Study of Memory in Medieval Culture* (Cambridge, 1990), 195-96, 199-200, 211-14. On oral composition, rhythmic prose and group reading in twelfth-century monastic culture, see the extraordinary study by Paul Saenger, "Silent Reading: Its Impact on Late Medieval Script and Society," *Viator* 13 (1982): 367-414; see 379-83. One should note, however, that such writers as Anselm and Bernard of Clairvaux carefully edited and supervised the publication of the written texts of their works.

[26] M. van Woerkum, "Florent Radewijns," *Dictionnaire de spiritualité* 5 (Paris, 1964): 433-34, traces a line from Radewijns through Gerard of Zutphen (†1398) and Jan Mombaer to Ignatius of Loyola. For the influence of Carthusian writers, including possibly Denys, upon Ignatius, see P.B. Spaapen, "Karthuizervroomheid en Ignatiaanse spiritualiteit," *Ons Geestelijk Erf* 30 (1956): 337-66, and 31 (1957): 129-49.

[27] For Epiney-Burgard's treatment of the treatise, see *Gérard Groote*, 258-65.

[28] *De quattuor generibus*, 48. On Geert's supposed "nominalism," see Epiney-Burgard, 33-34. For the terms *coniectura, verisimilia, similitudo, argumentum*, see Cicero, *De oratore* 2.74.299, *Orator* 36.126-27, *Partitiones oratoriae* 9.33-11.40, in *M. Tulli Ciceronis Rhetorica*, ed. A.S. Wilkins, 2 vols. (Oxford, 1902-3, reprt. 1969-70); *De inventione* 2.5.16, 2.32.99, with trans. H.M. Hubbell (Cambridge, Mass., 1968), 180, 264. For *coniectura*, see also Quintilian, *Institutionis oratoriae libri duodecim* 1.2.25, 3.16.15, 7.2.6, 7.3.25, 7.4.23, 8.4.26, ed. M. Winterbottom, 2 vols. (Oxford, 1970), 18, 145, 379, 394, 401, 454. A precise definition is found in *Inst.* 3.6.30 (148): "Coniectura dicta est a coniectu, id est derectione quadam rationis ad ueritatem, unde etiam somniorum atque omnium interpretes coniectores uocantur."

Post, characteristically, finds it extraneous.[29] Nevertheless, the appropriateness of the scriptural text to the theme of meditation becomes clear. In his Incarnation, Christ accomodated himself to the weakness of sensible human nature, which, Geert says, draws nourishment from "fictions" and "imagined things." Befitting the weakness of our nature, if we wish to enter the kingdom of heaven we must become like little children (Matthew 18:2-4), drinking the milk of babes, the food of the imagination, before presuming to eat the solid food of abstraction.[30]

Lest "the cloud of our eyes" and our "carnal and animal nature" be overwhelmed by exceeding light, God and the angels have revealed spiritual realities to us in corporeal forms, images, figures and figments (*figmentis*).[31] As Dionysius the Areopagite says, it is impossible for us to perceive the ray of divine light except through a variety of sacred veils prepared for us by the fatherly providence.[32] Alluding to Horace, Geert adds that the "holy fictions" of sacred Scripture no more deceive than the fictions of moral poets. Certainly, one must not accept the writings of the poets literally, according to the "naked sound" of their words, but rather one must realize that in poetic speech, the literal is figurative.[33] This example reveals Geert's bookishness, evident throughout his treatise.[34] His treatise does not, as one might expect, show four methods or degrees of meditation, but rather distingushes the kinds of books from which one may draw matter for meditation: Scripture, saints' lives and revelations, Scholastic texts and even poetic fictions.

Whatever images one meditates upon must be governed by, and referred to, the images of sacred Scripture. Alluding to Augustine's *De doctrina christiana*, Geert says that the images of Scripture have a special property: the things to which they refer themselves signify other realities too difficult for us to apprehend because they cannot be impressed on our senses.[35] Moreover, there is an hierarchy among scriptural images. The images and figures of the Old Testament books and of the Apocalypse, because they are prophetic shadows, must (like the writings of the poets) be read figuratively. Like the assertions of the doctors, their interpretation yields only conjectures and probable arguments, not necessary truths. The images of the Gospels and Christ's words and deeds, on the other hand, must always be received "purely and simply, according to the letter."[36] In this ordering of scriptural images,

---

[29] Post, 164-65.

[30] *De quattuor generibus*, 42,48.

[31] Ibid., 48-50, 52-54.

[32] Ibid., 102. Geert alludes to chap. 1 of ps.-Dionysius, *De caelesti hierarchia*, in *Dionysiaca: Recueill donnant l'ensemble des traductions latines des ouvrages attribuées au Denys l'Aréopage*, ed. P. Chevallier, 2 vols. (Brussels, 1937), 2: 733.

[33] Horace, *Ars poetica* 11.333-44, 11.361-65, with trans. by H. Rushton Fairclough (Cambridge, Mass., 1961), 476, 480.

[34] Epiney-Burgard, 57-59; Post, 98-99, 165. Geert was a zealous collector of books and an advocate of *originalia*, or manuscripts of complete texts by the fathers and other writers.

[35] *De quattuor generibus*, 52-54; cf. Augustine, *De doctrina christiana* 1.2.2, 2.1.1, 2.6.8, ed. J. Martin (CCSL 32: Turnhout, 1962), 7-8, 32-36.

[36] *De quattuor generibus*, 66-72 passim.

Geert provides a doctrinal and hermeneutical rationale for the priority of meditation upon Christ's life and Passion. His teaching draws together several medieval notions: the ancient exegetical principle that the New Testament fulfills and completes the Old; the Scholastic principle that only arguments based on the literal sense of Scripture yield certain theological conclusions; and perhaps, Anselm's distinction between the "pictures" of Scripture and "necessary reasons." His teaching also looks forward to "evangelical" religion, in his followers of the Modern Devotion and beyond.

Although meditation begins in imagination, and remains rooted there, it must rise to abstraction. Unlike Anselm, who associates faith with memory, Geert, reflecting Scholastic teaching, appropriates faith to the intellect. Faith, he says, does not operate in the imagination, which is formed by sensible sight, but in the intellectual power, which is remote from the phantasms of sensible forms, and which apprehends the common reasons and eternal causes of created realities.[37] We are able to believe that the Lord was born of a virgin named Mary because we know the "universal species and quiddities" of the terms, that is, we know what a 'virgin' is, what it means 'to be born', and what a proper noun is.[38] Because faith is received in the intellect (through hearing) and not in the imagination, one must detach oneself from images and signs, which should be "emptied out" (*evacuandum*), and pass through them to the universal realities they signify. Thus, although it is useful to imagine oneself as present to the words and deeds of Christ, one must be careful not to be deceived. Meditating upon Christ's Incarnation, one must pass through its corporeal images to the idea of God's love and humility, and meditating upon Christ's miracles, one must be led to consideration of God's omnipotence. Not surprisingly, Geert disapproves of such books as the *Meditationes de vita Christi*, which imagine details of Christ's life not recorded in Scripture. In sum, in "sincere meditations and devotions" founded on faith, "it is fitting that the lineaments and forms of corporeal things be purged, and that the rational soul (*animus*) turn to their species and quiddities."[39]

It is the teaching of Thomas Aquinas, not that of some "nominalist," that underlies Geert's psychology and theory of meditation.[40] According to Thomas' teaching, Geert can find no direct means for the emptying out of images that true meditation requires. On the one hand, although the signs and names in Scripture refer to particular realities, one cannot comprehend them immediately, since singulars cannot be apprehended except through universals;[41] on

---

[37] Ibid., 80-82.

[38] *De quattuor generibus*, 78; cf. Augustine, *De Trinitate libri XV* 8.5, ed. W.J. Mountain with Fr. Glorie (CCSL 50: Turnhout, 1978), 277.

[39] *De quattuor generibus*, 56, 58-60, 70, 76, 78.

[40] See Epiney-Burgard, 34.

[41] *De quattuor generibus*, 80-82. Cf. Thomas Aquinas, *Summa theologiae* 1a q.85 a.3 in corp.: "Est ergo dicendum quod cognitio singularium est prior quoad nos quam cognitio universalium, sicut cognitio sensitiva quam cognitio intellectiva. Sed tam secundum sensum quam secundum intellectum, cognitio magis communis est prior quam cognitio minus communis"; *ST* 1a q.86 a.1 in corp.: "Respondeo dicendum quod singulare in rebus materialibus intellectus noster directe et primo cognoscere non potest. Cuius ratio est, quia principium singularitatis in rebus materialibus est materia individualis; intellectus autem noster... intelligit abstrahendo speciem intelligibilem ab

the other hand, although understanding of Scripture requires abstraction, total detachment from singular images is impossible. Echoing Thomas' doctrine that the human mind must have recourse to phantasms in every cognitive act, Geert says that phantasms impress themselves so strongly on the mind that it habitually "runs back" (*recurrere*) to their origin in the exterior senses.[42] Following Aristotle and Cicero, he attributes this habit to the human mind's reliance on the dominant sense of sight. At a distance, in a seemingly more spiritual way, sight comprehends more properties of things than the other senses, and therefore is closest to the common sense.[43] And sight, in biblical terms, is the opposite of faith, upon which true meditation must be grounded.

At this point, Geert makes some singular and revealing remarks. Illustrating the mind's inability to think without phantasms by way of the more difficult example, he says that whenever learned men read or hear something, especially if it be abstract, they remember it by visualizing the books, the places in books, the very letters and syllables whereby they read and learned it the first time. Thus, although they think their meditations and thoughts to be abstract, they are no less imaginative than the reflections of unlettered folk, who visualize what they hear by recalling more pictorial images. In this matter philosophers particularly deceive themselves. When speaking of essences, natures, quiddities, matter, forms, genera and species, they believe that they philosophize through the intellect alone, but in fact their minds are turned to the sensible phantasms of letters.[44]

By necessity, Geert implies, unlettered folk practice an art of memory that employs vivid corporeal images to retain what they hear or wish to remember. Such an art was developed systematically by ancient orators and was adapted for many purposes by thinkers throughout the Middle Ages.[45] Denys the Carthusian incorporated this art as an element of meditation (see below). To the learned, however, Geert ascribes another form of the art of memory, which fastens ideas visually to their places in books. In the context of his theory, this kind of memory is advantageous: it acknowledges that the human mind cannot think without phantasms, but the spatial images of words and marks on a page are less likely than pictorial images to absorb the imagination and deter spiritual abstraction.

Geert's observation about the memory of the literate surely reflects his own experience of reading as a university student and afterwards. In general, it reflects enormous changes in medieval literary culture that occurred largely in the thirteenth century. These changes met

---

huiusmodi materia. Quod autem a materia individuali abstrahitur est universale. Unde intellectus noster directe non est cognoscitivus nisi universalium."

[42] *De quattuor generibus*, 60. Cf., Thomas Aquinas, e.g., *ST* 1a q.84 a.7 in corp.: "dicendum quod impossibile est intellectum nostrum, secundum praesentis vitae statum, quo passibili corpori coniungitur, aliquid intelligere in actu, nisi convertendo se ad phantasmata."

[43] *De quattuor generibus*, 82-84. Cf. Aristotle, *De sensu et sensibili* 1.437a; Cicero, *De oratore* 2.87.357 (ed. Wilkins): "acerrimum autem ex omnibus sensibus esse sensum videndi; qua re facillime animo teneri posse ea, quae perciperentur auribus aut cogitatione... ut res caecus et ab aspectus iudicio remotas conformatio quaedam et imago et figura ita notaret, ut ea, quae cogitando complecti vix possemus, intuendo quasi teneremus."

[44] *De quattuor generibus*, 86-90.

[45] Frances A. Yates, *The Art of Memory* (Harmondsworth: Peregrine Books, 1969), esp. 17-113.

the requirements of Scholastic thought and institutions. More and more, authors wrote rather than dictated their "original" texts, and reading became a silent, private activity.[46] Scholastic books, with their tables, headings, text-divisions, indices, intricate means of alphabetical localizing and cross-reference were designed to serve the visual memory and rapid use of their readers.[47] Geert Grote's treatise on meditation is addressed to readers accustomed to books of this kind. Indeed, he and his followers among the Devout taught that silent personal reading is the foundation of the spiritual life. Accordingly, the Devout, adapting visual formats and textual devices they saw in university books and preaching manuals, became leaders in the mass-production of well-marked, well-divided books, usually without illuminations. For the most part, their books were intended to organize materials for meditation.[48] One should note that Denys the Carthusian, who wrote the exemplars of his own texts, made apparatus to reading an integral feature of his compositions.[49] Geert Grote and he may have left the university seeking solitude, but they read in the manner of university men, and this shaped their methods of meditation.

The practices of meditation and book production by followers of the Modern Devotion come together extravagantly in the *Rosetum exercitiorum spiritualium et sacrarum meditationum*, composed by Jan Mombaer in the 1490s. In the edition published by J. Badius Ascensius and printed by Iehan Petit (Paris, 1510), the massive encyclopedia of materials for meditation is divided into two major parts, each of which is divided into *distinctiones*. The individual *Tituli* collected in the work are designated by roman numerals at the head of column A of each recto, and these are further divided sequentially by an alphabet, the divisions of which are numbered at the head of column B of each recto. Under each numbered division of the alphabet, the columns are again subdivided by the letters A-Z down the margins. There are further chapter and article divisions, and in various prefaces, Mombaer offers alternative thematic schemes of division and organization. The volume has manifold tables and word-subject indices, as well as several complicated memory diagrams.[50] Jan Mombaer's book is itself an object of meditation; one wonders whether its

---

[46] Saenger, "Silent Reading," 383-414, documents every aspect of this change wrought by Scholastic culture, and its spread outside the university.

[47] See the excellent study by Richard H. Rouse and Mary H. Rouse, *Preachers, Florilegia and Sermons: Studies on the «Manipulus florum» of Thomas of Ireland* (Toronto, 1979), and their essays collected in *Authentic Witnesses: Approaches to Medieval Texts and Manuscripts* (Notre Dame, 1991), 191-255.

[48] See Saenger, 401-3. For the character of books produced by the Devout, the Carthusians et al. in the late-medieval Rhineland and the Low Countries, see Rouse and Rouse, "Backgrounds to Print: Aspects of the Manuscript Book in Northern Europe of the Fifteenth Century," in *Authentic Witnesses*, 449-66. In this essay and in *Preachers*, 212-13, the authors note that the Devout used reference works designed as preaching aids, such as Thomas of Ireland's *Manipulus florum*, to compile their own texts. For an interesting study of the books of the Devout, see *Moderne Devotie: Figuren en Facetten. Tentoonstelling ter herdenking van sterfjaar van Geert Grote, 1384-1984: Catalogus*, ed. A.J. Geurts et al. (Nijmegen, 1984); for the *Manipulus florum*, see 152-53.

[49] For Denys' methods of composition and written memory, see Kent Emery, Jr., "Denys the Carthusian and the Invention of Preaching Materials," *Viator* 25 (1994): 378-409.

[50] I have used the copy at the Newberry Library, Chicago. No manuscript of the work is known to survive. The work was printed earlier in 1496 (Zwolle) and 1504 (Basel); see *Moderne Devotie*, 217-21 (P. Nissen). The *Rosetum*, "in quo etiam habetur materia predicabilis per totius anni circulum," indicates that the same methods that were first used for organizing preaching materials were later used for organizing *meditabilia*.

elaborate visual aspect does not defeat Geert Grote's intention in recommending a textual, local memory as a means to easier abstraction.

Geert Grote teaches that the effects of sight's obvious or subtle dominance can be mitigated by relying more on the other senses. Sight, which is the origin of knowledge (*scientia*), is the instrument of reason (*ratio*); faith comes through hearing (Romans 10:7). By itself, hearing cannot supply phantasms of singular visible objects; it yields knowledge only *in genere*. Thus, when one hears that Christ's Passion was bitter, one understands its bitterness only generally, no matter what phantasms one may form in the imagination. Precisely because of its inadequate imaginative resources, hearing far better than sight serves "pure faith" and spiritual understanding (*intellectus*), since things heard must adhere to the first truth (or nothing).[51] So too the crudest senses serve faith more reliably than sight. Sacred Scripture, especially in the Canticle, warrants the use of odor, taste and touch for speaking about the highest realities. Citing Bernard of Clairvaux, Geert conjectures that spiritual savor originates in the sense of taste.[52] Paradoxically, the least refined in the order of senses corresponds with the highest in the traditional order of gifts of the Spirit, and the most refined sense corresponds with the lowest in the order of gifts: *scientia* (sight), *intellectus* (hearing), *sapientia* (taste). Finally, Geert notes, the sacraments (especially the Sacrament of the altar), in which there is a special proportion between sensible sign and invisible grace, are received primarily through the senses of taste and touch.[53]

The use of the senses in meditation, then, is governed by a general principle: the less refined the sensible sign, the more efficacious it is for meditation, inasmuch as, unlike the philosopher, one will not be deceived by its apparent spirituality. This principle applies to images derived from reading. The further the sound of the words recedes from the "truth" (in terms of adequation to the rational object), the less the mind is allowed to linger in the letter. On this crucial point, Geert refers to the doctrine of "dissimilar similitudes" taught by Dionysius the Areopagite:

> Sed hoc etiam sciendum quod sicut negationes de Deo sunt affirmationibus veriores, sic dissimiliores similitudines et difformiores de Deo et spiritualibus rebus utiliores sunt, eo quod, nihil dignum Deo vel spiritualibus in se continentes, cogunt mentem hominis ab eis declinare et altius aspirare.[54]

By means of this anagogic technique, Geert Grote, much in the spirit of Thomas Aquinas himself, resolves the dilemma of human meditation on purely spiritual realities, caused by the

---

[51] *De quattuor generibus*, 80, 84, 96-98.

[52] Ibid., 102-6.

[53] Ibid., 102-4.

[54] *De quattuor generibus*, 54; cf. ps.-Dionysius, *De caelesti hierarchia* 2, in *Dionysiaca* 2: 759-63. See also Hugh of St.-Victor, *Expositio in Hierarchiam coelestem* (PL 175: 961, 988-89); Richard of St.-Victor, *In Apocalypsim Joannis* (PL 196: 686-90); Denys the Carthusian, *Commentaria in librum de Coelesti seu angelica hierarchia* (*Op. om.* 15: 32-34).

mind's inability to think without phantasms. And in this manner he introduces the simply devout to the *via negativa*.

***

In *Contra detestabilem cordis inordinationem*, Denys the Carthusian already displays the broad erudition and compiling method characteristic of all his writings. In the treatise, he "collates materials" (see below) about meditation from many authors, citing or quoting and excerpting verbatim from, among others, Anselm, Augustine, Basil, Bernard of Clairvaux, David of Augsburg, Fulgentius, the *Glossa ordinaria*, Gregory the Great, Hilary of Poitiers, Hugh of St.-Victor, Isidore of Seville, Jerome, John Cassian, John Climacus, John Damascene, Nicholas of Lyre, Peter Comestor's *Historia scholastica*, Peter Lombard, Richard of St.-Victor, Ubertino of Casali. The work otherwise shares the general features of the tradition of meditation I have outlined in Anselm and Geert Grote. For Denys, too, meditation comprises precisely the movement from memory and imagination to understanding and abstraction. As they were for Geert Grote, so also for Denys Thomas Aquinas and Dionysius the Areopagite are the chief authorities for the theory of meditation. Denys calls Thomas "patronum meum,"[55] and in this early writing he accepts Thomas' teaching that in every act of cognition the mind must have recourse to phantasms. Later in his career, he criticized Thomas for this doctrine.[56]

It is noteworthy that in their treatises on meditation, Geert Grote and Denys seldom if at all refer to Dionysius' *De mystica theologia*, relying instead upon *De caelesti hierarchia*. Meditation is not a practice of mystical theology, wherein by definition one must rise above all sensible and intelligible realities. Meditation belongs properly to symbolic theology, wherein one rises by means of created visible realities to the invisible realities of God (Romans 1:20).[57] Although in *Contra detestabilem* Denys uses the terms 'meditation' and 'contemplation' interchangeably, in other writings he distinguishes them sharply. A passage he excerpts from (ps.-)Hugh of St.-Victor, *Super Ecclesiasten*, expresses the distinction in terms of the difference between discursive scrutiny of images and intuitive vision. The text articulates the movement from memory and imagination (*cogitatio*) to rational abstraction (*meditatio*) to sight (*contemplatio*); meditation examines one thing at a time while contemplation sees all:

> Cogitatio est, quum mens notione rerum transitorie tangitur, quum ipsa res sua imagine subito praesentatur animo, vel per sensum ingrediens, vel a memoria

---

[55] *Contra detestabilem* a.8 (*Op. om.* 40: 202D').

[56] See Kent Emery, Jr., *"Sapientissimus Aristoteles* and *Theologicissimus Dionysius*: The Reading of Aristotle and the Understanding of Nature in Denys the Carthusian," in *Mensch und Natur im Mittelalter*, ed. A. Speer and A. Zimmermann (Miscellanea Mediaevalia 21/2: Berlin, 1992), 579-80; "Denys the Carthusian and the Doxography of Scholastic Theology," in *Ad litteram: Authoritative Texts and their Medieval Readers*, ed. M.D. Jordan and K. Emery, Jr. (Notre Dame, 1992), 347-48.

[57] Ps.-Dionysius, *De mystica theologia* 1 and 3, in *Dionysiaca* 1: 567-68, 587-88.

exsurgens. Meditatio autem est assidua et sagax retractio cogitationis, aliquid involutum explicare nitens, vel scrutans penetrare occultum. Contemplatio es perspicax et liber animi contuitus, in res perspiciendas usquequaque diffusus. Inte meditationem et contemplationem hoc interesse videtur, quod meditatio semper est de rebus ab intelligentia nostra occultis, contemplatio vero de rebus vel secundum naturam vel secundum nostram capacitatem manifestis; et quod meditatio semper circa unum aliquid rimandum occupatur, contemplatio autem ad multa vel etiam ad universa comprehendenda diffunditur. Meditatio itaque est actio animae curiosa et sagax ad investigandum obscura et perplexa; contemplatio vero est vivacitas illa intelligentiae quae cuncta in palam habens, manifesta visione comprehendit: et ita quoddamode quod meditatio quaerit, contemplatio possidet.[58]

In terms of these definitions, Denys' 'meditation' in *Contra detestabilem* presses unceasingly towards 'contemplation,' but he immediately retreats from its comprehensive vision to con sideration of single images and topics.

The full title of Denys' treatise (....*in Dei laudibus horisque canonicis, vel Lau Cartusiana*) reveals its monastic and liturgical context. The first work (*opus*) of the monk Denys says, is "to assist in the divine praises of God with all vigilance, purity of heart, and an illumined intellect." Divine praise is the beginning and end of the monk's life; "a fervent well-disciplined heart is its required means." The enemies of divine praise are "cogitatione supervacuae, otiosae, volatiles ac inanes." Because of the weakness of human nature, the mind cannot easily remain elevated; the *pondus* of the soul in this life is towards lower bodily things, and the mind wanders continuously among their images.[59] Denys' treatise offers means whereby to keep the mind elevated and to discipline the imagination.

In defining purity of heart as the aim of the monk, a purity vitiated by wandering thoughts, Denys follows the teaching of John Cassian, whose works he later translated ad *stilum facillimum.*[60] In the first *Collatio*, Cassian distinguishes between the monk's ultimat end, the kingdom of heaven, and his proximate end, or *scopos*, which is purity of heart. A this *scopos*, or fixed target, the monk should aim all the arrows of his prayer and thought.[6] Summarizing his teaching on this point, Cassian says that in divine praises it is common fo the memory to slip from one verse to another, never retaining any of them. Thus the soul is drawn from one psalm to another, from the Gospel to the Epistles of St. Paul, from these to the utterances of the prophets and thence to the spiritual histories. Unstable, vague, and always moving, the mind never examines nor judges fully any text, nor does it touch, taste give birth to, or possess the spiritual senses. Three things stabilize the mind: vigils meditations and prayers. In order for the mind to be stable in the time of prayer, it mus

---

[58] Denys, *De contemplatione* 2 a.5 (*Op. om.* 41: 240C-A'); ps.-Hugh of St.-Victor, *In Ecclesiasten Homili I* (PL 175: 116-17).

[59] *Contra detestabilem* Prooemium, a.23 (*Op. om.* 40: 193-94, 243A, 244C-D).

[60] *Translatio librorum Joannis Cassiani presbyteri ad stilum facillimum* (*Op. om.* 27).

[61] *Iohannis Cassiani Conlationes XXIII* 1.2-5, ed. Michael Petschenig (CSEL 13: Vienna, 1886), 10-11; c Denys, *Coll.* 1.2-5 (*Op. om.* 27: 136-37).

lready be formed "by thoughts that it has dwelt on before prayer."[62] This teaching explains he relation between Denys' elaborate meditations and the praise of God "in... laudibus orisque canonicis."

Cassian's *Collationes* were especially influential among the Carthusians and followers of he Modern Devotion. Geert Grote developed Cassian's themes throughout his writings; it vould seem also that the form of the *Collationes* was one source for the *rapiaria* and *ollatieboeken* wherein the Devout collected and arranged texts for their personal medita- ion.[63] Geert's successor, Florens Radewijns (1350-1400), begins his *Rapiarium «Omnes, nquit artes»* by excerpting Cassian's text concerning the monk's *scopos*.[64] Jan Mombaer esigned his various arts precisely to prevent wandering thoughts and thereby achieve purity f heart.[65] In his *Ratio seu methodus compendio perveniendi ad veram theologiam*, Erasmus ses the term *scopus* to designate the all-embracing "commonplace," Christ in head and 1embers, to which one should refer all scriptural passages.[66] All human arts, Cassian says, ave an end that directs their exercise; no less than these should the monk's reading and 1editation be ordered by such an end. For late medieval writers, Cassian's analogy was an uthority for the "methodic" use in meditation of techniques borrowed from the verbal arts. 'hese were amply developed by Wessel Gansfort (1419-89)[67] and Jan Mombaer; the 'arthusians too played an important role in the development of schematized meditation.[68]

In the traditional manner, Denys the Carthusian teaches that an illumined intellect requires pure heart, which is the effect of a disciplined imagination. The discipline of the nagination should befit man's created nature. Alluding to Dionysius' theory of hierarchical lumination, as interpreted by Thomas Aquinas,[69] Denys states that since the human intellect s situated between intelligible substances (the angels) and corporeal creatures, and since in

---

[62] Cassian, *Conlationes* 10.12-13 (CSEL 13: 306-7); cf. Denys, *Coll.* 10.13-14 (*Op. om.* 27: 265-66).

[63] Epiney-Burgard, 64-65; *Moderne Devotie*, 152-67 (Cassian, 160-61); Thom Mertens, "Rapiarium," *ictionnaire de spiritualité* 13 (Paris, 1987): 114-19.

[64] M.Th.P. van Woerkum, *Het Libellus «Omnes, inquit, artes». Een Rapiarium van Florentius Radewijns*, 3 ols. (Nijmegen, 1950), 2:1.

[65] *Rosetum* (1510), Titulus XX, Alphabetum XLVI, Prologus C-M.

[66] *Ratio seu Methodus*, in vol. 5 of *Desiderii Erasmi Roterodami Opera omnia*, ed. J. Clericus (Leiden, 1704; eprt. Hildesheim, 1962), 77, 83-88. Erasmus suggests the origin of the term *scopus* in the verbal arts, and the devout 1eaning of the term *rapiarium*: "Inter humanas disciplinas, aliae alium habent scopum. Apud Rhetorem, hoc spectas, copiose, splendideque dicas: apud Dialecticum, ut argute colligas, et adversarium illaquees. Hic primus et unicus bi scopus, hoc votum, hoc unum age, ut muteris, ut affleris, ut rapiaris, ut transformeris in ea quae discis" (77). ee Marjorie O'Rourke Boyle, *Erasmus on Language and Method in Theology* (Toronto, 1977), 72-81.

[67] Lee Daniel Snyder, *Wessel Gansfort and the Art of Meditation* (Ph.D. diss., Harvard University, 1966).

[68] Ludolph of Saxony developed systematic meditation on the Passion; see Walter Baier, *Untersuchungen zu en Passionsbetrachtungen in der Vita Christi des Ludolfs von Sachsen: Ein quellenkritischer Beitrag zu Leben und Jerk Ludolfs und zur Geschichte der Passionstheologie*, 3 vols. (Analecta Cartusiana 44/1-3: Salzburg, 1977). For udolph and Denys, see Emery, *Dionysii Cartusiensis.... Bibliotheca manuscripta* (CCCM 121: 129-31). For the arthusian contribution to the development of the meditation of the rosary, see Karl Joseph Klinkhammer, *Adolf von ssen und seine Werke: Der Rosenkranz in der geschichtlichen Situation seiner Enstehung und in bleibendum Anliegen uellenforschung* (Frankfurt, 1972).

[69] Ps.-Dionysius, *De caelesti hierarchia* 15, in *Dionysiaca* 2: 986-90. See Thomas Aquinas, *ST* 1a q.50 aa.1,3; .55 a.3; q.75 aa.1,5,7; q.76 a.1. See also Thomas' *Opusculum de humanitate Iesu Christi* a.1, prooemium, in vol. 7 of *Sancti Thomae Aquinatis... Opera omnia* (Parma, 1864; reprt. New York, 1950), 189.

this life it inclines more to the body of which it is the act of existence, the human mind can understand intelligible realities only through bodily images. Hence the human mind does not receive the illumination of superior substances directly, but knows only through sensible species; in the words of Dionysius, the mind cannot turn towards the divine ray except through a variety of sensible forms. Even the inspirations of the prophets were communicated through imaginative forms and figures. Again, Denys supports his teaching by the authority of Thomas Aquinas.[70] As he later criticized Thomas' doctrine of phantasms, so in later writings he argued that the human mind could receive direct spiritual illumination from superior Intelligences (or angels).[71] Even so, Thomas' teaching holds for ordinary cognition, and it is especially appropriate within the scope of the art of meditation, if not for mystical theology.

Accordingly, Denys teaches that the art of meditation involves a continual process of rising from images to abstraction, reverting to phantasms, and from those same phantasms rising once more to abstraction. When by weakness or inattention we fall from interior to exterior realities, Gregory the Great says, we should arise once more from the visible to the invisible exactly as we fell down, with the hand of consideration reaching up to the place where, by negligence, the wayward foot of love slipped. Thus we may return on high by the same steps by which we fell.[72] Insofar as one acquires the habit of returning from phantasm to abstraction (thereby reversing the inclination of our fallen nature), one experiences *in via* a foretaste of the felicity to come *in patria*. Happy is he, Denys says, who continually wipes away the phantasms and images occuring in his mind, and who, continually turning within himself and lifting up his mind to God, at last reaches the point where, to a certain extent, he is able to disregard images. If against his "will of willing" phantasms return like flies before his eyes, he should continue to brush them away; by habit he will become better at the practice everyday, provided that by the love of God and contempt of everything else he lays hold of the increase given him.[73]

Like Geert Grote, Denys distinguishes between the wholly abstract conceptions formed by faith alone and the spiritual realities communicated to the soul through a variety of sensible forms. Texts that Denys extracts from "Augustine" (actually Honorius of Autun), *De cognitione verae vitae*, illustrate the distinction. They also illustrate the circular movement of meditation, from abstraction rooted in faith to images, which must again be corrected by abstract consideration. Although by nature the intellect requires a local object, nevertheless

---

[70] *Contra detestabilem* a.1 (*Op. om.* 40: 195B'-96A); cf. ps.-Dionysius, *De caelesti hierarchia* 1, in *Dionysiaca* 2: 733. For the argument that the prophets (namely Jacob) did not see the essence of God, Denys quotes Thomas Aquinas, *4 Sent.* d.49 q.2 a.7 ad 2, directly: "Ad secundum dicendum, quod visio illa Jacob fuit imaginaria, vel corporalis. Dicitur tamen vidisse facie ad faciem, quia illa figura in qua ei apparuit Deus, facie ad faciem est ab eo visa" (in vol 7 of *Opera omnia*, Parma, 1211).

[71] Kent Emery, Jr., "Twofold Wisdom and Contemplation in Denys of Ryckel (Dionysius Cartusiensis, 1402-1471)," *The Journal of Medieval and Renaissance Studies* 18 (1988): 111-20.

[72] *Contra detestabilem* a.31 (*Op. om.* 40: 258B-D); Gregory the Great, *Moralia in Iob* 26.12, ed. M. Adriaen (CCSL 143b: Turnhout, 1985), 1277-79.

[73] *Contra detestabilem* a.27 (*Op. om.* 253B-C).

by faith we piously believe that the human soul has no dimension or extension. Indeed, we cannot properly conceive the soul except in relation to God, its exemplary cause. So by faith we believe that God is an uncircumscribed spirit present everywhere through his essence and power, possessing within himself, as in a point, all life, all wisdom, all eternity and all creatures.[74] Aptly does Alan (of Lille) call God "a sphere whose center is everywhere and whose circumference is nowhere."[75] According to his likeness, God created thousands upon thousands of angels who stand before him. The brilliance of these beings, who are temples of God, are thousands of times brighter than the sun that illumines the world. We may believe the same of the thousands upon thousands of human souls who enjoy beatitude. Now the soul is a *scintilla* of its divine cause. According to its intellectual nature and "magnitude" it virtually contains the whole circuit of the world within itself; having no spatial dimensions, by means of the intellect it is able to reduce the corporeal dimensions of the outer world to its own "smallness," or point. And when the mind rises above itself to the spiritual cosmos, and in one glance gazes upon the incomparable clarity and magnitude of the heavenly lights, of the angelic orders and blessed souls, it will discover a "light of all lights" radiating over them all, as much more brilliant than they as the sun is than the stars. This is the inaccessible light wherein the essence of God dwells, which satiates the angels and the blessed souls and illumines the contemplation of the clean of heart.[76] Denys remarks that, although this image of Augustine (Honorius) does not stray far from the truth, the conception it conveys is beyond the weak capacity of our minds. Moreover, one must be careful lest one be seduced too easily by such phantasms. It is well to remember the statement of Isidore of Seville, that neither the angels nor the blessed souls after the Resurrection ever attain a full comprehension of God's essence; this is reserved to the persons of the Trinity, and to the incarnate humanity of the Word, the second divine person.[77]

Such paradoxical conceptions (similar to those of Nicholas of Cusa)[78] more confound than establish comprehension. Lest our weak intellects be broken by, and err in, their difficulty, it is better that we contemplate God by means of similitudes and aenigmas used in sacred Scripture, which temper and proportion the most noble spiritual objects to our capacity. Meditation "examines one thing at a time" (ps.-Hugh of St.-Victor); so, Denys says,

---

[74] *Contra detestabilem* a.1 (*Op. om.* 40: 196D). Cf. Honorius of Autun, *De cognitione verae vitae* 7 (PL 40: 1010): "Deus spiritus est essentia invisibilis, omni creaturae incomprehensibilis, totam vitam, totam sapientiam, totam aeternitatem simul essentialiter possidens: vel ipsa vita, ipsa sapientia, ipsa veritas, ipsa justitia, ipsa aeternitas existens, omnem creaturam instar puncti in se continens." For the soul's lack of dimension and extension, see, e.g., Augustine, *De quantitate animae* 3 (PL 32: 1037): "Quamobrem quanta sit anima secundum inquisitionem hanc tibi respondere non possum; sed possum affirmare, neque illam longam esse, nec latam, nec robustam, neque aliquid horum quae in mensuris corporum quaeri solent."

[75] *Contra detestabilem* a.17 (*Op. om.* 40: 219D'); Alan of Lille, *Regulae de sacra theologia* 7 (PL 210: 627).

[76] *Contra detestabilem* a.2 (*Op. om.* 40: 196D-197B); Honorius, *De cognitione verae vitae* 8 (PL 40: 1011-12).

[77] *Contra detestabilem* a.2 (*Op. om.* 40: 197C-A'); Isidore of Seville, *Sententiarum liber I: De summo bono* (PL 83: 542).

[78] See, e.g., Nicholas of Cusa, *De docta ignorantia* 1.12-13, 1.23, 2.3, in vol. 1 of *Nicolai de Cusa Opera omnia*, ed. E. Hoffman and R. Klibansky (Heidelberger Akademie der Wissenschaften: Leipzig, 1932), 25-26, 46-47, 69.

IV

lest our intellect be seduced by various phantasms and discourses, we should bind together the images of our meditation and fix our thoughts on certain set objects.[79]

Denys' art of meditation relies upon two forms of memory: one is textual, recalling "discourses" of abstract reasoning, the other regards corporeal "similitudes," drawn from the Scriptures, which are manifestly "dissimilar" to the spiritual realities they convey. For an object of meditation Denys uses the term *palus*, a set stake employed as a mark or standard. He takes the term from a text in Ecclesiasticus (14:22-25):

> Blessed is the man who will continue in wisdom, and who will meditate on her justice, and will think in his mind on God's all-encompassing sight; who considers wisdom's ways in his heart, and understands her secrets, follows her path and remains in her ways; who looks through the windows, hears through the doors, and lodges near her house; and who, fixing a stake (*palum*) in her walls, sets up house nearby her.

In his later commentary on this text, Denys explains that the secrets of wisdom are the incomprehensible attributes of God, which one comes to understand through the illumination of the mystical senses of sacred Scripture. Through the windows of Scripture and the writings of holy authors, one acquires the clarity of divine illumination; through the doors of ecclesiastical sacraments one enters the kingdom of heaven. One fixes a stake (*palum*) in wisdom's walls when he stabilizes his intellect in the figures and tropes of Scripture or in created things through which God is known. These stand as walls between the seer and the one seen: "nunc enim videmus per speculum in aenigmate" (1 Corinthians 13:12).[80]

In a series of articles, Denys sets forth an ordered sequence of *pali* for meditation. These are anagogic in the exegetical sense: all of them pertain to heavenly mysteries and to the mysteries of the human being's final beatitude. As Denys says, the roots of the psalms are in heaven, so that when we recite them our conversation should be there.[81] He arranges the anagogic mysteries hierarchically and topically. His *pali* descend in order from God in three persons (a.4), to the Virgin Mary, who is exalted above all the angels (a.5), through the nine angelic orders (aa.6-11), and thence to the various conditions, joys, and privileges to be experienced by the blessed in soul and body (aa. 12-22). In relation to the human soul, Denys divides the anagogic mysteries generically, according to a formula used by Richard of St.-Victor, Bonaventure and others to expose degrees of being and corresponding degrees of spiritual perfection. The joyful vision of heaven is partaken in a threefold way, *supra se, intra se* and *sub se*. The vision of God, the Virgin Mary and the angelic hierarchies is above the soul, the experience of the glorified faculties is within it, and the experience of the glorified body is beneath it. Moreover, the beatified human person delights also in things

---

[79] *Contra detestabilem* aa.2-4 (*Op. om.* 40: 197A-D').

[80] Denys, *Enarratio in librum Ecclesiastici* a.14 (*Op. om.* 8: 85).

[81] *Contra detestabilem* a.1 (*Op. om.* 40: 195A-B).

extra se, in the manifold joys of the heavenly city, in the earth viewed from a divine perspective, and in the just punishments of the damned:

> Sancti in patria elevantes se supra se, gaudent de Dei visione; convertes se intra se et circa se, extra se et juxta se, et in coelo infra se, exulatant in hoc multifarie. Jam vero oculum reflectentes ad ea quae extra coelum sunt sub se, scilicet ad mundum et infernum, multiplex concipiunt gaudium.[82]

The articles concerning the anagogic *pali* of meditation are a compendium of Scholastic doctrine, in which Denys "locates" and paraphrases common teaching about the angelic hierarchies and the joys of the blessed. The articles concerning the angelic hierarchy present a synthesis of the teachings of the two great authorities on the topic, Dionysius the Areopagite and Gregory the Great, and Thomas Aquinas. Denys treats the joys of the blessed according to the conventional order of questions about them in theological *Summae* and commentaries on the fourth book of Peter Lombard's *Sentences*.[83] His hierarchical, conventional order of topics serves the memory as a ladder upon which one may situate objects of meditation. The individual articles are containers encapsulating summaries of the doctors' arguments. Throughout his writings Denys employed article titles as an aid to topical memory; he conceived his own commentaries on the *Sentences* as a "treasurechest" of materials that could be retrieved and abbreviated in other writings. Likewise, the order of questions in commentaries on the *Sentences* was subject to memory schemes.[84]

For each *palus* of meditation, Denys discovers appropriate anagogic signs, or "dissimilar similitudes," scattered throughout the Scriptures. Because they compel greater abstraction, such paradoxical images are most suitable for meditation upon heavenly realities. Thus, creatures of the lowest order may signify creatures of the highest. The differing properties of the nine stones enumerated in Ezechiel (28:12-13) and investigated in lapidaries, for example, serve well to signify the differing virtues of the nine angelic orders.[85] Other scriptural images dissolve in a famous paradox. Many texts in Scripture suggest that the heavenly city is built on a square foundation. At the same time, this city may rightly be imagined as circular, like the highest Empyrean heaven, which by its power encloses the lower spheres. According to these conflicting images, the heavenly city is something that reason cannot conceive to exist: a squared circle. But even though these images fail their object, they yet signify different qualities of the heavenly city: its stability, perfection and

---

[82] *Contra detestabilem* a.20 (*Op. om.* 40: 232C'-D'); see also a.16 (218D-219B). Cf. Richard of St.-Victor, *Benjamin maior* 74 (PL 196: 53), and Bonaventure, *Itinerarium mentis in Deum* 1,2,4, in vol. 5 of *Doctoris seraphici S. Bonventurae Opera omnia* (Quaracchi, 1891), 297.

[83] Cf. *Contra detestabilem* aa. 12-22 (*Op. om.* 40: 208-42) with Denys, *In librum IV^m Sententiarum* d.44 qq.3-7, d.49 qq.1-10 (*Op. om.* 25/1: 266-303, 392-450); Thomas Aquinas, *ST* Suppl. qq. 92-96.

[84] On these matters, see Emery, "The Doxography," 332-34; *Dionysii Cartusiensis… Bibliotheca manuscripta* (CCCM 121: 25-28, 47-49); "Denys the Carthusian and the Invention of Preaching Materials," 379-82; see 381 n. 18.

[85] *Contra detestabilem* a.6 (*Op. om.* 40: 199C'-200A).

influence.[86] Another heavenly mystery seems to contradict a fundamental law of nature. The subtlety of the glorified human body allows it to occupy simultaneously the place of another body, and thus pass through the spheres without suffering division. (Decent order, in accordance with divine wisdom and the divine will, however, requires that glorified bodies not occupy each other's place). This mystery is analogous to the mystery of the Sacrament of the altar, wherein Christ's body shares the same place with the accidents of bread and wine. Both are accounted for by an abstract principle stated in the first proposition of the *Liber de causis*. God, the first cause of all things, can preserve effects without secondary intermediate causes. Because they partake the divine virtue of omnipresence, Christ's body in the Sacrament and the glorified body can remain distinct from other bodies while occupying the same place.[87] What appears contradictory to sense and nature is an effect of the first principle of nature, the divine creative power.

The intellect, Denys says, is most likely to fail and to err regarding the highest object of contemplation or meditation, God in himself. A general rule stated by Gregory the Great especially applies to the mystery of the divine Trinity: "Whatever here we perceive of God is not him, but is something under him." Therefore, Denys touches only briefly (*pro tantilla*) upon the first *palus* of meditation, referring to the mysteries of the Trinity and the Incarnation by way of a "most tenuous similitude," the image of the Ancient of Days (Daniel 7:9-14) which, according to Dionysius, is one of the more remote names of God. The enthroned Ancient of Days, before whom the Son of Man intercedes, represents the "paternal substance" of the Father, and the stream of fire issuing from his face represents the Holy Spirit.[88]

Significantly, Denys treats the Trinity more fully when meditating upon the perfection of the soul's faculties in the beatific vision. This topic is especially important, for it establishes a continuity between what begins in faith, increases through understanding, and culminates in vision. Here Denys expresses his conviction that the faculty of intellect governs the spiritual life, *in via* and *in patria*. He thus rejects the priority of will and affection taught by so many spiritual masters, including Bernard of Clairvaux, William of St.-Thierry, Hugh of St.-Victor, Thomas Gallus, Bonaventure, the Carthusian Hugh of Balma, to name a few. Denys' intellectual notion of 'anagogy' contrasts with the notion of Hugh of Balma (fl. 1300) for example, who defines 'anagogy' as an aspiration of the affections.[89]

Concerning the beatific vision, Denys follows the teaching of Thomas Aquinas, although he seems to incorporate some notions (concerning God's presence in the beatified soul and the light of glory) of Henry of Ghent, whose teaching is otherwise quite different from Thomas'. Human beatitude consists formally in three endowments (*dotes*) or acts of

---

[86] Ibid. a. 17 (*Op. om.* 40: 219B-220B).

[87] Ibid. a. 13 (*Op. om.* 40: 212A'-D').

[88] *Contra detestabilem* a.4 (*Op. om.* 40: 197D'-198B'); cf., ps.-Dionysius, *De divinis nominibus* 10, in *Dionysiaca* 1: 482-94.

[89] Hugh of Balma, *Mystica theologia*, printed in vol. 8 of *S.R.E. cardinalis S. Bonaventurae... Opera omnia* ed A.C. Peltier (Paris, 1866), 1-53.

cognition, dilection and fruition bestowed upon the soul by God. In the soul's most elevated condition, perfection pertains first and foremost to its highest act; the intellect is the soul's most powerful faculty and intelligence is its most noble act; therefore the beatitude of the human soul consists principally in the cognitive act of vision, whereby it contemplates the divine persons and the divinity and humanity of Christ. As Thomas Aquinas teaches, therefore, the act of vision is essentially the soul's whole reward and and the substance of its beatitude. Because of the mutual interconnection among the acts of cognition, dilection and fruition, what is common to all three may be attributed to each one of them, but chiefly to vision, because it is, in a sense, the cause of the other two. Moreover, the distinction between the soul's beatific condition and its condition *in via* appears more obviously in relation to the vision of the intellect than to the dilection or fruition of the will. For the blessed see God without any obscuring medium, and not, as here, "per speculum et in aenigmate." Thus, in the beatific vision the soul does not see God "through a distance," as here, but through his very "presence" in the soul. God is anyway present essentially to all of his creatures; in the beatific vision, wherein every medium is withdrawn, he is present to the soul more immediately and manifestly. Yet a certain medium is necessary for the perfection of the intellect; this is called the "medium of the light of glory, by which the intellect is disposed and perfected for seeing God himself." But this "mediating medium" does not cause the deifying vision in the soul, nor does this vision require any other species or similitude informing the intellect.[90] The act of vision virtually contains the other acts of the beatified soul. By seeing or knowing God the soul loves him, by loving him it possesses him, and by possessing him it enjoys (*fruitur*) him. Thus, dilection proceeds from cognition, and fruition arises from both of them.[91]

Discourse about the soul's beatific act and habit *intra se* leads inevitably to consideration of its object *supra se*, the divine Trinity. As Denys says, beatific cognition is not the proper act of angels or human souls, but the act of the Son of God in them, for no one knows the Father except the Son and those to whom the Son reveals him (Matthew 6:27).[92] Denys first considers the relations among the persons of the Trinity by recourse to the traditional image of *lux, splendor, calor*. These are rooted in the single nature of light, but they may be distinguished according to the different formal significations of their terms (*vocabula*). The term 'light' suggests substance, the term 'splendor' the grace of light, and 'heat' the efficacy of light; so the Father is light by substance, the Son is "the splendor of the Father and the figure of his substance" (Hebrews 1:3), and the Spirit, who is a "consuming fire"

---

[90] On the presence of God in the soul in the beatific vision, the 'distance' of our sight here, and the adapting light of glory, cf. Henry of Ghent, *Quodlibet III* q.1, ed. J. Badius Ascensius in *Quodlibeta magistri Henrici Goethals a Gandauo....*, 2 vols. (Paris, 1518; reprt. Louvain, 1961), ff. 47r-48v.

[91] *Contra detestabilem* a.12 (*Op. om.* 40: 208C'-211D). On the teaching of Thomas Aquinas and other late thirteenth-century masters, including Henry of Ghent, see Edouard Wéber, "Eckhart et l'ontothéologisme: Histoire et conditions d'une rupture," in *Maître Eckhart à Paris: Une critique médiévale de l'ontothéologie*, ed. E. Zum Brunn et al. (Paris, 1984), 55-83. Unlike Thomas, Denys here does not speak of the divine essence as the "uncreated species" by which the soul sees God.

[92] For Thomas on this point, see Wéber, "Eckhart et l'ontothéologisme," 60-61.

(Deuteronomy 4:24, Hebrews 12:29), is his efficacy, or efficient will.[93]

Denys considers the object of the blessed soul *supra se* more extensively under many images of streams and rivers in the sacred Scriptures. Through these images he discerns the inexhaustible "flow of being" (*fluxus entis*) within the divine essence, and its outpouring diffusion and communication to every creature. Here Denys refers to a fundamental conception of Albert the Great and his followers in the Rhineland and the Low Countries, including Jan van Ruusbroec. Indeed, the terms of his expositions come directly from *De causis et processu universitatis* and other works by Albert the Great (*fluxus entis, influxus, fons luminis, fons fluminis, derivare-derivatio, emanare-emanatio, exuberare-exuberantia, redundare-redundantia, scaturire*, etc.).[94] "He showed me a river of the water of life, as splendid as crystal, proceeding from the throne of God and the Lamb" (Apocalypse 22:1), "a deep torrent, which could not be passed over" (Ezechiel 47:5). Denys comments:

> Quid aliter intelligi datur nobis per fluvium hunc, seu potius fluminis fontem, nisi fontale principium omnium entium, Deum? Cui in se ante omnem creaturam primo competit fluere et scaturire: quod intelligitur immanens fontis actus et communicatio in eo substantialis, propter suam bonitatem sibi innatam nec extra diffusam. Quum extra diffunditur, creare seu causare vel conservare dicitur: exemplo aquae materialis fontis, qui primo fluxum indeficientem in se manentem exuberare videtur, per cujus redundantiam postea procedunt rivuli, propter copiam innundantis aquae in thesauro ejus collectae. Omne igitur fluens, in fonte consideratum manens, necessario, ut sic, cum suo fonte ejusdem permanet naturae, indistans a fonte.[95]

There is a twofold "flow of emanation" (*fluxus emantionis*) issuing from the "riverbed" (*alveus*) of the divine essence. These emanations are "indistant" from the substance of their source (*fons*), because they do not flow beyond the identity and unity of the divine essence. Proceeding from, but remaining in, their unborn principle, the Father, they are eternal, wholly immanent acts, identical with the divine substance. As one may consider the processions of the divine persons under the image of *lux, lumen, calor*, so one may consider them under the threefold image, *fons, flumen, flux*. Formally, the term *fons* predicates "by reason of origin," the term *flumen* "by reason of the outflow" (*liquor*) from the source, and the term *flux* by "reason of the superabundance" (*exuberantia*) gushing forth from both of them. These images express a synonymy between light and being (divine being is constitutively intelligent being). Conceptually, their terms imply a closer nexus, or indistinction, between the source and its first emanation (the substance of light and the figure

---

[93] *Contra detestabilem* a.12 (*Op. om.* 40: 209A'-D').

[94] See Maria Rita Pagnoni-Sturlese, "A propos du néoplatonisme d'Albert le Grand: Aventures et mésaventures de quelque textes d'Albert dans le Commentaire sur Proclus de Berthold de Moosberg," *Archives de philosophie* 43 (1980): 635-54, esp. 644-53; Alain de Libera, *Albert le Grand et la philosophie* (Paris, 1990), 117-77, and *La mystique rhénane d'Albert le Grand à Maître Eckhart* (Paris, 1994), 141-45, 158-61 n. 106, 355-64 et passim; Jan van Ruusbroec, *De ornatu spiritualium nuptiarum* 3.4, Latin trans. by L. Surius in *D. Ioannis Rusbrochii... Opera omnia* (Cologne, 1552; reprt. Farnborough, Hants, 1967), 370-71.

[95] *Contra detestabilem* a.19 (*Op. om.* 40: 230B-C).

of its substance, the source of being and its outflow) than between the source and its second emanation (the substance of light and its heat, the source of being and its superabundance). Denys makes the conceptual distinction in abstract terms. The first divine "flow of emanation," the generation of the Son, proceeds by way of nature, whereas the second, the breathing forth (*spiratio*) of the Spirit, proceeds by way of will, or love. Thus, although both the Son and the Spirit are consubstantial with the Father, and equally share the fullness of divine being, conceptually (*secundum rationem intelligendi*) one may understand that an emanation by way of nature precedes an emanation by will, and that the procession of the Spirit presupposes the generation of the Son ("generationem Filii praesupponit jam factam").[96] Although in this passage Denys does not use the terms, one may infer that the generation of the Son is identical with the divine act of understanding, and that the procession of the Spirit presupposes the generation of the Son as an act of the rational will presupposes an act of intellect. Further on in the article Denys identifies the Son with the Wisdom of God, and in later writings, following Thomas Aquinas, he explicitly identifies the generation of the Son by nature with the divine act of understanding:

> Duae sunt emanationes in Deo ad intra: una intellectus et per modum naturae, alia voluntatis et per modum liberalitatis... quoniam intellectus et voluntas sunt digniores et simpliciores potentiae, quae... praecipue ac excelletissime sunt in Deo, cujus natura est intellectualis. Operatio quoque et emanatio ad intra per intellectum convenit ei per modum naturae, cujus est aliquid sibi simile procreare. Hinc productio Verbi aeterni, generatio nominatur, estque emanatio naturalis, in ratione conformationis consistens. Porro effluxio voluntatis ad intra est amoris productio, et vocatur activa spiratio, per modum liberalis donationis se habens, quia ad voluntatem spectant liberalitas, datio, amor, amplexus et unio.[97]

Since the Spirit "proceeds from the Father and the Son," and its procession presupposes the generation of the Son, the conceptual distinction between the first and second emanations in the Trinity, which posits a certain priority of the act of intellect in God and connotes a more intimate relation between the divine essence and intellect than between the divine essence and will, would seem to have some foundation *in re*; thus, the priority of cognition in the soul's beatific act is grounded in the very reality of its divine object and exemplar, the "flow of being" among the divine persons.[98]

The superabundant, immanent activity of the divine essence overflows into a third "flow of being," the procession of creatures from God. This flow is "extrafusus, nec introfusus... non immanens, sed transiens, qui consideratur ut extrafluxus, non ut influxus... temporalis

---

[96] Ibid. (230B-231B').

[97] Denys, *Elementatio theologica* prop. 20 (*Op. om.* 33: 128B-D); cf., *De contemplatione* 1 a.27 (*Op. om.* 41: 167B-168D). On Thomas' teaching concerning the intellectual generation of the Son, and its relation to the question of the soul's beatitude, see Wéber, "Eckhart et l'ontothéologisme," 40-54.

[98] Concerning this conceptual distinction in Thomas Aquinas, see Paul Vignaux, "Pour situer dans l'école une question de maître Eckhart: Interrogations et suggestions sur 'être', 'connaître' et 'vouloir' en Dieu," in *Maître Eckhart à Paris*, 141-54.

est, non aeternus." Denys discovers this flow *ad extra* in images from the book of
Ecclesiasticus. "Wisdom pours out in streams" (24:40), that is, God the Father created all
things through the Son, the Wisdom of God, the image of the invisible God, the firstborn of
every creature, in whom all things exist as one (Colossians 1:15-16; Proverbs 8:30). So the
being of creatures derives from the Father's knowledge of them in the divine Word, their
exemplar.[99] From the hidden wellspring (*alveus*) of the divine river flows a mighty
waterway (*trames aquae immensae*; Ecclesiasticus 24:41):

> Unde sicut trames a fluvio derivatur, ita temporalis processus creaturarum ab aeterno
> processu personarum. Semper enim id quod est primum, est causa eorum quae
> sequuntur, secundum Philosophum. Itaque fluxus seu processus primus, est causa et
> ratio processionis sequentis. Procedit etiam trames extra alveum fluminis, quia
> creatura extra divinam essentiae unitatem a Deo procedit, in qua personarum fluxus
> continetur sicut in alveo.[100]

Denys' metaphors are not only philosophic and mystical, but rhetorical as well. Through
his creating Word, God's goodness pours out on creatures in the same way that streams of
eloquence pour forth from the *copia rerum et verborum* stored up in the wise orator's
"treasurechest" (*thesaurus*) of invented matter (see n. 95 above).[101] This analogy between
the abundance of being flowing forth from the divine wellspring and the abundance of
concepts and words flowing forth from the orator's treasurechest of invented matter is the
governing metaphor of Wessel Gansfort's art of meditation.[102] Denys advises that one
should not despair if the "exercises of meditation and recollection" seem difficult at first, for
all arts are full of difficulties, but when by long practice they are acquired, they become easy.
Meditation then becomes second nature, as Jean Gerson teaches: "When he handed over the
precepts of eloquence, Cicero said that if one does not exercise them, he will scarcely
advance in the art, or will not advance at all; how much more should one observe the
precepts of praying to God." If one meditates continually, Gerson adds, everything he sees
or hears will become matter for his prayer. When he sees a swineherd, for example, he will
remember the parable of the prodigal son and his merciful father; when he sees an ulcerous
beggar, he will remember the parable of Lazarus and the rich man; when he sees the

---

[99] See Denys, *De contemplatione* 1 a.27 (*Op. om.* 41: 167D-A'): "Denique, quoniam Pater unico actu
intelligendi, se ipsum et cetera universa plenissime atque clarissime intelligit, hinc unico verbo se ipsum et cetera
omnia profert, ita quod tota Patris natura, excellentia seu majestas atque perfectio, in hoc unico suo Verbo aeterno
plene omnino continetur, repraesentatur, resplendet. Propterea Verbum hoc non jam dumtaxet est perfecta ac naturalis
imago Dei Patris, sed exemplar quoque ac ratio omnis entis creati."

[100] *Contra detestabilem* a.19 (*Op. om.* 40: 231C'-D').

[101] For *copia*, see Cicero, *De oratore* 1.12.50 and 3.31.25, *Brutus* 11.44, *Topica* 18.67 (in vol. 2 of *Rhetorica*,
ed. Wilkins); Quintilian, *Inst.* 1.8.17, 4.2.117, 7.1, 11.3.56, 12.4.1 (ed. Winterbottom, 57, 117, 222, 365, 664,
710). For *thesaurus*, see Quintilian, *Inst.* 11.2.1-2 (642). For *flumen orationis, flumen verborum*, see Cicero, *De
oratore* 2.45.188 and 3.15.62, *Orator* 16.52-53 (ed. Wilkins); Quintilian, *Inst.* 10.1.78 (583), and 10.1.61 (579):
"beatissima rerum uerborumque copia et uelut quodam eloquentiae flumine."

[102] This theme runs throughout Gansfort's *Scala meditationis*; see especially 1.7 and 1.19 ("Quod sicut in
oratione, sic et in opere nostro, semper finis constitutus attendendus est, ut digne exerceamur"), in *M. Wesseli
Ganfortii Gronigensis... Opera*, ed. (Groningen, 1614), 579, 583.

consolations received by the children of this world, he will meditate on the consolation that God has prepared for those who love him. "So your meditation will run through all things, and you will find everywhere most ample and ever-present material for your prayer."[103]

Denys'anagogic *pali* and abstract "discourses" may seem far removed from liturgical prayer, unless one recall Cassian's saying that in the time of prayer the mind must be formed by thoughts upon which it has previously dwelt. Because of human weakness, in vocal prayer and chanting one is seldom able to attend "actually" to everything he says or sings. The power of one's first intention, however, will render his prayer meritorious, although not as meritorious as if his attention were "always in act." Disciplined meditation outside vocal prayer serves both its intention and act. When before prayer one's mind is occupied with illicit intentions, as soon as one comes to choir, the images and "unclean species of corporeal things" he recently cogitated will erupt in his mind, obstruct his prayer, and render divine praise inefficacious.[104] Finally, the habit of abstract meditation is not contrary to vocal prayer, because the *oratio mentalis* is much more rapid than the voice.

In the latter articles of his treatise, Denys offers more popular techniques of meditation that are immediately applicable to the recitation of the liturgy. Adapting a motif from *De rhetorica divina* by William of Auvergne, he recommends an image easily remembered in choir: the golden altar of Apocalypse 8:3. This image properly signifies Christ's propitiatory sacrifice. Around this prop one should gather all of the objects of Christ's Incarnation and Passion; to this fixed stake he should bind all of his thoughts and affections; from this treasurechest he may withdraw the distinct articles of Christ's life and death, and apply them one-by-one to single nocturns, hours or psalms.[105] (Assigning stations of the Passion to each liturgical hour of the day was a common device in Books of Hours.) Several techniques accomodate meditation on the single verses of the psalms. While reciting them, one may imagine oneself in the heavenly company before the throne of God, attributing each verse to a different saint. Denys says that these should follow the order of saintly dignity or some personal order (I presume he means the generic order of the Litany, or the order of one's patrons).[106] Moreover, in reciting the psalms one may use the *ars digitorum*, which enlists the senses of sight and touch in the service of memory. By means of this art, one may localize points to be remembered on each of the joints, sections and tips of the four fingers of the left hand. By pressing the thumb at the right place, one can recall the point attached there. This technique, which "leads one by the hand to God," may be used in conjunction with the alphabet. Guided by the first letters of the psalm verses, one may direct superlative

---

[103] *Contra detestabilem* aa.29,31 (*Op. om.* 40: 255C-D, 258A'-D'); Jean Gerson, *De modo orandi* (Lettre-traité à son frère Jean, Prieur des Célestins de Lyon), in vol. 2 of *Oeuvres complètes*, ed. P. Glorieux (Paris, 1960), 173-74.

[104] *Contra detestabilem* a.23 (*Op. om.* 40: 243B'-D').

[105] *Contra detestabilem* a.24 (*Op. om.* 40: 246A'-248D); *Rethorica divina de oratione domini Guilermi Parisiensis* (Freiburg: Kilian Fischer, 1490-91), chap. 42, f. 45v^{a-b}.

[106] *Contra detestabilem* a.25 (*Op. om.* 40: 248A'-249D').

aspirations to God. If a verse begins with the letter D, for example, one might praise God as *Dulcissimus* or *Dilectissimus*, and so on. Or one might pray for a virtue corresponding to the first letter, or likewise invoke the name of a saint.[107] Denys probably read about the alphabetic, digital art in the *Alphabetum divini amoris*, variously and wrongly attributed to Jean Gerson, the Dominican John Nider (1380-1438), and the Carthusian Nicholas Kempf (†1497); the work seems to have been composed by a Carthusian, perhaps by John Egen of Würzburg. In any event, the author states that the digital art is practiced especially by Carthusians, who are accustomed to constitute the whole Psalter on their hands, reciting the psalms as if playing a cithern.[108] The art is presented with elaborate diagrams in the *Directorium solvendarum horarum per Chiropsalterium* by Jan Mombaer. Mombaer invests the hand with a storehouse of topics for meditation, organized by techniques of rhetorical invention and indexed alphabetically.[109]

In the end, Denys says, "the most fruitful manner of reciting the psalms is to attend to their sense, drawing all that is heard or read into affection, by which the heart is vehemently inflamed with the love of God." In divine praise, one's mind should agree with one's voice.[110] Happily, Carthusian custom prescribes a measured, deliberate, and unison recitation of the Offices, careful of points and pauses, that allows for sustained meditation and reflection. (The Order prescribed that liturgical books be carefully emended and punctuated, respectful of regional differences of pronunciation, to assure uniform recitation.)[111] For recollecting the proper attitude, Denys suggests a mnemonic verse:

> Quum Domino psallis, psallendo bis tria serves:
> Dirige cor sursum, profer bene, respice sensum;
> Sit mens sublimis, pes junctus, visus in imis.
> Dicas attente, dic totum supplici mente.
> Syncopa vitetur, versus non anticipetur,
> Donec finitus omnino sit bene primus....[112]

Perfected human souls rise to ranks equal with the angels in the celestial hierarchy. Carthusian life, which virtually contains all perfection within it, and teaches one to bury the flesh, to walk in the Spirit, to flee company and dwell in silence, is already an angelic status

---

[107] Ibid. a.26 (*Op. om.* 40: 250A-251D').

[108] The *Alphabetum* is printed in vol. 3 of *Joannis Gersonii Opera omnia*, ed. E. Du Pin (Antwerp, 1706), 770-99; see chap. 13, 788-91. On the date (1430s) and authorship, see Dennis D. Martin, *Fifteenth-Century Carthusian Reform: The World of Nicholas Kempf* (Leiden/New York, 1992), 306-7. Theodorus Petreius, *Bibliotheca Carthusiana, sive Illustrium sacri Cartusiensis ordinis scriptorum Catalogus* (Cologne, 1609; reprt. Farnborough, Hants, 1968), 162, attributes the work to John Egen of Würzburg.

[109] Mombaer, *Rosetum* (1510), Titulus V, Alphabetum XVIII-XIX; Debongnie, 172-81.

[110] *Contra detestabilem* Prooemium, a.26 (*Op. om.* 40: 193, 251B'-C').

[111] Mary A. Rouse and Richard H. Rouse, "Correction and Emendation of Texts in the Fifteenth Century and the Autograph of the *Opus pacis* of 'Oswaldus Anglicus'," in *Authentic Witnesses*, 427-47.

[112] *Contra detestabilem* a.23 (*Op. om.* 40: 245D'-246D). For the verse, see Hans Walther, *Initia carminum ac versuum medii aevi posterioris latinorum* (Göttingen, 1969), n° 3596.

of life. Like a well-composed art it provides a "direct, compendious pathway" to its end, the heavenly kingdom.[113] In a long passage that he excerpts from Henry Suso's *Horologium sapientiae*, Denys discovers a "succinct, most salutary formula" of perfection, which teaches how we can assiduously abstract and segregate our thoughts and affections from all created things. Wisdom tells her Disciple that one who seeks purity of heart should withdraw completely from the company of men and seize every occasion of solitude, which keeps one from excessive contact with sensible, worldly images.[114] Where better can one direct his life towards this *scopos*, purity of heart, than in the silence of the Charterhouse? External silence, however, is vain unless it gives birth to internal silence. As a "venerable father of our Order" teaches, in such silence God operates his most most noble work, creating in the soul the similitude of his divine simplicity. In internal silence one also becomes most like the invisible holy angels. Denys urges his soul to rest in internal silence with God, who is most pleased when the soul becomes "inactive (*otiosa*), naked, pure, and cleansed from every vice and phantasm," when it cogitates nothing and when it considers nothing.[115]

Denys the Carthusian's first treatise, *Contra detestabilem cordis inordinationem*, reveals that he was gifted with--and beset by--an extravagant imagination. In the solitude of the Charterhouse, he needed to struggle relentlessly against his wandering mind. Thomas Aquinas' doctrine concerning the necessary recourse to phantasms in every act of knowledge seems to have had pointed meaning for Denys. He combatted phantasms with phantasms, engaging in a program of voracious reading and restless writing, which focused his attention on every item, one after the other, in the universe of philosophic, theological and pious discourse. Wisdom's Disciple complains that life is short, and thousands are the books treating religious life, the vices and the virtues, and subtle questions. Denys' art was long; he read and wrote hundreds of such books. He gathered from the the books he read, and recorded in the books he wrote, abundant, life-giving images and discourses that fixed his mind on anagogic realities. Speaking of Denys and his works, Theodorus Petreius defines a fivefold activity of the monk: reading, *writing*, meditating, praying, contemplating.[116] In the very act of writing, whereby he digested, redisposed and localized what he read, Denys was able to practice an art of continuous meditation. From the start, however, he knew that all of his mental and written words were wholly inadequate to their divine object. "So delightful are the joys and so abundant are the goods in God, the ever-abiding, living and inexhaustible source (*fons*), and in his saints, who are inebriated by a torrent of enjoyment," Denys exclaims, "that if all intellectual creatures, and all rational souls ever created or to be

---

[113] *Contra detestabilem* a.23 (*Op. om.* 40: 243B-C). For the medieval notion of the art of dialectic as a "compendious pathway," see Neal Ward Gilbert, *Renaissance Concepts of Method* (New York, 1960), 55-58.

[114] *Contra detestabilem* a.28 (*Op. om.* 40: 253D-255B). The whole article is excerpted from *Heinrich Seuses Horologium sapientiae* 2.3, ed. Pius Künzle, O.P. (Spicelegium Friburgense 23: Freiburg Schweiz, 1977), 540-45.

[115] *Contra detestabilem* a.30 (*Op. om.* 40: 257D-258A). I have not identified the Carthusian author whose text on internal silence Denys quotes.

[116] Theodorus Petrius, *Bibliotheca Carthusiana*, 50.

created, were to have all of the fountains, rivers and oceans of the world as ink, and all of the heavens, multiplied by the number of intellectual spirits dwelling in them, as (sheets of) parchment, all of the oceans and rivers would run dry, and all of the heavens would be filled with letters, before even a small portion of the divine goodness and its joys contained in the plenitude of the fontal principle of divine light, existing there always in act, abounding within him and gushing forth beyond him, could ever be written down."[117]

---

[117] *Contra detestabilem* a.19 (*Op. om.* 40: 228C'-D').

V

FONDEMENTS THÉORIQUES DE LA RÉCEPTION DE LA BEAUTÉ SENSIBLE DANS LES ÉCRITS DE DENYS LE CHARTREUX (1402-1471)

Dans sa lettre aux frères cartusiens de Mont-Dieu[1], Guillaume de Saint-Thierry évoque brièvement la question de l'utilisation de la beauté artistique dans la vie érémitique. Ses arguments et ses exhortations font appel aux plus anciens thèmes de la tradition monastique. Le monastère est la cité de refuge pour qui cherche la simplicité. C'est au cœur de cette cité que l'on doit progresser de la condition d'homme-animal, dans laquelle nous sommes tous tombés par le péché, à la condition d'homme spirituel. Le cheminement, depuis la préoccupation des réalités extérieures jusqu'à la simplicité intérieure de l'esprit, correspond au pèlerinage de l'homme sur terre vers la demeure éternelle du Père. En règle générale, l'homme absorbé par les réalités intérieures méprisera et dédaignera les choses extérieures, tout comme les pèlerins de ce monde ou les soldats de la terre (Jb 7,1) ne construiront pas de maisons afin de s'y établir, mais habiteront dans des tentes qu'ils pourront abandonner d'un instant à l'autre[2]. Le moine est un nomade spirituel et son cadre privilégié le désert ou les régions incultes, plutôt qu'un jardin agréable et cultivé.

A la lumière de ces images, les préceptes de Guillaume, concernant la beauté sensible en général, et l'ornement artistique en particulier, vont presque de soi. Le moine doit se préoccuper de la beauté de l'âme, ce temple qui ne fut pas construit par les mains de l'homme. Les moines, qui font bâtir par les mains d'artisans

---

1. GUILLAUME DE SAINT-THIERRY, *Lettres aux frères du Mont-Dieu (Lettre d'or)*, éd. et trad. fr. par J. DÉCHANET, o.s.b., « Sources chrétiennes », 223, Paris, 1975.
2. *Ibid.*, 1, 147-50, p. 258-263.

V

habiles, des églises et des cellules qui sont de nature aromatique plutôt qu'érémitique, abandonnent l'exemple de la sainte simplicité que leurs pères leur ont transmis[3]. L'esprit préoccupé par les réalités intérieures, en vérité la seule et unique chose nécessaire, ne doit pas être distrait par des décorations superflues. Le cadre extérieur doit être en harmonie avec la préoccupation intérieure, c'est-à-dire qu'il doit être empreint de simplicité[4]. Les œuvres d'art peuvent retarder ou corrompre le progrès de la vie monastique, car l'attention portée à la beauté sensible « ralentit la détermination qui est propre à l'homme, et tend à efféminer l'esprit masculin[5] ». En résumé, quiconque s'attache à la beauté sensible redescend de l'état d'homme spirituel à l'état d'homme-animal, des sens intérieurs aux sens extérieurs, et confie l'ordre de sa maison intérieure à une « femme acariâtre » (Pr 21, 9 ; 25, 24), sa chair[6].

Guillaume concède, bien entendu, que certains peuvent user de tels choses, comme s'ils n'en usaient pas (1 Co 7, 31)[7]. Les choses qui sont belles dans leur propre ordre peuvent être employées à bon ou à mauvais escient. Ainsi les hommes spirituels savent tirer parti de la connaissance du monde visible et des arts, tels que l'éloquence, les lettres, la peinture et l'architecture ; ceux qui sont sous l'empire des sens feront un mauvais emploi de ces mêmes choses, pour satisfaire leur curiosité, leur plaisir et leur fierté[8]. Cependant, la prudence ascétique, qui tient compte de la condition affaiblie de l'homme et qui ne perd jamais de vue l'aboutissement, comprend que c'est « par le mépris, plutôt que par l'usage, que l'on parvient à extirper de tels attachements[9] ».

Trois siècles plus tard, le moine chartreux, Denys de Ryckel (1402-1471), acclamait les enseignements spirituels de cette « épître d'or » qui, pensait-il, avait été composée par Bernard de Clairvaux[10]. On ne peut concevoir que Denys qui, comme le déclare Huizinga, s'adonnait à un « ascétisme féroce » et qui prêchait sans cesse le mépris de ce monde[11] ait trouvé quoi que ce soit d'exceptionnel dans les paroles de Guillaume. Toutefois, Denys était prêt à encourager le bon emploi de la beauté sensible parmi ses frères cartusiens ; en effet, la recherche de l'attrait de la beauté est pour lui essentielle à la vie contemplative qui définit la vocation cartusienne. Je ne veux pas impliquer par là que les ensei-

3. *Ibid.*
4. *Ibid.*, 1, 153-54, p. 264-265.
5. *Ibid.*, 1, 152, p. 262-265.
6. *Ibid.*, 1, 138, p. 250-253.
7. *Ibid.*, 1, 153, p. 264-265.
8. *Ibid.*, 1, 58-59, p. 190-193.
9. *Ibid.*, 1, 152, p. 262-265.
10. Nous nous référons toujours à l'édition : *D. Dionysii Cartusiani Opera omnia*, Tournai, Montreuil, Parkminster, 1896-1913, 1935 (= *Op. om.*). Voir *De contemplatione*, 2-4, dans vol. XLI, p. 236-241.
11. J. HUIZINGA, *The Waning of the Middle Ages*, Garden City, NJ, 1954, p. 18.

gnements de Denys aient influencé directement les attitudes cartusiennes vis-à-vis de la beauté sensible ou artistique ; au contraire, tout semble démontrer que, dans ses préoccupations théoriques, il a été un cas unique dans l'Ordre[12]. Par ailleurs, les écrits de Denys présentent une vision exaltée de la beauté sensible, entièrement compatible avec le traditionnel ascétisme de son ordre ; bien qu'il n'aborde pas directement la question, Denys admet, par implication, qu'on puisse utiliser à bon escient la beauté artistique dans la vie érémitique.

Par rapport à Guillaume de Saint-Thierry, ce qui diffère dans les réflexions de Denys sur la beauté, c'est l'apprentissage scolastique et l'autorité du pseudo-Denys l'Aréopagite. Les deux ont un rapport. *Les Noms divins* du pseudo-Denys, qui traitent de questions fondamentales concernant les prédications sur Dieu, deviennent un texte méthodologique important chez les théologiens dans les écoles[13]. Le chapitre quatre de son œuvre, qui traite du nom de beauté, a fourni la base de la plupart des réflexions scolastiques sur le sujet[14]. Le pseudo-Denys est le « maître parmi les maîtres » pour Denys[15] ; les écrits de Denys sur la beauté sont, pour la plupart, une méditation élargie sur le chapitre quatre des *Noms divins*, dans laquelle il cite l'ancienne autorité de saint Augustin (plus particulièrement *De civitate Dei*) et la pensée des scolastiques qui se sont intéressés tout particulièrement au sujet de la beauté : Alexandre de Halès, Albert le Grand, Thomas d'Aquin et Ulric de Strasbourg[16]. Les divers enseignements recueillis des uns et des autres se rejoignent dans les écrits de Denys « comme les rivières d'un continent confluent dans l'estuaire », pour reprendre les mots de Huizinga[17]. L'art de Denys consiste

---

12. K. EMERY, Jr., « Twofold Wisdom and Contemplation in Denys of Ryckel (Dionysius Cartusiensis, 1402-1471) », *Journal of Medieval and Renaissance Studies* 18, 1988, p. 99-134.

13. H.F. DONDAINE, o.p., *Le Corpus dionysien de l'université de Paris au XIII*e *siècle*, Rome, 1952.

14. E. DE BRUYNE, *Etudes d'esthétique médiévale, III, le XIII*e *siècle*, Bruges, 1946, *passim*.

15. K. EMERY, Jr., « Twofold Wisdom », art. cité, p. 102-103.

16. HUGUES DE SAINT-VICTOR, *De operibus trium dierum (Didascalicon 7)*, PL 176 ; p. 811-838 ; ALEXANDRE DE HALES (aussi JEAN DE LA ROCHELLE et « CONSIDERANS »), « De creatura secundum qualitatem seu de pulchritudine creati, » *Summa theologica,*, II, notes 75-85, Ed. Quaracchi, 1928, p. 99-108 ; ALBERT LE GRAND, *Super Dionysium De divinis nominibus*, IV, notes 71-94, P. SIMON éd., Münster, 1972, p. 180-197 ; ULRIC DE STRASBOURG, *De summo bono*, II, tr. 3, IV, A. De Libera éd., *Corpus Philosophorum Teutonicorum Medii Aevi* 1.2 (1), Hambourg, 1987, p. 54-63. Pour les textes de THOMAS D'AQUIN, voir E. DE BRUYNE, *Études, III*, p. 278-346.

17. J. HUIZINGA, *op. cit.*, p. 189. Sur Denys le Chartreux et la beauté, voir O. ZÖCKLER, « Dionys des Kartäusers Schrift De venustate mundi », *Theologische Studien und Kritiken* 54, 1881, p. 636-665 ; A. RÖSLER, « Die Schrift des Kartäusers Dionysius De venustate mundi et pulchritudine Dei und der Schönheitsbegriff der Gegenwort », *Historischpolitisch Blatter für das katholische Deutschland* 149, 1912, p. 505-522 ; E. DE BRUYNE, *Geschiedenis van de Aesthetica de Middeleeuwen*, vol. 4, Anvers-Amsterdam, 1955, p. 470-483 ; R. ASSUNTO, *Die Theorie des Schönen im Mittelalter*, Cologne, 1963, p. 118-119, 191-193 ; J. MÖLLERFELD, s.j., « Die Schönheit des Menschen nach Dionys dem Kartäuser, » *Dr. L. Reypens Album*, dir. A. Ampe, Anvers, 1964, p. 229-240.

V

à réduire différentes autorités et divers entendements en consonance et en harmonie, et non pas en de nouvelles conceptions ;
mais si chacune des parties est familière, la beauté de l'ensemble
(*forma totius*)[18] est souvent unique.
   Guillaume de Saint-Thierry parle en même temps de l'utilisation de la connaissance du monde naturel et de la beauté artistique. Le premier principe enseigné par le pseudo-Denys est que la
beauté peut être convertie en termes d'être et de vérité. D'après
ce principe, la question concernant l'utilisation de la beauté sensible est la même que celle de l'utilisation de la connaissance naturelle ou philosophique. Généralement, à la fin du Moyen Age, les
moines chartreux se défiaient du recours à l'apprentissage scolastique, autant que Guillaume de Saint-Thierry se défiait du recours
à la beauté artistique[19]. De plus, bien que le pseudo-Denys fût
une autorité prééminente parmi les écrivains cartusiens de la fin
du Moyen Age, c'était sa *Théologie mystique* et non pas les *Noms
divins* qu'ils lisaient. Qui plus est, ils interprétaient la *Théologie
mystique* de façon à faire une comparaison affligeante entre la
théologie mystique et la théologie scolastique[20].
   En 1451, Denys accompagna le cardinal Nicolas de Cues durant
une partie de sa légation pontificale à travers les deux États
allemands[21]. A son retour, au cours des quelques années qui sui-
virent, il composa une suite de traités philosophiques, chacun
d'entre eux contenant une apologie implicite de son recours à
l'apprentissage scolastique[22]. Parmi ceux-ci, on trouve le *De
natura aeterni et veri Dei*, où, pour la première fois, il traite de
façon synthétique du sujet de la beauté[23]. Il composa cet ouvrage
aux environs de 1452, peu de temps avant le *De venustate mundi
et pulchritudine Dei*. Le premier traité est, pour ainsi dire, un commentaire sur les *Noms divins*[24] ; parmi les nombreux attributs
divins, Denys se penche sur la beauté de Dieu, qui est le fonde-
ment de toute beauté créée. Dans le second traité, Denys se penche non seulement sur la beauté divine, mais également sur la
beauté de l'ordre créé dans toute son immensité, depuis la matière
première presque inexistante, jusqu'à l'acte suprême de l'intelligence angélique.
   La rédaction du *De natura aeterni et veri Dei* est un acte d'ami-

---

18. DENYS LE CHARTREUX, *De venustate mundi et pulchritudine Dei*, a. 7, in *Op. om.*,
XXXIV, p. 233B-D.
   19. K. EMERY, Jr., « Twofold Wisdom », art. cité, p. 105-107, 128-130.
   20. *Ibid.*
   21. J. KOCH, *Nikolaus von Cues und seine Umwelt*, Heidelberg, 1948, p. 111-152 ;
D. SULLIVAN, « Nicholas of Cusa as Reformer : The Papel Legation to the Germanies,
1451-1452 », *Mediaeval Studies* 36, 1974, p. 383-428.
   22. K. EMERY, Jr., « Twofold Wisdom », art. cité, p. 107-110.
   23. DENYS LE CHARTREUX, *De natura veri et aeterni Dei*, in *Op. om.*, XXXIV, p. 11-97.
   24. Voir aussi, DENYS LE CHARTREUX, *Comm. in librum De divinis nominibus*, IV, a.
32-34, in *Op. om.*, XVI, p. 133-137.

tié spirituelle. Denys adresse son ouvrage à un confrère chartreux, qu'il appelle « *mi frater carissime, et in visceribus sincerissime caritatis unice praedilecte, atque super millia auri et argenti semper cordialissime praeamande*[25] ». En écrivant son ouvrage pour cet ami plus cher que tout autre, Denys, *parvus Dionysius*, imite « le divin et grand Denys », qui écrivait ses livres pour son cher Timothée. De plus, du fait qu'il connaît si bien l'esprit de son ami, son exercice spirituel et son affection, il peut être certain que ce qu'il écrit sera compris correctement[26].

Denys semble s'attacher, de manière presque excessive, à expliquer l'intention de son ouvrage ; l'explication, en fait, englobe les trois premiers articles. L'intention de l'ouvrage, déclare-t-il, est de découvrir la nature de Dieu, pas de n'importe quelle manière, mais à la manière de la raison naturelle. Cette procédure, employée par les anciens philosophes, s'élève des choses visibles de ce monde à une connaissance de la nature invisible de Dieu (Rm 19). Au cas où de telles réflexions pouvaient paraître pauvres, Denys les étaye par l'autorité de l'Écriture et des docteurs de l'Église catholique[27]. Les avantages que procure cet effort sont multiples. D'une part, nul ne parviendra à la vision béatifique, s'il n'adhère pas au bien suprême de cette vie, avec un amour plus fervent que celui de toutes les créatures. Parce que la connaissance montre à l'esprit ce qu'il doit aimer, une connaissance naturelle de Dieu dans ce monde est utile, en ce sens qu'elle nous mène à l'amour de Dieu. Par « connaissance naturelle », Denys entend ce que l'on peut obtenir d'une étude des créatures dans le monde naturel. Puisque les créatures sont des similitudes qui participent du Créateur, quiconque est doté de la connaissance naturelle tendra plus facilement à la contemplation de Dieu. C'est pour cette raison que les autorités monastiques que sont saint Cyril et saint Antoine approuvaient une telle connaissance[28].

En outre, la recherche de la connaissance naturelle de Dieu est tout particulièrement appropriée à la vocation cartusienne. Elle crée une habitude de l'âme, en fait une experte des choses spirituelles ; et ainsi, à tout instant, au milieu d'une tâche, quelle qu'elle soit, l'âme peut conduire le cœur vers Dieu et contempler la nature divine, tandis qu'elle transparaît à nos yeux dans les multiples choses de la Création[29]. De surcroît, le désir même de connaissance encourage une rigoureuse purification morale, car, comme le penseur monastique Jean Cassien nous l'enseigne, « *scientia ethica*

---

25. DENYS LE CHARTREUX, *De natura...*, *op. cit*, a. 3, p. 15A'-B'.
26. *Ibid.*, p. 15B'-C'.
27. *Ibid.*, a. 1, p. 13A-C'.
28. *Ibid.*, a. 2, p. 14A-A'.
29. *Ibid.*, p. 14A'-B'.

seu moralis » précède nécessairement « *scientia theorica seu contemplativa*[30] ».

Denys termine son argumentation par une autorité on ne peut plus concluante Jan Van Ruysbroek, qu'il appelle, dans un autre passage, « *alter Dyonisius* »[31]. Van Ruysbroek jouissait d'une grande autorité chez les fervents dévots, ceux qui étaient les plus susceptibles de se défier de l'intention de Denys. En s'adressant aux pieux au sein de son propre ordre, Denys répond aux dévots modernes et à ceux qui, comme Guillaume de Saint-Thierry, affirment douter de l'utilité de la connaissance du monde naturel. En dépit de son utilité manifeste, Denys reconnaît que de nombreuses personnes religieuses et dévotes, bien qu'ayant l'esprit vif, se soustraient au désir de la connaissance naturelle des choses divines, parce qu'elles constatent que nombre de ceux qui excellent dans une telle connaissance sont vaniteux, bouffis d'orgueil, remplis de vices, et de fervents adeptes de ce monde[32]. De telles personnes pieuses ne devraient pas s'en prendre à la connaissance, mais plutôt aux abus des « connaisseurs » ; elles devraient cultiver le savoir qui, comme le dit saint Augustin, contribue grandement à la charité[33].

Denys examine la beauté divine dans *De natura*, immédiatement après avoir étudié Dieu-Lumière ; autrement dit, sa discussion sur les attributs de Dieu, suit l'ordre des *Noms divins* du pseudo-Denys. La méthode de Denys, en accord avec son intention de s'élever jusqu'à l'invisible par le visible, est d'appliquer une série de définitions classiques de la beauté sensible à la beauté de Dieu. « La beauté des choses visibles est faite de deux qualités, à savoir d'un juste rapport ou d'une proportion agréable des parties entre elles et avec l'ensemble, et d'une suffusion appropriée de couleur et de lumière, informant ou décorant les parties du corps » (saint Augustin)[34]. Or les substances spirituelles ne comportent pas de parties ; elles ne sont pas non plus colorées ou infusées par la lumière sensible. Par analogie, cependant, ce qui fait la beauté des substances spirituelles, c'est la justesse et l'harmonie de leurs actes par rapport à leur essence, et leur cognition intellectuelle, qui illumine et embellit leurs opérations, tout comme la lumière sensible ou une couleur splendide illumine et embellit les mem-

---

30. *Ibid.*, p. 14D'-15B.
31. K. EMERY, Jr., « Twofold Wisdom », art. cité, p. 131-134.
32. K. EMERY. Jr., « Lovers of the World and Lovers of God and Neighbor : Spiritual Commonplaces and the Problem of Authorship in the Fifteenth Century », *Historia et Spiritualitas Cartusiensis Colloquii Quarti Internationalis Acta*, dir. J. De Grauwe, Destelbergen, 1983, p. 177-219.
33. DENYS LE CHARTREUX, *De natura...*, *op. cit.*, a. 3, p. 15D'-A'.
34. *Ibid.*, a. 57, p. 90B : « *Rerum praeterea visibilium pulchritudo in duobus consistit, videlicet, in debita habitudine seu convenienti proportione partium inter se et ad totum, et item in congrua superfusione coloris aut luminis partes corporis informantis ac decorantis.* » Voir CICERON, *Tusculanae disputationes*, 4, 13 et AUGUSTIN, *Epistola 3 ad Nebridium*.

bres d'un corps. La lumière, en effet, appartient plus proprement au domaine du spirituel plutôt qu'aux réalités sensibles[35]. Selon ce critère de la beauté, il apparaît clairement que Dieu est « *pulcher et vere pulcherrimus atque incomparabilis pulchritudinis* ». L'acte divin est *convenientissima*, co-naturel et consubstantiel avec l'essence divine ; l'intellect divin est la lumière inaccessible même, qui se fait intuition en elle-même et en toutes choses avec « une infinie limpidité et une sincérité invariable[36] ».

D'autres affirment qu'on qualifie de beau tout ce qui est plus lucide et plus pur[37]. Parce qu'il a déjà été établi que Dieu est unité la plus simple, pureté absolue et lumière essentielle, ou plutôt d'immense pureté de la lumière infinie, il va de soi que Dieu est « *pulcher et superpulcher atque pulcherrimus* [...] *pulchritudo substantialiter pulchra, speciositas infinita*[38] ».

Les deux définitions de la beauté exprimées précédemment et appliquées à Dieu sont objectives, en ce sens qu'elles signifient des propriétés (une harmonie de parties, de splendeur et de couleur) intrinsèques des choses existantes. Une autre définition de la beauté que Denys emprunte à saint Thomas d'Aquin[39] renforce cette interprétation, la relation avec un sujet, avec celui qui contemple. La beauté est ce qui plaît à la vue (« *pulchrum vocatur quod visui placet* »). Parce que Dieu est la vérité originelle et la sagesse non créée, de qui découlent toute vérité, toute illumination et tout acte de connaissance (*cognitio*), il est évident qu'il plaît infiniment à la vue intérieure des créatures intellectuelles, plus que tout autre bien. Il est donc juste que nous louions Dieu comme *decorus et super pulcherrimus*. Dans la contemplation de Dieu par lui-même, les aspects objectifs et subjectifs de la beauté sont parfaitement résolus. Aucun esprit de la création ne peut connaître la bonté divine, pour autant qu'on puisse la connaître, ou y prendre plaisir, si tant est qu'on puisse y prendre plaisir ; seul l'esprit infini et divin peut connaître entièrement et jouir pleinement de la nature divine. La relation entre l'esprit divin et l'essence divine est infiniment belle ; Dieu se considère comme « *bonum superpulchrum et sicut pulchritudinem superessentialem* », et prend plaisir à lui-même avec un contentement infini[40].

L'application faite par Denys de cette dernière définition de la beauté (« *quod visui placet* ») est fondamentale au développement ultérieur du sujet dans le *De venustate mundi et pulchritudine Dei*. En premier lieu, elle situe résolument la beauté comme étant une caractéristique essentielle de la vie contemplative. En deuxième

35. DENIS LE CHARTREUX, *De natura, op. cit.*, a. 55, p. 86C'-89C.
36. *Ibid.*, a. 57, p. 90B-D.
37. ULRICH DE STRASBOURG, *De summo bono, op. cit.*, 3, 4, p. 55.
38. DENYS LE CHARTREUX, *De natura..., op. cit.*, a. 57, p. 90C'-D'.
39. E. DE BRUYNE, *Études, III*, p. 282.
40. DENYS LE CHARTREUX, *De natura..., op. cit.*, a. 57, p. 90D-B'.

lieu, l'argument développé par Denys annonce une vision spécifiquement chrétienne de la beauté. Dans le *De natura*, Denys expose seulement cette connaissance qui peut être obtenue par la raison, à partir des réalités de la Création. Son application de la définition classique de la beauté sensible à la nature divine engendre cependant la vision d'une essence qui a la connaissance et prend infiniment plaisir à elle-même. C'est la relation trinitaire dans l'essence divine, entièrement révélée dans l'Écriture, qui établit la beauté particulière de l'univers de la Création, en y imprégnant son image et sa trace.

Denys achève son discours sur la beauté dans le *De natura* par un résumé de l'enseignement du pseudo-Denys et une référence à saint Thomas d'Aquin, les deux nous préparant au *De venustate mundi*. Selon les paroles de Denys l'Aréopagite, le « prince des théologiens », la bonté divine doit être louée comme étant le beau (*pulchrum*) et la beauté (*pulchritudo*). Alors que les deux diffèrent dans les choses de la Création, en tant que effet et cause, ils sont identiques en Dieu. Dans les créatures, nous qualifions de beau tout ce qui participe à la beauté ; la beauté, toutefois, est elle-même une participation à Dieu, la beauté première qui embellit toute chose. Toute beauté, toute belle chose préxiste uniformément, et par un lien causal, dans la beauté simple et supersubstantielle. De cette beauté naissent les concordances, les amitiés et les unions entre toutes choses (à savoir l'harmonie et la consonance du monde, tant admirées par les philosophes). La beauté est la cause efficiente et finale de toute chose, car toute chose naît pour la beauté et la désire comme finalité. D'après cela, on peut déduire que beauté et bonté sont une seule et même chose. Par ailleurs, la beauté est la cause exemplaire de toute chose dans le Verbe, qui détermine tout dans son espèce[41].

Dans le *De venustate mundi*, Denys reprend les principes résumés ici, pour établir la nature de la beauté sensible. Avec pertinence, dans le *De natura aeterni et veri Dei*, il ne développe pas la relation entre la beauté et le Verbe, qui est un aspect purement théologique. Cependant, son allusion à cette relation indique une association entre la beauté et le pouvoir cognitif. Cette association est explicite dans une référence finale à saint Thomas d'Aquin. Le bien et le beau, explique saint Thomas, sont une seule et même chose *secundum rem*, mais distincts *secundum rationem*. Le bien se rapporte au pouvoir d'appétence, dans la mesure où toute chose le désire ; le beau se rapporte au pouvoir cognitif, car le beau est ce qui plaît à l'œil[42]. C'est par cette distinction, qui est fonda-

---

41. *Ibid.*, p. 91D-D' ; Pseudo-Denys l'Aréopagite, *De divinis nominibus*, iv, trad. lat. par Jean Scot Érigène, *D. Dionysii Cartusiani, Op. om.*, vol. XVI, p. 106-107.
42. Denys le Chartreux, *De natura...*, *op. cit.*, a. 57, p. 91D' ; Thomas d'Aquin, *ST*, 1, q. 5, a. 4 *ad* 1.

mentale dans sa conception de la vie contemplative et de l'union mystique, que Denys commence le *De venustate mundi*.

Le *prooemium* au *De venustate mundi* indique que la recherche de la beauté, lorsqu'elle est bien comprise, est la même chose que l'ascension au *summum bonum*. Denys évoque la double autorité du pseudo-Denys et de saint Augustin. Dieu, qui est à la fois bonté pure, immense et on ne peut plus causale, ainsi que beauté distincte, idéale, illimitée, et qui survit par elle-même, apaise et satisfait chaque geste et chaque désir de l'âme, qu'il soit intellectuel ou volitif. Nulle chose créée ne peut apaiser l'esprit créé ; seule la beauté exemplaire non créée et sa splendeur infinie peuvent satisfaire au désir de l'esprit. Ainsi saint Augustin, citant le grand platonicien, Plotin, nous dit : « La contemplation de Dieu est une vision d'une telle beauté, digne de tant d'amour, que, dépourvus de cette vision, tous les autres biens, quels qu'ils soient, doivent être méprisés[43]. »

Cet exorde sous-entend des définitions et des distinctions déjà établies dans le *De natura aeterni et veri Dei* et réitérées dans le premier article du *De venustate mundi*. La beauté peut être convertie en transcendantaux, l'unique, le vrai, le bien et l'être (« *bonum, verum, unum pulchrum cum ente* ») ; ainsi toutes les choses sont belles par le fait même qu'elles sont. Denys l'Aréopagite prétend que la beauté est la cause exemplaire de toute chose dans le Verbe ; par conséquent, chaque chose créée est belle, dans la mesure où elle imite proportionnellement sa raison idéale et sa forme exemplaire dans la lumière et la sagesse de l'esprit divin. Comme dans l'esprit divin, dans l'esprit humain, la beauté relève du pouvoir cognitif. Pour cette raison, certains définissent la beauté comme étant ce que toute chose regarde ou connaît (« *adspiciunt et cognoscunt* »), c'est-à-dire ce qui, par son existence réelle, est capable de déplacer ou d'attirer le regard (*intuitum*) ou le coup d'œil (*adspectum*) du connaisseur[44]. Cette définition est très vaste, en ce sens qu'elle établit le rapport entre la beauté intrinsèque d'un objet et celui qui le contemple. Elle renvoie à une définition similaire d'Alexandre de Halès qui, à son tour, appelle une distinction différente encore entre le bien, le beau et l'être. L'être d'une chose lui est attribué par rapport à la cause efficiente ; on affirmera qu'elle est bonne par rapport à la cause finale, qu'elle est belle par rapport à la cause exemplaire ou formelle[45]. La beauté doit être rattachée à la cause exemplaire, en rapport avec la cause efficiente et la cause finale ; à la sagesse divine, en regard de la puissance et de la bonté divines ; au *ratio intelligendi*, pour

---

43. DENYS LE CHARTREUX, *De venustate mundi...*, *op. cit.*, prooem., p. 223 ; AUGUSTIN, *De civitate Dei*, 10.
44. DENYS LE CHARTREUX, *De venustate mundi...*, *op. cit.*, a. 1 p. 227A-C'.
45. *Ibid.*, a. 2, p. 227C'-228B ; ALEXANDRE DE HALÈS, *Summa theologica*, *op. cit.*, n° 103, p. 162-163.

ce qui est de la *causa subsistendi* et de l'*ordo vivendi* ; à la vérité, en regard de l'unique et du bien ; et au pouvoir cognitif humain, en regard des facultés de l'âme. Dans le sillage d'Alexandre de Halès, Denys fait une autre distinction entre le beau et le vrai[46]. La vérité est cette disposition inhérente à une forme par rapport à l'appréciation de l'esprit qui la conçoit. On dit des formes artificielles qu'elles sont vraies, lorsqu'elles correspondent aux formes conçues par l'esprit de l'artiste qui les produit ; on dit des formes naturelles qu'elles sont vraies, lorsqu'elles imitent, dans leur être, la forme idéale conçue par l'esprit du créateur. La beauté, en outre, est la disposition d'une forme par rapport à son apparence extérieure, tandis qu'elle apparaît, agréable et splendide (*conveniens et ornatum*), devant l'œil qui connaît ou qui voit[47]. Cette distinction finale suggère l'argumentation élargie du traité de Denys. Dieu révèle sa propre beauté et confère de la beauté à ses créatures, précisément dans le but suivant : afin d'attirer à lui l'esprit contemplatif. Quiconque aspire au vrai, et par cela même au bien, le fera parce qu'il aura été séduit par le beau.

Une série de distinctions, que Denys recueille chez Ulrich de Strasbourg, parmi la beauté créée et non créée, essentielle et accidentelle, corporelle et spirituelle, définit l'ascension vers la beauté en elle-même[48]. En matière de beauté corporelle, Denys examine la beauté des éléments, leurs mélanges, les corps célestes, les corps inanimés, les plantes et les animaux[49]. D'un bout à l'autre, il a recours à la définition de saint Augustin, dont il fait usage dans le *De natura* : la beauté des corps consiste en un accord entre leurs parties, avec une certaine douceur des couleurs. Il ajoute à cela, toujours dans le sillage d'Albert le Grand, un troisième critère : la dimension élégante et appropriée[50]. La beauté corporelle suprême est le corps humain, si harmonieux dans ses proportions, une matière noble, digne de la forme noble qui la représente, ou l'âme humaine[51].

Comme dans le *De natura*, Denys définit la beauté des créatures spirituelles par analogie avec les critères de la beauté corporelle. Cette autre distinction entre la beauté essentielle et la beauté accidentelle a trait uniquement aux créatures spirituelles. La beauté essentielle d'une créature est sa participation naturelle et spécifique à la nature divine. De par sa nature, l'âme humaine embrasse les perfections des autres âmes (*esse, vegetare, sentire, movere*)

---

46. DENYS LE CHARTREUX, *De venustate mundi...*, *op. cit.*, a. 2, p. 228B-D'.
47. *Ibid.*, a. 3, p. 229C-D ; ALEXANDRE DE HALÈS, *Summa theologica, op. cit.*, II, n. 75, p. 99.
48. DENYS LE CHARTREUX, *De venustate mundi...*, *op. cit.*, a. 4, p. 229C'-230D' ; ULRIC DE STRASBOURG, *De summo bono, op. cit.*, 3, IV, p. 60-63.
49. DENYS LE CHARTREUX, *De venustate mundi...*, *op. cit.*, a. 5-6, p. 230B'-232A'.
50. *Ibid.*, a. 5, p. 230B'-D' ; sur Albert le Grand, voir E. DE BRUYNE, *Études, III, op. cit.*, p. 168.
51. DENYS LE CHARTREUX, *De venustate mundi...*, *op. cit.*, a. 14, p. 240A-241A.

V

et s'associe aux esprits angéliques des substances séparées ; de plus, c'est une image de la Trinité, un sceau de la lumière non créée, dotée d'une forme indestructible et ordonnée à la vision béatifique du Créateur[52]. De même, à un niveau supérieur, l'esprit angélique participe à la lumière infinie et à l'acte pur de Dieu. Les âmes humaines ont en commun avec les esprits angéliques une certaine égalité. Les deux procèdent directement du même principe effectif, et tous deux retournent au même objet de béatitude. Ainsi, bien que les esprits angéliques soient plus nobles que l'âme humaine, par leur forme et leur nature spécifique, ils ne le sont pas en ce qui concerne leur finalité. Dans ce sens, on peut accepter les mots de saint Augustin (et de Plotin), qui déclaraient que rien ne se situe au-dessus de la nature de l'âme, si ce n'est Dieu. Sinon, cet adage semble contredire les enseignements du pseudo-Denys dans ses hiérarchies ecclésiastiques et célestes[53].

La beauté essentielle des créatures spirituelles ne peut décroître ou s'accroître. Ainsi, le pseudo-Denys déclare que même les démons restent beaux dans leurs pouvoirs naturels[54]. Par le péché, cependant, les créatures spirituelles peuvent se départir de la beauté accidentelle, qu'elles peuvent acquérir par des actes vertueux et recevoir par la grâce. Tout comme la beauté corporelle est faite d'une bonne concordance des parties entre elles et d'une coloration appropriée, de même la beauté des créatures spirituelles est faite d'une coordination harmonieuse des vertus naturelles, des grâces, et des dons de l'esprit, des béatitudes, etc. En outre, puisque la beauté relève tout particulièrement du pouvoir cognitif, éminemment beaux sont les actes contemplatifs de l'intellect, qui ne sont rien d'autre que certaines *luciformes fulgores* illustrant l'esprit[55]. C'est en ces mêmes termes que Denys expose les beautés de la *sponsa universalis* (ou Église), de la *sponsa particularis* (ou âme rationnelle) et de la *sponsa singularis* (ou Vierge Marie) dans un commentaire ultérieur sur le Cantique des Cantiques[56].

La beauté transparaît dans chacune des parties de l'univers (*forma partis*), mais l'univers est particulièrement beau dans l'harmonie et l'ordre de l'ensemble (*forma totius*)[57]. Denys décrit cette beauté à travers des passages empruntés à Hugues et Richard de Saint-Victor[58]. La beauté de l'univers s'étend même à diverses formes du mal qui, dans leur dépossession, contribuent cependant

---

52. *Ibid.*, a. 15, p. 241A-A'.
53. *Ibid.* ; Augustin, *De civitate Dei*, 10, 2 ; K. Emery, Jr. « Twofold Wisdom », art. cité, p. 114-115.
54. Pseudo-Denys l'Aréopagite, *De divinis nominibus, op. cit.*, IV, p. 118.
55. Denys le Chartreux, *De venustate mundi..., op. cit.*, a. 17-18, p. 242D-244A ; Alexandre de Halès, *Summa theologica, op. cit.*, I, n° 103, p. 163.
56. Denys le Chartreux, *Enarratio in Canticum Canticorum* (après 1457), in *Op. om.*, VII, p. 311A-312B, 316B'-317A, 320D-B', 364B, 367B'-368C, 375B, 377B'-D', 380B-C', 382D-D', etc.
57. Denys le Chartreux, *De venustate mundi..., op. cit.*, a. 7, p. 233B-D.
58. *Ibid.*, a. 10, p. 235A'-236D' ; Hugues de Saint-Victor, *De operibus trium dierum*.

à la beauté de l'ensemble, de par le contraste qu'elles présentent, et à la matière première, presque inexistante en acte, mais qui participe, d'une certaine façon, à l'idée du bien et du beau[59].

Quelle que soit la beauté de l'univers dans l'ordre harmonieux de ses parties, sa grandeur et son illustration hiérarchique aux multiples couleurs, elle est plus nette encore dans sa relation formelle avec la beauté divine. Pour expliquer plus en détail cette relation, Denys s'appuie sur des matériaux qu'il a déjà rassemblés sous deux questions, dans son commentaire sur les *Sentences*[60]. Bien que la beauté, l'attribut propre de Dieu, soit commune à chacune des personnes de la Trinité, elle devrait, cependant, selon une formule de saint Hilaire de Poitiers, être attribuée au Fils, le Verbe éternel : « *Aeternitas est in patre, species in imagine, usus in munere* ». Le terme *species* équivaut aux termes de « beauté » et de « forme ». Pour cette raison, tout ce qui participe à la forme est qualifié de beau[61]. Les choses créées sont déclarées belles, à la fois par rapport à leur cause exemplaire extrinsèque, et du fait de leur cause formelle ou formatrice intrinsèque, à savoir « une certaine impression et une certaine similitude de la forme idéale, qui confère beauté (*speciem*) et grâce (*decor*) à l'être[62] ». La beauté du Verbe divin, ou de l'espèce divine, peut, de la même manière, être contemplée en elle-même et par rapport aux créatures. (Notons que la beauté d'une créature existe tout d'abord dans sa relation avec Dieu, et ensuite par elle-même, alors que la beauté du Verbe existe tout d'abord par elle-même, et ensuite dans sa relation avec les créatures.) Le raisonnement de Denys suit celui de saint Bonaventure, dont il rapporte plus en détail les arguments dans son commentaire sur les *Sentences*. Le Fils est la similitude même du Père, dont il procède à la manière d'un acte cognitif. En tant qu'acte cognitif du Père, le Verbe contient en lui-même l'exemplaire et la raison de toute chose. En tant que similitude parfaite et exacte, le Fils est beau par rapport à celui qui l'exprime ; parce qu'il est la raison exemplaire de tout l'univers, il est, selon les mots de Boèce, « *pulchrum pulcherrimus ipse mundum mente gerens* » (*Cons.*, 3, met. 9). Par rapport au Père, le Fils possède la beauté de parfaite égalité ; par rapport aux créatures, il est l'*ars Dei, mundus archetypus*, « l'art rempli de raisons vivantes[63] ».

---

59. DENYS LE CHARTREUX, *De venustate mundi...*, *op. cit.*, a. 8-9, 11, p. 233B'-235D, 237A. Voir aussi ALEXANDRE DE HALÈS, *Summa theologica, op. cit.*, II, n. 77-79, 82, p. 100-102, 104-105.
60. DENYS LE CHARTREUX, *I Sent.*, d.3, q.4, in *Op. om.*, XIX, p. 235D-246D : « *Qualiter Trinitas adoranda repraesentetur, reluceat et cognoscatur in creaturis per vestigium* » *I Sent.*, d. 31, q.1, *Op. om.* 20, p. 312A-325A' : « *An appropriatio Hilarii, utpote quod in Patre est aeternitas, in imagine (id est Filio) est species, in munere (id est Spiritu Sancto) est usus, extet conveniens.* »
61. DENYS LE CHARTREUX, *De venustate mundi...*, *op. cit.*, a. 1, p. 227B-A'.
62. *Ibid.*, a. 2 p. 228C-D.
63. DENYS LE CHARTREUX, *I Sent.*, d. 31, q. 1, p. 312C'-313B ; *De venustate-mundi...*, *op. cit.*, a. 23, p. 248D'-249B'.

L'emploi équivoque du terme « *species* », qui signifie à la fois « beauté, principe formel, et image intellectuelle », permet à Denys de définir la relation exacte entre la beauté divine et la beauté créée. Le beauté du monde, déclare saint Augustin, descend de la beauté originelle exemplaire. De même, Isidore de Séville affirme que Dieu entend que sa beauté illimitée soit comprise à travers la beauté limitée des créatures. D'après ces affirmations, Denys conclut que la beauté créée est une certaine empreinte (*vestigium*) par laquelle on peut, de manière cognitive, prendre conscience (*notitia*) de la beauté non créée. Dans ce sens, le terme *vestigium* signifie principalement le *modus, species et ordo* des choses créées. Selon Alexandre de Halès, la beauté du monde repose principalement sur ces trois aspects[64].

En ce qui concerne la beauté qui subsiste dans les vestiges du monde, Denys fait la synthèse des enseignements d'Alexandre de Halès, de Bonaventure, de Pierre de Tarantaise et de Richard de Middleton, qu'il a rapportés dans son commentaire sur les *Sentences*[65]. *Motus, species et ordo* sont présents en toutes choses, selon une triple disposition ou relation par rapport à leur cause. Selon leur manière (*modus*) d'être, les créatures sont liées à leur cause efficiente, car Dieu limite et modifie chaque créature pour lui donner un certain genre. Selon leur espèce ou leur beauté essentielle, distincte ou spécifiée, les créatures sont liées à leur cause formelle et exemplaire. Selon leur ordre, ou leur inclination pour leur propre bien, les créatures sont liées à leur cause finale. La triade de saint Augustin[66], qui fait autorité, correspond à une autre triade proclamée dans le livre de la Sagesse (11, 21) : « *Omnia in numero, et pondere, et mensura constituiti* ». Nombre correspond à espèce, *pondus* à ordre, mesure à la manière (*modus*) d'être. Le texte de la Sagesse admet plusieurs interprétations harmonieuses (donc belles). Dieu a créé le monde selon le nombre, c'est-à-dire qu'il a constitué les créatures selon certains principes essentiels (le genre, la différence) qui désignent leur beauté essentielle. Seul Dieu est pure unité ; toutes les autres choses sont nombrées, parce qu'elles subissent une composition. Les créatures corporelles sont composées par la forme et par la matière ; les créatures spirituelles sont composées par l'acte et par la puissance (Avicenne) ; ou par *quo est* et *quod est* (Boèce), ou par *esse* et *essentia* (Thomas, Gilles de Rome), ou par *esse, posse* et *agere* (« divin pseudo-Denys »). On peut dire que Dieu « mesure » les choses, parce que les créatures ont une existence limitée ou parce que leur taille, ou leur aptitude à la perfection spirituelle, est finie. Finalement, on

---

64. DENYS LE CHARTREUX, *De venustate mundi...*, *op. cit.*, a. 7, p. 232B'-233B ; ALEXANDRE DE HALÈS, *Summa theologica, op. cit.*, II, n° 75, 81, p. 99, 103. Voir E. DE BRUYNE, *Études, III, op. cit.*, p. 97-100.

65. DENYS LE CHARTREUX, *I Sent.*, d.3, q.4, p. 239A'-240c, 242A-243D.

66. AUGUSTIN, *De Trinitate*, 6, 10 ; PIERRE LOMBARD, *Lib. I Sententiarum*, d. 3.

peut dire que toutes les choses ont du « poids » (*pondus*), parce qu'elles ont une inclination naturelle pour leur propre perfection, ou parce qu'elles restent à la place qui leur a été assignée[67].

Plus précisément, la beauté essentielle du monde, par conséquent, est constituée dans la relation qui existe entre la cause exemplaire et la forme spécifique créée, les termes correspondants du milieu de la triade divine (*aeternitas, species, usus*), et de la triade créée (*modus, species, ordo*). La beauté essentielle se rapporte aux genres et à l'espèce des choses, qui sont fixes, et ne peuvent s'accroître ou décroître, et non pas aux beautés individuelles et accidentelles, qui vont et viennent. Denys fixe son œil contemplatif sur la beauté abstraite des choses. Pour cette raison peut-être, lorsqu'il prend pour illustration son ascension à travers les beautés de ce monde, vers la fin du *De venustate mundi*, celle-ci nous semble seulement banale et livresque. Mais si c'est la beauté intelligible que l'on recherche, l'idée d'un phénix ou d'une licorne, puisée dans l'encyclopédie, s'avérera tout aussi utile que l'idée constituée à partir d'un oiseau ou d'un autre animal existant[68].

Le fait que Denys consacre un traité entier au sujet de la beauté va tout à fait de pair avec son approche rigoureusement intellectuelle de l'union contemplative, que j'ai abordée ailleurs[69]. Car la beauté est l'être transcendantal, puisqu'elle se prête à la contemplation du pouvoir cognitif. Il y a cependant, implicite dans l'ascension vers Dieu à travers la beauté, une sérieuse limite : l'ascension est définie par la capacité limitée de notre intellect. En termes plus concrets, le mode affirmatif des *Noms divins* doit céder le pas aux dénégations de la *Théologie mystique*, juste à l'endroit où la beauté des créatures semble finalement s'approcher de Dieu lui-même. Pour la plupart des écrivains cartusiens, confrères de Denys, qui, par routine, interprétaient la *via negativa* de façon affective, le problème est moindre : il suffit tout simplement de renoncer à l'intellect et de suivre l'affection, là où la vue ne peut se poser[70]. Pour Denys, manifestement, le problème est plus complexe. Si l'on ne peut, d'une certaine manière, « connaître » la beauté transcendantale, alors la beauté que l'on contemple peut être aussi bien un mirage qu'une image. Ironiquement, Umberto Eco cite une vision mystique de Denys de Rijkel pour illustrer le type d'expérience religieuse « qui fit des ravages dans la métaphysique de la beauté » à la fin du Moyen Age. Denys rapporte qu'il fut transporté « vers une sphère de lumière infinie [...] où l'incompréhensible Dieu était pareil à un désert immensément vaste, parfaitement plat, et incommensurable ». Nous pourrions alors, comme Eco, nous demander comment on peut contempler

---

67. Denys le Chartreux, *De venustate mundi...*, *op. cit.*, a. 13, p. 238D-239D.
68. *Ibid.*, a. 22, p. 247C'-D'.
69. K. Emery, Jr., « Twofold Wisdom », art. cité.
70. *Ibid.*, p. 105-107, 128-130.

l'ordre, la plénitude et la variété de l'univers, ou l'harmonie des attributs divins, si Dieu est perçu comme un abîme ou un désert incommensurable[71] ?

Dans le *De natura aeterni et veri Dei*, Denys consacre une série d'articles à la « question épineuse », celle de savoir si l'on peut ou non affirmer, de façon positive et substantiellement, quoi que ce soit sur Dieu[72]. Beaucoup d'arguments prouvent et beaucoup d'autorités confirment que la nature de Dieu est incompréhensible. Parce que la nature de Dieu est incompréhensible à la connaissance humaine, nos dénégations au sujet de la nature divine sont plus vraies que nos affirmations. Selon l'enseignement du pseudo-Denys, ratifié par Jean Damascène, Hugues de Saint-Victor, Van Ruysbroek et d'autres, aucun nom tiré du miroir des créatures ne peut signifier Dieu, tel qu'il est véritablement, mais seulement une certaine participation de la Création à la perfection divine. Comme chaque essence créée est infiniment éloignée de l'essence du Créateur, de même chaque forme intelligible est infiniment éloignée d'une représentation parfaite de la nature divine[73]. Ainsi donc, comme le rabbin Moïse Maimonide nous l'enseigne, chaque formulation positive au sujet de Dieu suggère déjà une dénégation. Lorsque nous disons, par exemple, que Dieu comprend, nous entendons par là que Dieu ne comprend pas à la manière qui est la nôtre[74].

Bien que la nature divine soit incompréhensible et inconnaissable, nous pouvons cependant posséder une véritable connaissance de Dieu. Certains noms — *esse, bonum, pulchrum*[75] — sont attribués, à juste titre et substantiellement, à Dieu. Ces noms ne désignent pas des attributs, tels qu'ils existent dans la nature divine, mais ils donnent à entendre que les perfections signifiées existent en Dieu d'une façon plus élevée[76]. Dans son traité *De contemplatione*, Denys soutient que la *via negationis* et la *via eminentiae* ne font qu'un. La *via eminentiae* assigne à Dieu les perfections que l'on trouve dans les créatures, non pas telles que (*quia*) elles existent dans les créatures, mais d'une façon plus sublime[77]. On ne peut comprendre de telles perfections divines, mais on peut, sans nul doute, savoir que (*quia*) elles existent infiniment en Dieu. Une affirmation éminente offre ainsi une perfection positive pour la contemplation, tout en préservant la véracité de la *via ablationis*. Dire que Dieu est corporel est tout simplement erroné ; dire qu'il est *superpulcherrimus* indique qu'il est, en effet, la beauté

---

71. U. Eco, *Art and Beauty in the Middle Ages,* trad. angl. par H. Bredin, New Haven et Londres, 1986, p. 90-91.
72. Denis le Chartreux, *De natura..., op. cit.,* a. 31-34, p. 53C-58C.
73. *Ibid.,* a. 33, p. 57A-A'.
74. *Ibid.,* a. 31, 33, p. 53C-A', 56D-C'.
75. *Ibid.,* a. 17, 55, p. 33C-35A, 86C'-89C.
76. *Ibid.,* a. 33, p. 57 A.
77. Denys le Chartreux, *De contemplatione* 3, a. 4, in *Op. om.* XLI, p. 258-259.

V

en soi, mais si infiniment beau qu'aucune créature ne peut comprendre cette beauté. Ainsi, comme Hugues de Saint-Victor l'explique, quoi que l'on puisse dire à propos de Dieu est en dessous de ce qu'il est ; néanmoins, on peut dire une chose à propos de Dieu, non pas en l'ayant atteint, mais en s'approchant de lui[78]. Les superlatifs, dont sont entrelacés les écrits de Denys, ne sont pas tant des exclamations pieuses que les instruments scientifiques, grâce auxquels on se rapproche de plus en plus de la contemplation de la nature divine.

L'infinité est un attribut intrinsèque et propre à Dieu[79], et en ce qui nous concerne, la cause principale de sa nature incompréhensible. La connaissance assimile celui qui connaît à ce qui est connu ; ainsi, il doit exister une certaine proportion entre les deux. Mais entre le fini et l'infini, il n'y a pas de proportion. Par conséquent, puisque Dieu est véritablement et intensivement immense, il dépasse infiniment notre connaissance. La nature divine ne connaît aucune limite, la puissance divine aucune restriction, la sagesse divine aucun nombre et la grandeur divine aucune fin. Toutes les propriétés simples, telles qu'elles existent en Dieu, échappent infiniment à notre esprit et à toute perspicacité créée[80]. Denys exprime l'infinité divine en des termes qui sont particulièrement adaptés à la spéculation de la fin du Moyen Age. L'essence divine est la puissance divine. La puissance divine n'a pas créé ni n'est capable de créer quoi que ce soit, de telle façon qu'elle ne puisse pas en créer infiniment plus. Comme la puissance divine absolue (*absolutam potestatem*) pourrait créer des mondes infinis, ainsi l'essence divine, s'il y avait des mondes infinis, n'y serait pas moins présente qu'elle ne l'est dans ce monde[81].

Néanmoins, pour qui l'étudie, la vérité de la divine infinité n'efface pas la valeur de la beauté créée. Denys réitère sa conception de la puissance infinie de Dieu dans le *De venustate mundi*. Même si la beauté essentielle de l'univers, selon les genres et les espaces, ne s'accroissait pas, Dieu pourrait multiplier à l'infini les espèces, particulièrement dans leur nature angélique. L'immense puissance divine n'a pas créé tant de choses qu'elle ne puisse produire infiniment plus de natures, infiniment plus excellentes. Pourtant le Dieu suprêmement libre (*superliberrimus*), selon sa profonde sagesse abyssale, insondable, on ne peut plus rationnelle (*rationabilissimam*), a créé toute chose dans la beauté du nombre, du poids et de la mesure[82]. Dieu nous a ainsi fait don d'une

78. DENYS LE CHARTREUX, *De natura...*, *op. cit.*, a. 34, p. 57C'-58B.
79. *Ibid.*, a. 24-25, p. 41-45.
80. *Ibid.*, a. 29, p. 50D'-51D'.
81. Au sujet de *potentia absoluta-potentia ordinata* à la fin du Moyen Age, voir H. OBERMAN, *The Harvest of Medieval Theology : Gabriel Biel and Late Medieval Nominalism*, Grand Rapids, Mi, 1967, p. 30-55 et *passim*.
82. DENYS LE CHARTREUX, *De venustate mundi*, *op. cit.*, a. 7, p. 233A'-B'.

beauté véritable et proportionnée, par laquelle il nous est possible de nous approcher de lui. Il ne faudrait pas non plus imaginer que Dieu nous ait refusé une partie de la beauté créée, comme si la puissance absolue de Dieu était réellement différente de celle qui a ordonné l'univers. Elles semblent seulement distinctes à notre raison limitée. C'est précisément parce que la nature divine est infinie que tous les attributs divins ne font qu'un en Dieu. Ainsi donc, la sagesse divine est identique à la plénitude de la puissance divine et, dans sa sagesse, Dieu a créé toute chose dans la beauté du nombre, du poids et de la mesure, pour notre contemplation.

Il est douteux que beaucoup de confrères chartreux de Denys l'aient suivi dans ses spéculations sur le rôle de la beauté dans la vie contemplative. A ma connaissance, il n'existe aucun exemplaire manuscrit du *De venustate mundi et pulchritudine Dei*. Ses derniers mots sur la beauté, en tout cas, renvoient au traditionnel ascétisme monastique. Parce que la beauté de Dieu est infiniment, et de façon incompréhensible, plus plaisante et plus digne d'amour que l'univers tout entier, comme sont insensés et stupides ceux qui aiment la beauté des choses créées, plus que le Créateur ; qui périssent dans le désir de l'attrait charnel (*decorem*), au lieu de désirer la beauté invariable (*speciositatum*) de la face divine ; qui prennent plus de plaisir dans la beauté des formes (*specie*) du monde, que dans la beauté gracieuse (*venustate*) de Dieu ; qui, finalement, parent le corps, bien plus qu'ils ne décorent l'âme de vertus[83]. On ne doit considérer les choses créées que dans la mesure où elles servent à aiguiser l'esprit à la contemplation du bien non créé. Denys conclut en reprenant l'enseignement rebattu de saint Augustin dans le *De doctrina christiana*. Certaines choses sont faites pour qu'on en use, d'autres pour qu'on en jouisse. Nous devons jouir de ces choses qui nous rendent bienheureux et faire usage de celles qui nous mènent à la béatitude. Dans cette vie mortelle, nous devons faire usage du monde et ne jamais en jouir ; de la Trinité seule, on doit jouir. Et, comme l'ajoute saint Augustin, seuls ceux qui meurent de ce monde verront Dieu[84].

Paradoxalement, le conseil ascétique de Denys appelle une implication positive : où, sinon dans une chartreuse, pourrait-on trouver des âmes qui soient mieux à même de discerner le bon usage de la beauté créée ? Pour un chartreux, au moins, la beauté de ce monde a conduit à une intuition de la

« Pulchritudo separata,
Infinita, incausata
Idealis et fontalis,

---

83. *Ibid.*, a. 25, p. 252B-D.
84. *Ibid.*, p. 252B'-235A ; AUGUSTIN, *De doctrina christiana*, 1,3-5 et *passim*.

324

Simplex ac substantialis
Es, o Deus radiose
Et prae cunctis gratiose[85]. »

85. DENYS LE CHARTREUX, *De laudibus superlaudabilis Dei,* in *Op. om.* XXXIV, p. 420D.

Twofold wisdom and contemplation in Denys of Ryckel (Dionysius Cartusiensis, 1402-1471)

"He who reads Dionysius the Carthusian reads everything." So runs a proverb in the sixteenth- and seventeenth-century world of sacred learning.[1] Denys of Ryckel (Dionysius Cartusiensis, 1402–1471) was the most prolific writer of the Middle Ages. His works, as Fr. Synan suggests, put the entire medieval tradition on the balance scale.[2] During forty years, he wrote commentaries on each book of Scripture; huge scholastic commentaries on Peter Lombard's *Sentences* and Boethius' *Consolation* as well as numerous independent philosophical and speculative theological treatises; commentaries on the corpus of pseudo-Dionysius and many independent treatises on mystical theology; commentaries on the works of Cassian and the *Scala paradisi* of Climacus and treatises on every topic of monastic life; an encyclopaedic *Summa de vitiis et virtutibus*, four model sermon sequences embracing over 700 sermons, and treatises addressed to each vocation in the Christian estates; juridical, reforming and apologetic works engaging all the controversies of the day.[3] Trained as a boy in an abbey school and in an-

Journal of Medieval and Renaissance Studies 18:1, Spring 1988. Copyright © 1988 by Duke University Press. CCC 0047-2573/88/$1.50

1. The modern edition of Denys's works, from which I cite, is *Doctoris ecstatici D. Dionysii Cartusiani opera omnia*, cura monachorum sacri ordinis Cartusiensis, 42 in 44 vols. (Montreuil, Tournai, Parkminster, 1896–1913, 1935). For the proverb, see Petrus Blomevenna's (1455-1536) "Epistola nuncupatoria" (*Op. om.* 1: LXXXVIII) and Johann Huizinga, *The Waning of the Middle Ages* (Garden City, 1954), 189. For the sixteenth-century edition (Cologne) of Denys's works, upon which the modern edition is based, and its editor, Dietrich Loher, see Gérald Chaix, *Réforme et contre-réforme catholiques. Recherches sur la Chartreuse de Cologne au XVIe siècle.* 3 vols. *Analecta Cartusiana* 80 (Salzburg, 1981), passim.
2. E. A. Synan, "Cardinal Virtues in the Cosmos of Saint Bonaventure," in *S. Bonaventura 1274-1974*, 3 (Grottaferrata, 1974): 21.
3. The scriptural commentaries are contained in *Op. om.* 1-14. The commentaries on Peter Lombard's *Sentences* are contained in *Op. om.* 19-25 bis. *Enarrationes in V libros De consolatione philosopiae B. Severini Boetii*, *Op. om.* 26; on this work, see P. Courcelle, *La Consolation de philosophie dans la tradition littéraire: Antécédents et postérité de Boèce* (Paris, 1967), 328–29, and Raymond Macken, "Denys the Carthusian, Commentator on Boethius's *De Consolatione Philosophiae*," *Analecta Cartusiana* 118 (1984) 1-70. The commentaries on the works of pseudo-Dionysius are contained in *Op. om.* 15-16. *Expositio librorum Joannis Climaci*, *Op. om.* 17, and *Translatio librorum Joannis Cassiani ad stilum facillimum*, *Op. om.* 18. The *Summa*

other inspired by the modern devotion, a student in the *via Thomae* at the University of Cologne and called "the last scholastic" by historians, a member of the strictest contemplative order and named the *Doctor ecstaticus* because of his mystical teaching and experience, an admirer of Petrarch and admired by northern humanists for his "stilus simplex," Denys encompasses in his person all of the spiritual currents of the late Middle Ages.[4]

Because of the enormous size of his corpus, studies of Denys's thought have tended to be partial in respect of genre, inattentive to chronology, and ahistorical in character.[5] If it is miraculous that one man wrote so much,[6] it would be more so for another to analyze it all. I think, however, that certain events occurring in the mid-fifteenth

---

de vitiis et virtutibus is in *Op. om.* 39: 7–242, and the sermon sequences in *Op. om.* 29–32.

4. Denys attended the Abbey school in Sint-Truiden and the school associated with the Brethren of the Common Life in Zwolle; see K. Swenden, "Dionysius van Rijkel, biographische Nota," *Ons Geestelijk Erf* 24 (1950): 170–81. For Denys's praise of Petrarch, see *Op. om.* 37: 495; for the humanist Alardus Amstelredamus' praise of Denys's simple style, see *Encomium D. Dionysii Carthusiani . . . autore Alardo Amstelredamo*, in *Operum minorum tomus primus* (Cologne, 1532).

5. The modern reprinting of Denys's works was carried out under the aegis of Leo XIII's encyclical letter, *Aeterni patris* (1879). Not surprisingly, early scholars focused on Denys's Thomistic commentaries and paraphrases and considered him a Thomist. See Karl Werner, *Der Endausgang der mittelalterlichen Scholastik, IV. I: Die Scholastik des späteren Mittelalters* (Vienna, 1887), 134–37, 206–62; R. Montagnani, O. Cart., "Doctor Angelicus et Doctor Ecstaticus seu Manuale Thomistarum," *Divus Thomas Piacenza* 6 (for 1899): 542–49, 602–7, 632–36, and Series altera 1 (1900): 54–68; K. Krogh-Tonning, *Der letzte Scholastiker: Eine Apologie* (Freiburg im Breisgau, 1904). In a valuable study, P. Teeuwen, *Dionysius de Karthuizer en de philosophisch-theologische Stroomingen aan de Keulsche Universiteit* (Brussels-Nijmegen, 1938), showed that Denys in fact held many positions counter to those of Thomas and characteristic of the Albertist school at the University of Cologne. (On the Albertists at Cologne, see the works cited in n. 48 below.) Teeuwen hypothesized a steady "evolution of doctrine" in Denys's work from an early Thomism to a mature Christian Platonism, and on this hypothesis, constructed an undated sequence for Denys's speculative works (pp. 33–34). This sequence has been proved wrong, in detail and desired effect. On solid evidence, Anselm Stoelen established a dated chronology of Denys's works; see his articles, "De Chronologie van de Werken van Dionysius de Karthuizer," *Sacris erudiri* 5 (1953): 361–401; "Recherches récentes sur Denys le Chartreux," *Revue d'ascétique et de mystique* 29 (1953): 250–58, and the chronology in "Denys le Chartreux," *Dictionnaire de spiritualité* 3 (Paris, 1957): 431–34. Among other things, Stoelen confirmed that Denys's major Thomistic work, *Summae fidei orthodoxae libri IV, alias Enterione, id est Medulla operum sancti Thomae* (*Op. om.* 17–18), was written in 1466, one of the last works Denys wrote (see "De Chronologie," 372). Teeuwen thought that this was Denys's first work. Denys's complicated relations to Thomist and Albertist traditions cannot be accounted for by a simple evolutionary theory.

6. For Denys's "miraculous" literary production, see Dietrich Loher's *Vita Dionysii Cartusiani* (*Op. om.* 1: XXIV–XXV), and the testimony of Sixtus Senensis (*Op. om.* 1: VI–VII).

century open a door to a properly historical understanding of Denys's work as a whole.

In 1446, twenty-three years after he had entered the Charterhouse at Roermond in Limburg, accusations were laid against Denys and another monk at the General Chapter. What these were specifically is not known to date. However, one may infer their nature, for probably in the same year (otherwise shortly before), Denys was constrained to write a *Protestatio ad superiorem suum*.[7] This document has the form of an apology; in it Denys petitions to be allowed to continue his study and writing. Doubtless, his constant literary activities caused certain irregularities in observance and required a commerce with the outside world unusual among Carthusians. Whatever, in the *Protestatio* Denys must explain "the reason why he has written commentaries in both Testaments and other works."[8]

Literary activity among fifteenth-century Carthusians is noteworthy, and a famous clause in the customaries provides for it.[9] Most of what late medieval Carthusians wrote can be categorized—in the terms of manuscript catalogues—as "opera ascetica et devotionalia." None occupied himself with speculative philosophy and theology as did Denys. Denys begins his apology with disclaimers. It is the duty of a monk, he knows, "to mourn and be illumined rather than to teach or to illumine." Nevertheless, it is true, he has expounded sacred Scripture and he is prepared to continue. His conscience tells him that he has not sought some vain or vile end, such as fame or temporal advantage. On the contrary, his heavy labor has taught him humility, meekness, and patience. At the end of the text, he answers the objec-

---

7. Stoelen, "De Chronologie," 394–400. Stoelen shows convincing reasons why the *Protestatio* could not have been written in 1469, as the printed text otherwise suggests. Mistranscription is probably the source of the error.

8. Denys's *Protestatio ad superiorem suum quo motivo sua in utrumque Testamentum conscripserit commertaria, operaque reliqua* is printed in *Op. om.* 1: LXXI–LXXII, and again in *Op. om.* 41: 625–26.

9. Guigo I, *Consuetudines* 28.3 (*PL* 153: 693–94). See the list of authors and titles in André Rayez, "Chartreux," *Dictionnaire de spiritualité* 2 (Paris, 1953): 760–64, 773–74. Besides Denys, the most voluminous fifteenth-century Carthusian authors were Joannes Hagen de Indagine and Jacobus (Paradisus) de Jüterbog. See J. Klapper, *Der Erfurter Kartäuser Johannes Hagen. Ein Reformetheologe des 15. Jahrhunderts*, 2 vols., *Erfurter theologische Studien* 9–10 (Leipzig, 1960–61); Heinrich Rüthing, "Jean Hagen de Indagine," *Dictionnaire de spiritualité* 8 (Paris, 1973): 543–52; Ludger Meier, O. F. M., *Die Werke des Erfurter Kartäusers Jakob von Jüterbog in ihrer handschriftlichen Überlieferung*, in *Beiträge zur Geschichte der Philosophie und Theologie des Mittelalters* 37.5 (Münster, 1955); Dieter Mertens, "Jacques de Paradiso," *Dictionnaire de spiritualité* 8 (Paris, 1973): 52–55.

tion that the great doctors and holy fathers have already expounded Scripture sufficiently. Citing Jerome, Augustine, and Jean Gerson, he responds that as exterior taste differs among different persons in different times, so interior taste; consequently, it is always apt to bring new dishes to the table of wisdom.[10] Denys frames his argument in the most appropriate terms: he has studied and written for his personal sanctification and the edification of others.

Likewise appropriately, Denys justifies his intellectual effort as a reduction to Scripture. In the middle of the text, however, without other explanation, he makes what I take to be a confession of crimes:

> I have been most studious and have read many authors, namely, [the commentaries] on the *Sentences* of Thomas, Albert, Alexander of Hales, Bonaventure, Peter of Tarantaise, Giles [of Rome], Richard of Middleton, Durand [of St. Pouurçain], and others. Also, the books of the saints: Jerome over all the prophets and many other volumes of his, Augustine, Ambrose, Gregory, Dionysius the Areopagite—my most elect teacher, Origen, Gregory Nazianzen, Cyril, Basil, Chrysostom, the Damascene, Boethius, Anselm, Bernard, Bede, Hugh [of St. Victor], Gerson, William of Paris. Besides, I have read all of the popular *Summas* and Chronicles, the whole of the law—canon and civil—as much as was worthwhile for me, many commentators on both Testaments, and whatever natural philosophers I have been able to obtain, Plato, Proclus, Aristotle, Avicenna, Algazel, Anaxagoras, Averroes, Alexander, Alfarabi, Abubacer, Avempace, Theophrastus, Themistius and others.[11]

10. *Protestatio* (*Op. om.* 41: 626).
11. *Protestatio* (*Op. om.* 41: 625-26): "exstiti studiosus, et multos legi auctores: scilicet super Sententias, Thomae, Alberti, Alexandri de Hales, Bonaventurae, Petri de Tarento, Aegidii, Richardi de Mediavilla, Durandi et aliorum. Libros etiam sanctorum: Hieronymi super omnes Prophetas, et alia multa volumina ejus, Augustini, Ambrosii, Gregorii, Dionysii Areopagitae doctoris mei electissimi, Origenis, Gregorii Nazianzeni, Cyrilli, Basilii, Chrysostomi, Damasceni, Boetii, Anselmi, Bernardi, Bedae, Hugonis, Gersonis, Guillelmi Parisiensis. Praeterea Summas omnes vulgares et Chronicas, totum Jus, canonicum et civile, quantum mihi conveniebat, multos commentatores utriusque Testamenti, et quidquid naturalium philosophorum habere potui, Platonis, Procli, Aristotelis, Avicennae, Algazelis, Anaxagorae, Averrois, Alexandri, Alphorabii, Abubatheris, Avempote, Theophrasti, Themistii, ac aliorum." Not included here, but included in a list which Denys made of his own works, are "domini anthisiodorensis, henrici de gandavo, ulrici, scoti et hanybalis" (Trier, Stadtbibliothek, Ms. 631/1562, f. 228r). These omissions in the *Protestatio* support Stoelen's argument for an early date for that work (see n. 7 above), and suggest that Denys prepared his *Sentences* commentaries over many years. The authors mentioned in the Trier Ms.

Indeed, Denys has read all of these and many more, all, as he says, to the mortification of sensuality and carnal desires.

Medieval thinkers are especially capable of simultaneous, multiple orders, so we need not think that Denys's avowal reducing all to Scripture is some kind of exoteric cover for an esoteric intent. It does seem appropriate that he should re-introduce "commentaries on both Testaments" before the list of heathen philosophers. Nevertheless, the signal clue of this text is the epithet for pseudo-Dionysius: "my most elect teacher." For indeed, pseudo-Dionysius is Denys's supreme authority, against whose teaching he measures the opinions of all others. Moreover, evident throughout his writing is another intellectual order inspired by pseudo-Dionysius. Within this order, the study of Scripture is the foundation for a progress that leads through scholastic to mystical theology.[12]

Denys was allowed to continue his work and in 1452 he resumed his scriptural commentary, immediately after a decisive turn in his career. Since he had entered the Order in 1423, Denys had never left the enclosure of the monastery; nor after 1452 would he ever again.[13] But from September 1451 to March 1452 he accompanied Cardinal Nicholas of Cusa on his Papal Legation through the Low Countries and the Rhineland.[14] This trip afforded visits to monastic centers of learning at Egmont, Liège, Mainz, and Trier (nearby the Cardinal's own Hospital), as well as to the university city of Cologne. In these places, Denys was able to see the kinds of books, not owned by his monastery, which he envied Gerson at Paris.[15] Moreover, there is

*

---

subsequently influenced Denys's thought in significant ways, prompting departures from Thomistic positions. By "popular *Summas* and Chronicles," Denys means such works as William Peraldus, *Summa virtutum et vitiorum*; Raymond of Pennafort, *Summa de poenitentia*; John of Freiburg, *Summa confessorum*; Bartholomew of Pisa, *Summa Pisana*; (ps)-Vincent of Beauvais, *Speculum historiale*.

12. I refer to pseudo-Dionysius' modes of theology, symbolic, intelligible (equated with "scholastic" in the late Middle Ages), and mystical. For Denys's treatment, see *inter alia*, *De contemplatione* 3.aa. 1–5 (*Op. om.* 41: 255–60). G. E. M. Vos de Wael, *De Mystica theologia van Dionysius mysticus in de Werken van Dionysius Carthusianus* (Nijmegen-Utrecht, 1942), 11–13, gives a long list of Denys's epithets of praise for pseudo-Dionysius.

13. Denys did leave his monastery in Roermond in 1465–66, when he became Prior of the new foundation of St. Sophia te Vught, near 's Hertogenbosch.

14. On this Legation, see Josef Koch, *Nikolaus von Cues und seine Umwelt* (Heidelberg, 1948), 111–52, and Donald Sullivan, "Nicholas of Cusa as Reformer: The Papal Legation to the Germanies, 1451–1452," *Mediaeval Studies* 36 (1974): 383–428.

15. *In Genesim* a. 3 (*Op. om.* 1: 12A'). For Denys's convent library at Roermond and its scarce holdings of speculative works, see the fine study of Peter J. A. Nissen,

strong reason to believe Denys was able to avail himself of Cusanus' splendid library.[16] Denys wrote at least three treatises for the Cardinal,[17] besides "multae epistolae," all seemingly lost.[18] Otherwise, Denys tells us that a great part of his extensive correspondence was concerned with obtaining the use of books; Cusanus opened his library to such exchange, at least by copy.[19] Like the modern devotionalists and Cusanus himself, Denys had a passion for *originalia*, or whole texts rather than collections.[20]

In any case, after returning from the Legation, Denys wrote three large philosophic works: Book I of *De lumine christianae theoriae* (ca. 1452), which treats the procession of all things from God and their reversion to him;[21] *De natura aeterni et veri Dei* (1452), which resumes the former's questions *de deo*; and *De puritate et felicitate animae* (ca. 1455), which resumes the questions *de anima* in the first treatise.[22] These works evince a first-hand acquaintance with a great number of philosophic texts. Especially notable are many references to Plato's *Meno* and *Phaedo* in the Latin translation of Aristippus.[23]

"Die Bibliothek der Kartause Bethleem zu Roermond: Ein Forschungsüberblick," *Analecta Cartusiana* 113.3 (Salzburg, 1985): 182–225.

16. J. Marx, *Verzeichnis der Handschriften-Sammlung des Hospitals zu Cues bei Bernkastel a. / Mosel* (Trier, 1905). Other mss. owned by Cusanus are extant in other libraries.

17. *Monopanton, seu Redactio omnium Epistolarum beati Pauli in unam* (*Op. om.* 14: 465–537); *Epilogatio in librum Job: Tractatulus de causa diversitatis eventuum humanorum* (*Op. om.* 5: 45–80); *Contra perfidiam Mahometi* (*Op. om.* 36: 231–442). It seems likely that Denys's *De auctoritate summi pontificis et generalis concilii* (*Op. om.* 36: 525–674) and *Contra vitia superstitionum* (*Op. om.* 36: 211–30) are also related to Cusanus.

18. For these letters, see the *Elenchus* of Denys's works (*Op. om.* 1: LXVIII).

19. See E. Vansteenberghe, *Autour de la docte ignorance. Une controverse sur la théologie mystique au XVe siècle*, in *Beiträge zur Geschichte der Philosophie des Mittelalters* 14.2–4 (Münster, 1915), passim, concerning Cusanus' lending books to the Benedictine monks of Tegernsee.

20. Raymond Klibansky, *The Continuity of the Platonic Tradition During the Middle Ages . . . together with Plato's Parmenides in the Middle Ages and the Renaissance* (first published, 1939, 1943; rev. ed. 1981, repr. Millwood, New York, 1982), 309; Georgette Epiney-Burgard, *Gerard Groote (1340–1384) et les débuts de la dévotion moderne* (Wiesbaden, 1970), 57–59.

21. *De lumine christianae theoriae* (*Op. om.* 33: 233–513). Henceforward cited *De lum.* For the date, see Stoelen, "De chronologie," 371.

22. *De natura aeterni et veri Dei* (*Op. om.* 34: 7–97—henceforward cited *De nat.*); *De puritate et felicitate animae* (*Op. om.* 40: 393–443—henceforward cited *De pur.*). For the dates, see Stoelen, "Denys le Chartreux," 433–34.

23. *Meno interprete Henrico Aristippo*, ed. Victor Kordeuter, (*Plato Latinus* 1, London, 1940); *Phaedo interprete Henrico Aristippo*, ed. L. Minio-Paluello (*Plato Latinus* 2, London, 1950). See, e.g., *De lum.* 1.a. 102 (*Op. om.* 33: 363C–365B). As is

Klibansky's survey of extant manuscripts of these texts suggests that Denys probably acquired them from Cusanus.[24] I think also that Denys saw a new copy of Proclus's *Elements of Theology* in the Latin translation of William of Moerbeke at Cusanus' hands,[25] and the Cardinal may have alerted him to Ambrogio Traversari's translations of the works of pseudo-Dionysius.[26]

At the same time, Cusanus was engaged in a correspondence and controversy that lasted nearly a decade.[27] In a letter written towards the end of 1452, the abbot of the Benedictine monastery of Tegernsee, Gaspar Aindorffer, asked the Cardinal's opinion on a question of mystical theology that perplexed the brothers: "Is the devout soul, without any previous or concomitant cognition of the intellect, able to attain God by affection alone through what is called the apex of the mind or synderesis?"[28] This is none other than the famous *quaestio unica* of the work *De triplici via*, written by the late thirteenth-century Carthusian Hugh of Balma.[29] Hugh's teaching in the affirmative represents the extreme pole of an affective interpretation of pseudo-Dionysius' mystical theology, first developed by Thomas Gallus (Vercellensis)

---

more common, Denys also refers to *Timaeus a Calcidio translatus*, ed. J. H. Waszink (*Plato Latinus* 4, London-Leiden, 1962). See 2, pp. 32–33, which Denys quotes directly in *De lum.* 1.a.56 (*Op. om.* 33: 299C–299A′).

24. Klibansky, 31, cites Bernkastel-Kues, Hospital, Ms. 177; see Marx, 164–65.

25. Klibansky, 31, cites Bernkastel-Kues, Hospital, Ms. 195; see Marx, 181–82. For Denys's redaction of Proclus's *Elementatio theologica*, see Helmut Boese, *Wilhelm von Moerbeke als Übersetzer der Stoicheiosis theologike des Proclus* (Heidelberg, 1985), 84–86. Boese's edition of Moerbeke's translation of the *Elements* (De Wulf-Mansion Centre, Leuven, 1987) has appeared too late for our use; we shall cite from the edition of C. Vansteenkiste, *Procli Elementario theologica translata a Guilelmo de Moerbeke (Textus ineditus)*, in *Tijdschrift voor Philosophie* 13 (1951): 263–302, 491–531; 14 (1952): 503–546. For Denys's use of Proclus in the late works, see J. Stiglmayr, "Neoplatonisches bei Dionysius dem Karthäuser," *Historisches Jahrbuch* 20 (1899): 367–88.

26. Denys followed Eriugena's translation of pseudo-Dionysius' four major works. He used Sarrazinus' translation for Epistles 1–8, 11, and Traversari's translation for Epistles 9–10. In his commentaries on *De coelesti hierarchia*, and *De ecclesiastica hierarchia*, Denys cites Traversari's translation (*Op. om.* 15: 8A′, 357C, 359C). In his commentary on *De divinis nominibus*, Denys says, referring to Traversari: "Sensum hujus difficilis intricatique loci alia translatio recentior et clarior, imo et aliarum frequenter quasi expositoria, evidentius sic expressit" (*Op. om.* 16: 72B′). Cusanus' copy of Traversari's translation (Ms. 43) does not contain the letters; see Marx, 39.

27. This controversy has been beautifully documented and analyzed by E. Vansteenberghe, *Autour de la docte ignorance*, cited n. 19 above.

28. "Gaspard Aindorffer à Cusa" (1452), ed. Vansteenberghe, 110.

29. This work is alternatively titled *Mystica theologia*, or "Viae Sion lugent." The text is printed in vol. 7 of *Sancti Bonaventurae opera omnia* (Rome, 1596), 699–730. For the *Quaestio unica*, see 726–30.

in the thirteenth century.[30] By Nicholas' and Denys's time, the affective interpretation of pseudo-Dionysius was standard, although not all pushed it so far as Hugh of Balma.

To Aindorffer, Cusanus responds briefly that the affections cannot be moved without some apprehension of the good in the intellect. He goes on to suggest a certain unity of love and cognition in the highest contemplation by way of "the coincidence of knowledge and ignorance, or learned ignorance," and to warn against the deception of raptures rooted in images or phantasms.[31] This is the germ of repeated responses to the monks on this point, which culminated in his composing *De visione Dei* for them.

In 1453 a monk of Tegernsee, Joannes Schlitpacher, forwarded to Cusanus a treatise on mystical theology by another disputant in the expanded controversy, the Carthusian prior Vincent of Aggsbach. Vincent is an intrepid defender of Hugh of Balma, whom he judges to be the correct interpreter of pseudo-Dionysius, and hence of mystical theology itself. In effect, Vincent's treatise is a diatribe against Jean Gerson, even though Gerson is an affective interpreter of mystical theology. Vincent excoriates Gerson for mixing scholastic and mystical theology, and for confusing contemplation and mystical union. All of Gerson's errors, Vincent says, derive from this bad habit. Chief among these is the opinion that there must be some cognitive act prior to affective union.[32]

Cusanus was asked by the monks to reply to Vincent, as was another consultant, the theologian Marquard Sprenger. Following Aquinas, Sprenger identified mystical theology with contemplation and the cognitive gift of wisdom, and disputed Hugh of Balma's interpretation of pseudo-Dionysius, suggesting that some of Hugh's teachings were dangerous.[33] Again taking the pen against his adversaries, Vincent accuses them both of the vices of Gerson; he is par-

30. See James Walsh, "*Sapientia christianorum*: The Doctrine of Thomas Gallus, Abbot of Vercelli, on Contemplation" (Ph.D. diss., Gregorian University, Rome, 1957).
31. "Cusa à Gaspard Aindorffer" (22 Sept. 1452), ed. Vansteenberghe, 111–12: "Impossibile est enim affectum moveri nisi per dilectionem, et quicquid diligitur non potest nisi sub ratione boni diligi. . . . Omne enim quod sub racione boni diligitur seu eligitur, non diligitur sine omni cognitione boni, quoniam sub racione boni diligitur. Inest igitur in omni tali dilectione qua quis vehitur in Deum, cognicio, licet quid sit id quod diligit ignoret. Est igitur coincidencia sciencie et ignorancie, seu docta ignorancia."
32. Vansteenberghe, 28–32, and Vincent of Aggsbach, "Traité contre Gerson" (1453), ed. Vansteenberghe, 189–201.
33. Vansteenberghe, 49–57.

ticularly outraged at Sprenger's identification of the gift of wisdom, common to all Christians, with the "sapientia Christianorum" of pseudo-Dionysius, reserved for a few simple and beloved disciples. Vincent moreover remarks that Thomas Aquinas has nothing to say about mystical theology in any of his works.[34]

In this whole affair, it is apparent that the monks of Tegernsee could never quite grasp Cusanus' notions of the "coincidence of opposites" and "learned ignorance." Cusanus seemed to realize this, for in 1455 he responded yet again to the monks in the most conventional terms:

> those who posit that affection can be borne or moved into an object which is wholly unknown [by the intellect] contradict Aristotle in *De anima* 3, who says that affection cannot be moved into its object unless the object be apprehended; the good, as apprehended, moves affection. Thus say all of the theologians, and St. Thomas in the questions *De veritate*, art. 5, concerning the justification of the impious.[35]

There is no evidence that Denys the Carthusian was directly involved in this controversy, although just before it began Cusanus sent the monks at Tegernsee a copy of one of his treatises.[36] However, the affair serves to reveal two things relevant to our considerations. First, it testifies the influence which the affective interpretation of mystical theology in general and the teachings of Hugh of Balma in particular held within the Carthusian Order. This evidence is corroborated elsewhere.[37] Secondly, probably because of his Thomistic training but perhaps for closer reasons, Denys's own teaching on contemplation and mystical theology falls strongly on the side of Cusanus and Sprenger. This is unusual among monastic circles of the late Middle Ages. It is Denys's rigorously intellectualist teaching on contemplation, I believe, and the huge intellectual preparation it approves, that are the source of his tensions in the Order.

34. Vansteenberghe, 58–65, and Vincent's texts, 204–218.
35. "Cusa à Bernard de Waging" (28 July 1455), ed. Vansteenberghe, 159–60: "Qui enim ponunt affectum in penitus ignotum ferri seu moveri, contradicunt Aristoteli, in 3° *De anima*, qui ait quod affectus non movetur in suum obiectum nisi apprehensum, bonum enim apprehensum movet affectum; et ita omnes theologi, et S.T. in questionibus veritatis de justificatione impij, articulo 5ᵗᵒ." Cusanus adds "de coincidencia motuum intellectus et affectus aliqua in sermonibus huius anni . . . lacius locutus sum."
36. The *Monopanton* (see n. 17 above); Vansteenberghe, 18, 109.
37. See, for example, Denis Dale Martin, "The Carthusian Nicholas Kempf: Monastic and Mystical Theology in the Fifteenth Century" (Ph.D. diss., Univ. of Waterloo, 1981), 202–16.

Indeed, it is in the treatise *De contemplatione libri III* that one discovers the seminal reasons of Denys's entire intellectual enterprise. Denys wrote this work over the years 1440–1445, that is, in the years just before he was constrained to make his *Protestatio*.[38] For Denys, a nature is defined by its highest possible act. Contemplation is the highest human act and all others must be related directly to it. Throughout his subsequent writings, Denys took every opportunity, however slight, to speak about contemplation. But *De contemplatione* remains his only independent treatise on his favorite topic. As such, the work holds a privileged place within Denys's corpus, and its teaching may serve as a measure against which to evaluate the development of his speculative positions.

At the beginning of *De contemplatione*, Denys discovers an hierarchical order of wisdom. Substantially, in itself, wisdom is the second person of the Trinity, the divine Word and truth of the Father. Human minds partake this wisdom in an ascending, threefold manner. First, they are capable of acquiring a natural, philosophic wisdom, which is the cognition of "immaterial, intellectual and immortal natures." Its highest perfection is the knowledge of "Deus super-simplicissimus."[39] The second kind of wisdom is called "supernatural," be-

---

38. For the date, see Stoelen, "Denys le Chartreux," 434.

39. As these terms imply, Denys understands that the object of metaphysics is God and the separated substances. Thus he accepts Averroes' and Albert's interpretation of Aristotle rather than Avicenna's and Thomas Aquinas's (the object of metaphysics is being as being). Concerning natural wisdom, Denys says: "et talis sapientia, secundum philosophos, principaliter est de ipso altissimo ente, Deo sublimi et benedicto; secundario quoque de substantiis separatis, de quibus Aristoteles in libro de Coelo et mundo testatur: Extra hunc mundum nihil est, nec vacuum, nec locus, nec tempus; sed sunt ibi quaedam entia simplicia, optimam vitam ducentia, et de suis sufficentia" (*De donis Spiritus Sancti* 2. a. 3, *Op. om.* 35: 177D–A'). In natural philosophy, only metaphysics is properly called wisdom: "Unde Philosophus solam metaphysicam ait sapientiam simpliciter nominandam, quum sit de primo universorum principio, ac separatis intelligentiis et divinis substantiis" (ibid., 2. a. 5, *Op. om.* 35: 179A). Because of its object, the highest natural wisdom or metaphysics is rightly called theology: "De qua summi philosophi pulchra ac mira, Augustino testante, indagati sunt. Nam et Aristoteles metaphysicam suam theologiam appellat ac sapientiam seu divinam scientiam. Liber quoque Procli Platonici, Elementatio theologica intitulatur" (ibid., 2. a. 2, *Op. om.* 35: 176A'). This understanding serves Denys's architechtonic well, wherein natural wisdom is the analogical image of supernatural wisdom, directed towards the same object but participated in a different manner: "sed theologia est nobilior illa, et de maxime speculabilibus, atque praecipue de his de quibus metaphysica in suo supremo, puta de Deo et substantiis separatis" (I *Sent.* q. *praevia* 2, *Op. om.* 19: 68A). The object of separated substances befits man's station in the hierarchy of created intellects: "ex naturis rerum secundum essentialia principia naturalemque proprietatem et legem ipsarum procedit. Ad hanc nempe sapientiam pertingit intellectus, sensibiles naturas

cause originally it was infused into the minds of men from above, revealing to them divine truths which otherwise they could not have known. Once given, however, these truths may be investigated by natural reason alone and may be acquired by human study. This kind of wisdom is a prevenient grace, or grace given for the benefit of others ("gratia gratis data"), since it can be attained by those lacking sanctifying grace and charity. Denys calls this wisdom "scholastic." Finally, the highest form of wisdom is supernatural properly speaking. It is the infused gift of wisdom, through which the human mind becomes connatural with divine things, discerns them intellectually in a clear intuition, and is conformed to them in the affections. This wisdom is "mystical."[40]

Denys makes the same distinction earlier in *De donis Spiritus sancti*, the first three tracts of which he composed in 1430 in preparation for his work on contemplation.[41] His distinction in this work reveals a personal dimension. As in *De contemplatione*, he distinguishes among wisdom itself, supernatural theological wisdom, and natural philosophical wisdom. The latter is itself theology, as Aristotle and Proclus teach.[42] Likewise, Denys subdivides supernatural wisdom into two, emphasizing that one of them may be performed without sanctifying grace, "since we see that many of the most proud and vain men abound in it and teach it to others."[43] This remark echoes the constant late medieval complaint made against school theology by modern devo-

---

supergrediens, atque in intellectualium essentiarum speculationem prodiens: est enim humanus intellectus creatus in umbra intelligentiae, secundum Isaac" (*De lum.* 1. a. 5, *Op. om.* 33: 240C–D). Denys's conception of metaphysics accords with his doctrine of natural felicity, discussed in the body of the present article. For the competing medieval views concerning the object of metaphysics, see Albert Zimmermann, *Ontologie oder Metaphysik? Die Diskussion über den Gegenstand der Metaphysik im 13. und 14. Jahrhundert. Texte und Untersuchungen* (Leiden-Köln, 1965); James Doig, *Aquinas on Metaphysics* (The Hague, 1972), 172–213; John F. Wippel, *The Metaphysical Thought of Godfrey of Fontaines: A Study in Late Thirteenth-Century Philosophy* (Washington, D.C., 1981), 2–15.

40. *De cont.* 1.a.2 (*Op. om.* 41: 137B–B′).

41. *De donis Spiritus Sancti* (*Op. om.* 35: 155–262). For the dates, see Stoelen, "De Chronologie," 362–63. This is the second work Denys wrote after entering the monastery. Its early date bespeaks the first intention of his study: to understand the contemplative act which defined his vocation. In 1446, Denys added a fourth tract to *De donis*, containing abbreviations of the teaching of various scholastic doctors.

42. *De donis* 2.a.1 (*Op. om.* 35: 175B′–176C′). See n. 39 above.

43. *De donis* 2.aa.2–5 (*Op. om.* 35: 176C′–179D). See 2.a.3 (177B′) concerning the evidence for wisdom without grace, "quum multi superbissimi atque vanissimi in ea abundent ac alios doceant."

tionalists, converts to the monastic life from the university, and even those who stayed in the university, like Gerson.[44] By his censure here, Denys as in the *Protestatio* distances his own activity from such sterility.

Denys reinforces the point in another threefold distinction among kinds of reading and study. There are those who read and study for the sake of disputation, who relish ingenious subtleties and difficulties for the sake of vainglory. Far better are those who read books meant to excite interior affection, expose one's imperfections, and provide an abridged way to perfection: "better indeed is a small knowledge with a virtuous life than an unworthy life with a copious science." This is the reading appropriate for monks, Denys adds. He thus concedes the argument of monastic advocates of the affections and Hugh of Balma. There are yet others, however, who read in order to abound in both knowledge and virtue. Such students benefit not only themselves but others. Denys's examples are the icons of the highest contemplative wisdom: Moses, David, Paul, John, and the "most glorious Dionysius the Areopagite." On a lower plane are certain "modern doctors": Thomas Aquinas, Albert, and Giles of Rome. This kind of study is appropriate for pastors, prelates, and members of the mendicant orders. Arguing tacitly on his own behalf and anticipating his argument in the *Protestatio*, Denys comments that although his rule of appropriate reading holds in general, in special cases a rule should not be given.[45]

To call attention to an ungraced, sterile reason would seem rather risky in a work which diligently searches the writings of heathen philosophers. Hence, in *De lumine* I Denys's distinction is only twofold, between natural, acquired philosophic wisdom and supernatural, infused theological wisdom.[46] Book I of *De lumine* treats the former and Book II the latter. To justify the pursuit of natural wisdom, Denys offers cosmological and noetic reasons, in accord with his constant principle that the order of knowing follows strictly the order of being. The study of natural wisdom serves Christian wisdom as creatures serve the creator; not wholly but in part natural wisdom represents supernatural wisdom as nature in part represents God. Truth ascertained

---

44. A good example of this common motif is Gerson's *Contra curiositatem studentium lectiones duae*, ed. P. Glorieux, *Œuvres complètes III: L'Œuvre magistrale* (Paris, 1962), 224–49. Martin, 141–66, gives a useful survey of the attitudes of Devotionalists and other figures.

45. *De donis* 1.a.2 (*Op. om.* 35: 160A'–161A).

46. *De lum.* 1.a.5 and 2. *Prœm.* (*Op. om.* 33: 239D'–240A, 385).

philosophically serves "to induce" the truths of faith, to assist in showing the certitude of things otherwise not demonstrable.[47]
What Denys means by "representation" and "induction" becomes
clearer in his elucidation of the order of nature to which the order of
knowing corresponds. The order of being is strictly hierarchical in all
of its dimensions.[48] In every order, an inferior nature is a certain

47. *De lum.* 1.a.6 (*Op. om.* 33: 240B–C'). See also Denys's *Elementatio theologica*,
prop. 1 (*Op. om.* 33:111A): "Quidquid in Elementatione philosophica de Deo inductum
est et probatum, in Elementatione hac theologica est tanquam verum et ratum prae-
supponendum."
48. The classic work on the hierarchy of being, but weak on medieval doctrines, is   ✱
Arthur O. Lovejoy, *The Great Chain of Being: A Study in the History of an Idea*
(Cambridge, Mass., 1936). A recent volume commemorates the work: *Jacob's Ladder
and the Tree of Life: Concepts of Hierarchy and the Great Chain of Being*, ed.
Marion Leathers Kuntz and Paul Grimley Kuntz (Bern-New York, 1986). The land-
mark study on metaphysical hierarchy in the Middle Ages is Edward P. Mahoney,
"Metaphysical Foundations of the Hierarchy of Being According to Some Late
Medieval and Renaissance Philosophers," in *Philosophies of Existence Ancient and
Medieval*, ed. Parviz Morewedge (New York, 1982), 165–257. Mahoney's notes (pp.
212–57) are an annotated bibliography on the subject. As one would expect from a
student of the *via antiqua*, Denys's understanding of the hierarchy of being follows
in the line of Albert the Great and Thomas Aquinas and is founded on the same
original sources: Proclus, pseudo-Dionysius, *Liber de causis* (Mahoney, 166–74, and
notes, pp. 214–30). Denys considers pseudo-Dionysius the author of his doctrine. The
seminal study is René Roques, *L'Univers dionysien: Structure hiérarchique du monde
selon le Pseudo-Denys* (Paris, 1954); see Mahoney, 218–19 n.5, for other studies. In
the present study, I suggest that Denys follows Proclus more closely than his thirteenth-century predecessors. For some deep influences of Proclus upon Denys, see
Werner Beierwaltes, "Philosophische Marginalien zu Proklos-Texten," *Philosophische
Rundschau* 10 (1962): 60–64. Denys's reading of Proclus must be studied in relation
to the thought of the German Dominican disciples of Albert the Great: Ulrich of
Strassburg, Dietrich of Freiberg and Berthold of Moosburg. Denys quotes Ulrich's
Summa de bono extensively throughout his *Sentences* commentary. He probably knew
Berthold's commentary on Proclus through Cusanus. Berthold's work is now being
edited: *Expositio super Elementationem theologicam Procli. Propositiones 184–211
De animabus*, ed. L. Sturlese (Rome, 1974); *Propositiones 1–13*, ed. M. R. Pagnoni-
Sturlese and L. Sturlese, and *Propositiones 14–34*, ed. M. R. Pagnoni-Sturlese, L. Stur-
lese, and B. Mojsisch, Corpus philosophorum teutonicorum medii aevi 6.1–2 (Ham-
burg, 1984–86). The scholarly literature on the Albertist school is now considerable.
See the chapters in Martin Grabmann, *Mittelalterliches Geistesleben*, 3 vols. (Munich,
1926; repr. Hildesheim-New York, 1975), concerning Ulrich of Strassburg (1: 147–
221), the influence of Albert the Great (2: 324–412), and Moerbeke's translations of
Proclus (2: 413–23); Ruedi Imbach, "Le (Néo-) platonisme médiéval, Proclus latin,
et l'école dominicaine allemande," *Revue de théologie et de philosophie* 110 (1978):
427–48; Mahoney cites other studies (pp. 221–22 n. 23). The seminal study of the
fifteenth-century Albertists at the University of Cologne is G. Meersseman, O.P.,
Geschichte des Albertismus, I: Die Pariser Anfänger des Kölner Albertismus (Paris,
1933); *II: Die ersten Kölner Kontroversen* (Rome, 1935). Recent studies are found
in the volume *Albert der Grosse. Seine Zeit, sein Werk, siene Wirkung*. Miscellanea
Mediavalia 14, ed. Albert Zimmermann (Berlin-New York, 1981); see Sophie Wlodek,
"Albert le Grand et les Albertistes du XVe siècle. Le problème des universaux," 193–
207; Jerzy B. Korolec, "Heymeric de Campo et sa vision néoplatonicienne de Dieu,"
208–16; Hans Gerhard Senger, "Albertismus? Überlegungen zur 'via Alberti' im 15. Jahr-

exemplification and image of the nature immediately superior. Thus, Isaac [Israeli] says that the second arises in the shadow of the first, and Aristotle, Proclus, and the author of the *Liber de causis* say that the heavenly soul is at once the example of a higher nature and the exemplar of a lower nature. Dionysius the Areopagite confirms this, saying that divine wisdom links up the termini of higher orders with the heads of lower orders. If the first God had not so constituted all things in congruity with himself and among themselves, a lower nature could never be a measure (*ratio*) whereby to know a higher essence, nor could one quiddity induce the notion of a higher species. For this reason, Isaac also says that the created human intellect rests in the shadow of an Intelligence.[49] By philosophic wisdom, the intellect rises above sensible natures to the speculation of intellectual essences. The direction of this argument allows one to understand that the speculation of intellectual essences will in turn aid the induction of the truths of faith. Further, the two orders of wisdom, while distinct, cannot be unconnected. As in the order of nature an Intelligence links up with the ones immediately above and below, so supernatural wisdom in its lowest register connects with natural wisdom in its highest: certitude about the "super-simplest God."

That Denys should allege pseudo-Dionysius to authorize the teaching of Proclus and the *Liber de causis* is for us a fine historical irony. Generally, Denys will not adduce theological authorities when treating what to his mind is a strictly philosophical issue, although he will refer to theologians when a philosophic doctrine has had some consequence among them. However, on matters of hierarchical order he must nearly always evoke pseudo-Dionysius, for none of the philoso-

---

hundert," 217–36. Heymericus de Campo was the leading Albertist at Cologne, a student of the art of Rámon Llull, a teacher of Nicholas of Cusa and possibly an acquaintance of Denys the Carthusian. A full bibliography is contained in the notes of J.-D. Caviglioli, "Les écrits d'Heymericus de Campo (1395–1460) sur les œuvres d'Aristote," *Freiburger Zeitschrift für Philosophie und Theologie* 28 (1981): 294–371. See as well the important article of Rudolf Haubst, "Albert, wie Cusanus ihn sah," in *Albertus Magnus. Doctor Universalis. 1280/1980*, ed. Gerbert Meyer and Albert Zimmermann (Mainz, 1980), 167–94.

49. *De lum.* 1.a.5 (*Op. om.* 33: 239D'–240C). See "Isaac Israeli *Liber de definicionibus*," ed. J. T. Muckle, *Archives d'histoire doctrinale et littéraire du moyen âge* (*AHDLMA*) 11 (1937–38): 313; Proclus, *Elem. theo.*, theorems 20–21, pp. 273–743; "Le *Liber de Causis*," ed. Adriaan Pattin, *Tijdschrift voor Philosophie* 4 (1966): 90–203; see props. 4, 13, pp. 142–44, 164–65. We cite the works of pseudo-Dionysius from Denys's *Op. om.*, where the various translations are conveniently printed; see *De div. nom.* 7 (*Op. om.* 16: 249).

phers ever got the rule of hierarchy quite right.[50] Thus, in this instance, Avicenna rightly discerned the general principles of hierarchy, but he wrongly inferred that each Intelligence created the one beneath; Plato correctly perceived that beings of a lower order are "certain resultants and resonances" of a higher one, participating in its being, but he wrongly thought that the highest order comprised separately existing ideal forms.[51]

In *De contemplatione*, Denys recapitulates the hierarchical nature of the human soul. The hierarchy terminates in the human mind, the lowest in the chain (*catena*) of intellectual substances.[52] As the Peripatetics say, in the beginning the human soul is a *tabula rasa*. Nonetheless, "since it is truly preserved in the gyro and order of intellectual essences, its nature is immortal and capable of true beatitude."[53] This contrapuntal formula hints at what is a central tension in Denys's philosophic writings. In a series of articles in *De lumine* and again in *De puritate* Denys struggles with the problem which Aristotle's concept of the soul as the substantial form of the body presents for the demonstration of the soul's immortality. That the soul is the form of the body was declared *de fide* in 1312; because of the Philosopher's firm teaching on this point, Denys praises him as the one among "the multitude of philosophers whose philosophy conforms most to Christian theory."[54] On the other hand, it is evident that the Philosopher's professed followers, whose doctrines Denys rehearses, most frequently went awry on the question of immortality. On this point, Denys is

50. One might refer here to some articles by E. von Ivánka, who argues for pseudo-Dionysius' Christian correction of Proclus and other neo-Platonists. See "La significication du Corpus Areopagiticum," *Recherches de science religieuse* 36 (1949): 5–24; " 'Teilhaben,' 'Hervorgang' und 'Hierarchie' bei Pseudo-Dionysius und bei Proklos (Der 'Neuplatonismus' des Pseudo-Dionysius)," in *Actes du XIe Congrès International de Philosophie* (Brussels-Amsterdam-Louvain, 1953), 153–58; "Zum Problem des christlichen Neuplatonismus. II. Inwieweit ist Pseudo-Dionysius Areopagita Neuplatoniker?" *Scholastik* 31 (1956): 387–93.

51. *De lum.* 1.a.5 (*Op. om.* 33: 240A–B). See *Timaeus a Calcidio translatus*, 21–33.

52. For the metaphor of the "chain," originating in philosophical allegorizations of Homer, see Mahoney, 212–14 n. 1. Denys calls the hierarchy of created intellects a *concatenatio*; see *De cont.* 1.a.6 (*Op. om.* 41: 141C).

53. *De cont.* 1.a.5 (*Op. om.* 41: 139B').

54. *De lum.* 1.a.92 (*Op. om.* 33: 347A). Denys specifies that Aristotle's pre-eminence lies in his understanding of the soul: "Hic igitur omnium Graecorum philosophorum sapientissimus Aristoteles, quidditatem animae investigans. . . . Claret denuo animam formam esse, non utique a formando vel foris manendo, sed ab informando. Unde animam definiens ait: Anima est actus primus, id est substantialis forma, corporis organici physici, vitam habentis in potentia" (347D–A').

strongly drawn to Proclus, producing a series of the latter's *theoremata* concerning the soul's self-reflexiveness, which entails its spiritual self-subsistence. These propositions, Denys says, "establish the beautiful rule which states: each thing acts according to the way it is substantiated."[55] In a text of *De contemplatione*, Denys points to the source of his mediation of the problem:

> the mind or rational soul, insofar as it is an immaterial, intellective, simple, volitive and free form, is called an image of the first mind, a small seal of the divine light, an immortal ray of the highest truth. Thus, since it is elevated above every time and continuum, it has a certain respect or face pointed directly and immediately towards the divine, celestial, and eternal, indeed to God the creator.[56]

These terms come from Avicenna, and were adopted by the early Franciscan theologians.[57] It is the higher face of the soul that links directly with the higher order of Intelligences; in its lower face, the soul acts as the substantial form of the body. Straightway, Denys tacitly corrects Avicenna's false inference concerning causality by adducing a proposition of Proclus, which he interprets in a Christian sense: "each thing is able to return (*reditivum*) to the source of its procession, to that by which it is caused and from which it flows forth.... Thus, since the soul originated from the highest God through creation, so only in him can it felicitate."[58] This does not mean, we shall see, that the soul's felicity suffers no mediation.

Denys grasps fully the implications of pseudo-Dionysius' teachings concerning the hierarchy of being. These he must confront in a famous

---

55. *De lum.* 1.a.98 (*Op. om.* 33: 356C–357A'). From Proclus, Denys cites theorems 15–16, 44–47, 83, 188–189. See Proclus, *Elem. theo.*, 271, 282–83, 296, 522–23.

56. *De cont.* 1.a.5 (*Op. om.* 41: 139C'–D'): "Itaque mens seu anima rationalis, in quantum est forma immaterialis, intellectiva, simplex, volitiva ac libera, appellatur primae mentis imago, divinae lucis signaculum, summae veritatis radius immortalis: sicque ut supra tempus atque continuum elevata, respectum quemdam seu vultum habet directe et immediate ad divina, coelestia atque aeterna, imo ad Deum creatorem."

57. Avicenna, *Liber de anima seu sextus de naturalibus* 1.5, ed. S. Van Riet (*Avicenna Latinus*, Louvain-Leiden, 1972), 93–94. See J. Rohmer, "Sur la doctrine franciscaine des deux faces de l'âme," *AHDLMA* 2 (1927): 73–77, and Etienne Gilson, "Les sources Gréco-Arabes de l'augustinisme avicennisant," *AHDLMA* 4 (1929–30): 57–62.

58. *De cont.* 1.a.5 (*Op. om.* 41: 139D'). Denys refers to Proclus, *Elem. theo.*, theorems 31, 34, pp. 278–79: "Omne procedens ab aliquo secundum essentiam convertitur ad illud a quo procedit.... Omne quod secundum naturam convertitur, ad illud facit conversionem, a quo et processum propriae subsistentiae habet."

question of mystical theology. That the angels are mediums between God and human minds is clear enough in Scripture and in the writing of "the most sacred chief of theologians, Dionysius." But Augustine says that there is no medium between the human mind and God, and that nothing save God is more sublime than the human mind. Augustine's statements are true, Denys says, insofar as the rational soul receives nature, grace, and glory immediately from God, and insofar as God is its ultimate felicity. Nevertheless, in terms of specific, formal dignity, the angelic Intelligences are more perfect than human minds and mediate between the soul and God. Denys concludes his articles on the nature of the soul in *De contemplatione* by remarking that in all of the teachings of philosophy the principles of being and of knowing are the same.[59] He understands this maxim in the strictest, isomorphic way. In light of the human soul's hierarchical situation, the meaning of this maxim would seem to be clear; whereas grace can elevate the mind directly to God, natural contemplation at its point of return will necessarily be mediated by higher Intelligences.

The implication is confirmed by the teaching of the "Peripatetics, Avicenna, Algazel, Averroes, Alfarabi and many others," who understood that the soul's felicity consists in the contemplation *quid est* of separated, intelligible substances. This teaching may be saved, Denys judges, if it be understood that the soul's natural beatitude does not stand fixed in the cognition of an Intelligence, but that such cognition makes it more apt for contemplation of the highest truth.[60] In Dionysian terms, confirmed by Proclus and the *Liber de causis*, the higher Intelligences purify, strengthen, and illumine philosophic knowledge of the first cause.[61]

59. *De cont.* 1.a.8 (*Op. om.* 41: 142D–D'). Augustine, *De Trinitate* 14.3 (ed. W. J. Mountain, CCSL 50a: 426); *De civitate Dei* 11.2 (ed. Bernard and Alphonse Kalb, CCSL 48: 322). Denys refers, of course, to pseudo-Dionysius' teaching in *De coel. hier.* This question of mystical theology does not involve the redemptive mediation of Christ, which is presumed in the order of grace. Christ is the gate—through whom all must pass—to the Father; no one rises to the divinity except through the humanity of Christ; all union with God presupposes incorporation in Christ's mystical body. Whether one may surpass the humanity, or must never cease to contemplate it, is a separate question, which, incidentally, I treat fully in my book, *Renaissance Dialectic and Renaissance Piety: Benet of Canfield's Rule of Perfection* (Binghamton, N.Y., 1987).

60. *De cont.* 1.a.9 (*Op. om.* 41: 143C–D).

61. *De lum.* 1.a.43 (*Op. om.* 33: 284C'–285B). Pseudo-Dionysius, *De coel. hier.* 7 (*Op. om.* 15: 118); Proclus, *Elem. theo.*, theorem 32, p. 278; *Liber de causis*, props. 4, 22, pp. 143–44, 183–84. See Albert the Great's paraphrase of *Liber de causis*, Tract. 2, c.23 (ed. Borgnet, *Opera omnia* 10:513–14) where the Dionysian terms are emphasized.

A commonplace states that natural wisdom lacks the love that makes supernatural wisdom savorous.[62] Denys counters this distinction by the testimony of Plato, Aristotle, and Plotinus (as reported in Macrobius),[63] who speak of the heroic virtues of the purged soul. Of course, natural wisdom engenders a love insufficient for salvation, because love is measured by the object of understanding.[64] Nonetheless, since natural contemplation embraces both knowledge and love, it justly represents or exemplifies the lineaments of supernatural contemplation.

In *De lumine*, Denys examines the procession of beings from God in the teachings of the Platonists and the Peripatetics, one by one. From each, he gathers useful principles and corrects one against the other. Most of the philosophers' errors concern the causality of secondary beings and the necessity of emanation. On this last point, Denys finds Avicebron's teaching concerning God's freedom especially helpful.[65] In conclusion, he educes from his materials a correct conception of the procession of beings:

What place causes in corporeal beings, order effects in spiritual beings. Accordingly, as among bodies what is more luminous diffuses its rays to the objects nearby, so a superior intellect strengthens and increases the light of its inferior. Moreover, the inferior Intelligence is moved to the form of the superior as the highest Intelligence is moved to the form of the first cause. Therefore, it is said in the *Liber de causis* that inferior Intelligences cast their intellectual glances and intelligent countenances towards the lights of superior Intelligences; the inferior, indeed, are converted to the superior. In this way one illustrates the other. Finally, in every order there is a certain contact between coordinates; accord-

---

62. For example, Marquard Sprenger distinguishes between the philosophical contemplation of the pagans, which is purely speculative, and that of Christians, where love holds the greater place. See Vansteenberghe, 51. Denys, *De cont.* 1.a.10 (*Op. om.* 41: 143C′) cites Hugh of St. Victor "super Angelicam hierarchiam" as making this distinction.

63. Macrobius, *Commentary on the Dream of Scipio*, trans. W. H. Stahl (New York, 1952), 1.8, pp. 120–29.

64. *De cont.* 1.a.10 (*Op. om.* 41: 143D′–144C).

65. *De lum.* 1.aa.27–40 (*Op. om.* 41: 264D–282D′). Denys treats Avicebron in 1.a.33 (273D′–274D′), of whom he says: "Etenim in multis philosophia ejus sublimis est, praesertim circa exitum universorum a primo; et ut posterius ostendetur, fidei in hoc vicinior est ipsa, quam sit quorumdam Peripateticorum traditio" (274C′-D′). See *Avencebrolis (Ibn Gebirol) Fons vitae ex Arabico in Latinum translatus ab Iohanne Hispano et Dominico Gundissalino*, ed. Clemens Baeumker in *Beiträge zur Geschichte der Philosophie des Mittelalters* 1 (Münster, 1895), esp. pp. 323–30.

ing to Isaac, the second stands in the shadow of the first. In separated spiritual creatures, this contact occurs because the superior Intelligence virtually contains and encloses the inferior Intelligence; truly, the inferior touches the superior by desiring it. In this manner, one Intelligence is conformed and united with another.[66]

The mind's conversion to the first principle follows the exigencies of this natural order of being. If all intellects come directly from the hand of God, it would seem that they return directly to him. But God's causality is wholly transcendent: as Proclus teaches, the first is outside every genus and in itself is unparticipated (*amethekton*).[67] Even those attributes which we know are predicated properly of God—*bonum, lumen, Esse*—we comprehend only by way of analogy to creatures.[68] No less than Christian sages, the philosophers understand that one best approaches God by means of negation. Denys cites texts from Alfarabi, Avicenna, Algazel, Proclus, the *Liber de causis*, and Apuleius (from Augustine).[69]

Having established the general principles of the procession of created intellects from God and conversion to him, Denys searches the philosophers' teachings on the contemplative felicity of the human

---

66. *De lum.* 1.a.86 (*Op. om.* 33: 339A'–C'): "Enimvero de illuminatione unius intelligentiae ab alia hoc verum: quia quod in corporalibus facit situs, agit in spiritualibus ordo. Unde sicut in corporibus quod luminosius est, radios diffundit ad situaliter ei objecta; sic superior intellectus confortat et auget lumen inferioris. Amplius, inferior intelligentia movetur ad formam superioris, sicut et suprema ad formam primae causae. Ideo in libro Causarum dicitur, quod intelligentiae inferiores projiciunt visus suos intellectuales et intelligentiales vultus ad lumina superiorum: inferiora enim convertuntur ad superiora. Sic igitur una illustrat aliam. Denuo, in ordine omni est quidam coordinatorum contactus, secundum Isaac: semper enim secundum subsistit in umbra primi. In separatis autem spiritualibus est contactus iste, per hoc quod superior intelligentia inferiorem concludit et virtute continet; inferior vero superiorem contingit quasi eam cupiens. Per hunc ergo modum una applicatur et unitur alteri." Isaac, *Liber de definicionibus*, 313, 317–18. *Liber de causis*, prop. 9, p. 160.

67. *De cont.* 3.a.7 (*Op. om.* 41: 262B'). Denys here cites Proclus, *Elem. theo.*, theorems 99, 123, pp. 301, 499–500. Denys cites these two Proclus texts to the same effect in *De lum.* 1.a.20 and 1.a.29 (*Op. om.* 33: 253C'–D', 268B').

68. On the positive names of God, their order, and predication, see *De cont.* 1.a.42 and 3.a.5 (*Op. om.* 41: 184C–185D, 260C–B'); *De lum.* 1.aa.16, 23–24, 28, 115 (*Op. om.* 33: 250A'–251D, 256A'–258C, 266D–A', 381C'–382D'); *De nat.* aa.15–18, 23, 31–34 (*Op. om.* 34: 29C'–36B, 40B'–41C, 53C–58C).

69. *De cont.* 3.a.7 (*Op. om.* 41: 262C–263A). *Algazel's Metaphysics. A Medieval Translation*, ed. J. T. Muckle, C.S.B. (Toronto, 1933), Tract 3, p. 62; Proclus, *Elem. theo.*, theorem 123, p. 499; *Liber de causis*, props. 5, 21, pp. 147, 181; Augustine, *De civ. Dei* 9.3 (*CCSL* 47: 250). Denys makes the same argument in *De lum.* 1.a.20 (*Op. om.* 33: 253B–254B').

soul. A being's highest virtue is the *ratio* which defines its species. The power of intellect defines the being of separated spiritual substances and the human soul. The soul's felicity, then, is intellectual contemplation of the first intelligible truth, insofar as it is congruent to its nature. Such contemplation includes love and delectation, but these are rooted primordially in the intellect, since the will is moved only insofar as the good which attracts it is understood. Thus, although what Boethius says is true, that "felicity is a perfect state which aggregates all goods, and does not consist in naked contemplation alone," nevertheless felicity *principaliformiter* resides in the intellect.[70]

Denys denies that felicity can be achieved through faith or demonstration. Nor can it be achieved amidst the perturbations of this life.[71] Alexander, Averroes, and Abubacer erred in thinking this, because of their denial of the soul's personal immortality and their false understandings of the agent and possible intellects.[72] These possibilities eliminated, the soul's natural felicity can be said to be attained only in its immortal, separated condition. Since nature does not frustrate, the soul's reasonable, natural desire for the tranquil contemplation of this condition cannot be in vain. Now, since no created intellect by its own power can attain the first God, the separated soul's natural contemplative felicity must needs consist in its conversion to the intellectual light of the lowest Intelligence, as Dionysius and Avicenna teach. By this light, the soul is more powerfully illumined, and more sincerely understands and more splendidly intuits the first truth. Asked whether the soul felicitates in the lowest Intelligence as in its end, Denys responds by restating the rule of hierarchical, mediating illumination of the first cause:

> According to Dionysius, Augustine, and Avicebron, what place causes in corporeal things, order effects in spiritual things. For the intellectual rays of the first light flow from the first intellects to the last in a most becoming order. Indeed, the light of the first intellect is the strongest, and is disproportionate to the capacities of lower created minds, until it is adapted for them through intermediary supercelestial souls, as is said in the *Liber de causis*. Since therefore the rational soul was created in the shadow of the lowest

---

70. *De lum.* 1.a.45 (*Op. om.* 33: 286B–287A′). *Boethii Philosophiae consolatio,* 3. pros. 2 (ed. Ludwig Bieler, *CCSL* 94: 38).
71. *De lum.* 1.a.46 (*Op. om.* 33: 287B′–289A).
72. *De lum.* 1.a.50 (*Op. om.* 33: 291D′–293C).

Intelligence, it is plain that the light of the lowest Intelligence is more fully proportionate to it, and that through the light of the lowest Intelligence the soul knows more distinctly and sublimely. This is so because the intellects of the first orders, since they are closer to the first intellect, understand more perfectly by means of fewer, more universal species, while the inferior intellects understand through many, more particular species, as the author of *Liber de causis* and Proclus attest. Whence the first intellect contemplates all things fully by means of one, most simple species; what is closer to the first intellect, assuredly, is more similar to it. Thus, the species of the first intellects do not descend into the soul except through intermediaries. . . . Thus, it is manifest that the natural beatitude of the separated soul must be placed in its contemplation of the Intelligence of the lowest order and union with its intellectual light.[73]

Denys thus affirms the idea the appearances of which he saved in *De contemplatione*. He does not mean to say that the felicity of the separated soul consists in contemplation of the lowest Intelligence, but rather that the soul can contemplate the first truth only "according to the analogy and mode of its proper species and . . . only through union with the proximate and immediate Intelligence."[74] Only supernatural grace, we shall see, enables the soul to transcend this rigorous natural order.

Denys finds authority for his teaching in Avicenna. Avicenna erred, too, concerning the nature of agent intellect and the intellectual mem-

---

73. *De lum.* 1.a.47 (*Op. om.* 33: 289A′–D′): "secundum Dionysium, Augustinum et Avicebron, quod in corporalibus agit situs, in spiritualibus efficit ordo. Intellectuales etenim radii primae lucis ordine decentissimo defluunt a primis intellectibus usque ad extremos: lumen quippe primi intellectus fortissimum est, et capacitatibus inferiorum [cr]eatarum mentium improportionatum, donec per intermedios supercoelestes animos ipsis coaptetur, ut in libro Causarum dicitur. Quoniam igitur rationalis anima in umbra ultimae intelligentiae creata est, palam fit quod lumen ultimae intelligentiae proportionatum est ei amplius: sic quod per ipsum distinctius cognoscit et sublimius. Cujus ratio est, quia ut auctor libri Causarum et Proclus attestantur, intellectus primorum ordinum, quo fuerint primo intellectui viciniores, eo universalioribus paucioribusque speciebus perfectius intelligunt, inferiores vero, per species particulariores et plures. Unde et primus intellectus una simplicissima specie omnia plene contemplatur: et ob id quod est ipsi vicinius, est utique et ei similius. Non igitur descendunt species primorum intellectuum in animam nisi per intermedios. . . . Nunc igitur manifestum est, quod per contemplationem intelligentiae imi ordinis, ac unionem ad ejus intellectuale lumen, sit naturalis beatitudo separatae animae statuenda." Pseudo-Dionysius, *De coel. hier.* 7, 10 (*Op. om.* 15: 118, 191); Proclus, *Elem. theo.*, theorems 60–62, pp. 287–88; *Liber de causis*, prop. 9, pp. 158–60.
74. *De lum.* 1.a.47 (*Op. om.* 33: 290A′).

ory. But of all the philosophers, Denys says, he spoke most sublimely on the soul's final felicity, which Aristotle did not determine.[75] In *De lumine* and throughout *De puritate* Denys develops Avicenna's teaching concerning the way in which the soul gradually becomes adept at intelligible contemplation of separated substances. For Denys, it is apparent, Avicenna most justly mediates Peripatetic and Platonist understandings of the soul.[76] Denys does not, however, take the usual Christian ploy of identifying Avicenna's agent intellect with God himself. Rather, he keeps the illumining intellect in its proper place, only he identifies it with an angelic Intelligence who illumines the soul's highest, natural contemplation. Denys is an example, then, not of an "Augustinisme avicennisant," but of a "Dionysianisme avicennisant."[77] If Avicenna cannot be saved, he can be granted rest. Surely, he was one of those philosophers, adorned with heroic virtues, who through habitual "abstraction from sensibles become adept at eminent speculation of metaphysical essences."[78] Such souls, free of all save original sin, rest in limbo content in natural felicity.[79]

From the standpoint of this doctrine of natural felicity, Denys sharply criticizes Thomas Aquinas' and Giles of Rome's teaching about the soul's natural desire for God, which he perceives to violate fundamental principles of nature and knowing. Denys introduces this criticism at strategic points in *De lumine*, and expands it three years later in *De puritate*.[80]

75. *De lum.* 1.a.48 (*Op. om.* 33: 290B′–291C′).
76. I intend to show Avicenna's role in an extended study of Denys's teaching on the soul.
77. See Gilson, "Les sources," 84–102, and "Pourquoi saint Thomas a critiqué saint Augustin," *AHDLMA* 1 (1926–27): 46–127. In "Les sources," 96 n.2, Gilson says: "Nous pensons à ce qu'Augustin a souvent répété. Dieu préside à l'âme humaine. "nulla natura interposita." En ce sens et sur ce point, Avicenne était en contradiction absolue avec l'augustinisme comme d'ailleurs avec toute philosophie chrétienne." With the last, on the authority of pseudo-Dionysius, Denys disagrees. See n. 59 above.
78. *De cont.* 3.a.7 (*Op. om.* 41: 263A): "Et respondendum, quod quidem praeclari philosophi naturalibus virtutibus decorati, qui se ad philosophicas considerationes totaliter extenderunt, atque per abstractionem a sensibilibus ad eminentem metaphysicalium essentiarum speculationem apti fuerunt, interdum ad summi Dei contemplationem quamdam praeclaram atque suavem perducti sunt, quantum per scientias acquisitas naturaleque lumen, per naturalem quoque Dei amorem et virtutes naturaliter adipiscibiles, fieri potuit."
79. *Elementatio philosophica*, prop. 159 (*Op. om.* 34: 231C′).
80. *De lum.* 1.aa.51–52, 2.aa.2–3, 56 (*Op. om.* 33: 293C–B′, 388C′–389A, 390C, 455B–B′); *De pur.* aa. 56–61 (*Op. om.* 40: 431–434C′). See Martin Beer, *Dionysius' des Kartäusers Lehre vom desiderium naturale des Menschen nach der Gottesschau*, Münchener Theologische Studien 2.28 (Munich, 1963), and Henri de Lubac, S.J., *The Mystery of the Supernatural*, trans. Rosemary Sheed (New York, 1967), 185–87.

Like Denys, Thomas held that every created perfection falls infinitely short of the divine essence and can only imperfectly represent its purity. From this, however, he drew conclusions opposite to Denys's. Knowledge of God through creatures is imperfect; every imperfect appetite seeks to perfect itself; hence, imperfect knowledge of God seeks its perfection, and the natural desire to know is not quieted until it rests in contemplation of the divine essence. Similarly, through creatures one can only know God in the manner *quia*; but what one knows *quia* he desires to know *quid est*; therefore, etc. Further, the nearer the mind comes to something, the more vehemently it desires it. Hence, the closer the human mind comes to the divine essence, the more intensely it desires perfect knowledge of it.[81] In short, it is the very inadequacy of philosophic knowledge that engenders desire for the vision of the divine essence.

Denys thinks that these arguments presuppose what they ought to prove, namely, that the soul in fact has a natural desire for the vision of the divine essence.[82] But nature does not tend to the impossible, nor does the created mind have a natural desire to see God as he is, the possibility of which no "pure philosopher" ever conceded. One desires knowledge *quid est* only insofar as the object allows and only insofar as one judges it possible. (Natural desire is perfectly measured by the understanding.) Now, whatever is inscribed in nature has been discussed by the philosophers, but no philosopher has ever spoken of an immediate vision of God or the desire for it. They knew that no natural desire remains vain, or longs for something impossible.[83] Besides this positive testimony of "pure" natural experience, Denys offers more philosophic rejoinders. "To each created mind belongs a vision of the divine light commensurate with the specific subsistence and substantial grade of its proper nature and species." Whereas a mediated vision of the divine essence may not be simply perfect, it is perfect according to the proportions and capacities of created intellects. Moreover, not only is the nature of a created intellect limited, its intellectual desire is contracted analogously to the nature from which it flows. In other

---

81. *De lum.* 1.a.51 (*Op. om.* 33: 293C–D′); *De pur.* a.57 (*Op. om.* 40: 431C′–432D). In these texts, Denys takes Thomas's arguments from *Summa contra gentiles* 3.50: see also 3.41–45, where Thomas rejects the possibility of knowing separated substances in this life, or of finding felicity in such knowledge. Denys refers to Giles of Rome's commentary on *De anima* 3.

82. *De lum.* 1.a.52 (*Op. om.* 33: 294B′).

83. *De pur.* a.56 (*Op. om.* 40: 431C); *De lum.* 2.a.56 (*Op. om.* 33: 455A′–B′).

words, natural desire follows the order of its species and does not extend beyond its capacity. Neither God nor nature frustrates the soul
by implanting in it a desire for something it cannot obtain. As Denys
declares often, "modus agendi parificatur modo essendi."[84]

Denys's arguments have a certain Aristotelian look, and to some
they appear to anticipate modern ideas of an autonomous natural
finality.[85] Their inspiration is quite different, however. Denys's arguments are founded on a strict hierarchical vision of nature, as taught
by pseudo-Dionysius and other ancient "theologians." This becomes
clearer in De puritate when Denys must confront, in a special article,
an argument that strikes close to his own principles. "A quo processio,
in id conversio"; but the soul is created immediately by God; therefore it cannot find bliss in anything save the immediate vision of God.[86]
On the contrary, Denys responds, all of the highest philosophers—
Aristotle, Plato, Proclus, the author of Liber de causis—assert that the
divine essence is unknowable to every created intellect. According to
them, no created mind can see the first Intelligence through a species
more clear than its own essence, or beyond its own natural power.
Thus, the vision of the divine nature is proportioned to the weakest
minds through a mediating order of intellectual substances. The lower
intellect, then, returns naturally to the intellect next above it, and
through it unites its powers to, and seeks to find bliss in the first source
of things.[87]

Denys does not intend to suggest that the order of nature closes the
human soul completely to the immediate experience of God. To prevent this inference, he resorts to a distinction which some modern historians (wrongly) think the distinguishing mark of nominalist thought.
All things serve the hierarchical law of God's "ordinata potentia,"
which he has instituted by means of his "absoluta potentia" in a
wholly free and wise manner. Nevertheless, in every created nature
there is a "certain innate, obediential power" by which the creature is
able to obey the command of the creator in those things which are
above nature. It is this power, related to God's supernatural bounty

84. De lum. 1.a.52, 2.a.56 (Op. om. 33: 294, 455D–A'); De pur. a.58 (Op. om. 40:
432C'–433A).
85. De Lubac, 187, while acknowledging the difference, says that Denys nevertheless "opened the way for Cajetan." With respect to this doctrine, Beer, 157, calls Denys
"der erste neuzeitlich denkende Theologe."
86. De pur. a.57 (Op. om. 40: 432A).
87. De pur. aa. 60–61 (Op. om. 40: 433A'–434A').

and absolute power, to which is assigned the capacity and desire for supernatural beatitude.[88] Such a desire cannot be natural, but arises only from a gift of grace.[89]

Denys's disagreement with Thomas is not minor, and it involves many others. Not all of these are explicit in *De lumine*, but their seeds are latent. For example, in this work Denys notes that "Avicenna, Albert, and many of the more solemn philosophers say that the soul in the condition of this life is able to gaze upon separated substances and to contemplate by intuition the quiddities of things without phantasms." Here Denys simply rehearses a few of Thomas's arguments against the notion.[90] In *De puritate*, he states the arguments on both sides,[91] but by the time of the *Elementatio philosophica* (1465), armed with new arguments of contemporary Albertists and Henry of Ghent, he states as propositions: "It is not necessary for man to look on some phantasm in every intellectual act," and "It does not seem contrary to the nature of the rational soul, nor impossible by nature, that in this life it be able to understand the *quid est* of a separated substance clearly and immediately."[92] Not only the gravity of his philosophic thought moved Denys's change. For it is the constant witness of Christian mystics that contemplation in its higher acts is without phantasms. Since Christian contemplation is the exemplar of natural contemplation, there must be something in the latter that exemplifies the higher forms of the former. Moreover, imageless contemplation in this life is considered a foretaste of the Christian's final beatitude; by proportion, there should be an analogous foretaste of final felicity in the mirror of natural wisdom.

As he proceeds to the consideration of supernatural wisdom in *De lumine*, Denys states clearly the usefulness of philosophic study. In the natural order, he says, the human soul does not become a contemplator of the highest and most difficult truths unless it exercise and adapt itself to natural wisdom and science. Philosophic exercise dis-

88. *De pur.* a.59 (*Op. om.* 40: 433B–D).
89. *De lum.* 2.a.2 (*Op. om.* 33: 388C′).
90. *De lum.* 1.a.100 (*Op. om.* 33: 362B).
91. *De pur.* a.17 (*Op. om.* 40: 406A′–407A).
92. *Elementatio philosophica*, prop. 45 (*Op. om.* 33: 57D–59C′): "Non est necesse hominem in omni actu intellectivo phantasma aliquod speculari"; prop. 75 (84C′–85A′): "Non videtur naturae rationalis animae repugnare, neque per naturam impossibile est, intelligere in hac vita substantiam separatam clare et immediate quantum ad quid est." Here Denys cites "Albertus in tractatu suo de Intellectu et intelligibili." See this work, 2.9, ed. A. Borgnet, *B. Alberti Magni Opera omnia* 9 (Paris, 1890), 316–17.

124

poses the intellect for the knowledge of truth above all reason. It renders the soul capable of such truth and enables the soul to strive for it more profoundly.[93] Philosophic abstraction, in short, is part of an ascetic regime that prepares the soul for the reception of spiritual experience.

The philosophic wisdom so amply unfolded in De lumine I Denys abridges and contextualizes in De contemplatione. Book I of De contemplatione treats the symbolic and intelligible affirmative theologies. It comprises Denys's fivefold classification of modes of contemplation, distinguished in descending order according to their formal objects: contemplation of the Trinity, of the superessential simple God, of the incarnate Word, of the gifts of grace, and of the gifts of nature.[94] Denys derives the architecture of this classification largely from Bonaventure and in part from Bernard, as is made clear in Book II, where he reports the classifications of various mystics and doctors (pseudo-Dionysius, Origen, Augustine, Bernard, Hugh and Richard of St. Victor, Thomas Aquinas, Bonaventure, Jan van Ruusbroec, Thomas Gallus, Guigo de Ponte).[95] Unlike Bonaventure, however, who relates contemplation of the incarnate Christ to that of the Trinity and God's highest name (goodness), Denys situates this contemplation in the mediate position. His fellow Carthusian, Guigo de Ponte,[96] may have inspired him in this, but in any case, such placement conforms more closely with the teaching of pseudo-Dionysius. Denys includes materials concerning natural wisdom under the second mode of contemplation of "the most simple deity."[97] One may attain this object by human reason; appropriately enough, in this treatise Denys emphasizes the assistance of sanctifying grace. By hierarchical rule, the two wisdoms convene here in their formal object—the natural at its apex, the supernatural at its beginning.

Denys identifies contemplation and mystical theology with the highest act of the gift of wisdom.[98] On the basis of these identities, he

93. De lum. 2.a.1 (Op. om. 33: 387C'-D').
94. De cont. 1.aa.26-71 (Op. om. 41: 165C'-229D').
95. De cont. 2.aa.1-11 (Op. om. 41: 231-53). Denys's treatment of pseudo-Dionysius here (232B-236B') is confined to the spiritual motions of the soul as treated by Thomas Aquinas in ST 2a2ae.q.180.a.6. The teaching of pseudo-Dionysius is the basis for Book III of De cont.
96. See De cont. 1.aa.8, 11 (Op. om. 41: 245B-247B', 252D'-253D'). Guigo de Ponte's De contemplatione has now been edited: Traité sur la contemplation, ed. and trans. into French by Philippe Dupont, 2 vols. Analecta Cartusiana 72 (Salzburg, 1985).
97. De cont. 1.aa.38-44 (Op. om. 41: 179B-188A).
98. De cont. 1.a.3. 3.a.10 (Op. om. 41: 138C, 265C-266C).

judges that mystical union pertains formally to the intellect. Christian contemplation, like its natural subordinate, virtually includes affection, which is the "formative complement" of vision in the intellect.[99] Denys's insistence on the priority of intellect in mystical union leads him to a formulation of the traditional threefold way quite different from the standard: the contemplative life exists dispositively in the purgative way, essentially or formally in the illuminative way, and *completive* in the unitive way.[100]

Denys's manner of formal-essential definition causes him to be far more exclusive than Thomas Aquinas in his attribution of contemplative union to the intellect. In *De donis*, Denys reports Thomas's determination of the question as to whether the gift of wisdom is speculative or practical. By means of his composite logic, Thomas concludes that "wisdom as a gift is not merely speculative but also practical" because it not only considers divine things in themselves but also consults them in directing human acts amidst contingent affairs.[101] For Denys, on the other hand, formally speaking, wisdom can only be either speculative or practical. In a contemplative life, acts amidst contingent affairs have no integral finality, but dispose immediately to their ultimate end, thereby making the same act essentially different than it would be in an active life. Rejoining Thomas, Denys adduces Henry of Ghent—rare in the early treatises: "a name is imposed from the final and proper end directly and properly intended; whence Henry of Ghent calls wisdom speculative absolutely."[102] For the same reason, Denys disagrees with Thomas's conclusion that the gift of understanding is partly speculative, partly practical; it too is wholly speculative, because "species or denomination is assigned with respect to the principal object and ultimate end."[103] Thomas likewise determines that the gift of science is primarily speculative, secondarily practical; to the contrary, keeping things formally distinct, Denys argues that the gift of science is wholly practical.[104] In each instance, he counters Thomas with the authority of Jan van Ruusbroec, about whom I shall speak presently.

In *De contemplatione*, Denys poses a series of questions concerning

99. *De cont.* 1.aa.7, 11 (*Op. om.* 41: 141C′, 144B′).
100. *De cont.* 3.a.14 (*Op. om.* 41: 270B′).
101. Thomas Aquinas, *ST* 2a2ae.q.45.a.3 *in corp.*
102. *De donis* 2.a.10 (*Op. om.* 35: 183D).
103. *De donis* 2.a.29 (*Op. om.* 35: 200A–B′). Thomas Aquinas, *ST* 2a2ae.q.8.a.3.
104. *De donis* 3.a.27 (*Op. om.* 35: 228C′–229D). Thomas Aquinas, *ST* 2a2ae.q.9.a.3.

the active and contemplative lives derived directly from a series of articles in Thomas's *Summa theologiae*. The same pattern of difference emerges. To Denys's mind, there is no such reality as a mixed life, which Thomas, on the other hand, said to be superior to either a strictly active or strictly contemplative one. Somewhat ironically, Denys takes his arguments from a question in the *Summa* where Thomas simply argues the sufficiency of the ancient division between active and contemplative lives. Augustine spoke of a leisured life (*otium*), a life occupied with external affairs (*negotium*), and a mixture of both. Any mean, however, is confected from the simple elements of its extremes, and is virtually comprehended by one or the other, depending upon which predominates. Moreover, all human concern pertains either to providing the necessities of this life (the active life) or to the consideration of truth (the contemplative life). As the human intellect is twofold, practical or speculative, so human life is twofold, active or contemplative. Again, as Aristotle says (*Eth.* 9), one most rejoices in what he most desires, and he wishes to live together with what he desires as with a friend. Men either principally intend exterior actions or the contemplation of truth, and thus their lives are either active or contemplative.

Denys's comments change the direction of this question. Not only does he exclude a mixed life but he also undermines any final distinction, for Christians, between active and contemplative lives. All of the acts of a Christian must refer to the end of the contemplative life, the cognition of truth *in patria*: "whatever we think, desire, speak about, do, or suffer we ought to refer to the beatific vision of God." The sincere cognition of God informed by charity cannot be referred to anything else, since it virtually includes delectation as its formative complement. The life of all Christians, then, must be contemplative; the active life assumes its species only from proximate ends. Thus, all true "friends" of God, religious or secular, endeavor to draw closer to the life of contemplation. In this remark, I think, Denys has in mind Ruusbroec's definition of the "friends" of God, "who cling to God by a loving and intimate adherence, extending themselves to spiritual taste and internal exercise." Finally, Denys notes, some acts often assigned to the active life, such as preaching or teaching sacred doctrine, actually have a greater propinquity to the contemplative life.[105]

105. *De cont.* 1.a.11 (*Op. om.* 41: 144A'–145D'). Thomas Aquinas, *ST* 2a2ae.q.179. aa.1–2. For Thomas's treatment of a threefold religious life, see *ST* 2a2ae.q.188.a.6.

In another question, Thomas concludes that the contemplative life may be said to consist in one act in the sense that, although many acts constitute such a life, these derive unity from the one act that completes them. This sounds well enough to Denys. However, Thomas, to argue his conclusion, refers to the distinction between simple angelic minds and human minds, which must proceed discursively to the truth by multiple acts.[106] With this Denys disagrees. The act which defines the contemplative life is simple, not an integral whole made up of many. Thomas's resolution

holds for contemplation of those things which are arrived at by way of inferior things through the inquiry of reason and study; it does not hold for more sublime contemplations, which radiating from the Holy Spirit above, are divinely infused, when God supernaturally touches, annoints, and illumines the mind. In such contemplations, the human mind acts in an angelic manner, which the great Dionysius calls deiform, because in a simple glance (*ictu*) and heaven-formed (*coeliformi*) gaze (*conspectu*) it discerns the truth.[107]

Finally, Thomas decides that the active life will not remain *in patria*.[108] On the contrary, Denys argues, Dionysius shows that the higher angels continually purify, illumine, and perfect the lower ones, and that the angels govern the ecclesiastical hierarchy. In the same way, the virtues of the active life exist virtually, in a more sublime way, in the souls of the blessed, and they flow downwards from the plenitude of the blessed souls' contemplation.[109]

Denys's treatment of these questions, I think, reveals his self-understanding. From the perspective of Thomas's teaching, Denys lived a mixed life of contemplation, preaching, and teaching. Such a life,

---

For Denys's allusion to Ruusbroec's distinction among mercenaries, faithful servants, secret friends, and hidden sons of God, see *De cont.* 3.a.23 (285D'–286D).

106. Thomas Aquinas, *ST* 2a2ae.q.180.a.3 *in corp.*

107. *De cont.* 1.a.12 (*Op. om.* 41: 146A'–B'): "Sed hoc locum habet in contemplationibus ad quas ab inferiori per rationis inquisitionem ac studium pervenitur; non autem in contemplationibus sublimioribus, quae Spiritu Sancto desuper radiante, coelitus infunduntur, Deo mentem supernaturaliter tangente, ungente ac illustrante. Nempe in talibus habet se mens humana angelico modo, et a magno Dionysio deiformis vocatur, quoniam simplici ictu ac coeliformi conspectu veritatem dignoscit."

108. Thomas Aquinas, *ST* 2a2ae.q.181.a.4.

109. *De cont.* 1.a.18 (*Op. om.* 41: 153D'–154D').

proper for mendicants, was improper among the strictly contemplative Carthusians. By a different logic, however, Denys argues that all of the works he engages in are comprehended virtually by the formal definition of the contemplative life in its highest, unified act. It is, after all, a principle of hierarchical operation that the higher effects more by means of fewer species.[110]

As is wont in mystical treatises, Book III of *De contemplatione* treats the highest form of contemplation. This is the negative way of pseudo-Dionysius, which is a mean between intelligible affirmative theology and the beatific vision.[111] In accordance with his general principles and like Nicholas of Cusa, Denys understands that the negative way yields some kind of cognition. The negative way denies our concepts as we conceive them analogically from creatures. Nevertheless, although we cannot comprehend the manner, we know that (*quia*) some divine attributes are predicated properly of God. Among these, besides goodness, light, and being, is infinity. Denys deduces God's infinity from his pure act of existence, which lacks the composition (*hyliathin*) that defines created spiritual substances. God is "truly, intrinsically, formally, intensively and perfectionately infinite. . . . This infinity is the first, intrinsic and most worthy property of God"; thus, he is incomparably and incomprehensibly greater than anything else, "since between the finite and the infinite there is no comparison or proportion." Elsewhere, Denys praises Avicebron and (uncharacteristically) Duns Scotus for their analyses of infinity as a positive divine attribute.[112] When we negate our analogical concepts, love penetrates where cognition cannot go. Instantaneously a new knowledge

---

110. See, e.g., *De lum.* 1.a.57 (*Op. om.* 33: 301A'–B'): "quod id quod virtus inferior facit per plura, superior facit per pauciora." Denys employs this principle throughout his writings; see n. 73 above.

111. This adapts Anselm's definition of theological understanding in general, which lies "inter fidem et speciem." See Anselm's commendation "ad Urbanum Papam II," in *Cur Deus Homo*, ed. F. S. Schmitt, *S. Anselmi Cantuariensis opera omnia* 2 (Edinburgh, 1946) 40.

112. *De cont.* 1.a.40 (*Op. om.* 41: 182D–A'); *De lum.* 1.a.17 (*Op. om.* 33: 251A'–252D); *De nat.* aa. 24–25 (*Op. om.* 34: 41D–44C). For Scotus's "very subtle and beautiful" teaching concerning God's infinity, see *De nat.* a.24 (42C'–43B). For the composition (*hyliathin*) of spiritual creatures, see *Liber de causis*, prop. 8, p. 157. In all the texts cited here, Denys also alleges *Liber de causis*, prop. 15, p. 168: "Omnes virtutes quibus non est finis, pendentes sunt per infinitum primum, quod est virtus virtutum." For some aspects of Denys's doctrine, see Raymond Macken, "The Intellectual Intuition of the Infinity of God in the Philosophy of Denys the Carthusian," *Franziskanische Studien* 68 (1985): 237–46.

is introduced to the mind, connecting it directly to God. The mind is then fixed in the divine light and infinity, contemplating it most limpidly, intuiting it most certainly, and completely dissolving in the fire of love.[113] As Ruusbroec says, we then intuit the abyssal clarity and divine nakedness without any image and beyond any manner.[114]

More than an instrumental dialectic, the experiential intuition of God's infinite goodness and being and blinding light negates our logical conceptions. By its very property, infinity negates, and so the dialectic of the negative way never rests in either of its poles. For Denys, as for Cusanus, theology is circular; that is, all of the divine attributes are infinitely identical in God.[115] Hence Denys never relents his criticism of Scotus and the *formalizantes* for their formal distinctions in God and their doctrine of the univocity of being.[116] At the same time, he sharply rebukes Thomas for misreading Maimonides, as if this "very great philosopher and theologian . . . absolutely and simply . . . taught that nothing could be said of God positively or substantially."[117] Likewise he criticizes Thomas for thinking that pseudo-Dionysius predicated light of God only metaphorically.[118]

Denys may now turn to the contemporary question: "whether mystical theology is essentially love or cognition." Denys summarily dismisses an affective interpretation of pseudo-Dionysius. He alludes to "a certain recent (*novellum*) doctor" who simple-mindedly distinguishes speculative and mystical theology by arguing that the subject of speculative theology is the intellect and its object the true, while

---

113. *De cont.* 3.a.5. (*Op. om.* 41: 259D′–260A).

114. *De cont.* 3.a.6 (*Op. om.* 41: 261D′–262B). Denys quotes here from Ruusbroec's "De sacramento altaris": cf. *Speculum aeternae salutis*, (alternate title), trans. L. Surius, *D. Ioannis Rusbrochii opera omnia* (Cologne, 1552; reprint. Farnborough-Hants, 1967), 39–40. Denys usually translates Ruusbroec's Netherlands himself, but we know that he used Geert Groote's Latin translation of *De ornatu spiritualis disponsationis*; see Epiney-Burgard, 125–33.

115. Nicholas of Cusa, *De docta ignorantia*, ed. E. Hoffmann and R. Klibansky, *Opera omnia* 1 (Leipzig, 1932) 2.3, pp. 71–72. For Denys on the divine attributes and their unity in God, see the texts cited in n. 68 above.

116. *De lum.* 1.aa.13, 57 (*Op. om.* 33: 247A′–248D, 301D–B′); *De nat.* a.35 (*Op. om.* 34: 59D′–61C).

117. *De nat.* a.31 (53D–54B′): "Verumtamen, quamvis B. Thomae non minimus imitator, amator et fautor exsistam, tamen salva in omnibus tanti Doctoris reverentia, quantum judicare praevaleo, has positiones, et maxime primam, videlicet Rabbi Moysis, qui erat maximus philosophus atque theologus, insufficienter resolvit, determinat, reprobat . . ." Denys supports Maimonides against Thomas by reference to pseudo-Dionysius.

118. *De nat.* a.55 (*Op. om.* 34: 87B).

the subject of mystical theology is the affective power and its object the good. The "recent doctor" is Jean Gerson.[119] The reason of the good, no less than the reason of the true, is an analogical concept negated by mystical theology. The object of mystical theology, in terms of the *via eminentiae* which reduces to the *via ablationis*, is the incomprehensible *superbonum*.[120] More reverently, Denys turns to the *quaestio unica* of Hugh of Balma. He disputes Hugh's interpretations of pseudo-Dionysius and multiplies arguments showing that the will can never proceed without a prior and coordinate act of intellect. Denys, nevertheless, "saves" the teaching of his Carthusian forebear, observing that acts of love can be so fervent and absorbing that they often obliterate awareness of the cognitive act sustaining them. Hugh also knew that the mind can be illustrated from above as well as by an ascending consideration of God's goodness in his creatures.[121]

If mystical union resided in the affections, it would necessarily be short, since without cognition the will would lose its object. Denys refers to texts by Gregory and Bernard which affirm that contemplative union is momentary. Thomas Aquinas likewise says that the highest contemplative act is brief, in the question of the *Summa* upon which Denys bases his article.[122] To the contrary, Denys argues, the act by its nature is almost inescapably long. Against Thomas and other authorities, he quotes a text from Ruusbroec:

> when we are transformed in the divine clarity, in the uncreated and eternal light, there we are forgetful of our very selves, and are one with it. Thus we live in it and it in us, although we remain distinct in substance. The clarity of God which we see within us has no beginning, end, time, place, manner, form, species or color. It entirely surrounds, comprehends, penetrates or passes through us, and opens our simple sight so widely, that

---

119. See *Ioannis Carlerii de Gerson De mystica theologia*, ed. André Combes (Lucca, 1958), 1.6.29, pp. 73–74: "speculativa (igitur) theologia est in potentia intellectiva, cuius obiectum est verum, misticam vero reponimus in potentia affectiva, cui pro obiecto bonum assignamus . . . obiectum speculative theologie est verum et mistice bonum."

120. *De cont.* 3.aa.3, 4, 14 (*Op. om.* 41: 357B′–C′, 258B′–259C, 269C′–270D′).

121. *De cont.* 3.a.15 (*Op. om.* 41: 271A–274D). For Hugh of Balma's text, see n. 34 above. Denys's remark that fervent love can obliterate awareness of cognition echoes Cusanus; see n. 35 above.

122. Thomas Aquinas, *ST* 2a2ae.q.180.a.8 *ad ob.* 6.

necessarily our eye stays open perpetually, and we are scarcely able to lose it.[123]

Denys adds that this contemplation engenders such a corresponding desire to persist in it, that it is not at all easy to recall the mind from its intuition.

Many times Ruusbroec contradicts the authority of Thomas, whom Denys otherwise calls "the most distinguished doctor among the moderns."[124] In a remarkable passage from *De donis*, Denys expresses Ruusbroec's authority:

I do not know how to name the marvelous man, master John Ruusbroec, except to say that as venerable Hugh of St. Victor is called another Augustine because of the eminence of his science, so this wondrous John may be named another Dionysius because of his most excellent wisdom. . . . Therefore, since this man had such great wisdom, worthily I call him the Divine Doctor, because he had no teacher but the Holy Spirit. For he was otherwise illiterate and an *idiota*, in the same way that the archapostles Peter and John are said by Luke to be illiterate in the Acts of the Apostles. Whence he wrote his books in the vernacular, the profundity and pith of which nevertheless, no one can wonder at fully enough. And since I am certain that this man was taught by the Holy Spirit, his authority with me is great.[125]

123. *De cont.* 3.a.16 (*Op. om.* 41: 261B'–C'): "Ubi translati et transformati fuerimus in claritate divina, videlicet luce aeterna et increata, ibi obliti sumus nostri ipsorum, et sumus unum cum ipsa: sicque vivimus in ipsa, et ipsa in nobis; semper tamen substantia divisi manemus. Claritas Dei quam videmus in nobis, non habet initium, finem, tempus, locum, viam semitam, formam, speciem, neque colorem. Ipsa nos totaliter circumsepsit, comprehendit, penetravit seu pertransiit, ac simplicem visum nostrum tam ample aperuit, quod oportet oculum nostrum perpetuo stare apertum, nec ipsum claudere possumus aut valemus." Denys quotes from "in libro de Sacramento altaris"; cf. Ruusbroec, *Speculum aeternae salutis*, trans. Surius, 41.

124. *De donis* 1.a.8 (*Op. om.* 35: 165C): "doctor inter modernos eximius"; *De cont.* 2.a.7 (*Op. om.* 41: 244B'): "insignem philosophum atque profundum egregiumque theologum."

125. *De donis* 2.a.13 (*Op. om.* 35: 184B'–D'): "Vir autem mirabilis, dominus Joannes Ruysbroeck: quem qualiter digne appellem ignoro, nisi ut quemadmodum venerabilis ille Hugo de S. Victore propter eminentem suam scientiam vocatus est alter Augustinus, sic Joannes iste mirabilis propter excellentissimam suam sapientiam nominetur alter Dionysius. . . . Quoniam igitur vir hic tantae sapientiae fuit, merito eum appello Doctorem divinum, quia instructorem non habuit nisi Spiritum Sanctum. Erat enim alias illiteratus ac idiota, eo utique modo quo Petrus et Joannes archiapostoli a Luca in Actibus Apostolorum illiterati fuisse narrantur. Unde et libros suos in vulgari conscripsit: quorum tamen profunditatem atque sententiam nemo ad plenum mirari

Elsewhere I have expounded the many dimensions to this text.[126] Suffice it to say that Ruusbroec participates the authority of pseudo-Dionysius, or the very authority of the "wisdom of Christians."

Since philosophic contemplation embraces every formal element of Christian contemplation, save elevating grace, their difference can only be one of degree. Paradoxically, the sublimity of the Christian contemplative vision, in comparison to the pagan achievement, is measured by sensible—or non-sensible—effects. Thus, Denys points out that the philosophers did not have raptures like the Christians, or none, surely, that lasted so long.[127] Strictly speaking, rapture or ecstasy is caused by a total abstraction of reason that so wholly occupies the soul, the mind cannot turn to any of its lower operations. Hence, in rapture the imaginative and sensible powers cease to operate.[128] We see the evidence for such sublime abstraction in the lives of the saints. Besides John, Paul, Mary Magdalene, Catherine of Siena, Elizabeth of Spalbeeck, Ruusbroec, and a host of others, Denys cites the example of Aquinas' levitations.[129] Against mockers of Christian religion like Porphyry, these ecstasies "demonstrate experimentally that the Christian law comes from the true God."[130]

Rapture is the necessary condition for the "culmen perfectionis" in this life, the transient vision *per speciem* of the divine essence. Like Augustine and Aquinas,[131] Denys concedes this experience to Moses and Paul, here and in his scriptural commentaries.[132] By condign reasons, he argues the same for the Virgin Mary.[133] Such a vision would

---

jam valet. Quoniam itaque certus sum virum istum a Spiritu Sancto instructum, propterea magna est ejus auctoritas apud me."

126. Kent Emery, Jr., "The Carthusians, Intermediaries for the Teaching of John Ruysbroeck during the Period of Early Reform and in the Counter-Reformation," *Analecta Cartusiana* 43 (Salzburg, 1979): 102–4. For the tradition of Ruusbroec's divine inspiration, see André Combes, *Essai sur la critique de Ruuysbroeck par Gerson* (4 vols., Paris, 1945–72), 2: 67–68, 84–98, and Joannes de Schoonhoven's *Epistola responsalis*, ed. Combes, in 1: 727–31.

127. *De cont.* 3.a.7 (*Op. om.* 41: 263B'–C').
128. *De cont.* 3.a.18 (*Op. om.* 41: 279B–C).
129. *De cont.* 3.a.19 (*Op. om.* 41: 279D'–281C').
130. *De cont.* 3.a.20 (*Op. om.* 41: 282B'–C').
131. Augustine, *De Genesi ad litteram* 12 (PL 34: 453–86); Thomas Aquinas, *ST*, 1.q.12.a.11 *ad* 2.
132. P. Alessio Martinelli, O.F.M., "La Visione di Dio 'per speciem' durante la presente vita secondo S. Dionigi il Certosino (1402–1471)," *Divinitas* 2 (1958): 371–408, esp. 390–94.
133. *De cont.* 3.a.24 (*Op. om.* 41: 287A'–B'). See Martinelli, 377–89; and P. Bonaventura Tonutti, O.F.M., *Mariologia Dionysii Cartusiani* (1402–1471) (Rome, 1953), 147–52.

require an abstraction yet more sublime than that of mystical union. Indeed, it would require virtual death, as various scriptural texts testify. Hence we must suppose that Moses and Paul "were abstracted completely from all actual life of the flesh and the senses."[134] That Thomas conceded these visions to Moses and Paul suggests his deference to traditional authority; he did so, it seems to me, rather to prove the rule of ordinary human cognition in light of its rare exceptions. For Denys, these experiences supply the final element in the paradigm of Christian wisdom, and he reads the evidence in another way. Thus, he refuses to deny the possibility of this vision to others. He notes that certain saints speak as if they had had the experience.[135] I think that he has Ruusbroec in mind.

De contemplatione ends with the testimony of Ruusbroec. In the perfected, deified state of the contemplative life, Denys says, the soul finds itself embraced in the life of the superessential Trinity, in the mutual, infinite delight and enjoyment of the infinite God, the eternally generated Word, and the spiration of love proceeding from them both. Here the soul expires in God, and is deiformally simplified, transformed, immersed, and absorbed in him. Denys remarks that Ruusbroec spoke often in this way. Only one who reads Ruusbroec's words superficially, like Gerson, would think that they meant the soul's created being to be converted into the ideal, uncreated being of God. This is a "most crude and foolish error." Ruusbroec did not speak of the consumption of the soul's being, but of the melioration of its manner of being.[136]

Mystical theology is the exemplar of speculative theology, and the latter exemplifies the former. The Trinity is the highest formal object of speculative theology and so it is, in an eminent way, in mystical theology. Herein lies the importance of Ruusbroec for Denys. Ruusbroec provides a trinitarian understanding of the mystical theology of pseudo-Dionysius. In mystical union, the soul does not penetrate to a unity behind trinity, as Eckhart seems to say, nor rise beyond trinitarian emanations, as many Platonists teach. In the mystical life beyond analogical concepts, it enters the very life of the three-in-one.

Through the mystical revival of the seventeenth century, Denys

134. *De cont.* 3.a.24 (*Op. om.* 41: 287A).
135. *De cont.* 3.a.24 (*Op. om.* 41: 287A'–B').
136. *De cont.* 3.a.25 (*Op. om.* 41: 288B–D'). Combes treats Gerson's criticism of Ruusbroec on this point throughout vol. 2 of *Essai*; see esp. pp. 108–121. The text of Gerson's first criticism is printed in *Essai* 1: 618–19.

134

the Carthusian was esteemed the master of contemplative tradition. Certainly, he testifies against the late medieval "divorce between (speculative) theology and mysticism."[137] Precisely because of his zeal for the contemplative life he searched the testimony of ancient philosophic tradition. In his eyes, the books of the Platonists—and the Peripatetics most akin to them—were a providential preparation for the supernatural wisdom of Christians. In a letter composed in 1489, Marsilio Ficino traced a line of Platonic teaching through the Latin Middle Ages. His list begins with Denys's "most elect teacher," Dionysius the Areopagite, and ends with the Carthusian's friend, Nicholas of Cusa. The list embraces Denys's preferred philosophic texts and authors: Boethius' *Consolation*, Avicebron's *De fonte vitae*, Alfarabi's *De causis* (sic), Proclus's *Elementatio theologiae*, Henry of Ghent, and Avicenna.[138] Denys rightly belongs in this company, as a final medieval witness to the continuity of the Platonic tradition.

137. François Vandenbroucke, "Le divorce entre théologie et mystique: Ses origines," *Nouvelle Revue théologique* 72 (1950): 372–89.
138. Ficino's letter is edited in Klibansky, 46–47. For the context of this letter and Ficino's conception of the history of philosophy, see Paul Oskar Kristeller, *The Philosophy of Marsilio Ficino*, trans. Virginia Conant (New York, 1943), 20–29.

Sapientissimus Aristoteles and Theologicissimus Dionysius
The Reading of Aristotle and the Understanding of Nature
in Denys the Carthusian

Nearly uninterrupted save for his daily religious obligations, the Carthusian monk Denys of Ryckel (Dionysius Cartusiensis, 1402—71) for 48 years conducted a life of study and writing in his monastery in Roermond.[1] Naturally enough, much of his enormous literary production comprises scriptural commentaries, commentaries on monastic works, ascetical, mystical and pastoral treatises.[2] More extraordinary for a monk of his time are his many volumes concerning scholastic philosophy and theology. These include his huge commentaries on the Sentences of Peter Lombard, on Boethius' De consolatione philosophiae, on all of the writings of Dionysius the Areopagite, and a number of works based on the various writings of Thomas Aquinas.[3] Drawing materials from these works of "invention", he composed as well a number of independent philosophical and speculative treatises and books.[4]

Denys' most extensive strictly philosophic work is Book I of De lumine christianae theoriae, written in mid-career (ca. 1452) shortly after his travels with Cardinal Nicholas of Cusa on a Papal Legation through the Germanies

---

[1] Denys entered the Charterhouse in Roermond in 1423; except for a sojourn with Nicholas of Cusa in 1451 on the Papal legation through the Low Countries and parts of Germany, and a short time in the newly founded Charterhouse in Vught near 's-Hertogenbosch towards the end of his life, he remained in Roermond until his death in 1471.

[2] For a full study of Denys' corpus, see my Dionysii Cartusiensis Bibliotheca manuscripta. I: Studia bibliographica, forthcoming. All citations of Denys' works are to Doctoris ecstatici D. Dionysii Cartusiani Opera omnia, 44 vols. in 42, ed. Carthusian Fathers, Montreuil-Tournai-Parkminster 1896—1935. The edition is henceforward cited: Op. om.

[3] The commentary on the Sentences is found in Op. om. 19—25bis; on Boethius in Op. 26; on Dionysius in Op. om. 15—16; the paraphrase of Thomas' Summa theologiae in Op. om. 17—18.

[4] Cf. K. Emery, Jr., Twofold Wisdom and Contemplation in Denys of Ryckel (Dionysius Cartusiensis, 1402—1471), in: The Journal of Medieval and Renaissance Studies 18 (1988) 99—134, and Denys the Carthusian and the Doxography of Scholastic Theology (henceforward The Doxography), forthcoming in: Ad litteram: Authoritative Texts and their Medieval Readers, ed. K. Emery, Jr. and M. D. Jordan, Notre Dame, Indiana 1991. Full bibliographies are given in the notes of these articles.

and the Low Countries.[5] This work treats the procession of all creatures from God; the theological Book II, based on Thomas Aquinas' Summa contra gentiles, treats their return. Book I shows a great erudition in the doctrines of Platonic and Peripatetic philosophers, Greek and Latin, ancient, Arabic and Jewish. Denys' approach is "eclectic", to philosophical advantage: without overt resort to theological authority, save decisive philosophical interventions by his *doctor electissimus* and *patronus specialissimus*, Dionysius the Areopagite,[6] he discerns a philosophical truth concordant with Christian theory in one philosopher or another, whose very disagreements are an instrument for coming to truth.

An even more impressive erudition and similar intent are displayed in his huge commentaries on the Sentences of Peter Lombard, composed over the whole course of his intellectual life and finished near its end (ca. 1464).[7] On each question, Denys presents the teaching of an array of scholastic teachers in carefully quoted or paraphrased extracts. These he arranges with or against each other as his sense of the resolutions suggests, appends comments or rejoinders to the selections, and at the end summarizes the discussion and responds to objections to the position he adopts. Without suppressing real differences, he seeks always to find a principle for consensus among the doctors, and is severe only with singular positions.[8] Denys distilled and summarized his personal philosophical and theological doctrines, derived from his reading of scholastic doctors, in two *compendia*, the Elementatio philosophica and Elementatio theologica (ca. 1464–65).[9] As their titles suggest, these are written in the form of declarative propositions with brief comments, in the manner of Proclus' Elementatio theologica.[10] One should turn to these works for Denys' final judgments.

For three years before entering the monastery (1421–24), Denys studied in the Arts faculty at Cologne in the *Bursa* recently founded by Henricus de Gorrichem (1420), later called the *Bursa montana* after its second Regent,

---

    [5] De lumine christianae theoriae (henceforward De lum.) in: Op. om. 33: 233–513. See Emery, Twofold Wisdom, 104–5. For the overall chronology of Denys' writings, see A. Stoelen, De Chronologie van de Werken van Dionysius de Karthuizer, in: Sacris erudiri 5 (1953) 250–58, and Denys le Chartreux, in: Dictionnaire de spiritualité 3 (1957) 431–34.

    [6] Denys calls Dionysius *"doctor meus electissimus"* in: Protestatio ad superiorem suum (Op. om. 41: 625–26) and *"specialissimus patronus"* in 2 Sent. d. 9. q. 3 (Op. om 21: 496C').

    [7] For the composition of the commentary on the Sentences, cf. Emery, The Doxography, and the Introduction to Dion. Cart. Bibl. man.

    [8] Emery, The Doxography.

    [9] The Elementatio philosophica (henceforward Elem. phil.) is published in: Op. om. 33: 21–104; the Elementatio theologica (henceforward Elem. theol.) in: Op. om. 33: 105–231.

    [10] Proclus, Elementatio theologica translata a Guillelmo de Morbecca, ed. H. Boese, Leuven 1987.

Gerardus ter Steghen de Monte.[11] Denys studied under Thomist teachers; he may have also come in contact with the group of "Albertists", just beginning to form at the University.[12] In any event, during the course of his career he adopted many of the distinctive positions of "*Albertus ac eius sequaces.*"[13] Accordant with his schooling in the *via antiqua*, Denys for the most part confines his scholastic sources to the thinkers of the thirteenth century; he read the works of recent or contemporary masters, but only rarely does he mention one by name.[14] He knew of the prevailing tradition of the fourteenth century, and in some instances, alludes to its authors. Influenced, however, by the realist schools at Cologne, he chose not to engage or consider the opinions of the *nominales*, whom he judged to deny the first principles of grammar and logic.[15]

In an excellent essay, Stefan Swieżawski traces a renewed esteem for Aristotle and return to his writings as the foundation of philosophy that spread throughout Europe in the fifteenth century. This development is somewhat remarkable, in light of the attitudes and free departures from the Philosopher's authority in the previous century. The recovery of Aristotle was encouraged and supported by ecclesiastical authorities, who wished to establish a unified philosophical and theological doctrine to

---

[11] A. Mougel, Denys le Chartreux: Sa vie, son rôle, une nouvelle édition de ses ouvrages, Montreuil-sur-Mer 1896, 13−15; P. Teeuwen, Dionysius de Karthuizer en de philosophisch-theologische Stroomingen aan de Keulsche Universiteit, Brussels-Nijmegen 1938, 15−18. Gerardus was a fellow student of Denys; he matriculated in the Bursa in 1421 and began teaching in the Arts Faculty in 1424. See also A. G. Weiler, Heinrich von Gorkum (+1431): Seine Stellung in der Philosphie und der Theologie des Spätmittelalters, Köln 1962, 39−55.

[12] "Albertism" was introduced at Cologne by Heymericus de Campo, who arrived in 1422; Heymericus, however, taught in the Bursa Laurentiana. See G. Meerseman, Geschichte des Albertismus. II: Die ersten Kölner Kontroversen, Rome 1935. The first dispute between Albertists and Thomists at Cologne (Heymericus and Geraedus de Monte) took place during Denys' time, in 1423 (Meerseman, 11−22). For the founder of the movement, Heimericus' Parisian teacher Iohannes de Novo Domo, see Z. Kaluza, Les querelles doctrinales à Paris: Nominalistes et realistes aux confins du XIVᶜ et du XVᶜ siecles. Bergamo 1988, 87−125. For a full biblioraphy, see Emery, Twofold Wisdom, 111−12 n. 48. The most specific account of Denys' teachers in now Emery, Dion. Cart. Bibl. man., in Chap. 1.   .

[13] Teeuwen, passim; R. Macken, Denys the Carthusian, Commentator on Boethius's De Consolatione Philosophiae, in: Analecta Cartusiana 118 (1984) 35−41, 49−51.

[14] In their Response to the Electors (1425), the Cologne Masters of the "via antiqua" listed as their preferred Doctors, Thomas Aquinas, Albert the Great, Alexander of Hales, Bonaventure, Giles of Rome, Scotus. These authors form the core — but not the sum — of Denys' Sentences commentaries. The text of the Cologne Masters is edited by F. Ehrle, Der Sentenzenkommentar Peters von Candia des Pisaner Papstes Alexanders V, in: Franziskanische Studien Beiheft 9, Münster 1925, 281−85; see 283 L. On Denys' tacit use of Iohannes de Novo Domo's writings "de esse et essentia", of Heymericus de Campo and Gerardus de Monte, see Teeuwen, 70−72, 75, and 77−79 passim.

[15] Kaluza, 92−95; Emery, The Doxography.

serve a reunified Christendom, so chaotically disturbed by the divisions in the fourteenth century. Those humanists, scholastic masters of arts and theologians who advocated Aristotle's restoration, and contributed to the effort, usually harmonized his teaching on crucial points with the neo-Platonists, and in turn, made the amalgam concordant with the doctrines of faith. This approach attained its summit at no other place than the Arts faculty and *Bursa Montana* at the University of Cologne, precisely where Denys the Carthusian received his education. Throughout the fifteenth century, teachers at Cologne were the most stubborn promoters of a Christian Aristotle. At the same time, the renewed regard for Aristotle stimulated the historical and philological researches of Cajetan, Pomponazzi and others. Their work, ironically, undermined the intention of the theological program, uncovering rather the discrepancies between Aristotelian teaching and the faith. Moreover, the historians often reached the invidious conclusion that Averroes and Alexander of Aphrodisias were the most reliable guides to the Philosopher's true intent. Cajetan, for example, concluded that Aristotle did not teach the immortality of the individual soul, that his remarks suggesting immortality referred only to the agent intellect, probably universal, and that there was no strong foundation in the Philosopher's texts for a possible intellect proper in man. In reaction, the masters at Cologne advanced Thomas Aquinas as the true interpreter of Aristotle, and zealously taught a unified philosophic-theological doctrine purportedly derived from Thomas and his mentor among the ancients. This approach has persisted in various Thomistic schools until our own day. [16]

Sentiment for the Christian Aristotle reached its summit among the Thomists at Cologne. Followers of Scotus, another branch of the *via antiqua*, maintained that Aristotle had said all there was to say in philosophy, and that philosophy strictly speaking was simply identical with Aristotle's writings. [17] Denys the Carthusian from time to time expresses such sentiments, at least through the voice of an authority. Jerome in his Regula, Denys says, said that Aristotle was, as it were, a great miracle in the whole

---

[16] S. Świeżawski, Les débuts de l'Aristotelisme chrétien moderne, in: Organon 7 (1970) 177—94; for Cajetan's conclusion, see 186. Cf. also Świeżawski, Le problème de la 'Via Antiqua' et de la 'Via Moderna' au XVe siècle et ses fondements idéologiques, in: Antiqui und Moderni: Miscellanea Mediaevalia 9, hg. A. Zimmermann, Berlin-New York 1974, 484—93; Kaluza, 105—6. The masters of the "via antiqua" at Cologne used the works of Thomas Aquinas in their teaching in the Arts faculty, as their Response to the Electors (1425) reveals: "... *dicimus quod Artium cum Facultate Theologie tam indissolubilis est connexio, quod per idem valere est, prohibere hujus doctrine usum in Artibus et in Theologia, et permittere in Theologia et in Artibus. Exempli gratia, Doctor Sanctus in omnibus summis suis utitur eisdem principiis, quibus usus est libros Philosophi exponendo, prout luce clarius constat cuilibet in ejus doctrina eruditio*" (Ehrle, 284 N). This explains Denys' remark that he studied in the "via Thomae" at Cologne, in 1 Sent. d. 8. q. 7 (Op. om. 19: 408D).

[17] Świeżawski, Les débuts, 183—4.

of nature, and seems to have been infused with whatever can be known naturally. Hence we say that Aristotle and the Peripatetics following him deviated the least from the truth of Christian faith, and were more rationally steeped in philosophy. As a corallary to his remark, Denys in another place adds that therefore it is not easy to withdraw from Aristotle, unless the authority of faith, Scripture or determination of the Church requires it.[18]

Denys did not write a commentary on any of Aristotle's works, one of the few *lacunae* in his corpus. He claims to have read whatever he was able in natural philosophy, among the Peripatetics, Aristotle, Avicenna, Algazel, Anaxagoras, Averroes, Alexander, Alfarabi, Abubacer, Avempace, Theophrastus, Themistius and others.[19] There is no strong reason to doubt him, for his works otherwise bear ample testimony that he read what he said he did. Surely he read through Aristotle's writings in school. The manuscripts that contain the treatise on universals, hitherto lost, attributed to him by his sixteenth-century editor, also contain commentaries on most of the works of Aristotle, as well as Porphyry's Isagoge and the Liber de sex principiis. The manuscripts were written by students of the *via antiqua*, and testify to the revival of the old curriculum in the fifteenth century.[20] Nevertheless, it is likely that Denys gained much information about Peripatetic teaching from the commentaries and paraphrases of Albert the Great, whom, in a comparison with Thomas Aquinas, he says to be more "eminently experienced in the doctrine of the Peripatetics."[21] Curiously, I have found no direct evidence that Denys read the Aristotelian commentaries of Thomas Aquinas. Whatever the case may be in regard to the Peripatetics, there is ample evidence that he read what was available of Plato and the writings of neo-Platonists in *originalia*, for he quotes their works amply and *verbatim*. His commentaries on Boethius and Dionysius the Areopagite were line-by-line.[22]

---

[18] 1 Sent. d. 3. q. 12 (Op. om. 19: 276C'): *"De quo Aristotele ait [Hieronymus] in Regula sua, qoud procul dubio fuit quasi grande miraculum in tota natura, et quod ei infusum videtur quidquid naturaliter sciri potest. Hinc Aristotelem et Peripateticos eum sequentes, dicimus a veritate fidei christianae minus deviasse, ac rationabilius fuisse philosophatos."* Cf. also 1 Sent. d. 3. q. 1 (Op. om. 19: 219C).

[19] Protestatio (Op. om. 41: 626). On the document, cf. Emery, Twofold Wisdom, 102—3. The Cologne masters (1425) explained that they used the commentators Averroes, Avicenna, Eustrachius, Boethius and Themistius, as well as Thomas, Albert, Giles of Rome and Buridan in expounding Aristotle for the students. Cf. Ehrle, 283.

[20] For these manuscripts, cf. Emery, Dion. Cart. Bibl. man., Chap. 3 1 NE 194. Weiler, 66—70, gives a good summary of the way the Aristotelian books were studied at Cologne.

[21] 2 Sent. d. 3. q. 3 (Op. om. 21: 211C): *Qui Albertus in doctrina Peripateticorum eminenter fuit exercitatus.* Denys' disposition of materials and opinions concerning the soul in Book 1 of De lum. is especially indebted to Albert the Great's Liber de natura et origine animae, in: Opera omnia 9, ed. Borgnet, Paris 1890, 375—434.

[22] Emery, Twofold Wisdom, 104—5 nn. 20—26.

Not surprisingly, because he was a contemplative monk, Denys' philosophical focus is directed to those questions that immediately concern God, the rational spirits and the human soul. Absolutely central to his understanding is his strict interpretation of the principle that, as is something's manner of being, so is its manner of act and operation: *"modus agendi parificatur modo essendi."* He adduces this principle over and over, on a variety of questions. He understands the orders of being and knowing to be perfectly parallel and symmetrical. Hence, not only can one deduce truths in the order of knowing from the order of being, but what is more interesting, their reciprocity allows one to deduce truths in the order of being from what is evident in the order of knowing. For example, influenced greatly by Avicenna among others, Denys came to affirm that one need not have recourse to phantasms in every act of knowledge, and that in this life it was possible to come to a knowledge according to the *quid est* of separated substances. In turn, the soul's capacity to achieve knowledge of this kind was for him perhaps the strongest argument for the human soul's immortality.[23]

Denys' conception of the strict reciprocity between the orders of being and knowing enabled as sharp a distinction between the twofold theological and philosophical wisdom as one might wish. Like the orders of knowing and being, the two orders are perfectly parallel and analogical, shape by shape. Thus, for example, the ancient philosophers of heroic virtue could attain a final philosophic beatitude in the soul's separated condition, analogous, if wholly remote from, the supernatural beatitude of Christians. By the same analogy, each order of wisdom has its preeminent authority. Not less among theologians, Denys remarks, is the authority of Dionysius than the authority of Aristotle among philosophers. But whereas Aristotle's authority necessarily is limited to natural wisdom, Dionysius' authority also penetrates the philosophical order. In his commentary on De divinis nominibus, Denys states explicitly what is evident throughout his writings: *"Summus et sanctus iste philosophus noster magnus Dionysius"* introduced into his theological books many things that he learned from philosophy or knew by natural light.[24] According to this perception, Denys freely invokes Dionysius on a number of questions in his philosophical writings, especially on matters pertaining to the hierarchical procession of beings from the First Principle.

Denys' definitions of nature likewise enabled the distinction. These he conveniently collects in a preliminary article of the Elementatio philosophica. First of all, the word "nature" designates the essence of a thing,

---

[23] Elem. phil., prop. 75 (Op. om. 33: 84C'−85A'), see Emery, Twofold Wisdom, 114−20.
[24] 1 Sent. d. 26. q. 1 (Op. om. 20: 403A'); In lib. De div. nom. c. 4. a. 30 (Op. om. 16: 130A−C). For the natural beatitude of the philosphers, see Emery, Twofold Wisdom, 114−20.

which defines its act or operation. In this sense, it comprehends divine as well as created being. The nexus between the two is established by the ideas or exemplar reasons in the divine mind, which are productive of the principles of created things. In a more limited sense, "nature" is taken to mean the specific quiddity of a thing, that which, in Boethius' terms, distinguishes its specific difference. To these formal definitions, Denys adds others pointing to the operation of nature as a whole. Nature is an innate power in things, which generates similars from similars, or it is an innate inclination, which, for example, causes light things to rise and heavy ones to fall. In physics, nature is considered as the principle of whatever state of motion or rest in which a thing stands. Materially, *naturalia* are whatever is treated by the natural and physical sciences. In general, the term "nature" designates whatever pertains to a thing by reason of its innate inclination or created constitution, so that whatever proceeds in the ordinary course of the created world may be called "natural", in a sense more extended than the natural realities treated in the science of physics. The term "nature" has its most extended meaning in relation to the noetic order, signifying all that the intellect is able to conceive, as Boethius teaches. In this collection, the emphasis is on metaphysical definitions of nature. Denys' insinuation of the divine ideas into the conventional catalogue, his focus on the quiditative and noetic definitions, allows for a natural, divine philosophy separate from, but propaedeutic to, supernatural wisdom.[25] The relations among the orders of being and knowing, the definitions of nature, and theology and philosphy are evident in Denys' statement of intention in Book I of De lumine christianae theoriae:

> Since, therefore, there exists a twofold wisdom, my intention in this work is to show, I do not say demonstrate, the certitude, induce the truth, and uncover the foundations of the knowledge and wisdom of those things which are handed over by faith, namely Christian theory. Since however the habit of the sciences conforms to the condition of things, as nature serves the Creator, so natural knowledge serves divine knowledge ... For this reason, therefore, it is first necessary to contemplate the nature of divine things according to natural wisdom.[26]

---

[25] Elem. phil., prop. 17 (Op. om. 33: 34C'—35B). Four of Denys' definitions come from Boethius, De persona et duabus naturis, c. 1, in: PL 64: 1341—42. Denys probably took the list from Thomas Aquinas, 2 Sent. d. 37. q. 1. a. 1, in: Scriptum super libros Sententiarum 2, ed. R. P. Mandonnet, Paris 1929, 943. Denys paraphrases this question, and quotes the definitions, in Creaturarum in ordine ad Deum consideratio theologica a. 122 (Op. om. 34: 201B'—C'). Neither Boethius nor Thomas includes reference to the divine ideas, and Denys cites as his source Hugh of St. Victor.

[26] De lum. 1. a. 6 (Op. om. 33: 240B'—C'): "*Duplici quidem igitur exsistente sapientia, praesentis operis intentio est, ejus quae per fidem traditur cognitionis et sapientiae, christianae videlicet theoriae, veritatem inducere, et fundamenta reserare, ipsiusque certitudinem ostendere, non dico demonstrare. Quoniam autem conformis est habitudo scientiarum habitudini rerum, sicut natura Conditori servit, sic naturalis agnitio divinae subservit agnitioni.*"

The conviction that these analogies compel — that there must be a knowledge in this life that corresponds to the soul's inherent separability — led Denys increasingly to distance himself from Thomas Aquinas. In teaching that every act of knowledge requires phantasms, Thomas moreover manifestly contradicted the authority of "the great and most divine Dionysius", no matter how often he adduced the well-known text from De caelesti hierarchia, stating that it is "impossible for us to gaze upon the divine ray, unless it be veiled in the various coverings of sensible forms."[27] In response, Denys invokes many other texts from Dionysius, and points out that the text in De caelesti hierarchia refers to the lower order of symbolic theology, not to the higher orders of intelligible and anagogic or mystical theology, whereby we are led *"ex radiatione theorici luminis intellectualisque radii et immaterialium essentiarum notitia, ad primae veritatis ac divinorum contemplationem."* To confirm this teaching, Denys, relying on Avicenna, distinguishes between the judgment of a thing's operation in its beginning and in the course of its development. In its first acts, the soul must rely upon phantasms in order to know; through the habit of science, however, the soul becomes more adept at abstract contemplation until it is able to consider intelligible realities without the assistance of sensible images.[28]

Denys can find philosophical authorities enough for his argument against Thomas, among both Platonists and Peripatetics. He is loathe to exclude Aristotle from the company, although he can find no definitive text in the Philosopher's writings to support him. His difficulty is evident, for he proceeds in a rather circular way, just as he accuses his adversaries. According to Aristotle in De anima and elsewhere, Denys says, if the soul were not able to have some intellectual operation free and immune from communion with the sensible, it would follow that the soul is inseparable from the body and therefore mortal. Many of Aristotle's followers, however, proved that the soul is immortal, especially those who taught that the soul can act without the aid of phantasms. As an afterthought, Denys adds that Aristotle himself seemed to think that the soul is immortal. If so, by reason of the relation between knowing and being, he must have judged that the soul can understand *"sine phantasmatum adspectione."* If those who deny human knowledge without phantasms, yet maintain the immortality of the soul, reply as they are wont to do, that the separated soul has a different manner of existence and therefore of knowing, they

---

[27] Pseudo-Dionysius, De cael. hier., trans. Eriugena, c. 1, printed in: Dion. Cart. Op. om. 15: 6.

[28] Elem. phil., prop. 45 (Op. om. 33: 57D—59C'). See also Denys' comments in 2 Sent. d. 7. q. 4 (Op. om. 21: 412B'—D'), and his strong criticism of Thomas' reading of Dionysius in his commentary on De mystica theologia (Op. om. 16: 487A'—490B). I treat this criticism in The Doxography.

beg the premise. For the soul's separated existence remains then to be proved, and this cannot be done unless it be shown that "existing in the body, the soul can have some act in which it neither communicates nor concurs with the body or any organic power, interior sense or phantasm."[29] Denys' criticism is cogent enough; it seems to me that the burden of proof rests with Thomas. Denys' stumbling occurs, rather, in his attempt to adduce Aristotle to his side, where the burden of proof lies with him.

With Thomas, however, Denys affirmed that the intellectual soul is the unique substantial form of the human composite. This doctrine is the most conformed to faith, and to his mind, has the clear authority of Aristotle. Denys recognizes the difficulties that led others to teach a plurality of forms, and these difficulties, we shall see, are not unlike his own.[30] In any event, Denys' most extended praise of Aristotle occurs in an article of De lumine christianae theoriae entitled, "the nature and substantial perfection of the rational soul according to Aristotle, in which it is proved that the intellectual essence is the substantial form of man and the first act of the body".[31] Here Denys recites a number of arguments, according to one conventional interpretation of Aristotle, for the union of the intellectual soul and body in man. Typically, he is drawn to arguments deriving from the relation between the soul's being and its acts. Universally, second act follows upon first act and presupposes it. To understand and reason discursively are second acts of the rational essence; they require in man a commensurate first act, and this is its rational nature. This rational nature is the substantial perfection of man, for otherwise to reason would not be an operation proper to him. Therefore, man's first and second acts must be "of the same and by the same." Everything whatsoever acts by means of that through which it is substantiated, and as is its being, so is its act, according to Aristotle in the Metaphysica. If therefore the intellectual form were not the substantial act of man, he would not at all by his own means be able to understand. Understanding would be accidental to his nature and would derive from a form subsistently separated from his nature. Form is act, however, according to the Philosopher, and every act flows from form. Manifestly man contemplates, knows and understands, and by nature he possesses the formal principle of these acts.[32]

Denys prefaces his recitation of Aristotle's teaching with what is both an encomium and apology for the Philosopher."Indeed, in all the multitude

---

[29] Elem. phil., prop. 45 (Op. om. 33: 58B—D): *"Hoc quippe restat probandum, quod anima possit separari a corpore; nec potest probari, nisi probetur quod exsistens in corpore, habeat actionem in qua non communicet neque concurrat corpus seu virtus organica, aut sensus interior ac phantasma."*

[30] Elem. phil., prop. 30 (Op. om. 33: 45B'—47B'): *"In eodem composito non nisi unam consistere formam substantialem, probabilis est opinio; quae tamen multis rationibus et experimentis videtur contraria."*

[31] De lum. 1. a. 92 (Op. om. 33: 346D'—348C').

[32] Ibid. (347D—348C').

of philosophers", he says, "one finds the philosophy of Aristotle to conform more to Christian theory, and to support it with firmer foundations." It is precisely the wisest of all the Greek philosophers (*"omnium Graecorum philosophorum sapientissimus Aristoteles"*) who lends support to the Christian understanding of the union of soul and body in man. Even in those other opinions where he happened to dissent from the teaching of faith, he was not ashamed to admit that his determination was not demonstrative, as is also the case for his arguments for the eternity of the world and the number of intelligences. True, he did seem to wish to demonstrate that the heavenly bodies were animated, which however, does not really oppose Christian faith, as Augustine manifestly shows. There are those, like Ambrose and Gregory of Nyssa, who say Aristotle proposed that God does not enter the governance of human affairs. Nevertheless, Aristotle did not manifestly and fully speak of this matter, and from what he did say, the opposite can be understood. Surely, some of his statements require an understanding of God's providence for man. He says, for example, that "contemplative and theoric men are the most loved by God", and in the Politica, that bestial and criminal men are incomparably worse than beasts themselves. Does this not imply that Aristotle thinks God would hate the latter as much as he loves the former? How does he think this difference could be shown, if he did not believe that God punishes the ones and rewards the others, inasmuch as he also openly teaches that the soul is immortal and wholly unable to pass from one body into another? One must be careful not to ascribe to Aristotle himself opinions held by some of his followers.[33]

These arguments make clear that Denys' esteem for Aristotle must rise or fall on the question of the immortality of the soul. Denys does not need Aristotle to prove the immortality of the soul; he can find enough convincing reasons in Plato, Proclus, Avicenna and Christian scholastics to support his own resolution.[34] What is at stake is Aristotle's authority and the unity of philosphic wisdom on the most fundamental points, or rather, the most fundamental point.

In De lumine, Denys defends the position that according to Aristotle, the rational soul is immortal. As is evident, he reads the pattern of his own conviction into the texts of the Philosopher. Because Aristotle taught that the formal cause, in which act and potency arise at the same time, is not prior to the caused, and because he taught that the human soul is the form of the body, some estimate that he concluded the soul to perish with the body. On the contrary, Aristotle said many things that imply the opposite. In De anima 1 he says that the intellect seems to be a certain

---

[33] Ibid. (347 A—D):"[*Aristoteles*] ait namque homines contemplativos et theoricos viros, amantissimos Deo." Aristotle, Eth. 10,8 (1179a 20—32); Polit. 1,2 (1253a 33—34).
[34] De lum. 1 aa. 98—99, 102 (Op. om. 33: 356C—361A', 363C'—365B).

incorruptible substance. Elsewhere he says that if the intellect is some proper operation of the soul, then it will not be destroyed. In De anima 3 he plainly teaches that the intellect is unmixed, and that the soul has an operation separate from matter. Further, in the same book he assigns to the agent intellect four properties: it is separable, unmixed, impassible and being in act. He also says that the possible intellect is unmixed and separable, so that it can receive all things. He denies, of course, that the possible intellect is being in act, as it is the opposite by definition. Further, contrary to the arguments of Averroes and Avicenna, it is clear that Aristotle understood both of these powers to inhere properly in man, since he says that it is necessary that there be in the soul something potential to all things, and something that is able to actuate this potency. Denys refers again to Aristotle's statement that the contemplative man is most beloved by God. What significance could this saying have, if after this life God did not confer some beatitude on such men, especially since in this life adversities inflict contemplative more than carnal men. Indeed the former are often oppressed, even killed by the latter. Moreover, it is proper for a friend to communicate and bestow goodnesses upon those whom he loves. What would his love for theoric men mean, if he withheld from them any retribution for the evils they suffered?[35]

These, of course, are not arguments for the immortality of the soul. The argument from Aristotle's *dictum* concerning contemplative men[36] provides only a presumption; citing Aristotle's statements concerning the separability and impassibility of the intellect, Denys prescinds from the obvious question of the intellect's relation to the human composite. Denys' article on Aristotle serves a rhetorical purpose within his longer argument, to distance the "chief of the Peripatetics" from the egregious errors of some of his followers, which could likewise be used against the Philosopher by his enemies. Denys concludes that those who say Aristotle to have thought the soul inseparable from the body do not speak well. The *nominales*, the modern descendents of Alexander of Aphrodisias' interpretation of Aristotle, not only deny that one can demonstrate the immortality of the soul from the principles of Aristotle's philosophy, but go so far as to say that such a demonstration is impossible to natural reason itself. No wonder they say this, for when they try to examine the nature of things, they turn only to terms and *sophismata*.[37]

---

[35] De lum. 1 a. 101 (Op. om. 33: 362D'—363B'). Aristotle, De anima 1,4 (408b 18—20, 29—30); 3,5 (430a 15—20).

[36] In 2 Sent. d. 17. q. 1. (Op. om. 22: 131C'—132A), Denys incorporates the idea, in his characteristic terms, in his recitation of Albert the Great. Albert's text, however, gives only the slightest suggestion of the argument. See his Summa theologiae 2a pars q. 77 tract. 13memb. 5, in: Opera omnia 33, ed. Borgnet, Paris 1895, 105. See also Albert the Great, Ethica 10 tract. 2 c. 6, in: Opera omnia 7, ed. Borgnet, Paris 1891, 633.

[37] De lum. 1 a. 101 (Op. om. 33: 363B'); see Emery, The Doxography.

Denys' résumé of Aristotle is part of a long series of articles reciting the positions of many Peripatetics and Platonists concerning the related problems of the soul's union with the body and its immortality. Against Avicenna's argument for a single agent intellect existing as a separated substance outside of man, Averroes' "rude, frivolous and irrational errors", and Alexander's opinion that the animating human soul is an harmonic form educed from matter, he strives to prove that these opinions are not only false in truth, but contrary to Aristotle, whom all invoke.[38] He criticizes, in turn, the problems of the Platonists over the union of soul and body, but approves their arguments for immortality, especially Proclus' "most subtle demonstrations" based on the soul's self-reflexiveness, which do not seem to entail other Platonic errors.[39]

The fluctuating state of the discussion, wherein each philosopher gets something right and something wrong, requires Denys to find solutions elsewhere. Those he adopts are characteristic, attempting to strengthen the two motives he searched in reading Aristotle: the reciprocity of the orders of being and knowing, and man's aspiration to a contemplative existence. Reversing his previous presentation, before turning to the soul's composition with the body, he first addresses its immortality. Here he tacitly adapts an argument from Albert the Great, which directs a famous motif in Aristotle's *Ethica* towards proof of the immortality of the soul. Every nature that seeks and discovers honorable, pious and religious goods, he declares, by nature is immortal. For every appetite arises by reason of a similitude between the desire and the desired. What is "honorable" (*honestus*) is defined as that which is desirable for its own sake, without essential consideration for its delight or utility. But no power acting only for the well-being of its corporeal harmony seeks such a good. Whence one sees no irrational animal rejoicing in the aspect of beautiful things, their sweetness of smell or sensible perception, except insofar as these relate to their utility or delight in satisfying corporeal appetites. Man alone among composed creatures delights in the beautiful and the good on account of their essential dignity and their own natural virtue. Thus, there is in the soul a power similar to these perpetual goods that is elevated above the harmony of the body and its material disposition. And the desire for these goods, rooted naturally in the soul, can operate more freely and purely when the soul exists separately, since then man requires fewer merely useful and delightful goods.[40]

---

[38] De lum. 1 aa. 94—96 (Op. om. 33: 351—55).

[39] De lum. 1 a. 98 (Op. om. 33: 356—57).

[40] De lum. 1 a. 99 (Op. om. 33: 358B—B'). Aristotle, Eth. 8.3—4. See Albert the Great, Liber de natura et origine animae, tract. 2 c. 6, in: Opera omnia 9, ed. Borgnet, Paris 1890, 411b—412b. For the importance of the aesthetic and the transcendental beauty in Denys' thought, see K. Emery, Jr., Fondements théoriques de la reception de la beauté sensible dans les écrits de Denys le Chartreux (1402—1471), in: Les Chartreux et l'art XIVᵉ—XVIIIᵉ siècles, ed. D. Le Blévec et Alain Girard, Paris 1989, 307—24.

Man's desire for pióus and religious goods shows the same thing. Here Denys mixes arguments based on man's innate desires and his manner of knowing. As Aristotle proves in Ethica 10, contemplative felicity is the highest good sought by every intellectual nature. Further, every contemplation of created things is directed towards the highest object possible to created minds in the natural order; as Averroes says, the question of the divine intellect is desired by all. It is common, therefore, to the intelligence and the rational soul, to felicitate in contemplative speculation of the first truth. Thus, it is necessary that there be in the soul some similitude to this highest nature. This similitude is either rooted in the soul insofar as it is joined to, and dependent upon the body, or as it is incorruptible and has nothing in common with the body. The former is impossible, for neither contemplative felicity nor communication with divine intellects can be achieved by any material power, nor is such capable of receiving the "sincere and universal species" in which such contemplation is enacted.[41]

Moreover, as Aristotle says, neither God nor nature frustrates, nor does nature institute anything it denies to perfect. But every intellect desires always to be. Every desire arises either through some previous apprehension, or through instinct. The soul's intellectual desire, called the will, arises from a previous apprehension in the intellect; thus, as the intellect understands the good, so the will desires it. Sense knows being only according to its aspect "here and know", and is therefore incapable of desiring being as it is in itself. The intellect, on the contrary, to which it is proper to know universally, knows being as perpetual, without determination to time. The will thus naturally seeks being in this way, and this desire would be frustrated by nature itself if the soul's existence were incapable of fulfilling such a desire.[42]

Indeed, nature acts with regard to possibilities so as to make things better. But the soul, through species and "scientific and sapiential habits", is able to achieve a conformity and relation to celestial souls. Indeed, in this respect, it can operate more perfectly and freely when separate from the body than when joined. The proof of this may be found in what is commonly observed: the more the soul withdraws from bodily cares and delights for study, science and the purity of abstraction, the more it draws closer to, and becomes more capable of, "sapiential contemplation of divine things and heavenly influences." Nor will the soul desirous and capable of such withdrawal perish with the body, for nothing is corrupted in precisely that in which resides its perfection. Material and organic

---

[41] De lum. 1 a. 99 (Op. om. 33: 359C – A'). Aristotle, Eth. 10,7.
[42] Ibid. (360C' – 361A).

VII

powers, on the other hand, such as sight, are not perfected in withdrawal, but in the temperance of harmony.[43]

These arguments, based on the soul's desire for divine contemplation and the soul's ability to pursue it, naturally enough are persuasive to Denys, who had intimate experience with the contemplative life. It should be made clear that he does not refer here to any implicit natural desire for the beatific vision, which he denies, but rather to a purely natural desire for abstract, philosophical contemplation, observed in heroic ancient men. This natural desire, he shows in a series of other articles, is frustrated in any but a separated condition of existence.[44]

Denys' arguments on behalf of the unity of soul and body follow the same pattern, but also involve the hierarchical situation of man in the universe. After affirming that the human intellect begins as a *tabula rasa*, in need of phantasms and sensitive powers in order to acquire the species and forms of things, he goes further to confirm, with Avicenna and Algazel, that in its permanent condition the soul is not as it is in its beginning, and he repeats the intellect's ability to become adept at wholly abstract contemplation. The soul's increasing nearness to spiritual forms and distance from matter, however, is not a local withdrawal or separation from the composite, but a degree of perfection or dignity, for forms are said to be nearer or farther from the fount of all forms to the extent that in their act they rise above the faculty of matter. It should be understood, then, that the perfection of superior powers comprehends within itself all of the perfections of lower powers, but in the higher manner of their own being, not in the lower manner of the powers comprehended. Hence, the vegetative and sensitive powers of the soul are comprehended in the soul in the manner of its rational nature. According to its inferior powers, the human soul informs the matter of the body; according to its rational being, the soul is joined to the body, not through its information or impression of matter, but rather through a certain attractive power (*tractum*) by which it draws the body to its nature and manner of being. The intellectual soul, then, is created in "the shadow of intelligence", as Isaac Israelita says, standing before the lowest intelligence in the hierarchy of being as color to light, according to Avicenna. At the same time, it is joined to matter in its being and essence, through those lower perfections and powers that it comprehends. Thus, the same being of the soul, in terms of the expansion of its power and the separate and divine capacities that flow from it, is said to be immaterial and "soul" alone, and in terms of the material and organic powers that it comprehends in its own manner,

---

[43] Ibid. (358D'—359A).
[44] De lum. 1 aa. 45—52 (Op. om. 33: 286—94). Emery, Twofold Wisdom, 117—23. See M. Beer, Dionysius' des Kartäusers Lehre vom 'desiderium naturale' des Menschen nach der Gottesschau, München 1963, esp. 154—89.

it is said to be material and of the whole composite. In this way, the human soul is "an horizon of forms, and a certain boundary between the corporeal and incorporeal."[45]

Despite his persistent intent, Denys could not finally save Aristotle's preeminent philosophic authority. His reading for the commentary on the Sentences confirmed the doubt evident in all of his efforts on Aristotle's behalf in De lumine. He confronts the problem of Aristotle and the immortality of the soul in a question of the second Book of the Sentences (d. 17. q. 1: *"An anima primi hominis vere sit creata"*). The author who compels his admission is Henry of Ghent, from whose Quodlibet IX q. 14 he extracts at length at the end of his comment.

Henry searches the reasons for the confusion among Aristotle's followers on the question of the soul. He concludes that there is no wonder for the confusion, since there are inherent contradictions in the Philosopher's thought, which for various reasons he never sought to resolve. Because Aristotle never affirmed certainly, as a principle, that the intellect is one in all men, or that it is diverse in diverse, or that the intellect is the substantial act and form of the body, or that it is not, speaking sometimes as if the one, other times as if the other, one cannot argue on the basis of any of his "naked propositions." Rather, one must search other fundamental principles of his philosophy in order to discover what his intention was. Here likewise, Henry's investigation reveals, one is left in doubt, for each possible construction of Aristotle's teaching on the soul creates a contradiction with one or another clear principle of his thought. It is evident that Aristotle did not assert clearly the intellect to be the form and act of matter, nor that in man there is some form that remains when the composite is corrupted. Hence it cannot be certain whether he understood there to be many intellectual souls of many men, or a unique intellect for all. If he thought that the intellect were not the form and act of matter, he necessarily would have needed to say that there is a unique intellect for all men, according to his undoubted principle that individuals are not multiplied in the same species except by matter. On the other hand, if he thought that the intellect were the act and form of matter, he would need to posit a single intellect for each, on the same principle of the multiplication of forms by individuation in matter. But in this instance, because he clearly thought that the world is eternal, and also that the intellect cannot be corrupted, he would need to concede an infinite number of actually existing separated souls. But Aristotle does not admit the possi-

---

[45] De. lum. 1 aa. 103—4 (Op. om. 33: 365—66, 366B'—D', 367A). *"Sit ipsa horizon formarum, et tanquam confinium quoddam corporeorum et incorporeorum"* (366B'). Cf. also Elem. phil., prop. 49 (Op. om. 33: 62A—D'). The source is Le "Liber de causis." Édition établie à l'aide de 90 manuscrits avec introduction en notes, ed. A. Pattin, in: Tijdschrift voor Filosofie 28 (1966) 50, 81.

bility of an infinite multitude in act. Thus, although it is certain that
Aristotle taught that the human soul is the form of the body, it is not
certain that he meant a soul that includes intellectual as well as vegetative
and sensitive powers. If he speaks only of the vegetative and sensitive
soul, it is then not clear how he thinks the act of understanding to pertain
to man. Further, in De caelo et mundo 1, Aristotle states expressly that
nothing is perpetual *a parte post* that was not perpetual *a parte ante*. Thus,
if he thought that souls remain after the body, he must have thought them
to be from eternity. But this contradicts other expressly stated principles,
which state that form does not precede matter in the composite, and again,
that there cannot be an infinite multitude existing in act. Thus, Henry
judges it probable that Aristotle inclined to the idea that the intellectual
principle is not the act and form of the body, and that therefore there is
one intellect in all men, inasmuch as this agrees with his deepest principles.
However, because he did not wish to assert openly what follows from this
conclusion, and was aware of further contradictions to his own teaching
involved in other consequences, he preferred to leave in doubt whether
the intellect is the form of the body, and thus multiplied according to the
number of bodies.[46]

Henry's discussion, which points out the futility of trying to determine
Aristotle's position on the soul by means of any express sayings, and alerts
one to the problems of assuming Aristotle meant that the intellectual soul
is the form of the human composite, caused Denys to revise his judgment,
however reluctantly. In the Elementatio philosophica, he states as a proposition: *"Difficile est vere exprimere quid Aristoteles senserit de animae rationalis
immortalitate."* A summary of Henry's argument is the heart of his comment. He still cannot concede, however, Henry's implication that Aristotle
could have held the "absurd, rude and false" opinion saying the intellect
to be the same number in all men. Here, his strongest rebuttal is allusion
to the Liber de morte et pomo, Liber de secretis secretorum, and "certain
letters", where the immortality of the soul is taught openly.[47] Already in
De lumine, Denys had acknowledged Aristotle's doubtful authorship of
these works, but then they were not very vital to his argument.[48]

---

[46] 2 Sent. d. 17. q. 1 (Op. om. 22: 132D—133C'). Cf. Henry of Ghent, Quodlibet IX q. 14,
in: Opera omnia Henrici de Gandavo 13, ed. R. Macken, 248—57. Aristotle, De caelo,
1,10 (279b 17—18, 33): Metaph. 12,4 (1070a 21—27); Phys. 3,5 (206a 7—8).

[47] Elem. phil., prop. 48 (Op. om. 33: 61—62). For the pseudo-Aristotelian Epistolae ad
Alexandrum, Liber de pomo and Secretum secretorum, cf. C. B. Schmitt and D. Knox,
Pseudo-Aristoteles Latinus: A Guide to Latin Works Falsely Attributed to Aristotle
Before 1500, London 1985, 32—33, 51—52, 54—75. For the "clear" statements in Liber
de pomo, cf. Aristotelis qui ferebatur Liber de pomo. Versio latina Manfredi, ed. M.
Plezia, Warszawa 1960, 49, 64. See n. 86 below.

[48] De lum. 1 a. 92 (Op. om. 33: 347C—D).

In his commentary on Boethius' De consolatione, finished shortly after (ca. 1465) the Elementationes, Denys again expresses wonder that "the most ingenious philosopher" could conceive such "an absurd and rude" error as the unity of intellect in all men. In defense, he refers to Aristotle's obscure remark in Metaphysica 12, that it cannot be excluded that in some things, act may remain after potency, and that if the soul is such, the intellect, not the whole, might so possibly remain. Henry of Ghent had dismissed this conditional statement as having no force in argument.[49] In his commentary on Boethius, Denys concedes a point he had not before; he states flatly that in De anima, Aristotle determines that it is necessary for man to regard phantasms in the act knowing. He saves the text by referring to a twofold interpretation, one of Thomas and Giles of Rome, understanding that a phantasm is required for every intellectual act, and another, saying that this is true only for the beginnings of science. For the latter, he alludes to "Albert and his followers, Ulrich and Henricus de Ballivis", and gives an example that he draws from the Albertists: as one who wishes to ascend to a roof or terrace requires a ladder, but when he arrives there, no longer has need of it, so the intellect needs phantasms to ascend, but can operate without them once it has acquired the habit of science.[50]

That Denys' mistrust of Aristotle went further than his verbal expressions is indicated by his comment on the immortality of the soul in the Elementatio philosophica. Here he mentions Aristotle only once, to the effect that the intellect is separated and unmixed. He praises Plato, "more divine than other philosophers", and the arguments for the soul's immortality in the Phaedo, Meno and Timaeus. Likewise, he quotes theorems of Proclus, and for the greater part of his comment, recites ten signs of the soul's immortality given by Avicenna. From his own arguments in De lumine, he states briefly the evidence of man's desire for the honorable, which nature does not frustrate.[51] In a concluding article on the human

---

[49] Henry of Ghent, Quodl. IX q. 14, ed. Macken, 248, 254. Aristotle, Metaph. 12,4 (1070a 24–25).

[50] Enarrationes in De cons. phil. 2 a. 14 (Op. om. 26: 219C–220D). Aristotle, De anima 1,1 (403a 8–9). Cf. Macken, Denys the Carthusian, 50–69; Teeuwen, 85. In: Did Denys the Carthusian Also Read Henricus Bate?, Bulletin de philosophie médiévale 32 (1990) 196–206, I argue that "Henricus de Ballivis", unidentified in previous literature, is Henricus Bate (1246–1310).

[51] Elem. phil., prop. 47 (Op. om. 33: 60B–61A). For Avicenna's ten signs of immortality, Denys refers to Liber VI de naturalibus; see 5a pars. c. 2, in: Avicenna Latinus: Liber de Anima seu Sextus de naturalibus, ed. S. Van Riet, Louvain-Leiden 1968, 81–101. Denys' direct source is surely from the writings of Albert the Great, who often repeated the ten signs. Cf. De anima lib. 3 tract. 2 cap. 14, in: Opera omnia 7.1 [Ed. Colon.], ed. C. Stroick, Münster 1968, 196–98; Summa de creaturis 2a pars q. 61. a. 2, in: Opera omnia 35, ed. Borgnet, Paris 1896, 521–31; Summa theologiae 2a pars tract. 13 q. 77 memb. 5, in: Opera omnia 33, ed. Borgnet, Paris 1895, 104–5.

VII

soul, he reinforces the notion of the soul as "a ligament and knot of higher and lower things" in the concatenated order of nature, "and an horizon or zone between them", by reference to texts of Proclus and "divine Dionysius."[52]

Denys confronted the corrosive problem of Aristotle's opinions on the human soul again and again in his inquiries. Henry of Ghent drew his attention as well to similar seeming contradictions or ambiguities in Aristotle concerning the eternity of the world, the providence of God and several other matters.[53] Of these, the difficulties Denys encountered in his consideration of the possibility of an eternal world had the most damaging effect on his regard for Aristotle.

Until the end of his career, Denys largely followed Thomas Aquinas on this question. As one would expect, he always treats the problem in the terms in which it was posed in thirteeth-century philosophy and theology. Nevertheless, as in at least one other crucial instance, he reaches into some fourteenth-century authors.[54] In his extended treatment in the commentary on the Sentences, besides his usual authors — William of Paris, Thomas Aquinas, Albert the Great, Ulrich of Strasbourg, Peter of Tarantaise, Bonaventure, Richard of Middleton, Durandus of St. Pourçain, the Quodlibeta of Henry of Ghent, Duns Scotus — Denys includes arguments from Peter of Candia (ca. 1340–1410) and Peter Aureoli (ca. 1280–1322).[55]

Reading his long treatments of the question, one can have little doubt that Denys thought the eternity of the world to be a sublime metaphysical concept. Not only can the possibilitiy be considered "absolutely" — that is, in terms of God's omnipotence — but the idea also has a real appro-

---

[52] Elem. phil., prop. 49 (Op. om. 33: 62A–D').

[53] Elem. phil., prop. 48, in: Op. om. 33: 61C.

[54] On the question of the unity and distinction of divine attributes. Cf. Emery, The Doxography.

[55] 2 Sent. d. 1. q. 4 (Op. om. 21: 68–89). In 85D'–87A, Denys gives a catalogue of 12 arguments attempting to prove the temporality of the world, which he says Henry of Ghent apparently (*"ut apparet"*) makes in his Summa, Peter of Candia also touches, and are likewise introduced by Peter Aureoli. The first 8 are reported by Petrus de Candia in 2 Sent. q. 1. a. 3 as reasons of those who say the eternity of the world is impossible; I consulted the text in Bruxelles. Bibliothèque Royale. 3699–3700 (Van den Gheyn 1555), ff. 115r^a–115v^b. Peter later cites 4 more instances ("instancias"), f. 117r^{a-b}, but these do not correspond to Denys' last 4 arguments or examples. Peter does not name the authors of the arguments. Peter Aureoli discusses some of these arguments (1–4, 8, 10) — but does not affirm them all — in 2 Sent. d. 1. q. 1. a. 2, in: Petri Aureoli ... Commentariorum in secundum Sententiarum tomus secundus [vol. 3 of 4 vol. set], Roma 1605, 12v^b–13r^a. I have not found anything similar in Henry of Ghent's Summa quaestionum ordinariarum, ed. J. Badius Ascensius, Paris 1520, reprt. 2 vols. St. Bonaventure, New York 1953. Henry mentions the question in passing in a. 52. q. 3, a. 59. q. 5, a. 68. q. 5, in: 2: ff. 58rD–58rI, 150rO–P, 230vT. It seems likely that Denys found the references to Henry's Summa and Peter Aureoli in an annotation in a manuscript of Peter of Candia's Super Sententias.

priateness in relation to the divine nature. In fact, Denys is constrained to accept the theoretical possiblility of an eternal world by his solution, reflecting the deepest tendencies of his thought, of a prior problem: the procession of creatures from God. In one sense, this is the foremost issue of Book I of De lumine, which has for its theme the *exitus* of creatures from God, and contains a long series of articles specifically on the manner of procession. For the design of these articles, Denys seems indebted to Albert the Great's paraphrase and comment on the Liber de causis, but he seems to have gathered his own materials.[56] Notably, Aristotle does not receive special attention on this important matter.

Denys first rehearses the emanation of all things from God according to the teaching of Plato in the Timaeus, and then of other Platonists. Their essential error, which he corrects first by Peripatetic arguments and then by Dionysius the Areopagite, is to posit *autobonitates* and ideal forms surrounding God, as it were, and thereby creating "a multitude of gods according to the descending chain of divine emanations."[57] Avicenna, who represents Peripatetic teaching, erred in arguing that because "nature is only determined to one", the divine emanation could have only one effect, a created intelligence, and so on down the chain of intelligences, so that in fact the world has many created creators. Moreover, the emanation of creatures from God is natural and therefore necessary; in passing, Denys remarks that accordingly, Avicenna taught that the world existed from eternity, so that God is prior to the world by an order of nature, not duration.[58]

Strategic among the doctrines of the philosophers is that of the "Platonist" Avicebron, who taught that creatures emanate freely from God, by means of the executive act of the divine will according to the exemplar reasons in the divine mind. Although Denys disputes Avicebron's doctrine of a spiritual matter composing spiritual creatures, he says that Avicebron's "philosophy is sublime in many things, especially about the going forth (*exitus*) of all things from the first being ... in which he is closer to faith than the tradition of certain Peripatetics."[59]

Summarizing the various positions of the philosophers, Denys distinguishes a manifold emanation: a "natural efflux" (*naturalis effluxio*), taught by Avicenna, Alfarabi, Algazel and other Peripatetics; a "free and artificial

---

[56] Cf. Albert the Great, Liber de causis et processu universitatis lib. 1 tract. 4, in: Opera omnia 10, ed. Borgnet, Paris 1891, 410—31.

[57] De lum. 1 aa. 30—32 (Op. 33: 269C—273C'); for the quotation, see a. 32 (273D).

[58] De lum. 1 a. 34 (Op. om. 33: 274D'—276B).

[59] De lum. 1 a. 33 (Op. om. 33: 273D'—274D', esp. 274C'—D'). Denys states that Albert calls Avicebron a Platonist "in libro de Mirabili scientia Dei." See Albert the Great, Summa theologiae 2 tract. 1 q. 4. a. 1. pt. 2, in: Opera omnia 32, ed. Borgnet, Paris 1895, 63b. See also Albert's Liber de causis 1 tract. 1 c. 5, in: Opera omnia 10, ed. Borgnet, 371a.

VII

diffusion" (*libera et artificialis diffusio*), taught by Avicebron; a "certain formal generation, or essential shining forth" (*formalis generatio, aut essentialis emicatio*), taught by Plato and his followers; or an "intellectual and sapiential emanation" (*intellectualis et sapientialis emanatio*). Employing an interesting term, he says that nothing prohibits these various processions, or aspects of them, "*coincidere in re.*"[60]

By means of this analysis and these distinctions, Denys preserves for Christian theory a doctrine of divine emanation, whereby creation is a free act implying no mutation of the divine will, befitting the dignity and according with the simplicity, eternity, infinite intelligence and diffusive goodness of the divine essence. He thus rejects the "natural efflux" taught by Avicenna, observing that "ingenious and subtle" philosophers were unable to distinguish the natural emanation from God *ad intra*, in the generation of the Son, from a voluntary emanation *ad extra*.[61] Significantly, he does not distinguish between an emanation *ad intra* and "creation" *ad extra*, as many Christian thinkers do, but rather preserves the term "emanation" for creation as well.[62] Such a free emanation *ad extra* well befits the dignity and nature of the divine essence. For all things act in respect of an end; the end of the first agent is the divine goodness, which God perfectly possesses outside of any other good; therefore, when he freely shares this goodness with others in creation, he acts in a way most worthily and honorably, and more excellently than he would if he acted necessarily. Moreover, the divine liberty acts not by reason of mutation, but by reason of non-obligation. Thus, to act freely does not derogate the simplicity by which God acts through his being or essence, upon which every creature depends. Avicenna's notion can be retained in a diminished sense, if one understands that the efflux of things from God is "natural" in that by means of it, creatures share in the substantial perfections of the divine nature, such as *esse, vivere et cognoscere*, in an analogical way.[63]

Whereas Denys rejects wholly the *essentialis emicatio* of Plato and his followers, he retains the other terms of his distinctions, concluding that the emanation of creatures from God is "sapiential", "free", and in a certain sense, "artificial."[64] Denys' motives for retaining the term "emanation" for creation are closely related to his understanding of the absolute

---

[60] De lum. 1 a. 35 (Op. om. 276C—B'). For the significance of Denys' use of the term "*coincidere*", see Stephan Meier, Von der Koinzidenz zur coincidentia oppositorum, Zum philosophiehistorischen Hintergrund des Cusanischen Koinzidenzgedankens, in: Die Philosphie im 14. und 15. Jahrhundert. In memoriam Konstanty Michalski (1879—1947), hg. O. Pluta, Amsterdam 1988, 333, 337.

[61] De lum. 1 a. 36 (Op. om. 33: 276D'—277A, 277A'—B').

[62] R. C. Dales, Medieval Discussions of the Eternity of the World, Leiden-New York-Köln 1990, 43, 166—67 (Henry of Ghent).

[63] De lum. 1 aa. 35, 37 (Op. om. 33: 278A, 279A—D, A'—D').

[64] De lum. 1 aa. 38—40 (Op. om. 33: 280—40).

simplicity of God and unity of the divine attributes, which he argues strenuously in all of his works, and to his vision of the strictly hierarchical operations and influences in nature, especially among intelligent beings. These are among the doctrines where the authority of Dionysius the Areopagite is most assertive. *"Divinissimus, sacratissimus et theologicissimus Dionysius"* spoke of the "incomparable and incomprehensible unity and simplicity of the deity, and most pure identity of the attributes", Denys notes, especially in De divinis nominibus.[65]

These reasons and this authority, as I have suggested, commit Denys to admit the possibility of an eternal world. In De lumine, where he treats the question in several articles, he quotes "the great Dionysius", who states that "God is not the cause of things once only, but always causes and produces things", in the sense that he is the eternal source of being and becoming, upon whom all things depend as the rays upon the sun, and without whose preservation they would perish in the blink of an eye.[66] In two articles that prepare for his solution, Denys follows the model, but not so directly the material, of Thomas' Summa contra gentiles, first stating the stronger reasons the philosophers have posited for an eternal world, then replying to each of them to show that a temporal creation can meet or surpass their best insights.[67] He begins by distinguishing between true eternity, according to Boethius "the perfect possession all at once of interminable life", and an eternity of extended duration, according to which apparently Aristotle thought that the world, motion and time were eternal. In the first sense it is wholly impossible for the world to be co-eternal with God; and Aristotle knew, as his statement in the Topica indicates, that in the second sense, the eternity of the world could not be demonstrated.[68]

Denys groups the arguments for the eternity of the world according to philosophical families. The argument that whatever acts through its being or essence, acts through its nature, but whatever acts through will, acts in view of something proposed, involving mutation, arises, Denys says,

---

[65] 1 Sent. d. 2. q. 2. (Op. om. 19: 174C): *"Insuper, divinissimus, sacratissimus et theologicissimus Dionysius, de summa et incomprehensibili Deitatis simplicitate et unitate atque attributorum identitate purissima, in variis tractat locis, praesertim in libro de Divinis nominibus."* For Denys on this topic, cf. Emery, The Doxography.

[66] De lum. 1 a. 103 (Op. om. 33: 379C—D). Denys seems to refer to De div. nom. c. 4, trans. Eriugena, in: Dion. Cart. Op. om. 16: 104—7. See also Denys' commentary, c. 4. aa. 29—33 (126A—137D').

[67] Cf. Thomas Aquinas, Summa contra gentiles 2 cc. 32—37, in: Opera omnia 13 [ed. Leon.], Roma 1918, 344—55.

[68] De lum. 1 a. 82 (Op. om. 33: 333D—A'). Thomas Aquinas, 2 Sent. d. 1. q. 1. a. 5, in: Scriptum 2, ed. Mandonnet, 33—34; Denys extracts the solution in 2 Sent. d. 1. q. 4 (Op. om. 21: 70B—C). The reference is to Aristotle's Topica 1,11 (104b). For the frequent equivocation of, and difficulty in relating the concepts of "eternity" and "infinite duration", cf. Dales, 17, 60—61, 88, 117—18, 185, 195, 257.

from the doctrine of Plato, and was often advanced by Proclus. That the divine goodness, like light, is naturally diffusive, and that what is natural to a thing is inseparable from it, is the principle from which Alfarabi, Algazel and Avicenna argue for the eternity of the world.[69] The strongest Aristotelian arguments, as Denys deduces them, relate to the divine dignity and goodness. Those which always cause are better than those which rarely, or only frequently cause. Likewise, to act now after not acting before requires a movement from potency to act; not only is God pure act, but that which is always in act is better than that which is not. Either God was willing and able to create the world from eternity, or he was able but did not will it, or he willed it but was not able. If the first, he made the world from eternity; if he was able but did not wish it, and then wished, there was some mutation, as in all willing and not willing; if he willed it but was not able, then he was not omnipotent. The second of these seems also to derogate the divine goodness, for envy is the reason for not bestowing what one is able, but the first is also the best and is far from envy.[70]

Although these arguments relate to Aristotelian principles, they are not those customarily adduced from the Philosopher in the medieval discussion of the problem.[71] Significantly, Denys invokes only one argument from the motion of the universe. The kind of argument he finds most forceful pertains to the divine nature. This accords with his admiration for Aristotle's "truest and most profound conclusion", the pure act of divine being.[72]

Denys' responses to these arguments derive from the principles he already stated concerning the emanation of creatures from God, and rely upon Boethius' notion of eternity. As a finite effect can flow from the incommensurate infinite, so a temporal emanation can flow from an incommensurate eternity; goodness and light are in God intellectually, and so they flow from him, not by natural necessity; the proposal of God's will is immobile in him, and because he "knows and disposes all things in a most simple intuition of the mind", it is not repugnant to his "incommutable simplicity" to institute and preordain the order, vicissitudes and times of works; that which operates freely is more perfect than that

---

[69] De lum. 1 a. 82 (Op. om. 33: 333B'—D'). Algazel, in fact, opposed the eternity of the world, but many, including Denys and his sources, confused Algazel's statement of opposing arguments for his own views. Cf. Dales, 44.

[70] De lum. 1 a. 82 (Op. om. 33: 334A—C').

[71] For the usual Aristotelian texts adduced, cf. Dales, 39—42.

[72] De lum. 1 a. 84 (Op. om. 33: 336D'). In another work, Denys says: *"Nec puto Aristotelem unquam tam subtile et utile verbum esse locutum, sicut quod dixit Deum esse purum actum: quod eum duodecimo Primae philosophiae dixisse recordor ... multa pulchra sequantur ex hoc".* Cf. De natura aeterni et veri Dei a. 20 (Op. om. 34: 38A', 37B'). Aristotle, Metaph. 12,7 (1072b 25—29).

which acts only naturally, and hence God's perfection shines more limpidly in created things which bear the seal of having been created in time rather than necessarily from eternity.[73] In other words, creation in time more manifestly displays the liberty and hence dignity of the divine nature. To the Aristotelian concern about mutation in the divine nature, Denys simply reverses the argument and says "the first is cause of the world not through some previous mutation, but simple emanation, and since God's act is his essence, it does not follow that it must first be moved in some way in creating something new."[74]

Denys' arguments uphold the divine freedom against the philosophers and justify the fittingness of creation in time; they do not at all deny the fittingness, perhaps only less in degree, of a creation, equally free, from eternity. Not surprisingly, Denys frequently repeats with Thomas that essentially, creation entails a priority of nature rather than a priority of time. His concluding article in De lumine on the subject yields exactly what one would expect. He affirms, of course, that since the world was in fact created in time, the question is one of "absolute possibility", and that the reasons purporting to show the eternity of the world are only probable. He refers once again to the distinction between effects that proceed from an agent according to mutation or motion, and those that proceed by "simple emanation." Most of the arguments supporting the possibility of an eternal world are evident in previous articles, and so need not be repeated. Hence, the article consists mainly of arguments "by certain doctors of our religion", chiefly of the "Order of Friars Minor", purporting to demonstrate the impossibility of an effect being created from eternity, and the responses to these. The arguments are those of Bonaventure and his followers, pointing out seeming contradictions involving infinity, the necessity of a creature created *ex nihilo* having *esse post non esse*, etc. Denys borrows his responses from Thomas' Contra gentiles. These dissolve the problem of a traversed infinity, and argue that an augmented, successive infinity, and a first man eternally prior in nature if not duration, etc., are not unthinkable.[75] Denys' resort to these arguments is simply convenient. His eye is steadfastly fixed on the infinite divine substance and the perfect unity of its perfections, in which the divine will is identical with the divine intellect, wisdom and expansive goodness. Although he often states that arguments on both sides are

---

[73] De lum. 1 a. 84 (Op. om. 33: 334D'−335C').
[74] Ibid. (335D').
[75] De lum. I a. 113 (Op. om. 33: 378C'−381A). For Bonaventure's arguments, cf. Dales, 91−96, and F. Van Steenberghen, Saint Bonaventure contre l'éternité du monde, in: Introduction à l'étude de la philosophie médiévale, Louvain-Paris 1974, 404−20. Denys' responses are taken from Thomas' Summa contra gentiles 2 c. 38, in: Opera omnia 13 [Ed. Leon.], 355−56; Thomas had made essentially the same responses in his commentary on the Sentences; cf. Dales, 97−101.

undemonstrable, not once in his protracted discussion does he refer to the intrinsic inscrutability of acts that depend solely on the divine will, a cornerstone of Thomas' arguments.[76] The most revealing item in the article is Denys' approval of a comment by Proclus, "the most profound of the Platonists", not for its conclusion, but for the invariable order of nature that it expresses: "It is manifest that intellect is desirable to all things, and all things proceed from intellect, and the whole world has substance from intellect; and if the world is perpetual, it does not therefore not proceed ... But it does always proceed and is perpetual according to essence, and is always turned towards [the First], and is in an indissoluble order. Indeed, the world is said to proceed always from the First, and always to be turned towards it, because it always depends upon it and is sustained by it."[77]

How little Aristotle has to do with all this. For Denys, the metaphysical authors of the doctrine are Avicenna and the neo-Platonists. He states this explicitly in the opening proposals of his question in the commentary on the Sentences, and by the end of the long question, Aristotle's status in the debate is considerably diminished. Denys proposes a series of arguments more explicit in the writings of Aristotle than those assigned to him in De lumine. Prime matter is ungenerated and incorruptible; the heavenly bodies lack the contrariety that brings corruption; if the world were created newly in time, there would need to have been a vacuum from eternity where the heavens now are; time is a flowing "now," which is defined by the end of a past "now" and the beginning of a future one. Many arguments similar to these are induced by Aristotle to prove the eternity of the world, Denys concludes, "but I omit them, because they prove nothing else except that the world did not begin by some first motion, natural mutation or variation of the first agent, not however that it did not begin through simple emanation from the invariable and most free Creator, who remaining in himself incommutable, in that 'now' and first instant of time created the world, which from eternity he decreed to

---

[76] Cf. Dales, 47, 178—79. Thomas acquired the argument from Maimonides.

[77] De lum. a. 113 (Op. om. 33: 379A—C): "... *manifestum, quod appetibile omnibus est intellectus, et procedunt omnia ab intellectu, et totus mundus ab intellectu substantiam habet; et si perpetuus est mundus, non ideo non procedit ... Sed et procedit semper et perpetuus est secundum essentiam, et conversus est semper et insolubilis secundum ordinem. Dicitur quippe mundus semper procedere a primo, et semper converti secundum eum, quia semper dependet et manutenetur ab eo.*" Cf. Proclus, Elementatio theologica 34, ed. Boese, 21—22. Denys has already quoted this text in 2 Sent. d. 1. q 7 ("Whether preservation is the same thing as creation"), and makes an interesting comment: "*Et si quis auctoritatem despiciat Procli tanquam Platonici, quid ad auctoritatem divini Dionysii respondebit, qui quarto capitulo de Divinis ait nominibus, quod Deus est bonitas summa, omnium productiva, non quasi nunc producens et nunc non causans, sed quoniam indesinenter omnium causa est et omnia causans?*" (Op. om. 21: 101A'—B'). Denys sensed the routine disregard for Platonic authority within scholastic discourse; for this reason, the acknowledged authority of the Areopagite is crucial for him.

himself to create." Such physical arguments dismissed, Denys can turn to the serious business of Avicenna, Algazel, Averroes and certain other Peripatetics, who introduced "more acute reasons than the Philosopher himself" for proving the eternity of the world.[78]

The restriction of Aristotle's arguments to the order of physics is a familiar item in the historically long debate, often used to accommodate the Philosopher;[79] Denys' use of the strategy has a somewhat different intention. It indicates his own, almost exclusively metaphysical consideration of the problem *ex parte Dei*, and also reflects, it seems to me, a common conception among fifteenth-century neo-Platonists, whereby Plato is *divinus metaphysicus*, master of the *sermo sapientiae*, Aristotle *physicus*, master of the *sermo scientiae*.[80] After summarizing arguments of the more acute Peripatetics, Denys cites an unusual argument of theological authority. Because it concerns the divine nature in relation to the angelic hierarchies,whose possible eternal existence is more evident than for other creatures, it has a certain attractiveness to him. The argument from appropriateness is stronger in its implication than its expression. "Many saints among the Greek doctors" say that intellectual creatures were created long before the sensible world, for it appears unbecoming that the highest and more than noble (*superoptima*) majesty through all of the centuries should have been without his ministers, and that the effusion of his liberality should have waited until the production of the sensible world. Despite the confusion between notions of eternity and long duration in this pious opinion, the implication is clear that it would be most becoming for God to rejoice with his ministers from eternity. Denys traces the idea to the likely source for the Greek fathers: Plato also asserted that God was elated when he produced the world, as Augustine recites. These and similar arguments, Denys concludes, are what human wisdom, or rather human fatuousness, can cogitate and fashion against the actual, immense wisdom of the Creator.[81]

Among the many resolutions he extracts, Denys seems most affected by Durandus of St. Pourçain. Durandus' arguments cause a subtle change from his previous positions. Durandus distinguishes between creatures, created successively, that are generated through motion or some mutation arising from it, and those permanent creatures that are created through a simple emanation. For his distinction, he employs the difference between true eternity and extended duration. The measure of permanent creatures, in whom to become and to be made are simultaneous, is an eternal, stable

---

[78] 2 Sent. d. 1. q. 4 (Op. om. 21: 68A'−D'). Cf. Aristotle, Phys. 4, 11−12 (219b−221a); 8,1 (250b−252b), etc.

[79] Dales, 57−58, 64−65, 68−70, 76 n. 64, etc.

[80] Swieżawski, Les débuts, 180.

[81] 2 Sent. d. 1. q. 4 (Op. om. 21: 69A−B').

VII

"now", which can co-exist with many temporal, flowing "nows". In such sudden (*subita*) act, nothing impedes that which is produced from co-existing with that which produces. The case of creatures generated successively, including men, is otherwise. Durandus produces a number of paradoxical arguments, reasoning that the completed (*acceptae*) revolutions of the heavenly bodies, no two of which can occur together, necessarily require a finite order with a first and last; that in human generation, there could not be infinite intermediaries between a presupposed first man and women and the most recently generated; and that if generation is presupposed from eternity, so also must be corruption, which is impossible, since corruption presupposes something corruptible prior to it in duration.[82]

Although Denys responds to some of these arguments, in his summary of the question in the Elementatio philosophica, he alludes to Durandus' distinction between permanent and successive things, and says that it is supported by "very strong reasons."[83] The impact of Durandus' argument is further indicated by a remark Denys makes in the course of his question in the Sentences: "Nevertheless, given that according to the opinion of some, the eternity of the world cannot be saved in the order of successive, generable and corruptible things, nor for the human creature, it does not follow from this, nevertheless, that absolutely speaking it cannot be saved for some creature of a permanent nature, especially angels."[84] In light of this distinction, whereas Denys defends the possibility of an eternal "world" in De lumine, in the Elementatio philosophica he restricts his proposition to some "creature."[85]

---

[82] Ibid. (73A—75B). Cf. Durandus of St. Pourçain, 2 Sent. d. 1. qq. 2—3, in: D. Durandi a sancto Portiano super Sententias theologicas Petri Lombardi, Paris 1539, 96vª H—O, 96vᵇ A, 97rᵇ N—97vª P, 97vª B—97vᵇ C. For similar arguments based on the distinction *"esse acceptum/esse accipiendum"*, cf. Dales, 185—89. In the related question, "Whether preservation is the same as creation", Denys approves Durandus' conclusion that since the measure of creation is a *"nunc stans"* able to coexist with many "temporal nows", it is not necessary for some new motion to precede creation or act of preservation. Thus, it is always true to think that in created things, as long as they exist, the act of creation and preservation is the same. Referring to the Condemnations of Etienne Tempier at Paris, Durandus goes on to say that what we may think, however, we must not say. Citing definitions of Plato and Augustine, Denys responds that Durandus' last position *"videtur esse duplicitas, dolus et falsitas, quum ea quae sunt in voce, sint notae et signa eorum quae sunt in mente."* See 2 Sent. d. 1. q. 8 (Op. om. 21: 101C'—102D). The article to which Durandus refers is n. 35 in R. Hissette, Enquête sur les 219 Articles condamnés à Paris le 7 Mars 1277, Louvain-Paris 1977; 73—74: *"Quod Deus numquam plus creavit intelligentiam quam modo creat"*, [error].

[83] Elem. phil. prop. 89 (Op. om. 33: 94C').

[84] 2 Sent. d. 1. q. 4 (Op. om. 21: 88A—C): *"Nihilo minus dato quod juxta quorumdam opinionem, opinio ista de mundi aeternitate salvari non posset in sucessivis et generabilibus et corruptibilibus, neque in creatura humana; ex hoc tamen non sequeretur, quod absolute loquendo salvari non posset de aliqua creatura permanentis naturae, praesertim de angelis."*

[85] De lum. 1 a. 103 (Op. om. 33: 378C'); Elem. phil. prop. 99 (Op. om. 33: 94C—D).

From Peter of Candia, Denys draws a catalogue of by then familiar arguments showing that an eternally existing world involves a number of contradictions to Aristotle's own tenets. For the most part, these are the arguments to which Denys responds in the conclusion. Peter of Candia introduces his list with the ironic remark that these are the arguments of Christian philosophers who wish to make Aristotle a theologian by showing that he could never have taught the world to have existed from eternity. It is impossible to traverse an infinity, which would be required if the world existed from eternity. There cannot be an infinite multitude in act, but if the world were eternal, there would be infinite souls in act. A pile of stones augmented each day would now be an infinite quantity. One infinite cannot be greater than another, or added to, as would be the case if there were infinite revolutions of the heavens, days, etc. If the world were eternal, the part would be equal to the whole, since there would be as many days as months, months as years, etc.[86]

Denys finally maintains his earliest opinion, that Thomas spoke more "truly" and "probably" than others on this matter. In his responses to opposite arguments, he amplifies Thomas' argument that infinite intermediaries between two terms are not unthinkable; argues that when time is said to be infinite, it is all of time together that is understood, even if each of its parts is finite; nor does there need to be an order among things in a "mere infinity." This was the mind of the Philosopher, Denys says, who about such things spoke more rationally than others. In such considerations, he adds, it is necessary to transcend imagination by imagining, as when speaking about time as a whole as different from its consideration in each of its single parts.[87] Denys means, I suppose, trying to imagine infinite duration from the perspective of the divine mind, for whom all times are at once.

---

[86] 2 Sent. d. 1. q 4 (Op. om. 21: 80C−D'). Denys draws this list from an earlier part of Peter of Candia's question in 2 Sent. q. 1. a. 3, in: Bruxelles. Bibl. Roy. 3699−3700, ff. 113r^a−v^b. Denys' wording of Peter's introductory remark is different from that given in the manuscript, or by Ehrle, 66−67: *"Sed aliqui theologi volunt aristotelem catholicum"* (f. 113r^a). Kaluza, 106, quotes the remark after Ehrle. Also interesting are Peter's remarks concerning the authorship of the Liber de pomo and De secretis secretorum; see the ms., f. 113r^b−113v^b, and Ehrle. The arguments listed by Peter were familiar; cf. Dales, 123−24, 185−89, 207, 211−12, etc.

[87] 2 Sent. d. 1. q. 4 (Op. om. 21: 87A−D'). Denys extracts from Thomas' commentary on the Sentences (n. 68 above), ST 1a q. 46. aa. 1−2, and briefly alludes to Summa contra gentiles (69B'−71B). Denys says that Peter of Candia seems to have favored the position of Thomas; in fact, Denys' final conclusion seems closer to Peter than to Thomas. Peter, who does not mention Thomas, concludes: *"Et sic apparet quod licet posicio illarum racionum posset sustineri non tamen per has raciones sufficienter et conuincenter probantur Dico ergo pro completo huius articuli quod quelibet istarum posicionum potest probabiliter sustineri."* (Bruxelles. Bibl. Roy. 3699−3700, f. 118v^a).

In the end, however, Denys does not exempt Aristotle from seeming contradiction. As before, the chief author of his doubts is Henry of Ghent. On the question as a whole, Denys' attitude towards Henry is ambiguous. He quotes extensively Henry's famous treatment of the question in Quodlibet I, qq. 7—8.[88] He cannot accept, however, the metaphysical foundations of Henry's arguments for the necessary temporality of the creature, or his distinction between the acts of creation and preservation. Thus, he rejects Henry's criticism of Augustine's example of the eternal footprint, often cited by those who maintained that creation and preservation are the same. In Henry's mind, this image is insufficient to show what its proponents wish, for in fact the image requires that there have been some motion before which the depression did not exist; thus the image, and the images of the sun and its rays, the object and its shadow are able to express only God's preservation of the creature, and cannot suggest a relation of Creator and creature.[89] For Denys, it is a fundamental tenet that the acts of creation and preservation are the same; on this point, he finds Thomas Aquinas' teaching "beautiful", conferring upon it one of his most approving adjectives. In the Elementatio philosophica, he retains the examples that Henry criticizes.[90] More disturbing for Denys is Henry's argument that, by definition, the creature is constituted by being and non-being, so that non-being should be conceived as pertaining to a creature prior to its being. This is weakly conceived, Denys says, for what is innate and pertains to a thing's nature cannot be destructive of that nature. It is certain that, because of the contrariety of its qualities, a composed creature bears the cause of its corruption. Likewise, every creature by nature depends unceasingly on the first cause for its preservation from falling into nothingness. It is also true that it pertains to every rational creature, by its own cause, to fail and to sin. Nevertheless, non-being does not

---

[88] 2 Sent. d. 1. q. 4 (75B—77B). Denys extracts Henry's solution; cf. Henry of Ghent, Quodlibet I qq. 7—8, ed. R. Macken, in: Henrici de Gandavo Opera omnia 5, Leuven 1979, 29—40; cf. also Macken, La temporalité radicale de la créature selon Henri de Gand, in: Rech. de Théo. anc. et méd. 38 (1971) 211—72.

[89] 2 Sent. d. 1. q. 4 (Op. om. 21: 88C—A'). Henry's criticism is recited in 75A'—C'. Cf. Henry of Ghent, Quodl. I qq. 7—8, ed. Macken, 29—32, 37—38; Macken, La temporalité, 224—26, 233; Dales, 166—67. Augustine's image of the eternal footprint, used to characterize the opinion of philosophers and not to support his own opinion, is found in De civitate Dei 10, 31. Thomas and others, however, used the image to suggest the possibility of an eternal act of creation. At the time of writing De lum. 1 a. 113 (Op. om. 33: 379C'—D'), Denys had already encountered Henry's distinction between creation and preservation and criticism of the image, but he did not know the author of the argument.

[90] In 2 Sent. d. 1. q. 7 (Op. om. 21: 97D'—102D'), Denys quotes Henry as the spokesman for the distinction (98A—A', from Quodl. I q. 7), and responds with Thomas' teaching in ST. 1a q. 104. aa. 1—2 and Contra gentiles 3 c. 65 (98B'—100A'). See nn. 77, 82 above, and Elem. phil., prop. 89 (Op. om. 33: 94B').

pertain to the creature *ex se*, as if non-being were a something. Thus non-being does not effectively corrupt, as it neither acts nor is.[91] Henry's formulation of the creature's inherent nonbeing, one might add, strikes at the heart of Dionysius the Areopagite's expression of the creature's irrefrangible natural being, which tends always to its preservation, and the consequent intrinsic goodness of even the fallen angels *in naturalibus*. In his commentary on De divinis nominibus, Denys admits that Dionysius spoke extremely, but with good reason, precisely to prevent any notion that the creature is composed of contrary principles.[92]

Denys, however, incorporates a different kind of argument by Henry in another question that impresses him more (Quodlibet IX q. 17: *"An secundum fundamenta Aristotelis sit dicendum, quod semper fuerit homo, et unus ab alio in infinitum"*).[93] He likewise incorporates the argument, not in his Elementatio philosophica, but in a corresponding proposition of his Elementatio theologica, where the problem is viewed from the perspective *de veritate rei*, and where Henry's argument serves to show that more difficulties arise from the teaching of philosophers on the creation of the world than in the teaching of theologians.[94]

According to the intention of Aristotle, Henry says, in infinity man is generated by man, nor will there be some man who is not generated by another prior to him, and this proceeds infinitely over an infinite time. This is true also of the individuals of other species, especially those that arise from composition. Although this was Aristotle's opinion, he nevertheless held at the same time, and states clearly in Metaphysica 12, that naturally and simply man is prior to his seed, so that seed essentially comes from man rather than the contrary. Likewise, in Metaphysica 9, he says that although sometimes potency may precede act, as in this given egg potency precedes the act of the hen that it generates, nevertheless simply, act precedes potency in diverse things, nor does the process proceed infinitely. Thus it seems, Henry comments, that it is necessary for Aristotle to propose some man or some men to have been produced by God immediately, and likewise for other first supposites.[95]

But in fact, Denys continues, Aristotle did not concede this; hence one might conclude that he did not really think the world to have existed

---

[91] 2 Sent. d. 1. q. 4 (Op. om. 21: 88A'—D'). Denys inadvertently here attributes the argument to Durandus, for the argument appears in his résumé of Henry (76B'—77A). Cf. Henry, Quodl. I qq. 7—8, ed. Macken, 33—40; Macken, La temporalité, 234—42; Dales, 166—70.

[92] Comm. in lib. De div. nom., c. 4. aa. 52—53 (Op. om. 16: 169B'—173A').

[93] 2 Sent. d. 1. q. 4 (Op. om. 21: 77B—C'). Cf. Henry of Ghent, Quodl. IX q. 17, ed. Macken, 285—87. Denys extracts the argument from the end of the solution; the title he gives the question is his own application.

[94] Elem. theol., prop. 90 (Op. om. 33: 183B—184C').

[95] 2 Sent. d. 1. q. 4 (Op. om. 21: 77B—C'); Elem. theol., prop. 90 (Op. om. 33: 183C'—184C). Aristotle, Metaph. 9,8 (1049b 4—27); Metaph. 12,7 (1072b 30—1073a 3).

eternally, which he did, or that he contradicted himself. This is not the only instance involving the same matter, for in Physica 3, Aristotle says that the infinite cannot be traversed, yet if the world should have existed from eternity, there would be many examples in which this principle could not hold. Finally, Denys cites once more the crux of an infinite multitude of existing souls.[96]

It is precisely because it reminds him of the most disturbing dilemma in Aristotle's teaching — the apparent requirement for an infinite multitude of separated souls — that Denys includes Henry's latest argument in the treatment of the eternity of the world. If this problem had been a worry for Thomas Aquinas,[97] it was an insuperable stumbling-block for Denys the Carthusian. It is not the idea itself of an infinite multitude that disturbs; Denys could entertain arguments on both sides of the concept. Rather, it is a hidden consequence in this particular example, which sets in apart from all the other dilemmas arising from the notion of infinity: either one must acknowledge that Aristotle contradicted himself, with all that this means for his authority as a natural philosopher, or one must affirm that he was consistent, teaching one intellect for all men, and that Averroes is the authentic interpreter of "the wisest of all of the Greek philosophers." In the end, Denys prefers to be charitable, conceding the contradictions, or at least confusions, rather than the reprehensible moral error. But his only remaining assurance on the matter are the clear statements Aristotle purportedly made in the Liber de pomo et morte, and his disbelief that a great philosopher could really think there to be one intellectual soul for all men.

It is the singular dilemma of an infinite multitude, then, that lends credibility to the idea that there are other contradictions in Aristotle's teaching. Recollection of this dilemma causes Denys to admit the cogency of Durandus of St. Pourçain's resolution,[98] and it is to this dilemma that he returns in his final observations in the commentary on the Sentences. Here he rejects the example of the infinite pile of stones as irrelevant, because quantity and magnitude are determinate (*certa*) in all natural things, according to Aristotle, and hence no creature is capable of an infinite augmentation of quantity. A similar principle, Denys says, would seem to apply to an actual multitude. Thus, if one should concede an infinite generation of men to have occurred from eternity, the most reasonable thing to conclude, as Plato did, would be that a finite number of souls

---

[96] Elem. theol., prop. 90 (Op. om. 33: 184C—C'). Aristotle, Phys. 3,6 (207a); 3,5 (206a 7—8); 3,6 (206a 20—21). Algazel was the author of this argument, which he himself rebutted; see Dales, 44.

[97] Dales, 44 n. 10, 101, 130—40. One wonders whether Thomas saw the same implications in the argument as Denys.

[98] As is evident in his comment in 2 Sent. d. 1. q. 4 (Op. om. 21: 88B—C).

eternally pass into the diverse bodies ceaselessly produced by generation. It is a wonder, therefore, that Avicenna unqualifiedly proposed that the world has existed from eternity, that generation is eternal, and thus infinite separated souls exist in act. In these, he was an heretic in his own law, preferring to follow philosophy, as the reading of the Koran and other Saracen books makes clear.[99]

The final effect of Denys' suspicion, aroused by the difficulties in the discussion of the eternity of the world, is to degrade Aristotle's stature in the hierarchy of philosophic authorities. To err on the process of divine causality is almost inevitable to natural philosophy without benefit of divine revelation. To err on the immortal nature of the individual human soul, on the other hand, is inexcusable, since the soul knows its immortality. To err on this point is likewise to err on the central issue of natural philosophy, for man is the knot that links together the hierarchical natural order of spiritual and corporeal substances. Avicenna, who beautifully taught the immortality of the soul, and at the same time taught that the generation of individuals is eternal, had the courage of his convictions and tolerated the idea of an infinite multitude. And Plato, in proposing the transmigration of immortal souls, and thereby avoiding an infinite multitude, was perhaps even more coherent.

Aristotle's demotion, and the demotion of the authority of those who would follow him, is unambiguous in a further question. In his discussion of the eternity of the world in the Elementatio theologica, Denys mentions in passing that among the inconveniences of Aristotle's teaching is his assertion that not only the heavenly bodies and elements, but also the species of composed and corruptible things are eternal.[100] Of all of the questions concerning the heavenly bodies, Denys is most emphatic about their composition with elemental matter. His response to the question is the same in both Elementationes and the commentary on the Sentences. Aristotle in De caelo et mundo, Denys notes, proposes that the heavenly bodies are composed of a nature, or quintessence, "more simple and noble" than the nature of the elements, "immune from all contrariety and elemental quality, so that neither heaviness nor lightness exists in them." He deduces this unique nature from their proper circular motion, and from their incorruptibility. On this point, however, Christian authority speaks with nearly a unanimous voice. Denys enlists a long line of fathers and scriptural commentators, whose authority he trusts more than "the damned philos-

---

[99] 2 Sent. d. 1. q. 4 (Op. om. 21: 88D'—89C). Aristotle, Phys. 3,7 (207b 15—20); Metaph. 12,7 (1973a 5—6). Denys wrote two large works on Islam: Contra perfidiam Mahometi, et contra multa dicta Sarracenorum (Op. om. 36: 231—442); Dialogus disputationis inter Christianum et Sarracenum (Op. om. 36: 443—500).

[100] Elem. theol., prop. 90 (Op. om. 33: 183C—D).

ophers."[101] He further queries the principle from which Aristotle deduced his conclusion: the single, circular motion of the spheres. Aristotle's arguments lack great vigor and are scarcely persuasive (*persuasiuncula*). Does not the element of fire in its sphere beneath the moon move naturally, not violently, in a circular motion? Is it true that simple natures only have one movement? Do not the lighter elements, air and fire, as Averroes and Avicenna attest, naturally move downwards when participating in the generation of composed things, in respect of the universal good of nature and the preservation of species? Likewise, does not water naturally move upwards in a water-clock (*clepsydra*) in order to avoid a vacuum? According to Ptolemy and other astronomers, the motions of the planets in their epicycles, retrogressions, eccentricities and stops are various and many. Do these various movements signify various natures among them? Is it unreasonable to argue that the heavenly bodies in their elemental nature are moderated, proportioned and tempered so that it is natural to them to move neither upwards nor downwards, but in a circular manner as their location and figure require in order to serve the good of the whole natural condition? Nor can one say that those who hold the heavenly bodies to be composed of elemental nature are ignorant of true philosophy, for such preeminent doctors as William of Paris, William of Auxerre and Alexander of Hales maintain that they are.[102]

Besides these, all of the scholastic doctors whom Denys reports in his commentary affirm the opinion of Aristotle. Most notable among these is Thomas Aquinas.[103] Among other things, at issue in this question is the manifold testimony of Scripture concerning the watery nature of the firmament above the heavens. As often, Thomas appeals to Moses' condescension to a rude and imbecilic people.[104] But even Thomas admits with Augustine, Denys says, that the authority of Scripture is greater than every capacity of human wit.[105] Moreover, against the massive authority of the Christian fathers, Thomas invokes the authority of Dionysius the

---

[101] Elem. phil., prop. 50 (Op. om. 33: 63C−A'): Ambrose, Augustine, Basil, reprove the position, as do the glorious doctors of the Church, Jerome, Athanasius, Gregory Nazienzen, Chrysostom, Cyril, Theophilus, Gregory of Nyssa, the most blessed Pope Gregory, and also John Damascene, Bede, Strabo, Rabanus Maurus and the Master of the Sentences. A similar list is produced in Elem. theol., prop. 60 (Op. om. 33: 160A−B), where also Denys adduces many scriptural texts, and again, in 2 Sent. d. 14. q. 2 (Op. om. 22: 60D−A'). Aristotle, De caelo 1,2.

[102] These queries are made in 2 Sent. d. 14. q. 2 (Op. om. 22: 60C'−61A), and repeated in Elem. phil., a. 50 (Op. om. 33: 63A−64C). For the water-clock, see Aristotle, De caelo 2,13 (294b 20−22).

[103] On this, cf. Thomas Litt, Les corps célestes dans l'univers de saint Thomas d'Aquin, Louvain-Paris 1963, 54−90 et passim.

[104] 2 Sent. d. 14. q. 2 (Op. om. 22: 57D'); Thomas Aquinas, ST 1a q. 68. a. 3.

[105] Elem. phil., prop. 50 (Op. om. 33: 64B').

Areopagite in De divinis nominibus 4: "the heavens and the stars are ungenerable and have an invariable substance." Thomas futher remarks that Dionysius followed Aristotle nearly everywhere, as is obvious to those who inspect his books carefully.[106] In one of his early works, based on Thomas' commentary on the second book of the Sentences, Denys lets this comment pass.[107] At this point in the Elementatio theologica, however, he responds with texts by "the divine and most sacred Dionysius, instructed by the apostle Paul", which expound the first and fourth days of creation, and he addresses Thomas' remark specifically:

To that which has been introduced, it should be said that the glorious prelate, doctor and martyr Dionysius in very many things departed from Aristotle, as in this matter. For he never conceded the world to have been from eternity, nor that its motion would continue perpetually. Indeed, as has now been shown, he said that on the first day the sun was made from unformed matter, and on the fourth day formed through the reception of a greater light and virtue. Thus it stands that he is not a follower of Aristotle concerning the substance, nature and invariability of the heavenly bodies. Nor did he say absolutely that the heavens were ungenerable, since in Genesis it is written: "These are the generations of heaven and earth." Finally, according to the philosophers also, the elements are not in themselves corruptible, nor newly generable; nor are the heavenly bodies properly corruptible, as mixed bodies that possess contrariety. Even so, every created thing is in some manner corruptible, indeed can be annihilated, and immediately would fall back into nothingness, as produced from nothing, should at any moment it be deprived of the preservation of the omnipotent God. Truly, also in many other things divine Dionysius followed Plato more than Aristotle, proposing good to be before being, and asserting that prime matter is a something good, although it is not a being.[108]

---

[106] 2 Sent. d. 14. q. 2 (Op. om. 22: 57D, B'); Thomas Aquinas, 2 Sent. d. 14. q. 1. a. 3, in: Scriptum 2, ed. Mandonnet, 349—51.

[107] Creaturarum in ordine ad Deum consideratio theologica a. 57 (Op. om. 34: 13C).

[108] Elem. theol., prop. 60 (Op. om. 33: 160C'—161B): "*Ad quod videtur dicendum, juxta nunc introducta, quod gloriosus praesul, doctor et martyr Dionysius, in valde multa ab Aristotele recessit, etiam in ista materia: quia nec coelum concessit ab aeterno fuisse, nec ejus motum perpetuo duraturum: imo, ut modo monstratum est, solem dixit primo die factum ex prima illa informi materia, et quarto die formatum per receptionem majoris lucis atque virtutis. Quo constat, quod Aristoteles non sit secutus circa substantiam et naturam ac invariabilitatem coelestium corporum. Nec dixit coelum prorsus ingenerabile esse, quum et in Genesi scriptum sit: Istae sunt generationes coeli et terrae* (Gen. 4: 2). *Denique etiam secundum philosophos, elementa non sunt quoad se tota corruptibilia, neque de novo generabilia; nec (juxta praehabita) coelestia corpora sunt proprie corruptibilia, eo modo quo mixta, in se contrarietatem habentia: quamvis omne creatum sit aliquo modo corruptibile, imo et annihilabile, atque confestim in nihilum relaberetur, sicut ex nihilo est productum, si ad momentum omnipotentis Dei conservatione destitueretur. At vero etiam in aliis multis divinus Dionysius Platonem magis quam Aristotelem est secutus, ponendo bonum ante ens, et asserendo quod materia prima sit quid bonum, quamvis non sit ens.*" Denys refers to De div. nom. c. 4, trans. Eriugena, in: Dion. Cart. Op. om. 16: 104—5; see his comment in c. 4 aa. 38—39 (Op. om. 16: 123C—128C'), where he concludes: "*Ex quibus verbis est evidens, quod S. Dionysius*

VII

Appropriately, Denys alludes to a text from Plato's Timaeus, showing that although by their elemental nature the heavenly bodies are intrinsically corruptible, nevertheless they will not be corrupted or dissolved because of the divine will:

> "O dii deorum, quorum opifex paterque ego. Opera siquidem vos mea, dissolubilia natura; me tamen ita volente, indissolubilia. Omne siquidem iunctum, natura dissolubile est: quapropter, quia facti generatique estis, immortales nequaquam nec indissolubiles estis. Nec tamen dissolvemini, quia voluntas mea maior est nexu vestro."

Denys remarks that Henry of Ghent, among others, greatly approved this text in his Quodlibeta. In the Elementatio philosophica, he states as a proposition: "Plato better than others seems to have indicated the cause of the incorruptibility of the heavenly bodies." [109]

Each of these inquiries, conducted over a lifetime of reading, ends in a Platonic authority. From the beginning, the inspiration of Denys' "most-elect teacher" worked to ambush the analogous authority of Aristotle, "the wisest of all of the Greek philosophers." Denys was constantly driven to search better philosophic authorities for establishing the concordances between natural and supernatural wisdom, no matter what he had learned in school. As he finally understands it, the heavens are deanimated, [110] the intermediate movers of the physical world are radically contingent, and left standing as the only spiritual creatures before God, and as the only created spiritual influences on the world, are human souls and the hierarchies of angels. Man is the only creature linking the spiritual and physical worlds, and there is no other composite substance in the universe more noble. Further, the workings of the human soul, more remarkable than Aristotle would allow, are themselves the best guide to the corresponding

---

in Scripturis studiosissimus, et in earum intelligentia ab Apostolis ac apostolicis viris, praesertim a Paulo ac Hierotheo instructus, ut ipsemet frequenter testatur, dies illos primae creationis rerum de quibus locutus est Moyses, intellexit et intelligendos edocuit de temporalibus et successivis diebus, in quorum quarto perhibuit solem factum ... Idcirco quod quidam doctores scholastici eam [expositionem Augustini] assertive sequuntur, non censetur laudabile ... Per hoc quoque quod asserit solem factum esse de luce illa, insinuat solem esse naturae elementaris" (128B'—C').

[109] Elem. theol., prop. 60 (Op. om. 33: 161B—A'); Elem. phil., prop. 52 (Op. om. 33: 66A—A'). The text of Plato is in Timaeus a Calcidio translatus, 2a pars, in: Plato Latinus 4, ed. R. Klibansky, 35. For Henry of Ghent, cf. e. g., Quodl. IX q. 16, ed Macken, 272.

[110] The "more excellent philosophers" truly taught that the heavenly bodies are properly animated; but how can bodies lacking sensitive powers be properly animated?; Thomas wavered on the question; Albert saw no necessary contradiction between the philosophers and saints, but in fact, there is no possible concordance *ad rem*; the doctrine poses inconveniences for faith: did any "noble souls" fall? or were some confirmed in grace? should we pray to them?; scriptural and patristic authority speak of only two spiritual creatures, men and angels; the position granting no kind of animation is "more secure", and besides, the proposition was condemned by Etienne Tempier at Paris. Cf. Elem. phil., prop. 53 (Op. om. 33: 66B'—68C'), and 2 Sent. d. 14. q. 4 (Op. om. 22: 67D—79D).

order of nature. Nicholas of Cusa observed that, "today, when the sect of Aristotle prevails ... it is like a miracle — like a change of cult — when someone, rejecting Aristotle, passes over to something higher."[111] It does not seem strange to me that Nicholas considered Denys the Carthusian a kindred spirit.

---

[111] Nicolaus Cusanus, Apologia doctae ignorantiae, hg. L. Gabriel, übersetz. W. Dupré, in: *
Nikolaus von Kues. Philosophisch-theologische Schriften 1, Wien 1964, 530: "*Unde, cum nunc Aristotelica secta praevaleat ... sit miraculo simile — sicuti sectae mutatio — reiecto Aristotele eos altius transilire.*" Quoted in Swieżawski, Les débuts, 179. In the work, Cusanus defends his thought against the attacks of the Heidelberg professor in the "*via antiqua*", Iohannes Wenck (ob. 1460); cf. A. Gabriel, "Via antiqua" and "via moderna" in the Fifteenth Century, in: Miscellanea Mediaevalia 9: Antiqui und Moderni, ed. A. Zimmermann, 441, 451.

VIII

Theology as a Science: The Teaching of
Denys of Ryckel (Dionysius Cartusiensis, 1402-1471)

Among the huge literary achievements of Denys of Ryckel (Dionysius Cartusiensis, 1402-1471), perhaps none is more remarkable than his commentaries on the *Libri Sententiarum* of Peter Lombard. In effect, these commentaries are an encyclopaedia of scholastic learning. The careful reader will observe, however, that Denys disposes the arguments of his authors dialectically, interprets them in the course of reporting them, and conducts them to his own resolution.

Denys's commentaries are not a school exercise. After completing a Master of Arts at the University of Cologne, he entered the Charterhouse at Roermond, where he stayed - save two brief periods - for the rest of his life. Anselm Stoelen dates the commentaries late in Denys's career, in the years 1459-64.[1] It is clear, however, that Denys began this work much earlier. Already in 1430 he had gathered teachings from various commentaries on the *Sentences* for his treatise *De donis Spiritus sancti*. In 1446 he made a book of additions to this treatise, drawn from commentaries he had read subsequently. Also in 1446 he wrote a letter to his Superior wherein he lists the commentators on the *Sentences* whom he had read. It seems, then, that Denys's commentaries were compiled over a life time. I judge that he wrote the preliminary questions to Book I of the *Sentences* around the year 1446, when he finished the additions to *De donis Spiritus sancti* and encountered the teaching of Durandus of St. Pourçain for the first time.[2]

---

[1] The modern edition of Denys's works is: *Doctoris ecstatici D. Dionysii Cartusiani Opera omnia*, cura monachorum sacri ord. Cart., 42 in 44 vols. (Montreuil, Tournai, Parkminster, 1896-1913, 1935). The *Sentences* commentaries are in vols. 19-25bis. For the chronology of Denys's works see Anselm Stoelen, "Denys le Chartreux," *Dictionnaire de spiritualité* 3 (Paris, 1957): 431-34. For several months in 1451-52 Denys accompanied Nicholas of Cusa on a Papal Legation through the Germanies; in 1466-67 he helped establish a Carthusian foundation near 's Hertogenbosch.

[2] The treatise *De donis Spiritus sancti* is in *Op. om.* 35: 155-262, and the *Protestatio ad superiorem suum* in *Op. om.* 41: 625-26. For the dates, see Anselm Stoelen, "De Chronologie van de Werken van Dionysius de Karthuizer," *Sacris erudiri* 5 (1953): 361-401, esp. 362-63, 394-400. In Book 4 of *De donis* (1446) Denys adds reports

In the Prooemium to his commentary on Book I of the *Sentences*, in order to define the kind of wisdom to be found in the work and in the commentaries upon it, Denys uses a distinction which he developed first in *De donis*, amplified in his signal treatise *De contemplatione* (1435-45), and again in his philosophic work, *De lumine christianae theoriae* (1452).[3] Properly, wisdom is "supersapientissimus Deus," in whom "esse et essentia, sapere et sapientia" are identical. Created minds participate in this wisdom in a manifold, hierarchical manner. In the highest degree, human minds are infused with the supernatural gift of wisdom. This gift is joined inseparably to sanctifying grace, and to a formed faith and a formed charity. At its highest reach it is the same as mystical theology, as defined by pseudo-Dionysius the Areopagite (Denys's "most-elect teacher").[4] The infused gift of wisdom yields an intuitive knowledge of divine things, an affection exactly commensurate to the knowledge, and a savor for, and connaturality with, the divine. Throughout his writings, more exclusively even than Thomas Aquinas, Denys argues that the gift of wisdom is speculative "essentialiter et principaliformiter."[5]

Besides this infused wisdom is a twofold "sapientia causata," or acquired wisdom. By means of the natural light of the intellect one can rise from the visible to the invisible, to a knowledge of separated substances and God. This is natural, philosophic wisdom, achieved by the greatest natural "theologians," Plato and Aristotle, Proclus and Avicenna.[6] Mediating the supernatural wisdom supernaturally received and the natural wisdom naturally acquired is a supernatural wisdom that may be naturally acquired. This wisdom is a knowledge of sacred Scripture. It is "supernatural" because of its origin and because it teaches truths which human reason could never otherwise discover. Once revealed, however, such

---

from the commentaries of Albert, Bonaventure, Peter of Tarantaise and Durandus of St. Pourçain.

[3] *De donis* 2.aa.1-5 (*Op. om.* 35: 175B'-79D); *De contemplatione* 1.a.2 (*Op. om.* 41: 137B-B'); *De lumine christianae theoriae* 1.a.5 (*Op. om.* 33: 239D'-40A).

[4] For pseudo-Dionysius, see *Protestatio* (*Op. om.* 41: 625-26). G. E. M. Vos de Wael, *De Mystica theologia van Dionysius mysticus in de Werken van Dionysius Carthusianus* (Nijmegen-Utrecht, 1942), pp. 11-13, supplies a list of Denys's epithets for the Areopagite.

[5] See my article (forthcoming), "Twofold Wisdom and Contemplation in Denys of Ryckel (Dionysius Cartusiensis, 1402-1471)," *Journal of Medieval and Renaissance Studies* 18 (1988).

[6] *De donis* 2.a.2 (*Op. om.* 35: 176A').

wisdom can be acquired by reason alone. Although it can be perfected by sanctifying grace, essentially it is a grace given for the good of others (*gratia gratis data*), ordained to the defense, persuasion and declaration of faith. An acquired knowledge of the truths of faith, one sees, is common to good and bad men, good and bad angels alike; it is this kind of wisdom, called "scholastic," that one finds in commentaries on the *Sentences*.[7]

The threefold distinction of wisdom in the Prooemium illumines Denys's treatment of the first preliminary question: "Whether theology be a science." Fr. Synan discusses in detail the objections which Denys presents against theology being a science.[8] These objections reflect the practice, after Thomas Aquinas, of measuring theology against the strictest Aristotelian criteria for scientific knowledge; since theology could but fail these, the question became nearly mute.[9] In a sense, Denys's arguments, which introduce a new perspective, revive the question.

Objections may be made against theology's unscientific matter - sacred Scripture - and against its unscientific form. Science treats universal, necessary objects whereas Scripture concerns particular, contingent, individual words and deeds. Science proceeds from or resolves into principles *per se nota*; since they are incomprehensible, the first principles of theology are nowise evident. Demonstration requires that the certitude of the principles be more evident than the conclusions; since the principles of theology cannot be evident, certain conclusions cannot be deduced from them. In sum, theology, though more sure than opinion, attains the credible but falls short of science.[10]

---

[7] 1 *Sent.* Prooem. (*Op. om.* 19: 37-38); *De cont.* 1.a.2 (*Op. om.* 41: 137B-B').

[8] E. A. Synan, "Sensibility and Science in Medieval Theology: The Witness of Durandus of Saint-Pourçain and Denis the Carthusian," *Knowledge and the Sciences in Medieval Philosophy.* Proceedings of the Eighth International Congress of Medieval Philosophy (S.I.E.P.M.) Helsinki 24-29 August 1987. Vol III. Eds. R. Työrinoja, A. I. Lehtinen, D. Føllesdal. Annals of the Finnish Society for Missiology and Ecumenics 55 (Helsinki 1990), pp. 531-539.

[9] Among many works, see Robert Guelluy, *Philosophie et théologie chez Guillaume d'Ockham* (Louvain-Paris, 1947), pp. 25-76 et passim; Camillo Dumont, S. J., *La théologie comme science chez les scolastiques du treizième siècle. Histoire de la question "Utrum theologia sit scientia" de 1230 à 1320* (Excerpt of Diss., Gregorian Univ.; Louvain, 1962); Paul Tihon, S. J., *Foi et théologie selon Godefroid de Fontaines* (Paris-Bruges, 1966), esp. pp. 31-49, 120-31.

[10] 1 *Sent.* q.præv.1 (*Op. om.* 19: 58B-59D).

Faithful to his early training, Denys responds to these objections by reciting the well-known resolution of Thomas Aquinas: as a subalternated natural science borrows its first principles from a higher one, so the theology of the faithful derives its first principles from the higher science of the blessed.[11] Denys's eventual resolution indicates that he understands the inadequacy of this analogy: the practitioner of a natural, subalternated science can, in principle, acquire the premises derived from the higher science.[12] For this and probably other reasons,[13] Denys does not allow Thomas to express the argument more fully, but rather adduces Richard of Middleton. As music draws its principles from arithmetic and perspective from geometry, so the theologian draws his principles from the science of God himself, to whom they are self-evident. The blessed gaze on these principles, which were in turn handed over to the prophets and apostles in incorporeal light. Hence, in itself theology is a science *simpliciter*. With respect to us, theology is a science in a qualified sense; presupposing first principles through faith, we can discover conclusions necessarily deriving from them. Admittedly, the conclusions of theology in this life cannot be as scientific as those of natural subalternated sciences, since their principles can be acquired with certain knowledge. Certainty in any subalternated science is relative to whatever "certain knowledge we can acquire of those sciences to which it is subalternated, and from those principles from which it proceeds."[14] Richard's formulation appears to be a probable source for Denys's acquired, supernatural wisdom; it also opens a window to illuminative experience from above.

Denys rightly allows Durandus of St. Pourçain (ca. 1270-1332) to make the counter argument, for Durandus, although he concludes that theology is a science "broadly speaking," empties the notion of any real meaning. The term "theology," he says, may be understood in a threefold sense. It may designate the habit by which one assents to the contents of

---

[11] Ibid. (59C-D); Thomas Aquinas, *ST* 1.q.1.

[12] See Tihon, pp. 121-24.

[13] Thomas's position, that the wayfarer can have no knowledge without the mediation of phantasms, which Denys will oppose, does not very well allow Denys's argument on this question; see Emery, "Twofold Wisdom." For the significance of Denys's perception that Richard follows Thomas, see Dumont, pp. 52-53.

[14] 1 *Sent.* q.*præv*.1 (*Op. om.* 19: 59D-D'). See Richard of Middleton, 1 *Sent. Prol.* q.2, in *Ricardi de Mediavilla ... Super quatuor libros Sententiarum*, 4 vols. (Brixen, 1591; reprt. Minerva Press, 1963), vol. 1, f. 5r.

sacred doctrine, in the same way that "natural philosophy" can mean a knowledge of what is in philosophical books. In this sense, "theology" seems no different than faith. Secondly, "theology" may signify the habit of strengthening and defending the faith by reference to principles truly knowable to human reason. This habit, it seems, excludes the virtue of faith. Finally, some use the term "theology" to stand for the habit of deducing conclusions from the articles of faith as from first principles. Stating an argument that Denys includes among the original objections, Durandus says that no conclusion can be firmer than the principle from which it is derived; the wayfarer can never say that it is impossible for an article of faith to be otherwise; hence no conclusion deduced from the articles of faith can be certain or necessary, as science requires.[15]

Durandus likewise deprives the articles of faith of their moral certitude. Some say that the articles of faith are verified by their author, who can neither deceive nor be deceived. But the wayfarer cannot be certain that God is their author. To know this certainly he would need to be a *comprehensor* of the divine Word, which he is not. Or maybe one imagines that God speaks directly to the wayfarer. If he did, he would need to communicate through sounds formed in some kind of created substance. Demons as well as God can form such sounds. Moreover, even if it could be ascertained in some general way that God authored the articles of faith, one could not transfer this general certainty to any particular article.[16]

Durandus's arguments rest on the premise that man's experience of revelation is always sense-bound, and they are meant to magnify the virtue of faith and the authority of the Church. Durandus's piety and positivism are evident in arguments which Denys reports elsewhere. We believe the articles of faith because they are revealed in the Scriptures. We believe in the Scriptures because we believe that they are inspired by God. We believe that the Scriptures are inspired by God because the Church says that they are. Denys summarizes Durandus's argument: "from first to last, the reason for believing everything else is the belief that the Church is governed by the Holy Spirit." If indeed God could speak

---

[15] 1 *Sent.* q.*præv.*1 (*Op. om.* 19: 60B'-61D'). See Durandus of St. Pourçain, *Prol. Sent.* q.1: 6-11, 21-25, 38-40, in *Durandi a Sancto Porciano ... in Petri Lombardi Sententias*, 2 vols. (Venice, 1571; reprt. Gregg Press, 1964), ff. 2v-4v.

[16] 1 *Sent.* q.*præv.*1 (*Op. om.* 19: 61D-C'); Durandus, *Prol. Sent.* q.1: 43-47 (ff. 4v-5r), and perhaps 2 *Sent.* d.7.q.4: 5 (f. 146r).

directly to man, Durandus reasons, whatever he told us must needs be true since by definition he cannot deceive; hence we would possess scientific knowledge of him and faith would be impossible.[17] Denys applauds Durandus's Catholic sensibility ("verba illa Durandi videntur catholice dicta"), but he admits that Scripture derives its authority from the Church in only a limited sense. "Causaliter et existentialiter" Scripture derives its authority directly from God. Moreover, through internal inspiration and the mediation of holy angels the prophets knew certainly that God spoke to them, and yet they had faith; likewise, Paul knew certainly that he was rapt to the third heaven and heard the secret words of God immediately, and yet he had faith; finally, the virgin Mary, although she had the faith of a wayfarer, yet knew *supercertissime* that the angel spoke to her, that she conceived the Son by the Holy Spirit and heard from him the truths of faith.[18] Significantly, Durandus argued that whatever Paul's experience, he could only remember it in some confused, imaginative way.[19]

Durandus's arguments, which implicitly deny man's immanent experience of spiritual realities, strike to the heart of Denys's thought. Denys formulates his initial response in terms of a threefold classification of visions commonplace in mystical literature.[20] It is not true that we must be *comprehensores* in order to know certainly that the articles of faith come from God; nor is it true that God can communicate directly with man only through some material sound. One can know certainly that God is the author of faith through "internal illustration, apparition and allocution"; or through the imaginative and intellectual powers at once, as - according to "divine Dionysius" - did the prophets through the ministry of angels; or finally, through the intellectual power alone, as did David in his "revelations" and "anagogic illuminations." In short, the Holy Spirit can certify supernatural realities in the mind, as he does in the visions,

---

[17] Reported by Denys in 3 *Sent.* d.24.q.*unica* (*Op. om.* 23: 420C'-21C). See Durandus, *Prol. Sent.* q.1: 44, 49 and q.3 (ff. 4v-5r, 6v-8r); 3 *Sent.* d.23.q.7: 12, and d.24.q.1: 8-9 (ff. 255v, 256v-257r).

[18] 3 *Sent.* d.24.q.*unica* (*Op. om.* 23: 420D-C').

[19] Durandus, *Prol. Sent.* q.3: 4, 11, 19 (ff. 7r-8r).

[20] Augustine, *De Genesi ad litteram* 12.7-37 (*CSEL* 28: 387-435). Cf. Hugh of St. Victor, *Comm. in Hier. coel.* 2.1 (*PL* 175: 941C-43B); Richard of St. Victor, *In Apocalypsim* 1.1 (*PL* 196: 686A-89A). See also Denys's classification in *De particulari judicio* a.26 (*Op. om.* 41: 462D-63C') and *Enarratio in Epist. I beati Joannis* a.6 (*Op. om.* 14: 43B'-44B').

raptures and ecstasies of mystical theology.[21] Arguing that faith and certain knowledge of the same object cannot co-exist in the same mind, Durandus states the principle that contraries, however modified, cannot unite. Denys asserts the opposite; one extreme may be reduced to its contrary by way of intermediaries. Accordingly, Durandus poses a dichotomy between the possessor's vision *per speciem* and the wayfarer's obscure faith, whereas here and elsewhere Denys proposes a mediating hierarchy of spiritual cognition extending from simple faith through mystical intuition to the transient vision of God face to face.[22] Acquired theological wisdom participates in this hierarchy, inasmuch as its origin is in the visions imparted to the prophets, the anagogic illuminations of David and the sights seen by Paul in ecstatic rapture.

Durandus reports and disapproves a "certain opinion" which argues, on the one hand, that the principles of a science must be evident, and, on the other hand, that theology can be a science properly speaking. According to this opinion, the articles of faith whence theology proceeds can be truly understood in a light that lies between faith and vision. Conclusions deduced from principles thus illumined are known truly. This argument is based on a twofold distinction in evidence. By the evidence of vision, one knows something nakedly and immediately as a rustic knows the eclipse of the sun. By the evidence of understanding (*intelligentiae*) one knows something not present through its distinct *ratio*, as an astronomer knows an eclipse. The latter is sufficient for understanding and is compatible with faith.[23] Durandus judges that a light between faith and vision is fictitious, and that such a light could not anyway co-exist with faith, which is obscure by definition. He wonders further why all students of theology are not privy to such light.[24]

The author of the opinion which Durandus reproves is Henry of Ghent.[25] At this point,[26] Denys does not know the author but the

[21] 1 *Sent.* q.prœv.1 (*Op. om.* 19: 62B-C). On rapture and ecstasy, see *De cont.* 3.aa.18-19 (*Op. om.* 41: 278A-81A').

[22] 1 *Sent.* q.prœv.1 (*Op. om.* 19: 65A-C, 66B-C'); Durandus, *Prol. Sent.* q.2: 19 (f. 6v). See Emery, "Twofold Wisdom."

[23] 1 *Sent.* q.prœv.1 (*Op. om.* 19: 64A'-65A). Durandus reports and rejects Henry of Ghent's teaching in *Prol. Sent.* q.2 (ff.5v-6v).

[24] 1 *Sent.* q.prœv.1 (*Op. om.* 19: 65A-C); Durandus, *Prol. Sent.* q.2: 12 (f. 6r).

[25] Henry of Ghent, *Quod.* 12.q.2, in *Quodlibeta magistri Henrici Goethals a Gandavo*, 2 vols. (Paris, 1518; reprt. Louvain, 1961), ff. 485r-86v. See Raymond Macken, "L'Illumination divine concernant les vérités révélées chez Henri de Gand," *Journal*

argument strikes a resonant chord. He interprets it in light of the contemplative theory which he established in *De donis Spiritus sancti* and *De contemplatione.* Whoever receives sanctifying grace partakes the gift of wisdom in some degree. Men of heroic virtue perfected in charity possess the gift in the supreme degree and by it are made familiar friends with God. The gift of wisdom directly touches uncreated wisdom, enabling one by an internal taste to judge divine things correctly. Moreover, the gift of understanding (*intellecius*) enables one to penetrate the truths of faith and to see them transparently. By this gift one discovers the coherence and inter-connectedness of the articles of faith so that nothing appears more reasonable or true. Denys here distinguishes between a demonstrative certitude (*quid est*) of the articles of faith, impossible to the wayfarer, and a rational certitude (*quia*) that they come from God which does not exclude faith.[27] He is scarcely surprised that not all theologians receive the illumination between faith and vision, for the ones who receive it are those

> who have continually experienced mystical theology. This illumination is not given only to those who study theology, nor to all of them, nor equally to the clever-minded, but rather to those who are more advanced in purity of heart and charity. One of these was brother Giles, [the companion of Francis], who did not like to say "I believe in God," but "I know God." And most of all the seraphic Francis [received this light].[28]

Thus, Denys interprets the understanding which, in Anselm's terms,[29] lies between faith and vision as the gift of understanding itself. He says elsewhere that this gift is

> a certain participation in the light of the divine intellect. Thus, as the light of the divine intellect, remaining one and simple, sees through and penetrates every truth intimately, so the light of the

---

philosophique 5 (1985): 261-71.

26 Denys does not mention Henry in his list of authors in the *Protestatio* (1446), nor does he name Henry in 1 *Sent.* q.*præv.*1.

27 1 *Sent.* q.*præv.*1 (*Op. om.* 19: 66D-A'). On theological knowledge *quia-quid est,* see 2 *Sent.* d.3.q.6 (*Op. om.* 21: 271D-D'). In arguments against subalternation, many scholastics denied certitude *quia* concerning the principles of faith; see Dumont, pp. 54-58, and Tihon, pp. 124-29.

28 1 *Sent.* q.*præv.*1 (*Op. om.* 19: 65C-C'). "Et communiter tales sunt omnes qui mysticam theologiam assidue experimentur. Hinc illuminatio ista non datur solis aut omnibus in theologia studentibus, seu æque ingeniosis, sed eis qui in puritate cordis et caritate magis proficiunt. Horum unus fuit sanctus frater Ægidius, qui noluit dicere, Credo in Deum; sed Scio Deum. Et maxime seraphicus ille Franciscus" (65B'-C').

29 Anselm, "Ad Urbanum Papam II," *Cur Deus homo,* ed. F. S. Schmitt in *S. Anselmi Cantuariensis Opera omnia* 2 (Edinburgh, 1946), p. 40.

gift of understanding in its way, by virtue of the uncreated light, so vehemently illumines the mind that through it, although it remains simple and one, it understands all of the truths of faith.[30]

Through the gift of understanding, then, the theologian in some measure participates in the science of the divine mind. Participation in this simple science allows one to discover the one in the many, to see how the new Law agrees with the old, and how the whole of Scripture accords with itself.[31] Herein lies the germ of Denys's response to objections against Scripture's particularity. The particulars in Scripture are not properly understood as such, but as signifying universal salvific mysteries. They also exemplify the universal attributes of God's providence, mercy, justice, omnipotence, etc, and are examples of human virtues.[32]

Denys resumes this dispute in 3 *Sent.* d.24 q. *unica*: "whether faith concerns only those things which are unknowable." By the time he composed this question, he had obtained a text of Henry of Ghent's *Quodlibeta* which he could comment on directly. Contrary to most doctors, Henry holds that some articles of faith may in some sense be proved or demonstrated, as some think Richard of St. Victor to have taught. Reasoned discourse (*disputatio*) is of two kinds. One kind seeks to demonstrate absolutely, without qualification. The articles of faith are beyond such demonstration. Another kind seeks to demonstrate suppositionally (*ad positionem*); starting from presupposed certain principles it discovers their necessary adjuncts. Some articles of faith can be "demonstrated" in this way. Presuming that certain articles are true and necessary, by means of natural reasoning one may attain conclusions about the faith which are truly understood and known. Some principles of faith, such as the Trinity, are eternal and absolutely necessary, although their reasons are known only to God; presupposed as first principles by faith, these can yield necessary conclusions. Other principles of faith, such as those pertaining to the sacraments or redemption, are not absolutely necessary, but suppose a determination of the divine will;

---

[30] *De donis* 2.a.27 (*Op. om.* 35: 198A-B): "sit quædam participatio luminis intellectus divini. Ideo, sicut lumen intellectus divini simplum unumque permanens, omnem veritatem perspicet et intime penetrat; ita et lumen doni intellectus suo modo, in virtute luminis increati, mentem tam vehementer illustret, ut per ipsum, quamvis simplex perseveret ac unum, omnia prædicta intelligat, cunctosque effectus prætactos obtineat."

[31] *De donis* 2.a.24 (*Op. om.* 35: 195A'-B').

[32] 1 *Sent.* q.præv.1 (*Op. om.* 19: 66D'-67A). Denys refers to Alexander of Hales, *Summa theologica, Tract. intro.* 1.2 (Quarrachi, 1924), and Richard of Middleton, 1 *Sent.* q.4.ad 4 (f. 7r).

presupposed as first principles by faith, these can yield only probable or convenient conclusions. Yet other truths - that God exists, that he is one - are not strictly speaking articles of faith, since they can be demonstrated by reason alone.[33]

Denys does not affirm Henry's arguments; he consents more to the opposite arguments of Thomas Aquinas, reported earlier in the question.[34] (Henry's theological science, nonetheless, sounds very much like Denys's acquired supernatural wisdom.) On the other hand, he confirms Henry's and Richard of St. Victor's statements that nothing is more certain than the truths of faith, and he wholly embraces the "solemn doctor's" argument that the articles of faith can be known in a light clearer than faith.[35] Denys draws Henry's sense to his own, alluding to the distinction between a supernatural wisdom supernaturally received and a supernatural wisdom naturally acquired which he makes in the Prooemium and elsewhere. Corresponding to this twofold wisdom is a twofold science. As the gift of wisdom is the supernatural habit of speculative judgment that accompanies the gift of understanding's apprehension of divine things, so the gift of science is the supernatural habit of judging created things in relation to God.[36] The supernatural gifts of wisdom, understanding and science, surely, are lights clearer than faith. Furthermore, acquired theological wisdom and science are also lights clearer than faith, as long as they are founded in faith and formed by sanctifying grace.[37] With these provisions, Denys accepts Henry's intention in the argument. Only when we understand the term "light of faith" in its broadest sense, to mean any light whatsoever that comes to the wayfarer in this life, can we say that there is no light higher than faith. Even then there are exceptions, such as the special privilege granted to Paul.[38]

To deny that there is a light higher than faith, to scoff at the idea and dismiss it as a fiction, as does Duns Scotus, "is not the mark of

---

[33] 3 *Sent.* d.24.q.*unica* (*Op. om.* 23: 422A-D); Henry of Ghent, *Quod.* 8.q.14 (ff. 324v-26r); Richard of St. Victor, *De Trinitate* 1.4 (*PL* 196: 892B-93A).

[34] 3 *Sent.* d.24.q.*unica* (*Op. om.* 23: 416A'-19C'). See Thomas Aquinas, 3 *Sent.* d.23.q.2, and *ST* 2a2ae.qq.1-2.

[35] 3 *Sent.* d.24.q.*unica* (*Op. om.* 23: 423D'-24D): Richard of St. Victor, *De Trin.* 1.2 (*PL* 196: 891C-92A); Henry of Ghent, *Quod.* 8.q.14 and 12.q.2 (ff. 325r-v, 485r-86v).

[36] *De donis* 3.aa.21-22 (*Op. om.* 35: 223C'-25D').

[37] 3 *Sent.* d.24.q.*unica* (*Op. om.* 23: 424B'-C').

[38] Ibid. (424D'-25A).

a subtle mind, but serves rather to demonstrate one's inexperience."[39] Furthermore, Duns Scotus's opinion is contrary to the whole of theological tradition. Concerning this light Augustine spoke in many writings; so have the most eminent doctors, Alexander, Thomas, Albert, William of Paris, William of Auxerre, Peter of Tarantaise and Ulrich of Strassburg. Notably, the "devout and sweet doctor Bonaventure wrote diffusely about this light, its degrees and species, in many works." Even certain outstanding philosophers, like Plato, discovered something about it. Decisively, the highest authorities of Christian wisdom testify to its reality. In his book on *Mystical Theology* "altissimus, divinissimus, sacratissimus et theologicissimus Dionysius" spoke evidently concerning this light; likewise did the Canon Regular Jan van Ruusbroec, "a man wonderfully taught and anointed from above, very expert in all devotional and internal exercises."[40]

Many pious men in the late Middle Ages willingly conceded the unscientific character of theology, to the advantage of a blind and heroic faith or a piety of the will and the affections. Unlike these, in order to establish theology as a science, Denys goes beyond the conventional boundaries of the scholastic debate and adduces the testimony of mystical tradition. To his mind the analogy between natural and theological science is more than a justifiable manner of speaking. Because it contemplates the first cause and separated substances directly, metaphysics in the natural order is called wisdom *simpliciter*. This wisdom first judges its own content, and then through its "most common and causal principles" it judges lower sciences. Likewise in the supernatural order, and in a way more true, the gift of wisdom (identical with mystical theology) judges what pertains to itself, and then through the illumination of its "divine reasons, laws and standards judges all lower sciences."[41] As a subalternated science scholastic theology borrows its first principles from the higher science of the blessed. But it need not adopt them blindly, with no cognition of them at all. In this life the saints and more holy

---

[39] Ibid. (425D'-26A).

[40] 3 *Sent.* d.24.q.unica (*Op. om.* 23: 425A'-26B'). As evidence for the philosophers, Denys cites Augustine quoting Apuleius about Plato in *De civitate Dei* 9.16 (*CCSL* 47: 264). On Denys's response, see J. Beumer, *Theologie als Glaubensverständnis* (Würzburg, 1953), pp. 110-16; on the special authority of Ruusbroec, see *De donis* 2.a.13 (*Op. om.* 35: 184B'-D'), and Emery, "Twofold Wisdom."

[41] *De donis* 2.a.5 (*Op. om.* 35: 179B-D).

teachers, at least, to some degree participate in the higher light of beatific science, if only briefly.

Denys indicates how full this participation can be by his several references to the rapture of St. Paul, to whom, with the virgin Mary, he grants the transient vision of God *per speciem* in this life. He seems also to concede the possibility to others.[42] In both questions from the *Sentences* which we have considered, Denys refers to an interpretation of Job 36:32-33, "Deus in manibus abscondit lucem," made by "holy father Bernard" (actually William of St. Thierry) in his *Epistola ad Cartusienses domus Montis Dei*. This text suggest that God sometimes concedes to his beloved, in the course of this life, a glimpse of the light of his face, so that the soul will be enkindled to desire "the full possession and vision of eternal light." In this light, Denys says, "the truths of faith are discerned evidently, wholly and indubitably."[43] In his own commentary on the Book of Job, Denys devotes an entire article to this verse. The light which God now reveals, now conceals to his special friends, in order to excite in them a desire for their eternal inheritance,

> is not, properly and most subtly speaking, really the same thing as the light of grace (that is, sanctifying grace, which is a certain light), as some say, nor is it charity, nor the gift of wisdom, nor an act belonging to it or elicited from it, nor something habitual and lodged in the soul, nor is it a prophecy. It is, rather, a certain actual flash (*fulgor*) of the divine light, beating down upon the face of the created mind, shining over it, ineffably clarifying and illumining it in such a way that, as the light of glory in heaven disposes to the beatific vision, so this light elevates, actuates and clarifies the mind for contemplation, mystical intuition and the highest perfection possible in this life.[44]

---

[42] *De cont.* 3.a.24 (*Op. om.* 41: 287A'-B'). See P. Alessio Martinelli, O. F. M., "La Visione di Dio *per speciem* durante la presente vita secondo S. Dionigi il Certosino (1402-1471)," *Divinitas* 2 (1958): 371-408.

[43] 1 *Sent.* q.præv.1 (*Op. om.* 19: 66A-B); 3 *Sent.* d.24.q.unica (*Op. om.* 23: 426B-C); *De fonte lucis ac semitis via* a.16 (*Op. om.* 41: 114D'-16C'). For "Bernard," see William of St. Thierry, *Epistola* 2.3.268-71, ed. Jean Déchanet, O. S. B., *Lettre aux frères du Mont-Dieu (Lettre d'or)*. Sources chrétiennes 223 (Paris, 1975), pp. 256-61.

[44] *Enarratio in librum Job* a.65 (*Op. om.* 4: 686B-89C'). "Porro lux ista ... proprie ac subtilissime de ea loquendo, non est, ut dicitur, realiter idem quod lumen gratiæ (id est ipsa gratia gratificans, quæ lumen quoddam est), nec caritas, nec donum sapientiæ, nec proprius atque elicitus actus ipsius, nec aliquid habituale et fixum in anima, sicut nec prophetia; sed actualis quidam fulgor lucis divinæ, vultui mentis creatæ instantanee desuper incidens, superque fulgens, ineffabiliter eam clarificans et perlustans, ita quod sicut in patria lumen gloriæ disponit ad beatificam visionem, ita lux ista elevat, actuat atque clarificat ad præfatam contemplationem, mysticam intuitionem, huicque vitæ possibilem altissimam perfectionem" (687D'-88B).

388

The scientific habit of theology belongs properly to the blessed *in patria*. Some wayfarers, it would seem, participate in this habit more than others. The testimonies of God's special friends should be enough to certify the first principles of theology for those clever-minded ones who investigate supernatural wisdom in a natural, acquired way.[45]

---

[45] The notion of the special, or familiar, or secret "friends" of God occurs throughout Denys's writing, and was a set topic of late medieval spirituality. See the distinctions in *De cont.* 3.a.23 (*Op. om.* 41: 285B-86B), where Denys refers to Cassian, (Ruusbroec), Gerson. In 1 *Sent.* q.*præv.*1 (*Op. om.* 19: 65D) Denys speaks of "consiliarii et secretarii Dei, et familiares ejus amici"; the metaphor may derive from Alan of Lille, *De planctu naturæ* (*PL* 210: 450D).

IX

Denys the Carthusian and the Doxography of Scholastic Theology

"QUIDQUID RECIPITUR, ad modum recipientis recipitur." What is received by Denys of Ryckel (Dionysius Cartusiensis, 1402–1471) is nearly the whole tradition of Christian thought and practice up to his time. Denys's literary production embraces scriptural, monastic, speculative, mystical, apologetic, canonical, and pastoral works. In this study I shall focus upon Denys's reading of scholastic theology. But one must read Denys's scholastic writings in the broad context of his hierarchically ordered corpus. The rule of faith that he discovered in his scriptural commentaries governs his scholastic thinking, which is likewise guided by, and perfected in, the visions of mystical theology. The order in which Denys executed his literary works follows in outline the order of his intellectual intention. His first work after entering the Charterhouse of Roermond in Limburg in 1424 concerns the Carthusian life.[1] Significantly, his first speculative work is a treatise on the gifts of the Holy Spirit.[2] Thereafter, between the years 1434–1457, he produced commentaries on each book of Scripture. These commentaries expound Scripture according to the traditional four senses, and make an encyclopedia of comments of the fathers and doctors. They provided Denys a storehouse of material to be distributed among other works, and supplied him with a complete set of scriptural references with attached interpretations.[3]

Denys's enormous scholastic erudition is all the more remarkable inasmuch as he did not receive a full university education. He studied only in the arts faculty at the University of Cologne, where in 1421 he matriculated in the *Bursa* founded by Henricus de Gorrichem (ob. 1431), later named the *Bursa Montana* after its second Regent, the Thomist Gerardus de Monte (Gerardus ter Steghen).[4] Denys received a Master of Arts degree in 1424, whereupon he immediately entered the monastery. While at Cologne he wrote a treatise, *De ente et essentia,* now lost. He may also have written a treatise on universals attributed to him by his sixteenth-century editor, undiscovered until recently.[5] We know the character of the first treatise from a remark Denys makes many years later in his *Sentences* commentary:

> When I was studying in my youth and I was instructed in the *via Thomae,* I rather thought that *esse* and *essentia* should be really distinguished. At the time I compiled (*compilavi*) a certain treatise on the matter. I wish that I had it now, for I would correct it. In the meantime, having more carefully considered the matter, often in the past as now, I am convinced that, more truly and probably, the two do not really differ.[6]

* Happily, I have discovered three manuscript copies of the treatise on universals of which Denys's editor spoke. Although his authorship must be proved, there are signs of authenticity. The text is a compendium of realist teaching on universals, and in each case was copied by fifteenth-century students of the *via antiqua.*[7]

Denys conceives his intellectual effort within a threefold hierarchical ordering of wisdom that he proposes from his earliest works until his last treatises and commentaries.[8] The order is neatly summarized in one of his last works, *Elementatio theologica, seu Compendium theologiae,* written about 1465.[9]

Properly speaking, the eternal Son of the Father is uncreated wisdom, which every created wisdom reflects. The uncreated wisdom is distributed to created minds eminently through the gifts of the Holy Spirit. The human mind ascends toward the uncreated wisdom in a threefold manner. First, one may ascend through a natural, philosophic wisdom, the highest act of which is the contemplative felicity about which Aristotle speaks in the tenth Book of the *Ethics.* Aristotle calls this "theology" in the *Metaphysics.* Second, there is a supernatural, theological wisdom which good and bad, elect and reprobate alike may acquire. Although founded in Revelation, it is expanded by human inquiry. This acquired wisdom, called "scholastic," is among the charismatic graces bestowed for the good of others (*dona gratiae gratis datae*). Those possess this wisdom who have knowledge of Scripture and are erudite in the theological books of the saints and doctors. Third, strictly speaking, supernatural wisdom is a sanctifying grace and is formed by a savorous awareness (*notitia*) of the divine that is identical with the gift of wisdom. In its highest degree and condition, this wisdom is called "mystical theology" by the "divine Dionysius" the Areopagite.[10]

The order of wisdom engenders an order of theological literacy. The eternal Word or uncreated wisdom diffuses itself in a covering (*tegumen*) and in shadows whereby its infinite luminosity is proportioned to the weakness of human capacity. Hence the evangelical doctrine of Scripture is wrapped in various similitudes, parables, and figures suited to our way of knowing, which ascends from sensible images to a knowledge of immaterial realities and a love of the divine. From the source of Christ's teachings in the four Gospels derive the countless volumes of the saints and Catholic teachers. These pour into a mighty river of lucid water in the *Liber Sententiarum*, compiled (*compilatus*) from the books of the fathers by Peter Lombard. From this river branch so many streams of science in the commentaries and writings of scholastic doctors. In his own *Sentences* commentary, Denys adds, he has attempted to reunite the tributary waters in a single flow: in four huge volumes he has collected in one place the sapiential statements of the outstanding scholastic commentators on the *Sentences*.[11]

Denys's account of the order and course of wisdom, one should note, follows a temporal as well as a logical or natural order. This order of wisdom also suggests a hierarchy of authorities that Denys follows closely throughout his writings. Sacred Scripture is the highest authority, but because of its condescending obscurity it is the most difficult to penetrate and more often than not is the object of dispute. Scripture is a symbolic theology whose meaning becomes evident through intellectual and mystical probings. After Scripture the statements and lives of the saints are authoritative. Who these saints are is indicated by a list Denys writes in the *Protestatio ad superiorem suum* (*c.* 1440–41): Augustine, Ambrose, Gregory, Origen, Gregory Nazianzen, Cyril, Basil, Chrysostom, John Damascene, Boethius, Anselm, Bernard, Bede, Hugh of St. Victor, Jean Gerson, and William of Paris.[12] The greatest authority among the saints is Denys's "most-elect teacher," Dionysius the Areopagite, whose *Mystical Theology* defines and names the highest form of wisdom. For Denys, the teaching of the Areopagite provides a rule of thought analogous to Scripture's rule of faith. With Denys, it is seldom a matter of disputing the Areopagite, but simply of determining what he says.

After the authority of the fathers belongs the authority of scholastic doctors. Their authority is only as strong as their arguments, evaluated in the light of Scripture and mystical theology. Among scholastics, Thomas Aquinas has a certain preeminence, not because his arguments are always the best — sometimes he erred outstandingly — but because he was the only saint among them.[13] Finally, the authority of philosophers rotates from school to school, depending on how much on any given question they adumbrate the truths of Scripture and mystical theology. Proclus' uncanny resonance with Dionysius, for example, assures him Denys's high esteem.[14]

In a remarkably clear way, Denys's ordering of wisdom determined the chronological sequence and generic pattern of his philosophical and scholastic writings. His first mature effort of this kind was *De lumine christianae theoriae,* composed around 1451–1452.[15] Book 1 of this work treats natural, philosophic wisdom, Book 2 supernatural, theological wisdom. Whereas the arguments of the advocates for a Proclean order of Thomas's *Summa theologiae* seem forced,[16] such an order for Denys's *De lumine* is explicit. In the Prooemium, Denys explains that his two-part work is arranged according to the way things go out from the first cause and then return to it. He concludes the introduction with a theorem from Proclus: "Omne causatum et manet in sua causa, et procedit ab ipsa, et convertitur ad ipsam."[17] Book 1 assembles an impressive collection of texts from the philosophers; although these are drawn largely from primary sources, Denys is guided by the digests of Albert the Great, whom he calls the "most skilled" in the doctrines of the Peripatetics.[18] Book 2 on the other hand, draws almost exclusively from one source: for the most part it is a résumé of Thomas's *Summa contra gentiles.*[19] Closely related to *De lumine* Book 1 are two works composed in 1452 and 1455. *De natura aeterni et veri Dei* synthetizes the questions concerning God in *De lumine,* and *De puritate et felicitate animae* does the same for the questions concerning the soul.[20]

Two works bespeak Denys's early attachment to the teaching of Thomas. The *Dialogion de fide (c.* 1432), written in a simple dialogue form for novices, adheres closely to Thomas; the treatise *Creaturarum in ordine ad Deum consideratio theologica* abridges Thomas's commentary on the second Book of the *Sentences.*[21] More problematic is Denys's massive paraphrase of Thomas's *Summa theologiae,* composed at the end of his life in 1466, long after he had rejected key tenets of Thomas's thought.[22] Its title is: *Summa fidei orthodoxae, alias Enterione, id est Medulla operum sancti Thomae.* The Greek neologisms in this and Denys's first Thomistic work point to a certain *lumen orientale,* transmitted through Proclus and Dionysius, that suffuses his interpretation of

Thomas. The chronology of these works and their generic form, as well as Denys's accustomed disposition of Thomas's opinions in the *Sentences* commentary, suggest that he thought Thomas to be the best starting point for scholastic exercise and an apt teacher for beginners.

Denys's most ambitious scholastic work is the enormous commentary on the *Sentences* of Peter Lombard. Since he never entered the theology faculty, Denys's commentary is not a youthful, public, university exercise, but a private undertaking that he composed progressively over a lifetime in the solitude of the monastery. He finished around 1464. The accumulating materials extracted from commentary after commentary supplied Denys with a treasure-chest of texts which he thence redistributed appropriately throughout his other works. The private character of Denys's effort is indicated by the fact that, in eight years of searching his manuscripts, I have not found one medieval copy of even a part of the commentary, nor is the title registered in a single ancient library list of the many I have consulted. The autograph volumes, now lost, may be the only copy that ever existed. In the Prooemium to the work, however, Denys speaks about how difficult it was, and the great labor it took, to acquire the books of the many doctors he recites.[23] It seems likely, therefore, that before writing a final fair copy, he wrote down extracts in many other pages. Perhaps some of these will turn up as an anonymous abbreviation of one scholastic doctor or another.

In his *Sentences* commentary, Denys speaks *recitative* and *elective*. In two epitomes of the commentary, written in 1464–65, he speaks *assertive*.[24] In the *Elementatio philosophica* and *Elementatio theologica* he separates what he judges to be the distinctive philosophic and theological issues in the *Sentences*. As the titles of these works suggest, Denys imitates the form of Proclus' *Elements of Theology:* under declarative propositions, imitating Proclus' theorems, he organizes a concatenation of arguments. These works serve as an index to the *Sentences* commentary and are the most direct sources for Denys's independent judgments.

These syncopated works of philosophy and theology prepared Denys for his final, arduous acts of wisdom. Around 1465 he wrote a large commentary on *De consolatione philosophiae* of "noster fidelis Boetius."[25] Denys considers *De consolatione* to be a philosophic work in its literal sense. But Boethius is a Christian who tacitly holds the rule of faith in his mind. Denys unfolds the latent conformity of the work to the mysteries of redemption in "mystical" readings that he appends to his literal comments. Finally, in the years 1466–68, Denys produced his crowning achievement: commentaries on all the works of Dionysius the Areopagite.[26]

In the Prooemium to his commentary on the *Sentences,* Denys expands on the historical progress of wisdom. Although the wisdom accessible to the mind *in via* is meager in comparison to the light *in patria,* nevertheless over time it has become very great. Gregory says that as the progress of wisdom increased in the times before the Savior, so it has continued to increase in the times afterwards. Thus, the wisdom revealed in the time of evangelical law, first through Christ, then through the sending of the Holy Spirit and the Apostles and Evangelists, has steadily grown through the holy fathers and again through the Catholic teachers and scholastics. Especially during the time when Master Peter Lombard assembled his *Sentences* was there a great outpouring in the elucidation of wisdom. The Prophet Isaias foresaw this when he said: "the earth is filled with the knowledge of the Lord" (Is 11:9). What was concealed has been brought to light; the difficulties of Scripture have been untangled; objections to the Faith have been resolved. And indeed, not only the difficulties of Scripture but the obscurities in the writings of the holy fathers have been subtly discussed, magisterially declared, and led to their full Catholic meaning by the Master and those illustrious Catholic men who have written so gloriously over the *Sentences.*[27]

Such praise for an old textbook and its commentators, such confidence in the progress of wisdom, written by a former schoolboy among the Brethren of the Common Life who lived as a monk during the waning of the Middle Ages and the harvest of nominalist religiosity, disturbs somewhat our conventional and emergent historiographies. In balance, we shall see, Denys admits a recent diminution. Through his *Sentences* commentary, by returning to more authentic sources, he aspires to the regeneration of Christian wisdom in his time.

Denys's commentary comprises sizeable recitations and extracts of the arguments and determinations of an array of scholastic doctors. What Denys extracts — usually the conclusion or solution of the argument — he quotes nearly *verbatim* or paraphrases closely. His artful abridgments show a good understanding of his authors. In each recitation he searches the *motivae,* or guiding principles, of the resolution. He explains his procedure in the Prooemium. First he will present the responses of the more famous doctors, Thomas, Albert, Alexander of Hales, Bonaventure, and Henry of Ghent. Afterwards he will present the more outstanding followers, such as Peter of Taran-

taise or Richard of Middleton, who seem to follow Thomas but sometimes disagree with him. Finally, he will report the responses of the
greater doctors and their followers on the other side of the question.
Included here, almost invariably, is Duns Scotus. Denys does not limit
himself to writings on the *Sentences;* where apposite, he will extract from
Summae and other treatises. Accordingly, Denys always recites from
Thomas's *Summa theologiae* after he records the resolution in the *Scriptum;* sometimes he adds something from *Contra gentiles* or the disputed
questions. Likewise he regularly includes material from Henry of
Ghent's quodlibetal questions and Ulrich of Strassburg's *Summa de
bono.*[28]

The form of Denys's compilation does not hang loosely on the
order of questions in the *Sentences.* He calls his work a *collectaneum* or
collectio that gathers into one volume the writings of the scholastic commentators, just as the Lombard collected into one text the words and
teachings of the fathers. Thus, Denys says, his commentary is a "reduction of the scholastic doctors into one"; this rubric is nearly identical
to that of the *Monopanton,* composed for Nicholas of Cusa, which reduces
all of the verses of Paul's Epistles to one continuous text.[29] Denys's
commentary follows the model of the Lombard's book, since it is at
once large and compendious. It is large because it contains a great
quantity of material; it is compendious because of its form. "The *sententia,*" Avicenna declares, "is the most decisive and definite utterance."[30]

Denys's reduction to unity is more than literary. As it descends
from above, the simple, uncreated wisdom becomes more and more
diverse. Whereas the cognitive act of mystical theology is extraordi-
narily unified,[31] the lower degree of scholastic learning is necessarily
various. This variety, however, has its own becomingness:

> There are diverse and various opinions in scholastic materials,
> and it is delightful to know something about all of them. Fre-
> quently, indeed, in order to clarify the conscience, it is whole-
> some to know the teachings of diverse doctors. Nor should one
> cling pertinaciously or incautiously to the opinion of any one
> doctor, as those sometimes do who read only one doctor, or only
> a few of them. Moreover, many useful and beautiful things are
> found in the writings of one doctor that are not found in the
> writings of another.[32]

In light of the scattering of the divine wisdom, eclecticism is a sapiential method and prudential judgment founded on the nature and order
of human cognition.

Denys's irenic attitude does not embrace everyone. He remarks that countless books have been written on the *Sentences* and are still being written. Alas, too many books have been written; by the endless multiplication of their writings, certain recent, less eminent authors have caused the writings of ancient, superior authors to be read less.[33] The inflated currency of the fourteenth century, in other words, has driven out the good coin of the thirteenth-century ancients. Durandus of St. Pourçain is the only fourteenth-century writer whom Denys adduces regularly.

Doubtless, Denys's attitude was affected in general by his schooling at Cologne, but I think that it is possible to point to more specific sources. Recently, Zenon Kaluza has brilliantly documented the origins of the negative attitude towards fourteenth-century thinkers in the early fifteenth century, tracing it to the writings of Jean Gerson and the Parisian master in the arts faculty, Iohannes de Nova Domo (Jan van Nieuwenhuyze). For reasons of piety and a desire to cleanse from theology the terminology of artistic study, Gerson censured the theological endeavors of the *secta nominalium*. Gerson continually urged the theology faculty to return to the writings of earlier masters, specifically, the writings of Thomas, Albert, Bonaventure, Henry of Ghent, and Durandus of St. Pourçain. This is a short-list of Denys's scholastic authorities. Gerson reserved even more aversion for the advocates of the formal distinction, whom he called *formalizantes*. As Kaluza amply demonstrates, Gerson's aversion stems from his understanding of Dionysius the Areopagite's teaching in the *Mystical Theology*.[34] Denys was well acquainted with Gerson, whose works he classifies as written in the manner of the saints.[35] Denys disputes Gerson's affective, anti-intellectual interpretation of mystical theology and dismisses his clumsy reading of Jan van Ruusbroec, whom he considers "another Dionysius."[36] Nevertheless, he confers upon Gerson considerable authority in the lower registers of knowledge and, like him, attacks the formal distinction.

Closer yet to Denys's attitude are Iohannes de Nova Domo's strictures against the *nominales*. Iohannes's grammatical and logical writings, via Heimericus de Campo, migrated to Cologne just at the time Denys studied there (1422).[37] Later, albeit silently, Denys employs Iohannes's texts in his comments on the distinction between *esse* and *essentia*.[38] Iohannes's principle with respect to the *nominales* is simple and decisive: "contra negantes principia non est disputandum." In logic, the nominalists deny the reality of the universal outside the soul; but the universal "is the principle of art and science, indeed, the first, for-mal object of adequation that every science investigates, and when we do not look upon it, we cannot conceive or understand anything at all."[39] Likewise, in grammar the nominalists deny the *modos signifi-candi,* which are the first principles of correct speech.[40]

Denys does not expressly state Iohannes de Nova Domo's prin-ciple, but he certainly applies it. In his philosophic works, the nomi-nalists are mentioned a few times in connection with the doctrine of the immortality of the soul. For Denys, this doctrine is central in establishing the strict analogy between natural and supernatural wisdom.[41] Surveying the various arguments of the Peripatetics on the question, he analyzes the position of Alexander of Aphrodisias, Aver-roës and Abubather who, because they deny the personal immortality of the soul, place in this life whatever felicity is possible to human beings. At the end of his analysis Denys adds:

> There are certain philosophers of the present time, who are phi-losophers in name only, who think that Alexander philosophized best about the nature of the soul. Not unreasonably did Albert couple Alexander with those rude and unlearned (*rudibus et in-doctis*) philosophers because he alone among outstanding philoso-phers said that the intellectual power is destructible.[42]

Elsewhere Denys observes that certain *solemn* philosophers argue that Aristotle taught the soul to be inseparable from the body. There are other, not so solemn philosophers, Denys adds, called *nominales,* who agree with Alexander of Aphrodisias that neither Aristotle nor natural reason itself can demonstrate the immortality of the soul. No wonder they assert this, "because when they should look upon the na-tures and properties of things, they repeatedly turn to terms and so-phismata."[43] For this reason they are sometimes called *terminalistae.*[44]

The opinions of the nominalists, then, are unworthy of serious consideration because they never attain the level of philosophy. Denys thus distinguishes them from "solemn" philosophers who otherwise reach the conclusion that Aristotle did not demonstrate the immor-tality of the soul. Indeed, he eventually came to declare, as a proposi-tion in the *Elementatio philosophica,* that "it is truly difficult to express what Aristotle thought about the immortality of the soul." He draws his arguments in support of this proposition from the "solemn doctor" himself, Henry of Ghent, who had persuaded him of the fluctuations and ambiguities in Aristotle's words.[45]

As the subphilosophic nominalists fail in the first principles of logic, so they fail in the first principles of grammar. In his treatment of the *Sentences* question, "Whether whatever God knew once, he knows and will always know," Denys affirms the arguments of Bonaventure and Thomas. Both trace the arguments to grammatical principles. Those who maintain that God will always know as true what he once knew are called *nominales* because they suppose the unity of the name for the thing signified in such declensions as "albus, alba, album," and in such utterances as "Socrates runs," "Socrates ran." Rather, Bonaventure says, they should distinguish between speaking grammatically, as they do, and speaking logically, whereby different modes of signification designate corresponding differences in the manner of being. Similarly, Thomas distinguishes between speaking materially, with reference to the intentional object of reason, and speaking significantly, with reference to the being of a thing and its various conditions. In significant speech, changes in consignification point to changes in the condition of a thing's being. Thomas notes that the old position of the *nominales* has been rejected by most of the "moderns."[46]

Bonaventure's and Thomas's remarks lead Denys to make his contribution to the vexed taxonomy of the terms "ancient" and "modern." At the end of the question he exclaims how truly Aristotle said that the same opinions are repeated infinitely. Those who William of Auxerre, Bonaventure, and Thomas called *nominales* are now called *terministae,* because they speak only about terms and concepts instead of the natures of things. Whereas Thomas called the *nominales* "ancients," they are now called "moderns," because their teaching has reappeared in recent times. The "moderns" in William of Auxerre's day were called *reales,* and their followers today are called *realistae.* The realists are now called "ancients," because constant in the truth, they follow "the path of the ancient and true Peripatetics."[47]

Today we would more likely label Denys a "Platonist" than a "Peripatetic," but then he considered the author of *Liber de causis* and Avicenna authentic Peripatetics. (Denys doubts Thomas Aquinas's identification of Dionysius the Areopagite as a Peripatetic, however.)[48] Surely our terms "Platonist" and "Aristotelian" are as shifting as the medieval usage of the terms "ancients" and "moderns." In any event, Denys's allegiance to "the ancient and true Peripatetics" and their thirteenth-century followers raises further questions about his judgment of later developments in the theology faculty. In the *Elementatio philosophica,* he reports Henry of Ghent's statement that Aristotle stumbled on questions concerning the eternity of the world, divine providence, the unity of intellect in the human species, and the immortality of the soul.[49] Henry's remark points to the famous Parisian Condemnations of 1277. Before turning to Denys's encounter with these, I shall make some preliminary observations.

Because he lived and worked in the happy seclusion of the Charterhouse, in speculative matters Denys never needed to engage in *viva voce* dispute; nor, because he was not a licensed master of theology, did he need to work under the direct surveillance of ecclesiastical authority. Denys's scholasticism was a literary affair, rather like most of ours: he did his thinking in a network of old texts, which he analyzed privately, set in relation to one another in a personal disposition, and explained in writings that may or may not be read. His several personal confrontations with authorities took place within a monastic ambit, over issues of the religious life. But in speculative matters he was free. He rejected every simply positive notion of ecclesiastical authority. We do not believe the Scriptures because the Church tells us they are inspired by God. Rather, the Scriptures derive their authority "causaliter et exsistentialiter" directly from uncreated wisdom.[50] Thus, a reason of the Scriptures is always there to be discovered, difficult though it may be to discern. Ecclesiastical pronouncements, in turn, are the more binding the more they bear the marks of intrinsic authority, that is, the more evidently they relate to the analogies of faith and right thinking.

Denys confronts the Condemnations of 1277 in the writings of Richard of Middleton and Henry of Ghent, over a limited set of problems concerning angelic situation, locomotion, and individuation, the causality and nature of heavenly bodies, and the "double truth." When he first addresses the question of angelic situation in his *Sentences* commentary, Denys prefers Thomas's argument that, because of their purely spiritual composition, angels can be said to be in a place only by virtue of their action upon a body. Angels are limited by a determined range of power and influence, not by spatial dimensions. Only in passing, in his recitation of Richard of Middleton, does Denys mention that Thomas's position seems to agree with an article condemned at Paris.[51] In a later question, however, he recites the arguments of Henry of Ghent. Henry's first argument reaches the same conclusion as Thomas's, albeit in a typically more complicated way. Denys comments that Henry must add to his response because his first conclusion falls directly under an article condemned by Lord Stephen (Étienne Tempier) at Paris: "Substantiam intellectualem (videlicet angelum aut intelligentiam) non esse in loco nisi per suam operationem: error."[52] Henry's involved, subsequent arguments indirectly confirm the older conclusion that Denys prefers. Henry explores several arguments that would enable one to say that a spiritual substance is determined to a place in some other way than by its action upon a body. None of these arguments survives Henry's criticism of them, and in the end he is forced to confess simply that "unless one believes, he will not understand" (Is 7:9).[53] In response to Henry's statements, Denys notes that many who lived after Bishop Stephen simply acquiesced in the decision of Paris, conceding that an angel is somehow in a place by reason of its substance, even when it does not act upon a body. But Thomas, Albert, and most of the ancient Parisian doctors who preceded Stephen thought otherwise. Since Stephen's decision is difficult to comprehend, many who have come after him — especially those outside Paris — do not pay any attention to the excommunication. They say that a bishop's jurisdiction does not extend beyond his diocese.[54] In short, because it does not square with intrinsic criteria of thought (namely, what follows from the purely spiritual nature of angels), and because it collides with more ancient authorities, this particular article of condemnation looks like modern nonsense.

On the other hand, Denys firmly maintains that angels move, and move through a medium. Against opponents who argue the contrary, such as Durandus of St. Pourçain, he multiplies scriptural and patristic authorities.[55] Thus he upholds Lord Stephen's article: "Quod substantiae separatae non possunt moveri ab extremo in extremum nec per medium seu in medium, nisi quia possunt velle operari in eis: error."[56] Those who argue that angels do not actually move often sound dangerously like the ancient Peripatetics, Denys says, who taught that Intelligences are immobile in their place and operation.[57]

Denys encounters this opinion in the writings of Albert the Great, in a way that involves a far more serious error. From Albert's *Sentences* commentary and *De quatuor coaequaevis* he extracts arguments affirming that angels move from place to place through a medium, and when they are in one place they are not in another. Albert catalogues four errors on this question, including the opinion of Averroës and Maimonides that angels never move because they are unmoving movers of the spheres, through which they influence human hearts and senses.[58] Denys remarks that Albert's words here sound more Catholic than what he says in his commentary on the *Liber de causis*.

There Albert proves by manifold arguments exactly what he otherwise condemns: the Intelligences do not move; each is the first mover
in its own order, and remaining immobile, moves the orb or its con-
joined soul as the desired moves the desiring. Some may claim, Denys
continues, that in the commentary on the *Sentences* Albert speaks as
a theologian, but that in his commentary on the *Liber de causis* he
speaks as an expositor, defender, and imitator of the Peripatetics and
as a natural philosopher. Indeed, Albert himself says in the latter
work that he defends the opinion of the Peripatetics denying that an
Intelligence is limited to any place and affirming that each Intelligence is always everywhere. Albert speaks often in this way, as does
his student Ulrich of Strassburg. To say that "this is true according
to natural reason or the teaching of the philosophers or the tradition
of the Peripatetics, but not according to Scripture or the documents
of faith, as if there could be two truths contrary to one another" is
exactly the manner of speaking condemned by Lord Stephen at Paris.
Whatever is contrary to Christian faith must simply and absolutely
be denied as false, Denys concludes.[59] On this crucial issue, then, he
is willing enough to evoke the Condemnations; but one should also
note that the "double truth" strikes near the heart of Denys's vision
of wisdom, wherein the philosophic truths of the natural order yield
a perfectly isomorphic analogy to the theological truths of the supernatural order.[60] Denys's eclectic attitude enabled him always to find
some proportionate teaching among the philosophers, and thus preserve the analogy.

Concerning angelic individuation, right reason and ecclesiastical authority are in perfect accord. Denys considers this problem in
two questions of his *Sentences* commentary. In the first, he addresses
the underlying philosophical issues. Thomas's teaching, in *De esse et
essentia* and elsewhere, moves the question. The cause of individuation in any species is the specified or designated matter (*materia sig-
nata*), determined in quantitative dimensions, that enters into composition with form to make the essence of a thing.[61] Denys responds
with a chain of arguments that are recapitulated in the *Elementatio
philosophica*. In general, his determination is governed by the hierarchical principle that the higher reality effects more than the lower one.
More specifically, his argument follows Henry of Ghent. He relies upon
Henry's distinction between the *esse essentiae* of a being, defined by its
relation to the exemplar cause, and its *esse actualis exsistentiae*, produced
by the efficient cause. These are intentionally distinct in the mind of

340

God, understood as distinct by human reason, but really the same in the existing creature.[62]

The reason for the individuation of a thing, Denys says, is its *esse hoc aliquid*. Because each thing has only one specific and substantial being, it follows that its *esse* and *hoc esse* are really identical, distinguishable only by reason. The extrinsic, effective principle of any individual reality is the cause that produces or creates it. The individual is the end reality of the creative act, for to suffer, to act, and to become pertain only to supposites or singular things. It is the intellect that confers universality upon beings. Nothing abstracted by the intellect — neither form nor matter — can be the cause of actual, existential, real being (*esse actuale, exsistentiale, reale*). Hence, a reality is determined or singularized by reason of its very existential being, for being belongs first to supposites. Thus, no logical principle abstracted from actual being, neither matter, nor this matter, nor quantity, can be the cause of the individuation of a form.[63]

To assert that matter or specified matter (*materia designata*) is the principle of individuation, Denys continues, seems to be an uncultivated way of speaking. The specified matter is what is individuated, not the principle of individuation. In itself, matter is the least determined, the most potential and confused; how then can it be the cause of determination and individuation? Form is what is said to distinguish, determine, and beautify the confusion of matter. Moreover, first composition precedes second composition, that is, the composition of substantial form with its matter precedes the composition of the matter with its accidents. Hence, matter is specified by its composition with substantial form before it is determined further by accidents of quantity and quality. Moreover, since form may be understood as *esse* no less communicable to many than matter, there is no greater reason for considering matter to be the principle of individuation than form. Finally, as in abstraction form is considered to confer *esse* on matter, so in reality it must be *this form* that confers *esse* on *this matter*. In any real being, form individuates and determines far more than matter.[64]

Having established the general, philosophical principles, Denys turns to the theological problem of angelic individuation in the next question of the *Sentences*.[65] Here he disputes two opinions. The first, represented by Thomas, argues that because only matter can individuate a species, and because matter does not enter the composition of angelic natures, there are as many angelic species as there are individuals. Elsewhere Denys remarks that those who hold this opinion follow the words of Aristotle "too immoderately."[66] A second opinion, represented by Albert the Great, argues that all angels are of the same species.[67] Against these opinions Denys sets the arguments of Henry of Ghent. Since a creature is individuated by its *esse actualis exsistentiae,* even though lacking composition with matter an angelic species can yet be individuated by means of a purely spiritual composition. Every created essence participates *esse,* and the essence of an angel or Intelligence becomes a person or supposite by no other reason than by the fact that it has spiritual *esse* as an actually subsisting effect of God's creative act. *Esse* adds nothing to essence save a relation to the efficient cause.[68]

Henry confirms his argument by reference to three articles condemned at Paris; Denys makes these his own in the *Elementatio theologica:* (1)"God cannot multiply individuals in a species without matter: error"; (2)"Forms do not undergo division except by matter, error, unless this be understood of forms educed from the potentiality of matter"; (3)"Because Intelligences do not possess matter, God cannot make many of them in the same species: error."[69] Somewhat disingenuously, in light of his previous restrictions, Denys reinforces and extends the authority of these condemnations, pronounced by "Lord Stephen, Bishop of Paris and outstanding doctor in theology, with the approval of all of the doctors of the theology faculty."[70] Denys saves Thomas from the condemnation in the only way he can: chronologically. If Thomas had lived at the time these articles were condemned, or afterwards, he would not knowingly have defended anything contrary to them. How unbecoming it is, then, for any Thomist (*Thomistam*) now to defend a position that so many solemn doctors contradict with good reasons.[71]

In his own response, Denys enacts Henry of Ghent's principle within the hierarchical order of spiritual realities. Although angels are simple forms subsisting as supposites, no one thinks that they are pure acts of being. Rather, they are more or less mixed with some potency as they are more or less distant from the pure act. "Divine Dionysius" affirms that *esse, posse,* and *agere* are diverse in angelic natures, and Boethius says that *quo est* and *quod est* differ in them. These need not be really distinct in the angelic nature, however. One and the same essence is called *quo est, esse,* or "act" insofar as it participates the first pure act; it is called *quod est* or "potency" insofar as it falls away from the purity of the first act. Hence, one may easily understand how angels receive genus and specific difference. Angels are not equal in act or formality; each degree of essential perfection, measured by nearness to the pure act, constitutes a special species, and likewise each degree of essential perfection constitutes a specific difference.[72]

Henry's and Denys's arguments establish the possibility of individuation within an angelic species; they do not establish the fact. Denys is sensitive to the arguments of Ulrich of Strassburg, who otherwise reaches the same conclusion as Thomas, because they rely on the authority of Dionysius the Areopagite.[73] Dionysius says in the *Celestial Hierarchy* that illuminations descend from superior to inferior angels, not only from hierarchy to hierarchy, but from the highest to the mean to the lowest angel in the same order.[74] Does this mean, Denys asks, that each angel is distinct in essential perfection, or only in accidental perfection? He allows that he does not fully understand what "the leader among theologians" (*princeps ille theologorum*), "the most sacred Dionysius," intends in the text. Thus, he will not dare assert that all angels must convene in the same *species specialissima*.[75] Finally, he judges it more probable that angels in the same choir or order share the same species. He adds, however, that in questions about the holy angels, those most "worthy substances, our lords, rulers, helpers, protectors and guardians," one must be careful lest he offend, by incautious assertion and contentious disputation, before their benign and beautiful faces.[76] Only dimly can one discern those beings higher in the order of Intelligences.

Denys's final remark on angelic individuation, in the *Elementatio theologica,* looks to the lowest being in the order of Intelligences. Because the human soul is an individual form that is the term of God's real, creative act, "the opinion affirming that rational souls are individuated by their bodies is nothing."[77]

Questions concerning individuation touch directly the spiritual realities of angelic beings and the human soul; the formal distinction among the divine attributes, proposed by Duns Scotus, touches directly the spiritual reality of God. No less strenuously than Gerson, Denys rejects the formal distinction. He engages the distinction already in his earlier philosophic works. In *De lumine christianae theoriae* he identifies the distinction as arising among doctors of the Franciscan order, now called *formalistae.* Without naming the author, he presents an abbreviated argument for the distinction from Francis of Meyronnes.[78] In this work, Denys appears to follow the opinion of Alexander of Hales that no distinction among divine attributes can be understood except in terms of God's relations to creatures.[79] Denys takes up the question again in *De natura aeterni et veri Dei,* written for a beloved Carthusian confrère. Here, appropriately, after adducing a few arguments from Aristotle and Proclus, he multiplies authorities of the saints against the distinction.[80]

In these works, Denys bases his arguments upon the absolute simplicity of divine *esse,* and the simplicity of the divine act of knowing; he founds the perceived diversity among attributes in the diverse manner of the human knower: "cognitio enim fit secundum naturam cognoscentis." Denys's arguments are only indicative; evidently he was making more extensive preparation to treat the question. The results of his preparation are manifest in the *Sentences* question: "Whether the distinction among divine attributes is real, or formal, or only by reason." This question is the longest in his entire commentary; in it, he displays even more than his usual erudition.[81]

To expound the massive argumentation of this question would require a monograph. But in any case, it is Denys's disposition of recited authorities — in other words, his doxography — that most fully reveals his thought. At the beginning of the question, he announces the intensification of his usual procedure. This question, he says, is one of the outstanding difficulties of the theology faculty, provoking dissension, minute inquiry, and out-and-out combat. For this reason he must linger over the material, and with extreme care adduce the words of the doctors.[82]

Denys first presents the writings of Thomas Aquinas, whose position remains largely his own: distinctions among the divine attributes are perceived by reason alone, although they have a real foundation in the plenitude of perfection in the simple divine *esse.*[83] Denys, however, here omits a statement by Thomas in a later article that will play an important role in the further unfolding of the question. The distinction among divine attributes derives from reason and intellect, Thomas states, but not in the reason of the human intellect alone, but also in the reason of the angelic and divine intellects.[84]

Denys follows Thomas with the arguments of doctors whose conclusion is essentially the same, Peter of Tarantaise and Richard of Middleton.[85] He further reports certain objections of Giles of Rome against Thomas's expression, answering each of them and striving to show that Giles has misread what Thomas says. Giles anyway reaches the same conclusion as Thomas.[86] Denys next recites the similar opinions of Alexander of Hales, Bonaventure, and William of Auxerre.

These hold that the plurality of divine attributes is only a distinction of reason, understood in terms of God's many relations to created perfections. If, unlike Thomas, these doctors do not speak of the foundation of attributes in the divine perfection, they perhaps even more affirm the divine simplicity.[87]

Denys concludes the first movement of his question with the teaching of Albert the Great. He has postponed Albert because a slight variance from Thomas's position seems to echo Alexander of Hales's understanding. The difference between Thomas and Albert, Denys notes, has been magnified by Albert's contemporary followers. They say that Thomas posits a *distinctio rationis rationabilis* among the divine attributes, whereas Albert posits only a *distinctio rationis ratiocinantis.* Denys tests this against Albert's texts, does not find the difference, and reconciles the teaching of the two doctors.[88] Throughout his recitation of the ancient doctors, Denys makes every effort to find the underlying unity of their teaching in order to set them in a common front against Duns Scotus. Before turning to Scotus, however, Denys will put forward the arguments of one who seems to occupy a middle ground, and who introduces the decisive new element in the discussion: Henry of Ghent.[89]

With utmost care, Denys rehearses Henry's version of the tradtional argument. Considered in terms of God's relations *ad extra* to creatures, the plurality of ideas correspond to *imitabilitates* of the divine nature. These exist indistinct in act in God, and are known by him in all of their diversity in a single act of comprehension corresponding at once to the simplicity of his nature and the multiplicity of his relations to creatures. God knows this multiplicity *a priori,* according to the plenitude of his divine perfection; the created intellect, by a natural light, knows this multiplicity of conceptions *a posteriori,* according to the multitude of created perfections.[90]

At this point, Henry enlarges his argument by a distinction among corresponding terms. Until now, he has spoken of a plurality of "ideas" corresponding to perfections participated by creatures; now he will speak of "attributes" corresponding to perfections considered absolutely, that is, perfections considered abstractly as what it is better to have than not to have. These may be said to exist independently in God, without reference to creatures. Among them there is a certain plurality, known to the divine intellect *ad intra.* This plurality derives from the plurality of personal, trinitarian emanations, for all the divine attributes may be reduced to intellect and its operations (e.g., wisdom) or will and its operations (e.g., goodness). Now, from eternity God knows himself as true and thereby generates the Word, and loves himself as good, and thereby breathes forth the Spirit. Hence from eternity the divine reason knows a distinction of absolute perfections; through the divine light, the minds of the Blessed also perceive this distinction. This distinction, however, is no more real than the personal distinction to which it relates. One may now fill in the corresponding sets of terms. As by a natural, philosophic light the created intellect may discern a plurality of ideas corresponding to the many ways creatures partake the simple *esse* of God *ad extra* by virtue of being created, so by a supernatural, theological light the created intellect may discern a plurality of attributes corresponding to perfections, reducible to the divine persons, existing absolutely in God *ad intra* and bestowed upon creatures in gracious *bene esse*.[91]

Denys makes no immediate response to Henry's resolution, which, it seems to me, owes its structure to the movement from Book 5 to Book 6 in Bonaventure's *Itinerarium*.[92] Later in the question Denys aligns Henry with the ancient doctors, remarking that Henry goes beyond them all, showing how there is a distinction of reason among the divine attributes not only in the human mind, but in the uncreated intellect and the conceptions of the Blessed as well. Denys adds that Henry's position seems more reasonable than Alexander's, which posits a distinction only in relation to creatures.[93] Later in his *Sentences* commentary Denys adopts Henry's doctrine of a special, supernatural illumination of theological verities.[94] After reading Henry, he no longer treats this question concerning the divine attributes as a philosophical one; after the *Sentences* commentary, he assigns it to the *Elementatio theologica*.[95]

According to Denys's disposition of the question, Henry's determination gives rise to the formal distinction in Duns Scotus. Denys affords Scotus ample space to speak his case, although not so much as Henry of Ghent.[96] For Scotus, the crux of the question is this: Henry argues that there is a distinction *ad intra* of divine attributes related to the distinction of personal emanations, saying that this is a distinction understood by the divine reason. But the distinction among personal emanations is real. No real distinction presupposes a merely rational one, as no real being presupposes a mere *ens rationis*. A real being is distinguished from an *ens rationis* precisely because it exists independently of any action of intellect upon it. An *ens rationis*, then, is posterior to real being; thus, the distinction of divine attributes that derives from really distinct personal emanations must in some way be *ex natura rei*.[97] Elsewhere, Denys rejects Scotus's notion of a real, absolute distinction among the properties of the divine persons upon which Scotus founds his objection to Henry.[98] For now, he follows Scotus's explorations, which lead Scotus to conclude that although the divine attributes are not really distinct, there is a certain non-identity and formal difference among them *ex natura rei* before any consideration of the intellect, divine or human. This distinction is signified by a formal distinction, which lies between real and rational distinctions.[99]

Here Denys takes an unexpected turn, leading the reader into an obscure, textual forest. To clarify the many difficulties of Scotus's teaching, he resorts to a compiler no less able than himself: Peter of Candia. Here, finally, in the heat of battle, Denys enlists troops from the fourteenth century. From Peter of Candia's encyclopedia of opinions, he seizes now welcome arguments of William of Ockham and Gregory of Rimini against the formal distinction among divine attributes. He selects only those arguments, of course, that deny the formal distinction and affirm the divine simplicity. He could not accept, for example, William of Ockham's conclusion that the divine attributes are only mental signs or concepts and have no real foundation in the divine essence.[100] After all has been said, Denys — like the ancients before him and many after — cannot find a formal distinction between a real or a rational distinction.[101]

Reciting Francis of Meyronnes's ("the leader of the Scotists") manifold distinctions about the distinction, Denys gives the *formalistae* one more chance.[102] He counters Francis, finally, with Durandus of St. Pourçain. Durandus brings the question back down the ladder it has climbed. First he denies the formal distinction; then Henry of Ghent's distinction in the divine mind; then Thomas's foundation for the plurality of attributes in the plenitude of divine perfection. With Alexander, Durandus concludes that there is only a distinction of reason among the attributes corresponding to God's relations with things really distinct in creatures.[103]

Denys has allowed the ancient scholastics to show the truth, the moderns to expose falsehood. Scotus is the inventor of a novelty never thought of by "the holy doctors and most-excellent masters of theology who went before him."[104] The authorities Scotus invokes in fact all militate against him. To prove this, and to affirm the absolute divine simplicity and identity of attributes in the divine *esse,* Denys calls forth his own authorities, among the philosophers, Aristotle, Proclus, the *Liber de causis,* and among the saints, Augustine, Bernard, Anselm, and most of all, "divinissimus, sacratissimus et theologicissimus Dionysius."[105]

Three concluding remarks point to the deep reasons for Denys's hostility to the formal distinction. In his commentary on the *Sentences,* Denys says that those who put forward a formal distinction in God have not "subtly enough contemplated the divine simplicity, in which undoubtedly every perfection is contained, not formally as they imagine to themselves, but supereminently as divine Dionysius teaches."[106] Similarly, he judges in the *Elementatio theologica* that the formalists have not attained to "sincere contemplation."[107] In *De natura aeterni et veri Dei,* after citing his reasons and authorities against a formal distinction among attributes in God, he counsels his beloved confrère. The divine simplicity is something that can be talked about and believed, but can be seen only by the pure in heart. Let us therefore not be empty assertors about it, as many are, but rather sincere contemplators of it, as — alas — too few are. Let us then simplify our hearts, and fasten them on the unchanging good, for all perfection consists in a deiform simplification and loving conversion to the simplicity of the divine mind.[108] This text draws a full circle from Denys's first monastic work, which treats purity of heart,[109] to the great Dionysian commentaries.

The *nominales* never pass beyond the concepts that their terms signify; nor, in fact, do the *formalistae,* who, worse, reify their concepts and project them into the divine mind. At the root of their errors is their mistaken notion of the univocity of the concept of being.[110] Only an analogical understanding of being at once preserves the transcendence of divine *esse* and shows the human soul a way to ascend towards God. It also establishes what Denys calls "the beautiful rule" of knowing: "modus agendi sequitur modum essendi, et proprietas actionis, naturam agentis."[111] According to this principle, the human soul's spiritual individuation, assuring its separate substantiality, allows for the spiritual cognitions of mystical theology testified to by the saints and verified in Denys's own experience. In his commentary on the Areopagite's *Mystical Theology,* Denys teaches that in the highest form of union possible in this life, the soul, although not attaining a vision of God *quid est* through an uncreated species, may yet attain an intuition of God *quia est* above every created species.[112]

In this context Denys reproves Thomas's oft-repeated statement that the soul must return to a phantasm in every act of cognition. Even more than a disagreement over speculative principles, Denys's difference with Thomas is a matter of interpretation: interpretation of the words of "the most blessed Dionysius." To support his position, Thomas frequently alleges a text from the *Celestial Hierarchy:* "the divine ray cannot enlighten us unless it is wrapped up in the various veils of sensible forms."[113] This text refers only to the first information of the soul, Denys says.[114] Among other reasons, this is why Thomas is suited for beginners. What does Thomas think the saint means at the beginning of the *Mystical Theology* when he says: "In mystical visions, rise up in an absolute ascent beyond all things, detached from them all, to the ray of the supersubstantial obscurity, withdrawing absolutely from all things by means of a forceful beating down and abandoning of the senses and intellectual acts, all sensible and intelligible realities, and all existing things, even yourself." Certainly one cannot rise above intelligible realities if he cannot rise above sensible ones.[115] In the same chapter Dionysius says: "the sole cause of all things truly appears without veils to those who transcend all unclean and material realities, and all of the supercelestial souls." Do you hear what he says, Denys asks, he says *incircumvelate.* And if in this intuition one must rise above even the most-pure angelic minds, how much more must he rise above the lowly material phantasm? If what Thomas says is true, then what David (Ps 1:8, 2 Kings 23:2–4) and the saints have said about anagogic, purely mental contemplation and the illustrations of the Holy Spirit cannot be true.[116]

Perhaps ironically, Denys of Ryckel, who so loved the ancients, anticipated in one sense the most modern: for the human mind, save mystical vision, truth is foremost a matter of interpretation. Of course, Denys thought himself to be measured by authoritative texts, rather than to measure them according to slight disclosures of mundane experience. Even so, he apparently has had his modern readers. Several features of his scholastic doxography may have a familiar ring. Students at Toronto were sometimes told how a line of French scholars, from Victor Cousin to Étienne Gilson, as a first step of inquiry surveyed the topography of a question in Denys's commentary on the *Sentences.* They dipped less often, it would seem, into the pages of mystical theology. Remotely and unknowingly, in any event, we may all have partaken Denys the Carthusian's textuality and his disposition of medieval scholastic discourse.

NOTES

1. Denys's first monastic writing (before 1430) is *Contra detestabilem cordis inordinationem in Dei laudibus horisque canonicis vel Laus Cartusiana* (*Opera omnia* 40:191–259). See Kent Emery, Jr., "Denys of Ryckel and Traditions of Meditation: Contra detestabilem cordis inordinationem" in *Spiritualität Heute und Gestern,* Analecta Cartusiana 35/3 (Salzburg, 1983), 69–89.

2. *De donis Spiritus Sancti* (*Opera omnia* 35:155–262). The first three tracts were written around 1430; the fourth tract was compiled about 1446.

3. The scriptural commentaries are published in *Opera omnia* 1–14. For their chronology, see A. Stoelen, "De Chronologie van de Werken van Dionysius de Karthuizer: De eerste Werken en de Schriftuurkommentaren," *Sacris erudiri* 5 (1953): 361–401.

4. P. Teeuwen, *Dionysius de Karthuizer en de philosophisch-theologische stroomingen aan de Keulsche Universiteit* (Brussels and Nijmegen, 1938), 15–18. A more detailed account of Denys's career at Cologne is given in my *Dionysii Cartusiensis Opera selecta 1* (*Prolegomena*). *Bibliotheca manuscripta 1A: Studia bibliographica* (CCCM 121 [1991]: 15–18).

5. See Emery, *Dionysii Cartusiensis . . . Bibliotheca manuscripta 1A* (CCCM 121:122–128).

6. *Sent.* 1.8.7 (*Opera omnia* 19:408D): "Postremo, quamvis in adolescentia dum eram in studio, et in via Thomae instruerer, potius sensi quod esse et essentia distinguerentur realiter (unde et tunc de illa materia quemdam tractatulum compilavi: quem utinam nunc haberem, quia corrigerem); interim tamen diligentius considerando, non solum hac vice, sed et ante frequenter, verius ac probabilius ratus sum quod non realiter ab invicem differant."

7. The three manuscripts are now in Prague. The manuscripts, and   *
the evidence for and against Denys's authorship, are discussed in Emery, *Dionysii Cartusiensis . . . Bibliotheca manuscripta 1A* (CCCM 121:122–126).

8. See Kent Emery, Jr., "Twofold Wisdom and Contemplation in Denys of Ryckel (Dionysius Cartusiensis, 1402–1471)," *Journal of Medieval and Renaissance Studies* 18 (1988): 99–134.

9. *Opera omnia* 33:105–231. For the date, see A. Stoelen, "Denys le Chartreux," *Dictionnaire de spiritualité* 3 (Paris, 1957), 433.

10. *Elem. theol.* prooemium (*Opera omnia* 33:111–112).

11. Ibid. (112).

12. *Protestatio ad superiorem suum* (*Opera omnia* 1:LXXI).

13. In *De sacramento altaris* 28 (*Opera omnia* 35:425A'), Denys says that Thomas is "Doctor ille inter doctores scholasticos praecipue sanctitatis, illuminationis et auctoritatis." In his early *Contra detestabilem* 8 (*Opera omnia* 40:202D'), he calls Thomas "meum patronem." In *De donis* 1.8 (*Opera omnia*

350

35:165C), he calls Thomas "doctor inter modernos eximius," and in *De contemplatione* 2.7 (*Opera omnia* 41:244B') he calls him "insignem philosophum atque profundum egregiumque theologum."

14. See Emery, "Twofold Wisdom," 105, 111-117; Werner Beierwaltes, "Philosophische Marginalien zu Proklos-Texten," *Philosophische Rundschau* 10 (1962): 60-64.

15. *Opera omnia* 33:233-513. For the date, see Stoelen, "De Chronologie," 371.

16. I refer to the argument for the neo-Platonic, *exitus-reditus* structure of the *Summa* in M.-D. Chenu, O. P., "Le plan de la Somme théologique de S. Thomas," *Revue Thomiste* 45 (1939): 93-107, and in *Introduction a l'étude de Saint Thomas d'Aquin* (Montreal and Paris, 1954), 255-276. For a review of subsequent arguments and criticisms, see Otto Hermann Pesch, "Um den Plan der Summa theologiae des hl. Thomas von Aquin," in *Thomas von Aquin,* ed. Klaus Bernath (Darmstadt, 1978), 1:411-37. The pattern fits Denys's two-book *De lumine* easily.

17. *De lumine* 1 prooemium (*Opera omnia* 33:235). I cite the edition in C. Vansteenkiste, "Procli Elementatio theologica translata a Guilelmo de Moerbeke (Textus Ineditus)," *Tijdschrift voor Philosophie* 13 (1951): 263-302, 491-531 and 14 (1952): 503-546. The edition of Moerbeke's translation by H. Boese (Leuven, 1987), was unavailable to me at the time of writing. Denys here combines *Elementatio* theoremata 30-31: "Omne quod ab aliquo producitur immediate, manet in producente et procedit ab ipso; Omne procedens ab aliquo secundum essentiam convertitur ad illud a quo procedit" (Vansteenkiste 13:278).

18. *Sent.* 2.3.3 (*Opera omnia* 21:221C-D). It is a common formula of fifteenth-century Albertists that Albert "longius et profundius laboravit" than others in the doctrine of the Peripatetics; see Zenon Kaluza, *Les querelles doctrinales à Paris: Nominalistes et réalistes aux confins du XIVe et du XVe siècles* (Bergamo, 1988), 122.

19. See Teeuwen, *Dionysius de Karthuizer,* 131-135.

20. *De natura aeterni et veri Dei* (hereafter *De nat.*) is printed in *Opera omnia* 34:7-97; *De puritate et felicitate animae* (hereafter *De pur.*) is printed in *Opera omnia* 40:393-443. For the dates, see Stoelen, "Denys le Chartreux," 433-434.

21. The *Dialogion de fide catholica contra gentiles* is printed in *Opera omnia* 18:269-530; *Creaturarum in ordine ad Deum consideratio theologica* is printed in *Opera omnia* 34:99-221. See Teeuwen, *Dionysius de Karthuizer,* 110-124.

22. Stoelen, "De Chronologie," 372.

23. *Sent.* 1 prooemium (*Opera omnia* 19:37).

24. Denys applies this terminology to Peter of Candia in *Sent.* 1.2.2 (*Opera omnia* 19:167C').

25. Denys's commentary on *De consolatione* is printed in *Opera omnia*

26. For the epithet, see *Elementatio philosophica* 81 and *De lumine* 2.52 (*Opera*

omnia 33:89C, 439C). In *De lumine* 1.68 (*Opera omnia* 33:314C) Denys says of Boethius: "Noster autem Boetius . . . subtilissimam atque veracem induxit de rerum regimine philosophiam." For Denys, Boethius is the model for the Christian philosopher, strictly speaking, as distinct from the theologian. For Denys's rather modern conception of Christian philosophy, evident in this typology of Boethius, see Emery, "Twofold Wisdom."

26. Denys's commentaries on the works of pseudo-Dionysius are printed in *Opera omnia* 15–16. These include the various Latin translations of ps-Dionysius's writings, and I shall cite from them.

27. *Sent.* 1 prooemium (*Opera omnia* 19:36).

28. Ibid. (37).

29. *Sent.* 1 prooemium (*Opera omnia* 19:36). In the list of his works contained in Trier, Stadtbibliothek Hs. 631/1562 4°, the title for the work is "Super quatuor libros sentenciarum scripta doctorum scholasticorum reducendo in unum" (f. 227r). Denys's *Monopanton* (*Opera omnia* 14:465–537) is a work "Epistolas beatissimi Pauli quasi in unam redigendo epistolam" (467).

30. *Sent.* 1 prooemium and expositio prologi (*Opera omnia* 19:36, 57A′–B′).

31. See Emery, "Twofold Wisdom."

32. *Sent.* 1 prooemium (*Opera omnia* 19:37): "scholasticorum materiarum in quibus sunt opiniones variae ac diversae; estque delectabile de omnibus aliquid scire. Imo frequenter pro serenatione conscientiae, est salubre diversorum doctorum doctrinas agnoscere, nec opinioni unius incaute aut pertinaciter inhaerere, sicut interdum his accidit qui pauca aut unum dumtaxat doctorem legerunt. Multa quoque pulchra atque utilia inveniuntur in uno doctore, quae in scriptis non habentur alterius."

33. *Sent.* 1 prooemium (*Opera omnia* 19:36).

34. I refer to Kaluza's *Les querelles doctrinales*. Kaluza delineates Gerson's attitudes on 13–86, and gathers in Appendix 1, 127–144, texts of Gerson's remarks on the Scotists.

35. *Protestatio ad superiorem suum* (*Opera omnia* 1:LXXI), where Denys lists Gerson among the "saints" and not the doctors. The classification is formal.

36. See Emery, "Twofold Wisdom," 130–133 and notes.

37. The original study of Iohannes de Nova Domo, Heimericus de Campo, and the Cologne Albertists is: G. Meersseman, *Geschichte des Albertismus, 1: Die Pariser Anfänge des Kölner Albertismus* (Paris, 1933), and *2: Die ersten Kölner Kontroversen* (Rome, 1935). My "Twofold Wisdom," 111–112, n. 48, gives subsequent bibliography. See also Kaluza's notes, 107–120.

38. Teeuwen, *Dionysius de Karthuizer,* 70–72, 75, 92, 98.

39. Kaluza, *Les querelles doctrinales,* 94–95. The text comes from the preface of Iohannes's *De universali reali,* which may have been added by a la-

ter writer. It conforms, however, to statements throughout Iohannes's works.

40. Kaluza, *Les querelles doctrinales,* 92–94. The fifteenth-century revival of the *modi significandi* by Gerson, Iohannes de Nova Domo, Heimericus de Campo, Denys, and others merits further study.

41. Emery, "Twofold Wisdom," 110–111, 118–120, 123–124, and throughout. For a fuller study of Denys's concern for the philosophic demonstrability of the immortality of the soul, see Emery *"Sapientissimus Aristoteles* and *Theologicissimus Dionysius:* The Reading of Aristotle and the Understanding of Nature in Denys the Carthusian," in *Mensch und Natur im Mittelalter,* ed. A. Zimmermann and A. Speer, Miscellanea Mediaevalia 21/2 (Berlin, and New York, 1922), 572–606.

42. *De lumine* 1.50 (*Opera omnia* 33:292C'): "Sunt autem et praesentis temporis quidam, vel re vel potius nomine tantum philosophi, qui Alexandrum de natura animae optime philosophatum reputant: quem tamen Albertus rudibus et indoctis philosophis non irrationabiliter comparavit, eo quod solus inter omnes egregios philosophos, intellectualem virtutem destructibilem dixit." Gerson likewise adopted Albert's doxography linking the ancient Epicureans and modern *nominales,* projected it to the terminists, and termed them "rudes" (Kaluza, *Les querelles doctrinales,* 14–15, 39–40, and throughout). In *Dialogus disputationis Christianum et Sarracenum* 10 (*Opera omnia* 36:468C'), Denys joins the terms invidiously: "Mahon autem secutus est quosdam Epicureos rudissimosque philosophos, qui felicitatem hominis in delectationibus sensualibus gustus et tactus constituerunt."

43. *De lumine* 1.101 (*Opera omnia* 33:363C'–D').

44. *De pur.* 64 (*Opera omnia* 34:436D).

45. *Elem. phil.* 98 (*Opera omnia* 33:61A–62A). Denys quotes Henry of Ghent, *Quodl. 9* q. 14 (Macken, 247–248). For Henry's influence upon Denys in this matter, see Emery, *"Sapientissimus Aristoteles."*

46. *Sent.* 1.41.4 (*Opera omnia* 20:551B–555A'). Denys recites Bonaventure, *Sent.* 1.41.2.2 (*Opera omnia* 1:739–41); Thomas Aquinas, *Sent.* 1.41.5 (Mandonnet and Moos 1:375–76) and *Summa theologiae* 1.14. ad 3. Iohannes de Nova Domo traced most of the terminists' errors to their expansion of material supposition to the exclusion of "simple" supposition; see Kaluza, *Les querelles doctrinales,* 103–105.

47. *Sent.* 1.41.4 (*Opera omnia* 20:554D'–555A'). William of Auxerre's classification is reported by Denys in *Sent.* 1.39.1 (*Opera omnia* 20:469B–D); see William of Auxerre, *Summa* 1.9.2 (Ribaillier, 1:180–81).

48. Denys says that of all the Peripatetics, Aristotle and his followers, Avicenna spoke most profoundly about human felicity; see *De lumine* 1.48 (*Opera omnia* 33:290B'–291C'). In *Sent.* 1.8.6 (*Opera omnia* 19:390A), Denys states: "quamvis liber de Causis ex libro Procli sit sumptus, tamen ut ait Thomas in suo commento super librum de Causis, auctor libri de Causis Peripateticus fuit, non Platonicus." Following Thomas Aquinas, both Ger-

son and Iohannes de Nova Domo identify pseudo-Dionysius as a Peripatetic; see Kaluza, *Les querelles doctrinales,* 47, 123. Denys demurs on this point in the late *Elem. theol.* 60 (*Opera omnia* 33:160C'): "Interim his objici potest quod Thomas in Scripto secundi affirmat, beatissimum Dionysium Aristotelem esse secutum pene in omnibus . . . Ad quod videtur dicendum . . . quod gloriosus praesul, doctor et martyr Dionysius, in valde multis ab Aristotelis recessit."

49. *Elem. phil.* 98 (*Opera omnia* 33:61B–C). See Emery, *"Sapientissimus Aristoteles."*

50. See *Sent.* 3.24.unica (*Opera omnia* 23:420C'–421C), where Denys responds to the opinion of Durandus of St. Pourçain that in relation to us, the authority of Scripture is based solely on the Church's word that it is inspired. See Kent Emery, Jr., "Theology as a Science: The Teaching of Denys of Ryckel," in *Knowledge and Sciences in Medieval Philosophy: The Proceedings of the Eighth International Congress of Medieval Philosophy* (S.I.E.P.M.), vol. 3, ed. R. Työrinoja, A. I. Lehtinen, and D. Føllesdal (Helsinki, 1990), 196–206.

51. *Sent.* 1.37.3 (*Opera omnia* 20:450C'–455A'). Denys recites the solutions of Thomas Aquinas, *Sent.* 1.37.3.1–2 (Mandonnet and Moos 1:869–875), and Richard of Middleton, *Sent.* 1.37.2.1 (1:325–326).

52. See Tempier, Parisian Condemnations 204 (CUP 1:554).

53. *Sent.* 2.2.5 (*Opera omnia* 21:168B–170C'). Denys nicely abbreviates the solution of Henry of Ghent, *Quodl. 2* q. 9 (Wielockx, 58–72).

54. *Sent.* 2.2.5 (*Opera omnia* 21:170C'–B); see also *Elem. theol.* 86 (*Opera omnia* 33:180A'–D'). By reporting what others say, Denys's rejection of the Parisian article is indirect and refers to geographical, not temporal, extent.

55. *Sent.* 1.37.3 (*Opera omnia* 20:458C'–459D').

56. Tempier, Parisian Condemnations 204 (CUP 1:554): "Quod substantiae separatae sunt alicubi per operationem; et quod non possunt moveri ab extremo in extremum, nec in medium, nisi quia possunt velle operari aut in medio, aut in extremis. — Error, si intelligatur, sine operatione substantiam non esse in loco, nec transire de loco ad locum."

57. *Sent.* 2.2.6 (*Opera omnia* 21:177D'–178A).

58. *Sent.* 1.37.4 (*Opera omnia* 20:466B'–468A'). Denys recites from Albert the Great, *Sent.* 1.37.24 (*Opera* 26:264–266) and *Summa de creaturis* 1: *De quatuor coaequaevis* 4.59.1–3 (*Opera* 34:621–631).

59. *Sent.* 1.37.4 (*Opera omnia* 20:468A'–469A). Denys recites Albert the Great, *Liber de causis et processu universitatis* 2.2.3 (*Opera* 10:482–84). Denys (468C'–D') also quotes exactly from Albert's *Liber* 2.2.1 (*Opera* 10:477–78): "Peripaticorum enim his rationem defendimus, qui negant intelligentiam loco diffiniri: dicentes omnem intelligentiam esse ubique et semper." In condemning the double manner of speaking, Denys would seem to refer to Tempier, Parisian Condemnations 90, 146 (CUP 1:548, 552).

60. Emery, "Twofold Wisdom," 123–125 and throughout.

61. *Sent.* 2.3.2 (*Opera omnia* 21:216B–C).

62. Denys resumes at length Henry of Ghent's teaching concerning the distinction between *esse* and *essentia* in spiritual beings in *Sent.* 1.8.7 (*Opera omnia* 19:405D–408A′). There he extracts from Henry's *Quodl. 1* q. 9 (Macken, 48–56) and alludes to *Quodl. 10* q. 7, where, he says, Henry "de hac ipsa materia multo diffusius scribit." Later, in *Sent.* 2.3.1 (*Opera omnia* 21:191B′–196D), Denys again extracts generously from Henry's teaching on the matter, this time from *Quodl. 3* q. 9 (Badius Ascensius, fols. 60v–61v) and from *Quodl. 10* q. 7 (Macken, 145–197). Denys's own arguments in *Sent.* 2.3.2 (*Opera omnia* 21:216C–217A′) are based on these earlier treatments. In conclusion, Denys says (217D–A′): "Istud scholastice dictum sit, ut studiosis praebeatur inquisitionis acutioris occasio. Nec enim in opinabilibus istis materiis, in quibus etiam magni tam diversimode opinantur, aliquid cum temeraria assertione est proferendum aut quasi certitudinaliter determinandum: quanquam nonnulli in talibus nimis assertive loquantur, quasi ipsi soli sano ac praecellenti pollerent ingenio."

63. *Elem. phil.* 38 (*Opera omnia* 33:44B–A′).

64. Ibid. (44A′–C′).

65. *Sent.* 2.3.3 (*Opera omnia* 21:217D′–237D): "An omnes angeli sint eiusdem speciei."

66. *Sent.* 2.3.3 (*Opera omnia* 21:220C–221C′). Denys extracts from Thomas Aquinas, *Sent.* 2.3.1.4 (Mandonnet and Moos 2:97–98) and *Summa theologiae* 1.50.4. Denys makes his remark in *Elem. theol.* 64 (*Opera omnia* 33:164B).

67. *Sent.* 2.3.3 (*Opera omnia* 21:221C–222B′); Albert the Great, *Summa theologiae* 2.2.8 (*Opera* 32:137–38).

68. *Sent.* 2.3.3 (*Opera omnia* 21:225D–226A′). Denys extracts from Henry of Ghent, *Quodl. 2* q. 8 (Wielockx, 43–52) and alludes to *Quodl. 11* q. 1 (Badius Ascensius, fols. 438r–439v).

69. *Sent.* 2.3.3 (*Opera omnia* 21:225B′–C′); *Elem. theol.* 64 (*Opera omnia* 33:164D–A′). Denys quotes the Parisian articles directly from Henry of Ghent, *Quodl. 2* q. 8 (Wielockx, 45); see Tempier, Parisian Condemnations 96, 191, 81 (CUP 1:549, 554, 548).

70. *Elem. theol.* 64 (*Opera omnia* 33:164D).

71. *Sent.* 2.3.3 (*Opera omnia* 21:226D–A′).

72. Ibid. (228D′–229A).

73. Ibid. (222B–D′).

74. Ps-Dionysius, *De coelesti hierarchia* 10, trans. Eriugena (in *Opera omnia* 15:190–91).

75. *Sent.* 2.3.3 (*Opera omnia* 21:229A–C).

76. Ibid.

77. *Elem. theol.* 64 (*Opera omnia* 33:164D′–165D′).

78. *De lumine* 1.13 (*Opera omnia* 33:247A′–248D), Denys remarks that

advocates of the formal distinction try to demonstrate it in a fourfold way: "per viam divisionis . . . per viam definitionis . . . per viam oppositionis . . . Quarta via . . . est demonstrationis via." This distinction comes from the third part of Francis of Meyronnes's treatment in *Sent.* 1.8.1 (fol. 44r^a–44v^a, c–i). Like Gerson, Denys in his writings views the distinction through the perspective of ps-Dionysius's teaching about the divine transcendence in the *Mystical Theology* and engages Duns Scotus and Francis of Meyronnes chiefly in their arguments over *Sent.* 1.8, which concerns the divine attributes (see Kaluza, *Les querelles doctrinales,* 53). Denys certainly read Gerson's *Contra vanam curiositatem* and his *Notulae* over mystical theology at an early date; it is in these texts that Gerson most often makes his strictures against the Scotists (see Kaluza, Appendix 1, 127–144). Thus, Gerson's writings may have first alerted Denys to the "danger" of the formal distinction. Denys, however, is nowhere as "superficial" (Kaluza's word) as Gerson in his understanding of his opponents' arguments; he attends their words carefully. He certainly does not, as Gerson does, classify Henry of Ghent among the formalists with Duns Scotus (Kaluza, 60). The rest of my study will make this evident.

79. *De lumine* 1.57 (*Opera omnia* 33:299B'–301B'; see esp. 301B–C).

80. *De nat.* 35 (*Opera omnia* 34:58D–61C).

81. *Sent.* 1.2.2 (*Opera omnia* 19:149–77).

82. Ibid. (149C').

83. *Sent.* 1.2.2 (*Opera omnia* 19:149C'–152C'); Thomas Aquinas, *Sent.* 1.2.1 (Mandonnet and Moos 1:66–71) and *Summa theologiae* 1.13.

84. Thomas Aquinas, *Sent.* 1.36.2.2 ad 2 (Mandonnet and Moos 1:842): "quamvis relationes quae sunt Dei ad creaturam, realiter in creatura fundentur, tamen secundum rationem et intellectum in Deo etiam sunt; intellectum autem dico non tantum humanum, sed etiam angelicum et divinum."

85. *Sent.* 1.2.2 (*Opera omnia* 19:153A–154A').

86. Ibid. (154A'–155A).

87. *Sent.* 1.2.2 (*Opera omnia* 19:155A'–D'). Denys extracts from the conclusion of Bonaventure, *Sent.* 1.35.3 (*Opera* 1:608), and the solution of Alexander of Hales, *Summa theologica* 1.1.3.1.4 (1:130–131, n.80).

88. *Sent.* 1.2.2 (*Opera omnia* 19:155D'–156D'); Albert the Great, *Sent.* 1.8.3 (*Opera* 25:224–25).

89. Denys quotes at length from Henry of Ghent, *Quodl.* 5 q. 1 (Badius Ascensius, fols. 150v–154r). He extracts from all the parts of the argument, not just the solution.

90. *Sent.* 1.2.2 (*Opera omnia* 19:157A–158B).

91. Ibid. (157D'–159B; answers to objections, 159C–162A).

92. Bonaventure, *Itinerarium mentis in Deum* 5–6 (*Opera* 5:308–12). In chapter 5, Bonaventure considers God as *Esse,* the divine simplicity, and divine attributes; this is the way of Moses, the Old Testament, and of philosophy. Rising higher, in chapter 6 he considers the Trinity of Persons under

the name of *Bonum;* this is the way of Paul, his disciple Dionysius, and in general, of Revelation.

93. *Sent.* 1.2.2 (*Opera omnia* 19:171C'-172B).

94. See Raymond Macken, "L'illumination divine concernant les vérités révélées chez Henri de Gand," *Journal philosophique* 5 (1985): 261-271; Emery, "Theology as a Science."

95. *Elem. theol.* 25 (*Opera omnia* 33:131C-133D'): "Inter attributa divinae naturae non est realis neque formalis distinctio, sed rationis dumtaxat; nec praeter ac ultra personalem distinctionem est ponenda in divinis ulla distinctio ex rei natura, ut aliqui opinantur."

96. *Sent.* 1.2.2 (*Opera omnia* 19:162C-164B). Denys quotes Scotus from the *Opus Oxoniense.* He follows Scotus's text very carefully and traces all of the parts and turns of the argument. Compare Scotus, *Ordinatio* 1.8.1.4 (*Opera* 4:230-68 nos. 157-209).

97. *Sent.* 1.2.2 (*Opera omnia* 19:162A'-B').

98. *Sent.* 1.36.2 (*Opera omnia* 20:213B-215A'); *Elem. theol.* 36 (*Opera omnia* 33:133D'-134D').

99. *Sent.* 1.2.2 (*Opera omnia* 19:163D-164D').

100. *Sent.* 1.2.2 (*Opera omnia* 19:164A'-167C'). Denys takes the opinions of Gregory of Rimini and William of Ockham from the text of Peter of Candia. There is yet no complete printed edition of Peter's commentary on the *Sentences,* but introductory materials have been edited by S. F. Brown in "Peter of Candia's Sermons in Praise of Peter Lombard," in *Studies Honoring Ignatius Charles Brady* (St. Bonaventure, N. Y., 1976), 141-176, and in "Peter of Candia's Hundred-Year History of Theology," *Medieval Philosophy and Theology* 1 (1991): 175-190. See also the study by F. Ehrle, *Die Sentenzenkommentar Peters von Candia,* Franziskanische Studien 9 (Munster, 1925). Peter paraphrases (166D-D') William of Ockham's responses in *Sent.* 1.2.1-2 (*Opera* 2:17-20, 61-69) and quotes directly (167B'-D') from his argument against Scotus and William Alnwick in *Sent.* 1.2.1 (*Opera* 2:14.8-16). From Gregory of Rimini Peter reports "septem rationes contra Scoti opinionem" (166D'-167B'); see Gregory, *Sent.* 1.8.1.2 (fols. 66v^a-67r^a, L-Q, A-C). Denys remarks that Peter favors the position of Scotus (167C'). Although Denys can admit William's logical arguments and authorities against Scotus, he could not affirm the underlying principle of his resolution: "dico quod non sunt nisi quidam conceptus vel signa quae possunt vere praedicari de Deo, et magis proprie deberent dici conceptus attributales vel nomina attributalia quam perfectiones attributales. . . . Et ideo dico quod attributa divina quae sunt plura non sunt realiter essentia divina, sed attributa, quae sunt conceptus" (*Sent.* 1.2.2, in *Opera* 2:61, 66). Denys only alludes to this argument (166C'), which does not serve his own. In *Elem. theol.* 25 (*Opera omnia* 33:133C'-D'), Denys notes that William concedes formal distinction among the personal trinitarian relations and the divine essence, but not among the at-

tributes; see William of Ockham, *Sent.* 1.2.11 (*Opera* 2:358–79). William does not admit formal distinctions in creatures.

101. *Elem. theol.* 25 (*Opera omnia* 33:131B'–C'): ". . . inter distinctionem realem et rationis non videtur media esse: quoniam idem et multa, idem et differens, passiones et proprietates sunt entis; sed nil est nec esse potest nisi ens reale, quod habet esse praeter operationem animae, et ens rationis, quod habet esse per solam animae actionem: ergo praeter distinctionem realem et rationis alia non est. — Praeterea, quidquid convenit rei ex sua natura, convenit ei remota omni operatione intellectus. Si igitur inter attributa Dei sit formalis distinctio ex rei natura, omni operatione intellectus seclusa, illa esset realis: quod nullus admittit. — Insuper, non est sine necessitate ponenda in eodem pluralitas." Denys will adopt the principle of economy when useful.

102. *Sent.* 1.2.2 (*Opera omnia* 19:164A', 167D'–169C'). Here Denys reports all four parts of Francis of Meyronnes's question, *Sent.* 1.8.1–2 (fols. 43r^a–44v^a): "primo, quid sit distinctio; secundo, quot modis sumatur; tertio, qualiter possit investigari; quarto an in divinis sit distinctio" (167D').

103. *Sent.* 1.2.2 (*Opera omnia* 19:169C'–171B'). Denys extracts generously from Durandus of St. Pourçain, *Sent.* 1.2.2 (fol. 18r^a–v^b nos. 7–15).

104. Sent. 1.2.2 (*Opera omnia* 19:173C'–D').

105. Ibid. (172C'–D').

106. Ibid. (177D–A').

107. *Elem. theol.* 25 (*Opera omnia* 33:133C'–D').

108. *De nat.* 35 (*Opera omnia* 34:61B'–C'). Despite the tenor of this advice, Denys is not counseling a resort to simple piety. The work in fact is intended to urge upon the modern devout the importance of intellectual inquiry and speculative thought. See Emery, "Fondements théoriques de la réception de la beauté sensible dans les écrits de Denys le Chartreux (1402–1471)," in *Les Chartreux et l'art XIVe–XVIIIe-siècles: Actes du Colloque de Villeneuve-lès-Avignon*, ed. D. Le Blévec and A. Girard (Paris, 1989), 310–314.

109. See Emery, "Denys of Ryckel and Traditions of Meditation," 80–82.

110. Against Duns Scotus's doctrine of the univocity of the concept of being between God and creatures, Denys affirms the teaching of Henry of Ghent and adds his own arguments in *Sent.* 1.3.1 (*Opera omnia* 19:217D'–220C). He treats the topic again in *Sent.* 1.8.6 (*Opera omnia* 19:390D'–401B): "An Deo conveniat ratio universalis, seu generis aut speciei." There he concludes: "quam inconviens et absurda sit quorumdam opinio, dicentium quod ens non solum univoce de Deo et creaturis dicatur, sed item quod Deus sit in praedicamento ac genere, in tantum ut quidam dixisse legatur, quod Deus seu divina essentia in quantum quidditas, non est dignior quam quidditas asini: quod auribus vere religiosis detestabiliter sonat, et honorificentiae superdignissimi Dei contrariatur, de quo cum omni reverentia et timore loqui debemus . . . ut beatissimus Dionysius et Damascenus affirment. . . . Itaque

358

dico quod divina essentia in quantum quidditas, secundum quod quidditas convenit ei, non solum quidditate asini, sed etiam quidditate excellentissimi angeli, in infinitum praestantior est. Nec in hoc simile est de Deo et creaturis . . . de Deo tamen majestatis et excellentiae penitus infinitae loqui sic nefas est" (400A–D). Again, Denys's concern is the unknowable transcendence of God, as taught by ps-Dionysius. In *Elem. theol.* 84 *(Opera omnia* 33:91C–D), Denys asks: if the more profound philosophers declared God to be above and outside of every genus, "quanto magis Christianos hoc fari faterique decet, cum et divinus ac magnus Dionysius, praesertim in libro de Mystica theologia, tam evidenter edoceat hoc?" See also *De lumine* 1.82–83 *(Opera omnia* 33:255A'–257C); *De nat.* 61 *(Opera omnia* 34:95D–96B'); and, as the problem relates directly to mystical theology, *Difficultatum praecipuarum absolutiones* (in ps-Dionysius's *De myst. theol.*) 2 *(Opera omnia* 16:486D–487A').

111. *Diff. praecip. absol.* 2 *(Opera omnia* 16:489D), and throughout Denys's writings.

112. *Diff. praecip. absol.* 2 *(Opera omnia* 16:487A'–488C). For Denys's doctrine concerning the highest mystical cognition, see Emery, "Twofold Wisdom," 124–133.

113. Ps-Dionysius, *De coel. hier.* 1, trans. Eriugena (in *Opera omnia* 15:6).

114. *Diff. praecip. absol.* 2 *(Opera omnia* 16:489B'–C'). On this issue, see Emery, "Twofold Wisdom" and *"Sapientissimus Aristoteles,"* throughout, and "Did Denys the Carthusian Also Read Henricus Bate? *Bulletin de philosophie médiévale* 32 (1990): 196–206.

115. *Diff. praecip. absol.* 2 *(Opera omnia* 16:489C'–D').

116. Ibid. (490A–B).

SCHOLASTIC EDITIONS CITED

Albert the Great. *Sancti Alberti Magni . . . Opera omnia.* Edited by A. Borgnet. 38 vols. Paris, 1890–99.

Alexander of Hales. *Doctoris irrefragabilis Alexandri de Hales Summa theologica.* Edited by Fathers of the College of St. Bonaventure. 4 vols. (vol. 4 in 2 pts.), with 2 vols. of indices. Quaracchi, 1924–29.

Bonaventure. *Doctoris seraphici s. Bonaventurae Opera omnia.* Edited by Fathers of the College of St. Bonaventure. 10 vols. Quaracchi, 1882–1901.

Denys the Carthusian. *Doctoris ecstatici D. Dionysii Cartusiani Opera omnia.* Edited by Monks of the Carthusian Order. 42 vols. in 44. Montreuil-Tournai-Parkminster, 1896–1913, 1935. (Cited as *Opera omnia*)

Duns Scotus, John. *Doctoris subtilis et mariani Ioannis Duns Scoti . . . Opera omnia.* Edited by C. Balić and others, 18 vols. to date. Vatican City, 1950–.

Durandus of St. Pourçain. *D. Durandi a Sancto Porciano . . . in Petri Lombardi*

Sententias theologicas Commentariorum libri IIII. 2 vols. in continuous foliation. Venice, 1571; reprinted Gregg Press, N. J., 1964.

Francis of Meyronnes. *In libros Sententiarum, Quodlibeta, Tractatus Formalita-
tum . . . De univocatione.* Venice, 1520; reprinted Frankfurt/Main, 1966.

Gregory of Rimini. *Gregorii Ariminensis O. E. S. A. Super primum et secundum
Sententiarum.* Venice, 1522; reprinted St. Bonaventure, N. Y., Louvain,
and Paderborn, 1955.

Henry of Ghent. *Henrici de Gandavo Opera omnia.* Leuven, 1979–.

————. V: *Quodlibet I.* Edited by R. Macken, 1979.

————. VI: *Quodlibet II.* Edited by R. Wielockx, 1983.

————. XIII: *Quodlibet IX.* Edited by R. Macken, 1983.

————. XIV: *Quodlibet X.* Edited by R. Macken, 1981.

————. *Quodlibeta Magistri Henrici Goethals a Gandavo.* Edited I. Badius Ascensius. 2 vols. in continuous foliation. Paris, 1518; reprinted Louvain,
1961.

Richard of Middleton. *Super quatuor libros Sententiarum.* 4 vols. Brescia, 1591;
reprinted Frankfurt/Main, 1963.

Tempier, Étienne. Parisian Condemnations of 1277: Edited by H. Denifle
and E. Chatelain in vol. 1, n. 473, pp. 543–558 of *Chartularium Universitatis Parisiensis.* 4 vols. Paris, 1889–97. (Cited as CUP.)

Thomas Aquinas. *Scriptum super libros Sententiarum.* Edited by P. Mandonnet
and M. F. Moos. 4 vols. Paris, 1929–1947.

William of Auxerre. *Magistri Guillelmi Altissiodorensis Summa aurea.* Edited by
J. Ribaillier. 4 vols. (vols. 2–3 in 2 pts.). Spicilegium Bonaventurianum
16–20. Paris and Grottaferrata, 1980–87.

William of Ockham. *Guillelmi de Ockham Opera philosophica et theologica.* Edited
by members of the Franciscan Institute, St. Bonaventure University.
10 vols. St. Bonaventure, N.Y., 1967–86. I cite from vol. 2: *Scriptum
in librum primum Sententiarum Ordinatio.* Edited by G. Gál and S. Brown,
1970.

X

DENYS THE CARTHUSIAN AND THE INVENTION OF PREACHING MATERIALS

A common opinion holds that Denys of Ryckel (Dionysius Cartusiensis, 1402–1471), monk of the Charterhouse in Roermond in the eastern Netherlands, was the most prolific writer of the Middle Ages. "I would not believe it possible that one author could produce so many books, among which are many huge volumes," says Denys's sixteenth-century editor, Dirk Loër, "unless I had seen them in his own hand, and seen that they had the same inventive power *(ingenium)*, style, and character." Moreover, Loër adds, Denys "copied, corrected, illuminated, rubricated, and bound his books himself."[1] The seventeenth-century Carthusian bibliographer, Theodorus Petreius, asserts that "so great is the bulk of Denys's works, that in the number of his books he far surpassed Aurelius Augustine, having no use of an amanuensis at all."[2] Denys the Carthusian's literary achievement appears even greater when one considers the range of his writings, which embrace every medieval genre of Christian literature: biblical commentaries, Scholastic and mystical commentaries and treatises, monastic, pastoral, and juridical works of every kind.[3] Cursory reading among Denys's works reveals the truth of another adage: "He who reads Denys the Carthusian reads everything."[4] An apology concerning his literary activities, which Denys wrote to his prior in mid-career (1440s), expresses the range of his reading among the fathers, monas-

---

[1] Denys's works are cited from *Doctoris ecstatici D. Dionysii Cartusiani Opera omnia*, ed. Carthusians, 42 vols. in 44 (Montreuil 1896–1935). For Loër's statement, see *Vita Dionysii Cartusiani* (ibid. 1.xxiv). In his *Epistola nuncupatoria* to Denys's commentaries on the four major prophets (ibid. 8.309–310), Loër witnesses the condition of the autograph manuscripts and Denys's activity as a one-man scriptorium (reading, composing, writing, revising, and correcting): "Maxime vero id in eo admirandum, imo et stupendum est, unde tempus illi suppetere potuerit tot exarandi libros, tamque immensa volumina. . . . Quae nisi manus illius, quod character proprius testatur, hodieque conscripta, revisa identidem atque correcta extarent, quis unquam crederet monachum unum . . . tot tam insignium solidorumque voluminum monumenta, posteritati donare potuisse? Est eapropter miraculi ei loco tribuendum (si legendi, scribendi, orandi in eo exercitia singulatim spectentur), tantum cuivis horum vacasse, ut impossibile videatur operam dare potuisse reliquis."

[2] Theodorus Petreius, *Bibliotheca Cartusiana, sive Illustrium sacri Cartusiensis ordinis scriptorum Catalogus* (Cologne 1609; repr. Farnborough 1968) 51.

[3] For a *Novus Elenchus* of Denys's writings, with a repertory of manuscripts, see Kent Emery, Jr., *Dionysii Cartusiensis Opera selecta* 1 *(Prolegomena): Bibliotheca manuscripta 1A–1B, Studia bibliographica*, Corpus christianorum continuatio mediaeualis (CCCM) 121–121A (Turnhout 1991) 218–257.

[4] Petrus Blomevenna, *Epistola nuncupatoria* to Denys's commentary on Genesis (Denys [n. 1 above] 1.lxxxviii). Petrus adds (xcii) that Denys's writings more than double the number of Augustine's.

Reprinted from *Viator* 25 (Berkely, Calif., 1994), pp. 377–409. Copyright © 1994 by The Regents of the University of California Press.

X

tic writers, Scholastic doctors, and ancient and medieval natural philosophers. The list, while long, scarcely comprehends all of the writers quoted or cited in his works.[5]

Investigation of the artistic means Denys employed to produce his massive corpus uncovers other—somewhat surprising—dimensions of his thought and religious and literary activity. In this essay, I propose a series of closely related theses. (1) Denys derived the techniques for assembling and organizing his writings from methods devised in the thirteenth century for discovering and ordering materials to aid preaching. (2) Although in general one witnesses among fifteenth-century Carthusians an increase in pastoral concern and activity extending beyond the traditional understanding of the order's strictly contemplative vocation, Denys's production of sermons, of works intended to serve preachers, and of works conceived according to the analogy of apostolic instruction and persuasion is no less exceptional for a Carthusian monk than his study and writing of Scholastic philosophy and theology. (3) At a deeper level than rhetorical order, Denys's organization of moral materials and the particular emphases of his moral teaching bespeak his highly intellectual conception of the Christian life, and assume that philosophic and doctrinal speculation plays an integral role in the progress of moral and saintly performance. (4) Accordingly, Denys presumed that a reasonable presentation of the evidence of the tradition of Christian teaching sufficed for moral persuasion and practice, insofar as a human teacher could assist them.

In its strongly intellectual character, Denys's moral teaching seems to run counter to the prevailing attitudes of late medieval Christian writers (including Carthusians) as commonly characterized by modern historians, who discern in their teaching a nexus among "nominalist" theology, affective piety, and either a positivistic or subjective morality and devotion.[6] Whether the exception proves the rule requires much broader study. In any event, Denys the Carthusian's writings yield an abundant late medieval harvest of *moralia* and *praedicabilia* from an unexpected quarter and in an unexpected manner.

READING AND WRITING AMONG LATE MEDIEVAL CARTHUSIANS

Denys's literary production may be seen within the context of developments within the Carthusian Order in the late Middle Ages. Originally, in accordance with the order's eremitic and ascetic ideals, Charterhouses were built in remote "deserts" or "wildernesses." In the fourteenth and fifteenth centuries, however, because of their renown for purity of observance at a time when other religious foundations were perceived to be in a state of decline, the Carthusians experienced their greatest period of

---

[5]Denys's *Protestatio ad superiorem suum* is printed, ibid. 1.lxxi–lxxii, and again in 41.625–626. Anselm Stoelen, "De Chronologie van de Werken van Dionysius de Karthuizer," *Sacris erudiri* 5 (1953) 394–400, corrects the printed text, dating the *Protestatio* in 1441. Harald Dickerhof, "Kartäusisches Apostolat in Leben und Werk des Dionysius von Rijkel (1402/3–1471)," in *Festgabe Heinz Hürten zum 60. Geburtstag*, ed. Dickerhof (Frankfurt a.M. 1988) 193–194, thinks that 1446 is an equally plausible date for the text. For comment on the text, see Kent Emery, Jr., "Twofold Wisdom and Contemplation in Denys of Ryckel (Dionysius Cartusiensis, 1402–1471)," *Journal of Medieval and Renaissance Studies* 18 (1988) 101–103.

[6]A representative of this historical reading is the recent pertinent book by Dennis D. Martin, *Fifteenth-Century Carthusian Reform: The World of Nicholas Kempf*, Studies in the History of Christian Thought 49 (Leiden 1992).

expansion, esteem, and influence. The order was patronized by the rich and powerful; Charterhouses were now built near or in the midst of cities. Inescapably, Char-
termonks found themselves more involved in the affairs of the world, and they
encountered what historians have called "urban temptations."[7] Not surprisingly, at
the time of this expansion and in these new conditions, there was a great outpouring
of literature by Carthusian authors, several of whom, besides Denys, were prolific.[8]
Moreover, many of the men who now entered the order, like Denys, had received a
university education, and they carried their learning into their monastic life.[9] As one
would expect, most of the literature written by late medieval Carthusian authors treats
monastic matters, comprising scriptural, liturgical, ascetic, devotional, and mystical
works. Like his confrères, Denys produced many of these.

Many of the writings by late medieval Carthusian monks—perhaps most of them—
may be called "compilations." In a recent essay, Richard and Mary Rouse have shown
the wide semantic range of the term *compilatio* and explored its application to various kinds of compositions in the Middle Ages. They have warned against speaking
loosely, as if the term "compilation" designated a well-defined literary genre, and
they stress the distinction between the intentions of authors, on the one hand, and the
disposition of received texts by readers, users, copyists, and patrons, on the other.[10]
This distinction sheds light on the compiling methods of many Carthusian writers in
the late Middle Ages.[11] The literary activity of a Carthusian monk involved mainly the
gathering, copying, and disseminating of texts. The origin of Carthusian "compilations" would seem to lie in personal collections of reading material, made by the
individual monk for his own edification and for his meditation. Such writings, of
course, when bound and placed in the library, could serve the instruction and piety
of brethren in the monastery and, in the usual medieval way, the writings were often
copied and circulated among other religious houses. In this manner, what frequently
originated as personal collections became "works," whose "author" was either known
or guessed.

Perhaps influenced by Carthusian example, adherents of the Modern Devotion de-

---

[7]For these developments, see the essays in *La naissance des chartreuses*, Actes du VIe Colloque d'histoire
et de spiritualité cartusiennes, Grenoble, 12–15 septembre 1984, ed. Bernard Bligny and Gérald Chaix
(Grenoble 1984). Dickerhof (n. 5 above) 187–212 discusses the order's turn to pastoral activities in the
fifteenth century, and interprets Denys's "apostolic" works in light of the change. The order's acceptance
of art in the Charterhouses in the late Middle Ages seems parallel to the development; see the volume *Les
Chartreux et l'art, XIVe–XVIIIe siècles*, Actes du Colloque de Villeneuve-lès-Avignon, ed. Daniel Le Blevic
and Alain Girard (Paris 1989), esp. K. Emery, Jr., "Fondements théoriques de la reception de la beauté
sensible dans les écrits de Denys le Chartreux," 307–324.

[8]Most notably, Jacobus de Jüterbog and Joannes Hagen de Indagine. See J. Klapper, *Der Erfurter Kartäuser Johannes Hagen: Ein Reformtheologe des 15. Jahrhunderts*, 2 vols., Erfurter theologische Studien 9–10
(Leipzig 1960–1961), and Ludger Meier, O.F.M., *Die Werke des Erfurter Kartäusers Jakob von Jüterbog
in ihrer handschriftlichen Überlieferung*, in Beiträge zur Geschichte der Philosophie und Theologie des Mittelalters 37/5 (Münster 1955).

[9]For the details of Denys's university education, see Emery (n. 3 above) 121.15–18, and P. Teeuwen,
Dionysius de Karthuizer en de philosophisch-theologische stromingen ann de Keulsche Universiteit (Brussels 1938).

[10]R. H. Rouse and M. A. Rouse, "*Ordinatio* and *Compilatio* Revisited," in *Ad litteram: Authoritative
Texts and Their Medieval Readers*, ed. Mark D. Jordan and Kent Emery, Jr. (Notre Dame 1992) 113–134.

[11]See studies of the Carthusians Henry Arnold of Alfeld, James of Gruitrode, and Henry of Kalker in
Emery (n. 3 above) 121A.375–399, 445–459, 540–548, 588–615.

X

veloped the practice of making personal collections *(rapiaria)* for their meditation. In more elaborate form, Devout authors composed works of ''methodic meditation'' using techniques of organization and memory developed earlier by mendicant authors for the production and disposition of preaching materials.[12] Likewise elaborately, Denys the Carthusian employed in his writings organizational methods that were most notably developed for the production of preaching materials;[13] and he saw in them not only a means by which to execute his literary program, but also an instrument for more profound understanding.[14] Moreover, the evidence presented in this paper and elsewhere suggests that from their initial composition Denys intended his ''compilations'' as works for teaching others. Whereas Carthusian writings commonly circulated anonymously, Denys is usually identified as the author in manuscript copies of his works. Conversely, anonymous Carthusian writings were often falsely attributed to Denys. The preservation of his autograph manuscripts as a treasure in the Charterhouse library in Roermond also suggests his perceived ''authorial'' status.[15]

Elsewhere I have treated Denys's ''compiling'' and ''collecting'' method in his philosophic and speculative works, whereby he constructed his writings from the texts of many authors that he quoted or paraphrased and disposed to his own ends. The materials that he gathered in amplified form in one work he abbreviated in

[12]For personal collections of the Devout, see M. Th. P. van Woerkum, *Het Libellus ''Omnes, inquit, artes'': Een Rapiarium van Florentius Radewijns,* 3 vols. (Nijmegen 1950); P. Bange, ''Rapiaria en Collatieboeken,'' in *Moderne Devotie: Figuren en facetten,* exhibit commemorating the death of Geert Grote, 1384–1984, ed. A. J. Geerts (Nijmegen 1984) 152–167; Thom Mertens, ''Rapiarium,'' *Dictionnaire de spiritualité* 13 (Paris 1987) 114–119. For the influence of organizational methods of preaching aids on meditational works of the Devout, see Richard H. Rouse and Mary A. Rouse, *Preachers, Florilegia and Sermons: Studies on the ''Manipulus florum'' of Thomas of Ireland* (Toronto 1979) 212–213. The most extravagant witness is Joannes Mauburnus, *Rosetum exercitatiorum spiritualium et sacrarum meditationum,* written ca. 1490–1494, published Paris 1510. The Carthusian contribution to methodic meditation is studied by B. Spaapan, S.J., ''Karthuizer-vroomheid en Ignatiaanse spiritualiteit,'' *Ons Geestelijk Erf* 30 (1956) 337–366, and 31 (1957) 129–149. For Denys in relation to this tradition, see Kent Emery, Jr., ''Denys of Ryckel and Traditions of Meditation: *Contra detestabilem cordis inordinationem,''* in *Spiritualität Heute und Gestern* 3, Analecta Cartusiana 35/3 (Salzburg 1984) 69–89.

[13]I refer to the distinctions, concordances, exempla collections, summas of vices and virtues, florilegia, preaching summas, etc., and the organizational techniques they employed, developed especially in the thirteenth century. See, among others, D. L. d'Avray, *The Preaching of the Friars: Sermons Diffused from Paris before 1300* (Oxford 1985) 64–90; Jean Longère, *La prédication médiévale* (Paris 1983) 177–202; A. J. Minnis, *Medieval Theory of Authorship,* ed. 2 (Philadelphia 1988) 145–159 *(forma tractatus);* Mary A. Rouse and Richard H. Rouse, *''Statim invenire:* Schools, Preachers, and New Attitudes to the Page,'' and ''The Development of Research Tools in the Thirteenth Century,'' in *Authentic Witnesses: Approaches to Medieval Texts and Manuscripts* (Notre Dame 1991) 191–255; and iidem (n. 12 above) 3–42.

[14]In *1 Sent.* prooem. (Denys [n. 1 above] 19.37), Denys states reasons why the collection and consideration of scholastic writings by many doctors, rather than studying only one or a few, is advantageous to understanding. See the discussion in Kent Emery, Jr., ''Denys the Carthusian and the Doxography of Scholastic Theology,'' in Jordan and Emery (n. 10 above) 329–334; also idem (n. 3 above) 121.19–28, 47–50, and passim.

[15]I treat Denys's authorial status, the autograph manuscripts, etc., in the various chapters in CCCM 121, and provide studies of the spurious attributions to Denys—mostly ''compilations,'' mostly by other Carthusian writers—in CCCM 121A. For the relationship between compilations and spurious or anonymous circulation, see K. Emery, Jr., ''Lovers of the World and Lovers of God and Neighbor: Spiritual Commonplaces and the Problem of Authorship in the Fifteenth Century,'' in *Historia et spiritualitas cartusiensis,* Colloqui Quarti Internationalis Acta: Gandavi-Antverpiae-Brugis 16–19 Sept. 1982, ed. Jan de Grauwe (Destelbergen 1983) 177–219.

X

another. For Denys the activities of reading, copying, and composing were nearly simultaneous.[16]

Moreover, Denys's own works constituted an accumulating library that provided materials for further writing. In effect, his corpus represents a large memory system in which materials are stored and ordered for easy location and retrieval, or "recycling," into other writings. In this technique of literary production, he was anticipated by thirteenth-century composers of preaching materials, notably Vincent of Beauvais.[17] As a result, each of Denys's works is an index to many others. Memorization of the scriptures and of the order of questions in the *Sentences* is the key to this indexing. As a memory-aid, he composed an *Epitome sive nobiliores sententiae totius Bibliae*, which gleans key verses from each chapter of each book of the scriptures; sometimes appended to the verses are reminders of interpretations or apposite themes.[18] The sententious article titles of Denys's writings, which in the manuscripts sometimes appear as a finding guide at the head of the work, likewise serve the memory.[19] There is also evidence that in certain circumstances he recorded on wax tablets extracts of books he saw, which he later entered into his compositions.[20] Surely, Denys often relied on his memory and mnemonic devices; primarily, however, he laid out and organized his memory, gathered from the books he laboriously acquired and diligently searched, directly on his written pages, especially in his great "collections" or storehouses of material.[21]

[16]For Denys's compilation of his *Sentences* commentaries, see Kent Emery, Jr., "Theology as a Science: The Teaching of Denys of Ryckel (Dionysius Cartusiensis, 1402–1471)," in *Knowledge and Science in Medieval Philosophy* 3, ed. R. Työrinoja et al. (Helsinki 1990) 376–388 at 376; idem (n. 14 above) 331–334; idem (n. 3 above) 121.19–28, 47–50, and passim.

[17]See Robert J. Schneider, "Vincent of Beauvais' *Opus universale de statu principis*: A Reconstruction of Its History and Contents," in *Vincent de Beauvais: Intentions et réceptions d'une oeuvre encyclopédique au Moyen Age*, ed. M. Paulmier-Foucart, S. Lusignan, and A. Nadeau (Montreal 1990) 285–299.

[18]The *Epitome* is printed, Denys (n. 1 above) 14.539–707. For the sixteenth-century edition of Denys's works, the Cologne professor of theology and law, humanist Arnoldus Vesaliensis (Arnoldus Halderen de Wesalia, d. 1534), prepared mnemonic tables and schemata for remembering the contents of the *Sentences* (printed, ibid. 19.13–33, 21.5–29, 23.5–23, 24.5–28). While not by Denys, Arnoldus's tables show that such schemata were used. For Arnoldus, see Hermann Keussen, *Die Matrikel der Universität Köln*, 3 vols. (Bonn 1928–1931) 2.513 no. 450, 89.

[19]For Denys's article titles, see Emery (n. 3 above) 121.48–49; on chapter titles as a memorative and finding device, Rouse and Rouse (n. 13 above) 197–198.

[20]Concerning Denys's visiting of libraries while on the papal legation (1451) with Nicholas of Cusa, Loër states: "Et est hoc in illo prorsus admirabile, quod quidquid uspiam alienis iisdemque raris ex codicibus lectione collegerat, non aliter atque ad tabulam signasset, tenaci memoria retineret" (Denys [n. 1 above] 8.310). For the use of wax tablets, see Richard H. Rouse and Mary A. Rouse, "The Vocabulary of Wax Tablets," in *Vocabulaire du livre et de l'écriture au moyen âge*, Études sur le vocabulaire intellectuel du Moyen Age 2: Actes de la table ronde, Paris 24–26 septembre 1987, ed. Olga Weijers (Turnhout 1989) 220–230, and Mary J. Carruthers, *The Book of Memory: A Study of Memory in Medieval Culture* (Cambridge 1990) 195–196, 204–205, 211–213. Whether Denys actually traveled with Cusanus for any significant period of time has now been put into question by Erich Meuthen, "Nikolaus von Kues und Dionysius der Kärtauser" (forthcoming).

[21]For purposes of meditation, Denys employed techniques of artificial memory; see Emery (n. 12 above). Carruthers (n. 20 above) seems to argue the priority of artificial/mental memory throughout the Middle Ages. In her treatment of page-layout, she equivocates, often leaving the impression that the ordering of manuscript pages is an expression of a prior ordering, in the author's mind, by means of artificial memory devices. Rouse and Rouse (n. 13 above) 191–219 suggest that various means of text division, apparatus, indexing, and text-marking by the thirteenth century largely replaced sole reliance on artificial memory. For Denys's

Among his Carthusian brethren in particular and late medieval monastic writers in general, Denys was exceptional in his study of, and writing about, Scholastic theology and natural philosophy. This interest bespeaks his rigorously intellectual understanding of mystical theology, in opposition to the affective understanding prevailing in monastic circles. Denys thought that piety, in principle, must be founded on a disciplined understanding, and he desired to overcome a prejudice against Scholastic thinking widespread among the devout of his time and a growing divorce between piety and religious speculation.[22] No less exceptional and uncharacteristic is his production of sermons and works that may justly be called preaching materials and preaching aids.

Preaching materials themselves constitute a large part of Denys's writing. He wrote four model sermon sequences—"de tempore et de sanctis ad saeculares, de tempore et de sanctis ad religiosos"—comprising over 900 sermons (ca. 1452).[23] Besides these, he wrote a sequence of six sermons on the Eucharist and he preached sermons in chapter and to general chapters of the Carthusians and Franciscans. The recently discovered sermons preached by Denys in chapter reveal how he adapted material that he originally preached within his monastery for the more general purposes of his model sequences.[24] Inserted among the sermons in the printed editions, but probably circulated separately in manuscript, is an *enarratio* on the Passion of Christ "ex quatuor Evangelistis collecta et sumpta," made to supply materials for popular preaching (1452–1457; see Appendix below).[25] To provide preaching materials, he composed a large *Summa de vitiis et virtutibus* in two books (ca. 1453), and another special treatise, *De doctrina et regulis vitae christianorum* (ca. 1455).[26] The compound title of the

---

use of the terms *collectio, collectum-collecta, collectarium*, see Kent Emery, Jr., "Monastic *Collectaria* from the Abbey of St. Trudo (Limburg) and the Reception of Writings by Denys the Carthusian," in *Literature and Religion in the Later Middle Ages: Philological Essays in Honor of Siegfried Wenzel*, ed. John A. Alford and Richard Newhauser (Binghamton, forthcoming).

[22] I have addressed this topic explicitly, in Emery (n. 5 above); idem (n. 7 above) 310–311; and idem (n. 3 above) 121.19–21, 121A.614–615 and 702–710.

[23] The sermon sequences are printed, Denys (n. 1 above) vols. 29–32; for the incipits, see Emery (n. 3 above) 121.264–334. For each Sunday, feast, and ferial celebration, Denys provides expositions of the Epistle and Gospel, followed by appropriately thematic sermons. As Anselm Stoelen, "Denys le Chartreaux," *Dictionnaire de spiritualité* 3 (Paris 1957) 433 suggests, surely many of the individual sermons were composed before the collections were put together around 1452. On model sermon sequences as preaching aids, see especially d'Avray (n. 13 above) 81–131. That Denys conceived such collections as aids to parish priests is suggested by an instruction he gives priests in *De doctrina et regulis vitae christianorum* 2 a.4 (n. 1 above) 39.531B'–C': "Quarto studeat suos domesticos idonee regere, totamque suam parochiam, quibus potissime festis diebus atque dominicis sermocinetur, Evangelium exponat, et de credendis ac agendis instruat in ecclesia congregatos."

[24] Denys, *Sermones sex de venerabili sacramento* (n. 1 above) 35.453–476; Emery (n. 3 above) 121.234 no. 78. On the sermons or *collationes* for the Franciscan general chapter, and those preached to Carthusians, see Emery op. cit. 121.119–121, 150–155, 241–242 no. 114, 249–250 no. 149.

[25] Denys, *Passio D. N. Jesu Christi iuxta textum quatuor Evangelistarum*, printed among the sermons *de sanctis* (n. 1 above) 31.425–546. For the date, see Stoelen (n. 23 above) 433.

[26] Denys's *Summa* is printed (n. 1 above) 39.7–242, and *De doct. et reg.* 39.497–572. See Emery (n. 3 above) 121.243 no. 115, 248 no. 145. For the dates, Stoelen (n. 23 above) 434. The Fourth Lateran Council (1215) established a close connection between preaching and the practice of sacramental confession. Penitential summas designed for confessors also served preachers, who were to preach primarily the vices and virtues to the people. See among others Roberto Rusconi, "De la prédication à la confession: Transmission et contrôle de modèles de comportement au XIIIe siècle," in *Faire croire: Modalités de la diffusion et de la réception*

latter, alluding to the authoritative preaching works of Augustine and Gregory,[27] reveals its intent. The title—and the very conception of the work—may also owe something to Alan of Lille.[28] In his *Summa* and *De doctrina*, Denys alludes to many other treatises he wrote that contain materials for preaching. In his moral writings as in his Scholastic works, he exhibits a "compiling" method, following ample precedent.

DENYS'S GLOSS ON WRITING AND PREACHING IN THE CARTHUSIAN LIFE

In writing for the instruction and persuasion of those outside the monastery, Denys went beyond the traditional conception of his Carthusian vocation. It was not the part of a contemplative monk to instruct or preach to others. Denys's reflections on his own activity in writing model sermons and preaching materials reveal a certain vocational ambivalence. In Thomas Aquinas's teaching concerning the perfection of a mixed life, which embraces prayer and contemplation and the preaching to, and teaching of, others, Denys encountered a doctrine of religious life that well described his own, if not the particular vocation of the order to which he was professed. As he needed to justify his interest in philosophy and Scholastic theology,[29] so he needed to justify his writing of preaching materials.

Denys acknowledges that it is the duty of a monk to be "purged, illumined, and perfected," not to "purify, illumine, and perfect others," which is a special privilege of the four mendicant orders,[30] and that monks should read books that expose one's imperfections and excite affection rather than those that abound in knowledge: "better indeed is a virtuous life with little knowledge than an unworthy life with copious science." There are others, however, who read in order to abound in both knowledge

---

des messages religieux du XIIe au XVe siècle, Collection de l'Ecole française de Rome 51 (Rome 1981) 67–85, and Leonard E. Boyle, O.P., "Summae confessorum," in *Les genres littéraires dans les sources théologiques et philosophiques médiévales: Définition, critique et exploitation*, Actes du Colloque international de Louvain-la-Neuve, 25–27 mai 1981 (Louvain-la-Neuve 1982) 227–237. The focus on preaching against the vices and the close bond between preaching and the sacrament of confession continued until the end of the Middle Ages; see Hervé Martin, *Le métier de prédicateur en France septentrionale à la fin du Moyen Age (1350–1520)* (Paris 1988) 369–392. For Denys, the materials on vices and virtues that serve as the basis of preaching are the same as serve confessors in instructing and hearing confessions; see Denys, *Summa* 2 a.49 (n. 1 above) 39.239D'–240A', and more extensively, his *De vita et regimine curatorum* aa.36–39, ibid. 37.283D'–289B'. Besides the vices and virtues, layfolk needed to be preached especially the Ten Commandments, the Creed, and the Pater Noster. In *Summa* 2 aa.37–40 (ibid. 39.220D'–229A), Denys compiles materials on the decalogue from various doctors and summas; see also *De doct. et reg.* a.8 reg.1, 4 (ibid. 39.517C'–518C, 520C–D'). Denys's brief commentaries on the Apostles' Creed, the Ten Commandments, and the Pater Noster are inserted in *De vita curatorum* aa.19–27, 41 (ibid. 37.248C–264D, 290D–292D), and the commentary on the Ten Commandments is reiterated in *De laudabili coniugatorum* aa.20–27 (ibid. 38.84A–92C).

[27] I refer to Augustine's *De doctrina christiana* and Gregory's *Regula pastoralis*.

[28] Denys does not mention Alan of Lille, but his *De doct. et reg.* contains all but two of the categories *ad status* in Alan's *De arte praedicatoria* (PL 210.109–198): "Ad oratores seu advocatos" and "Ad somnolentes." Alan's distinction of *sompnus*, however, appears in Denys's *1 Adv. Sermo* 1 ([n. 1 above] 29.11A'–B'). Denys also knew Alan's *Regulae theologicae* (PL 210.617–684), but his rules for the moral life are more rhetorical than Alan's scientific conception of them.

[29] Emery (n. 5 above) 101–103, and idem (n. 14 above).

[30] Denys, *De doct. et reg.* 1 a.6 (n. 1 above) 39.534B'–D', and *Protestatio* (ibid. 41.626).

and virtue. As examples, Denys cites Moses, David, Paul, John, Dionysius the Areopagite, and in a lower order, the "modern doctors" Thomas Aquinas, Albert the Great, and Giles of Rome. This kind of study is most appropriate for prelates, pastors, and members of the mendicant orders, whose appointed duty it is to lead others to God by teaching and preaching. With some self-reflection, Denys adds that although his rule of reading holds in general, in special cases no rule should be applied.[31]

In his first treatise (1430), an encomium of Carthusian life, Denys argues that the preacher's aureole is ordinarily awarded to prelates. This star *(stella)*, however, is bestowed upon those who actually preach, not just upon those who hold an appointment to preach or who merely belong to a preaching order. Thus, the preacher's aureole is a reward not only for officially appointed preachers, but for "whosoever licitly and meritoriously may exercise this act" and for those who write about sacred doctrine, for "to put together writings *(scripta componere)* is a certain kind of teaching." To support his claim, Denys refers to the famous Carthusian statute from Guigo I's *Consuetudines*: "We set aside certain periods of the day for works of manual labor, most of all for the writing of books *(scribendis libris)*, for as our statutes say, all whom we receive we teach to write, if they are able."[32]

Likewise, in his first scriptural commentary on the Psalms of David (1434), Denys says that those receive the preacher's aureole who may never preach to the people with their mouths, but who expound sacred Scripture and put together theological books ("seu de theologia codices componendo").[33] In *De vita et fine solitarii* (ca. 1440–1445), speaking of the monk's work in his cell, he again refers to Guigo I's statute: "Writing, however, is the most noble among the corporal works of the monk, insofar as those to whom we may not preach or teach by the tongue, we may edify, as readers, in books we write out *(libris conscriptis)* and by the preaching material we bequeath to them. This our Statute more fully discloses."[34]

One will remark the equivocation in these texts among composing, compiling, and copying books, which in Denys's mind are nearly one activity. The equivocation represents more Denys's interpretation of the statute than the statute itself, which refers to the copying of books as a useful occupation of the monk when he rests from his primary spiritual activities of reading, meditating, praying, and contemplating.[35] Denys must confront the ambiguity of his own activities when addressing the traditional question of the relative merits of the active and contemplative lives. In the early *De praeconio et dignitate Mariae* (ca. 1432–1435), he affirms that the contemplative life is more noble than the active life, but adds—with the teaching of Thomas Aquinas probably in mind—"nevertheless, a conduct *(conversatio)* embracing the perfection of each life

---

[31]Denys, *De donis Spiritus Sancti* 1 a.2 (ibid. 35.160A′–161A), written ca. 1430 (Stoelen [n. 5 above] 362–363, and [n. 23 above] 433). On this text, see Emery (n. 5 above) 109–110.

[32]Denys, *Contra detestabilem cordis inordinationem, vel Laus Cartusiana* aa.14, 23 (n. 1 above) 40.213–216A, 242D′–243A. Guigo I, *Consuetudines* 28.2–4, in *Coutumes de Chartreuses*, ed. and trans. a Carthusian, Sources Chrétiennes 313 (Paris 1984) 222–225: "Omnes enim pene quos suscipimus, si fieri potest scribere docemus . . . ut quia ore non possumus, dei verbum manibus predicemus. Quot enim libros scribimus, tot nobis veritatis praecones videmur."

[33]Denys's commentary *In Psalmos* a.7 (n. 1 above) 5.286B′–C′; Emery (n. 3 above) 121.221–222 no. 18.

[34]Denys, *De vita et fine solitarii* 1 a.21 (n. 1 above) 38.286B′–C′.

[35]The fourfold activity of the (Carthusian) monk is defined in Guigo II, *Scala claustralium*, ed. Edmund Colledge, O.S.A., and James Walsh, S.J., with a French translation by a Carthusian monk, *Lettre sur la vie contemplative (L'échelle des moines): Douze méditations*, Sources Chrétiennes 163 (Paris 1970).

constitutes the highest life."[36] In his commentary on Luke (ca. 1452), expounding the relation between Mary and Martha, he distinguishes among works of the active life. The contemplative life is superior to an active life constituted by wholly corporeal works, as are the exterior works of mercy. There are other works belonging to an active life, however, such as preaching and interpreting Scripture, that are more spiritual and have contemplation as a prerequisite. Prelates and those who teach others exercise these works and join together contemplative and active lives. Some, Denys says, hold the opinion that this kind of life is higher than a strictly contemplative life, because it seems to include the perfections of both lives.[37]

Denys had already used this distinction between corporeal and spiritual works of the active life in De contemplatione (1440–1445), where he addresses the question of the merits of the two lives in more detail. Here he again alludes to active works that have contemplation as their prerequisite: preaching the Word of God, correcting those who err, interpreting the scriptures for others, converting others, listening to confessions and publicly praying for others. As in his commentary on Luke, he notes that some think a life including these acts is superior to the contemplative life alone, and he adds that, properly understood, the opinion is probably correct. Furthermore, a text of Dionysius the Areopagite affirms that the most divine act for a human being is to cooperate in leading souls back to God. The spiritual works of the active life (preaching, interpreting Scripture, fraternal correction, etc.) not only must flow out of contemplation, they in turn incite the one who practices them to a more vehement love and contemplation of divine realities. When in solitude one silently cogitates what he teaches or preaches, contemplation and love are not diminished but increased.[38] In this way Denys brings his own extensive writing activity and "preaching works" into the precinct of his strictly contemplative vocation. In other articles of De contemplatione, he resolves this personal issue by reference to hierarchical principles in the writings of pseudo-Dionysius, whereby the works of the active life can be said to be contained "virtually" in the contemplative life; and ultimately he denies any "mixed life" as a real third term between active and contemplative lives.[39]

Elements of these arguments are amplified in the Prooemium to Denys's Summa de vitiis et virtutibus. The materials which constitute this Prooemium are likewise distributed in blocks elsewhere, in his commentary on the Epistle of James, which provides the scriptural incipit for the Summa ("He who converts a sinner from the error of his way will save his soul, etc.," James 5.20);[40] in the sermon on the Epistle of James for Rogation days;[41] and in the Prooemium to the Sermones de tempore ad saeculares.[42]

---

[36]Denys, De praeconio 2 a.11 (n. 1 above) 35.217C'. For the date, see Anselm Stoelen, "Recherches recents sur Denys le Chartreux," Revue d'ascétique et de mystique 29 (1953) 252–258. For Thomas Aquinas on the active, contemplative, and mixed lives, see Summa theologiae (henceforward ST) 2a2ae qq.179–182 and q.188 a.6.

[37]Denys's commentary In Lucam a.28 (n. 1 above) 12.25C–A'.

[38]Denys, De contemplatione 1 a.14 (ibid. 41.150D–C'). Denys cites ps.-Dionysius, De coelesti hierarchia 3.

[39]Emery (n. 5 above) 126–128.

[40]Denys, In Epistolam Jacobi a.7 (n. 1 above) 13.610D–D'; according to Stoelen (n. 23 above) 434, written after 1452.

[41]Denys, In diebus Rogationum, Enarratio in Epistolam (n. 1 above) 32.74D–75B'.

[42]Denys, Sermones de tempore prooem. (ibid. 29.1–3).

In each instance, the arguments and authorities are expanded or contracted as appropriate, and the phrasing is often verbatim.

Considering the words of James, Denys states: If it is so great to convert one sinner, how much greater it is to intend the conversion of many and to scatter everywhere the word of God. "Divine Dionysius" says that, of all divine things, the most divine is to cooperate with God in leading souls back to himself; Gregory says that the sacrifice most pleasing to God is a zeal for souls; we may infer from Bernard that Christ is most pleased with one who by benign exhortation, virtuous example, and apt teaching recalls another from diabolic deception.[43] Denys indicates his own share in this work:

> And so, since it is so deiform, wholesome, and meritorious to instruct, exhort, correct, convert, and save others by preaching, by how much the less I—who by my professed religion am enclosed and cannot go out and do not have the privilege of preaching—am able to accomplish these things by speaking, by that much more I wish to do them by writing, collecting, and composing *(scribendo, colligendo, dictando)*. To some extent I have already done this by compiling *(compilando)* sermons *de tempore* and *de sanctis* for both seculars and religious.[44]

Denys adds that he was compelled to write his *Summa* by a "learned, religious, and fervent" Franciscan preacher, in the fruit of whose lips he hopes to share by giving him the materials he has assembled. This Franciscan was probably Jan Brugman (1400–1473), the most renowned preacher of his day in the Low Countries.[45] For him also Denys may have composed the *Sermones ad saeculares*,[46] and certainly *De doctrina et regulis vitae christianorum*. In the Prooemium to the latter work he praises Brugman by way of etymology. As Jan Brugman's first name indicates, he is a "vessel of grace"; rightly also is he named *vir pontis*, for by his fervent words and example he constructs

---

[43]Denys, *Summa* 1 prooem. (ibid. 39.14D–A'). Denys's sentence from ps.-Dionysius seems to be drawn from *De coelesti hierarchia* c.3, trans. Eriugena, printed in Denys's *Opera* 15.65–66; see Denys's comments at ibid. 70C'–D', 74B–C. For Gregory the Great, see *Hom. in Hiezechielem* 1.12, ed. M. Adriaen, CCSL 142 (Turnhout 1971) 200; for Bernard of Clairvaux, see *Sermo in Conversione S. Pauli*, in *S. Bernardi Opera*, ed. J. Leclercq and H. Rochais (Rome 1966) 4.328.

[44]Denys, *Summa* 1 prooem. (n. 1 above) 39.15B–D. Since Denys did not have secretaries (see above at nn. 1–2), I have translated *dictando* in the broad sense, "composing."

[45]For Jan Brugman, see W. Moll, *Johannes Brugman en het Godsdienstig leven onzer vaderen in de vijftiende eeuw*, 2 vols. (Amsterdam 1854). For Denys and Brugman, see 1.70–81. A more recent study is F. A. H. van den Hombergh, *Leven en Werk van Jan Brugman O.F.M. (+ / – 1400–1473), met een uitgave van twee van zijn tractaten*, Teksten en Documenten: Het Instituut voor Middeleeuwse Geschiedenis, Rijksuniversiteit te Utrecht 6 (Groningen 1967), esp. 25, 61–62, 76. Van den Hombergh documents references to Denys in Brugman's *Devotus tractatus . . . ad exercicia passionis Domini*, 166 *(De doct. et reg.)*, 242 *(De passione Domini dialogus)*. After speaking of his sermons *de tempore et de sanctis* in his introduction to the *Summa*, Denys (n. 1 above) 39.15C adds: "attamen ista adjicere quasi compellor, utpote instantissime ad hoc rogatus sum a viro erudito, religioso ac fervido Ordinis S. Francisci, secundum carnem propinquo, atque secundum spiritum multum propinquiori, sperans particeps inveniri fructus labiorum illius, si forte ex isto opusculo potuerit aliquantulum adiuvari."

[46]In *Sermo* 3 for the feast of St. George, Denys (n. 1 above) 32.10C, after explaining that he has already written on the observance of the Sabbath in other works, adds: "Verumtamen de observatione sabbati, id est, quae opera sint diebus festivis illicita, et quae licita, nunc aliqua sunt addenda: praesertim quoniam vir religiosus, cuius intuitu et amore ista scribuntur, instanter rogavit de hoc plenius aliqua introduci." Curiously, this text is repeated verbatim in *Summa* 2 a.37 (ibid. 39.221B), indicating the connection between this work and the *Sermones ad saeculares*, and, it would seem, their common recipient. Denys compiled materials on the observance of the Sabbath and feasts in *Summa* 2 aa.37–40 (ibid. 39.220D'–229A: Aquinas, Bonaventure, Durandus of Champagne, Peter of Tarantaise, Hugh Ripelin, Gerson, Henry of Friemar, et al.).

for the faithful a bridge conducting them from the bitterness and evils of the stormy sea of this life to the sweet and tranquil port of eternal salvation. Brugman, in turn, is Deny's bridge to the people; by providing materials for him, Denys once removed may cooperate with the "more than most glorious, exalted, and all-powerful creator" in leading souls to their source and salvation.[47]

The Collected Materials and Guiding Topics of Denys's Preaching Works

In his *Summa de vitiis*, Denys says that he does not propose to speak with Scholastic subtlety, but with a religious simplicity, devotion, and fervor that will serve an audience of lay people and commonfolk. Likewise, for the sake of brevity he will not insert anything from the detailed expositions of the doctors that does not serve the people directly.[48] In fact, the *Summa* seems very "Scholastic" in the broad sense, containing a heap of arguments, sayings, and authorities. What Denys means, I think, is that he will not reproduce the dialectical argumentation which he so skillfully recites in his commentaries on the *Sentences*. Even so, he often cites Scholastic works and moral arguments by Alexander of Hales, Bonaventure, Albert the Great, Thomas Aquinas, Peter of Tarantaise, Richard of Middleton, and Durandus of St. Pourçain. Yet in the *Summa*, Denys also cites and draws extracts from what he calls "popular summas" *(Summas vulgares)*: William Peraldus's *Summa virtutum et vitiorum*; Raymond of Pennafort's *Summa de poenitentia et matrimonio*; William of Paris's *Libri de poenitentia, De fide, De universo* and *De sacramentali*; John of Freiburg's *Summa confessorum*; the *Compendium theologicae veritatis* by Hugh Ripelin of Strasbourg, which Denys ascribes to the Augustinian Thomas of Strasbourg; the *Summa de casibus* of Bartholomew of Pisa; Durandus of Champagne's *Summa pro confessionibus audiendis*, and others.[49] Besides his Scholastic and moral sources, Denys makes extensive use of the monastic, ascetic works of Cassian and Climacus, Bernard of Clairvaux, David of Augsburg's *De profectu religiosorum*, and more recent writings by Jean Gerson and

---

[47]Denys, *De doct. et reg.* 1 prooem. (ibid. 39.500–501).

[48]Denys, *Summa* 1 a.1, 2 a.7 (ibid. 39.15A'–B', 170C'–D').

[49]For the Dominicans William Peraldus, Raymond of Pennafort, Hugh Ripelin of Strasbourg (d. 1268), John of Freiburg (d. 1304), Bartholomew of Pisa (d. 1347), see Thomas Kaeppeli, O.P., *Scriptores Ordinis Praedicatorum medii aevi*, 3 vols. (Rome, 1970–) 1.157–165 no. 436, 430–436 no. 2344, 2.133–142 no. 1622, 260–269 no. 1982, 3.250 nos. 3407–3408. The casuistic summas are discussed in Pierre Michaud-Quantin, *Sommes de casuistique et manuels de confession du moyen âge (XII–XVI siècles)*, Analecta mediaevalia namurcensia 13 (Louvain 1962) 35–52, 60–62. Adolar Zumkeller, *Manuskripte von Werken der Autoren des Augustiner-Eremitenordens in mitteleuropäische Bibliotheken*, Cassiciacum 20 (Würzburg 1966) 382 notes that many manuscripts falsely ascribe Hugh of Ripelin's *Compendium* to the Augustinian Thomas of Strasbourg, as did Denys. For the titles of William of Paris (Auvergne) cited by Denys, see Friedrich Stegmüller, *Repertorium commentariorum in Sententias Petri Lombardi*, 2 vols. (Würzburg 1947) 1.127–129 no. 284. For the Franciscan Durandus of Champagne (Durandus Campanus, fl. 1340s) and his *Summa collectionum pro confessionibus audiendis*, see *Histoire littéraire de la France* 30 (Paris 1888) 302–333, and Johannes Dietterle, "Die Summa confessorum (sive de casibus conscientiae) . . . II: Die Summae confessorum des 14. und 15. Jahrhunderts bis zum Supplementum des Nicolaus ab Ausmo," *Zeitschrift für Kirchengeschichte* 27 (1906) 70–83. Denys's library in Roermond did not own any of these summas. Interestingly, however, Nicholas of Cusa, from whom Denys may have borrowed books, owned copies of William of Paris's *Tractatus de fide et legibus, De poenitentia*, John of Freiburg's *Summa confessorum*, Raymond of Pennafort's *Summa de casibus*, and the *Summa Pisanella*; see J. Marx, *Verzeichnis der Handschriften-Sammlung des Hospitals zu Cues bei Bernkastel a. /Mosel* (Trier 1905) 94–96, 259–260, and 264–268, MSS 94, 266, 273, 275.

X

Henry of Friemar.[50] In his *Protestatio ad superiorem suum*, Denys avers that he has read "the whole of the law—canon and civil—as much as was worthwhile" for him.[51] Throughout his moral writings he extracts materials from the sources of civil and canon law, and in some writings (on simony, benefices, the status of general councils, etc.) legal materials are especially prominent. It is evident, however, that he pillaged many of the Scholastic and legal materials found in his moral works from the "popular" moral summas—especially, it would seem, from the *Summa* of John of Freiburg— where they were already conveniently digested.[52] But he just as often quotes from the *originalia* of the Scholastic doctors, from whose works he was gathering texts for his commentaries on the *Sentences* throughout his career.[53] The sources I have mentioned are not all.

The leading authority in Denys's *Summa* is Thomas Aquinas, whose writings, especially the *Summa theologiae*, he cites directly: "All of these things are expressed copi-

[50]Denys used the works of Cassian and Climacus directly; he had already made his "translation" of the works of Cassian about 1450, and his commentary on Climacus about 1453 (n. 1 above) vols. 27–28; Stoelen (n. 23 above) 433; Emery (n. 3 above) 121.229–230 nos. 52–53, 121A.447–448 n. 5. Likewise, David of Augsburg's *De profectu religiosorum* is cited and extracted directly. Bernard of Clairvaux is another matter; he is cited and quoted often, but there are seldom references to titles. Denys himself speaks of a *Flores Bernardi*. Brian Patrick McGuire, "Denys of Ryckel's Debt to Bernard of Clairvaux," in *Die Ausbreitung kartäusischen Lebens und Geistes im Mittelalter*, Analecta Cartusiana 63/1 (1990) 13–34, suggests that Denys probably used a florilegium of Bernard, but also knew original texts. In *Summa* 2 a.40 (n. 1 above) 39.228B–D', Denys quotes from "tractatu illo notabili de Decem praeceptis, qui incipit, Audi, Israel," by Henry of Friemar. See Morton W. Bloomfield et al., *Incipits of Latin Works on the Virtues and Vices, 1100–1500 A.D. . . .* (Cambridge, Mass. 1979) 59 no. 0526; Bertrand-Georges Guyot, "Quelques aspects de la typologie des commentaires sur le *Credo* et le *Décalogue*," in *Les genres* (n. 26 above) 244–248. Nicholas of Cusa owned three copies of this text; see Marx (n. 49 above) 6–7, 70–74, and 101, MSS 7, 64, 100.

[51]Denys, *Protestatio* (n. 1 above) 1.lxxi.

[52]To many materials drawn from Raymond of Pennafort, John of Freiburg added selections from the Dominican masters, Thomas Aquinas, Peter of Tarantaise, Albert the Great, and Ulrich of Strasbourg. Bartholomew of Pisa and Durandus of Champagne, in turn, took materials from John's *Summa*. In the following places in his *Summa*, Denys seems to refer to Thomas and other doctors as reported in the summas of John of Freiburg, Bartholomew of Pisa, or Durandus of Champagne: "Thomas loco praeallegato, Joannes quoque in Summa confessorum, et Bartholomaeus in Summa Pisana, conscribunt" (1 a.32, Denys [n. 1 above] 39.75D'). Cf. 1 a.12 (35D), 1 a.21 (53D), 1 a.34 (78B, A'–B'), 1 a.40 (85C), 1 a.81 (142D), 1 a.86 (153C–D). Denys several times cites the *Quodlibeta* of Thomas Aquinas (1 a.10, 2 aa.8–9; 294B–D', 321C–C'), which is another sign suggesting that he plundered John of Freiburg's *Summa*; see Leonard E. Boyle, "The Quodlibets of St. Thomas and Pastoral Care," *The Thomist* 38 (1974) 232–256, esp. 252–256. A summary formula, resonant of the style of his intermediary sources, indicates that Denys extracted from excerpts of the "authentic doctors" found in popular moral summas: "De qua re S. Thomas in secunda secundae . . . tractat, Albertus quoque in diversis tractatibus; ceterisque doctores in Summis suis satis concorditer scribunt" (1 a.3; 313C).

[53]Denys's commentaries on the *Sentences* were put together finally between 1459 and 1464. In these he begins nearly every question with extracts or reports from Thomas's *Scriptum* and *Summa theologiae*. In his first three treatises on the gifts on the Holy Spirit (n. 1 above) 35.155–246, written in 1430, Denys extracts directly from the works of Thomas and Bonaventure; in the fourth treatise, compiled in 1446, he adds more extracts from Bonaventure, Albert the Great, Peter of Tarantaise, and Durandus of St. Pourçain, and mentions that he has also read Alexander of Hales on the gifts (ibid. 247–262). These are precisely the Scholastics who figure in the *Summa de vitiis et virtutibus*. See also the list of Scholastic doctors in the *Protestatio* of the 1440s (ibid. 1.lxxi). For now, I conclude that in the *Summa*, where the citation and text suggest it, Denys is using the "original" text. And this is most often the case for citations to Thomas Aquinas. But when Denys extracts from Scholastic "originals," and when he extracts from "popular summas" in his moral works, will need to be distinguished in the *apparatus fontium* of critical editions.

ously in the Summas of the doctors, of Durandus, John and others, but I cite Thomas more often because he is a famous and holy teacher."[54] Although he sometimes differs decisively from Thomas and corrects him on a number of speculative issues,[55] in moral matters he seldom departs from the "holy doctor" *(doctor sanctus)*.

Denys's preference may reflect in part the special authority Thomas's pastoral teaching enjoyed in the fifteenth century, especially in Germany and the Low Countries. Cardinal Nicholas of Cusa promoted pastoral *opuscula* written by Thomas and recommended their use by parish priests, and his prescription was enacted in provincial councils (1451–1452).[56] Denys's preference for Thomas's moral teaching, however, has more intrinsic grounds: the conviction that human moral behavior must have a rational foundation. Moreover, Denys seems to have received the moral teaching of the *Summa theologiae* in the manner Thomas probably intended, as a strengthening—and sometimes correction—of the pedagogy of older moral summas.[57] Thus, for example, having recited Peraldus's vivid account of the evils of dancing, Bridget of Sweden's damning revelations about it, and James of Varazze's forceful condemnations, Denys refers to Thomas's teaching on licit recreation *(eutrapelia)* in order to argue that dancing is not always a mortal sin, although most times it is. He thus advises that one should be careful about preaching that dancing is always a mortal sin. Those who dance will probably not stop, whatever is preached to them; consequently, if they continue to dance thinking it a mortal sin, it will indeed be so, even in those instances when it would otherwise be only venial.[58]

Denys disagrees with Thomas on at least one crucial point of *moralia*, however. On the conscience, Denys says, Thomas speaks elegantly, as "a man truly and specially illumined by God." Thomas argues correctly that conscience obliges, not by its own power, but in virtue of divine precept, that is, insofar as one thinks something should be done or avoided because it is commanded or prohibited by God. Denys, however, withdraws from Thomas's conclusion that even an erring conscience obliges, and he disagrees flatly with the opinion that, in indifferent matters, the dictate of an erring conscience binds more than the command of a prelate. With Bonaventure, Denys argues that in all doubtful and indifferent matters one should always prefer the judgment of his superior to his own, for the authority of a superior is more evidently founded in law and divine precept than the dictate of a doubtful conscience. If one

[54]Denys, *De vita curatorum* a.12 (n. 1 above) 37.238A'.

[55]See Emery (n. 5 above) 120–123, 125–128; Kent Emery, Jr., "Did Denys the Carthusian also Read Henricus Bate?" *Bulletin de philosophie médiévale* 32 (1990) 196–206; idem, "*Sapientissimus Aristoteles* and *Theologicissimus Dionysius*: The Reading of Aristotle and the Understanding of Nature in Denys the Carthusian," in *Miscellanea Mediaevalia* 21/2: *Mensch und Natur im Mittelalter*, ed. Andreas Spear and Albert Zimmermann (Berlin 1992) 572–606; and idem (n. 14 above).

[56]Erich Meuthen, "Thomas von Aquin auf den Provinzialkonzilien zu Mainz und Köln 1451 und 1452," in *Köln, Stadt und Bistum in Kirche und Reich des Mittelalters: Festschrift für Odilo Engels zum 65. Geburtstag*, ed. Hanna Vollrath and Stefan Weinfurter (Cologne 1993) 641–658.

[57]Leonard E. Boyle, O.P., *The Setting of the "Summa theologiae" of St. Thomas*, Etienne Gilson Series 5 (Toronto 1982). See also René-Antoine Gauthier, O.P., intro. to *St. Thomas d'Aquin: Somme contre les Gentils* (Paris 1993) 173–174.

[58]Denys, *Summa* 1 aa.80–81 (n. 1 above) 39.140–144B; Aquinas, ST 2a2ae q.168 a.2. Denys also cites opinions of Albert the Great (in the *Summa Pisana*) and Durandus of Champagne, confirming that dancing is not always a mortal sin. Denys's monastery owned a copy of James of Varazze's *Sermones de sanctis*: see Lucidius Verschueren, O.F.M., *De Bibliotheek der Kartuizers van Roermond* (Tilburg 1941) 50 no. 53.

could always refuse obedience on the ground of conscience, he would often excuse and deceive himself. One's obligation toward an erring conscience is to reform it.[59]

Denys's disagreement with Thomas serves his rigorous interpretation of the maxim that "ignorance of the law is no excuse." "Ignorance of the law" means ignorance of what pertains to one's specific condition in life, profession, or vocation. Ignorance of a fact may be excused, but only ignorance of an unusual fact, the knowledge of which is hard to come by.[60] For this reason the people should be diligently instructed, lest they have an erroneous conscience or be ignorant of the precepts, statutes, and ordinances pertaining to their vocation and state in life; these they must come to love, and they must seek eagerly to hear, inquire, and learn about them.[61]

In two articles of his *Summa de virtutibus*, Denys outlines his whole program of preaching materials. His words point to many titles of his writings, and indicate the extent to which *praedicabilia* constitute his corpus. In the article entitled "Certain general documents appropriately mixed into every sermon," he says that all those things that concern charity, piety, and the avoidance of vice pertain to every Christian. All must be exhorted to fervent love, mutual charity, peace, the spiritual and corporal works of mercy, patience, justice, the progress of the virtues, and so on. So that he may more fully persuade his hearers, the preacher of the heavenly word must impress in his memory the authorities of Scripture, refer to them often in his sermons, and inculcate them in the hearts of his listeners. For this purpose, the authorities and exhortations of Saint Paul are especially apt. Paul mixes these in his Epistles, with variations in the order and form of words. At this point, Denys provides a small collection of Paul's exhortations.[62] Denys says further that, in every sermon, the faithful should be exhorted to consider mutual charity and peace, the last things, the recollection of the Passion, the benefits bestowed upon creatures by God, the avoidance of mortal sin, the fruitful use of time, the daily examination of conscience, the custody of heart, and the progress of the virtues.[63] These topics correspond directly to a number of works Denys wrote, some originally intended for novices and a monastic audience, but each containing materials "preachable" to all and any: *De gaudio spirituali*, *De pace interna*, *De quatuor novissimis*, *De modo recordationis dominicae Passionis*, *De munificentia et beneficiis Dei*, *De fructuosa temporis deductione*, *De custodia cordis et profectu spirituali*, and *De remediis tentationum*.[64]

[59]Denys, *Summa* 2 a.48 (n. 1 above) 39.238C-D'. In *2 Sent.* d.39 q.3 (ibid. 22.523B'-528D'), where he addresses the question, "Whether conscience binds or obliges, whether correct or erroneous?" Denys recites the opinions of Alexander of Hales, Bonaventure, and Henry of Ghent and sets them against Thomas (and Peter of Tarantaise) on this point.

[60]Denys, *Summa* 2 a.48 (n. 1 above) 39.239B-C.

[61]*Summa* 2 a.48 (ibid. 238C-D'); Denys, *De doct. et reg.* prooem. (ibid. 500-501).

[62]Denys, *Summa* 2 a.50 (ibid. 240D'-241B'). At the beginning of the *Summa*, 1 aa.3-5 (ibid. 507B-514C), Denys makes a number of small scriptural collections, "ex apostolicis documentis, ex Epistolis Pauli, ex Evangelio," and at the end (514C) adds: "Ad ista insuper comprobanda possent ex Epistolis beatorum Jacobi ac Joannis plura induci, quorum iam sententia competenter est tacta; quae et infra suis poterunt locis commemorari." For a manuscript containing "collections" of linked texts, topically arranged, from Paul, the canonical Epistles, Acts, the four Gospels, the Apocalypse and the Wisdom books, the first of which (and perhaps others) was composed by Denys, see Kent Emery, Jr., "Copyists, Text-Collectors and Authors in Some Late Medieval Monastic Manuscripts," forthcoming. The collections are said to be "useful for preachers."

[63]Denys, *Summa* 2 a.50 (n. 1 above) 39.241C'-D'.

[64]*De gaudio* and *De pace* are printed as one work (Denys [n. 1 above] 40.503-581; see Emery [n. 3 above] 121.247 nos. 138-139); *De quatuor novissimis*, written between 1455 and 1459 (Denys 41.489-594; Emery

It is especially important that every Christian know what sin is, the various reasons why it is abominable, its effects, and the differences between mortal and venial sin. Articles 3–22 of the *Summa de vitiis* treat these topics; the same materials are expanded or contracted in corresponding articles of a separate treatise entitled *De gravitate et enormitate peccati*.[65]

The article in the *Summa de virtutibus* concerning "general documents" for preaching is followed by another, entitled "How diverse sorts of people must be instructed diversely." This article draws attention to one of the most significant features of Denys's body of preaching materials. His writings represent an extraordinary late medieval flourishing of the sermons *ad status* tradition.[66] Denys's very habit of thinking is especially congenial to this kind of literary work. In his Scholastic works, he thinks in terms of "essential definitions," a way of thinking that accounts for many of his differences from his early "patron," Thomas Aquinas.[67] Johan Huizinga perceptively remarked Denys's habit of conceiving natural and social realities in terms of distinct "entities" and "essences."[68] Likewise, I believe, this style of thinking led him to conceive moral teaching as an art, whereby sets of specific rules are generated from general principles or maxims. His model sermon sequences are divided generically, *ad saeculares* and *ad religiosos*.[69] The *Summa de vitiis et virtutibus* treats the general moral

---

121.249 no. 147); *De munificentia*, written ca. 1430–1435 (Denys 34.291–325; Emery 121.233 no. 67); *De fructuosa* (Denys 40.51–71; Emery 121.245 no. 128); *De custodia* (Denys 40.467–502; Emery 121.247 no. 137); *De remediis*, written ca. 1455 (Denys 40.117–189; Emery 121.246 no. 132). For the dates, see Stoelen (n. 23 above) 433–434. The work entitled *De modo recordationis dominicae passionis*, mentioned in old lists of Denys's writings, seems to be lost. Denys, however, wrote several other works on the Passion, and material concerning ways of meditating the Passion is distributed through several treatises. See Emery 121.129–131, 156–157. For works and subject matter that Denys recommended for novices, see Emery 121.36. Layfolk and religious novices share the first degree of charity; see below.

[65]Denys, *Summa* 1 a.3 (n. 1 above) 39.16B′–18A′ corresponds to *De gravitate* a.4 (ibid. 368C–369C); cf. *Summa* 1 a.8 (ibid. 28C–29B′) and *De gravitate* a.3 (ibid. 367C–368C); *Summa* 1 a.9 (ibid. 29C′–31C) condenses aa.5–9 of *De gravitate* (ibid. 369D–375B′); *Summa* 1 aa.10–14 (ibid. 31D–39A) correspond to aa.11–14, 17 of *De gravitate* (ibid. 376D–380B′, 382D′–384B); *Summa* 1 a.16 (ibid. 40D′–43B) corresponds to *De gravitate* a.19 (ibid. 387B′–388B′). The date of *De gravitate* is uncertain, but it seems to have been written before the *Summa*.

[66]On *ad status* sermon collections of the thirteenth century, see among others David L. d'Avray, "The Transformation of the Medieval Sermon," D.Phil. thesis (Oxford 1976) 134–211; Maria Corti, "Structures idéologiques et structures sémiotiques dans les sermones ad status du XIIIe siècle," in *Archéologie du signe*, Recueils d'études médiévales 3, ed. Lucie Brind'Amour and Eugene Vance (Toronto 1983) 143–163. D'Avray (n. 13 above) 127 notes that "major *ad status* collections are few in number" (notably, Jacques de Vitry, Humbert of Romans, and Guibert of Tournai), and Martin (n. 26 above) 396–401 speaks of "l'éclipse relative des sermons 'ad status' " in the later Middle Ages. Rusconi (n. 26 above) 84 makes a suggestive remark concerning the relationship between the *casus* organization of the moral summas and the conception of the sermons *ad status*: "Cet aménagement progressif des *Summae* pénitentielles selon les répartitions juridiques des *casus* correspond à l'aménagement d'un modèle social totalisant analogue à celui qui s'épanouit dans les *sermones ad status*, le nouveau genre de prédication en vogue durant les premières décennies du XIIIe siècle." The relation is certainly evident in Denys.

[67]Emery (n. 5 above) 125–127.

[68]J(ohan) Huizinga, *The Waning of the Middle Ages*, trans. F. Hopman (New York 1954) 209–210, 215–216, 220–221, 264.   *

[69]D'Avray (n. 13 above) 123–126 concludes that generally "the line between clerical and popular preaching was a faint one, easy to cross when a model sermon collection was being put together . . . ; model sermon collections were a multi-purpose genre, which could provide reading matter for clerics and sermons to be preached to them as well as sermons for lay congregations." Denys's strict generic distinction would thus seem to be less common, although typical for him for reasons stated here and elsewhere in the essay.

teaching that underlies all preaching. The greater part of Denys's other preaching materials are defined specifically, *ad status*. In the *Summa*, Denys states that each person must be informed about what specially pertains to his state in life. Hence, one must instruct married people about how they must behave in seeking and rendering the debt of the flesh, how they must behave with mutual love, how they can perform the marriage act without sin, the reciprocal obligations between husband and wife, and so on. We shall see that instruction on marriage holds a pivotal place in all moral instruction. Likewise, parents must be instructed on their duties to their children, children on their duties to their parents, the commonfolk must learn their duties to their spiritual and secular superiors, and ecclesiastical and civil rulers, judges, and princes must also be instructed in their responsibilities. At this point, Denys remarks: "Concerning these special documents, however, I shall not prosecute further in a special manner, because I have already written about them specially in other places *(aliis locis)*, especially in the treatise *De regimine curatorum*, and in the book *De laudabili vita coniugatorum"* (both written before 1450).[70]

The two titles to which Denys refers embrace the moral life in a general way, showing, on the one hand, what a pastor must know in order to instruct his flock, and, on the other hand, what layfolk—whose condition is defined generically by the state of marriage—must learn.[71] Denys defines the particular duties and "rules" of various states of life with more specific difference in a series of other treatises. Logically, these treatises derive first from the general teaching of the *Summa de vitiis et virtutibus*, and thence from the subgeneric *De regimine curatorum* and *De laudabili vita coniugatorum*. Thus, in individual treatises Denys treats the rule of life for bishops and other prelates, for archdeacons, canons, legates, monastic visitors, princes, princesses, nobles, civil rulers, soldiers, merchants, and for the special states superior to marriage, virgins and widows.[72] These do not include his treatises on the monastic life in general and

---

[70]Denys, *Summa* 2 a.51 (n. 1 above) 39.241D'–242C'. Stoelen (n. 23 above) 434 says that *De vita et regimine curatorum* ([n. 1 above] 37.217–336) and *De laudabili vita coniugatorum* (ibid. 38.55–117) were written before 1450, the first of Denys's series of lives *ad status*. See Emery (n. 3 above) 121.236–237 no. 91, 238 no. 99.

[71]In his preface to the *Sermones de tempore ad saeculares* (n. 1 above) 29.1, Denys states the reciprocal relation between pastor and flock. The chief duty of the curate is to illumine his charges about what pertains to salvation, what they ought to do and to avoid, etc. In turn, the layperson must seek out the law from the priest, learn the precepts and documents of divine law, and acquire information about every ambiguity and perplexity. The pastor must know the intricacies of moral teaching, and layfolk must acquire a casuistic sense.

[72]Stoelen does not specify the date or sequence of Denys's various *Vitae*. In *De doct. et reg.* (n. 1 above) 39.523D, 526A, 530B, 533B', 558A, 569D', Denys refers to the following works, indicating that they were written between ca. 1450 (the date of *De vita curatorum* and *De vita coniugatorum*) and ca. 1455 (the date of *De doct. et reg.*): *De vita et regimine archidiaconorum* (ibid. 37.111–162); *De vita et regimine praesulum* (37.7–110; mentioned in *De vita archidiac.* 37.154B); *De vita canonicorum*, *De vita et regimine principum*, *Directorium vitae nobilium* (37.163–207, 373–497, 519–563, 565–583); *De regimine politiae* (38.7–54); *De vita militarium* (37.565–583; cites *De reg. pol.* and *De vita et reg. princ.*, 581B). The last three treatises appear to extract appropriate materials from the more comprehensive *De vita et reg. princ.* The following, not mentioned in *De doct. et reg.*, would seem to have been written after 1455: *De regimine praelatorum* (37.59–110); *De laudabili vita virginum* (38.157–178); *De laudabili vita viduarum* (38.119–142); *De vita mercatorum et iusto pretio rerum Dialogus* (37.585–605). In *De doct. et reg.*, Denys gives no rules for virgins and widows, but does for merchants. Denys wrote *De vita et regimine principissae Dialogus* (37.499–518), dedicated to Isabella of Portugal, in 1467. The date of *De doctrina scholarium* (37.337–371) is uncertain. This work concerns the schooling of young boys, with an eye to a program of church

the solitary life of monks and nuns in particular.[73] The same materials, in expanded or abbreviated form, revolve through all of these treatises, as appropriate and as the general topic heading requires. Moreover, they are reduced to precepts, ordinances, or *regulae* for every state in life in *De doctrina et regulis vitae christianorum*. And that is not all. The same materials are expanded or abbreviated from "places" in Denys's *Sentences* commentary or scriptural commentaries, and they are woven into individual sermons in the model sequences.

How Denys locates and recycles texts is illustrated by his movement of materials on marriage from one work, treatise, or sermon to another. The proper use of the marriage act, the reciprocal duties of husband and wife, and parents' responsibilities toward their children are subjects treated amply in *De vita coniugatorum*; this material about marriage is reduced in *De vita curatorum*, as just one of the items about which lay people should be instructed; likewise it is reduced in the treatises for princes and nobles, and codified in sets of rules in *De doctrina et regulis*. The storehouse for materials concerning the nature of marriage and its right use is Denys's commentary on 4 *Sentences* distinctions 26–31, where he recites, comments upon, and analyzes the arguments of many doctors.[74]

Denys expects married people to govern their sexual behavior with a philosophic self-control. In order for the conjugal act to be free from all veniality, both parties must be instructed in the fine points of its right use, during times of menstruation, of pregnancy, of religious holidays. Further, they must know the rules for determining when the act, should it be motivated by concupiscence, is mortal or venial. If it is not prudent to preach some of these matters publicly, the priest must communicate them privately, and married people, in turn, are obliged precisely to inquire about doubts of this kind. Ignorance of the law is no excuse.[75]

Denys himself demonstrates how his collected materials are useful for preaching. In his sermons on marriage, he simplifies and abbreviates the materials he has gathered on the subject in his commentaries, moral summas, *Vitae*, and special treatises. As

---

reform; see Harald Dickerhof, "Schule, religiöse Erziehung und Kirchenreform in den pädagogischen Schriften des Kartäusers Dionysius von Rijkel," in *Ecclesia Militans: Studien zur Konzilien und Reformationsgeschichte Remigius Bäumer zum 70. Geburtstag gewidmet* 2: *Zur Reformationsgeschichte*, ed. Walter Brandmüller et al. (Paderborn 1988) 17–51. For all of these works, see Emery (n. 3 above) 121.236–238 nos. 86–89, 91–101. The works entitled *De officio legati* and *De actu visitationis* are lost (see Emery 121.253 nos. 173–174).

[73] *De reformatione claustralium*, *De reformatione monialium*, *De vita et fine solitarii*, *De laude et commendatione vitae solitariae*, *De vita inclusarum*, *De professione monastica*; Denys (n. 1 above) 38.209–409, 547–582; Emery (n. 3 above) 121.239–240, 245 nos. 105–109, 126.

[74] Cf. Denys, *De vita coniugatorum* aa.5–14 ([n. 1 above] 38.62D–74C); *De vita curatorum* aa.31–32 (37.271B–277C'); *De vita principum* 2 aa.3–12 (37.418C–430D'); *Directorium nobilium* a.34 (37.560D–561B'); *De doct. et reg.* 2 aa.7–9 (39.536A–541D'). For his pastoral works, Denys especially adapts materials treated in *4 Sent.* d.26 q.1, "Whether marriage is a natural and licit work, and also an act of virtue, that may be exercised without sin?" (25.60A–63D'); d.31 q. unica, "Whether the three goods of marriage *(fides, proles, sacramentum)* can make the marriage act honest, and whether they sufficiently excuse it from all sin?" (ibid. 109C–113A'); d.32 q. unica, "Whether both married partners are required by precept to render the marriage debt to one another, irrespective of time; and if not, when they are obliged to do so, and when not?" (ibid. 116A–120A'). For a full study of Denys on marriage, see Hans-Günther Gruber, *Christliches Eheverständnis im 15. Jahrhundert: Eine moralgeschichtliche Untersuchung zur Ehelehre Dionysius' des Kartäusers*, Studien zur Geschichte der katholischen Moraltheologie 29 (Regensburg 1989).

[75] Denys, *Summa* 2 a.51 (n. 1 above) 39.241D'–242B.

X

stated, marriage defines the lay state generically; analogically it embraces the life of Christians in every estate. This is evident in the sermons for the Third Sunday after the Nativity, based on the Gospel text: "Nuptiae factae sunt in Cana" (John 2.1–11).[76] Denys's method in the sermon sequences is to expound the Epistle and Gospel of the day, and to explain them further by connecting or linking *(annectendo)* a series of sermons to them.[77] The base sermon for the Third Sunday after the Nativity is a homiletic, line-by-line commentary on the Gospel; Denys transposes it directly from his literal commentary on the Gospel of John. The remaining five sermons are based on the moralization of the text in that commentary.[78] The second sermon announces the theme of the threefold nuptials, the first matter treated in the commentary's moralization. According to the distinction, there are *nuptiae carnales, nuptiae spirituales*, and *nuptiae aeternales*, or the beatific fruition of the saints in heaven. The *nuptiae spirituales* are divided into the *nuptiae mysteriales*, or the marriage between the Word and human nature in the hypostatic union, and the *nuptiae gratiales seu internales*. These last are subdivided into three: the marriage between God and the church, or the *sponsa universalis*; between God and the individual soul, or the *sponsa particularis*; between God and the Virgin Mary, or the *sponsa singularis*.[79] These are the express terms of analysis in Denys's manifold commentary on the Canticle of Canticles.[80]

These distinctions generate the sermons that follow. The third sermon treats carnal, sacramental marriage, neatly abbreviating material stored in the commentary on the *Sentences*, codified in *De vita curatorum*, amplified in *De vita coniugatorum* and condensed in *De doctrina et regulis*.[81] The fourth sermon is the last *ad saeculares*. It lifts its distinction—the six water urns which Christ commanded to be filled—from the moralization in the scriptural commentary, but gives significations different from those found there. In this sermon the water urns signify, appropriately enough, six initial steps of the spiritual life: contrition, confession, satisfaction, forgiveness of injuries, the corporal and spiritual works of mercy, and prayer.[82]

Two sermons for religious on the same Gospel are also based on the moralization in the scriptural commentary. The first resumes the theme of the threefold nuptials,

[76]D. L. d'Avray and M. Tausche, "Marriage Sermons in *Ad status* Collections of the Central Middle Ages," *Archives d'histoire doctrinale et littéraire du Moyen Age* 47 (1980) 71–119, state that by "far the largest and most important genre of marriage sermons" is on this Gospel pericope (71). Denys develops nearly all of the *topoi* of marriage sermons mentioned by d'Avray and Tausche. He may well have read or used one of the famous *ad status* collections, but his similarity to them on this topic stems rather, I think, from common Scholastic and moral sources.
[77]See the prefaces to the sequences *ad saeculares* (Denys [n. 1 above] 29.3, 31.2). The sequences *ad religiosos* were made on the model of those *ad saeculares* (29.5,31.4).
[78]Denys, *3 Nativ. in Evangelium* (ibid. 29.182A–186A'); *In Joannem* a.7 (12.312B–317B').
[79]Denys, *3 Nativ. Sermo* 2 (ibid. 29.186A–188D').
[80]See Denys, *In Canticum Canticorum* prooem., a.4 (ibid. 7.291, 312D–313B).
[81]Denys, *3 Nativ. Sermo* 3 (ibid. 29.189A–193B'). The topics are the obligations of husband to wife and wife to husband; man as head of the wife; carnal, social, and spiritual love between spouses; the carnal debt and the three goods of marriage; when the marital act is free from sin, when mortal, when venial; times when the marital debt must and must not be rendered; fraternal correction. Cf. *De vita curatorum* a.31 (37.271B–274A'); *De vita coniugatorum* aa.5–6 (38.62D–65D); *De doct. et reg.* 2 aa.7–8 (39.536A–540A); *1 Sent.* d.26 q.1, d.31 q. unica, d.32 q. unica (25.61D–B', 62A–C, 110A'–112A', 117B–118A, 118D'–119D'). Denys's main source on the carnal debt is Thomas Aquinas.
[82]Denys, *3 Nativ. Sermo* 4 (ibid. 29.193B–195C').

appropriately focusing on the graceful, internal marriage between Christ and the *sponsa particularis*, or the individual soul. The final sermon resumes the theme of the six water urns, assigned the significations which they have in the moralization of the Gospel commentary. The urns signify the six powers of the soul, each filled with a twofold perfection of nature and grace.[83] Denys's preaching materials merely touch things which a preacher can develop more amply.[84] Accordingly, in this model sermon the urns signify the outline of a sixfold ascent to mystical union fully developed in *De contemplatione*. The sermon's formulas of the relations between nature and grace are derived from pages of argumentation in Denys's commentary on the *Sentences*.

In his sermon concerning carnal and sacramental marriage, Denys adduces "documents" from Augustine, which state that a wife must correct her husband if she knows him to be an adulterer, even though he is her head. She must first try to persuade her husband by charitable admonishing, then by sharp scolding; if these fail, she should invoke the coercion and intervention of church authorities and have recourse to the advice of holy men, and to God by prayer. Augustine provides a model dialogue between wife and husband in such circumstances:

> *Husband*: We are men, you are a woman.
> *Wife*: If you are a man, conquer your libido.
> *Husband*: We are lords, you are helpmeets.
> *Wife*: A man does not have the power over his body, but the wife does (1 Cor. 7.4).
> *Husband*: We are the heads, you are the members.
> *Wife*: If you are the head, do not wish to go where you do not wish your members to follow.[85]

Fraternal correction and avoiding rash, incautious judgment are likewise major themes of Denys's moral teaching and preaching. Indeed, for Denys fraternal correction and preaching are nearly synonymous. As the little dialogue between husband and wife suggests, those in every state of life—inferiors as well as superiors—are obliged to practice this form of "preaching" when necessary. Denys recycles throughout his corpus materials he has gathered on fraternal correction.[86] Fraternal correction is a universal precept of the evangelical law: it binds superiors in justice and subordinates in charity. Prelates must enact the precept with their subordinates, pastors with their flock, princes with their subjects, parents with their children, teachers with their students, and religious among themselves. Denys wishes everyone to correct and preach to everyone else, for the universal perfection of the body of Christ. Since one who would correct another must be worthy of doing so, and all must receive correction gladly, reciprocal charity will govern human relations and all will therefore advance

[83]Denys, *3 Nativ. Sermones* 6–7 (ibid. 29.198A–202B); *In Joannem* a.7 (12.317B–B').

[84]In *De doct. et reg.* 2 a.4 (ibid. 39.530D), Denys says that Jan Brugman "dumtaxet petiit tangi quae sibi in sermocinationibus suis amplius potuerunt deservire."

[85]Denys, *3 Nativ. Sermo* 3 (ibid. 29.192C'–193B). Denys cites (pseudo?) Augustine "in libro quinquagesimo Homiliarum."

[86]Special articles concerning fraternal correction and avoiding rash judgment are found in Denys, *Summa* 1 a.89, 2 a.41 (ibid. 39.156D'–160B', 229A–230D'); *De vita praesulum* a.31, *De reg. praelatorum* aa.17–19, *De vita curatorum* a.33, *De vita principum* 2 a.2 (37.43C–44A', 85D–89D', 277C'–280C', 416C'–418C); *De reg. politiae* a.13, *De vita coniugatorum* a.19 (38.26D'–27A, 83A'–84A); *De doctrina scholarium* aa.8–9, 19 (37.349D'–352D, 361D'–363C); *De vita et fine solitarii* 1 a.34, *De laude et commendatione vitae solitariae* a.36, *In Tertiam Regulam S. Francisci* a.38 (38.289B–290D', 361B–362C', 498D'–500D).

toward perfection. Sometime before he wrote his *Vitae*, Denys collected a special treatise on this subject, *De modo iudicandi et corripiendi*.[87] The scriptural texts he gathers for this theme derive from the scriptural commentaries, where they are expounded accordingly, and they are expanded again in the appropriate sermons.[88] In every context, Denys quotes approvingly William of Auxerre's opinion that nearly the whole world perishes for two reasons, fornication or the failure to fulfill the precept of fraternal correction.[89]

In two treatises *De simonia*, which sparked a widespread controversy involving his Carthusian brethren and the faculties of theology and both laws at the University of Cologne, Denys did not fail to correct the opinions of his former teacher at the university. He in turn was criticized, not only for his determination of the question at issue, but for his deficiencies on points of fraternal correction.[90]

THE SPECULATIVE FORM OF DENYS'S MORAL TEACHING

For the purpose of reducing materials scattered throughout his writings to a series of general precepts for every Christian and then to special precepts for each state of Christian life, in *De doctrina et regulis vitae christianorum* Denys adopts an old instrument of topical logic, the *regula*, or maxim-like principle around which many particulars can be organized and a body of knowledge ordered. According to its sense in the writings of Cicero, Quintilian, and Boethius, and as developed by medieval theologians, the *regula* is a standard against which one may measure the rectitude of thought, speech, or human behavior. Medieval jurists organized particular laws and statutes around *regulae*, or summarizing general principles, from which they could draw arguments and which served to test the sense and application of a law to cases and circumstances.[91] In Denys's treatise, the rules at once gauge the scope of materials on any special topic for the preacher and serve as standards of moral behavior for those to whom he

[87]Denys, *De modo iudicandi et corripiendi* (ibid. 40.7–49); Emery (n. 3 above) 121.243 no. 121. This work, written in the 1440s, predates the series of *Vitae*, the *Summa* and *De doct. et reg.*, and the completion of the sermon sequences (it is mentioned in *De vita curatorum*, 37.280C'). It is the original storehouse for material on the topic.

[88]Among Denys's *Sermones de tempore* are several that treat fraternal correction or rash judgment especially: *3 Adv. Sermones* 1, 4 ([n. 1 above] 29.68D–70B', 81A–83D'); *4 Trin. Sermones* 4, 6–7, *15 Trin. Sermo* 5, *22 Trin. Sermo* 3 (30.214A–218A', 220A–225D', 456A–458C', 594A–596D'). Materials concerning the topics are inserted in sermons for the feasts of St. Nicholas, St. Stephen, St. Vincent, the Chair of Peter (31.36D–37B, 178D–D', 294A–C', 350D'–351D); and for Rogation days, the Ascension, the Visitation, St. Mary Magdalene, St. Luke, St. Martin, the Dedication of a Church (32.74D'–75B', 92B–93A, 237A–A', 264A'–265A, 497A'–C', 564C–B', 693B'–D'). The subject is treated throughout the scriptural commentaries. In *4 Sent.* d.19 q. unica, Denys collects new materials on fraternal correction (24.528B–533C) from the *Sentences* commentaries of Albert, Thomas, Richard of Middleton, and the *Quodlibeta* of Henry of Ghent. Here he refers to several of his *Vitae* and his treatise *De modo iud. et corr.* (ibid. 531B–C).

[89]Denys, *Summa* 1 a.21, 2 a.41 (ibid. 39.54A–B, 230A'–C'). Cf. William of Auxerre, *Summa aurea* 3 tract. 53 c. 1, ed. Jean Ribaillier, Spicilegium Bonaventurianum 18B (Paris 1966) 1036–1038.

[90]Emery (n. 3 above) 121.207–217.

[91]I treat the rhetorical and theological notions of "rule" and "rectitude," and their ancient and medieval sources, in K. Emery, Jr., *Renaissance Dialectic and Renaissance Piety: Benet of Canfield's Rule of Perfection*, Medieval and Renaissance Texts and Studies 50 (Binghamton 1987) 43–44, 53–55, and passim. For the legal *regulae*, see Peter Stein, *Regulae iuris: From Juristic Rules to Legal Maxims* (Edinburgh 1966).

preaches. Their sententious expression serves the memory of both. The burden of knowledge is almost as great for any Christian as it is for the preacher, who must preach to every condition. Layfolk must know not only the general obligations pertaining to all, but the singular things they are obliged to by reason of their particular conditions in life.

Denys's rules are conceived "essentially," according to the specific differences of lives in the Body of Christ. Existentially, however, each Christian's life falls under several categories. One and the same person, for example, is obliged to some things insofar as he or she is a Christian, to others insofar as he is a prince or judge, to others insofar as he is the head of a family, to others insofar as he or she is married, and to yet others insofar as he or she is subject to a spiritual father and is a son or daughter of the church.[92] For this reason, under the ruling exemplar of each station of life, Denys subordinates precepts pertaining essentially, as governing standards, to other kinds of life and social roles.

Brief and succinct rules, Denys says, are the most instructive, most easily memorized and most fitting to moral teaching, which is the more nearly perfect the more it descends to particular conclusions.[93] In character with his speculative bent, Denys lays a metaphysical foundation for his rule-generating moral art. Both the general and particular rules of the moral life are established on the most universal principles, as Denys makes clear when treating the general definition of sin in his *Summa de vitiis*. According to Dionysius the Areopagite, sin is a withdrawal of the rational creature from a right ordination toward the creator. Right order requires that the lower be subordinated to the higher, and through the higher be reduced to its beatific end. Speaking of the angels in his book *De quatuor coaequaevis*, Albert the Great says that all sin deviates from the standard of right reason (*recta ratio*), "which is a participation of the eternal law and a seal of the light of the divine face." Likewise, Avicenna and Algazel in their *Metaphysics* say that a creature possesses the truth of its being insofar as it conforms to its institution, idea, and exemplary form in the divine mind. Anselm teaches this likewise in *De veritate*, as does Thomas Aquinas in the *Summa theologiae* and his own *De veritate*. A creature lives rightly, then, "insofar as his behavior or action accords with, and is assimilated to, the dictates or judgment of the eternal law, which bears witness to the origin, cause, institutor, measure, and rule of all justice, sanctity, and virtue." Rightly did Augustine praise the Platonists in Book 8 of *De civitate Dei* for discovering the correct order of relations among the "causa subsistendi, ratio intelligendi, et ordo vivendi," which correspond to natural, rational, and moral philosophy.[94]

Denys's teaching concerning the constitution of the human moral act in his Scholastic writings is thoroughly intellectualist.[95] The same understanding pervades his pastoral writings. The final beatitude one attains in the next life is proportionate to the degree of charity one attains in this life.[96] But, according to the natural workings of the soul,

[92]Denys, *De doct. et reg.* prooem. (n. 1 above) 39.500.
[93]Ibid. a.8 (ibid. 517B'–C').
[94]Denys, *Summa* 1 a.3 (ibid. 39.16B'–18A').
[95]A full study of the human moral act in Denys's writings is Norbert Maginot, *Der Actus humanus moralis unter dem Einfluss des Heiligen Geistes nach Dionysius Carthusianus*, Münchner theologische Studien 35 (Munich 1968).
[96]Denys, *De doct. et reg.* 1 a.8 reg. 3 (n. 1 above) 39.519A'.

the degree of love in the will is commensurate to the degree of understanding in the intellect: as Aristotle says, the will is moved by the good known in the intellect. The strict relation between cognition and love that pertains in the natural order pertains throughout the supernatural order as well, in every degree of Christian living. Consequently, the exact scope of Denys's moral, pastoral, and homiletic writings must be defined in relation to the threefold hierarchical order of wisdom that he expounds throughout his works.

The philosophers exercised a natural wisdom, especially in their first "divine" philosophy (metaphysics), or "theology," as they called it. Christian Scholastic theologians practice a supernatural wisdom naturally acquired, which is a grace given for the benefit of others, whereby they reasonably explain and prove the truths revealed in sacred Scripture. The essential character of Scholastic theology, which deduces conclusions from the contents of revelation, does not require its practitioner to be in a state of sanctifying grace. Supernatural wisdom properly speaking, however, is a sanctifying grace; it is identical with the gift of wisdom and mystical theology.[97]

By natural reason, heroic ancient philosophers were able to discover the natural law and lead lives of true, naturally acquired virtue. The natural law discovered by reason is sufficient to indicate that God should be loved above all things. As Isaac Israelita says in his *Liber definitionum*, "The fame of God is sublime and most celebrated. Indeed, we know, read, or hear nothing about God except what is honorable, excellent, and lovable. If, therefore, we sometimes love something that we have never seen, about which by rumor alone we perceive something great, by how much more we should love God, concerning whom we have heard so many good things."[98] The happiness of the heroic philosopher, however, is confined to whatever happiness he can derive from a life of virtue in itself and from the limited philosophic contemplation of the first principle.[99]

The supernatural end above all natural scrutiny requires a proportionate means, supernatural grace. Denys rejects the opinion that grace, on the one hand, and the virtues and charity, on the other, are the same thing; like Thomas Aquinas and Bonaventure in the *Breviloquium*, he argues a real distinction between them. As a creature is constituted in its natural being through its substantial form, and then through acquired habits and powers it is prepared for its natural operations, so the rational creature is constituted in its deiform supernatural being through sanctifying grace, which it then exercises in the virtues and gifts. Grace establishes the creature in a new ontological relation to its creator. Thus Bonaventure says that as the productive principle gives natural life to the creature's first being and second act or operation, so the restorative principle of grace gives to the spirit its *esse gratuitum* or *esse spirituale*, which flows into its operations by way of various habits and gifts. The subject of grace, then, is the essence of the rational soul, not one of its distinct faculties or powers, which are rather the subjects of the virtues.[100]

---

[97]I have treated this scheme in Denys's works: Emery (n. 5 above) 108–113 and passim, (n. 16 above) 377–378, and (n. 14 above) 328–329.

[98]Denys, *Summa* 2 aa.7, 13 (n. 1 above) 39.171D–B', 182B'–C'. Cf. J. T. Muckle, ed., "Isaac Israeli: Liber de definicionibus," *Archives d'histoire doctrinale et littéraire du Moyen Age* 11 (1937–1938) 326–327 (and 305?).

[99]Emery (n. 5 above) 117–123, and idem, "Henricus Bate" (n. 55 above).

[100]Denys, *Summa* 2 a.1 ([n. 1 above] 39.161C'–163A). Aquinas, ST 1a2ae q.110 aa.2–3; Bonaventure,

X

Faith is a cognitive virtue, its subject the faculty of intellect, which thence moves the will to commensurate love and charity. "Faith is a ray of the first uncreated truth, the seed *(inchoatio)* of the future beatific vision, the eye of the mind, directing it so that it may know toward what it should order all of its works and in what it ought to fix its intention."[101] Faith bestows upon the intellect a habit of cognition higher than discursive reason, whereby it may consent to things that transcend reason "by an intuition of God and by the authority of Scripture."[102]

The theological science that derives from Scripture and explains faith is essentially speculative. In one of the preliminary questions to his commentary on the *Sentences*, Denys recites opinions of several doctors concerning the *forma tractandi* of sacred Scripture. Among his selections, he includes an influential argument of Alexander of Hales. Whereas the manner of the natural sciences is "definitivus, divisivus et collectivus," as befits the comprehension of human reason, the manner of sacred Scripture, which Christian theology ought to follow, is poetic and rhetorical—"praeceptivus, exemplificativus, exhortativus, revelativus, orativus"—as befits its intention to excite affection and piety.[103] Alastair Minnis suggests that Alexander's treatment of the various *modus sacrae Scripturae*, addressed to men in various conditions under the law and in states of sin and grace, "lies behind the production and collection of 'sermons for different states.'"[104] This cannot be true regarding Denys's extensive *ad status* materials, for he rejects the conclusion upon which Alexander's teaching is based: that theology is an affective more than a speculative science.[105]

In another opinion reported by Denys, Bonaventure argues that a "modus perscrutatorius seu inquisitivus," as found in Peter Lombard's *Sentences*, is appropriate to theology. Such a manner of proceeding is useful for refuting arguments against the faith, for strengthening the faith of the weak by means of probable arguments, and for delighting the understanding of the perfect.[106] Significantly, Denys does not report Bonaventure's argument in the *Breviloquium* that the manner of sacred Scripture proceeds more by example, precept, exhortation, praise, blame, prohibition, and promise than by ratiocinative argument.[107] It is Thomas Aquinas, Denys says, who speaks most "beautifully" *(pulchre)* about Scripture's manner of discourse. Consistent with his conclusion that theology is a speculative science and with the teaching of Dionysius the

---

Breviloquium 5.4–6, in *Doctoris Seraphici S. Bonaventurae Opera omnia*, 11 vols. in 28 (Quaracchi 1882–1902) 5.256–260. In both the *Summa* (op. cit. 162A'–B') and *2 Sent.* d.26 q.1 (22.323B'–324B, 325D'–326B), Denys remarks an apparent difference in Bonaventure's teaching in the *Breviloquium* and in his commentary on the *Sentences*. See Bonaventure, *2 Sent.* d.27 q.2, *Opera* 2.656–658.

[101]Denys, *Summa* 2 a.6 (n. 1 above) 39.171B.

[102]The intellectual intuition bestowed by faith (and perfected by wisdom) gives one certainty "that" *(quia)* something is true, not the reason "why" *(propter quid)* something is true, or knowledge of its essence *(quid est)*. See Emery (n. 5 above) 128–129, (n. 16 above), and (n. 14 above) 347–348; and for the philosophic principle, Raymond Macken, "The Intellectual Intuition of God in the Philosophy of Denys the Carthusian," *Franziskanische Studien* 68 (1985) 237–246.

[103]Denys, *1 Sent.* praevia quaestiuncula (n. 1 above) 19.89A'–90A–D; see the *Summa Halensis* Tract. introduct. q.1 c.4 aa.1–3, in *Doctoris irrefragabilis Alexandri de Hales Summa theologica* 1 (Quaracchi 1924) 8–10.

[104]Minnis (n. 13 above) 119–138 at 137–138. Rusconi's remark (n. 66 above) seems more germane.

[105]Denys treats this topic in *1 Sent.* q. praevia 2 (n. 1 above) 19.67B'–74D'. See Emery (n. 16 above).

[106]Denys, *1 Sent.* praevia quaestiuncula (n. 1 above) 19.89A'–90A; Bonaventure, *1 Sent.* prooem. q.2 (n. 100 above) 1.10–11.

[107]Bonaventure, *Breviloquium* prol. 5 (n. 100 above) 5.206–207. See Minnis (n. 13 above) 127.

Areopagite, Thomas argues that the reason for the "poetic or symbolic or parabolic" manner of Scripture is more noetic than exhortatory: transcendent divine wisdom must proportion itself to the capacity of human reason, which understands by means of sensible realities. Further, according to a threefold scheme similar to Bonaventure's, Thomas says that Scripture provides different models of theological discourse. When theology intends to refute error, it argues by way of authorities, reasons, and "natural similitudes." Likewise, it is "argumentative" when it serves contemplation of the truth; the scriptures sometimes adopt this mode, and it may be observed "in the original writings of the saints, and in the Book of *Sentences*, which, as it were, conflates these writings." When theology intends to instruct morals, it adopts a manner "praeceptivus, comminatorius et promissivus, et narrativus exemplorum."[108] Denys follows Thomas's scheme in his moral and preaching works; although these are based on Scholastic teaching, he does not speak *scholastice* in them, but rather addresses the various states of Christian life with precepts, rules, exhortations, and examples.

Alexander of Hales distinguishes the natural, philosophic "science perfecting cognition according to truth," which operates by means of intellectual sight, and the Christian theological "science moving the affection to the good," which operates by means of an affective savor that produces virtue.[109] Denys disputes both parts of the distinction. Neither theological science nor philosophic wisdom necessarily includes affection, nor do they necessarily induce charity or love in the will. Moreover, philosophic wisdom, in its own order, as much as theological science provides reasons and motives for loving God above all. The "more elegant philosophers" were not satisfied with naked cognition alone, as may be proved by many statements of Aristotle, Plato, the Platonists, Avicenna, Algazel, and others. As a grace given for the benefit of others, theological science can be possessed by good and bad alike, as experience proves. In itself, theology is a science that is unformed: it is not always joined to charity, nor does it necessarily inflame the soul, include affection, or possess internal savor. Scholastic theology in itself, therefore, is as unformed and naked as the "theology" of the philosophers. For both philosophers and Scholastic theologians alike, that one ought to love God above all is an inference made by reason that must be enacted by a separate act of will, according to the distinction of powers in the soul. Love of God, then, is not something inseparable from knowledge of God, as Alexander and others imply when they say that Christian theology, as distinguished from natural wisdom, is an affective science.[110]

In contrast, the gift of supernatural wisdom, identical with mystical theology and contemplation, necessarily engenders charity in the will. The gift of wisdom, bestowed upon the intellect, is essentially speculative and distinct from the virtue of charity,

---

[108]Denys, *1 Sent.* praevia quaestiuncula (n. 1 above) 19.90D–91A; Aquinas, *1 Sent.* prol. q.1 a.5, in *Scriptum super libros Sententiarum*, ed. R. P. Mandonnet, 1 (Paris 1929) 17–18. Denys too saw his Scholastic commentaries as serving contemplation; see Emery (n. 5 above) and idem (n. 14 above).

[109]Denys, *1 Sent.* q. praev. 2 (n. 1 above) 19.68C′–69B; Alexander of Hales, *Summa* Tract. introduct. q.1 c.4 a.1 (n. 103 above) 1.8.

[110]Denys, *1 Sent.* q. praev. 2 ([n. 1 above] 19.72D′–73D′). Denys sums up those with whom he disagrees (and whose opinions he has recited): "Ostensum est enim, qualiter secundum Aegidium et Albertum, theologia sit scientia affectiva; et quod secundum Alexandrum, sit cognitio non solum illuminans intellectum, sed etiam accendens affectum; et quod secundum Bonaventuram ac Petrum, includit notitiam et affectum. Quibus videtur repugnare quod dictum est supra, hanc sapientiam seu theologiam esse donum gratiae gratis datae, ita quod bonis et malis potest inesse" (ibid. 72D′–73A).

bestowed upon the will. But the two are inseparably joined; charity is the necessary complement and completion of the cognition granted by the gift of wisdom.[111] All Christians in a state of grace partake the gift of wisdom and the virtue of charity in some degree.

There is, moreover, a hierarchical threefold order of charity exactly proportionate to the threefold order of the gift of supernatural wisdom. In *De doctrina et regulis*, because he had already "collected" a special treatise on the subject, Denys passes over briefly the gifts of the Holy Spirit, concerning which "many beautiful things can be said."[112] In his earlier treatise on the gifts, he elaborates the threefold order of the supernatural gift of wisdom that engenders a threefold order of charity. The first degree of the gift of wisdom, pertaining to beginners, enables one to judge created realities rightly in relation to God, and to dispose and regulate human and external affairs according to divine laws, precepts, and counsels. The second degree, pertaining to the proficient, enables one to spurn all the allurements of the flesh and delights of the world, and to endeavor to fix all of one's powers "in the clear and savorous specula-tion of divine realities." The third degree, pertaining to the perfect, completely quiets the passions and reforms the exterior man, so that the mind may be wholly engaged in contemplation of divine realities, insofar as possible in this life.[113] The terms of these distinctions suggest that moral instruction pertains directly to the first degree of "faith-ful servants" and is still pertinent to the "secret friends" of God in the second degree, but is no longer so necessary for the "beloved sons of God" partaking the third degree of the gift of wisdom.[114]

Appropriately, Denys treats the threefold order of charity in his *Summa de virtu-tibus* and other moral works. Like the degrees of supernatural wisdom, the degrees of charity pertain to beginners, proficient, and perfect. According to the first degree, one loves God so that he seeks nothing contrary to charity, fulfills all that the precepts of charity require, and avoids mortal sin. This degree especially pertains to those living in the world. According to the second degree, one fulfills not only the precepts of God and the church, but performs works of supererogation. Those who partake this degree strive to avoid all venial sin and desire to be dissolved in God. This state pertains espe-cially to religious, but it is not impossible for laymen, if they behave with such care that they are not inordinately occupied with any temporal good, including the mar-riage bed. The third degree of wisdom seems possible only for those in the religious life. Those who partake this degree love God in such a way that without interruption they are actually borne into God and live in him. Because of the fragility of the body, they may not accomplish uninterrupted union fully in this life, but they may accom-plish it *semiplene*. Those who attain this degree of charity "are so far adorned with the gift of wisdom, that in the apex of the mind they stand, as it were, in contact with

---

[111]Emery (n. 5 above) 109–110, 124–132, (n. 16 above) 377–378, (n. 14 above) 217–328.

[112]Denys, *De doct. et reg.* 2 a.8 reg.7 (n. 1 above) 39.521C–A'.

[113]Denys, *De donis Spiritus Sancti* 2 a.16 (ibid. 35.188D'–190B). See also *De contemplatione* 1 a.44 (41.186C–188A), where Denys states that the degrees of wisdom and degrees of charity are the same.

[114]Denys, *De donis* (ibid. 41.189D'–190A). The terms "ad fideles servos, secretos amicos, filios caris-simos" Denys takes from Jan van Ruusbroec's *De perfectione filiorum Dei*. On Ruusbroec's influence on Denys, see Kent Emery, Jr., "The Carthusians, Intermediaries for the Teaching of John Ruysbroeck dur-ing the Period of Early Reform and in the Counter-Reformation," in *Miscellanea Cartusiensia* 4, Analecta Cartusiana 42 (Salzburg 1979) 100–129; idem (n. 5 above) 131–133.

the Sun of justice and sempiternal wisdom, by which they are frequently and abundantly illumined, vehemently inflamed, mercifully seized, and immersed and absorbed in the riches of the glory of God.''[115]

In sum, according to his understanding of the relation between intellect and will in every degree of natural and supernatural life, Denys's moral pedagogy *(ordo vivendi)* must be based on truth founded in the order of being *(causa subsistendi)* and discovered by the intellect *(ratio intelligendi)*. As charity is the proportionate complement of wisdom, so Denys's pastoral works are the complement of his speculative writings. In his moral works, he strives to persuade all to virtue and to elicit the charity possessed by all the faithful by means of a preceptive, exhortatory, and exemplary discourse addressed to each condition of Christian life. In principle, perfection in the moral life opens the way to mystical theology and contemplation, the crown of Christian wisdom toward which the whole Christian life is directed.

The severity of Denys's standards, expectations, and ascetic examples is explained in part by a singular conclusion that he reaches against the common opinion of the Scholastic doctors, including Thomas Aquinas. On the authority of Scripture and the fathers, and by the experience of "many holy, most illumined, and perfect men," who heartily deplore and speak bitterly about their venial sins, Denys maintains that venial sins diminish charity in the soul. Venial sin, absolutely speaking, does not participate in the strict definition of sin, which is a direct transgression of the divine law. Yet venial sin participates in the general definition of sin as a turning away of the rational mind from God, and insofar as it participates in this definition, it participates in the effects of sin. In themselves, venial sins may be slight, but their danger lies in their repetition and number, the increasing burden of which weighs down the soul and its virtuous operations. Although venial sins cannot annul a gratuitous virtue, they do slacken, diminish, and debilitate charity, and thereby dispose the soul to mortal sin. By the same degrees that charity may grow and increase (as Scholastic theologians teach), it may slacken and decrease, until it is extinguished.[116]

Denys elaborates the effects of venial sin in the *Summa* and *De gravitate et enormitate peccati*, and delineates its decline into mortal sin. There are many who are satis-

---

[115]Denys, *Summa* 2 a.12 ([n. 1 above] 39.279C'–181A'). Denys says, "de ista materia in multis sermonibus dicta sunt plurima" (ibid. 29.351D). See *Quinquagesima Sermo* 3 (29.351B–D); *1 Trin. Sermo* 1, *8 Trin. Sermo* 3 (30.131B–A', 408C'–409B'); *Feria 2 Pent. Sermo* 5, *Comm. Confessoris Pontificis Sermo* 3 (32.119B–122C', 635A–636A). The material finds its way into articles of treatises: *Elementatio theologica* prop. 102 (33.224B'–D'); *De munificentia et beneficiis Dei* a.15 (34.306C'–D'); *Inflammatorium divini amoris* a.1 (41.318D–320B') In *De sacramento altaris* a.18 (35.408D'–410C') the three degrees of charity correspond to three degrees of devotion, in *De gaudio spirituali* a.12 to three degrees of joy, and in *De pace interna* 1.8 to three degrees of peace (40.527B'–528C, 562C'–563D). In the *Summa* (39.181A–A') and the sermon for *Feria 2 Pent.* (32.120B'–121B) Denys quotes his sources for the motif: David of Augsburg, *De profectu religiosorum*, and Augustine, *Super primam Joannis canonicam.*

[116]Denys, *1 Sent.* d.17 q.9 (ibid. 20.54B–64C'). Denys's personal response to the question (ibid. 59C'–64C') is one of the longest in his *Sentences* commentaries. His authorities are scriptural and patristic (Augustine, Caesarius, Eusebius) and he responds directly to the contrary arguments of Albert and Thomas. He is able to adduce William of Auxerre to his side. Perhaps the Devout writer, Gerard Zerbolt of Zutphen (1367–1398), is one of the "holy and perfect men" to whom Denys alludes. In his enormously popular *De spiritualibus ascensionibus* (ed., with Dutch trans. H. Mahieu, S.T.D. [Bruges 1941]), Gerard speaks of man's three "descents": into original sin with Adam, into impurity of heart, and into mortal sin. The structure of the work and Gerard's discourse make it clear that "impurity of heart" is equivalent to venial sin. And from impurity of heart one slides into mortal sin; see Gerard cc. 4–5, ed. Mahieu 24–30.

fied to abstain from mortal sin and avoid hell. Such do not strive to avoid venial sin, they do not keep custody of their hearts, and they do not seek perfection, but are content with mediocrity in serving God; they thus remain in a state of torpor and negligence.[117] They do not realize their danger, for if one does not progress, one regresses. Venial sin is a certain deviation from the ultimate end, if not a complete withdrawal from it; it is an inordinate attachment to created temporal goods without regard to God, if not a love of them that equals or exceeds love of the creator. Venial sin produces the following effects in the soul: it obscures the light of reason and diminishes the beauty of the mind; correspondingly, it weakens charity in the will and diminishes its actual fervor; it thus weighs down the powers of the soul and disables the practice of the virtues, retarding spiritual progress; it makes one subject to a greater penal satisfaction in this world and in purgatory (in hell venial sin is punished *per accidens* on account of the mortal sin to which it is annexed); it robs one of internal consolation and the sweet taste of familiarity with God; it retards one's entry into glory, since no one will be glorified until all of his venial sins are purged; further, inasmuch as it lessens merit before God, it diminishes one's final state of felicity; worst of all, it disposes one to mortal sin and the loss of the good altogether.[118]

Denys cites the *Compendium theologicae veritatis* to show how venial sin slides into mortal sin in four ways: first, by way of conscience, since whatever is committed against conscience, even if the conscience is erroneous and the deed is in fact venial, leads to Gehenna; second, by complacency, whereby the venial delight one takes in creatures can increase until it becomes so intense that it overpowers delight in divine charity; third, by disposition, since frequent lapses into venial sin dispose one to mortal sin; fourth, by way of progress, for if venial delight is not repudiated when it first arises, it can progress to mortal sin, as it does when venial delight in the first motions of the soul swells until it yields consent. Hence, some say that guilt begins in cogitation, increases in delight, is perfected in consent, and is consummated in action.[119]

Beginners in the first degree of charity must follow the example of the more proficient and the perfect, who daily emend and consume their venial sins through contrition, self-castigation, fervent charity, supererogatory works of virtue, patience in adversity, prayer, and so on. In light of the danger of venial sin, it is not enough to preach a minimal virtue; and since "laughter, joking, verbosity, levity, and laxity" are perilous venialities,[120] it would seem better that the preacher not insert "entertaining" *exempla* in his sermons, nor virtuoso displays of text division, both of which might arouse disorderly delight in his hearers—and in himself.[121]

As the performance of moral virtue is proportionate to what can be known about the final cause and object, so it is proportionate to the perfection of its exemplar cause. The perfection of law is commensurate to the status of the lawgiver. Thus the law of Christ is more perfect than the natural law discovered by the gentiles and revealed to

[117]Denys, *Summa* 1 a.16, *De grav.* a.19 (n. 1 above) 39.42B', 387B'–C'..

[118]Denys, *Summa* 1 a.16, *De grav.* a.19 (ibid. 40D'–42B, 387B'–388B'). This catalog of effects in great part derives from Hugh Ripelin's *Compendium theologicae veritatis* 3 c. 13, in *D. Alberti Magni . . . Opera omnia*, ed. Borgnet, 34 (Paris 1895) 103–104.

[119]Denys, *Summa* 1 a.19 (n. 1 above) 39.47A'–48D; Hugh Ripelin c. 12 (n. 118 above) 102.

[120]Denys, *Summa* 1 a.16 (n. 1 above) 39.42B–C, B'–C'.

[121]See Denys's comment on the division of text for exposition in his commentary on Boethius's *De consolatione* (ibid. 26.22), where, however, he does not raise a moral issue.

Moses. The "great philosopher" Avicenna was able to discern that Christ was far more moral and wise than the prophet Mohammed. Thus, all the faithful are bound to the evangelical law of Christ, and, as Augustine says, to the full spirituality and exemplarity of Christ from the moment of his Incarnation until his Passion, each "according to the measure, degree, and requirements of his vocation."[122]

In this perspective, Denys's rules *ad status* are the measures of a high perfection, and—*proh dolor!*—of a deviant deformity. Viewed against the perfection of the church as revealed in the metaphors of the Canticle and other scriptures, the present condition of the church is monstrous.[123] The visions of Saint Bridget, wherein Christ complains to the heavenly army about the vicious life of Christians from top to bottom, of the pope, cardinals, archbishops, bishops, priests, secular princes, judges, and common folk, are a dire warning.[124] The higher one's degree, state, prelature, order, or dignity, the greater his guilt in wrongdoing, the more deserving his ruin, the more blameworthy *(vituperabilior)* his negligence and damnable his carnality. Of course, one should be prudent speaking about clerics to lay people, who themselves are blameworthy enough.[125] Most damnable and most wicked are those members of the mendicant orders who, plunged in vice, presume to preach publicly to others. What they assert with their words, they deny with their lives; as Thomas Aquinas says, they empty out and trample the true meaning of Scripture, and they sin damnably.[126] Having granted the mendicants some of their arguments concerning the superiority of a mixed active and contemplative life, Denys has earned the right to hold them to their words.

The spirit of prophetic reform pervades all of Denys's works, and several treatises address the conventional fifteenth-century reform topics.[127] The last part of *De doctrina et regulis* consists of typical characters, drawn from Aristotle's *Politics* and the *De regimine principum* by Giles of Rome, of the various conditions and states of life: youth, old age, women, nobles, the rich, the powerful and civic rulers, soldiers, merchants. These characters portray praiseworthy and blameworthy traits, providing material for preaching in the *genus demonstrativum*. They show up, properly distributed, in the several *Vitae*.[128]

---

[122]Denys, *De doct. et reg.* 1 aa.1–2 (ibid. 39.503A–505A').

[123]Ibid. aa.6–7 (514C–517A').

[124]Denys, *Summa* 1 a.23 (ibid. 39.58D–B').

[125]Ibid. 58B', and *De doct. et reg.* 2 a.4 (ibid. 39.530C').

[126]Denys, *De doct. et reg.* 2 a.6 (ibid. 39.535A'–B').

[127]Besides the treatises of monastic reform, against simony and the plurality of benefices mentioned elsewhere in the essay, Denys wrote three treatises concerning the relation between council and pope, and *Contra superstitiones* (ibid. 36.211–230, 525–674); Emery (n. 3 above) 121.232 no. 62, 235–236 nos. 83–85.

[128]Denys, *De doct. et reg.* 2 aa.18–25: nobles, the rich, the powerful, youth, the old, women, soldiers, merchants ([n. 1 above] 39.558B–572B'). Cf. *De regimine et vita principum* 2 aa.4, 10, 3 aa.12–15: women, youth, nobles, the rich, the powerful, the old (37.419C–420D, 425D'–427D', 447D'–452B'); *Directorium nobilium* a.32: women (37.558A'–559C); *De vita coniugatorum* a.9: women (38.67A'–68D). See also *De vita militarium* aa.4, 10: soldiers (37.571B'–572C, 578C'–580A'). Giles of Rome in *De regimine principum libri III* lib. 1 pt. 4 cc. 1–7 (ed. Hieronymus Samaritanius [1607; repr. Darmstadt 1967] 188–213) treats the "mores laudabiles et vituperabiles . . . eorum qui sunt in statu" (youth, the old, nobles, the rich, civic rulers). Denys exploited this work in his various *Vitae*; in his own *De regimine et vita principum* 1 a.1 (37.377A), he contrasts Giles's work with his: "Aegidius de Roma . . . scripsit volumen, in quo philosophice magis quam theologice loquitur ac procedit: imo in toto opere illo (si bene recordor) nusquam sacram allegat Scripturam, sed in omnibus Aristotelem copiose allegat. Ego autem theologice potius quam philosophice intendo procedere: quo enim sacra Scriptura dignior atque sublimior est quam philosophica doctrina, eo

The requirements for all are great, but then again the possibilities for perfection are exalted. All must live without mortal sin. As the apostle John says, no one in this life is without venial sin (1 John 1.8), which is an "obliquity," "tortuosity," or *incurvatio* from divine rectitude.[129] Nonetheless, for short spaces of time in this life it is possible to be without venial sin. An adult who has just been baptized, for example, is without sin in the time immediately after; more wonderful are those "heroic and perfect men," whom one reads about in the *Vitae patrum*, who, perfected in charity, were wont to be in continuous rapture, up to fourteen days at a time. Those advanced in charity shun not only mortal sin but every attachment to temporal concerns and to relatives and spouses that impedes perfection. Such charity is usually found among religious, but it can be attained by laymen, "who have wives as not having them, and who use the world as not using it" (1 Cor. 7.29, 31). While difficult, this is not impossible to the all-powerful God, who has bestowed the special grace on several in the world, such as David, Hezekiah, and Joshua in the Old Testament, and in more recent times on Elizabeth of Thuringia, daughter of the king of Hungary. Moreover, it is recorded in the *Vitae patrum* that Anthony, after years of ascetic warfare in solitude, discovered that he did not have charity to the measure of a certain tanner living in Alexandria.[130]

Throughout Denys's writings, examples from the *Vitae patrum* instruct both religious and lay. "Opposites laid next to each other expose each more clearly." The virtues of the desert fathers provoke those who hear about them to aim high and to follow their footsteps. By comparing ourselves to them, we learn to be humble and to despise ourselves.[131] To this end, Denys "collected" his *De exemplis et documentis authenticis*, wherein from the works of Cassian and Climacus he excerpts examples and sayings of the fathers not found in the *Vitae patrum*. He compiled these while preparing his translation "ad stilum facillimum" of the works of Cassian and commentary on John Climacus.[132]

COLLECTION AND MORAL PERSUASION

A collecting method, the act of preaching "by hand," and the theme of fraternal correction are inseparably bound together in Denys's *Contra pluralitatem beneficiorum*,

---

ad exhortandum, arguendum, docendum et inflammandum est aptior et omnino potentior." Besides being more sublime in its object, the discourse of Christian moral theology is more compelling and affective than the discourse of philosophical ethics. The idea of using psychological characters as aids to Christian preaching comes ultimately from Gregory the Great's *Regula pastoralis* 3.

[129]Denys, *De doct. et reg.* 1 prooem. (n. 1 above) 39.499. For the terms, from Gregory the Great and Bonaventure, see Emery (n. 91 above) 53, 276 nn. 244, 248.

[130]Denys, *Summa* 2 a.12, *De doct. et reg.* 1 prooem., a.8 reg.3 (n. 1 above) 39.180A–C, 499–500, 519C′–D′.

[131]Denys, *De doct. et reg.* 1 a.7, *De exemplis et documentis authenticis* prooem. (ibid. 39.515C′, 579).

[132]Denys, *De exemplis* is printed, ibid. 573–621; Emery (n. 3 above) 121.230 no. 55. For the works on Cassian and Climacus, and their dates (ca. 1450, 1453), see n. 50 above. Concerning *De exemplis*, Denys says, "Praeterea, collectio ista (reor) non erit superflua: quoniam libros Cassiani ac Climaci multi raro aut nunquam legunt, sive ex sua tarditate, sive es sua simplicitate, quoniam libri illi sunt aliqualiter armati atque difficilis stili, et modus ipse loquendi frequenter obscurus est. Idcirco in isto opusculo uti intendo plano ac facillimo stilo" (575).

ex dictis authenticis.[133] Denys is moved to write this treatise because certain "friends most dear" to him have acquired many benefices, when one would suffice, and do not seem to realize what spiritual danger they are in; some of them have fallen into such hardness of mind that they will not listen to anything said against possessing a plurality of ecclesiastical benefices. It is tempting to think that, among others, Denys may have had his friend Nicholas of Cusa in mind.[134] Lest one think that he has presumed too much in criticizing those who exceed him in "rank, age, and knowledge," Denys appeals to the universal duty of charitable correction. Moreover, since he is writing as an inferior, he casts his arguments in a form more likely to persuade a superior than his own reasonings and expressions. He simply collects authoritative texts on the subject, which should be as binding on one of high rank and knowledge as on anyone else:

> So that the method of my [work] may be firmer and my argument more unanswerable, and lest someone be able to argue my feebleness of presumption or novelty, I shall adduce nothing but the authorities, reasons, writings, and sayings of the holy fathers and solemn and authentic doctors, inserting nothing of my own, except perhaps sometimes in order to clarify those things that have been written.[135]

The first introductory articles, concerning the behavior that all Christians must practice and how exemplary and virtuous their lives must be, the perfection of the evangelical law, and the right behavior of canons and priests, are drawn from materials in Denys's *Summa*, *Vitae*, and other moral works. Thereafter he follows his intention strictly, adducing the proper materials, among others, "ex his quae in libro Universalis boni conscripta sunt, ex dictis Guillelmi Parisiensis episcopi, ex dictis S. Thomae, ex Summa virtutum et vitiorum, ex Summa Udalrici, ex scriptis S. Bernardi, ex dictis sanctorum patrum." More than his own exhortation, this assembly of authoritative and reasonable documents might persuade "the excellence of the most beloved" friends for whom he has written his treatise.[136]

Throughout Denys's works, one finds articles composed "ex dictis et scriptis" of fathers, saints, and doctors. These "collections" are themselves effective preachments. For Denys, the *modus inveniendi* readily becomes the *modus proferendi*; what is most important to his persuasion is the apt placement and disposition of the materials he has compiled. Fittingly, Denys applies his methods of invention and disposition to the words and writings of the greatest Christian preacher himself. The work which lays bare the skeleton of his method—and which more than any other brought him fame in his day—is the *Monopanton*, or "redaction of all the Epistles of Paul into one." To reduce all the Epistles to one continuous text, Denys "mixes together and moderates . . . those words and places which seem to sound more alike, accord well, and coincide" ("eaque loca ac verba contemperando et commiscendo, quae amplius consonare, coincidere, et concordare videntur"). He distributes these linked texts into appropriately titled special chapters. The titles indicate the leading topics of Denys's preaching materials; for example, "Against rash and disorderly judgment; On charitable and just

---

[133]Denys (n. 1 above) 39.243–282; Emery (n. 3 above) 121.242 no. 116. Presumably written before *De vita praesulum* (aa.32–33), *De vita archidiaconorum* (aa.26–27), and *De vita canonicorum* (a.22), all of which contain articles based on this material (Denys 37.44A'–46A', 154A'–159C, 199D–200D').

[134]E. Vansteenberghe, "Nicolas de Cusa," *Dictionnaire de théologie catholique* 11.1 (1931) 602.

[135]Denys, *Contra plural. benefic.* a.1 (n. 1 above) 39.247A'–248C at 247C'–248A.

[136]Ibid. a.19 (282A').

fraternal correction; On effective arguments of evangelical preaching; How married people ought to behave, and the continence of virgins and widows; How parents ought to behave toward their offspring, and vice versa; How superiors ought to behave toward subordinates and vice versa; Certain teachings regarding prelates, and how they ought to instruct diverse sorts diversely.''[137] By means of internal alphabetical signs corresponding to marginal citations, the *Monopanton* incorporates a cross-index to the Epistles it redisposes. This apparatus is copied faithfully in most of the manuscripts. Denys dedicates his work to Cardinal Nicholas of Cusa, on the occasion of his papal legation through Germany and the Low Countries. Cusanus, who provided copies of Denys's work for the monks of Tegernsee and Melk,[138] seemingly admired its invention, or ''coincident'' logic, which Denys used otherwise to reduce nearly the whole medieval library to a single body of preaching materials.

APPENDIX

Reasonable Piety and Popular Preaching: A Crux for an Encyclopedic Monk

Denys the Carthusian's collected works represent a comprehensive literary program, which attempts to gather all of the pertinent traditional matter on a subject and to dispose it according to general organizing principles and to undergird it with a consistent, coherent rationale. Such a large synthesizing effort, combining popular and elite elements, is bound to encounter stress points.

As I have suggested in this essay and argued in others, Denys's literary enterprise was meant to serve a reform of the beliefs and practices of the Christian people of his time. The reform of sincere piety is always a delicate matter; one must be careful lest, in amending beloved devotions and religious attitudes, one actually cause the love of God to diminish in people's hearts, which is the opposite of what one intends. Denys's reforming predecessor, Jean Gerson, had already faced this problem in his attempts to alter, or prohibit, pious practices that had scant theological foundation.

Denys encountered this question directly in his *Passio domini nostri Iesu Christi iuxta textum quatuor Evangelistarum* (*Opera* 31.425–546), a concordance of the four Gospel texts on the Passion with a running commentary designed to serve preachers. The intent of the work is to establish preaching about the Passion squarely upon the scriptural texts and their authoritative interpretation. Such was not always the practice of popular preachers when treating the highly emotional, highly effective (and affective) subject of the Passion.

At the end of his commentary (ibid. 513A–517A'), Denys addresses the subject of a pious text extremely popular among preachers of the Passion: *Dialogus beatae Mariae et Anselmi de Passione Domini*, falsely attributed to Anselm of Canterbury.[139] Besides its persuasively affective quality, the work carried the authority of a saint and prominent theologian.

---

[137]Denys, *Monopanton, seu Redactio omnium Epistolarum beati Pauli in unam ad materias* (ibid. 14.465–537; see 467); Emery (n. 3 above) 121.226 no. 39.

[138]Munich, Bayerische Staatsbibliothek Clm 18199 fols. 118ra–148rb; Melk, Stiftsbibliothek MS 878 (722. N 6) fols. 104–169v; Emery (n. 3 above) 121.134–135, 187–188.

[139]PL 159.271–290. The text of the *Dialogus* or *Interrogatio* is closely related to the *De planctu Mariae*,

Denys states that his exposition of the Gospel texts "according to the order of the history of Christ's Passion" ought to suffice as an aid for popular preaching about the topic. He is constrained to add other materials, however, in order to clarify the minds of preachers. He observes that preachers are wont to mix into their sermons about the Passion materials drawn from a certain *libellus*, which reports a dialogue (or *collocutio*) between the Virgin and Saint Anselm. He says that the material from this text provokes among listeners much pious devotion, compassion, and sorrow, "sometimes more," he adds ironically, "than the [scriptural] history of Christ's Passion itself" (ibid. 513A–B).

There are a number of questions to be asked about this book and preachers' use of it. In discussing them, Denys proceeds in a "scholastic manner of inquiry," while avoiding all incautious assertion (ibid. 513D–A'). In other words, the *Dialogus* requires analysis before promotion.

Objections against the work are comprehended by two doubts: Did the dialogue between Mary and Anselm literally take place, or is it a literary fiction, like the dialogue between "a devout Dominican" (Henry Suso) and divine Wisdom in the book entitled *Horologium sapientiae*? And, was "the holy and wise man" Anselm in fact the author of the book? (ibid. 513B–A').

These questions about the authenticity and veracity of the dialogue arise because many of the details concerning the Passion, reported by Mary to Anselm, do not accord with, and even seem to contradict, the divinely inspired Gospel accounts. Denys carefully sets out the factual discrepancies in the form of objections (ibid. 513A'–515B). In response, he first addresses the underlying issue. He notes that Anselm, "a man of great wisdom and virtue," from his youth was a very devout and fervent lover of the Virgin. Therefore, if he indeed asserted that Mary revealed these things to him, he can be trusted. On the other hand, Denys states, he would not dare assert that Anselm said these things, nor that he actually wrote the book. Moreover, Denys says that he has never found any other "authentic doctor" who reported such things (ibid. 515B–C). In light of Denys's voracious reading, this is a considerable testimony.

Nevertheless, because so many preachers solemnly introduce materials from this dialogue into their sermons, and because their listeners are so moved by its words, neither will Denys dare affirm that the little book is a fiction or mixed with falsehood. Therefore, the best course seems to be to "save the appearances" of the dialogue's discrepancies with the Gospel accounts and discover how they may be "piously understood," always submitting one's judgment to those who are wiser and to the church (ibid. 515C–A'). Denys offers his interpretations with one cautionary condition. Preachers who use the materials from the book must not assert absolutely in their hearts that the dialogue between Mary and Anselm actually occurred; rather, they must apply to the work only "a certain pious estimation, or conjecture or probability," as the chancellor of Paris, Jean Gerson, teaches in his treatise entitled *De gradibus certitudinis* (ibid. 515D–A').[140]

Denys's responses to each objection adopt the following strategies. He offers different rhetorical means for interpreting some of the questionable statements in the dialogue, so that they do not so clearly contradict the Gospels. He posits the possibility of errors in the manuscript transmission of the text, which produced the seeming discrepancies.[141] He points out that some of the details, while absent from Scripture, do not essentially contradict the facts reported in the

---

falsely attributed to Augustine and more often to Bernard. The *De planctu*, in turn, is an extract from the *De laudibus sanctae Dei genitricis* composed by the Cistercian abbot Ogier of Lucedio (Ogerius, Oglerius de Trino, 1136–1214). The *Dialogus*, then, is a thirteenth-century work deriving ultimately from Ogier's *De laudibus*. See H. Barré, "Le *Planctus Mariae* attribué à saint Bernard," *Revue d'ascétique et de mystique* 28 (1952) 243–266; for the work's influence, see Fidèle de Ros, O.F.M. Cap., "Le *Planctus Mariae* du Pseudo-Anselme à Suso et à Louis de Grenade," *Revue d'ascét. et de myst.* 25 (1949) 270–283.

[140]Entitled *Quae veritates sint de necessitate salutis credendae* in *Jean Gerson: Oeuvres complètes*, ed. P. Glorieux, 6 (Paris 1965) 181–189.

[141]The PL edition (n. 139 above) presents many variant readings.

Gospels, and that the Evangelists themselves state that they did not report everything Christ said and did (ibid. 515A'–516B).

Mary's fervent wish that Christ be spared the ordeal of his Passion, recounted with great effect in the *Dialogus* and inspiring powerful maternal sentiments among listeners, provides greater difficulty. Authoritative theological opinion, confirmed by Scripture, holds that Mary foresaw the necessary suffering of her son and willed its salvific consequences. On this point, Denys resorts to a spiritual psychology, likewise traditionally employed to confirm the fully human suffering of Christ on the cross and to interpret the meaning of his last words. Although the "God-bearing and most illumined Virgin always and ever knew most certainly, by act or habit, that her son would be most cruelly killed, and by his death would redeem humankind,"[142] it is possible that Mary was so "vehemently absorbed in the affect of compassion" in her "inferior reason" that she did not at the time actually consider what she otherwise habitually knew, and was able to wish circumstantially something contrary to what she knew "absolutely, with deliberate reason" (ibid. 516B–D). To support his argument, Denys quotes texts by Paulinus of Nola and John Chrysostom (ibid. 516A'–D')

Denys's treatment of the *Dialogus*, it seems to me, is revealing in several ways. First, he firmly believes that true piety must be based on authoritative sources and that the letter of the New Testament should not be violated, whatever the prospects of benign effects. Secondly, the historical question of authorship is an important one, inseparable from the question of "authentic teaching." Thirdly, he is sensitive to the issue of theologically correct piety, however well-intentioned the devout may be and however fervent their devotion. Fourthly, preaching must be evaluated in terms of its foundations as much as in terms of its effects. In all of these respects, Denys appears "forward-looking."

Nevertheless, he finds a way to accommodate what was obviously an effective, if ambiguous, source of piety and love of God. Gerson's "grades of certainty," conceived to address the same questions, provided Denys with an instrument whereby to preserve a rational hold on the matter. In the end, he accedes to common practice and tacitly admits a radical principle enunciated by Augustine in *De doctrina christiana*: All the scriptures serve charity, and they are read faithfully when they serve this end, whatever the pious reader's disregard for the strict sense of the letter. Those who have perfect charity, indeed, no longer have need of Scripture. Because in fact many people are inflamed by the narrative of "Anselm's" text and moved by it to great compassion, in the following article of his own work Denys extracts passages from the *Dialogus* for the use of preachers (ibid. 516B–519D'). Although he will not expressly affirm that the dialogue is "mixed with falsehood," he excerpts its least misleading, more sober passages— "the best of pseudo-Anselm," as it were.

---

[142]For Denys's highly mystical understanding of Mary's habitual vision, see Bonaventura Tonutti, O.F.M., *Mariologia Dionysii Cartusiani (1402–1471)* (Rome 1953) 147–152; and Alessio Martinelli, O.F.M., "La Visione di Dio 'per speciem' durante la presente vita seconda Dionigi il Certosino (1402–1471)," *Divinitas* 2 (1958) 377–389.

MYSTICISM AND THE COINCIDENCE OF OPPOSITES IN SIXTEENTH- AND SEVENTEENTH-CENTURY FRANCE

The seventeenth century in France was *le grand siècle* for what contemporaries defined precisely as "mystical theology." Ever since the writings of pseudo-Dionysius had been introduced into the Latin west, and especially after the twelfth century, the term *mystica theologia* had become part of the common vocabulary of theological discourse. By the beginning of the modern period, the term had come to designate a specialized genre of theology, treating the soul's intimate union with God, which was usually contrasted with the scholastic theology of the universities.[1]

For many in the late Middle Ages, the distinction between mystical and scholastic theology signified a sharp difference between a wholly affective union with God, and an attempt to understand God and his works according to the laws of human reason. In an oft-quoted text of his *De mystica theologia*, from which the genre took its name, pseudo-Dionysius urged his disciple to abandon every act of the senses and of the intellect in order to rise in an unknowing manner above all sensible and intelligible things to the one who is above all essence and knowledge.[2] Medieval commentators customarily construed this text to mean that one must finally abandon all intellectual speculation for a purely affective movement of the will towards God.[3] Most medieval theologians, like Bonaventure, gave intellectual speculation an important place in preparation for this final affective act; others, however, excluded speculation from mystical theology. The influential Carthusian writer Hugh of Balma (fl. 1300), whose *Mystica theologia* circulated under the name of Bonaventure, completely divorced scholastic and mystical theology, and taught that affective union with God required neither a preceding nor concomitant act of the intellect. Such an act, indeed, would hinder union.[4]

---

[1] Michel de Certeau, "'Mystique' au XVIIe siècle: Le Problème du langage 'mystique'," in *L'Homme devant Dieu: Mélanges offerts au père Henri de Lubac* (Paris, 1964), 267-91.

[2] *De mystica theologia*, 1, in *Dionysiaca: Recueil donnant l'ensemble des traductions latines des ouvrages attribués au Denys de l'Aréopagite*, I (Paris, 1937), 567-68.

[3] Thomas Gallus (Vercellensis †1246) seems to have fixed this affective interpretation in the Middle Ages. See Robert Javelet, "Thomas Gallus ou les écritures dans une dialectique mystique," in *L'Homme devant Dieu*, 99-110. The authoritative study of Thomas remains James Walsh, "Sapientia christianorum: The Doctrine of Thomas Gallus, Abbot of Vercelli, on Contemplation" (Ph.D. Diss, Gregorian University, Rome, 1957).

[4] Hugh of Balma, *Mystica theologia*, in *Opera omnia sancti Bonaventurae* VII (Rome, 1586-96), 699-730. See especially the *Questio unica*, 726-30. See also, Anselme Stoelen, "Hugues de Balma," *Dictionnaire de spiritualité*, VII (Paris, 1969), 859-73; Kent Emery, Jr., "Benet of Canfield: Counter-Reformation Spirituality and its Mediaeval Origins" (Ph.D. Diss., University of Toronto, 1976), 213-21.

Reprinted from the *Journal of the History of Ideas* 45, no. 1 (Baltimore, Md., 1984), pp. 3–23, by permission of Duke University Press.

4

Hugh's interpretation of pseudo-Dionysius gave rise to a widespread anti-scholastic, anti-intellectual prejudice among monks and other spiritual persons. In the fifteenth century, Nicholas of Cusa needed to confront this attitude directly, and to assert the role of speculation within mystical theology itself. Cusanus did so by stressing the intellectual character of the negative dialectic found in pseudo-Dionysius' mystical theology.[5] Within the context of mystical theology, of the ascent to the infinite God, Cusanus developed his famous principle of the coincidence of opposites.

As modern studies have shown, the French *humanistae theologizantes*[6] Jacques Lefèvre d'Etaples (1460-1563), Josse Clichtove (1472-1543), and Charles de Bovelles (1479-1553) admired the medieval mystics in general and Nicholas of Cusa in particular.[7] The encyclopaedic programs of learning which these erudites put forward were directed to contemplation and mystical theology. Lefèvre's prefatory epistles to Richard of St. Victor's *De superdivina Trinitate* (1510) and Nicholas of Cusa's *Opera* (1514) indicate that his order of studies was organized according to a hierarchical, threefold division of sensible, rational, and mystical theology corresponding to a hierarchy of powers in the soul: imaginative, rational, and intellectual. The pattern of a threefold division of theology, suggested in the writings of pseudo-Dionysius, was fully developed by a long line of medieval writers before Lefèvre.[8] In one text, Lefèvre recommends the

---

[5] E. Vansteenberghe, *Autour de la Docte Ignorance. Une controverse sur la théologie mystique au XVe siècle*. Beiträge zur Geschichte der Philosophie des Mittelalters, XV (1915). On Cusanus' role in the recovery of the paradoxical dialectic of Plato's *Parmenides*, and consequent reinterpretation of pseudo-Dionysius, see R. Klibansky, "Plato's Parmenides in the Middle Ages and the Renaissance," *Mediaeval and Renaissance Studies*, 1 (1941-43), 281-330. On Cusanus as mystical theologian, and his teaching on the role of speculation in mystical theology, see M.L. Führer, "Purgation, Illumination and Perfection in Nicholas of Cusa," *Downside Review*, 98 (1980), 169-89.

[6] This was a term of opprobrium coined by Noël Beda for Erasmus and Lefèvre. See Eugene F. Rice, Jr., "The Humanist Idea of Christian Antiquity: Lefèvre d'Etaples and his Circle," in *French Humanism, 1470-1600*, ed. Werner L. Gundersheimer (New York, 1966), 174.

[7] Eugene F. Rice, Jr., "Jacques Lefèvre d'Etaples and the Medieval Christian Mystics," in *Florilegium Historiale: Essays Presented to Wallace K. Ferguson* (Toronto, 1971), 88-124. For Bovelles, see Joseph M. Victor, *Charles de Bovelles, 1479-1553: An Intellectual Biography* (Geneva, 1978), 13-25, 57-71 (Lull and Cusanus), 167-78, *et passim*.

[8] See Lefèvre's prefatory epistle to Richard of St. Victor's *De Trinitate* in *The Prefatory Epistles of Jacques Lefèvre d'Etaples*, ed. Eugene F. Rice, Jr. (New York, 1972), 224-27, esp. 224. See also the prefatory epistle to the *Opera* of Cusanus, 343-47, esp. 346. For the tradition of the three modes of theology, initiated by pseudo-Dionysius (for example, *De mys. theo.*, 3: 584-93) and developed by a long line of medieval authors, see Emery, "Benet of Canfield," (*op. cit.*, n.4 above), 148-249. Neat *loci* of the tradition are found in Bonaventure, *Itinerarium mentis in Deum* in *Opera omnia*, 10 vols (1882-1902), V (Quaracchi, 1891), I, 7, 298, and *De reductione artium ad theologiam* in *Opera omnia*, V, 5, 321. Many writers related mystical theology to a purely affective *apex mentis*. The source of Lefèvre's threefold division (imagination, reason, intellect), which denotes the role of speculation in the highest, mystical mode of theology, is Richard of St. Victor,

content of such a threefold order of studies. One should begin, he says, with a study of the natural philosophy and metaphysics of Aristotle, proceed to a reading of Scripture and the fathers, and finally strive for the heights of contemplation. In contemplation one should be instructed by Dionysius, Nicholas of Cusa, and "others like them."[9]

The typological relation between Aristotle and Cusanus, expressed in the text above, is revealing. Elsewhere in his writings Lefèvre distinguishes two philosophies, one "rational" and the other "intellectual."[10] As the terms imply, this twofold division of philosophy is related to the threefold division of theology, the two highest modes of which are rational and intellectual. The relation of the two divisions is clear in Lefèvre's preface to Charles de Bovelles' *In artem oppositorum introductio* (1501). Here Lefèvre associates rational philosophy with Aristotle, the higher intellectual philosophy with Cusanus and other mystics. Lefèvre says that the Aristotelian disciplines should not be scorned; they are necessary for one who wishes to rise from the sensible world and imagination to the "second degree of rational philosophy." But if Aristotle represents the life of studies, Pythagoras, the exemplar of a higher philosophy, represents the death of them. One experiences death in intellectual philosophy because there he discovers silence instead of words. Thus, whereas in rational philosophy, typified by Aristotle, one finds many words, in intellectual philosophy, typified by Paul, Dionysius, and Nicholas of Cusa, silence is act and speech is privation.[11]

There is much to remark in this text. First, it is worth observing that the medieval theologian Hugh of St. Victor likewise praised Pythagoras, because his definition of philosophy acknowledged that wisdom lies deeply hidden from the human mind.[12] Secondly, in his preface to the *Opera* of Cusanus, Lefèvre states that the highest, intellectual mode of theology *in silentio docet*, the second, rational mode *in sermonis modestia*, and the lowest, imaginative mode *in multiloquio perstrepit*.[13] Since his terms for the modes of philosophy and the modes of theology are convertible, it appears that Lefèvre did not sharply distinguish them, and that the former provided the means for the latter. Indeed, Lefèvre's distinction between intellectual and rational philosophy echoes one made by pseudo-

---

Benjamin major (De arca mystica) I, 3, *PL* 196.66-67. (Richard uses the term *intelligentia.*) On the significance of the three modes in the thought of Lefèvre, see Augustin Renaudet, *Préréforme et humanisme à Paris pendant les premières guerres d'Italie (1494-1517)*. 2nd ed. (Paris, 1953), 376-77, 521, 597-99, 663-64, *et passim*. On the scheme *sensus, imaginatio, ratio, intellectus, intelligentia,* originating in Proclus, see E. von Ivànka, *Platonismus in der Philosophie des Mittelalters* (Darmstadt, 1969), 147-60.

[9] E.F. Rice, Jr., "The Humanist Idea of Christian Antiquity," 163-64.

[10] Renaudet, 410-12.

[11] *Prefatory Epistles*, 96.

[12] *Didascalicon,* I, 3, *PL* 176.742-43.

[13] *Prefatory Epistles,* 346.

6

Dionysius between a mystical theology of a few words and a symbolic theology of many.[14] Hugh of Balma characteristically develops the same contrast; for him the words of mystical theology are few because when one rises to the *apex* of the affections all discourse ceases.[15] After Lefèvre, the seventeenth-century Capuchin mystic Joseph du Tremblay (1577-1638) distinguishes between a contracted mystical theology and a verbally expanded scholastic theology.[16]

In Lefèvre's program of studies, the natural philosophy of Aristotle, whereby one might discern in sensible nature secret signs pointing to the intelligible world and divine things,[17] occupied an intermediate place in the ascent towards God, and supplied the logic for a rational theology that conducts man from sensible to intelligible realities. In his prefaces to Lefèvre's paraphrases of Aristotle, urging the spiritual importance of studying Aristotle, Josse Clichtove adopts the terms of the old commonplace of the book of nature used by the Victorines, Bonaventure, and other medieval mystics. The whole world, Clichtove says, is a mirror in which one may contemplate *vestigia* of the divine majesty. By contemplating these sensible images, one may ascend, as if by a ladder, to a knowledge of heavenly things.[18] As a modern scholar observes, for Lefèvre and Clichtove Aristotle's philosophy, and the logic upon which it was founded, served as an instrument of *askesis* preparatory to mysticism, and the study of physics was a step in an *itinerarium mentis in Deum*.[19]

But even if purified of the distortions of medieval commentators, Aristotelian logic and philosophy were inadequate for conducting man to the highest contemplative wisdom. The *ars oppositorum* of Cusanus served this purpose in Lefèvre's mind.[20] Cusanus' logic of the coincidence of opposites, rooted in the divine infinity, is a fit instrument for contemplative silence. In terms of the usual operations of reason the principle is privative, since it deprives the mind of its rational concepts (called

---

[14] *De mys. theo.*, 1, 572-74.

[15] Hugh of Balma, *Mys. theo.*, 1, 1, 700; 2, 2, 704.

[16] See *Le Resserré et l'étendu: Introduction à Joseph du Tremblay l'éminence grise*, I. *Herméneutique et logique, Etudes Franciscaines*, 19 (suppl. ann. 1969), 26, *et passim*.

[17] See Lefèvre's preface to Aristotle's *Physics, Prefatory Epistles*, 5-7. See Renaudet, 145-48.

[18] Josse Clichtove to Etienne Poncher, *Préfatory Epistles*, 97-100, esp. 98. See also Clichtove's commentary on Lefèvre's preface, *Prefatory Epistles*, 7-8, and Renaudet's remarks, 412. In Bonaventure's *Itin.*, self-knowledge, that is, knowledge of the "intelligible" reality of the human soul, stands between knowledge of the sensible world (below the soul) and God (above the soul). For the classification pertinent to Clichtove's text, see *Itin.* 1, 296-99.

[19] Jean-Pierre Massaut, *Josse Clichtove: L'Humanisme et la réforme du clergé*, I (Paris, 1968), 189,272; 180-94, 270-74. Throughout his study, Massaut notes the remarkable revival of twelfth-century themes by Lefèvre and Clichtove.

[20] Renaudet, 134-35, 378-80, 417-20, 506, 661-64, *et passim*. These pages also note the influence of Ramón Lull.

verba mentis by Cusanus).[21] Lefèvre performed the humanist task of editing the texts of Cusanus; his younger colleague Charles de Bovelles composed philosophic and theological works which applied and developed the principles found in them. Like Lefèvre, Bovelles related a twofold rational and intellectual philosophy to a threefold theology.[22] In his works of mystical theology, for which his other works were propaedeutic, Bovelles employed the *ars oppositorum* which he had gathered from Cusanus, and from Cusanus' predecessor in the matter, Ramón Lull. Such a logic allowed for speculation within mystical theology and at the same time respected the incomprehensibility of God's infinite nature.[23] In conclusion, it would seem that within Lefèvre's circle, the logics of Lull and Cusanus supplied the means whereby to account for the mystical experience above reason, and to interpret the writings of medieval mystics, many of whose works Lefèvre edited, and many of whom were *illiterati*, or in the paradoxical sense, *idiotae*.[24] Moreover, we should note that according to Lefèvre's hierarchical disposition of knowledge, Cusanus' intellectual philosophy does not contradict but rather transcends Aristotle's rational philosophy, in the same way that mystical theology transcends scholastic theology.

There is evidence, we shall see, that despite a drastically changed religious climate provoked by the Reformation, the thought of Lefèvre and Bovelles exerted an influence among mystical writers in late sixteenth and early seventeenth-century France. By then the Counter-Reformation

---

[21] Cusanus gives a variation on the threefold modes, an ascent from *vox* to *verbum mentis* to *Verbum*. *De docta ignorantia*, ed. E. Hoffman and R. Klibansky, *Opera omnia*, I (Leipzig, 1932), III, 11, 152-54.

[22] Victor, *Charles de Bovelles*, 71, 125-26, *et passim*.

[23] *Ibid.*, 145, 167-78. Victor corrects the early opinion of Eugene F. Rice, Jr., *The Renaissance Idea of Wisdom* (Cambridge, Mass. 1958), 196-223, that Bovelles moralized and secularized Cusanus' mystical notion of wisdom. Lefèvre appreciated Lull, and edited several of his mystical works. See notes 19 and 23. Charles de Bovelles was interested in Lull's art, which he associated with Cusanus', as a method for philosophy and theology: see Joseph M. Victor, "The Revival of Lullism at Paris, 1499-1516," *Renaissance Quarterly*, **28** (1975), 504-34, esp. 519-30. This association was well founded, since it is clear that Lull's writings directly influenced Cusanus. See P.E.W. Platzeck, "El lulismo en las obras del Cardinal N. Krebs de Cusa," *Revista Espanola de Teologia* (1940-41), 731-65; (1942), 257-324; M. Honecker, "Lullus-Handschriften aus dem Besitz des Kardinals Nicolaus von Cues," *Spanische Forschungen des Görres-Gesellschaft*, 6 (1937), 252-309; E. Colomer, *Nikolaus von Kues und Raimund Lull* (Berlin, 1961).

[24] Renaudet, 521, 597-600, 621-23, 635-37. Renaudet says that in his famous commentary, Lefèvre used the teachings of the mystics as aids for interpreting Paul. For the mystical texts Lefèvre edited, see Rice, "Jacques Lefèvre d'Etaples and the Medieval Christian Mystics," *op. cit.* Lefèvre uses the terms *illiteratus* and *idiota* in his prefaces to Lull's *Liber de laudibus beatissime virginis Marie, Philosophia amoris*, and *Contemplationes idiotae* (the second part of which Lefèvre translated into French), and in his preface to Jordaen's Latin translation of Ruysbroeck, *De ornatu spiritualium nuptiarum*. See *Prefatory Epistles*, 77, 277, 375, 412.

was well under way. New spiritual doctrines which accompanied that international movement had passed into France. Among the many spiritual currents of the times, however, modern historians recognize an indigenous French school of spirituality, which one authority calls "l'école abstraite."[25] Ironically, the founder of this "French school" was an English exile and Catholic convert, the Capuchin Benet of Canfield (1562-1610).[26] Benet's most important work, the *Règle de perfection*, inspired Cardinal de Bérulle, Madame Acarie, Joseph du Tremblay, and other leading figures of the Catholic revival in seventeenth-century France. Perhaps because the activities of the Jesuits were severely restricted there, the Capuchins (Benet's order) were pre-eminent among the new religious orders in France.[27] The Capuchins were a reform of an old order, the Franciscans, and they strove to continue and revive medieval traditions of thought and practice. The teaching of Benet of Canfield, and of his like-minded confrère Laurent de Paris (1563?-1631), provides an interesting example of the way in which newer ideas were assimilated to older, medieval ones.

Even though, in accordance with Franciscan tradition, Benet and Laurent teach that mystical theology is essentially affective, the one propounding a doctrine of "conformity to the will of God," the other a doctrine of "pure love," their doctrines have strong, speculative elements. For both, the principle of the coincidence of opposites is central. Although Benet never refers to the principle by name, its exercise is ubiquitous in the *Règle de perfection*. Laurent names the principle and cites its author.

Benet of Canfield composed the *Règle* around 1593; it circulated in manuscript until it was printed in English, French, and Latin versions in 1609-1610.[28] Benet wrote the work in French, translated the first two

[25] Louis Cognet, *La Spiritualité moderne: I. L'Essor, 1500-1650* (Paris, 1966), 233-73.

[26] Henri Bremond, *A Literary History of Religious Thought in France: II. The Coming of Mysticism (1590-1620)*, trans. K. L. Montgomery (London, 1930), 111-25; Aldous Huxley, *Grey Eminence: A Study in Religion and Politics* (New York, 1941), 62-66, 91-104; Optat de Veghel, *Benoît de Canfield (1562-1610): Sa vie, sa doctrine et son influence* (Rome, 1949); Paul Mommaers, "Benoît de Canfeld; Sa terminologie 'essentielle',", *Revue d'histoire de la spiritualité*, **47** (1971), 421-54, **48** (1972), 27-68; "Benoît de Canfeld et ses sources flamandes," *ibid.*, **48** (1972), 401-434, **49** (1973), 37-66; Cognet, 242-58, 262-72; Emery, "Benet of Canfield".

[27] Godefroy de Paris, *Les Frères mineurs capucins en France: Histoire de la province de Paris*, 2 vols (Paris, 1937-39, 1950); P. Raoul, *Histoire des frères mineurs capucins de la province de Paris (1601-1660)* (Blois, 1965). For the Capuchins' associations with neo-Platonizing circles at the French court, see Frances A. Yates, "Religious Processions in Paris, 1583-4," in *Astraea: The Imperial Theme in the Sixteenth Century* (London, 1975), 173-207; Emery, 251-315.

[28] Optat de Veghel, 400-422. The English version of *The Rule* contains only the first two books. See William Fitch (Benet of Canfield), *The Rule of Perfection* (Rouen, 1609), repr. English Recusant Literature 1558-1640, selected and edited by D.M. Rogers, vol. 10 (Scolar Press, 1970). Citations from Books I and II in the body of the paper are from this edition.

books into English, and the whole (comprising three books) into Latin. The 1610 French edition, printed at Paris, is the authorized form of the text, upon which the many subsequent reprintings were based.[29]

The principle of the coincidence of opposites is implicit in Benet's formal intention to "reduce" and "abridge" the "whole spirituall life" to one "only point": the "will of God," which is God's essence (I, 1, 1). Benet's *reductio* is akin to the reductions of Eriugena, Ramón Lull, and Bonaventure. He applies the method of reduction to the spiritual and moral life, leading each spiritual and corporal act into immediate union with God. Benet's upward movement of reduction has a corresponding downward movement of division.[30] Benet divides the will of God as it descends to man into three stages of the spiritual life: supereminent or superessential, interior, and exterior. In speaking of this division of God's will, Benet carefully eschews "scholasticall divisions" which are merely conceptions of the human mind. Benet's division is "mysticall," for although the will of God appears differently to souls in different stages of the spiritual life, nevertheless, the three manifestations of God's will (exterior, interior, and essential) "are one and the same will in God" (I, 4, 28-29). Benet's method of division and reduction, like that of Eriugena and Ramón Lull, is grounded on the essential identity of God's attributes in the divine unity, in this instance, the identity between the will of God and the divine essence.[31] God's will, one with his very essence, manifests itself variously in the multiple, created world in which the soul operates during this life.

Benet's reduction of the "whole spirituall life" to one "only point" has another, more practical aim. In the sixteenth century the Christian enjoying the fruit of spiritual thought in the Middle Ages was offered a multitude of spiritual doctrines, many of which appeared to conflict. In order to avoid confusion and to simplify, Benet proposes a spiritual method which "contains" and "comprehends" all the others (I, 2, 10-20). The *Règle de perfection*, in other words, is a *complicatio* of all Catholic traditions of contemplation.

The principle of the coincidence of opposites is most evident in Book III, controverted among Benet's contemporaries as it is today among modern scholars. In Book III, Benet treats the supereminent, or superessential life wherein the soul is united immediately to the divine will.

---

[29] *Reigle [sic] de perfection* (1610; repr. Lyons, 1653). My citations and translations from Book III in the body of the paper are from this edition.

[30] Guy-H. Allard, "La Technique de la *reductio* chez Bonaventure," in *S. Bonaventura, 1274-1974*, II (Grottaferrata, 1974), 395-416.

[31] Frances Yates, "Ramon Lull and John Scotus Erigena," *Journal of the Warburg and Courtauld Institutes*, 23 (1960), 1-44; Louis Sala-Molins, *La Philosophie de l'amour chez Raymond Lulle* (Paris, 1974), 50-95; and esp. E. Colomer, *De la edad media al renacimiento (Ramón Lull-Nicholás de Cusa-Juan Pico della Mirandola)* (Barcelona, 1975), 109-112, 159-66, 185-89, 219-23, *et passim*.

This highest form of spiritual life entails an amazing series of reconcil-iations. In the supereminent life the active and contemplative lives are united, as are the traditional mystic contemplation without images and contemplation of the Passion. This latter, apparent contradiction has led Jean Orcibal to conclude that the chapters in the *Règle* concerning the Passion are a subsequent addition requested by Benet's superiors and reflecting an "evolution" of his spirituality.[32] Whether Orcibal's hypoth-esis be wholly correct, and there is reason to doubt that it is,[33] Benet's reconciliation between contemplation with and without images is but one of a series of the coincidence of opposites, all of which are founded on yet another, that between the "All" of the creator and the "nothing" of the creature. This coincidence, in turn, is rooted in the identity of the will of God with the divine essence.

Benet's identification of the will of God with the divine essence recalls the principle, crucial in the thought of Nicholas of Cusa, that theology is circular, that is, that all of God's attributes are inseparable in the divine unity. Interestingly, in *De docta ignorantia* Cusanus states the principle in a text where he identifies God's will and omnipotence, and suggests that the creature is "utterly nothing," having less being in relation to the infinity of God than an accident in relation to substance.[34] From the identity of attributes in God, Benet of Canfield draws the same two conclusions. Furthermore, Eusebio Colomer contends that Nicholas de-rives the principle of the coincidence of opposites from the identity of divine attributes.[35] Benet of Canfield will follow Nicholas in this too.

Benet establishes the identity of the will of God with God's essence in Book III, chapter 1 of the *Règle*. In contrast to the exterior and interior will of God, appearing to man in sensible images and intelligible species, the "essential will" of God is "purely spirit and life, totally abstract, and stripped bare of all forms and images of created things, corporal or spiritual, temporal or eternal." As such, human reason cannot apprehend it, since "it is nothing other than God himself" (III, 1, 218-19). To demonstrate this identity, Benet produces several arguments. First, he alludes to a text from Bonaventure: since there is nothing in God which is not God, and since will exists in God, the will of God must be God.[36] Secondly, if God's will were not his essence, there would be some po-tentiality in God, and God would not be *pure act*, as most doctors teach. Thirdly, if God's will were not his essence, there would be something in one part of him that is not in another, and God could not be said to be

[32] Jean Orcibal, "'La Règle de perfection' de Benoît de Canfield: a t'elle été interpolée?" *Divinitas,* 2(1967), 845-74.

[33] Emery, 72-147, *et passim.*

[34] *De doct. ign.,* II, 3, 71-72.

[35] Colomer, *De la edad media al renacimiento,* 185-89. Colomer, 159-66, shows that Cusanus inherited the principle that theology is circular from Ramón Lull.

[36] Bonaventure, *In primum librum Sententiarum, Opera omnia* I (Quaracchi, 1882), d.8, p.2, q.4, 3 *ad opp.,* 173; d.45, a.1, q.1, 798-99.

"infinitely perfect in all perfection." Thus, one would needs say that there is some limit to God's will and to his essence. Hence, both will and essence would be finite and not infinite, if finite limited, if limited created, and if created, then they are not the creator. Finally, in Anselmian fashion, Benet argues that if God's will were not infinite, someone would have had to limit it, and that one would be greater than God, *ad infinitum*. However, both the will of God and the divine essence are infinite, and since there cannot be two infinities, the will of God must be identical with God's essence (III, 1, 219-20).

To support his reasoning, Benet adduces several authorities. He quotes Hilary concerning the absence of composition in God, Peter Lombard concerning God's simplicity, and Augustine and Boethius concerning God's substantial unity (III, 1, 221-23). Fundamentally, however, Benet's arguments follow from two main premises, God's pure act of being and his infinity. From the same two premises Benet later deduces the All of God and the nothing of the creature. Considering God in terms of his pure act and infinity serves Benet's spiritual doctrine well. As Bonaventure teaches, being is not predicated metaphorically of God, for *qui est* is a proper name for God.[37] Hence, when one speaks of God's being, he speaks properly of God's essence, as Benet intends in the third book of the *Règle de perfection*. Bonaventure's discourses concerning God's pure act of being, we shall see, are the primary source for the doctrine of All and nothing developed by Benet and other Capuchin writers. Appropriately, in his emblem for the *Règle de perfection* Benet inscribes the unpronounceable *tetragrammaton* on the face of the sun which represents God's essence and will.[38] The notion of the infinity of God is useful to Benet's purpose, for it defies conceptions formed by the human imagination and reason. Moreover, God's infinity implies the relative nothingness of the creature, for how can the finite be something when the infinite is everything? At this point, we might note that according to Bovelles' modern commentator, the two names that apply best to God in Bovelles' mystical theology are "being and infinity."[39]

Benet's arguments are more suggestive than rigorous. Nor did Benet intend otherwise. After asserting the identity of God's will with God's essence, Benet admonishes the reader not to seek or contemplate the divine will "under some images, forms, or similitudes, however spiritual or subtle they may be" because all such images are unworthy of their object (III, 1, 224). Benet does not wish the contemplative, who must rise above all images, to risk complacence in intellectual species. It is probably for this reason that Benet does not use the arguments of Bonaventure, or, unlike his Capuchin confrère Laurent de Paris, those of

[37] I *Sent.*, d.22, q.3, 394-97.
[38] *Reigle de perfection*, "Explication de ceste Figure". On the *tetragrammaton* see Cusanus, *De doct. ign.*, I, 24, 48-49.
[39] Victor, *Charles de Bovelles*, 177.

Thomas Aquinas, which demonstrate the convertibility of the divine will and the divine essence.[40] "Scholasticall" reasonings like these suggest to the imagination, if not to the intellect, that there are divisions among God's acts.

From God's infinite, undivided act of being Benet deduces the most extreme coincidence of opposites conceivable, that between All and nothing. In the Franciscan manner, Benet does not develop this doctrine for purely speculative reasons but rather for ascetic and moral ones. It is necessary therefore, to interpret Benet's doctrine of All and nothing in the light of his contemplative teaching.

Benet distinguishes two forms of contemplation in the supereminent life which, although they differ in their "accidents" or in the soul's experience, are nevertheless one in "essence." The first of these, which Benet calls *passive annihilation*, is the effect of the "actual drawing of God." It occurs in ecstasy, when the soul is drawn above the senses and intellectual powers into immediate union with God in the *apex mentis*.[41] Inspired by the psychology and trinitarian exemplarism of John Ruysbroeck,[42] Benet teaches that the immediate union between God and the *apex mentis* produces certain effects which flow into the three faculties of the soul. In the will, the only faculty capable in this life of extending to God immediately, the soul experiences a "flowing of fervent desires into God." In the intellect, the soul is purged of all images and experiences a total "denuding of spirit." Finally, in the memory, the soul recollects a "continual nearness and close vision" of its "object and blessed final end" (III, 4, 235; see III, 4-7, 235-67). Although in this contemplation the soul does not see God's essence face to face, it does perceive that God is the immediate "source and foundation" of the illumination it receives, that God is more present to the soul than it is to itself, and that the soul

dwells, resides and lives uniquely in him, and not at all in itself, whence it follows that the soul is all in God, all God's, all for God and all God, and

---

[40] Bonaventure, I *Sent.*, d.45, a.1, q.1-2, 797-802; Thomas Aquinas, *Summa theologiae*, I, q.19, a.1, 3,5; Laurent de Paris, *Le Palais de l'amour divin entre Jésus et l'âme chrestienne* (Paris, 1614), 318, 957-58. All citations and translations from Laurent's text in the body of the paper are from this edition.

[41] On this term which Benet uses, see E. van Ivánka *Plato Christianus* (Einsieden, 1964), 315-51.

[42] On Ruysbroeck and Benet, see Mommaers, "Benoît de Canfeld et ses sources flamandes," *Revue d'histoire de la spiritualité*, **48** (1972), 401-434, **49** (1973), 37-66; Emery, 432-40. Lefèvre d'Etaples published Ruysbroeck's *De ornatu spiritualium nuptiarum libri tres*, trans. William Jordaens (c.1360) (Paris, 1512). Benet and Laurent, however, probably read the work in the translation by the Carthusian Laurentius Surius, *Ioannis Rusbrochii Opera omnia* (Cologne, 1552; repr. Farnborough-Hants, Eng., 1967), 303-372. The Capuchins' Carthusian friend, Richard Beaucousin, translated Ruysbroeck's work into French from Surius' Latin: *L'Ornament des nopces [sic] spirituelles* (Toulouse, 1606).

nothing in itself, nothing of itself, nothing for itself, nothing itself; it is all in the spirit, will, light and power of God, and nothing in its own spirit, will, light, and natural power (III, 6, 259).

Thus although the intellect does not comprehend God's essence, in experiencing the soul's nothingness, it intuits the All of God's existence.

Such elevated moments of contemplation do not perdure in this life. However, it is possible, Benet teaches, to maintain a perpetual, habitual, and immediate union with the will of God. Benet's second form of contemplation, *active annihilation*, preserves the essence, if not the experience of ecstatic union, even while one is immersed in the sensible world and engaged in the duties of the active life. But whereas in passive annihilation intuition of God's All and the creature's nothing is the effect of union, in active annihilation this intuition is a means to union. Active annihilation is "more remote from feeling, more supernatural, more naked, and more perfect" than passive annihilation. Passive annihilation takes place when the soul is elevated, stripped bare, and drawn outside itself by the "actual drawing of the will of God." In active annihilation, the soul is drawn solely by the "virtual drawing of God" by which it remains united to God when "impeded exteriorly with images and occupied in affairs." During active annihilation an extraordinary coincidence of opposites occurs: exterior things are rendered interior, "corporeal things become spiritual and natural things become supernatural" (III, 8, 267-68).

The practice of active annihilation depends upon the knowledge that there is nothing else but the essential will of God. One acquires this knowledge through the "light of a pure, simple, naked, and habitual faith, aided by reason, ratified and confirmed by experience, and not subject to the senses, . . . but indeed contrary to them" (III, 12, 300). This light reveals to the soul that God is All and the creature nothing, a truth so paradoxical that it confounds conception, and thus annihilates the very act of intellect that tries to comprehend it. In this way, the soul suffers the same "denuding of spirit" that it does, by another means, in passive annihilation.

As Benet says, the "naked faith" in one's nothingness before the All of God is "aided by reason." To this purpose Benet advances another series of philosophic and theological arguments. Again, Benet reasons from God's pure act of being and infinity. It is a well known maxim, Benet points out, that being and goodness are convertible. Scripture says, however, that no one is good except God (Luke, 18:19); it follows, therefore, that no one has being except God. For this reason, God revealed his name to Moses as *Ego sum qui sum*. Moreover, God is infinite. If the creature were something, however, God would not be so, for his being would end where the creature's begins. Benet confirms these rapid deductions with a text from Bonaventure who himself quotes Jerome:

"God alone truly is, compared to whose essence our being is nothing" (III, 8, 269-70).[43]

Benet's reasoning here is as abbreviated as elsewhere, and doubtless for the same reasons. In order to impress the truth of God's All and the creature's nothing in the soul of the reader, a truth one cannot adequately express "by words," Benet prefers another device. In the tradition of pseudo-Dionysius and other neo-Platonic, Christian contemplatives, Benet uses a "dissimilar similitude," which does not allow confusion of the image with the object.[44] A creature, Benet says, is nothing but a "pure dependency" on God. In relation to God, a creature is as rays of light are in relation to the sun. As the rays of the sun depend entirely on their origin without whose continual communication and sustaining they would not be able to subsist, so the creature depends entirely on the creator without whose continual maintenance the creature would not be able to be. As the rays of the sun, therefore, must be referred entirely to the sun, so the creature must be referred to the creator, according to the maxim, "all being which is such through participation, must be referred to the being which is such by essence." When the sun withdraws, its rays disappear; likewise, if God were to withdraw from the creature, the creature would vanish. Nevertheless, although there is nothing in the creature but God, as there is nothing in rays of light but the sun, the creature, considered in itself, is not God. Rather, like rays in relation to their origin, the creature is a certain "dependency" or "spark" of God's being. When one considers a creature in itself, it appears to be something; but when one contemplates the creature in relation to God, it is nothing (III, 8, 272-273):

for as the sun assumes and appropriates to itself all its rays as beams issuing and going out from it, and as when it recalls them to their origin, its great light swallows them up and annihilates them and reduces them to nothing; so likewise the creator assumes and appropriates the creature to himself, as some spark gone out from him, and recalls it to himself as to its center and origin, and in his infinity he annihilates it and reduces it to nothing. (III, 8, 274).

Thus, although the creature may be considered apart from God as something, it is "nothing considered in the immensity of God, and in his infinite being."

Benet's similitude provokes two reactions among commentators. Those who wish to save Benet's orthodoxy say that he confuses the

---

[43] Bonaventure, I *Sent.*, d.8, p.1, a.1, q.1, *arg. pro aff.* 1, 150; d.22, q.3, *arg. con.* 4, 395.

[44] For medieval commentary on this theme, see, for example, Hugh of St. Victor, *Exposition in Hierarchiam Coelestem, PL* 175.961, 988-89; Richard of St. Victor, *In Apocalypsim Joannis, PL* 196.686-90; Dionysius Cartusianus, *Commentaria in librum de Coelesti seu Angelica Hierarchia, Opera omnia* XV (Tournai. 1902), 32-34. See also E.H. Gombrich, "*Icones Symbolicae:* Philosophies of Symbolism and their Bearing on Art," in *Symbolic Images: Studies in the Art of the Renaissance* (New York, 1972), 145-60.

psychological and ontologic orders.[45] Others argue that Benet verges towards pantheism.[46] Neither view, I believe is correct. On the one hand, in active annihilation the knowledge of the All of God and the nothingness of the creature is not a subjective experience but an objective truth upon which to base practice. On the other hand, as we shall see, the main source for Benet's doctrine is impeccably orthodox. None the less, one can understand the confusion of commentators. Judged in terms of Aristotelian logic, the above text is at least ill-sounding. Perhaps, however, the nothingness of the creature in relation to God might better be understood in terms of the coincidence of opposites.

The analogy of light and its diffusion of rays, applied to spiritual progress, has a long tradition among mystical writers.[47] Benet knew this tradition well. However, his precise use of the analogy in the above text, applied to the relative being of the creature, has, I think, a specific source. In arguing the creature's nothingness, Benet alludes explicitly to only one authority: Bonaventure. Indeed, Bonaventure uses this analogy in a work not properly mystical, his commentary on the *Sentences*, and there in the context of an argument similar to Benet's. When commenting upon a question concerning God's presence in all things, Bonaventure makes a triple distinction among the ways in which one thing may be united to another. First, one thing may be united to another through a *presence, dependence,* and a *concomitance* in matter, as the virtue (power) of a liquid is united to its matter. Secondly, one thing may be united to another immaterially, through a *presence* and *dependence,* as the soul is united to the body. Thirdly, one thing may be united to another in a purely immaterial and independent way, as the sun is present to the air in the radius of its light. It is in this third manner, Bonaventure says, that God is present in all things.[48]

The omnipresence of God, as understood by Bonaventure, elucidates Benet's doctrine of All and nothing. Bonaventure's influence upon Benet of Canfield is not unexpected. Although Capuchin scholastics were eclectic, Bonaventure nevertheless was the official doctor of the Order.[49] Perhaps more important, the spiritual teaching of Bonaventure was the basis for training Capuchin novices.[50] Bonaventure's influence upon Benet on the immediate questions is confirmed by the writings of Benet's fellow Capuchin, Laurent de Paris. Benet and Laurent lived at the same time

[45] Optat de Veghel, 293-94, 316n.1.

[46] Jean Orcibal, "Divinisation," *Dictionnaire de spiritualité,* III (Paris, 1957), 1446-52.

[47] Emery, 148-249, *passim.*

[48] I *Sent.,* d.37, a.1, q.1, 638-39.

[49] Camille Bérubé, "Les Capuchins à l'école de saint Bonaventure," *Collectanea Franciscana,* 44 (1974), 275-330.

[50] Louis Prunières, "Tradition bonaventurienne et spiritualité capucine en France au XVIIe siècle," *Collectanea Franciscana,* 44 (1974), 355-86.

in the convent of St. Honoré in Paris. If not written first, Laurent de Paris' *Le Palais d'amour divin* was printed in 1602-1603 before the *Règle de perfection*. The doctrine of the two works could not be more similar. Because of the similarity of their teaching, Benet and Laurent were coupled by friend and foe alike in a prolonged controversy over contemplation.[51] In response to this controversy, Laurent added treatises to a new edition of *Le Palais d'amour divin* in 1614.[52] These treatises amplify, with reason and authority, themes already present in the earlier edition.[53]

Although the *Règle de perfection* and *Le Palais d'amour divin* develop the same themes, the style of the two works is completely different. Where Benet is elliptical, Laurent is prolix. As a result, one finds explicit in Laurent's *Le Palais* what is usually implicit in Benet's cryptic *Règle*. In particular, in Laurent's work one will discover that the doctrine of the creator's All and the creature's nothing is an inference drawn from Bonaventure's teachings concerning God's pure act of being and consequent presence in all things.

Laurent de Paris' indebtedness to Bonaventure is evident in three treatises of *Le Palais d'amour* which treat a triad of divine attributes, Beauty, Truth, and Goodness.[54] On this subject Laurent either quotes or paraphrases closely long passages from chapters five and six of Bonaventure's *Itinerarium mentis in Deum*. On the principle that the divine attributes are convertible, Laurent identifies the divine Beauty with Being, which Bonaventure teaches to be the first name of God. Following closely chapter five of the *Itinerarium,* Laurent argues that Being-in-itself is so certain that it cannot be thought not to be. Hence, Being is the first thing noticed in the mind, for one can in no wise know created things, which suffer potentiality and privation, without knowing first that Being which is pure-in-act. In order to account for the mind's blindness to Being pure-in-act, Laurent borrows Bonaventure's analogy. As the physical eye loses itself in the variety of color so that it does not attend to the source of its light, so the mind, dispersed in a multitude of phantasms, does not see the act of Being upon which all created beings depend. From God's pure act of being, Laurent again following Bonaventure deduces that

---

[51] Jean Orcibal, *La Rencontre du carmel thérésien avec les mystiques du nord* (Paris, 1959).

[52] See note 40, above.

[53] Dubois-Quinard, 65-81.

[54] The usual scholastic triad is *unum, verum, bonum.* Laurent converts beauty and being, and these convertibles are added to truth and goodness. Laurent's immediate source is probably Dionysius Cartusianus, *De venustate mundi et pulchritudine Dei, Opera omnia,* XXXIV (Tournai), esp. a.1, 227-28, a.3, 229. Why Laurent uses the names Beauty, Truth, Goodness, when in fact he speaks of being, truth, goodness, is curious, since Paul Oskar Kristeller, "The Modern System of the Arts", repr. in *Renaissance Thought and the Arts* (Princeton, 1980) 167, has shown that the triad beauty, truth, goodness—as triad—seems to be an invention of the nineteenth century.

God is first, eternal, most simple, most actual, most perfect, and supremely one (127, 419-23).[55] Laurent concludes from these divine attributes that God is All to all created things, not as their formal essence but as the "most excellent cause of all the essences." Laurent, in the *Itinerarium*, finds expression for God being All to all things without being any of them; because God is perfect and immense he is within all things but not contained by them, outside all things but not excluded, above all things but not aloof, below all things but not humbled (127, 428).[56]

Bonaventure's terse formula expressing God's presence in, yet separation from, all things, implies the coincidence of opposites between the All of the creator and the nothing of the creature. Laurent de Paris defines the sense in which God is All in a special treatise concerning God's omnipresence, which in effect explicates Bonaventure's formula. As well as relying upon the *Itinerarium*, Laurent's treatise draws more detailed arguments from Bonaventure's commentary on the *Sentences*.[57]

Commentators on the *Sentences,* including Bonaventure, declare that God is in all things according to his *presence, power,* and *essence.* Laurent emphasizes the last of these, since it is through his essence, his pure act of being, that God is most intimately present to created things. Nothing is more intimate to a creature than its being, and creatures receive their being immediately from God. Because creatures depend upon God's being not only for their creation but for their preservation as long as they exist, God is present, essentially and intimately, in all of them, and in all of their acts (131, dup. pag. 465).[58]

God is intimately present to creatures at all times; so also is he in all places, for God gives places whatever being they possess, and the potency they have for giving place. Of course, God does not occupy place as a body does; rather, he is everywhere at once by virtue of his spiritual immensity.[59] God's immensity and extensive power are identical with his essence; thus, where he is present through his immensity, he is present through his whole essence (131, dup. pag. 466). Laurent distinguishes in Bonaventure's terms: whereas bodies occupy place by filling "the emptiness of distance," God gives place its being by filling the "emptiness of essence" (132, dup. pag. 468).[60] Properly speaking, as Bonaventure says, God is substantially present to all creatures by reason of the "indistance of his essence" (133, 471-73).[61] From these terms of Bonaventure it is a

[55] Bonaventure, *Itin.*, V, 308-310.

[56] *Ibid.,* V, 8, 310.

[57] I *Sent.,* d.37, p.1, 632-34 (text of Peter Lombard); 637-51 (Bonaventure's commentary).

[58] Bonaventure, I *Sent.,* d.37, p.1, a.1, q.1, 638-39.

[59] *Ibid.,* d.37, p.1, a.1, q.2; a.2, q.1-2, 640-645.

[60] *Ibid.,* d.37, p.1, a.1, q.2, 641.

[61] *Ibid.,* d.37, p.1, a.3, q.2, 647-49.

short step to a formula which but for a word is Cusanus': God may be called the "essence, indeed the superessence of all essences" (132, dup. pag. 468).[62] Laurent summarizes God's omnipresence in a traditional formula which he cites from Bonaventure's *Itinerarium:* God is an intelligible sphere whose center is everywhere and circumference nowhere (132, dup. pag. 467).[63]

Laurent defines the creature's nothingness as corollary to God's omnipresence, in another special treatise devoted to the topic. Here Laurent again acknowledges his debt to Bonaventure, and adds that his current topic might well be included in the treatise on God's omnipresence (145, 573). If God is independent, absolute, self-subsistent, and infinite Being, then one must necessarily conclude that a creature is "a pure, actual, total, continual, universal, essential dependence," in short, a "nothing" (145, 573). While God is the first of all things, man is the last in creation; while God is independent, man is wholly dependent; while God is absolute, man is subject to a thousand relations. Thus, man, who holds his being entirely from another, is nothing in himself, as is evident "by analogy and relation to him who alone is" (145, 575). Man's created being, then, is merely an effect of God's being, in much the same way that rays of light are effects of the sun that preserves them (133, dup. pag. 473). Benet of Canfield, we shall remember, refers to the same maxim, and develops the same similitude.

Like Benet of Canfield, therefore, Laurent de Paris deduces the creature's nothingness from the pure act of God's being. Benet did likewise from the infinity of God. Laurent too avails himself of this principle. His treatise on the divine Beauty, we have pointed out, is almost entirely a paraphrase of chapter five of Bonaventure's *Itinerarium*. Significantly, the only material in this treatise not taken from the *Itinerarium* concerns the divine infinity. Laurent states in this regard, without direct warrant of Bonaventure, that infinity is the "first and most intrinsic property" of God's grandeur (127, 424). It would seem that Laurent de Paris, and by implication Benet of Canfield, found this notion elsewhere than in Bonaventure.

In moving from consideration of Being to the second of the divine attributes, Truth, Laurent deviates from the progress of Bonaventure's *Itinerarium*. Bonaventure proceeds immediately from God's first name, Being, to his second, Goodness, which is God's third attribute in Laurent's scheme. It is precisely in the treatise on Truth, insinuated between Bonaventure's meditations on God's Being and Goodness, that the idea of divine infinity is most prominent in *Le Palais d'amour divin*.

[62] *De doct. ign.*, I, 16, 32: "omnium essentiarum simplicissima essentia".

[63] Bonaventure, *Itin.*, V, 8, 310. See *De doct. Ing.* I, 12, 25; I, 23, 46-47. The ultimate source of the maxim is pseudo-Hermes Trismegistus, *Liber XXIV philosophorum*. See Marie Thérèse d'Alverny, *Catalogus Translationum et Commentariorum* (Washington, 1960), 151-54.

Alluding to texts of pseudo-Dionysius, Laurent asserts that God is totally incomprehensible to the human intellect. Man's intellect, like his being, is impotent in relation to God. In fact, it cannot even grasp essentially created objects proportionate to it. This weakness of the human intellect is a consequence of God's All and the creature's nothingness. If one wishes to know the truth of created being, it is necessary to know God who is the "fontal and ideal" cause of all things, who causes all things to be and subsist, and who is more intimate to created things than they are to themselves. Such knowledge is impossible, since God is infinite, and man's finite mind cannot therefore grasp God (128, 433). Truth presents itself to the human mind in a multiplicity of things and operations. However, just as one cannot know numbers without first knowing the unity from which they unfold, so one cannot know the multitude of created things without knowing the unity upon which they depend. This unity, in Laurent's words, is "coincident" with Truth itself (128, 433-34). Elsewhere in *Le Palais d'amour* Laurent likewise speaks of God as the "numeral unity, the fountain of all numbers"; in God's being all creatures participate as all subsequent numbers unfold from the number one. God, in these terms, is the "punctual beginning" and "supereminent point of the whole universe" (301, 804-805). This idea reflects Cusanus, who in *De docta ignorantia* conceives God's infinite unity as a point.[64] In light of this arithmetical analogy, it would seem that the one "only point" to which Benet of Canfield reduces the spiritual life is more than a rhetorical adage.

The order of knowing follows the order of being. Thus, as a creature cannot wholly possess its own being, so in knowing it cannot adequately comprehend the being of other creatures. No matter how much one believes himself to know something, Laurent says, he knows that he could know it more truly. One realizes that, with a more penetrating eye, he can see visible objects yet more clearly; in truth, no visible object can be seen perfectly except by an eye infinite in power. The same may be said concerning intellectual sight. There is no circle so great, for example, that one could not conceive a greater, unless it be infinite, and this transcends imagination. Thus, not able to know infinite truth, one cannot even comprehend the truth of created essences, for these are radically contingent upon the "superessential," infinite Being. Laurent gives one more illustration. Whoever would know the virtue of a seed, which produces the roots, ears, stems, and leaves of a plant, must know its "seminal reason." This, however, is lost in the eternal reason, which causes the seed to subsist. In not knowing this Truth about a thing, one does not properly know it at all (128, 434).

Students of Nicholas of Cusa (d. 1464) will recognize these *formulae*, both in sound and sense, as coming from *De docta ignorantia* and *De*

---

[64] *De doct. ign.*, II, 3, 69.

visione Dei.[65] Laurent, concluding his discussion of man's impotent knowledge, confirms the association. The only real knowledge man can have, Laurent says, is that he knows nothing. This knowledge Laurent calls "the great science of learned ignorance" (128, 434). It appears that Laurent de Paris and Benet of Canfield, in deducing the creature's nothingness from God's pure act of his infinity, join the thought of Nicholas of Cusa to that of Bonaventure. Indeed, once alerted to the influence of Nicholas, one will discover that Benet's argument for the nothingness of the creature following from God's infinity resembles closely a text in *De visione Dei.*[66]

In a final contemplation of God's encompassing being, Laurent once more quotes his favorite text from Bonaventure's *Itinerarium.* This time, however, he adds a significant clause. God is above all without being elevated, below all without being beneath, outside of all without being foreclosed, within all, without being enclosed: in short, God is "the coincidence of all opposition and contrariety" (212, 663). For the only time in his work of over 1200 pages, Laurent de Paris cites Nicholas of Cusa in the margin.

Benet's and Laurent's synthesis of Bonaventure and Cusanus does not seem extrinsic or imposed. E. H. Cousins has shown that the coincidence of opposites was operative in Bonaventure's theology, and that Cusanus' thought indeed resembles Bonaventure's.[67] Lefèvre d'Etaples and Charles de Bovelles did not think that Cusanus' intellectual philosophy contradicted Aristotle's rational philosophy. Like Lefèvre and Bovelles, Benet and Laurent located the principle of the coincidence of opposites in mystical theology. Consequently, they perceived no contradiction between Cusanus' speculations and Bonaventure's many hierarchical, metaphysical conceptions. Contrary to what some notable moderns contend,[68] they did not consider God's essential infinity to efface the traditional hierarcy of being. Following Bonaventure,[69] Laurent de Paris carefully distinguishes God's uniform presence in all things, considered

---

[65] *Ibid.,* II, 3, 70-71; *De visione Dei,* ed. Jacobus Faber Stapulensis (Paris, 1514; repr. Frankfurt/Main, 1962, vol. 1), I, 99v; VII, 101v-102r; IX, 103r-v.

[66] *De visione Dei,* XIII, 105v. It is interesting that the seventeenth-century English Antinomian, Giles Randall, translated both the third book of Benet's *Règle (A Bright-Starre leading to and containing in Christ our Perfection,* London, 1646), and, in the same year, Nicholas' *De Visione (The Single Eye, entitled the Vision of God,* London, 1646).

[67] Ewert H. Cousins, "The Coincidence of Opposites in the Christology of St. Bonaventure," *Franciscan Studies,* **28** (1968), 27-45; "La 'Coincidentia Oppositorum' dans la théologie de Bonaventure," *Etudes franciscaines,* **18** (suppl. ann., 1968), 15-31; "Bonaventure, the Coincidence of Opposites and Nicholas of Cusa," in *Studies Honoring Ignatius Charles Brady Friar Minor,* ed. R. Almagno and C. Harkins (St. Bonaventure, N.Y., 1976), 177-97.

[68] Ernst Cassirer, *Individuum und Kosmos in der Philosophie der Renaissance* (Leipzig, 1927). See the remarks of Paul E. Sigmund, *Nicholas of Cusa and Medieval Political Thought* (Cambridge, Mass., 1963), 244-60.

[69] *I Sent.,* d.37, p.1, a.3, q.2, 646-47.

with respect to his infinite divine being, from his unequal presence in all things, considered in regard to his finite created effects (132, 468).

The influence of Bonaventure and Cusanus upon Benet and Laurent does not preclude a possible, intervening source for their teaching concerning the relation between creator and creature. If Charles de Bovelles did not directly influence (we have no explicit evidence), he surely anticipated the Capuchins' doctrine of All and nothing. In his work *De nihilo* (1511), largely influenced in its method by Cusanus, and in subsequent theological treatises, Bovelles conceived the relation between creator and creature logically as the relation between a positive term and its opposite negation. Since he defined God as essentially infinite being, Bovelles concluded that creation stood in relation to the creator as nonbeing or nothingness in relation to absolute being. Like Benet and Laurent, Bovelles deduced God's omnipresence from the divine infinity, which sustains the being of creatures against an underlying nothingness; as Joseph Victor observes, in such a doctrine the being of creatures is marked by a radical contingency and instability.[70] Among his many arguments for the nothingness of creatures, Laurent de Paris states the radical contingency of creatures in logical terms close to Bovelles'. This time citing Duns Scotus (II *Sent.*, d.50, qq. 4 & 5), Laurent states that the "relation of real and essential dependency, identical, really and essentially, with the creature itself" is the relation between a merely privative term (nothing) and the opposite, positive term by which it is defined. Only by means of its opposite "conserving, principle, and final term . . . namely God, self-subsistent Being" is the creature able to subsist (579). It is worth remarking that in this text Laurent evokes another authority, medieval and Franciscan, who predicated infinity positively and substantially of God.[71]

If there is no proportion between the infinite and the finite, between All and nothing, what then is the mean between God and his creation? Bovelles resolves the problem logically, by means of species of comparisons drawn chiefly from the works of Ramón Lull.[72] Benet and Laurent relied on their usual sources. Cousins has shown how terms of opposition in Bonaventure find their mean in the person of Christ.[73] Similarly, Christ is the mean between creator and created world in Nicholas of Cusa.[74] So also is he for Laurent de Paris and Benet of Canfield.

[70] Victor, *Charles de Bovelles*, 149-53, esp. 149. For Cusanus' *formulae* for the "nothingness" of creatures, see *De doct. ign.*, I, 16, pp. 30-32, I, 24, pp. 48-51, II, 3, pp. 69-72.

[71] Étienne Gilson, *Jean Duns Scot: Introduction à ses positions fundamentales* (Paris, 1952), 116-215. Victor, "The Revival of Lullism," 517-18, notes that many linked Lull and Duns Scotus, Lull and Bonaventure.

[72] Victor, *Charles de Bovelles*, 150-51.

[73] Cousins, "The Coincidence of Opposites in the Christology of St. Bonaventure," *loc. cit.*, 37-45.

[74] *De doct. ignorantia*, III, 2-6, 123-39; Cousins, "Bonaventure . . . and Nicholas of Cusa," 191-97.

When contemplating Goodness, the third of the triad of divine attributes, Laurent de Paris returns to paraphrasing Bonaventure's *Itinerarium*. Laurent deduces, like Bonaventure, the generation of the Son and the procession of the Spirit from the diffusive nature of Goodness, God's most proper name (129, 445-50).[75] But if the expansion of Goodness is marvelous *ad intra,* it is in a sense more so *ad extra.* God expresses his Goodness most fully in the union between God and man in Christ. This union achieves a final reconciliation of opposites. In the God-man, Laurent says quoting Bonaventure, one sees the primal first joined to the last of all, the eternal joined with the temporal, the most simple with the most composite, the most actual with the most suffering and altered, the most immense with the littlest, and the perfectly one with the individual composed and distinguished from all others (129, 451).[76] God's Goodness, revealed in the Incarnation, is even more manifest when one considers especially Christ's Passion, Laurent adds, for here one sees God united with the nadir of existence. Paradoxically, therefore, contemplation of God's highest name, Goodness, leads to contemplation of the greatest humiliation.

As contemplation of Christ is for Bonaventure and Laurent de Paris a necessary corollary to the highest form of contemplation, so it is for Benet of Canfield. Benet unites contemplation of the Passion to the contemplation of All and nothing. Although Benet states often that one must abandon all images in contemplation, in both passive annihilation, where images are anyway impossible, and in active annihilation he regularly excepts the Passion from this rule. In the first place the Passion is a special image, since in it "the inaccessible light is proportioned to man's capacity" (III, 20, 385). Although abstract images of the divinity seem more perfect than the image of the Passion, they are not really so, for they are one's own making, whereas the image of the Passion is given to man by God (III, 20, 383-85). Abstract images induce speculation; only the Passion, the image of God's love, can transform the soul in "fervor and living flames" (III, 20, 379).

Contemplation of the Passion pertains properly to active annihilation, and reveals in visible form the All of God united to the nothingness of the creature. It is important, Benet teaches, that one contemplate Christ's divinity and humanity together. Contemplating this way, one sees in a single person, as Bonaventure says, "the first and the last, the highest and the lowest, the circumference and its center, namely the book written without and within" (III, 20, 295-96).[77] Specifically, the paradox of the cross is the paradox of All and nothing. One sees on the cross the Son of God who, having assumed the form of a servant, "is annihilated and made nothing, as man is nothing" (III, 8, 270). We have remarked that

---

[75] Bonaventure, *Itinerarium,* VI, 310-12.

[76] *Ibid.,* VI, 5, 311.

[77] *Ibid.,* VI, 7, 312.

awareness of the All of God and the nothingness of the creature annihilates the very act of reason that tries to comprehend it. Likewise, correct contemplation of the Passion simultaneously admits corporal images and annihilates them:

in order to resolve this, it is necessary to rise above reason to faith, which looking at this man, recognizes him for God who is without form or image. And although the imagination represents the form of a man, nevertheless faith, transcending all sense and imagination, does not see any form since it sees God in such a way that, although we have the representation of a crucifix, the immensity of faith absorbs and annihilates it (III, 17, 357-58).

Christ on the cross, then, transcends all contradictions, or, to use Benet's words, the Passion is "the book wherein contrary propositions are reconciled" (III, 17, 353-54). For Benet of Canfield, Christ is the coincidence of opposites in whom God and redeemed man, that which is All and that which by nature is nothing, become one.

Primarily through the labors of Lefèvre d'Etaples and Charles de Bovelles, Nicholas of Cusa achieved authority as a doctor of mystical theology in early modern France. His principle of the coincidence of opposites supplied the sufficient reason for the mystical practice of the Capuchin friars, Benet of Canfield and Laurent de Paris. Capuchin enthusiasm for Cusanus continued through the seventeenth century.[78] And the essential point of Benet's and Laurent's mystical *ars oppositorum* entered the *Pensées* of another Frenchman:

What, after all, is man in nature? A nothing in comparison with the infinite, an all in comparison with the infinitely small, a midpoint between nothing and everything. . . . The finite is annihilated in the presence of the infinite, and becomes a pure nothing. So is our spirit before God; so is our justice before the divine justice. . . It requires as much to reach the nothing as the all, and one leads to the other. These extremes meet and reunite in God, and in God alone. . . The reality of things is an infinite sphere whose center is everywhere and circumference nowhere. In the end, it is the greatest sensible mark of God's omnipotence that our imagination is lost in this thought.[79]

[78] See Charles Chesneau, *Le Père Yves de Paris et son temps (1590-1678),* II (Meaux, 1946), 82-85, *et passim.*
[79] Blaise Pascal, *Pensées,* Texte de L'Edition Brunschvicg (Paris, 1951), II, 72, 87-90; III, 233, 134. See Rosalie L. Colie, *Paradoxia Epidemica: The Renaissance Tradition of Paradox* (Princeton, 1966), 252-72.

ADDENDA ET CORRIGENDA

V: Fondements théoriques de la réception de la beauté sensible dans les écrits de Denys le Chartreux (1402–1471)

Page 310, lines 21–22: 'les deux états allemands'; *read* 'les Pays Bas et l'Allemagne'. See the note to essay VI, pages 103–4, below.

VI: Twofold Wisdom and Contemplation in Denys of Ryckel (Dionysius Cartusiensis, 1402–1471)

Denys' interpretation of the Peripatetic philosophical tradition, its relation to mystical theology, and several particular arguments, all treated in this essay, seem generally to be related to the thought of Albert the Great and his followers in late medieval Germany (see pages 111–12, note 48, of this essay). For excellent studies of Albert and his deep influence on late-medieval philosophers and mystical theologians, concerning especially the soul and the knowledge of God, see Alain de Libera, *Albert le Grand et la philosophie* (Paris, 1990), and *La mystique rhénane d'Albert le Grand à Maître Eckhart* (Paris, 1994; reédition of *Introduction à la mystique rhénane*, Paris, 1984). That Denys was well-read in the philosophical and theological writings of Albert the Great is evident (see essay VII, pages 583, 588–90 et *passim*; essay IX, pages 330, 338-39). It is doubtful that Denys had much contact with the 'Albertists' at the University of Cologne while he studied there; see my *Dionysii Cartusiensis Opera selecta (Prolegomena). Bibliotheca manuscripta 1A: Studia bibliographica* (Corpus Christianorum Continuatio Mediaeualis 121: Turnhout, 1991), 16. Later, however, he obtained writings of Albertists at Cologne and adopted some of their key positions in disputes with Thomists; see the work by P. Teeuwen cited in this essay (page 100, note 5); essay VII, pages 579–80; essay IX, pages 334–35 (Iohannes de Nova Domo); A[driaan] Pattin, 'Le *Tractatus de homine* de Jean de Malines: Contribution à l'histoire de l'Albertisme à l'université de Cologne', *Tijdschrift voor Filosofie* 39 (1977): 3–89, esp. 4–5. Denys also read a thirteenth-century sourcebook for fifteenth-century Albertists; see my 'Did Denys the Carthusian Also Read Henricus Bate?' *Bulletin de philosophie médiévale* 32 (1990): 196–206. Through what channels Denys came into contact with Albertist thinkers and writings remains unknown, but it is clear that throughout his life he kept abreast of events and developments at the University of Cologne; see *Dionysii Cartusiensis . . . Studia bibliographica* (CCCM 121: 28–29, 207–17).

Pages 103–4: Concerning Denys and the Papal Legation conducted by Nicholas of Cusa, see now Erich Meuthen, 'Nikolaus von Kues und Dionysius der Kartäuser', in *EN KAI ΠΛΗΘΟΣ. Einheit und Vielheit. Festschrift für Karl Bormann zum 65.*

Geburtstag, hrsg. A.Th. Khoury und L. Hagemann (Religionswissenschaftliche Studien 30: Würzburg, 1993), 100–20. Modern scholars commonly have stated, as I have done here, that Denys travelled on the Legation with Cusanus for several months. In his extensive archival research, Meuthen finds no documentary evidence that Denys accompanied Nicholas on the Legation for any length of time, although the two probably met in Roermond in September 1451. Meuthen argues that the story of Denys' extended travels with Nicholas was created by his hagiographers and biographers (Pieter Doorlant, Dirk Loër); thence the story passed into modern scholarship. Presuming their conversations during the Legation, Louis Dupré, 'The Mystical Theology of Cusanus's *De visione Dei*', in *Eros and Eris: Contributions to a Hermeneutical Phenomenology. Liber amicorum for Adriaan Peperzak*, ed. P.J.M. van Tongeren et al. (Dordrecht/Boston, 1992), 105–17, esp. 108-9, conjectures that Denys introduced Cusanus to the writings of Jan van Ruusbroec. For a summary of the literary evidence concerning Denys and Nicholas, see my *Dionysii Cartusiensis . . . Studia bibliographica* (CCCM 121: 133–35). There is no surviving evidence of an extensive correspondence between Denys and Nicholas; saving new discoveries, the statement that they corresponded in 'many letters' seems to be an error of Denys' early bibliographers. The negative evidence concerning the Legation and the correspondence only raises more questions. For Denys did dedicate two writings to Cusanus, addressing him as *reverendus praeceptor, praediletissimus pater*, etc., and at least two other works by Denys seem to be associated with the Cardinal. What then were their contacts?

VII: *Sapientissimus Aristoteles* and *Theologicissimus Dionysius*: The Reading of Aristotle and the Understanding of Nature in Denys the Carthusian

Page 606, note 111: The proper title of the essay by Astrik L. Gabriel is: '*Via Antiqua* and *Via Moderna* and the Migration of Paris Students and Masters to the German Universities in the Fifteenth Century'. The essay, with expanded bibliography, is reprinted in Astrik L. Gabriel, *The Paris Studium: Robert of Sorbonne and his Legacy. Interuniversity Exchange between the German, Cracow and Louvain Universities and that of Paris in the Late Medieval and Humanistic Period. Selected Studies*, with a preface by James J. John (Texts and Studies in the History of Medieval Education 19: Frankfurt am Main, 1992), 113–67.

IX: Denys the Carthusian and the Doxography of Scholastic Theology

Page 328, lines 14–18, and page 349, note 7: In his list of Denys' writings (1532/35), Denys' editor, Dirk Loër, cites a work titled *De scientia universalium*, and gives an incipit from Aristotle, *De caelo* (and *De animalibus*). In *Dionysii Cartusiensis . . . Studia bibliographica* (CCCM 121: 122-26), I discuss a treatise on universals having this incipit found in three manuscripts now in Prague. The text in these manuscripts bears characteristic external marks of Denys' writings: it has a prologue, it is divided into 'articles', and its explicit is close to Denys' identifying signature. I conclude, however, that attribution of this writing to Denys is doubtful. Denys nowhere mentions the treatise, and although Dirk Loër must have seen a copy, he never published it. Perhaps he was at first misled by the external similarities. Maarten J.F.M. Hoenen, *Speculum philosophiae medii aevi: Die Handschriftensammlung des Dominikaners Georg Schwartz (†nach 1484)* (Bochumer Studien zur Philosophie 22: Amsterdam/Philadelphia, 1994), 80–82, has found a copy of selected articles from this treatise in Eichstätt, Universitätsbibliothek, Cod. St 686, ff. 257v–261r. Hoenen dismisses the possibility of Denys' authorship, but gives no indication as to the origin of the text. Moreover, in a footnote (81–82 n. 12) he wholly misrepresents my analysis in *Studia bibliographica*, as if I had attributed the work to Denys on the basis of an Aristotelian tag-incipit, when in fact I concluded, as stated above, that Denys probably did not write such a treatise, and that Loër's attribution was probably erroneous.

Page 335, line 13: 'Abubather'; *read* 'Abubacer'. 'Abubather' is the orthography in the printed edition of Denys the Carthusian's works.

Page 358, under SCHOLASTIC EDITIONS CITED: The proper title of Borgnet's edition of the works of Albert the Great is *B. Alberti Magni Ratisbonensis episcopi, Ordinis praedicatorum, Opera omnia*, 38 vols. (Paris: L. Vives, 1890–99).

X: Denys the Carthusian and the Invention of Preaching Materials

A newly-published doctoral dissertation, Dirk Wassermann, *Dionysius der Kartäuser: Einführung in Werk und Gedankenwelt* (Analecta Cartusiana 133: Salzburg, 1996), is especially relevant to this essay. Wassermann emphasizes the theme of personal and corporate *reformatio* as central to Denys' thought and writings.

Page 391, note 68: There is a new edition and translation, by Rodney J. Payton and Ulrich Mammitzsch, of Johan Huizinga, *The Autumn of the Middle Ages* (Chicago: University of Chicago Press, 1996). Payton and Mammitzsch restore crucial passages from Huizinga's second Dutch edition (and in the German translation) that were omitted in Hopman's English translation. The new editors and translators provide an informative introduction and add notes of their own.

INDEX NOMINUM

This index cites names of persons mentioned in the body of the texts of the articles. In some instances, I cite authors discussed in the notes. The index omits the name of Jesus Christ.

DATE DUE
